Microsoft® Office
Project Server 2003
UNLEASHED

QuantumPM

800 East 96th Street, Indianapolis, Indiana 46240

Microsoft® Office Project Server 2003 Unleashed

International Standard Book Number: 0-672-32743-0

Library of Congress Catalog Card Number: 20055901779

Printed in the United States of America

First Printing: June 2005

08   07   06   05   4   3   2

Trademarks

Warning and Disclaimer

Bulk Sales

Que Publishing offers excellent discounts on this book when ordered in quantity for bulk purchases or special sales. For more information, please contact

U.S. Corporate and Government Sales
1-800-382-3419
corpsales@pearsontechgroup.com

For sales outside the United States, please contact

International Sales
international@pearsoned.com

Associate Publisher
Greg Wiegand

Acquisitions Editor
Stephanie J. McComb

Development Editor
Mark Renfrow

Managing Editor
Charlotte Clapp

Project Editor
Mandie Frank

Copy Editor
Geneil Breeze

Indexer
Ken Johnson

Proofreader
Jessica McCarty

Technical Editor
Brian Kennemer

Publishing Coordinator
Sharry Lee Gregory

Multimedia Developer
Dan Scherf

Designer
Gary Adair

Page Layout
Kelly Maish

Contents at a Glance

Introduction 1

Part I   Enterprise Project Management Overview
  1   Enterprise Project Management—The Philosophy 11
  2   Using Microsoft Office Project 2003 As an Enterprise Project
       Management Solution 27
  3   Knowing Product Limits and Overcoming Them 39

Part II   Planning Your Enterprise Project Management Implementation
  4   Planning the Organizational Processes 57
  5   Understanding Project Server Architecture 83
  6   Designing the Enterprise Project Management Solution
       Architecture Details 109

Part III   Implementing Microsoft Office Project Server 2003
  7   Enterprise Project Management System Deployment Considerations 137
  8   Establishing Security Model Settings 143
  9   Enterprise Global Codes 163
 10   Creating Project Web Access Project and Resource Views 209
 11   Completing the Implementation and Configuration 239

Part IV   Validating the Microsoft Office Project Server 2003 Implementation
 12   Microsoft Office Project Server 2003 Validation 259
 13   Troubleshooting Business Process Implementation in the Application ... 277

Part V   Using Microsoft Office Project Web Access 2003
 14   Project Web Access Collaboration 293
 15   Time Tracking in Project Web Access 317
 16   Using Project and Resource Centers 345
 17   Portfolio Management Using Portfolio Analyzer and
       Portfolio Modeler 393
 18   Risks, Issues, and Documents Using Windows SharePoint
       Services (WSS) 441
 19   Using the Project Web Access Admin Menu Tab 477

Part VI   Using Microsoft Office Project Professional 2003 Enterprise Features

20   Building Custom Enterprise Configuration 537

21   Building Project Team and Resource Substitution 563

22   Project Team Collaboration 589

Part VII   Enterprise Project Management Integration with Microsoft Office Applications

23   Project Web Access and Project Professional Integration with Office 615

24   Project Workspace Integration with Office 635

Part VIII Server Maintenance and Configuration Management

25   Server Maintenance and Configuration Management 651

26   Capacity Planning 683

Part IX   Industry Configuration Examples

27   Industry Examples for Microsoft Office Project 2003 Configuration 701

Part X   Customizing Microsoft Office Project Server 2003

28   Enterprise Project Management Customization 731

29   Extending Enterprise Project Management Through Customization
        Overview 793

        Index 811

Table of Contents

Introduction to Enterprise Project Management   **1**

Why We Wrote This Book 1

How This Book Is Organized 1

Part I—Enterprise Project Management Overview 2

Part II—Planning Your Enterprise Project Management
Implementation 2

Part III—Implementing Microsoft Office Project Server 2003 2

Part IV—Validating the Microsoft Office Project Server 2003
Implementation 3

Part V—Using Microsoft Office Project Web Access 2003 3

Part VI—Using Microsoft Office Project Professional 2003
Enterprise Features 4

Part VII—Enterprise Project Management Integration with Microsoft
Office Applications 4

Part VIII—Server Maintenance and Configuration Management 4

Part IX—Industry Configuration Examples 4

Part X—Customizing Microsoft Office Project Server 2003 4

Who Should Read This Book 5

Business Managers and Leaders 5

Project and Resource Managers 5

Project Server Administrators 6

Technologists and Implementers 6

Special Features of This Book 6

Terms Included in This Book 6

Part I   **Enterprise Project Management Overview**

  1   **Enterprise Project Management—The Philosophy**   **11**

Defining Enterprise Project Management 12

Think Enterprise 14

Manage the Organizational Change 14

Emphasize Process over Technology 18

Align with the Six Pillars of EPM 19

Understanding the EPM Impacts on Your Organization 20

New Ways to Communicate 21

New Opportunities 22

Leadership Team Capabilities 23

Project Manager and Project Team Interaction 24

Focus on Project Management Skills 24

Set Realistic Expectations for Your EPM Implementation 25

Best Practices 26

**2   Using Microsoft Office Project 2003 As an Enterprise Project
Management Solution   27**

Major Features of Microsoft Project Web Access 2003 27
  Scheduling with Microsoft Project Professional 29
  Reviewing Portfolio Schedules with Project Web Access 30
  Centralized Storage of Project Schedule Data 31
  Resource Management and the Enterprise Global Resource Pool 31
  Centralized Storage of Risks, Issues, and Documents 32
  The Project Workspace 32
Understanding the Features of Project Server 2003 33
  Project Server Interfaces 33
  Architecture Overview 33
  Project Web Access 34
  Microsoft Project Professional 35
  Windows SharePoint Services 35
  Overview of Project Server Configuration and Settings 36
Best Practices 37

3   Knowing Product Limits and Overcoming Them   39

Augmentation Areas of Microsoft Office Project Server 2003 40
  Project Timesheets Versus Labor Timesheets 41
  Resource Commitment Management Versus Usage Management 42
  Budgeting and Forecasting Concepts 42
  Strategic Portfolio Support 42
  Methodology Support 43
  Standardization Validation and Support 43
  Interdependency Management (Vendor Management) 43
  Lightweight Project Management Support 44
  Governance and Project Initiation 45
An Overview of Third-Party Add-Ins 45
  Custom Component Object Model Add-Ins 45
  QuantumPM Schedule Auditor 45
  Extending Project Web Access with Enterprise Project
    Knowledge Suite 47
  ProSight Portfolios Bridge 50
  Micro-Frame Program Manager 51
  Risk+ for Risk Management 51
  Microsoft-Provided Downloads 52
  CMD to Manage Process Workflow 52
  Overview of the Project Guide and Customization 52
Best Practices 54

Part II   Planning Your Enterprise Project Management Implementation

4   Planning the Organizational Processes   57

Planning—Six Pillars of EPM...58
   Pillar 1: Project Management...58
   Pillar 2: Resource Management...61
   Pillar 3: Collaboration Management..64
   Pillar 4: Artifact Management...66
   Pillar 5: Organizational Readiness..68
   Pillar 6: Operational Principles..69
Defining Your EPM Scope..70
   Managing EPM Rollout Expectations..70
   Generic Phases of EPM Deployment...71
   Capturing EPM Feature Requirements...78
   Communicating the Implementation Strategy..80
Best Practices...81

5   Understanding Project Server Architecture   83

Software Components..85
   Client Tier...85
   Application Tier..87
   Project Server 2003 Services..93
   Project Server Email Layer...95
   Project Server Database Tier...95
Microsoft EPM Solution Architecture...98
   Number of Users and Their Roles in Your Organization.........................98
   Your Projects and Their Characteristics..99
   Usage Patterns...100
   Feature Usage Across Your Organization...100
Scalability..100
   Network Performance...102
   Database Server Performance...102
   Project Server Security Usage...102
   Project Server Data Usage..102
Network/System Security...103
   User Authentication..103
   Implementing Secure Sockets Layer (SSL)...104
   Project Server 2003 Security Model..105
Best Practices...107

**6   Designing the Enterprise Project Management Solution
       Architecture Details   109**

Reviewing the Business Requirements...109
Server Hardware...111

Network Topology and Architecture 114
    Network Latency and Bandwidth 114
    Using Multiple NIC Cards or NIC Teaming 115
    Wide Area Networks (WAN) 116
    EPM Solution for Users in Multiple Geographic Locations 117
    EPM Solution Deployment in Trusted and Nontrusted
      Domain Environments and Extranets 118
    EPM Deployment in Trusted Domains 119
    EPM Deployment in Nontrusted Domains 121
    Extranet Configurations for EPM Solutions 124
    Using Terminal Services As Part of an EPM Solution 126
Hyperthreading 127
Software Prerequisites 128
    Microsoft Office Project 2003 Software Product and Version
      Requirements 128
    Client-Side Requirements 129
    Server-Side Requirements 130
Multiple Configurations 130
    Multiple Project Server Instances and Edit Site Utility 131
    Virtualizing EPM Solution Infrastructure 132
Best Practices 134

Part III   Implementing Microsoft Office Project Server 2003

7   Enterprise Project Management System Deployment Considerations   137
Introduction to EPM Solution Deployment 137
    Security Models 137
    Enterprise Global Codes 138
    Views 138
    Calendars 138
    Timesheet Setup 138
Installing Prerequisites 138
    Get Professional Assistance 138
    Establish a Program Management Office 139
    Training 139
    Architecture 140
    Establish Standards 140
    Incremental Deployment 140
    Conduct a Pilot Deployment 141
    Integrate with Business Systems 141
    Integrate with Business Processes 141
    Sell the Solution 142
Best Practices 142

8 Establishing Security Model Settings   **143**

Server Configuration—Features 144
    Allow/Deny 145
    Selecting Features 145
Identifying Roles 147
Security Templates 147
    Creating Security Templates 147
Security Groups 149
    Creating Groups 149
    Setting Global Permissions for Members of This Group 151
Creating Categories 151
    Creating Categorics 151
    Category Name and Description 153
    Users and Groups 153
    Projects: Select the Projects That Users in This Category
        Can View 154
    Resources: Select the Resources Whose Information Can/
        Cannot Be Viewed by Users in This Category 156
    Project Center Views 158
    Optional Category Configuration 159
Associating Groups and Categories 160
    The Case for Multiple Categories 160
Assigning Resources to Proper Groups 161
    Managing Users 161
Best Practices 162
    Security Design Recommendations 162

9 Enterprise Global Codes   **163**

Overview of the Enterprise Outline Codes and Fields 163
Project Outline Codes 169
    Planning Enterprise Project Outline Codes 169
    Defining Enterprise Project Outline Codes 170
    Using Enterprise Project Outline Codes 172
Resource Outline Codes 173
    Planning Enterprise Resource Outline Codes 174
    Defining Enterprise Resource Outline Codes 176
    Defining Skills for Your Enterprise Resources 176
    Using Enterprise Resource Outline Codes 178
Resource Breakdown Structure 185
    Planning and Defining RBS Hierarchy 185
    Using RBS 190
    RBS and Project Server Security 190
Enterprise Resource Pool 191
    Building the Enterprise Resource Pool 192
    Working with the Enterprise Resource Pool 194
    Enterprise Resource Pool and Active Directory Synchronization 199

Enterprise Task Outline Codes 201
    Planning Enterprise Task Outline Codes 202
    Defining Enterprise Task Outline Codes 202
    Using Enterprise Task Outline Codes 203
Enterprise Custom Fields, Formulas, and Graphic Indicators 204
    Overview of Enterprise Custom Fields 205
    Defining Enterprise Custom Fields 205
Best Practices 207

10   Creating Project Web Access Project and Resource Views   209

Project Web Access Project and Resource Views 209
    Project Center Views 210
    Project Views 214
    Resource Center Views 218
    Assignment Views 222
Portfolio Analyzer Views 225
    Creating and Modifying Portfolio Analyzer Views 227
Managing Views Using Project Web Access Client 235
Microsoft Project Professional Views 236
    Creating and Modifying Views in Project Professional Client 237
    Managing Views in Microsoft Project Professional 237
Additional Recommended Readings 238
Best Practices 238

11   Completing the Implementation and Configuration   239

Using Administrative Projects 240
    Administrative Project Considerations 241
Managing Enterprise Project and Resource Calendars 247
    Managing Enterprise Project Calendars 248
Performing Enterprise Global Backup and Restore 251
    Backing Up Enterprise Global Template Data 251
Timesheet Setup 252
    Specify the Default Method for Reporting Progress on Tasks 252
    Lock Down Defaults 253
    Time Period Settings 253
    Define Current Tasks 255
Best Practices 255

Part IV   Validating the Microsoft Office Project Server 2003 Implementation

12   Microsoft Office Project Server 2003 Validation   259

Introduction to Validation 259
    Level 1—Technology 259
    Level 2—Basic Project Server Configuration 260
    Level 3—Business Process Validation 260
    Conclusion 260

Level 1—Technology Validation 261
    Server Operating Systems Validation 261
    Network Systems Validation 262
    Application Installation Validation 264
Level 2—Basic Project Server Configuration 273
    User Role Validation 273
    Security Setup Validation 273
    Data Access Validation 273
Level 3—Business Process Validation 274
    User Role Configuration 274
    Validate Business Process Test Scenarios 274
    Database Cleanup 274
Best Practices 275

13 Troubleshooting Business Process Implementation in the Application   277
Common Implementation Issues, Causes, and Suggested Remedies 277
    Project Web Access Administrator Account Does Not Work As
      Expected 277
    Cannot Create Project Web Access Windows-Authenticated
      Accounts 278
    Timesheets Do Not Show Expected Data Entry Mode 278
    Project Managers Cannot Open a Schedule in Project
      Professional 2003 When Clicking on the Project in Line
      in Project Web Access 279
    Resource Managers Cannot See Any Resource Information 279
    Some Users Can Access Project Portfolio Feature Although
      They Are Not Supposed to See It 279
    Project Portfolio Security Issue 280
    User Cannot See the Projects and Resources According to
      His Group Security Permissions 280
    User Cannot Save a Project Schedule As a Template 280
    User Does Not Receive Email Notification When She Has
      Been Assigned a New Task 281
    User Cannot See Documents, Risks, and Issues 281
    User Cannot Delegate Tasks 282
    User Cannot Create a New Task and Insert It Into Any
      Available Project 282
    Users Cannot Assign Themselves to an Existing Task in
      Projects That Have Been Published to Project Server 282
    Users Cannot Manage Status Report Requests 283
    User Cannot Create and Manage To-Do Lists 283
    User Cannot Find a Specific Task That He Was Working
      on in His Timesheet 284
    User Cannot Add a New Resource to His Project/Organization 284

Team Member Did Not Get His Task Assignment on the
Timesheet Page, Although the Project Manager Saved
the Project Schedule...284
Project Managers Cannot Change the Method for Reporting
Progress on Projects...284
Project Managers Cannot Save the Baseline...........................285
Issues with Mapping of Business Process in the Project Server 2003.......285
Troubleshooting the Resource Allocation Process......................285
Troubleshooting Data Accuracy: Data Presented in the
Database Is Inconsistent with Reality..............................286
Troubleshooting Portfolio Analyzer: Data Is Not in Sync
with the Information from Project or Resource Center...............287
Troubleshooting Incorrect Results for Projects in Progress
When You Use the Portfolio Modeler or the Resource
Substitution Wizard...287
Troubleshooting Adjust Actuals: Cannot Change the
Remaining Work Field When Adjusting Actuals.......................288
Troubleshooting the Updates: Cannot View All Past
Task Updates..288
Troubleshooting the Application of Rules: Setting the
Rule Produces Unexpected Results..................................288
Troubleshooting Duplicate Global.mpt Files...........................288
Troubleshooting Versions: I Cannot Delete the Published
Version...289
Troubleshooting Resource Calendars: Tasks Extend Their
Duration Unexpectedly...289
Best Practices...290

Part V   Using Microsoft Office Project Web Access 2003

14   Project Web Access Collaboration   293
Using PWA..293
Using PWA Functions..294
PWA Data Creation..297
Using PWA to Its Full Advantage....................................298
Accessing PWA..299
Navigating PWA...301
Using the Home Page..302
Changing Your Password...302
Alert Me on the Home Page (Email Reminders)........................302
Working with PWA Offline...303
Microsoft Outlook and PWA Integration..............................305
Managing Alerts..305
Exchanging Textual Information Using Status Reports....................307
Alert Me for Status Reports..308
Status Reports Based on Role/Permissions...........................308

Requesting Status Reports...308
Submitting Status Reports...310
Viewing and Compiling Submitted Status Reports............313
Edit or Delete an Existing Status Report.......................314
Miscellaneous Reports..314
Using the Status Reports Archive.................................314
Best Practices..315

15   Time Tracking in Project Web Access   317
Using the Tasks Page to Record Actual Work....................317
The Timesheet Update Cycle..319
Timesheet Format and Setup.......................................320
Different Tracking Methods for Timesheets.....................320
Viewing Data on the Timesheet....................................321
Entering Time on Tasks...325
Alert Me...328
Creating a New Task...328
Assigning Myself to a New Task...................................330
Delegating Tasks..331
Viewing and Reporting on Your Tasks from Your Outlook
    Calendar...332
Notifying Your Manager of Nonproject Time..................333
Printing the Timesheet/Using Excel..............................334
Customizing the Timesheet..336
Using the Updates Page...336
General Information About Using the Updates Page..........339
Setting Rules...341
Viewing History...342
Adjusting Time and Managerial Timesheet Review and
    Approval...343
Best Practices..344

16   Using Project and Resource Centers   345
Understanding the Project Center.....................................345
Using Project Center Views..347
Using Save Link to Create Custom Personal Views............352
Using the Build Team Function.....................................353
Edit Projects in Project Center.....................................360
Open Projects from Project Center...............................361
Gantt Chart Zoom Icon...363
Gantt Chart Go to Task Icon..363
Project Center Printing..364
Project Center Export to Excel......................................365
Viewing Project Details..366
Collaboration Using Project Center...............................367
Analyze Projects in Portfolio Analyzer..........................371

Model Projects with Portfolio Modeler 371
Working with To-Do Lists 371
Check in My Projects 375
Managing Administrative Projects 376
Understanding the Resource Center 377
Using Resource Center Views 378
Printing from the Resource Center 383
Export to Excel from Resource Center 383
Using the Save Link to Create Custom and Personal Views 385
View Availability 385
Edit Resources 388
Opening the Enterprise Resource Pool 389
Analyzing Resources in Portfolio Analyzer 390
Viewing Resource Assignments 390
Adjusting Actuals 391
Best Practices 392

17   Portfolio Management Using Portfolio Analyzer and
     Portfolio Modeler   393
Analyzing Portfolio Data in the Portfolio Analyzer 394
Building and Changing Portfolio Analyzer Views 395
Manipulating Portfolio Analyzer Views 422
Using Portfolio Modeler to Analyze Projects 424
Creating a Model 424
Viewing and Analyzing Data in a Model 429
Manipulating Models and What-If Analysis 432
Best Practices 440

18   Risks, Issues, and Documents Using Windows SharePoint
     Services (WSS)   441
Collaboration Using Windows SharePoint Services 442
Permissions in WSS 444
Building Templates 447
Modifying Settings 447
Risks 454
Risk Summaries 455
Creating Risks 455
Linking List Items to Tasks 458
Editing, Deleting, and Alert Me Actions on Risks 459
Issues 462
Issues Summaries 463
Creating Issues 463
Editing, Deleting, and Alert Me Actions on Issues 465
Viewing and Reporting Issue Items 465
Documents 468
Uploading or Creating a Document 470
New Folder, Filter, and Other Actions in a Document List 471

Actions on Documents 472
Actions on the Document Library from the Side Pane 474
Best Practices 476

19   Using the Project Web Access Admin Menu Tab   477
Admin Overview 478
Using the Manage Users and Groups Function 480
Managing Users 480
Managing Groups 485
Using the Manage Security Function 488
Managing Categories 488
Managing Security Templates 491
Setting Project Server Authentication Mode 493
Using the Manage Views Page 494
Adding a Project View 496
Adding a Project Center View 498
Adding an Assignment View 499
Adding a Resource Center View 501
Adding a Portfolio Analyzer View 502
Managing the Timesheet View 503
Copying, Deleting, and Modifying a View 505
Using the Additional Views Function 506
Using the Server Configuration Function 506
Setting Enterprise Features 507
Defining PWA Menus 509
Adding a Top-Level Menu 510
Using the Manage Windows SharePoint Services (WSS) Function 512
Connecting to Windows SharePoint Server 512
Setting Site Provisioning 513
Managing SharePoint Sites 514
Using the Manage Enterprise Features Function 516
The Update Resource Tables and OLAP Cube 517
Check In Enterprise Projects 520
Check In Enterprise Resources 521
Using Versions 521
Using the Customize Project Web Access Function 524
The Tracking Settings Function 524
Gantt Chart Formats 524
Grouping Formats 525
The Home Page Format Function 528
Notification and Reminders 529
Using the Clean Up the Project Server Database Function 531
Deleting Task Assignment Data 531
The About Microsoft Office Project Server 2003 Page 534
Best Practices 534

Part VI   Using Microsoft Office Project Professional 2003 Enterprise Features

20   Building Custom Enterprise Configuration   537

Introduction to Microsoft Office Project Professional 537

Enterprise Options 538

   Microsoft Office Project Server Accounts 538

   Tools Plus Options 541

   Using the Organizer 550

   Tools Plus Enterprise Options 552

Customizing the Enterprise Global Template 555

   Setting the Currency Symbol 555

   Customizing Enterprise Fields 556

   Adding Custom Objects 560

Best Practices 561

21   Building Project Team and Resource Substitution   563

Building Project Teams 563

   Identifying the Right Resources for Your Project 565

   Adding Generic Resources to Your Project Team 571

   Adding Individual Resources to Your Project Team 572

   Matching Skills of Generic Resources with Individual Resources ... 573

   How the Resource Matching Feature Works 574

   Replacing Existing Project Resources 575

   Removing Team Members from a Project 575

   Using the Build Team Feature in a Wide Area Network

      Environment 576

Performing Resource Substitution 576

   Skill-Based Scheduling Overview 577

   Preparing to Use the Resource Substitution Wizard 577

   Limitations of the Resource Substitution Wizard 579

   Using the Resource Substitution Wizard 580

Best Practices 587

22   Project Team Collaboration   589

Overview of Collaboration Features 589

Team Collaboration in Small Organizations 590

Team Collaboration in Large Organizations 591

Effective Use of Project Team Collaboration Tools 593

Team Collaboration on Management of Risks 594

   Risk Overview 594

   Risk Tracking Using Project Server 596

   Collaboration Features for Risk Management in Project

      Professional 597

Collaboration Features for Issues Management 597

   Overview of Issues Management 597

   Issue Tracking Using Project Server 597

   Viewing and Creating Issues in Project Professional 598

Collaboration Features for Documents Management 598
  Documents Management—A Stringent Necessity for Any
    Project Team 599
  Options for Document Collaboration 599
  How to Improve the Document Collaboration Process 601
  Using Document Libraries 604
  Viewing Documents in Project Professional 604
Updating Project Progress 605
  Tracking Project Changes 605
  Updating Project Progress Workflow 606
  Updating and Saving Task Changes into Project Schedules 607
Best Practices 612

Part VII   **Enterprise Project Management Integration with Microsoft Office**
            Applications

   23   **Project Web Access and Project Professional Integration with Office**   **615**
         Project Web Access and Project Professional with Individual Office
           Applications 616
           Project Web Access Integration with Outlook 616
           PWA Integration with Excel 622
           Project Professional Integration with Visio 627
         Best Practices 633

   24   **Project Workspace Integration with Office**   **635**
         The Project Workspace and Shared Office Integration 635
           Saving a Document to a Workspace 636
           Saving a Document, Versioning, and Check-In/Check-Out 640
           Web Discussions 642
         Integration with Individual Office Applications 642
           Project Workspace Integration with Outlook 642
           Project Workspace Integration with Excel 645
         Best Practices 647

Part VIII   **Server Maintenance and Configuration Management**

   25   **Server Maintenance and Configuration Management**   **651**
         Server Components Overview 651
           Active Directory and Windows Server 2003 652
           Internet Information Services (IIS) 6.0 652
           Structured Query Language (SQL) Server 2000 652
           Analysis Services (AS) 653
           Session Manager 653
           Views Processor (VP) 653
           Windows SharePoint Services (WSS) 653

Monitoring Project Server and Windows SharePoint Services 654
    Windows 2003 Server Log File Monitoring 654
    Real-Time Monitoring 654
    Internet Information Services (IIS) Log File Monitoring 656
    Monitoring SQL Server 2000 658
    Analysis Services Monitoring 660
Maintaining Project Server 2003 SQL Server Databases 662
    Database Lists and Functions 662
    Database Settings 662
    Simple Recovery Considerations 662
    Full Recovery Considerations 662
    Database Maintenance Plans 663
    Ensuring That the Maintenance Plan Worked 667
Disaster Recovery 667
Testing and Troubleshooting 668
    The Application and Client Layers 668
Managing Terminal Services 675
    Terminal Services Versus a Virtual Private Network (VPN) 675
    Benefits of Using Terminal Services for Project Server 2003 675
    Considerations for Implementing Terminal Services 676
    Installation Order and Application Server Mode 677
    Group Policy and the Group Policy Management
      Console (GPMC) 677
Patching 679
    Windows Server 2003 Patch Management 680
    Applying Hotfixes and Service Packs to Project Server 2003 680
    Microsoft Baseline Security Analyzer Tool 681
Best Practices 682

26 Capacity Planning   683
System Hardware/Architecture Instance Design 685
    User Numbers and Types 686
    User Location and Connectivity 687
    Peak/Heavy Usage Scenarios 687
    Network Environment 688
    Server Environment 689
    Data Complexity 690
    Client-Side Environment 691
    Data Storage Requirements 691
    Miscellaneous Advanced Areas 693
Planning for Growth 693
Monitoring for Growth 694
Ongoing System Concerns 695
    New Software Releases 695
    Information Life Cycle—Archive and Retention Policies 696

Business Need Changes...696
System Customization—Special Needs.............................696
Federation...696
Best Practices...698

Part IX   Industry Configuration Examples

27   Industry Examples for Microsoft Office Project 2003 Configuration   701

Customizing Project Web Access and Views Configuration 701
Managed Time Periods Versus Nonmanaged Time Periods 702
Tracking Settings 702
Locking Down Defaults 702
Project Web Access and Portfolio Analyzer Views 702
Customizing Enterprise Global Custom Outline Codes 703
Generic Enterprise Outline Codes for Projects 705
Project Location 705
Project Status...705
Grouping Projects By Project Type 706
Grouping Projects By Sponsoring Division 707
Project Performing Division...707
Project Priority 707
Custom Outline Code for Resources 707
Resources by RBS 708
Resources by Location 708
Resources by Skill Set...708
Resources by Certification 709
Resources by Type...709
Examples of Generic Enterprise Custom Fields.................................709
Enterprise Custom Field: Schedule Indicator...........................709
Enterprise Custom Field: Budget Indicator 710
Research and Development Examples 711
Project Location 711
Project Status...711
Project Life Cycle..712
Resource RBS...712
Resource Skill Set..712
Resource Role..713
Government Agency Examples 713
Project Type...713
Project Strategic Alignment 714
Project Funding...714
Project Areas...714
Project Scope 715
Air Industry Examples 715
Project Portfolio Sector 715
Project by Aircraft Manufacturer..716

Project Portfolio by Global Alliances 716
Projects by Aircraft Type 716
Resource Skill Set 716
Healthcare Sector Examples 717
Projects by Healthcare Area 717
Projects by Branch 717
Projects and Resources by Sector 718
Resource Skill Set Classification 718
Oil and Gas Industry Examples 718
Project Location 718
Projects by Type of Capital Expenditures 719
Projects and Resources by Area of Capital Expenditures 719
Project Area 719
Project Status 720
Project Phase 720
Resources Skill Set 720
Construction Industry Examples 721
Project Status 721
Project Phase 722
Projects by Types of Construction 722
Projects by Construction Component 722
Resources by Skill Set 722
Resources by Construction Management Position 723
Resources by Core Construction Skills 723
Pharmaceuticals/Biopharmaceuticals Industry Examples 724
Project Phase 724
Projects by Core Technologies 724
Projects by Emerging Biopharmaceuticals 725
Projects by Core Support Area 725
Resource Distribution of Medical and Clinical Staff 725
Resources by Skill Set 725
Information Technology Examples 726
Project Location 726
Project Status 726
Project Life Cycle 727
Project Portfolio by Area 727
Resources by Skill Set 727
Best Practices 728

Part X   Customizing Microsoft Office Project Server 2003

28   Enterprise Project Management Customization   731

Windows SharePoint Services Customizing the Project Workspace 732
    WSS Project Workspace Customization 732
    Saving Custom List As a Template 754
    Creating Nonproject-Related WSS Sites 756
    Server-Side WSS Customization Overview 758
Customizing PWA 766
    URL Parameters 767
    Modifying the Stylesheet 767
    Modifying Menus 767
    Adding New Pages Using ASP 770
    Adding New Pages Using Another Language 774
    How to Customize One Instance and Not Others 778
Using VBA Macros 779
    Recording Macros 779
    Assigning the Macro to a Toolbar Button 781
    Viewing and Editing VBA Code 782
    Debugging VBA Code 785
    The Project Object Model 786
    Security and Certificates 787
    The Tip of the Iceberg 791
Best Practices 791

**29   Extending Enterprise Project Management Through
Customization Overview   793**

Secure Access to Project Server Data Through the Project Data Service ...793
    When to Use the PDS 794
    How to Use the PDS 795
    Limitations of the PDS 800
    PWA Web Parts 800
Extending the Cube 800
    OLAP Cube Basics 800
    The Portfolio Analyzer to Display Cube Data 802
    Cube Extension Build Process 803
    Overview of the Cube Build Breakout Object 804
    Debugging the Cube Extension 806
SharePoint Portal Integration 807
    Connecting EPM to SharePoint Portal Server 807
Best Practices 809

Index   811

About the Authors

Unlike most books, this one was not written by an individual or a group of two or three experts. Instead, it was written by a large and diverse group of people from QuantumPM, LLC (QPM). The authors are undeniable experts; they have used this software within our organization and have helped hundreds of customers install and configure the software for their organizations. In addition, the QPM team works closely with the Microsoft team to support the rollout of the product and to provide input for future versions.

QuantumPM, LLC is a consulting firm specializing in strategic and tactical project management services. The company's focus is improvement of organizational bottom lines through effective project and portfolio management, targeting a balance of philosophy and tools. To this end, QuantumPM works closely with Microsoft, Inc. as a Premier Project Partner and with the Project Management Institute as a Registered Education Provider and active participant in standards development and various local chapter activities. These partnerships allow QuantumPM to provide state-of-the-art products and services to our customers.

The authors of the book include people from a variety of roles within the organization. They brought their unique perspectives to this effort and hope to have provided you with a great balance of technical and operational material based on many years of practical application of the product. Following are the QuantumPM team members who worked many long hours to develop the contents of this book:

- Our project manager and miracle worker who managed to get us all to deliver our work as promised: Genie Peshkova.

- Members of our sales and marketing teams who help our customers understand the capabilities of the software as a part of a complete solution for their needs: Greg Bailey, Karla Ferguson, Jim Patterson, and Crystal Trevino.

- Members of our operations staff who manage our internal administrative projects and keep things running smoothly: Laurie Dawkins and Jennifer Rollins.

- Members of our technical staff who help customers with system architecture, scalability and capacity planning, and other system administration decisions. They also keep this software running smoothly in our customer-hosted environment as well as our own internal environment: Tony Blackburn and Katie Stewart.

- Members of our project management consulting team who work together to provide solutions for our customers: Claudia Baca, Boris Bazant, Robert Bowman, Steve Drevon, Cristian Filip, Scott Footlik, Herman Gaines, Patti Jansen, Brian Musgrave, and Russ Young.

- Members of our development team who create custom solutions to enhance the capabilities of Microsoft's Enterprise Project Management software: Danny Allen, Adam Berle, Bruce Johnson, and Ethan Young.

- The project sponsors and founders of QPM: Kris Athey and Rose Blackburn.

About the Technical Editors

Two very important people were involved in making this book technically accurate and ensuring that it flows properly from beginning to end. Because this book is the first in-depth review of Microsoft Office Project Server, the task was no small feat.

Genie Peshkova was born and raised in Voronezh, Russia, located 500 kilometers south of Moscow. She is fluent in both Russian and English. At 17, she was working for LogicBay Corporation as a quality assurance specialist. During that time she also did consulting for RelexUS as a technical writer. Genie has a computer science degree from Colorado School of Mines and comes from a tradition of computer science specialists in her family (both her mother, Oksana, and father, Anatoly, have master's degrees). Genie started at QuantumPM in 2002 and by the age of 22 became the youngest project manager there. She was also immediately exposed to and gained knowledge of Microsoft Office Project Server, assisting in QuantumPM's effort in the writing of a couple of chapters in Que Publishing's *Special Edition Using Microsoft Office Project 2003*. Genie currently lives in Denver, Colorado, with her fiancé, Joe.

Brian Kennemer has worked with Microsoft Office Project 2003 and its predecessor products for almost 10 years. He has been recognized by Microsoft as one of a select group of Most Valued Professionals (MVP) for his knowledge and contribution to the user community. He is a longtime associate of QuantumPM, LLC, representing the organization in a variety of venues and providing support to the consulting staff. He is currently working as a senior trainer and consultant for Electronic Arts, the leading developer and publisher of interactive entertainment software for personal computers and advanced entertainment systems. Brian is an active member of the local Puget Sound Chapter of the Microsoft Project Users Group (MPUG) and a columnist for the MPUG newsletter. Brian lives near Seattle, Washington, with his wife, Alicia, his daughter, Alivia, and his two sons, Riley and Jesse.

Dedication

This book is dedicated to two very important groups of people: our customers and our families.

Our customers are the best. They challenge us daily as we learn about their environments and help them to map the capabilities of this software to their needs. They have helped us come up with creative solutions to overcome the limitations of the tools. We are much better consultants because of them.

Our families have been tremendously supportive and patient during the creation of this book. They supported us through empty periods of writer's block and anxious days when customer work took precedence over writing.

—The QPM Team

Acknowledgments

Over the past several years, we have worked closely with the Microsoft Office Project team. This group of people has helped us understand their plans for the product and the inner workings of the software. They continually seek advice on the future direction of this product set and have listened carefully to our input and that of the customers to design a product that provides enterprise capabilities and yet is easy to use. They have encouraged us to expand this book to show not only the capabilities of the software but also to highlight its limitations so that the customer experience is the best it can be.

This product is not intended to meet all the possible needs of all customers. Microsoft works hard to encourage third-party vendors to create add-on features and capabilities that extend the usefulness of the product. In Chapter 3, "Knowing Product Limits and Overcoming Them," you will see some of the many possible products that extend the capabilities of the software. QPM would like to thank Microsoft for working with us and helping us present more robust solutions to our customers.

QuantumPM would also like to acknowledge the hard-working staff at Sams Publishing who have helped make this book what it is today. We would specifically like to thank Stephanie McComb, acquisitions editor; Mark Renfrow, development editor; Mandie Frank, project editor; and Geneil Breeze, copy editor for their patience, collaboration, and efforts. It has been our pleasure working with them on a project of such a large scale.

We Want to Hear from You!

As the reader of this book, *you* are our most important critic and commentator. We value your opinion and want to know what we're doing right, what we could do better, what areas you'd like to see us publish in, and any other words of wisdom you're willing to pass our way.

As an associate publisher for Sams Publishing, I welcome your comments. You can email or write me directly to let me know what you did or didn't like about this book—as well as what we can do to make our books better.

Please note that I cannot help you with technical problems related to the topic of this book. We do have a User Services group, however, where I will forward specific technical questions related to the book.

When you write, please be sure to include this book's title and author as well as your name, email address, and phone number. I will carefully review your comments and share them with the author and editors who worked on the book.

> feedback@quepublishing.com

Mail: Greg Wiegand
        Associate Publisher
        Sams Publishing
        800 East 96th Street
        Indianapolis, IN 46240 USA

For more information about this book or another Sams Publishing title, visit our website at www.quepublishing.com. Type the ISBN (excluding hyphens) or the title of a book in the Search field to find the page you're looking for.

Introduction to Enterprise Project Management

Throughout this book, you will see that Enterprise Project Management (also called Enterprise Portfolio Management) is made up of two components—Philosophy and Tool. Although the book is primarily technical in nature, it is impossible to separate the technology from the environment in which it works. This software is not a "silver bullet" that will solve all process problems. Although it is great software, it has limitations, and the primary one is that it is only as good as the processes that surround the tool.

Why We Wrote This Book

The Sams Publishing *Unleashed* series is intended for both beginner and intermediate audiences. The primary purpose of this book is to provide knowledge to the reader of the capabilities of Microsoft Office Project Server 2003, a robust Enterprise Project Management (EPM) software application. It does not provide a step-by-step cookbook answer but rather provides the logic and approach that should be used for implementing a complex project management software product.

The material covered in this book is simple enough for a beginner to understand but also allows you to grow with the book as more advanced topics are covered as well.

The intermediate user will find that the material is new and interesting and provides practical tips, tricks, and guidelines based on this team's experience of hundreds of successful EPM installations and implementations for thousands of users.

This book is comprehensive enough to be a source of powerful and meaningful information but is not meant to be a "cradle-to-grave" guide of all things possible with this software. (It does need to fit in a briefcase or next to your desk!)

The team is excited to offer you the opportunity to get into the consultants' heads and get some practical and real-world examples on how to plan, install, configure, deploy, and manage an EPM implementation.

How This Book Is Organized

This book is divided into 10 parts designed to be of interest to a wide variety of readers. Some of the chapters focus on planning and organization, whereas others are focused on technology details. The following information should help you decide which chapters are important for your role.

Part I—Enterprise Project Management Overview

Part I is an introduction to the software application and to the philosophy of approach to EPM. It is intended for all audiences to provide context for successfully planning and managing the EPM environment.

Chapter 1, "Enterprise Project Management—The Philosophy," describes enterprise thinking and what it takes to be successful with deployment of a software tool. The tool is not a silver bullet that will solve all problems regarding people, process, and environment.

Chapter 2, "Using Microsoft Office Project 2003 As an Enterprise Project Management Solution," is an overview of the major features of the EPM tool and how these features are integrated within the tool.

Chapter 3, "Knowing Product Limits and Overcoming Them," addresses the limitations of the tool. Although feature-rich, the tool does have limits and will not fit all organizations with the "out-of-the-box" functionality. Chapter 3 addresses these limits and provides an overview of other tools available to meet specific needs and custom approaches to solving specific problems.

Part II—Planning Your Enterprise Project Management Implementation

Chapter 4, "Planning the Organizational Processes," helps the reader approach the implementation of this tool realistically.

Chapter 5, "Understanding Project Server Architecture," provides the high-level view of the software components, the solution architecture, and considerations for scalability and security.

Chapter 6, "Designing the Enterprise Project Management Solution Architecture Details," provides an in-depth look at design requirements that need to be considered when planning an EPM implementation.

Part III—Implementing Microsoft Office Project Server 2003

Chapter 7, "Enterprise Project Management System Deployment Considerations," focuses on the key components of the software that will be configured to match the business processes and standards of the organization. Because the software is highly configurable, it is important for the team to spend planning time making sure that the configuration decisions are appropriate to the organization's maturity and its capacity to manage change.

Chapter 8, "Establishing Security Model Settings," addresses the security options and capabilities of the software. This important chapter helps the reader create a security model that is both robust and flexible so that it does not require a great deal of administrative time to maintain.

Chapter 9, "Enterprise Global Codes," describes the core configuration elements of the software. Configuration models vary from organization to organization based on the complexity of the setup and the needs of the business. This chapter discusses the options available for the user.

Chapter 10, "Creating Project Web Access Project and Resource Views," explains how an organization can set up views of the data that will meet the needs of different users of the system. The data within the system can be depicted in an almost limitless variety of views.

Chapter 11, "Completing the Implementation and Configuration," describes the final components that need to be considered when developing a robust solution for the organization. It includes discussions of calendar uses, time reporting methods, and administration projects.

Part IV—Validating the Microsoft Office Project Server 2003 Implementation

Chapter 12, "Microsoft Office Project Server 2003 Validation," stresses the importance of performing thorough testing of all the system components and configuration to ensure that the system produces the expected results. Special attention must be paid to the roles and permissions, the security model, and the business and operational processes that surround this software.

Chapter 13, "Troubleshooting Business Process Implementation in the Application," provides a guide to common problems and their potential causes.

Part V—Using Microsoft Office Project Web Access 2003

Chapter 14, "Project Web Access Collaboration," discusses the capabilities of the system from a user perspective and provides insight into how the Project Web Access (PWA) interface can be used to improve the way in which the organization gets its work done.

Chapter 15, "Time Tracking in Project Web Access," describes the capabilities provided in the system and the various methods that can be used to measure project progress. The chapter includes information regarding entry and approval of project progress.

Chapter 16, "Using Project and Resource Centers," helps users understand how to use the software to manage their project and resource data.

Chapter 17, "Portfolio Management Using Portfolio Analyzer and Portfolio Modeler," helps users understand how to manipulate the data in the system to help them make business decisions and determine the real-time status of projects and portfolios of project or resource data.

Chapter 18, "Risks, Issues, and Documents Using Windows SharePoint Services (WSS)," describes the capabilities of the system to help the project teams with day-to-day management of their projects and project artifacts.

Chapter 19, "Using the Project Web Access Admin Menu Tab," describes the administrative capabilities managed via PWA. Although some portions of the software are administered via Microsoft Office Project Professional 2003, many of them can be administered via PWA.

Part VI—Using Microsoft Office Project Professional 2003 Enterprise Features

Chapter 20, "Building Custom Enterprise Configuration," provides information regarding the enterprise features built into the desktop scheduling engine of this software. These features are controlled by the application administrator of the system. Additional topics in this section include publication and version features.

Chapter 21, "Building Project Team and Resource Substitution," describes the resource management features of the desktop software that help the project manager build and manage the project team.

Chapter 22, "Project Team Collaboration," provides insight regarding the project team collaboration features that the tool provides for risk management, issue management, project progress tracking, and document management.

Part VII—Enterprise Project Management Integration with Microsoft Office Applications

Chapter 23, "Project Web Access and Project Professional Integration with Office," describes the features of the software that allow integration between this software and other Microsoft Office software, such as Outlook, Excel, and Visio.

Chapter 24, "Project Workspace Integration with Office," describes how the software is used to enhance team communication via web discussions and document sharing.

Part VIII—Server Maintenance and Configuration Management

Chapter 25, "Server Maintenance and Configuration Management," provides a technical description of the server components and the typical maintenance activities that should be set up for proper management of the servers and the data they contain.

Chapter 26, "Capacity Planning," provides information on how to plan for and monitor growth of the system as usage of the software expands through the organization. It addresses different methods of system management as well as ongoing support requirements.

Part IX—Industry Configuration Examples

Chapter 27, "Industry Examples for Microsoft Office Project 2003 Configuration," was written to provide the user with a variety of examples of how we have seen the system configured for different industry verticals and applications. It is not meant to be a complete picture of all possible configurations but rather to serve as a set of possibilities.

Part X—Customizing Microsoft Office Project Server 2003

Chapter 28, "Enterprise Project Management Customization," provides some insight into methods and approaches to customization when the organization decides that it needs additional capabilities not available from the basic system.

Chapter 29, "Extending Enterprise Project Management Through Customization Overview," explains the application programming interface (also known as Project Data Services or PDS) and also provides information regarding other common customization requests such as integration with SharePoint Portal Services and extension of the OLAP cube.

Who Should Read This Book

This book is intended to be a comprehensive guide to the implementation and use of Microsoft Office Project Server 2003. As such, portions of this book will be of more interest to one set of users than another. The following information should help readers determine which parts are most applicable to their needs.

Business Managers and Leaders

Leadership within the organization should pay special attention to Part I, Chapter 4 from Part II, and Part V. These components will help you understand how this product can be used to help your organization and will also help you understand the features that will be of most direct benefit to you. They will help you to sponsor and plan a successful deployment of the software and enable you to understand the evolutionary aspects of creating and refining the data within the system. The software is intended to support good project and portfolio management processes, and it will not be effective if effective processes are not in place.

Project and Resource Managers

This book is also intended to provide essential guidance and instruction for project and resource managers. The people in these positions play key roles in the success of the implementation and ongoing operation of Microsoft Project Server 2003. If performing one of these roles, you need to familiarize yourself with the capabilities of the system. It is important that you can perform your role effectively within the system. Also, given the enterprise focus and collaborative nature of the system, it is critical that you understand how to perform these roles in relation to the other roles being performed in the system.

There is also content in the book especially targeted and useful to those performing a resource manager role. Especially in matrix organizations, this role needs to be performed well to effectively plan, manage, and deliver projects using Microsoft Project Server 2003. Resource management can ultimately determine whether a project gets delivered as planned. To that end, the resource manager's knowledge of the features of the system, and how to best interact with the project manager, project team members, and other project participants is critical.

Project managers and resource managers represent two of the most important roles in both successfully delivering projects and in effectively managing them using Microsoft Project Server 2003. The material contained in this book provides guidance and key insights into enhancing and maximizing effectiveness and increasing the likelihood of a successful outcome in these areas. Project and resource managers provide the key planning, scheduling, and resource data that are the foundational details for all the information in Microsoft Office Project Server 2003. They also manage, and keep current, all of this detail during the operational life cycle of a project.

Part I, Chapter 4 from Part II, Part V, Part VI, and Part VII will be the most useful to project and resource managers.

Project Server Administrators

Because the application administration capabilities of this product are extensive, Project Server administrators will find most parts of this book useful. They need to be familiar with the administrative capabilities but also will find that they are better able to deal with the end users of the tool if they understand the various user roles and how they interact with the software. Even the parts focused on customization will help administrators understand the product limitations.

Technologists and Implementers

Technologists and implementers bring a new and exciting role to Project Server 2003 (EPM). They do more than install, enhance, configure, and maintain the system components; they aid in the definition of the Enterprise Project Management solution of an organization.

Implementers are the Project Server experts who supply in-depth knowledge of configuration and technology. The best implementers understand the discipline of project management and how it interacts with business processes. Technologists' responsibilities range from development of the system architecture to development of software and web interfaces and integration with or management of the databases. Each of these roles will find useful material throughout the book.

Special Features of This Book

Included with this book is a CD that contains all the written content of the book plus several additional features that we hope you will find useful. The additional materials are a trial version of QuantumPM's Schedule Auditor software, EPK Suite software that provides some great solutions for specific areas of portfolio management, EPM Workshop webcasts that will get you familiar with different materials available, and technical scripts that complement some of the more technical chapters of the book.

Terms Included in This Book

Microsoft Office Project Server 2003, *Microsoft Office Project Professional 2003*, and *Microsoft Office Project Web Access 2003* are the official product names for the EPM solution. Although these names are used to describe the product throughout this book, you will also see the products referenced by shortened versions of their names. The server product is generally referenced simply as Project Server, or Server, the desktop tool often is referred to as Project Professional, and the web interface is typically abbreviated as PWA.

Enterprise Project Management (EPM) is another name that Microsoft has chosen to describe the entire set of products in the software package.

> **NOTE**
>
> For a detailed explanation of EPM philosophy and EPM tools, see Chapters 1 and 2.

EPM is also used in many contexts to mean *Enterprise Portfolio Management* and *Enterprise Program Management*. Unfortunately, the terms are often used interchangeably, and this causes considerable confusion and long, philosophical arguments about the "correct" use of the terms. For purposes of this book, the authors have chosen to stay with the definition used by Microsoft for its product. We do, however, offer the following definitions for the terms *project*, *program*, and *portfolio* in the hope that these definitions will assist the reader in understanding the intent of the configuration options found throughout the book.

- **Project**—According to Harold Kerzner, in *Project Management: A Systems Approach to Planning, Scheduling, and Controlling*, a *project* is a series of activities that have a specific objective, defined start/end dates, and funding limits, and that consume resources. Using this definition, it is easy to see how most of an organization's resources (outside a regular operational context) are focused toward project work. Microsoft's EPM product, however, has also enabled organizations to "projectize" operational work as administrative projects so that true resource utilization is possible.

> **NOTE**
>
> For a detailed explanation of administrative projects, see Chapter 11.

- **Program**—There are many definitions and uses of this term in the project management context. The differences vary by organization and individual. There are so many definitions that it is difficult to provide a definition. For purposes of this context, however, a *program* is a grouping of projects related to each other in some manner. The relationship may be organizational or functional, or it may refer to a group of projects that have been subdivided for ease of execution. Any and all of these relationships can be managed and depicted with the EPM software.

- **Portfolio**—Portfolio management moves project and program management to the enterprise level. The concept has received a great deal of attention in recent years from many organizations including software developers and standards bodies. The authors of this book define portfolio management as the ongoing and proactive planning, execution, and control of the *future* of an enterprise. It is evolutionary and is based on a continuous improvement model. In the context of the EPM tool, portfolio management enables the organization to oversee and manage its projects, programs, and operational activities.

PART I

Enterprise Project Management Overview

IN THIS PART

CHAPTER 1   Enterprise Project Management—
The Philosophy   11

CHAPTER 2   Using Microsoft Office Project 2003 As an
Enterprise Project Management Solution   27

CHAPTER 3   Knowing Product Limits and
Overcoming Them   39

Enterprise Project Management—The Philosophy

IN THIS CHAPTER

- Defining Enterprise Project Management

- Understanding the EPM Impacts on Your Organization

- Best Practices

As mentioned in the Introduction, the primary purpose of this book is to provide knowledge to the reader of the capabilities of Microsoft Office Project Server 2003, a robust Enterprise Project Management (EPM) software application. Although the vast majority of this book focuses on the features and capabilities of the software, this chapter focuses on the organization, environment, and high-level processes surrounding the software. The goal of this chapter is to highlight key planning requirements and other critical success factors to EPM software deployment and most importantly, for successful use of this powerful tool. These items are not related to the hardware, software, or networking environments. They are related to the people and the process side of the equation.

Unlike many enterprise applications, successful adoption and use of this software is highly dependent on successful management of the domain knowledge and the processes used by the organization to manage its work. Implementing an EPM solution requires project management thinking. This is a complex project, and it should be planned and executed using good project management techniques and supported by strong executive leadership.

The Standish Group, a leading analyst group for the IT sector, has been performing research with major corporations for the past nine years on the success or failure record of IT projects. They published their initial results, which were very poor, in 1994 in the "Chaos Report." In their most recently released report, things have improved. Schedule overruns were significantly lower in 2000 than they had been in 1994 (down from 222% to 63%). Cost overruns are also down by similar margins. The Standish Group attributes these changes to a variety of things, including better tools, higher skill levels, and better management processes. Although this is good news, they also point out that there is still a lot of room for improvement. Many projects still fail to meet expectations, and the Standish Group attributes these failures to "lack of skilled project management and executive support."

The good news is that improvements in tools, skills, and processes are making a difference. The bad news is that most of the failures are linked to the softer skills of executive and project management leadership. The material in this chapter is provided to help put the implementation of EPM software in context of the overall goals of the organization.

Defining Enterprise Project Management

Enterprise Project Management (EPM) is more than just technology; it is a way of doing business, and it affects organizational structure and behavior. Although EPM is a relatively new discipline, many organizations around the world have adopted EPM best practices. In 2004, the Project Management Institute (PMI) released a new standard called the Organizational Project Management Maturity Model (OPM3). OPM3 is defined as "the consistent application of knowledge, skills, tools, and techniques to organization and project activities to achieve the aims of an organization through projects."

The OPM3 standard defines best practices for project, program, and portfolio management at an organizational level. Tools such as Project Server 2003 provide great benefits to organizations attempting to improve their project management maturity in many ways. These tools provide an easier method to manage and share data, enforce standard methods and procedures, collaborate, and provide visibility to the organization. As shown in Figure 1.1, it is the combination of people, business process, organization, and tools that provide a total EPM solution.

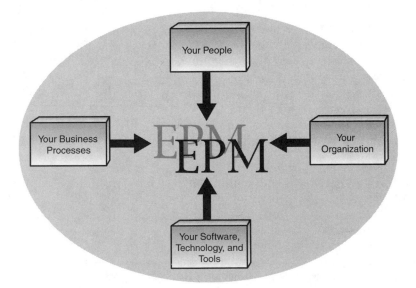

FIGURE 1.1   EPM as a total solution.

To ensure success with your EPM solution, you must understand the impact of the software within the organization and must plan for changes to all four of these components.

> **NOTE**
>
> You can find details about OPM3 by visiting the PMI website at http://pmi.org.

Because this book focuses on an EPM tool and not on process or people, the discussion of organizational project management maturity is discussed lightly. However, it is critically important that your organization understand the importance of project management maturity in overall success. Enterprise thinking should guide your decisions on how much of the capabilities of the software your organization can embrace at any point in time. An evolutionary approach provides the best opportunity for success. Because of their experience with the project management domain and software in a variety of industries and applications, you should look to industry resources and Microsoft Project Partners for assistance when you begin this effort.

Successful implementations of EPM require organizations to look not just at software features and integration but also at the impact of managing projects across the organization.

- What are the best ways to run projects across your organization? Are projects run consistently?

- Are they measured consistently?

- How are projects contrasted against each other, and is this the best way to do it?

- What processes and best practices do you have in place to support projects?

A lack of project management best practices, a lack of resources, and a lack of portfolio management review processes are the root causes of many problems, which compounded lead to aspects of project failures. If you are preparing for an EPM implementation, take a close look at your people, processes, and tools.

There is no one-size-fits-all-instant-cookie-cutter process. A process is a guide or a roadmap. A successful implementation and adoption of EPM across your organization will encompass people and processes. Take an extensive look at your processes:

- Do you have processes in place?

- If so, how long have they been in place? Are they outdated?

- Do your processes map to current roles and workflow?

- How do tools impact your process?

- Are some of your processes across multiple software applications?

- Do the processes result in desirable outcomes?

Re-evaluating and putting good processes in place is key to a successful EPM solution and required enterprise thinking.

Think Enterprise

Enterprise thinking allows an organization to look at its mix of projects and operational work as a portfolio that can and should be managed as a whole. This type of approach cannot happen all at once, however, so an evolutionary approach makes the most sense because it allows an organization to gain success and a return on their investment much earlier than an all or nothing approach can do. The organization should determine what problems it needs to solve most urgently and focus on those. The areas causing the most pain should be evident fairly quickly. The following categories of questions are typical problem areas in many organizations:

- **Resource contention**—Are resources working on too many projects at the same time? Do you know how much work is actually forecast for the next three months? Six months? Do you have too few (or too many) people in certain skill areas?

- **Project quality**—How do you know when a project is in trouble? Are projects typically delivered late or over budget? Do the projects meet the customer expectations? Are project problems caused by lack of project management skills, problems with scope management, resources, or other items?

- **Key projects continually slip because of maintenance requirements**—How much of the work in your organization is planned rather than reactive? How is the portfolio of work divided? What percentage of resource effort is focused on the highest priorities of the organization?

Microsoft has found that the customers who are most successful in deploying its software have done so in an evolutionary manner matched to the maturity level of the organization. Microsoft has developed a series of three workshops focused on enterprise thinking for project management. The three workshops, Envisioning, Planning, and Implementation, were developed to help customers understand the core capabilities of the Project Server 2003 software and its potential benefits in their organizations and to understand the organizational drivers related to EPM so that they can implement the software and associated processes effectively. Microsoft Project Partners deliver these workshops in an iterative manner to match the maturity of the organizations and their capacity to absorb change.

Manage the Organizational Change

The main failure point for an EPM implementation has little to do with the correct installation of the software and a great deal to do with getting the humans in an organization to change the way they work. This EPM solution is going to require that people do things differently than they do today. The change may be as simple as using a newer version of Microsoft Project. It may be as complicated as migrating from a different project management solution or introducing the use of a project management tool for the first time. Either way, the personnel in your organization will be required to change the way they work. This may cause confusion and stress. Understanding and utilizing an organizational change methodology will make your implementation go more smoothly. The following brief look at organizational change is intended to be an appetizer to the full course of what you should plan for your EPM deployment.

> **NOTE**
>
> We gratefully acknowledge Dr. William Casey and Executive Leadership Group, Inc., for their permission in the use of this material. Learn more about this Organizational Change Framework at www.executiveleadershipgroup.com.

The Framework

The Framework of Organizational Change contains a five-phased approach to planning, executing, and sustaining the changes that you will require your organization to make as depicted in Figure 1.2. The diagram depicts two major components of organizational change: the hard change (the project) and the soft change (the change process).

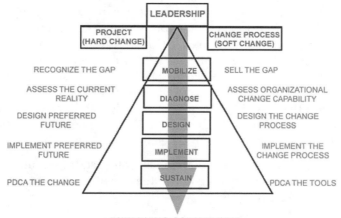

FIGURE 1.2   Organizational change model.

The left side of the diagram shows the hard change, or the tangible activities that can be managed in a project schedule. For an EPM implementation, this side of the framework represents the actual EPM implementation project plan that you put into place to deploy your EPM solution. It contains activities such as acquiring software, acquiring hardware, installing Project Server 2003, and so on. The left side is called the hard change because it is tangible and can be easily represented with tasks on the schedule for your EPM implementation.

The right side of the diagram is the change process, or the soft change. It is focused on activities such as documenting why you are making the change, communicating on a regular basis to the personnel who will be using the system, creating buy-in, gauging where people are in the process, and so on. The term *soft change* is used because the work is much more difficult to represent in a schedule. The activities involved here are more subtle. They influence the way the organization will think about the change as well as how fast they will adopt the EPM solution.

Notice that leadership is depicted in the middle of Figure 1.2. Both sides of the change model require leadership from the organization as well as leadership from the EPM project manager to make both the implementation and the adoption of the system work properly.

Using this framework you will plan both sides of the EPM solution implementation—both the hard changes and the soft changes. The next sections discuss the types of activities performed in each of the five phases of the Framework of Organizational Change. In each of the five phases you have work to do for both the hard and the soft changes.

The Mobilize Phase

The Mobilize phase is all about recognizing the need for change and mobilizing the rest of the organization to deal with it. In this phase the EPM project manager works with the leadership team to understand why the organization has decided to implement an EPM solution. You need to understand the two different spectrums of why this change is being addressed. You need to understand both the compelling threat and the compelling vision. The *compelling threat* describes what you are trying to eliminate from your organization. It may include problems such as the inability to know what projects are being worked on, where your project resources are at any given time, and so on. The *compelling vision* is the future desired state that the leadership sees when the EPM solution is implemented— project data at your fingertips, resources working on the right projects for the organization, projects completing as predicted, and so on. You want both ends of the spectrum because different people are motivated by different things.

After the compelling threat and vision are defined, you need to communicate the vision and the threat to the organization. Everyone in the organization needs to realize that change is needed and wanted and why.

Other activities performed in the Mobilize phase are

- Hard change—Officially initiating the project

- Soft change—Developing the change strategy that will be used throughout the rest of the project

The Diagnose Phase

After the change is recognized, you must diagnose the current reality to understand the shortfalls that need to be addressed. Ask yourself, "Does the organization have the capability to change?" Like a doctor, you will diagnose the health of the organization and determine what the organization must change to successfully implement a major change such as this.

The organizational change methodology uses the following set of transformational tools to determine the diagnosis. A sample set of the information that needs to be determined with each tool is included.

- **Measurement**—What measurements and metrics exist that will either help or hinder the change? Does the organization have existing metrics? How good is the organization at collecting data? How will you tell whether the new solution has been adopted?

- **Organizational structure**—What organizational structure and processes exist that either help or hinder the change? Is there an executive accountable for this EPM implementation project? Is the organizational design aligned to support this goal?

- **Communication**—What are the typical existing methods of communication that either help or hinder the change? What communication vehicles are currently used? Do these communication vehicles work? Do the employees trust what they hear?

- **Accountability structures**—What are the activities that managers use that produce accountability? Do managers discuss expectations with their subordinates? How skilled are the managers at this dialog? Are consequences based on performance?

- **Rewards and recognition**—What formal and informal rewards and recognition programs are in effect that will either help or hinder the change? What does it take to get promoted in this organization? What rewards can be provided? Are people recognized for good performance? Are rewards linked to performance?

- **Involvement**—What employee participation programs exist that will either help or hinder the change? Which groups will experience the greatest impact from the change? What is the past experience with employee involvement? How skilled is the organization at employee involvement?

- **Education and training**—What skill deficits will be experienced because of the change? What educational and training programs exist that will either help or hinder the change? Will there be a delay between training and the use of the new skills? What other tools or job aids exist or need to be created? Is there a budget for training?

- **Resourcing**—What resources will be available to staff the change? Do you have the capability to recruit and hire? How long does it take to acquire a resource? Are the current resources capable of doing the required work?

These tools are used to determine the areas that are properly set up as well as those in which the organization needs to change to be successful.

When your diagnosis is complete you perform other activities in the Diagnose phase:

- **Soft change**—Document your findings and update your change strategy based on your findings.

- **Hard change**—Develop the scope statement and build your requirements for the EPM implementation.

The Design Phase

You now know what shortfalls need to be addressed based on your findings from the Diagnosis phase. It is now time to design your change process, as well as the project:

- **Soft change**—Design a series of tasks based on your findings in the Diagnosis phase that will help the adoption of the EPM solution.

- **Hard change**—Develop the rest of the planning elements for your project including the project schedule and project plan. Include the soft change tasks in the schedule where appropriate.

The Implement Phase

During the Implement phase you now implement your carefully planned change program and your project:

- **Soft change**—You now complete the tasks that you outlined in the Design phase while continually taking a poll of what the personnel in the department are thinking about the change and how they will work with the EPM solution.

- **Hard change**—Here is where you implement the EPM solution using the steps, hints, and tips outlined in this book.

The Sustain Phase

After you complete your initial implementation of the EPM solution, you need to monitor what has been accomplished to make sure that the system is consistently used the way you planned. Stability is achieved by continual correction of any imbalances that you find. During the Sustain phase, the organization should establish a continual process improvement cycle to ensure the long-term quality of the solution. The acronym, PDCA, popularized by W. Edwards Deming in his Quality Control teachings, stands for the four components of the cycle: Plan, Do, Check, Act. As in each of the earlier phases, work is required on both the hard and the soft changes:

- **Soft change**—Monitor the usage of the system and watch for people bypassing it or perhaps doing things the way they used to. Continue utilizing the transformational tools to sustain the change.

- **Hard change**—You have completed the installation of Microsoft Project 2003. Now is the time to review your lessons learned from the project.

Emphasize Process over Technology

Successfully applying an EPM approach requires that both the business process framework, which supports enterprise thinking, and the technology infrastructure, which enables these business processes, be fully analyzed and understood prior to implementation. A piecemeal or ill-considered approach to either (or both) does not serve the needs of the organization and is likely to lead to an unsatisfactory outcome.

As the subsequent introduction to the six pillars of EPM further illustrates, the business processes and the technologies that enable them are, to an extent, interdependent. You must analyze and understand how the business manages projects and communicates performance to determine how the various technologies that constitute the EPM will be optimally implemented to support these processes, and, in turn, you must understand what the EPM technologies can do for your organization to take advantage of its technical capabilities. Although it is true that an understanding of the available EPM technologies can lead to epiphanies about underlying business processes, keep in mind that the EPM technology is not a driver—it is an enabler. An EPM tool exists to enable the business processes, not drive them.

This book discusses both the EPM technology and business processes. It is the considered, intelligent application of both EPM technologies and enterprise thinking that leads to success in managing projects. The business processes that relate to the features within the EPM toolset are defined in the following section.

Align with the Six Pillars of EPM

Your EPM planning activities require technical changes to your hardware and software in addition to nontechnical business process changes across your organization. This section provides an introduction on how to decompose the EPM implementation into manageable segments that Microsoft calls the *six pillars of EPM*.

Each of the six pillars of EPM is a convenient description that reminds you of how business processes relate directly to technology and operation of Project Server 2003. Affected technology includes Project Web Access (PWA), Microsoft Project Professional, Microsoft Outlook, and so on. Your EPM implementation should address each of the six pillars, briefly described in the following sections.

Pillar 1—Project Management

Every EPM implementation includes the business processes and disciplines related to project management. Project Server 2003 technology stores project schedule data in a centralized SQL Server database so that these schedules can be viewed within the PWA Projects tab. The PWA Projects tab includes several functions directly related to business processes needed to define and manage individual project schedules within the context of program portfolios. Your project management business processes must address activities such as initiate, plan, execute, audit, and close projects. People throughout your organization can then effectively use PWA and Microsoft Project technology.

Pillar 2—Resource Management

You need to decide whether the EPM implementation will include resource management business processes. Project Server 2003 enables all your resources to be stored within the Enterprise Global Resource Pool so that every project schedule can use those resources within task assignments. The PWA Resource tab allows resource managers and project managers to examine information about resources and work-loading assignments across all projects stored within the Project Server 2003 database. Your business practices are critical and have a direct relationship to the use of PWA and Project Professional.

Pillar 3—Collaboration Management

Every organization uses communication strategies to share information, report status, coordinate project teams, and so on. Project Server 2003 includes several features to help project teams communicate important information among team members and throughout the organization. PWA and Microsoft Project include functions such as tasks, updates, status reports, and alerts to automatically send email and alert messages when certain events occur. Your business processes must also provide organizational guidance about the roles people have and how each person is responsible to use electronic collaboration technology.

Pillar 4—Artifact Management

Every project produces a variety of important artifacts that are part of overall project deliverables. Project Server 2003 automatically creates document storage repositories as project managers use Microsoft Project to publish schedules to the database. PWA then provides a convenient set of functions such as documents, issues, and risks so that project teams can store and maintain artifacts associated with a project. Your business processes should provide guidance to people throughout the organization so that everyone knows how to find and manage project artifacts.

Pillar 5—Organizational Readiness

Project Server 2003 includes a sophisticated mix of technology to manage projects, resources, collaboration, and artifacts. People in your organization need a variety of skills to effectively use this technology throughout the life cycle of each project. Implementing EPM also has a significant impact on business processes as you move from "old" methods to changed techniques to manage projects. You need to assess the needs for initial training and postimplementation support. Everyone across the organization will need follow-up support, sometimes called *mentoring*. If your organization cannot use the EPM technology and business processes, your risk of failure is high.

Pillar 6—Operational Principles

The Project Server 2003 technology uses a complex mix of Microsoft technology that requires your operations support people to have special skills to install and maintain. Your PWA and Microsoft Project application administrators also play an important part in overall operations support as they set enterprise global codes and standards. You need to establish business requirements that create technology and applications management principles that address the business needs of the organization. These operational principles are then used to build technology and application training and procedures.

▶ **SEE** "Planning—Six Pillars of EPM," **PAGE 58**.

Understanding the EPM Impacts on Your Organization

What does enterprise project management mean to an organization? On any given day, organizations face decision points on how to best manage their business. It is a daily attempt to measure risk, weigh outcomes, balance the budget, meet deadlines, and measure return on investment. Whether your business functions are in terms of projects, initiatives, to-do lists, or objectives, there is a "body of work" that needs to be accomplished. How do you evaluate and weigh the decisions that cross your desk daily? The impacts on an organization are many and varied.

New Ways to Communicate

Organizations are living in a sea of information, both relevant and irrelevant, that comes at you in a variety of ways, at a rapid rate of speed. The lines of communication and collaboration are blurred. Although technology provides numerous communication options, when dealing with projects, employee productivity can quickly become tied to a paper process. Making sure that project team members, contractors, subcontractors, and so on have copies of materials related to the project can quickly become time consuming. Emailing project team members documents can also become cumbersome due to revisions and versioning. Making sure that information is available and current is also difficult due to iterations and keeping track of who has received what documents.

With the dawning of computers and multiple file formats the mantra was that we are moving to a "paperless environment." Is paper going away? Not necessarily, but the way in which we access and reference information is ever-changing. You may receive an email with an attached .pdf file, access a collaborative web page workspace, look up information via a search mechanism through a portal, or search past archives for keywords to find information or documents.

Running effective projects requires dynamic communication and increased agility. By nature, projects have iterations and cycles where information is updated or modified. Technology has opened the door to options now available to disseminate that information designed to enhance the way we work and collaborate.

EPM technology offers an alternative way to share and view information. Many technologies enable users to share, view, access, and store documents. EPM technology focuses on how project teams collaborate to access and share project documentation with executives, stakeholders, clients, team members, and partners. The following items are examples of how project data can now be shared:

- Instead of emailing a project schedule, the project schedule can now be viewed and updated through a web browser.

- You may view the project schedule without having the software application in which it was created loaded on your computer.

- All information relating to a project can now be posted on a connected website and can be secured and viewed through a web link.

- Project team members and stakeholders can now update information or see online versioning of documents.

- Project managers can get updated status and do reporting through semi-real-time reporting.

- Resources can be easily assigned to tasks as viewed through a web browser.

- Team members do not need to update the same data in multiple places.

- Teams located across different locations can view information without having to send it via an email.

A virtual workspace is now at your fingertips. Although, you may still opt to print a document, you don't have to.

Technology is a vast horizon. Every day we face challenges with new solutions, but the art of communication is still that—an art. Technology expands our options for communication but is not a replacement for communication and collaboration. In its purest form, collaboration is comprised of two or more people working together to achieve a common goal, or to create mutual value.

Communication is not a one-way street. Many people send an email and assume that because it was received, something is going to happen. For a variety of reasons, people tend to hide behind technology and do not effectively communicate. But if you look behind a successful project, you will find a project team and manager who have successfully figured out how to communicate and collaborate with each other, with project stakeholders, with executives, with partners, and with other contractors or vendors. They have also figured out how to move relevant information effectively across the team.

New Opportunities

EPM encompasses how work is defined, who is identified to do the work, how work is managed, when work is to be done, how work is progressing, and what issues or possibilities are on the horizon. EPM impacts organizations through processes, people (resources), tools, and work (projects). All these elements working together create an organizational solution.

When an EPM solution is implemented, you see the following types of benefits:

- Dispersed or local teams of people working together on projects are now able to view project data, input project data, and contribute to project knowledge and discussions via a web browser. This enables streamlined communication and creates an environment that facilitates large amounts of data.

- Business leaders can set strategic company direction and ensure the alignment of projects with that strategy. A portfolio of projects can be analyzed and viewed as a composite or by an individual project to see progression of work, risk, and budget. You can evaluate your organization's mix of projects and risks.

- A Project Management Office (PMO) can more easily drive standardization and best practices in how projects are run, enabling consistent evaluation of projects. The PMO can now compare apples to apples, and oranges to oranges.

Microsoft has stated that "companies are transforming from environments with inconsistent project management practices and tools to managing a portfolio of project with integrated, organization-wide tools. Industry forecasts consistently show growing demand for enterprise project management applications as companies recognize the importance of project management to reduce costs, improve processes, and maintain their competitive advantage. With increased economic and competitive pressures...a range of organizations are now adopting EPM to gain process and collaborative efficiencies throughout their organizations." (Microsoft, Microsoft Office Project—Enterprise Project Management Solution, "Microsoft Leadership in Enterprise Project Management, Microsoft Office EPM Solution Customer Research Report," November, 2003.)

Leadership Team Capabilities

As business leaders, you need to have a view of the work going on within your organization and how that work is accomplished across a variety of levels. An EPM solution helps business leaders make informed decisions for their organizations. The data available can help them do the following:

- Understand the costs of project success or failure.

- Obtain a realistic view of time to market and completion of projects.

- Align the portfolio of projects with corporate strategy.

- Discontinue projects that are of high risk or are out of alignment with the corporate strategy.

- Prioritize and manage projects.

- Set strategic direction.

- Decrease time to market for products.

- Build in the voice of the customer.

EPM can assist Leadership Teams in drawing focus through dashboard views, reports, and metrics, enabling you to respond to changes in business direction. According to "New Problems, New Solutions: Making Portfolio Management More Effective" (published in Research Technology Management Volume 43, Number 2, Cooper, Edgett, and Kleinschmidt, 2000), some of the questions addressed by EPM through project and portfolio management include the following:

- Are the projects aligned with business strategy?

- Is the portfolio of projects balanced?

- Does the organization have the right number of projects?

- Does the portfolio contain projects with high value?

- Does project spending reflect the business's strategy?

- Are resources balanced effectively?

- Are projects prioritized appropriately?

- Do I have the needed information to decide when it is time to cancel a project?

The ability to be agile in the day-to-day work environment and improve business performance is addressed through EPM. Consistent business metrics and the ability to align work with strategic priorities is a step forward in understanding and maximizing the value to your business.

Project Manager and Project Team Interaction

The project manager and the project team need the ability to interact with each other, their stakeholders, and their clients. Some of the benefits for this group include

- Improved communications both locally and for geographically dispersed locations
- Easier project coordination, collaboration, and execution
- Centralized and version-controlled document management
- Easier methods to share information and coordinate effort
- Improved productivity
- Improved methods to update information

A project team that is functioning smoothly has mastered effective ways to communicate and to facilitate information sharing. EPM can make their work that much easier.

Focus on Project Management Skills

Organizations look at the role of project manager in different ways. In general, a project manager is responsible for managing the overall delivery of a project. The primary role of the project manager is to guide the project team to successful delivery of a project based on quality, time, budget, and scope. This includes communicating the project business objectives and having a clear vision of how to achieve those objectives. Project managers must resolve conflict among the differing objectives and individuals across their projects. They also communicate key information to sponsors and stakeholders regarding the project.

Project managers build schedules and typically use a tool such as Microsoft Project to do so. With an EPM tool, there are many more functions that a project manager can perform in an automated fashion using the tools. The tool itself is a framework. Within that framework, it is possible to standardize processes and promote project best practices regarding the use of the tool and the process of project management. The tool can be used to enhance project communication and coordination, but it is not a replacement for a strong project manager. When projects fail, it is almost never the fault of a project management tool. The reasons are many and varied but directly dependent on the skills of the individual project manager.

Project management is more than Gantt charts, team coordination, and status reports. It is a disciplined approach to getting "work" done—completing projects that translate business strategies into results. Although an EPM tool can assist project managers, it cannot guarantee successful projects.

Project management is a recognized discipline that crosses industries from manufacturing to aerospace to retail, and numerous businesses from small to global in scale. People, organizations, and industries arrive at the role of project manager through different paths. If you've traveled down the path of accidental project manager, seek out resources and training to guide you.

Project management success is a balance across time, resources, results, and perceptions. It is a skilled project manager that orchestrates and guides a successful project.

Set Realistic Expectations for Your EPM Implementation

EPM is a dynamic decision process. As the saying goes, Rome wasn't built in a day. The same can be said for your organizational approach to EPM. It takes time to visualize, plan, and implement an EPM solution.

The Gartner Group has stated "through 2005, 40% of enterprise-level projects will be stalled at some point to address problems caused by team members providing duplicate skills, and team member roles being too vaguely defined. (Pat Phelan, Ned Fray, Gartner, Inc., "Avoiding Failure in Large IT Projects: New Risk and Project Management Imperatives," July 18, 2002.)

Giga, a wholly owned subsidiary of Forrester Research, Inc., expects to see an annual 15% per year increase in formal project management practices during the next five years. (Margo Visitacion, "Project Management Best Practices: Key Processes and Common Sense," January 2003.)

As these industry analysts have predicted, QuantumPM has seen a great deal of energy around the concept of EPM over the past several years. The interest intensified when Microsoft entered the EPM tool space in 2002 with its initial release of Project Server. For project management specialists such as QuantumPM, this attention was gratifying even though it was accompanied by unreasonable expectations that the software would eliminate all the pain that organizations were feeling in project management.

The organizations that have been most successful with their EPM deployments have had one important thing in common. All of them set reasonable goals based on their individual project management maturity levels and their ability to adapt to change. They formed the goals into an evolutionary set of plans, executed the plans, and established a sustainable continuous improvement process.

One of the most successful organizations began its journey at the lowest level of maturity. None of its work was managed via projects; the organization had no project managers on staff and had never used a scheduling tool. Its customers were angry about missed deadlines and runaway costs.

Three years later, this same organization has a clear picture of its entire portfolio of work. The organization meets its deadlines and has excellent communications set up with customers to manage any problems. The organization is confident enough in its plans and data to allow its customers to have direct access to view the projects.

It was not an easy journey for this organization, but it was realistic about what is possible and has worked tirelessly to reach its goals.

The starting point for organizations will vary, but the formula for success is the same for all. Understand and plan for incremental successes. Plan and run your EPM implementation as a project using project management processes and best practices. Project management maturity is developed over time. Take a realistic look at your organization, assess where your organization is today, and plan the roadmap for your outcome.

Best Practices

At the end of each chapter in this book, the authors present key ideas that they believe are most important and pertinent to the topics in the chapter. This section outlines the best practices recommended for the EPM philosophy considerations:

- Establish and run the EPM implementation as a project. An EPM implementation is a complex project and must be run as such. Designate a strong project manager and make sure that your team has the industry expertise, in both the project management domain and in the Microsoft software, to accomplish the project.

- Use an evolutionary approach. Your EPM implementation will probably roll out in phases, initially using simple strategies that become more complex as your EPM business processes and technology mature. Develop an overall project plan that describes each rollout phase and which parts of the technology will be used within those phases. This project plan should include a phased rollout schedule, communications plan, EPM team definition, scope statement, and audience for periodic broadcasts to the EPM community. This strategy minimizes uncertainty, anxiety, and frustration that may develop throughout the organization as you plan, develop, and roll out your EPM implementation.

- Focus on the changes to the people, process, and organization. Your decisions and approach to this large organizational change affect people, processes, and business structure. Pay as much attention to the organizational environment as you do to the technical environment.

- Strive for excellence in project management skills. No software tool guarantees success. The domain of project management is complex and requires highly skilled individuals. Make sure that the people who perform this role are capable and well trained.

- Set realistic expectations. Your EPM implementation will take time. Plan it in an evolutionary manner so that immediate gains are possible. Do not expect full capability to occur immediately.

CHAPTER 2

Using Microsoft Office Project 2003 As an Enterprise Project Management Solution

IN THIS CHAPTER

- Major Features of Microsoft Project Web Access 2003
- Understanding the Features of Project Server 2003
- Best Practices

The Enterprise Project Management (EPM) solution from Microsoft builds on the strengths of Microsoft Project 98 and 2000. Whereas the first two were desktop applications, designed to fulfill the needs of project managers to plan and manage their projects, Project 2002 and subsequently Project 2003 raise the bar and provide the project management community with an enterprise solution. Microsoft Office Project 2003 now has three major components: Project Professional 2003, Project Web Access 2003, and Project Server 2003. Major features for each of these three components are discussed in this chapter.

Major Features of Microsoft Project Web Access 2003

The Microsoft Project 2003 solution is a role-based application suite. Almost any business role in the organization can be mapped in the system. Out of the box, Project 2003 defines seven default roles and permissions based on those roles. Under these conditions, some users will have access to Project Web Access (PWA) only, whereas other users may have access to Project Professional, as well. For instance, a project manager may access and change project schedule data in Project Professional, but a programmer who has been designated as a team member cannot. Your organization may choose to use all or some of the roles, define additional custom roles, and also define what security permissions these roles have when accessing or viewing enterprise project data.

The general interface to PWA and Project Professional reflects the style of other Office applications, such as Word, Excel, or Visio. This makes Project 2003 more intuitive and easier for people to learn and use.

Project Professional gives users the flexibility to use the application for development of nonenterprise project schedules, as well as development of project schedules that will be part of the organizationwide repository of projects. Project Professional allows you to perform the following tasks:

- Use predefined enterprise templates to build schedules, such as all new project schedules are conforming to enterprise project management methodology.

- Include methodology tasks into the schedules you build to accurately reflect the type of project you are creating.

- Assign resources to project tasks based on their skills and monitor their work progress on those tasks.

- Baseline the schedule and keep it updated. Project 2003 allows you to save up to 10 versions of the baseline, providing you with the ability to compare different options or to track the evolution of the project plan from one phase to another.

- Save updates into the schedule, enabling project managers to update the progress of the tasks with values sent by team members assigned directly from PWA.

- Use various viewing and reporting tools in Project Professional. All the reporting capabilities and features included in previous versions are preserved and enhanced.

- Create a Work Breakdown Structure (WBS) chart using Visio. This enhances the view that project managers have over the overall scope of the projects. This is a simple and efficient way to make sure that no task in the WBS is missed.

Naturally, Project Professional offers backward compatibility, allowing users to read .mpp files from previous versions and formats including Microsoft Project 98, Microsoft Project 2000, or Microsoft Access database files.

NOTE

It is worth mentioning that the SQL database structure has been changed to provide for better scalability and enhanced storage to support new features.

Project Professional comes with an updated and improved access point for Help and training. You can now search for topics either locally, on your machine, or on the Web.

Project Professional now offers the option for using the Project Guide, which provides a step-by-step process for creating schedules, managing resources, tracking, and reporting on projects. An important feature is that this Project Guide can be easily customized to reflect the project management methodology for use in your organization.

Scheduling with Microsoft Project Professional

Project Professional is the tool that project managers will use to do most of the detailed work on their projects such as planning new tasks, tracking status, and assigning new resources. As a project manager, you will be entering the scheduling information in Project Professional and keeping it updated.

It is important to remember that one of your duties as a project manager is to ensure accuracy and integrity of the schedule data. You can then review the project-related data from different perspectives using available reports. Although PWA enables the communication between project managers and team members, Project Professional is the application used for project schedule development, update, baseline, and review.

As a general recommendation, only portfolio and project managers should have Project Professional installed on their desktops.

Project Professional helps users integrate their project schedules with specific methodologies for use in each organization. Usually, developing a project schedule is an iterative process, especially until the project manager sets the baseline.

With the introduction of the Project Guide, Project Professional can help you with initial steps to create a schedule:

- **Scope definition**—Defining what you are trying to do, establishing the measures of success and the definition of "done." Especially important at this stage of planning is to clearly identify the scope of the project and to make sure that all stakeholders agree on it. Associating notes and documents with tasks in Project Professional can help the project team to better understand the requirements of the job and clearly define what constitutes a 100% completion of the task.

- **Project schedule development**—Using enterprise templates, project managers can build project schedules in accordance with the methodology employed by each organization. Inclusion of methodology into the schedules you build accurately reflects the type of project you are creating. Project Professional supports various types of enterprise templates as well as local templates. This way, project managers have the flexibility to choose from the templates that make the most sense for their project.

- **Creation of a network diagram**—With the help of Project Professional you can now easily build a network diagram and identify the main pieces of your project and how they relate to each other. Using Project Professional integration with Visio you can also easily determine your WBS.

- **Resource assignment**—Essential to any project schedule is the assignment of resources to tasks. The Project Professional solution uses the Enterprise Resource Pool, which stores all generic and individual resources available to project managers in the organization. This way, project managers do not need to maintain a local Resource Sheet anymore.

▶ **SEE** "Building Project Team and Resource Substitution," **PAGE 563**.

- **Estimate the effort**—After the scope of the project is correctly identified, you need to determine how long each task will take and how much it will cost. Project Professional allows project and resource managers to set the duration, units, and work amount required for each task from each resource to complete the task.

- **Schedule assessment**—In the planning stage of a project, you may need to assess the schedule and modify it a few times to satisfy as many constraints as possible. Project Professional's scheduling assessment tools make this task much easier to perform.

- **Baseline the project schedule**—When the initial schedule is stable, it should be baselined. Project Professional creates a record of the planned tasks, dates, and effort. It also has the capability of storing up to 10 different versions of the baseline. This is particularly important to anyone in the project management community who needs to consider all the trade-offs of different options available.

After a project is defined and scheduled, you must track your progress to know how the project is doing and make decisions regarding the execution of the project. Tracking is an iterative process. You constantly track progress, make decisions based on the actual data, and update the schedule until project completion. Project Professional interacts with PWA so that project managers will receive information regarding progress on the tasks directly from resources assigned. This is important because the overall status of the project is determined by the progress of each individual task.

Finally, Project Professional can help you generate meaningful reports that present project information based on the parameters you want to see or analyze. You can generate a variety of reports based on the data you enter while creating your project plan, enabling project managers to develop more realistic project schedules.

Reviewing Portfolio Schedules with Project Web Access

One of the most important features of Project 2003 is the Project Center in PWA. This is the place where project and portfolio managers, as well as executives, get information regarding the status of their projects and the overall portfolio.

Tracking and measuring the work results is an essential part of portfolio management. Various views in the Project Center can generate a wealth of information regarding the status of a project portfolio as well as information regarding individual projects. The Project Center provides project managers and management personnel a way to analyze variances and trends to easily view details on various projects, including a quick view for earned value and plan variance.

The Project Center provides excellent portfolio management capabilities through Portfolio Analyzer and Portfolio Modeler. Through the Portfolio Analyzer, executives can see graphical and chart reports regarding projects and resource utilization. Using Portfolio Modeler, users can build models that involve multiple projects and perform "what-if" analysis using various scenarios.

The Project Center in Project 2003 can be customized to respond to almost all reporting needs of an organization. It can be configured to present a variety of reports, including the project schedule and status at any time in the project life cycle. Some of the most common reports that can be easily generated using Project Center capabilities are

- Reporting progress against the project plan
- Current activities/critical tasks
- Earned value analysis
- Budget and schedule variance

It is important that you understand that the Project Center elevates the visibility of your project at the enterprise level, and you need to keep your project's status and data up-to-date and as accurate as possible according to the processes set up in your organization to generate the correct portfolio reports.

Centralized Storage of Project Schedule Data

The Project 2003 solution leverages Microsoft SQL database functionality to store all project information. With versions previous to Project 2002 it was difficult for portfolio managers and executives to store, retrieve, and share information regarding project schedules because these files were stored on different local or shared drives.

With the introduction of the EPM solution, project schedules are now centrally stored in a database repository that can be easily accessed by anyone with sufficient rights and permissions. This database now stores information about project tasks, resources and their assignments, and custom fields and outline codes.

The centralized storage of project schedule data means that users no longer have to save the project schedules on their local or shared drives. Centralized storage of project schedule data allows users to have access to the most recent project schedule, thus eliminating the possibility of confusion and versioning problems.

Resource Management and the Enterprise Global Resource Pool

One of the most important features of Project 2003 is the resource management capability. Project 2003 uses a single Enterprise Global Resource Pool that allows project and resource managers to easily share resources across the enterprise, check their availability, and forecast resource demands.

With the release of Project 2002, and continuing in Project 2003, Microsoft introduces the concept of generic resources, which allows assignment of tasks to unnamed resources. By doing so, project and resource managers can forecast the demand based on availability of specific skills rather than on availability of named resources.

Equally important, Project 2003 enables a better synchronization of resources with the enterprise project portfolio, which permits identification of potential resource bottlenecks long before they occur. Early identification of a potential problem and assessment of its impact on the project portfolio drives better decisions when trade-offs are being considered.

Raising the visibility of resource allocation at the enterprise level facilitates the collaboration between project and resource managers and provides for a fact-based dialog between the two groups.

▶ **SEE** "Enterprise Resource Pool," **PAGE 191**.

Centralized Storage of Risks, Issues, and Documents

A common reason that some projects fail is the lack of communication within the project structure. Development of a good Communications plan is key to ensuring project success, and Project 2003 supports many information distribution methods based on the requirements of your Communications plan, such as the following:

- Risks management

- Issues management

- Documents management

Risk management is the art and science of identifying, analyzing, and responding to risk factors throughout the life of a project and in the best interest of its objectives. Project 2003 allows managers, executives, and team members to share information regarding project risks to minimize their potential effect on the project and provides ongoing management of identified risks through use of the Risks page in PWA.

The Issues page in PWA allows you to document and easily communicate new issues, issue updates, and resolutions with all project stakeholders.

The Documents page in PWA allows you to keep project documents in one place, in logically organized folders, and provide version management with check-in and check-out capabilities.

▶ **SEE** "Risks, Issues, and Documents Using Windows SharePoint Services (WSS)," **PAGE 441**.

Also, PWA facilitates communication between project stakeholders through use of status reports. The Status Reports page allows you to create status report templates for your team and allows your team to easily respond to your status reports.

▶ **SEE** "Project Web Access Collaboration," **PAGE 293**.

The Project Workspace

In Project 2003, each project may have its own project workspace. A project workspace is created for each project schedule in the form of a project website. Project workspace leverages the Windows SharePoint Services technology, and it is a way to enhance communication between project team members. Usually in the Project workspace, project managers may list announcements and events; store a project's documentation; and also navigate to the Issues, Risks, and Documents pages for the project. Included in the events section is the capability to establish attendees, determine objectives, and use templates to create a meeting agenda. Many more features are similar to this events feature, which you and your project team will want to explore.

A useful feature available is that the project manager may insert additional web parts from PWA or from other areas, and you can also insert links and pictures, as needed.

▶ **SEE** "Windows SharePoint Services Customizing the Project Workspace," **PAGE 732**.

Understanding the Features of Project Server 2003

Project Server 2003 is a complex tool that requires a thorough understanding of both the technical and the business sides of EPM for its implementation. When considering Project Server 2003, it is important to understand its interfaces, architecture, components, configurations, settings, and the security model.

Project Server Interfaces

There are two interfaces to Project Server 2003: Project Professional and PWA.

Project Professional is where the project managers do most of the detailed work on their project, such as planning new tasks, tracking status, and assigning new resources. Project managers enter the scheduling information in Project Professional and keep it updated. Project managers use Project Professional to assign resources to tasks and track progress with updates received from project team members via PWA. Project Professional 2003 maintains the look and feel of earlier versions, as well as all nonenterprise features.

PWA is the other interface where project managers can communicate about projects with the team members, and team members can communicate with project managers. All team members, including executives and managers, who want to view project or resource data need to have access to PWA.

Architecture Overview

The Microsoft Project 2003 EPM solution is based on four key elements: Project Professional, PWA, SQL Server 2000, and Windows SharePoint Services. All these components are kept synchronized by Project Server 2003.

Figure 2.1 shows the links between these three components.

Project Professional is the application that allows project managers to develop and update their project schedules.

PWA is the web interface for team members, resource managers, and other project stakeholders that allows them to review information about the project plan, send updates to the project manager, or communicate with other members of the team.

Microsoft SQL Server 2000 is used to centrally store information and data about projects and resources. It also serves as a data repository for generating reports.

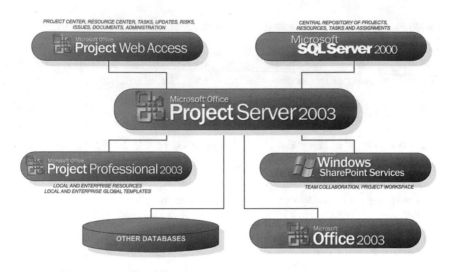

FIGURE 2.1   Project 2003 architecture.

Windows SharePoint Services is the application used to store project documentation, issues, risks, and certain information about tasks. Windows SharePoint Services provides an extensive customizable interface, which allows each project manager to tailor it to the specific needs of her team.

Project Server 2003 establishes the link between these components and makes it possible to link to other Office applications, as well as to other enterprise systems.

Project Web Access

The following list presents some of the features available in PWA. As previously noted, Project 2003 is a role-based system and, as such, different users will have access to different features and functions dependent on their role in the organization. PWA allows users to

- Approve project progress updates (actuals) via the Updates function.
- Review and analyze projects via the Project Center.
- Review and analyze resource allocation and information via the Resource Center.
- Create, delete, and manage status reports using the Status Reports page.
- Manage issues and risks through the Issues and Risks pages.
- Create and manage documents associated with the project via the Documents page.
- As a team member, update actual work progress and review and update schedule changes through the Tasks page.
- As a portfolio manager or executive, access Portfolio Analyzer and Portfolio Modeler to generate reports based on the parameters that you require and perform the "what-if" analysis.

In addition, PWA serves as the primary interface for system administration, which is done by accessing the Admin page.

The Admin page allows the system administrator to configure PWA, establish the roles of individuals and assign them the appropriate permissions, and configure the enterprise views and reports. It is important to note that only qualified individuals should have access to this page because it contains information and settings vital to good functioning of the system.

▶ **SEE** Part V, "Using Microsoft Office Project Web Access 2003," **PAGE 291**.

Microsoft Project Professional

Project Professional is the application that allows project managers to

- Build any new project schedules or update existing ones.

- Baseline the schedule and keep it updated.

- Build the project team, assign resources to project tasks, and monitor their work on those tasks.

- Review and update the project schedule with information received via PWA.

- Use various viewing and reporting tools in Project Professional to generate reports and presentations.

- Import project files and resources into the enterprise database.

Project Professional is also the application that allows system administrators to build and configure the Enterprise Global template. The Enterprise Global template provides the backbone structure for enterprise project schedule templates, and it is used to configure Enterprise Custom Fields and Outline Codes.

Through Project Professional, you can also access the Enterprise Global Resource Pool that stores information about all resources in the database, generic and named.

It is also important to remember that only system administrators should have access to modify the Enterprise Global template or Enterprise Global Resource Pool.

▶ **SEE** Part VI, "Using Microsoft Office Project Professional 2003 Enterprise Features," **PAGE 535**.

Windows SharePoint Services

Windows SharePoint Services facilitates communication among various project stakeholders. Using Windows SharePoint Services, you can do the following:

- Document the identification, analysis, and responses to the risk events that could positively or negatively affect your project. This feature is available to you in the Risks page of PWA.

- Document current issues relevant to your project, allowing you to prioritize and manage issue resolutions. This feature is available to you in the Issues page of PWA.

- Create document libraries containing project documents via the Documents page. You can create libraries specific to your project, and you can use a public library where you can store general organizational information that crosses individual project lines or standard corporate documents.

- Modify project workspace using a variety of customizable lists and libraries to facilitate organized and robust information sharing among team members.

Windows SharePoint Services also makes possible the management of the project workspace, which facilitates interaction and communication between project team members.

▶ **SEE** "Windows SharePoint Services Customizing the Project Workspace," **PAGE 732**.

Overview of Project Server Configuration and Settings

For your enterprise to make best use of the Project 2003 solution, you must set up and configure the system properly. This includes mapping your business process into the system, ensuring that the information in the database is accurate, and making sure that users can perform in the system those tasks required by their business role in the organization.

The following list presents the main areas that must be covered in the initial setup and configuration of the system:

- **Project Server 2003 security model**—Proper setup of the security model ensures that all users of the system can perform those tasks dictated by the organization's business process.

  ▶ **SEE** "Establishing Security Model Settings," **PAGE 143**.

- **Set up the Enterprise Global Resource Pool**—This is particularly important because Project 2003 bases its functional philosophy on the sharing of resources by multiple projects.

  ▶ **SEE** "Building Project Team and Resource Substitution," **PAGE 563**.

- **Set up the calendars for resources and projects**—Determines resource allocation and availability and constitutes the basis for accurate resource requirements forecast.

  ▶ **SEE** "Completing the Implementation and Configuration," **PAGE 239**.

- **Set up time tracking methods for projects**—Review the available options and choose the tracking method applicable to your organization.

  ▶ **SEE** "Time Tracking in Project Web Access," **PAGE 317**.

- **Configuration of Enterprise Global Template and Project Codes**—Determines enterprise settings for a number of features available and the way users can view and report data in the Project and Resource Centers.

  ▶ **SEE** "Enterprise Global Codes," **PAGE 163**.

- **Configuration of administrative settings**—Determines the behavior of certain functions and features available, such as the preferred method for updating the OLAP cube, automatic or manual creation of project workspaces, and so on.

  ▶ **SEE** "Using the Project Web Access Admin Menu Tab," **PAGE 477**.

> **NOTE**
>
> It is important that you read and understand the *Microsoft Administrator's Guide* before you start configuring Project Server 2003.

Best Practices

An EPM application, such as Microsoft Office Project Server 2003, is a complex system that consists of not only the technical components but also the tight integration of business processes and tools. It is important to

- Understand the architecture and components of Microsoft Project 2003.

- Plan your EPM implementation based on the business processes of your organization and the capability of the system.

- Get familiar with the *Microsoft Project Server 2003 Administrator's Guide* to understand the various implications of the system.

- Consider all Microsoft Project 2003 components and choose the appropriate implementation of those components based on your organization's needs.

- Take time to learn, plan, and manage your EPM application to provide a successful tool that will assist you in enforcing your organization's standards and support your entire project portfolio.

Knowing Product Limits and Overcoming Them

IN THIS CHAPTER

- Augmentation Areas of Microsoft Office Project Server 2003

- An Overview of Third-Party Add-Ins

- Best Practices

Microsoft Office Project Server 2003 is Microsoft's second-generation application for enterprise management. Unlike other enterprise management applications, Project Server evolved from the bottom up (desktop to enterprise) instead of top down. Microsoft added enterprise functionality and support for the project team while remaining true to the project managers and the desktop scheduling engine that is the de facto standard. This bottom-up approach provides a more solid foundation as a product, allowing project and task level detail to flow/aggregate up to support enterprise views. This reduces or removes potential inconsistencies of multiple subjective interpretation levels before reports reach executives. The top-down approach is good for high-level planning, but doesn't automatically break down into logical entities. It is easier to add the top than to add the bottom; having said that, Project Server 2003 still has room to grow to cover the top.

Fortunately, Microsoft Project has always had a commitment to be open to the solution developer community, allowing the market to evolve its own add-ins and solutions. Microsoft has continued this tradition into the enterprise world via an open database schema and incorporation of the Project Data Service (PDS) application programmer interface (API). This chapter discusses some of the areas where Microsoft's product is still growing and where the solution developer community has risen to the challenge.

> **TIP**
>
> This chapter addresses enterprise concepts and function areas that are either not currently addressed or not completely addressed in Project Server 2003. But, don't forget that one of the first challenges encountered during an implementation is the technical complexity of the solution. Microsoft's EPM solution is a blend of multiple Microsoft servers, technologies, and applications (IIS, SQL Server, ASP, XML/SOAP, ActiveX, and desktop applications). A vast amount of technical and implementation information is available online; however, the fastest, most cost-effective approach to getting up and running is to look up a registered Microsoft Project Partner on the Microsoft website, especially if you don't have all the prerequisite application and domain knowledge in-house.

Augmentation Areas of Microsoft Office Project Server 2003

The following list shows some of the augmentation areas that have been noted in the client community. Many solutions exist for each of these areas, and the "right" solution must be selected on a case-by-case basis. The intent of this chapter is not to solve your particular need but rather to identify the common augmentation areas, give you a little background on each, and provide you with one of possibly many alternatives that exist. Using customization instead of a third-party product is also an option in each of these areas and may in fact be the right option for your case. It is recommended, however, that you check out the third-party products before beginning customization as a matter of due diligence. The augmentation areas and issues are

- Project timesheets versus labor timesheets

- Resource commitment management versus usage management

- Budgeting and forecasting concepts

- Strategic portfolio support

- Methodology support

- Standardization validation and support

- Interdependency management (vendor management)

- Lightweight project management support

- Governance and project initiation

Each of these areas is further touched on in the following paragraphs. Some of the third-party applications mentioned here are also discussed in Chapter 10, "Creating Project Web Access Project and Resource Views."

> **TIP**
>
> The third-party add-in world is continuously changing. Because of the openness of the Project Server EPM solution, it is possible for outstanding ideas to be implemented by small as well as large companies. For more information about the third-party products mentioned here, or to see other third-party products, go to http://www.quantumpm.com, a site that will be updated regularly.

Project Timesheets Versus Labor Timesheets

Timesheets are generally thought of as an extension of punch clocks, used for checking into a job and checking out of a job. They are usually thought of as determining pay and vacation. These are *labor timesheets*, and they support payroll and finance. *Project timesheets* are used to track the status of tasks. This is a totally different concept. Capturing project time and labor time through one input mechanism (to avoid dual entry) is what many companies strive for. If both project and labor concepts are to be supported, project timesheets (out of the box) can be used to capture all time (including vacation, sick, and other administrative time) and the data then aggregated to support payroll and finance needs.

In most cases, labor timesheets cannot practically be the single entry point because they don't easily support time collection at any more detail than the project level. Project timesheets support a much lower level of detail that can be used in support of actual effort and task status for use in earned value and other calculations. On the other hand, the drawbacks to using project timesheets are in the discipline required of the team members and the extra work necessary for categorizing the information and aggregating it for fiscal/financial reporting needs. Team members must have a clear understanding of their scheduled tasks and the discipline to track them because they must enter time at the lowest level tasks created by their project manager. This level of understanding and tracking discipline is not necessarily as easy to achieve as it sounds. The project manager creates these tasks (usually for effort estimation purposes), and a common issue is that the team member does not understand the task breakdown or perform the work in the same breakdown manner used by the project manager. Both of these cases lead to incorrect input, frustration, and pushback from the team members.

A simple measure of this is the surprise initially reflected by team members when they see the number of tasks they have been assigned on the project timesheet. Many companies manage this with a combination of process and training, and for many companies this level of detail is exactly what they want. However, other companies find it easier to use a third-party product that addresses this in a more direct way. EPK Timesheets is a third-party add-in that allows you to plan to whatever task level you want and designate where (and at what level) you want to collect team member effort hours while still allowing the capture of percent complete on the remaining tasks. (This neatly supports the varying levels of detail desired for both project and labor time collection in a component that cleanly replaces the out-of-the-box project timesheet.)

> **NOTE**
>
> Many timesheet vendors say that they have integration with Microsoft Project. Be careful to evaluate them against the concepts discussed here and your particular needs.

Resource Commitment Management Versus Usage Management

Project Server provides excellent mechanisms in support of individual team member utilization and management across all projects. However, some companies want an additional, higher layer of resource management referred to here as *contract commitment*. In fact, many products don't directly support contract commitment, and it is frequently accommodated through totally separate mechanisms. Consider the case where you require a contract resource to perform two duties (one on each of two independent projects). Each project manager is told that she has a commitment for the resource for 20 hours a week (and the project will be charged 20 hours a week for that resource). This is a *resource commitment*. The project manager then manages the resource at the hour level within that 50% utilization commitment.

If project manager A is using the total of 50% commitment, but project manager B has the resource assigned to tasks totaling only 25% of that resource instead of 50%, Project Server's total utilization reporting will show 25% availability of the resource, when in fact that resource is fully committed. In many companies this "commitment" concept is handled completely independently (outside the scheduling tool). This is an area in which standalone spreadsheets or customization and process are frequently used. Third-party applications such as EPK Resources and components of ProSight can also be leveraged.

Budgeting and Forecasting Concepts

Budgeting and forecasting can be accommodated in the out-of-the box solution but are frequently customized to support individual company needs. This is because many companies have a yearly budgeting and forecasting process that occurs prior to detailed schedule-based effort estimates and is more in support of staffing prediction at a functional department level. Customization and third-party add-in applications such as EPK Resources and ProSight provide great benefits.

> **NOTE**
>
> Departments are formed in companies for different reasons. *Functional departments* are formed to isolate and manage specific skill sets more efficiently across the company. An example on a highway construction project would be an environmental department. Such a department would supply trained resources in environmental impact assessments. These resources would be leveraged at specific times and locations during the project. Managing the hiring, training, and availability of these resources is a function of immediate and predicted need.

Strategic Portfolio Support

Project Server provides project level attributes and display filtering and grouping on these attributes for reporting purposes. These mechanisms provide basic portfolio support. More advanced management can be set up simply by using the Windows SharePoint Services (WSS) project subwebs, in combination with Microsoft SharePoint Portal and some web part customization. This can create more advanced, company-specific solutions. If an organization requires more strategic/analytic capability to support its governance and portfolio management processes, products such as ProSight and EPK Portfolio provide different and more general packaged solutions in this area.

Methodology Support

Project Professional and Project Server (with its WSS project subweb support) are excellent tools for team development and collaboration, but what about supporting standardization on a project life cycle methodology? Project Professional has the feature-set called the *Project Guide*, which can be designed like a series of web pages with phase gates to lead project managers through a methodology. Microsoft does not promote any specific methodology out of the box. Microsoft leaves that for clients to incorporate either by using their own methodology or by using a methodology provided by the Microsoft partner community.

CMD's Symphony is a third-party add-in that provides methodologies and an infrastructure for accessing these methodologies. This add-in embeds an infrastructure into both Project Professional and Project Web Access (PWA) that directly supports knowledge base definitions around specific roles, tasks, and deliverables, as well as standard document libraries available to prepopulate project templates or pull in as needed. CMD is tightly integrated with WSS. In addition, CMD has prepackaged methodology-specific support (role definition, document templates, project and task knowledge base, and so on) that can be used immediately or customized for your methodology.

Standardization Validation and Support

Companies trying to get a handle on and report consolidated status across multiple projects sooner or later must achieve some level of standardization within and across those projects. Comparing the status of a project in which every task is three months long with a project in which every task is 20 hours long is misleading and can lead to poor executive decisions. Project standards are created to address this inconsistency. As soon as a standard is created, compliance checking should follow. Tools to check compliance are rare or one-of.

Two are available from QuantumPM: Quantum Schedule Auditor (QSA) and Quantum Portfolio Auditor (QPA). QSA is a Project Professional add-in that allows the project manager to self-audit his own schedules. It comes prepackaged with a set of configurable tests but can be extended as needed. QPA performs similar testing across designated project sets within the Project Server database repository.

Interdependency Management (Vendor Management)

When implementing Project Server, a fundamental question of what is a project arises. In many instances, wrapped up in this question is who is responsible for the planning and status of this set of work. The sets quickly become the de facto definition of a project.

This is a tremendous oversimplification, but it speaks to the fact that at some point you will make a decision as to whether to have large projects with few or no interdependencies between them or small projects with many interdependencies.

A highway project can be a single project plan with thousands of tasks. The project manager becomes more of a vendor manager, requesting and getting individual task sets and status from various road crews, material vendors, environment assessment, regulation impact teams, and so on. It can also be many individual project plans, each maintained by the most appropriate responsible party, with the interdependencies and higher level critical paths managed in an integrated plan by the overall project manager.

Many variations are within and around the spectrum defined by these two scenarios. Each variation is caused by the current mechanisms and requirements used by each company and vendor. Microsoft Project provides some of the functions necessary to handle these scenarios (inter-project dependencies and master projects for rolling the information up). However, Microsoft Project does not have simple, rigorous process that (out of the box) combines these easily together for handling program level critical path and interdependency planning, management and reporting. We have frequently encountered this and the best solution is to define the process that best fits your needs or current practice. This is often enough. A small amount of customization can support the process that you define and re-enforce collection, handoff, and reporting if required.

Lightweight Project Management Support

Few organizations truly have project management skills and processes infused through their organization at a consistent level. This is because most companies rely on individual project manager skill rather than a standardized skill (supported through training) and standards. Most, if not all organizations, have individual project manager skills that range from highly technical and tool savvy to nontechnical but people savvy. This spectrum encompasses managing hundreds of thousands of tasks within a technical tool to napkin-based to-do lists. Both skill sets have their places.

Project Professional is a tool with capabilities to accommodate large, complex project rigor and smaller, softer management efforts. The range of project management skills supported by Project Professional can itself be an issue, analogous to wanting to build a bird house for the first time and going to a hardware store and getting confused by all the tools and materials that could be used for your project. Tool and process training is required to keep focus on the aspects of the tool you want to use. When the number of project managers or their role changes, it can cause consistency issues within an organization. Training and discipline can be augmented by customization or third-party tools. The reason that third-party tools such as EPK Time are helpful is because they let you tailor the level or resolution you acquire information at on a case-by-case basis. This allows some project managers to go deep into the science, whereas others can support their current processes and depth, providing the opportunity to grow the latter into the former over time. Customization is usually helpful because it helps to remove the distraction of the bells and whistles that are not used.

Governance and Project Initiation

Governance is the name of the function that, through visibility into current activities and knowledge of corporate goals, provides prioritization of ongoing activities, approval of new activities, and validation of old or ending activities. A prime governance point is project initiation. Initiating projects and governing them differs from company to company and is mostly a process. Technical pieces available for incorporation into the process may come from various areas. Microsoft has a project initiation example available for free download. EPK Portfolio has a project initiation component available with it as well. Other third-party solutions have their own style of support for project initiation. Usually, some small level of customization is required. Report visibility into governance is typically covered for the processes that the third-party tools incorporate, but most require some tailoring or customization to fit your needs.

An Overview of Third-Party Add-Ins

The needs and methods of organizations in industry today are just as diverse as the personalities of individual people. This implies different perspectives on how to manage different needs for reporting and different requirements for the complexity of management tools.

Microsoft-developed applications, such as Office and Project 2003, tackle diversity head on by opening up the functionality to custom development. The Microsoft Project 2003 software system has the capability to be customized on multiple levels, ranging from the database to Project Professional to Project Server. An abundance of tools also are available to you as third-party add-ins, some of which are discussed in this section.

This section looks at several tools, add-ins, and complementary software packages that can be used in conjunction with Microsoft Project 2003. Keep in mind that this is not a comprehensive listing of add-ins. Many others not mentioned here enhance Microsoft Project both on the server and the desktop level.

Custom Component Object Model Add-Ins

The Microsoft Office suite delivers an easy method for developers to create third-party add-ins that reside in the Office applications themselves. They provide users with additional features, such as custom toolbars, buttons, and menus. They can then interface with the application to create reports, simplify tasks, or automate the application itself.

The application can register these add-ins because they are exposed over the component object model (COM). Any developer who can produce a COM component is capable of creating a COM add-in.

QuantumPM Schedule Auditor

Sometimes looking at project schedules within Project does not give you an adequate overview of the current health of the project. Often various regulations, methodologies, or standards are in place that are unique to an organization's project management office. Here, a need for a reporting tool becomes apparent. One such reporting tool is the QuantumPM Schedule Auditor (QSA).

QSA is a COM add-in for Project Professional. It compiles information about a project schedule to produce an easy-to-read HTML report. The out-of-the-box utility contains four areas of *checks*, or categories, of a project schedule that are analyzed:

- Tasks

- Resources

- Schedule

- Calendar

The utility has a completely modular design, allowing the user to easily add new checks as they are released, or a developer to add checks he has created. Each check has a set of user-configurable criteria that can be tailored toward an organization's business rules.

Some Key Checks

QSA comes with 17 different checks by default. Here, some key checks are outlined:

- **Predecessors and Successors**—Looks for tasks missing either, except the first and last task

- **Specified Names**—Searches for predefined required task names, such as "Mid-Project Review"

- **Duplicate Resource Entries**—Looks for possible duplicate resource names, such as "M Smith" and "Martin Smith"

- **Generic Entries**—Looks for resources not associated with a person, such as "Engineering Department"

- **Over Allocation**—Checks for the overallocation of a resource

- **Baselined Tasks**—Makes sure that all tasks are baselined

- **Correct Milestones**—Looks for 0 effort/duration tasks that aren't milestones

- **Holidays and Vacations**—Matches a list of known holidays against a calendar

Each check produces a graphical indicator on the summary page of the report that specifies OK, warning, or error, as shown in Figure 3.1. The details of the check can subsequently be examined by navigating to the detail section of the report.

The summary page also lists the 10 most heavily used resources, as well as the top 20 critical path tasks of the schedule. Because the report is generated in HTML, it can easily be placed on a website for quick access by team members.

For more information on QSA, visit http://www.QuantumPM.com.

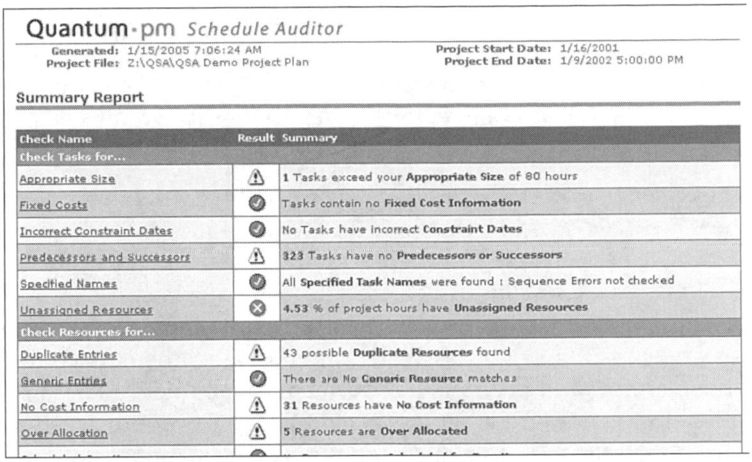

FIGURE 3.1   Intuitive colorful graphical indicators summarize each check.

Extending Project Web Access with Enterprise Project Knowledge Suite

In addition to add-ins for the desktop project application, add-ins are also available for Project Server. One such add-in is the Enterprise Project Knowledge (EPK) Suite by EPK Group, LLC.

EPK provides three modules that enhance the out-of-the-box functionality of PWA:

- EPK-Portfolio

- EPK-Resources

- EPK-Time

This functionality seamlessly integrates with PWA (including security), delivering features commonly yearned for by users of PWA.

The aim of these modules is to add new capabilities around portfolio, resource, and time management and improve performance and reporting capabilities of Project Server, regardless of your organization's level of project management experience. Each module functions similarly to PWA, but the views contain more powerful filtering, grouping, and drill-down capabilities. The views are also more pleasing to the eye by using colors that easily distinguish differences within the data.

The Enterprise Project Knowledge–Portfolio

The EPK-Portfolio module (see Figure 3.2) boosts your project management and reporting capabilities by providing integrated portfolio management from within the Project Server 2003 environment. EPK-Portfolio allows organizations to perform top-down planning, budgeting, and management of projects and nonproject-related activities. Additionally, organizations can perform portfolio management activities such as aligning projects with strategic objectives and managing them through a structured management process from the idea stage through authorization to close-out. The progression of an initiative through its stages is workflow-based with the capability to define and control information that needs to be collected, as well as approval/rejection actions that need to be performed for each step.

One of the unique benefits of EPK-Portfolio is the capability to define a "work activity" from PWA. These are called *portfolio items (PIs)* in EPK-Portfolio and information (that is, metadata) can be assigned to these without the need to create a Project file and publish to Project Server. These portfolio items can be used to create a Project file for Project Professional after the PI has transitioned through the work flow "stages" in your EPK environment. Conversely, existing projects in Project Server can be linked to PIs to take advantage of the planning and portfolio management capabilities of the EPK software. You can also place tasks under these portfolio items in EPK-Portfolio, called *work items*. Here again, you gain all the reporting and portfolio management capabilities available in the tool without the need to create a Project file and publish to Project Server.

Organizations can also establish time-phased hierarchical budgets for user-defined cost categories and generic resources associated with projects. Labor items can be planned by hours, costs, or full-time equivalents (FTEs). Organizations have the capability to roll up, filter, and group budgeted costs as well as perform "what if" analysis to support planning activities. Budgets can be compared to actuals collected from Project Server 2003 projects or costs imported from external systems. The Projects Explorer feature also allows users to perform advanced sort, group, and filter functions with aesthetically appealing graphic options.

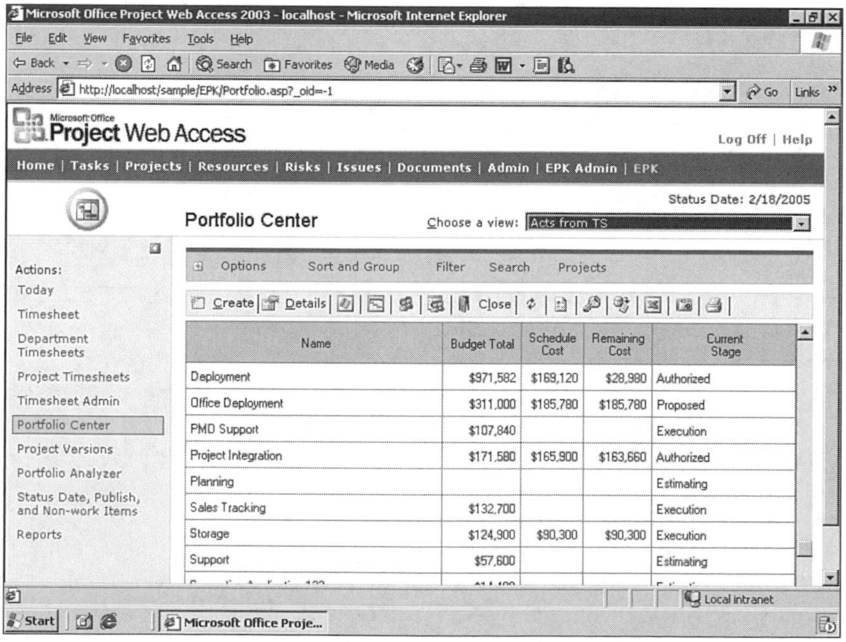

FIGURE 3.2   View more informative data in EPK-Portfolio.

Besides the project reporting and navigation mechanism, EPK-Portfolio allows organizations to identify and monitor nonproject-related work, such as support and operations, initiatives, proposals, and investment opportunities. It eliminates the need to create unique work plans or administrative projects.

To top off all this functionality, it also provides a convenient method for creating new projects through PWA.

Enterprise Project Knowledge–Time

The EPK-Time module (see Figure 3.3) provides complete timekeeping functionality at any level within or even outside a project. It more or less removes the dependency of timesheets with published project work plans, allowing time to be recorded without first requiring project work schedule to be created in Project Professional.

EPK-Time gives greater control over management, allowing both resource managers and project managers to view and approve time for tasks. Task status and hours accrued against those tasks are held independently, so more control is given to managers to designate status. This time reporting functionality is also extended to allow reporting on a summary task and project level.

EPK-Time also makes tracking administrative and nonproject work easier. You are given a central location to record time accrued for items such as holidays, vacations, and sick time.

Time spent on nonproject work, such as maintenance or support work, can also be recorded, thus giving a full picture of where time is spent.

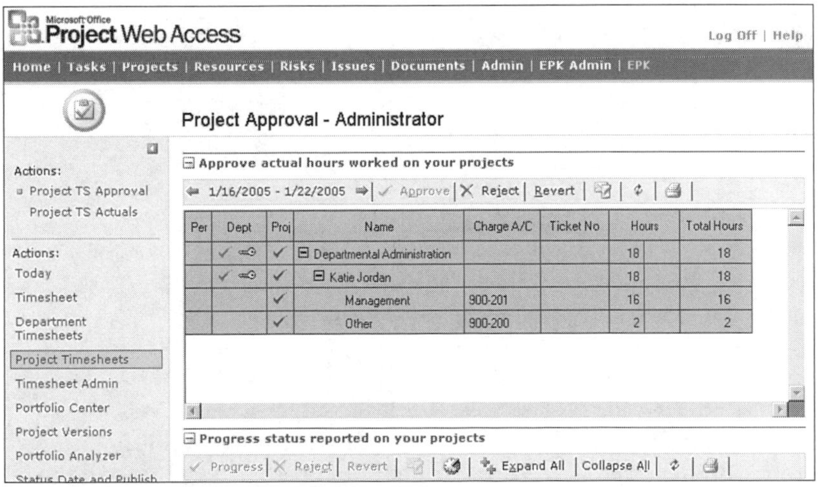

FIGURE 3.3   Manage time with the EPK-Time interface in PWA.

Enterprise Project Knowledge–Resources

EPK-Resources allows management to plan and allocate resources at a summary level without requiring a direct link to project work plans. Generic resources can be used for high-level planning, and an organization can look at resource availability across project, administrative, and nonproject work.

You now have a comprehensive resource availability tool. Instead of just project assignments, EPK-Resources covers all work, giving a realistic picture of availability factoring in nonproject and administrative work.

Resource allocation can also be planned more efficiently by assisting the process of staffing incoming work and efforts.

All this can be done through a web-based interface that functions much like a spreadsheet.

Enterprise Project Knowledge–Collaborate

EPK-Collaborate is the newest module of the EPK Suite that allows WSS sites for EPK portfolio items (PIs) and Project schedules linked to these PIs. It allows viewing of WSS items such as documents, issues, and risks across sites. Using EPK-Collaborate, you can jump to the WSS site from your EPK timesheet. This functionality was a missing link between the portfolio management of Project Server and collaborative functionality of WSS. EPK-Collaborate provides the capability to view WSS sites across your portfolio, further supporting the concept of EPM.

Administration

All views, configuration items, and fields can be managed through a central EPK admin page reminiscent of PWA's admin page. From here, you can maintain fiscal calendars, manage timesheet periods and limits, and specify nonproject work.

> **NOTE**
>
> More information about EPK can be found at http://www.QuantumPM.com and also at http://www.EPKGroup.com.

ProSight Portfolios Bridge

ProSight Portfolios is a tool designed to manage investment portfolios for large organizations. It helps CEOs and team members alike make business decisions based on importance and interdependencies of various investments.

Bridge to Project Server

The ProSight Portfolios Bridge for Microsoft Project Server 2003 creates a link between ProSight Portfolio and Project Server. The Bridge provides the capability for portfolio managers to cross-reference data, either through the project API or through the OLAP cube.

Information can be imported from a project as an investment, or vice versa. The project and portfolio data and life cycle are then correlated to each other to provide further insight into projects as a whole.

This information can be used to track not only the status and health of a particular project but also the necessity and comparative benefit as well. This can help in planning what projects get the attention of your company's resources.

> **NOTE**
>
> More information about ProSight Portfolios and the Project Server Bridge can be found at http://www.ProSight.com.

Micro-Frame Program Manager

The Micro-Frame Program Manager (MPM) is an Earned Value Management solution frequently used in industries such as aerospace and defense. It uses an integrated pricing engine with an earned value model to report a project's current performance and predict the amount of work and cost required for completion.

MPM is a complete program management application that can import data from projects created in Project Professional. It can then use this data to track a project throughout the entire management life.

The major advantage of this solution is its capability to forecast project costs and completion times. It is frequently seen in government areas as part of an approved process to calculate project and program earned value.

> **NOTE**
>
> More information about MPM can be found at http://www.BusinessEngine.com.

Risk+ for Risk Management

Risk identification and quantification can become a difficult and abstract process for managing projects. One tool that can be used to quantify cost and schedule uncertainty is Risk+ by C/S Solutions, Inc.

This add-in integrates with Microsoft Project to analyze the probability of completing a project on time and within budget by using the proven Monte Carlo–based simulation technique.

Charts and histograms can be generated to further understand potential impacts of risks and the tasks that have a high probability of hindering a project's completion.

All this is done with an interface that is easy and convenient to use within Microsoft Project.

> **NOTE**
>
> More information about Risk+ software can be found at the C/S Solutions website at http://www.cs-solutions.com/.

Microsoft-Provided Downloads

> **TIP**
>
> Microsoft also provides multiple add-ins. Add-ins for all the Microsoft Office Suites are available from http://office.microsoft.com. It is recommended that you visit this site regularly for the latest updates and new tools.

CMD to Manage Process Workflow

CMD Symphony™, created by CMD Corporation, is an add-in to Project Server that provides the capability to manage process workflow and project content through the use of industry and organizational best practices and methodologies. The product is particularly useful for defining and enforcing organizational standards for enterprise project management because it enables an organization to create well-defined repeatable work flows, complete with templates and examples available to the entire project team when needed. Organizations can create, customize, and publish the knowledge content of their methodology from within Microsoft Project. The best practices or methods library, built as an extension of the enterprise templates, has a flexible design to support all types of projects within an organization: marketing campaigns, product development, process maturity (CMM, Six Sigma, and so on), software engineering, event management, and IT deployments. The CMD Symphony Suite includes three products that together provide a data repository and access from either Project Professional or PWA:

- Process Manager is built inside Project Professional and includes facilities for authoring and customizing best practices, generating project plans from the best practices library, creating and maintaining shared standard work product examples and templates (stored in SharePoint Services [SPS]), defining and maintaining roles and responsibilities, and managing project deliverables.

- Insight is built inside PWA and allows all project stakeholders to view the detailed requirements of the tasks assigned to them over the web. It includes best practices views across multiple projects and assignments, task-specific roles and responsibilities, reference materials, and deliverables across tasks and projects.

- Symphony Server is built as an extension of Project Server. It is the repository of all the knowledge content for project process management including best practices.

> **NOTE**
>
> See http://www.cmdcorp.com/ for more information on CMD's products.

Overview of the Project Guide and Customization

The project guide was originally introduced in Microsoft Project 2002, and its features were extended for Project 2003. This tool offers step-through wizards and instructions that assist the user with common activities within Project Professional. These activities include creating tasks, assigning resources, defining the project, and reporting information to others on your team. The guide is also customizable, providing a tool to help users maintain business rules while developing a project schedule.

The project guide consists of three major screen elements:

- **Project guide toolbar**—A toolbar in Project Professional that assists in navigation to various wizards and instructions of the project guide.

- **Side pane**—The meat of the guide. It contains all the instructions, wizards, and accompanying information to the current assisted activity.

- **View area**—The various views, such as the Gantt chart, that display all the project data as well as custom views.

The project guide is a great learning aide for users who are new to Microsoft Project or who may not know how to perform a certain task. When a user feels she no longer needs the guide's assistance, it can be turned off from the project guide toolbar.

> **TIP**
>
> If the project guide toolbar is not visible, you can add it by right-clicking the blank space of another toolbar. The project guide toolbar contains the button to enable or disable the project guide.

The guide is not limited to assisting new users with common tasks. Using HTML, it can be customized to help direct project management activities that should follow standardized practices tailored to the need of an organization.

The beauty of the project guide is it allows the developer to concentrate on the fine-grained project details, lifting the burden of knowing these from the high-level user. The customized guide can show the user coarse-grained information about a project in relation to their business practices, as opposed to the abstract detailed level of project data. This is done with the familiar format of HTML to display project data in the view area, by controlling the application object model behind the scenes.

Custom guide screens, project goals, and custom project views can all be created or changed by a developer familiar with XML, HTML, DHTML, and scripting. The guide structure and content are specified in XML and are therefore intuitive to anyone with XML/HTML experience. Detailed instructions and examples of how to customize the project guide are available for download from MSDN. The Project Guide 101 Software Development Kit (SDK) contains these examples and a detailed compiled help document.

All the default project guide files are installed with Project Professional and reside in the library pjintl.dll. These files can be accessed using the gbui:// protocol, which is explained in more detail in Project Guide 101.

Custom project guides must be enabled within Project by setting the reference to its main page in the interface tab of Project Professional's Option dialog.

Best Practices

- Microsoft Office Project Server 2003 provides an excellent basis for building on, and many higher-end corporate business scenarios can be fulfilled using the functionality inherent in Project Server 2003 in combination with third-party applications and project partner expertise.

- Check out the third-party add-ins available in the market prior to beginning any Project Server customization because the solution you are looking for may already exist.

- When addressing problem areas in your organization, first examine whether these problems are going to be fixed by implementing a process or whether they relate more to a technology issue; this will help you find the ultimate solution.

- Take time to analyze the needs of your organization to find the appropriate third-party or other solution.

PART II

Planning Your Enterprise Project Management Implementation

IN THIS PART

CHAPTER 4   Planning the Organizational Processes   57

CHAPTER 5   Understanding Project Server Architecture   83

CHAPTER 6   Designing the Enterprise Project
Management Solution Architecture Details   109

CHAPTER 4

Planning the Organizational Processes

IN THIS CHAPTER

- Planning—Six Pillars of EPM
- Defining Your EPM Scope
- Best Practices

Generally, Enterprise Project Management (EPM) is an organizationwide managerial philosophy based on the principle that an organization's goals are achievable through a web of simultaneous projects. This often calls for a systematic approach and includes corporate strategy projects, operational improvements, and organizational transformation, as well as traditional development projects.

Making an EPM solution a reality means developing a structure aimed at transforming the organization into a more dynamic, project-driven enterprise. For that to happen, the initial phase of the deployment needs to be well grounded so that subsequent implementation phases are carried out successfully.

Deployment of an EPM solution involves participation of representatives from all departments. Ideally, deployment efforts must be coordinated by the Project Management Office (PMO). If your organization does not have a PMO, the deployment of an EPM solution could be coordinated by the Information Technology (IT) department.

Independent of the coordinating structure in the organization, the EPM deployment project must follow the project governance rules established in your company. These rules should clearly define who the ultimate approval authority in the organization is and who will approve moving the project from one phase to the next.

Project management books teach that to be successful, any project must have a clearly defined scope. An EPM solution deployment project makes no exception. Defining the boundaries of the project is not easy. What will be included and what will be excluded from the scope of the project must be established up front.

Defining the scope of the deployment helps the organization manage expectations of end users of the system or those of the sponsors. It helps set the appropriate criteria for project acceptance and determines how the project should be measured.

Planning—Six Pillars of EPM

EPM is much more than just the installation of technology tools such as Microsoft Office Project Server 2003, Microsoft Project Professional, Microsoft Outlook, and so on. Implementing EPM has an impact on your technology and the organization, so you need to plan for those impacts.

This section explains the principles of the six pillars of EPM so that you can plan for each in an organized way. Each of the pillars provides a convenient mechanism to address business processes and the relationship of business processes to Project Server 2003 technology.

Figure 4.1 shows the Project Web Access (PWA) user interface used as a reference within each of the six pillars.

FIGURE 4.1   PWA references the six pillars of EPM in the top navigation menu.

Project Professional technology is used to establish many EPM standards, so Project Professional is an important part of your EPM implementation. Figure 4.2 is also referenced within the descriptions of the six pillars.

FIGURE 4.2   Project Professional functions are part of the six pillars of EPM.

Pillar 1: Project Management

Project management business processes are an important aspect of a successful EPM implementation. As you plan your overall implementation, consider how people throughout the organization will apply project management disciplines such as those found within the guidelines of the Project Management Institute (PMI). The project management guidance you provide your organization will help people use the EPM technology in a coordinated way.

The project management business processes guide people throughout the organization on how to use the technology of Project Server 2003. Software functions such as the PWA Project Center are directly related to the business processes you establish. Figure 4.3 shows the PWA Project Center that contains several functions enabling users to see project schedules within portfolio rollout views. Those views have certain characteristics, including color bands for project groups, data columns such as work and dates, and possibly colored graphic icons that indicate conditions such as project health.

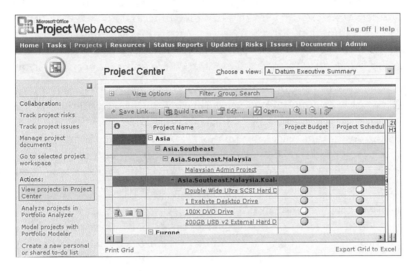

FIGURE 4.3   The Projects tab in PWA is part of the Project Management pillar.

The Project Center also includes additional features such as Portfolio Analyzer, Portfolio Modeler, To Do lists, Build Team, and so on. You need to plan your project management business processes that will provide guidance to your organization on how to use these features. You also need to specify how the PWA and Project Professional standards will control how project data is established for display within the Project Center functions.

The EPM project management plan should address each of the following technology items:

- **PWA user security roles**—Defined by groups, categories, and security templates that control the permissions each user has to use features and access data within PWA and Project Professional. Individual users can belong to multiple groups, therefore providing them access to a broad range of information. These security settings are a critical part of the overall implementation success because these settings also control which features are enabled or disabled for the entire system.

- **Project Professional Enterprise Global settings**—Define the key operating standards for people who use Project Professional. The Enterprise Global settings also define key attributes about projects, resources, and tasks. These global settings, therefore, allow classification of projects based on which attributes each project has when the schedule is published into the Project Server database repository. The attached project attributes are then used within Project Center views to group, filter, and search for projects. The Enterprise Global settings also establish common operating conditions for Project Professional users who use standards such as views, tables, calendars, defined data columns, Visual Basic for Applications macros, and so forth.

- **PWA Project Center views**—Defined and controlled within the Admin tab, where the administrators use the view maintenance functions to create named views with data columns important for portfolio and detailed project management. The view definitions can also use the Enterprise Global settings to show graphical indicators based on a project health metric set within each published project schedule.

- **Portfolio Analyzer views**—Allow people with sufficient privileges to view a sophisticated mix of project and resource information within PivotTable and graphical chart formats. The definition of these views is controlled within the PWA Admin tab where the view author places information into each view. The mix of information within these views can include data defined within the Enterprise Global settings. Each view can contain information such as project life cycle, sponsor organization, planned work, baseline work, actual cost, and other measurements.

- **Portfolio Modeler**—A special tool that enables portfolio managers to do what-if scenarios when Enterprise Global resources create bottleneck conditions across multiple projects. Portfolio models can be predefined so that the models can be easily accessed and used within the Project Center functions.

The EPM project management plan should also address common business processes that provide guidance to people throughout the organization. These business processes may include the following:

- **Project initiation**—The process used to create and classify new projects. This should include how to develop a Work Breakdown Structure (WBS) with appropriate estimates of work effort for each task, how to create milestones, how to assign resources to tasks, when to baseline tasks, and so forth.

- **Project status**—Describes how project teams periodically update status and report time for assigned tasks. This business process should also set expectations about reporting status.

- **Project and task codes**—Provide guidance on which Enterprise Global project and task codes should be used when setting project and task attributes.

- **Auditing projects**—Includes methods for determining whether project schedules comply with enterprise standards.

- **Earned value reporting**—Describes the responsibilities of project managers to evaluate progress compared to baseline information.

- **Schedule change management**—Determines how authorized project schedule changes should be incorporated.

- **Conducting project review meetings**—Provides guidance to project managers and team members on conducting review meetings. This can also provide guidance on what kinds of notes to take and roles of people during a meeting.

- **Managing project jeopardy conditions**—Defines how to identify key jeopardy conditions and how to report those to appropriate managers.

  ▶ **SEE** "Establishing Security Model Settings," **PAGE 143**.

  ▶ **SEE** "Enterprise Global Codes," **PAGE 163**.

  ▶ **SEE** "Creating Project Web Access Project and Resource Views," **PAGE 209**.

  ▶ **SEE** "Using Project and Resource Centers," **PAGE 345**.

Pillar 2: Resource Management

Resource management business processes also have a direct impact on which Project Server technology features will be used by your organization. Project and resource managers within your organization may already be using some form of resource management business processes, but you definitely need to review those practices as part of the EPM implementation.

The PWA Resource Center contains several major technology features that help resource managers understand how resources are assigned to projects and what the overall resource loading factors are across multiple projects. Resource managers can examine the Enterprise Global Resource Pool and attributes associated with each resource within the pool.

The Resource Center is also the entry point for functions such as View Availability, View Resource Assignments, Portfolio Analyzer, and so on. You need to design your business processes and the Project Server configuration settings, such as security, to determine how these features will be used and who is allowed to use those features. Figure 4.4 illustrates Resource Center functions.

Your business processes also provide guidance for resource managers who use Project Professional to define and manage the Enterprise Global Resource Pool. The resource managers set and maintain other resource attributes such as the RBS for each resource.

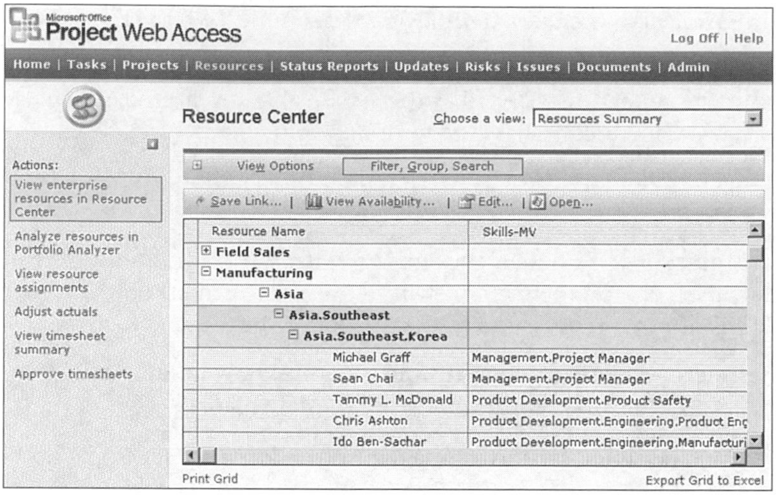

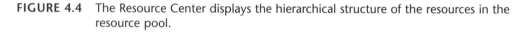

FIGURE 4.4   The Resource Center displays the hierarchical structure of the resources in the resource pool.

The EPM resource management plan should address each of the following technology items:

- **Defining the Enterprise Global Resource Pool**—This is a critical and central part of the Project Server implementation because all the project schedules use entities from this center resource pool. Each entry within the Enterprise Global Resource Pool contains information such as resource name, Active Directory account identifier, email address, monetary rates, working calendars, and so on.

- **Enterprise Global Resource Outline Codes**—Establishes centralized attributes about each resource in the enterprise. These attributes include RBS, location, skills, and so on. Also note that the RBS is part of the PWA security model that grants access to project and resource information and views. This means that you must pay special attention to developing the RBS code definitions.

- **Resource Center views**—Managed within the PWA Admin tab so that the administrators create named views with information available for each resource within the Enterprise Global Resource Pool.

- **Portfolio Analyzer views**—Can be structured to show resource-centric information important for staff and resource managers. These views can contain a wide variety of data including planned work for each resource over a span of time, actual work reported, baseline work, and so on.

- **Project Center build team**—Provides a mechanism to add resources from the Enterprise Global Resource Pool to the team list within each project schedule. This function allows project managers or resource managers to find appropriate resources that match certain predefined attributes. The build team also provides methods to do resource substitution on tasks within a project schedule. This is particularly helpful when matching from generic to named resources based on outline code attributes.

- **View resource assignments**—Enables staff and resource managers to see the task assignments for each resource. Certain people are granted permission by the PWA administrators to use this feature.

- **Resource availability**—Enables resource managers and staff managers to inspect the overall workload and remaining availability for each resource. This feature is also closely related to the Portfolio Analyzer views because availability information is produced when the OLAP cube is regenerated.

The EPM resource management plan should also address common business processes that provide guidance to people throughout the organization. These businesses processes may include

- **Modifying the Enterprise Global Resource Pool**—Should instruct resource managers how to add and modify resources and the attributes about resources.

- **Defining Enterprise Global Resource Codes**—A major part of the overall configuration to enable resource management functions such as finding resources that match skills criteria, substituting one resource for another with similar attributes, and so on.

- **Analyzing resource workloads**—Provides guidance for staff and resource managers so that they can use PWA and Project Professional tools to determine whether resources are over- or underloaded.

- **Deleting and deactivating resources**—Tells the staff and resource managers how resources will be handled when they leave the organization or become unavailable to work on projects.

- **Assigning resources to project teams**—Provides guidance for project managers and resource managers on how to find and use appropriate resources from the Enterprise Global Resource Pool. This should also describe appropriate negotiation and communication methods for the identifiable resources.

- **Substituting resources within project schedules**—Instructs resource managers and project managers how to replace resources assigned to project schedule tasks. This may also reference step-by-step actions to take within Project Professional functions.

- **Assigning resources to project schedule tasks**—Provides guidance so that project managers and resource managers can understand what happens within Project Professional and PWA when resources are assigned to working tasks. This business process should also provide best-practices guidance—for example, don't assign resources to summary or milestone tasks, don't create local resources, and so on.

  ▶ SEE "Enterprise Global Codes," **PAGE 163**.

  ▶ SEE "Using Project and Resource Centers," **PAGE 345**.

Pillar 3: Collaboration Management

The success of every project greatly depends on how the project teams share information and take responsibility for delivering results. Project teams can use Project Server technology such as status reports, email alerts, timesheet notifications, and other functions to communicate project activities and deliverables. Figure 4.5 shows an example of a PWA status report.

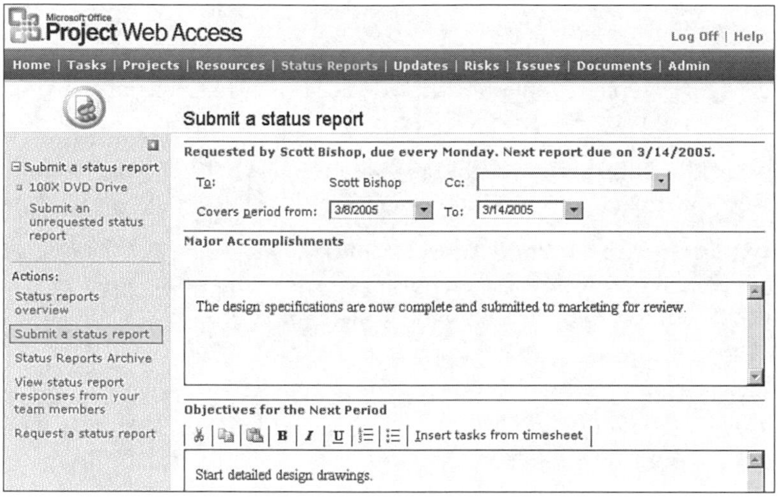

FIGURE 4.5   Status reports allow team members to effectively communicate progress to the project manager.

You should design business processes to guide people in the use of this technology. The business processes are critical to coordinate how the teams communicate among each other and with others throughout the organization. The business process guidance you provide reduces the overall risk to a successful implementation because teams understand their responsibilities to effectively communicate. Figure 4.6 shows an example of how a team member reports actual hours worked using the Project Web Access Tasks Timesheet function.

The EPM collaboration management plan should address each of the following technology items:

- **PWA status reports**—Allow team members to submit written status reports to project or resource managers. These reports can be placed on a request timer so that the reports are automatically broadcast at certain time intervals.

- **Tasks timesheets**—The primary method for project teams to report actual work for assigned project tasks. The originating project manager is automatically notified when the team members submit their timesheet for update into the project schedules.

- **Message alerts**—Enable each PWA user to establish how he should be notified about certain events—for example, a new task assignment, request for status reports, alerts when documents change, and so on.

- **Project Professional collaboration functions**—The primary method used by project managers to publish project schedules into the Project Server database repository and also notify team members about task assignments.

- **Resource Center timesheet summary**—Enables resource and staff managers to review timesheet data for resources they manage.

- **Resource Center approve timesheets**—Can be turned on whereby resource and staff managers can review submitted timesheets for approval and subsequent updates by the project managers.

- **Outlook integration**—Enables team members to use Outlook functions to submit timesheets to the project managers.

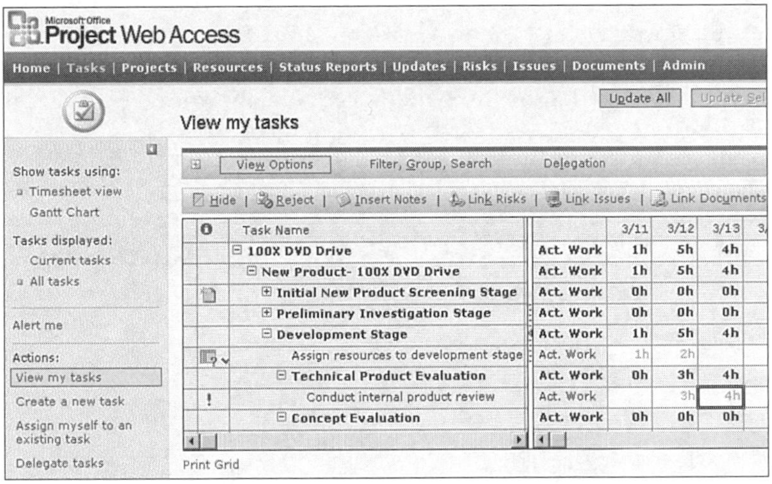

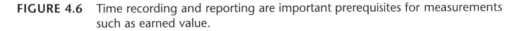

FIGURE 4.6   Time recording and reporting are important prerequisites for measurements such as earned value.

The EPM collaboration management plan should also address common business processes that provide guidance to people throughout the organization. These business processes may include

- **Issuing project status reports**—Provide guidance about what type of status reports should be submitted and when those status reports are due.

- **Tracking and reporting time**—Defines an operating framework whereby team members, resource managers, project managers, and other managers understand how time reporting is managed.

- **Administering lockdown time periods**—Provides a method to protect previously submitted timesheets that may be linked to accounting and billing systems.

- **Reporting administrative time**—Instructs team members how to partition their reported time that is not part of assigned project work.

- **Adjusting and correcting timesheets**—Defines who within the organization has permission to alter or submit timesheet information for other people. This business process also provides guidance regarding linked accounting and billing systems.

  ▶ **SEE** "Project Web Access Collaboration," **PAGE 293**.

  ▶ **SEE** "Time Tracking in Project Web Access," **PAGE 317**.

Pillar 4: Artifact Management

Many project artifacts are documents such as design specifications, quality control inspections, and other documentation regarding projects. Typical Project Server implementations include the use of Windows SharePoint Services technology to store documentation for each project schedule published within the database repository.

PWA includes the Documents tab, shown in Figure 4.7, as the entry point to store and review documents that can include Word, Excel, PowerPoint, Visio, PDF, and other document types. PWA also includes the Risks and Issues tabs, shown in Figure 4.8, which allow project teams to record and manage those types of project artifacts.

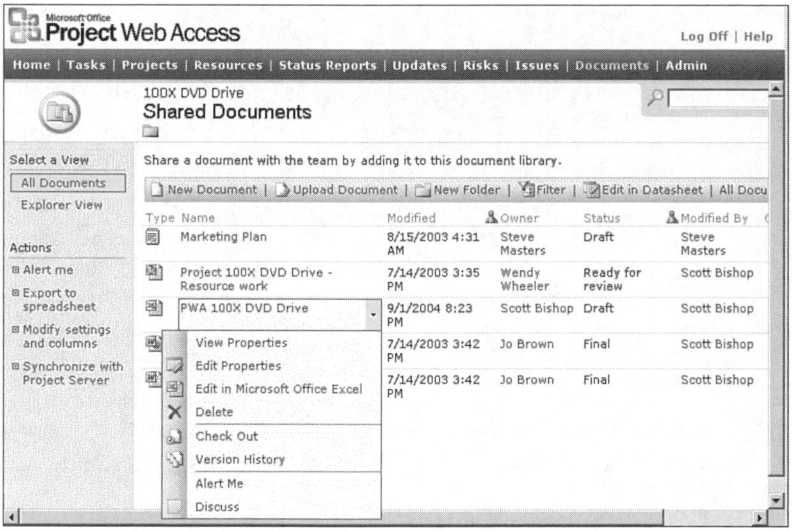

FIGURE 4.7   Note the different actions you can perform within the Documents tab in PWA.

You should define business processes that instruct your organization about using PWA functions such as Documents, Risks, and Issues, so that everyone knows where to find project artifacts. This guidance should address simple situations such as who has the ability to edit documents, how will documents be named, and the difference between a risk versus an issue.

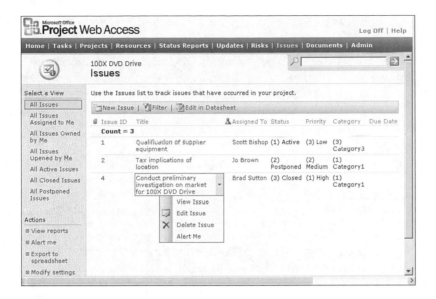

FIGURE 4.8   The PWA Issues tab provides a list of issues and their parameters for each project.

The EPM artifact management plan should address each of the following PWA technology items:

- **Documents**—Enables project teams to store documents such as Excel, Word, PowerPoint, and others within a project-specific repository. The documents can be directly associated with individual tasks within the project schedule.

- **Issues**—Functions allow the teams to define and manage issues about the project or about individual tasks within the schedule. Each issue can be assigned to a team member who seeks to answer questions raised within the issue.

- **Risks**—Similar in principle to issues except that each risk also has probability and cost effect factors defined as part of the risk. Risks can also be specifically assigned to a person and associated with a schedule task.

The EPM artifact management plan should also address common business processes that provide guidance to people throughout the organization. These business processes may include

- **Creating and managing project document folders**—Provides uniform standard guidance so that each project team uses the same general strategy to define and manage document subfolders. This guidance provides a common framework so that all PWA system users can recognize and find project information.

- **Editing and saving document versions**—A set of steps that helps team members open, edit, and save documents so that the document versions are retained.

- **Defining issues and risks**—Helps the organization understand how to define an issue and the conditions for which an issue becomes a project risk.

- **Measuring risks**—Helps people throughout the organization understand how to determine whether risks are becoming more or less critical as time or events transpire.

Pillar 5: Organizational Readiness

The fifth pillar of EPM is just as important as the other five pillars because if your organization is not ready to use the EPM business processes and technology, your implementation is at a high risk of failure. The essence of organizational readiness is to ensure that your organization can use the EPM technology within the context of your business environment.

The technology is much more sophisticated than simple desktop project management techniques that may have been used prior to Project Server implementation. The business processes needed are also more comprehensive and will require everyone across your organization to learn how to exercise those business processes while using the software.

You need an implementation rollout plan that addresses analogous conditions:

- **Comprehensive project implementation strategy**—Addresses all six pillars of EPM in addition to a phased rollout schedule.

- **Business process training**—Ensures that everyone knows how to apply business processes to manage EPM information.

- **Project Management Office (PMO) training**—Ensures that the PMO experts can help develop, set, and audit use of the EPM standards.

- **Testing and validation training**—Trains people who will validate and confirm that the implementation works as designed.

- **Training for project and resource managers**—Delivers the necessary knowledge to project and resource managers, so that they know how to use PWA and Project Professional to fulfill their responsibilities.

- **General management training**—Intended for other managers so that they are aware of what data the system holds and how to use software functions to review that data.

- **Training for technology support people**—The support personnel installs and maintains the EPM core technology such as Windows 2003, Windows SharePoint Services, SQL Server, SQL Analysis Server, networking, and so on.

- **Training for team members**—Ensures that the team members understand their responsibilities.

Each of these items should be addressed as you plan the EPM implementation across your organizations.

Pillar 6: Operational Principles

Another important part of a successful EPM implementation is the strategies needed to ensure that the EPM system is maintained in a manner consistent with the business's operational requirements. Before you install the software technology, develop a plan for how you will control the configuration and data over a long period of time.

After you install Project Server and Project Professional, the PMO or others will have the security permissions to alter the PWA and Project Professional settings. You need to decide how to implement configuration management control so that the systems don't suddenly change without a clear understanding of why. Configuration management of the PWA and Project Professional settings is an important aspect of maintaining the overall health of the EPM system.

Your EPM implementation plan should also address system availability, maintenance schedules for hardware and software, database backup and recovery, network recovery, and so forth. Each of these factors should be included within your EPM implementation plan.

The EPM operational principles plan should address sustaining maintenance and change control for each of the following technology and business process items:

- **PWA view generation and maintenance**—Controls the primary definition of PWA and Project Professional views. Daily operational stability of these views is important to ensure that people can get the information they need over a period of time. The PWA administrators need configuration management strategies to prevent unintentional effects on business processes when view details change.

- **PWA operating conditions**—Settings controlled within the Admin tab. The administrators can establish how certain Project Server features behave. These general settings also control Project Server functions—for example, email alerts, Windows SharePoint Services subsite provisioning, additional URL links on the home page, additional URL links within each PWA menu tab, and so on.

- **PWA security management**—A central control mechanism within Project Server. Strong management oversight is needed to ensure that only authorized people can view or change information. Therefore, the PWA security settings must also be managed through change control procedures.

- **Enterprise Global standards**—Settings are critical to every Project Server implementation. Some types of changes can have dramatic and immediate effects on the entire EPM implementation. Some types of changes can even completely disable or destabilize the Project Server installation. Change management controls should be designed to protect these Enterprise Global standards.

- **SQL backup and restore**—Procedures are needed to ensure the operational stability of the databases used by Project Server 2003. Configuration management and control of the databases are critical.

- **Windows SharePoint Services site management**—Also an important part of long-term stability of the EPM implementation. The technology and end-user community must understand how Project Server uses programmatic controls to manage Windows SharePoint Services subsites.

- **Windows operating system service packs and hotfixes**—These are a natural part of computing in today's world of technology. But some service packs and hotfixes may be detrimental to Project Server 2003 and Project Professional. You need to establish change controls for the server operating systems.

- **End-user desktop configuration control**—Also important so that end users have a stable and reliable application environment. Some application add-ins for Internet Explorer and Project Professional may be incompatible with PWA or Project Server in general. Therefore, you need to define the allowable applications.

- **Network management and security**—Is also a critical spoke in the EPM wheel because without a healthy network, there is no need for the EPM technology. Consider how your business practices require the network and then design the sustaining maintenance plan. If the network uses some form of load-balancing appliances for the Project Server system, you need to ensure that those appliances and the configuration settings are captured so that they can be restored if a failure occurs.

Defining Your EPM Scope

Making EPM a reality means developing a system aimed at transforming the organization into a more dynamic, project-driven enterprise. For that to happen, it is important to manage the organizational expectations of the EPM. An EPM solution is more than just the implementation of a project management software. It involves changing the way projects are planned, tracked, and controlled to ensure consistency throughout the organization. The EPM solution calls for the application of standards and principles at the organizational level and not only at the project level.

Managing EPM Rollout Expectations

It is important for the organization to understand the intent of deploying an EPM, which is to create an integrated structure linking functional departments with program teams.

The organization can expect that project managers, together with functional managers, portfolio managers, and executives, will identify the best practices and most suited project management methodology for the organization in the context of the EPM solution. Identification of roles and responsibilities of each party may ultimately be embedded in a governance agreement.

The *governance agreement* defines the organizational operational principles for project management, including the following:

- Role of the sponsor, project manager, and functional managers

- Budget authority allocated to the project manager

- Scope authority allocated to the project manager

- Change management process (describes how change will be accepted into the project)

- Resource allocation governance (describes how resources will be allocated from functional areas)

An important part of managing the EPM rollout expectations is to make sure that EPM stakeholders, and the organization in general, understand the organization's current project management terminology and processes. These processes, structures, and terms must be mapped into the Microsoft Project 2003 system, and the team must identify, review, and map any necessary business process changes required to leverage the new technology.

It is also important for managers and executives to understand that by participating in an enterprise system, some of the ways they were doing business so far may not apply anymore because an EPM solution seeks to standardize methods, procedures, rules, and structures throughout the organization.

Stakeholders must be aware of the fact that by implementing an EPM solution they gain access to a wealth of information and data not available to them before. Also, data reporting is now more complex, and it relies on the discipline of each participant in the project management process. The beauty of an EPM solution is that it makes it easier to spot project issues, and it increases the visibility of all projects and resources, and their assignments at the organizational level.

The organization must identify in the beginning all common business practices, structures, and terms for projects and resources and also identify gaps that must be closed for users to fully leverage the EPM solution functions.

Deploying an EPM solution requires the discipline of all participants and a long-term commitment to project management practice. It cannot be emphasized enough that introducing an EPM solution requires planning and regular review of the system to make sure that it reflects the organizational reality at all times.

Defining the scope of the deployment helps the organization manage expectations of end users of the system and those of the sponsors. It helps set the appropriate criteria for project acceptance and determines how the project should be measured.

Generic Phases of EPM Deployment

Most organizations that consider deployment of an EPM solution have developed for their project activities a certain methodology that varies according to the industry they operate in.

▶ **SEE** "Industry Examples for Microsoft Office Project 2003 Configuration," **PAGE 701**.

The following example of phases of deployment is generic and is not meant to override any existing methodology. Its intent is merely to give organizations considering an EPM deployment the necessary guidance and assurance of their own methodology.

Generally speaking, a project goes through the following phases and their corresponding stages:

- **Concept phase**—Includes the concept proposal stage and the planning stage.

- **Prototype phase**—Includes the design and development stage and the testing and verification stage.

- **Pilot phase**—Includes the preproduction validation stage and transition to the production stage.

- **Production phase**—Includes the launch stage.

- **Post-launch evaluation phase**—Includes lessons learned and administrative closure of the project.

The following sections describe what each phase should contain from the perspective of Microsoft Project 2003 deployment.

> **CAUTION**
>
> Bear in mind that this methodology is not specific to Microsoft Project 2003 deployment; it can be applied to any EPM solution.

Concept Phase: Concept Proposal Stage

During this stage, the project is being identified, and the organization recognizes the inception of the project. Also, an evaluation team is formed, and stakeholders agree on a project team that will manage the EPM solution deployment.

The intent here is to create an integrated structure linking functional departments with the project team. Together with other project managers and functional managers, the EPM project management team will identify roles and responsibilities for each party, including the following:

- Who is the sponsor of the project and what the role of the sponsor is. The project sponsor has the ultimate responsibility for the success of the project and usually is the primary liaison with the senior leadership team of the organization.

- Who is the project manager and what the role of the project manager is. The project manager has the responsibility for daily management of the project, ensuring that all interested parties stay informed at all times and also ensuring that appropriate actions are taken, as planned or in response to an unplanned event.

- Who are the team members and what their specific roles are. Team members have specific responsibilities covering the areas of software installation, networking, process and methodology, configuration, communications, and training.

Depending on the size of the organization and the size of the deployment, the number of stakeholders may vary largely from one organization to another.

At this point, the project charter is developed and agreed on. The project charter provides answers to questions such as the following:

- What is the budget authority allocated to the project manager?

- What is the scope authority allocated to the project manager?

- What is the change management process (describes how change will be accepted into the project)?

- What is the resource allocation governance model (describes how resources will be allocated from functional areas)?

In line with the roles and responsibilities assigned to each member of the project team, a responsibility assignment matrix may be developed to facilitate communication among project team members.

DEVELOPMENT OF A GAP ANALYSIS DOCUMENT

During the concept proposal stage, the organization formulates and describes the EPM solution concept and presents the technology requirements and availability. The resulting finding can be incorporated in a *gap analysis document*.

The goal of the gap analysis is to investigate and question what often passes for accepted fact and compare it with the practical reality of real-world experience in the business-technology arena within the organization.

From a technical perspective, the gap analysis presents the current status of the hardware (workstations, network, security features, and so on), their compatibility with MSP, and actions that must be taken to ensure proper and correct use of MSP.

From a business process point of view, the gap analysis identifies the functional business requirements. Although Microsoft Project 2003 is fully customizable to suit the desired project management methodology, a thorough analysis of the methodology and business operating model is required to assess the compatibility of the software with existing processes.

This stage is also marked by the development of the preliminary EPM solution targets (preliminary requirements and solution target). Understanding that it is impossible to determine accurately up front all the requirements of an EPM solution, the team will nevertheless try to gather as much information as possible from all stakeholders and develop a requirements document that constitutes the starting point for developing the EPM solution in terms of data, functionality, and access.

This stage also sees the development of the scope statement. To clearly define the scope you also need to state the assumptions made and the constraints surrounding the project. Each of these assumptions should be documented and followed up at a later date to validate the scope. If the assumption is false, it may have an impact on the scope. Constraints should also be documented and reviewed regularly to ensure the continued applicability of the existing ones and to identify potential new constraints.

Definition of the scope can be done in various ways. The most prevalent methods are to define the scope by identifying the deliverables or by defining the functionality and data.

When definition of the scope is done using the deliverables method, it is likely that project stakeholders will not be absolutely clear on all the deliverables, and you will need to make generic assumptions. For example, you might not know exactly what views will be required, but you allow for five unspecified Project Center views and three views for the Resource Center.

The other approach is to define the scope by definition of the functionality and data. The process is likely to capture what end users expect to see in an EPM system. The goal is to get the end users to formalize their requirements for information in a structured manner. This approach does not capture data that may be required to technically make the system work but does identify what the functionality is that the EPM system must provide to the end users.

The project team puts together a preliminary project plan and a business case that is submitted for the organization's approval. The plan should include the preliminary project schedule, budget, scope statement, risks and issues management, communication plan, human resource management, and a procurement plan.

Recommended documentation for approval and transition to the next stage include project charter, gap analysis, preliminary requirements and solution target, and project plan.

When approved, the project should move to the next stage: planning.

Concept Phase: Planning Stage

The planning stage is marked by refining and finalizing the requirements and solution target document and the project plan with all its components.

The project team establishes what projects and functional departments will be part of the pilot deployment and what period of time the pilot will run.

This stage focuses on technical and business aspects of the EPM solution. An important part of the business process assessment is the necessity that the project team understand the organization's current project management terminology and processes.

During this stage the organization finalizes the technical requirements and initiates purchasing and/or redeployment of the necessary hardware and software. In regard to the necessary hardware, you must consider that the project will have a pilot phase and a production phase, and that the hardware necessary for the pilot may be different from the one required for the full production deployment. You must make decisions regarding the application architecture and consider alternatives and trade-offs related to hosting, single versus multiple server implementation, federation, and process implications.

This stage is marked by finalization of the design and configuration document. This document contains the functional data and technical requirements. This document focuses on items such as hardware and software configuration, user and group roles, security settings, categories, views, server configuration, calendar settings, required views for Project and

Resource Center, Portfolio Analyzer views, time capture, use of administrative projects, and so on.

During this stage, the EPM project team must establish a feedback mechanism to capture items that need to be reviewed and/or modified. These items include installation and configuration settings, procedures, guidelines and instructions, and roles and responsibilities.

The project plan also includes plan items for the organizational rollout of the system. The same methodology that governs the pilot deployment applies to the organizationwide deployment. The EPM project management team must also document the strategy for deployment. One of the most important aspects of successful deployment is having the discipline to document key elements of the project.

Recommended documentation for exiting this stage and transitioning into the next are the final configuration and design document and the updated project plan.

Prototype Phase: Design and Development

This stage is marked by the actual build of the system and the configuration of Project Server 2003. This is the time when you install the hardware and software and configure the system. It is important that when you install the system to keep a log of all the steps and actions performed (installation log and notes). This can be helpful in case the installation is not successful or in case you need to debug certain aspects. It also serves as the baseline for the system and may help you in identifying potential areas for improvement in the future.

The project team must develop at this stage a testing and verification checklist. This document contains items that need to be monitored, tested, and verified during the next phase.

At the end of the prototype phase, the deployment team should have the EPM system built according to the configuration and design document, and have an updated plan for the testing and verification stage of the prototype. Also at the end of this stage, all users who will be part of the prototype verification and testing must be properly trained in the use of the system.

Recommended documentation for transitioning to the next stage are the installation log and notes, the configuration and design document (reviewed and updated, if necessary), an updated project plan, and the testing and verification checklist.

Prototype Phase: Testing and Verification

This stage is represented by actual use of the system in real life. During this period, the project implementation team meets regularly to assess the system and its use. The checklist of items that need to be monitored, tested, and verified represents the main point of reference for the general health of the system.

Also, during this period some changes will need to be made immediately, whereas others can be addressed at the end of the pilot, as a group. The reason for addressing these changes at the end of the pilot is that by then all users and stakeholders will have gained a better understanding of the system and will be in a better position to assess various changes and their impact.

During the prototype stage, the project management team should review the organizationwide rollout plan and submit it for approval of the company leadership. This plan must start with a production pilot and continue with the full production deployment. The production pilot stage is needed to ensure a transition period where the organization is getting ready for deployment and when all the procedures and methodologies are aligned with the business goals of the company.

After the prototype period has elapsed, the EPM deployment project team should review the operation of the system from a technical perspective and from a functional one. The technical review should include aspects regarding hardware performance, networking issues, and interface with other systems. The functional review should tackle issues such as mapping of business processes in the system, security rights and privileges for different groups and users, review of categories and enterprise views, and so on.

Any procedures and methodologies developed for this phase should be aligned with the corporate standards and business processes and document best practices.

Recommended documentation at the end of this stage includes the final design and configuration document and an updated project plan.

Pilot Phase: Pilot Production

This is the last stage before the EPM solution is fully deployed to the entire organization. You have two options here: You can either deploy the system all at once to the entire project management community of your organization, or choose a phased approach where each project team or functional department is brought into the system sequentially, one by one.

There is no good or bad approach to the full production deployment. Both approaches are valid and can be used successfully. The decision for one option or the other depends on multiple factors, such as corporate strategy, training plan for all users, availability of resources and support, and so on.

The focus of this stage is to validate the hardware, network configuration, and security settings. At this point of the deployment, the system should be stable and fully configured from a business model perspective. The deployment team may consider items such as server configuration and performance characteristics to ensure a proper maintenance procedure for the SQL server, monitoring the growth of the SharePoint sites, and so on.

One critical item for this stage is the development of the corporatewide training and support program. Training for end users should be scheduled according to their role:

- **Executives**—Managers in the executive ranks of an organization are often much occupied, and trainers should look for strategies to accommodate executives' busy schedules and to provide training without exposing potential gaps in the use of technology.

- **Portfolio managers**—These people focus on how individual projects combine into a composite of projects and have a specific set of training requirements, such as portfolio modeler and analyzer.

- **Resource managers**—Usually, members of this group are focused on allocating individual resources to various projects. Their key concern is to understand whether resources are allocated properly, what is the future demand for their function, and what trade-offs are available to them.

- **Project managers**—These people are typically involved in tactical activities linked to their projects. Members of this group must be provided with quality training to ensure that all features of the system available to them are adequately used to reap the great value provided by an EPM solution.

- **Project team members**—This group must be trained to use the collaboration features of the system and to perform the update functions required by project managers within project schedules.

At the end of this stage the recommended documentation for the project team includes the updated design and configuration document, the training and support plan, system hardware specification, and an updated project plan.

Launch Phase: Production Deployment

This stage represents the culmination of the efforts of the project team. Usually, this is the time when the Project Office takes over the responsibility of the system maintenance. The EPM implementation team ensures that all the users are properly trained, that the project implementation documentation is properly handed over to the Project Office team, and that the system performs according to specification.

It is not unusual to have some glitches, but most of them should be easily rectified with minimum inconvenience to users.

From this point forward the Project Office regularly checks the project database (Project Server) to ensure that the following occurs:

- All projects are properly scheduled and are updated regularly to reflect reality.

- Projects and tasks have adequately progressed.

- Each project task is properly resourced, understanding that any task may have one or more resources assigned. These resources may be generic or specific names.

- Costs are properly allocated to tasks.

- All project schedules must have a baseline and be updated periodically. Use of Work Breakdown Structure must be enforced and used consistently.

- All projects in different portfolios are grouped in the views based on basic health checkpoints and relevant groupings, such as location, percent complete, budget and schedule indicators, and so on.

- A change against the system configuration or a service pack or any other activity that effects a material change that directly or indirectly affects system behavior will be proposed and communicated to all Project Server implementation and maintenance teams. This includes but is not limited to systems administration, desktop deployment, SQL administration, systems security, operations, and training.

- A proper maintenance backup plan is in place, and the backup media is usable.

- All updates and service packs are properly applied to ensure proper functioning of the system.

At the end of the production deployment stage, recommended documentation includes the final design and configuration document, system architecture, and maintenance plan.

Post-Launch Evaluation Phase

After the system has been deployed in production to the entire project management community, the Project Office oversees the implementation of those methods and procedures that are most needed and are critical for the success of any project.

The PMO seeks out and "institutionalizes" best practices from within the organization, from consultants, and from industry symposiums and user group conferences.

Improved efficiency and accuracy in project plan development can be obtained by the development and utilization of methodologies that provide project template and estimate models for different types of projects. As projects progress, the PMO checks the "health" of the project by reviewing the details of the project plan so that deviations from project objectives can be corrected before serious impacts to the project occur.

The PMO takes responsibility for a professionally trained force of project managers. This should be accomplished through project management concept training leading to Project Management Professional (PMP) certification, EPM tool training, and training in soft skills such as leadership and team building. A close working relationship must be established with the Human Resources and Training departments.

This stage is marked by an evaluation of the project and the official handover to the Project Office of the EPM system. As an organization, you should obtain feedback from all stakeholders and document all lessons learned.

Capturing EPM Feature Requirements

Capturing the EPM feature requirements is an important step in making sure that the organization designs a good, solid system, capable of responding to the needs of the project management community.

It is important to understand that all EPM stakeholders must participate in the gathering of feature requirements so as to make sure that all relevant functions are considered.

These requirements must be captured and properly documented. The document may contain the following elements:

- Purpose of the EPM solution
- Problem definition
- Business objectives

- Initial approach
- Assumptions and constraints

When capturing the requirements a number of items should be carefully considered:

- **Enterprise Global template settings**—It is important to define these and make sure that all stakeholders agree because these settings determine the look and feel of the project schedules for the entire organization.

- **Calendars and Resource Pool settings**— Determining enterprise settings for project and resource calendars is paramount because this affects the scheduling and leveling calculations performed by Microsoft Project.

- **Enterprise Custom Fields and Outline Codes**—The primary goal for developing a coding structure within the Enterprise Global is to create attributes that are helpful in searching, finding, and selecting projects and resources. When considering development of custom fields and outline codes, focus on the key attributes. It is not necessary to create an exhaustive list for each project and/or resource. It is only necessary to cite the attributes that will assist decision-making when it is time to search, group, report, and select projects and resources. Also, avoid duplicating nonessential project or resource information that can be found using other sources (telephone numbers, office cubicle locations, and so on). During the process of defining these global code requirements, the deployment team must consider which project and resource attribute codes should be mandatory. Project 2003 allows for the required entry of some types of project and resource codes. The benefit of requiring an attribute code entry is that all projects or resources will be treated uniformly and consistently.

- **Project schedule templates definition**—Project templates used for scheduling purposes must align well with the methodology in terms of tasks and milestones, and must have generic resources assigned to tasks. Also, the schedule template should contain linked tasks and recommended durations.

- **Time reporting processes**—Project 2003 could have the greatest impact on people who have not maintained detailed records of activities in the past. They will be most uncomfortable with using the system because they must be more precise in every aspect of their daily work habits. The largest change may appear in the way project schedules are structured and how people track and report the time they spend on daily working activities.

- **Versioning and baseline requirements**—This represents, in many organizations, a strong cultural shift because it must be synchronized with the organization's project management methodology that defines when a project should be baselined and who has the authority to change it.

- **Reporting structure and how data should be displayed**—Ultimately, a good implementation of an EPM solution means that all reports created are accurate and meaningful to the stakeholders. In other words, a good report helps translate the data existent in the system into useful information for the user.

It is important to understand that every organization has specific needs and requirements for deploying an EPM solution. Nevertheless, following a documented and structured approach to the definition of feature requirements is always a good and recommended practice.

Communicating the Implementation Strategy

It is unanimously accepted that communication plays a major role in the life of any organization. When an organization decides to deploy an EPM solution, it is important that the project implementation team develop a responsibility assignment matrix and a communication plan that will be reviewed periodically for accuracy. Communication is of the utmost importance in every stage of an EPM implementation. The mere acts of communicating and listening will be interpreted by employees and stakeholders as a form of respect, which alone causes a great deal of value through a shift toward more positive attitudes.

The project implementation team must understand that deployment of an EPM solution also involves a strong cultural shift toward a more disciplined organization.

After the EPM implementation project is approved, it is important to establish the project management team and to assign the roles and responsibilities for each team member. These roles must be communicated to all stakeholders together with the project plan.

Project management team members are responsible for ensuring proper communication with the other team members and to the rest of the organization, within the appropriate limits dictated by the project implementation communication plan.

Following is an example of roles and responsibilities when communicating the implementation strategy:

- The project sponsor has the ultimate responsibility for the success of the project and fulfills the role of primary liaison with the leadership of the organization.

- The project manager has the responsibility for daily management of the project, ensuring that all interested parties stay informed at all times, and also ensuring that appropriate actions are being taken, as planned or in response to an unplanned event.

- Project team members are responsible for checking regularly with project managers to ensure that all tasks and issues are resolved in time.

- A communication specialist advises the project team on methods and ways of communicating within the project team and with the rest of the organization. Usually, this role is fulfilled by a member of the Human Resources department.

Communication of the EPM implementation progress must be done regularly in a structured manner. It is important to understand that communication of the progress to the organization must be done by only one individual. This ensures that everybody receives the same coherent and coordinated message. Having two or more people communicate the progress of the project or its strategy may lead to confusion and ultimately may significantly delay the implementation schedule.

A good communication strategy is part of ensuring a successful EPM implementation and must not be overlooked when planning the deployment.

Best Practices

- **Always develop a proper project schedule**—You must be realistic in estimating the durations and level of effort. No two EPM deployments are the same, and the particulars of each organization should dictate the duration and effort of the project.

- **Never skip stages and phases**—In doing so, you miss capturing important data and information, and you increase the risk of failure, which translates ultimately into lost opportunities and cost overrun.

- **Change control**—Make sure that you place the design and configuration document and the system architecture under strict change control.

- **Proper training**—Make sure that proper training is provided to all users.

- **Proper project documentation**—Make sure that your business processes map properly in the system and that all procedures and methodologies are properly documented.

- **Benefits of six pillars**—Planning activities for the EPM implementation are often considered drudgery, so this critical step, planning, is often trivialized or, worse, overlooked completely. When you address the six pillars of EPM as described in this chapter, you become more confident in the overall implementation. This leads to gaining stronger support from people across the organization.

- **Communicate the plan**—Don't forget to build a communications plan about the implementation. Make sure that you stick to it, even though you may think it's not needed. If other people do not understand the benefits of EPM, they may undermine your EPM efforts.

- **Scope control**—People throughout the organization may attempt to request more functionality to the EPM implementation than your organization is capable of handling. You need to be patient and structure a multiphase rollout of the technology and business processes. If you try to do too much on the first rollout, you are setting expectations that may be too great.

4

CHAPTER 5

Understanding Project Server Architecture

IN THIS CHAPTER

- Software Components
- Microsoft EPM Solution Architecture
- Scalability
- Network/System Security
- Best Practices

Implementation of an Enterprise Project Management (EPM) solution is a complex undertaking and includes a lot more than the technology installation and configuration. As one of our colleagues said, "It is not rocket science, but it is not trivial and simple either."

Prior to implementing and configuring the EPM system, develop your EMP Solution Vision and Initiative Roadmap. This roadmap will guide you through all phases of the EPM solution implementation initiative and help you manage client expectations.

Implementation of an EPM solution is also about organizational culture change. You should identify and manage the organizational impacts to ensure successful EPM solution implementation.

This chapter explains what exactly Microsoft Office Project Server 2003 is in reasonably simple terms.

The EPM solution, based on Microsoft Office Project Server 2003, is designed as a three-tier system. The EPM solution has a client tier, an application tier, and a database tier. Each tier of the EPM solution has unique components and provides unique functionality, as illustrated in Figure 5.1.

Components of each tier provide for availability and scalability, enabling companies of any size to manage projects of a wide range of sizes and levels of complexity. To deal with varying availability and scalability requirements and needs, where you are able to size and configure the application and database tiers of your EPM solution, see Figure 5.2.

Logical Architecture of Project Server 2003

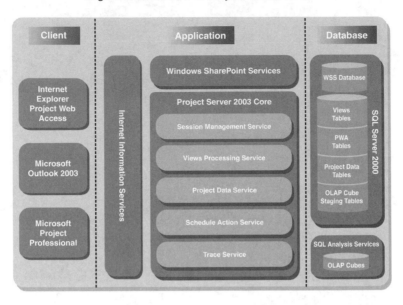

FIGURE 5.1   The logical schema of all three tiers of the Microsoft Enterprise Project Management (EPM) solution and how they fit together.

EPM Architecture Components

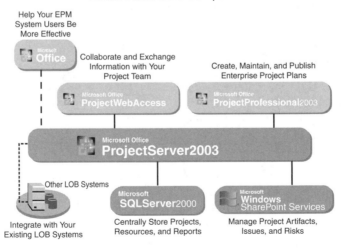

FIGURE 5.2   The architecture of the Microsoft EPM solution and how it maps to different requirements and needs of a typical organization.

Software Components

The EPM solution, based on Microsoft Office Project Server 2003, is designed as a three-tier system. This section describes software components for each tier.

Client Tier

You have some choices when it comes to what client application you use and when you use it. The client application you select mainly depends on your role in the organization and the task at hand. Are you a project manager who needs to adjust a project plan and reassign some of the resources on the project team, or are you a team member who needs to update and submit a timesheet for the current reporting period? The answer to this question determines what client application you use.

The client tier of the EPM solution includes Microsoft Office Outlook, Microsoft Office Project Professional 2003, Microsoft Office Project Web Access (PWA) client, and, possibly, any custom applications you may have developed to customize or extend the EPM solution.

Microsoft Office Project Professional 2003

Project Professional is a desktop application designed to enable project managers to create, edit, track, manage, and publish projects. In addition to scheduling and tracking tools, Project Professional provides project managers with enterprise resource and project portfolio management capabilities.

> **NOTE**
>
> Project Server administrators will also use the Project Professional client to define and maintain components of the Enterprise Global template, which is a central tool for defining, maintaining, and enforcing corporate standards.

Microsoft Office Outlook

Project Server 2003 facilitates integration with Microsoft Office Outlook 2003. There are two integration points for Outlook.

The first integration point relates to email-generated reminders and notifications. Users can receive email reminders generated by an email server running the SMTP service that are based on the task assignments status and email notifications based on various events in their Inbox. Email reminders and notifications also can be received by other email clients such as Outlook Express or Eudora.

The second integration point is the integration of project task assignments with Outlook calendar items. Users can download the Microsoft Office Project add-in for Outlook from their home page in PWA. Subsequently, users can synchronize tasks from projects saved to the Project Server database directly with the Outlook calendar. The tasks are then visible in the Outlook as calendar items, and users can use the Microsoft Outlook calendar to track and submit the task assignments status.

▶ **SEE** "Project Web Access and Project Professional Integration with Office," **PAGE 615**.

Microsoft Office Project Web Access (PWA)

PWA 2003 is a web-based client designed for users who do not require the ability to directly edit, manipulate, and maintain project plans. These users can have roles of resource managers, executives, or team members in the organization.

PWA provides access to the following set of features:

- Personalized home page
- Timesheets
- Project and resource views
- Status reports

- Document libraries
- Issues tracking
- Risk events
- Project Server administration

NOTE

Not all features may be available to all users. The final set of features available through the PWA interface depends on the user role and permission set associated with that role.

The PWA client consists of a set of Microsoft ActiveX controls and Hypertext Markup Language (HTML) pages presented to users by means of Active Server Pages (ASP). The first time a user accesses the server running Project Server through the PWA client, the ActiveX controls are downloaded and installed. To install and enable PWA on the client machine, the user must have the necessary Windows system permissions—log on to your computer as local administrator—to install the ActiveX controls.

Office Web Components

Project Server 2003 requires that EPM solution users who will be using the Portfolio Analyzer views feature have Microsoft Office 2003 Web Components installed on their client computers. You can install Office 2003 Web Components in one of two ways:

- By installing one or more Microsoft Office 2003 applications, such as Outlook, or by installing Project Professional 2003.

- By downloading the Microsoft Office 2003 Web Controls the first time that you access PWA.

NOTE

The Portfolio Analyzer functionality depends and is built on the Microsoft Office Web Components; specifically it requires Microsoft Office 2003 Web Components.

If the client machine being used to access the Portfolio Analyzer feature does not have Microsoft Office 2003 installed, on the first access a dialog box appears and offers the opportunity to install a runtime version of the Microsoft Office 2003 Web Components. If this option is not accepted, the Portfolio Analyzer views are unavailable. If this option is accepted and the installation is successful, the Portfolio Analyzer views are available. However, the runtime version of the Microsoft Office 2003 Web Components does not support the "interactive mode" of Portfolio Analyzer. This essentially is the capability to modify and maintain the Portfolio Analyzer view.

To create or modify the Portfolio Analyzer view, the user requires a full installation of Microsoft Office 2003 Web Components.

Line of Business Applications

Many organizations use other enterprise line of business (LOB) applications or develop their own custom applications to handle business-specific processes and requirements. The examples of LOB enterprise systems are human resources application suites such as PeopleSoft Enterprise or financial and accounting applications such as mySAP Business Suite.

These applications integrate with Project Server 2003 via the Project Data Service (PDS). The PDS is a web service hosted within Internet Information Services (IIS) that also serves as an extensible XML-based API for Project Server 2003.

▶ **SEE** "Extending Enterprise Project Management Through Customization," **PAGE 793**.

Application Tier

The application layer of the Microsoft EPM solution based on Project Server 2003 is comprised of three layers:

- The web-based front-end application layer, which is integrated with IIS and other Microsoft EPM solution components such as Microsoft Windows SharePoint Services (WSS).

- The Services layer, which provides additional services to other EPM solution components such as the Session Manager service.

- The optional email layer, used for reminders and notifications.

Web-Based Front-End Application Layer

The web-based front-end application layer has three components:

- Microsoft Office Project Server 2003

- Microsoft Windows SharePoint Services (WSS)

- Project Data Service (PDS)

Figure 5.3 displays the architecture of the Microsoft EPM solution application layer and how it communicates with other components of the Microsoft EPM solution.

Logical Architecture

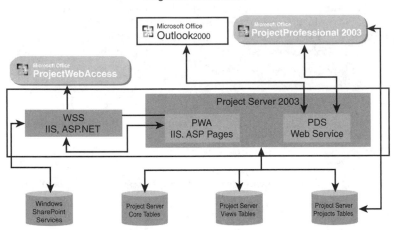

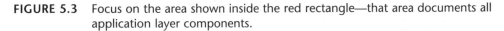

FIGURE 5.3   Focus on the area shown inside the red rectangle—that area documents all application layer components.

Each of these application layer components is dependent on IIS. One of the important considerations is how to deploy the components in the web-based front-end application layer when you are preparing plans for your Project Server 2003 configuration.

Microsoft Office Project Server 2003

Project Server 2003 is the central component of a Microsoft EPM solution and was designed as a highly scalable web-based server application that can communicate with several client tier applications, as well as the underlying Microsoft Windows Server 2000/2003 platform and Microsoft SQL Server 2000.

You can install Project Server 2003 on a single server or in a load-balanced server cluster to provide for future availability and scalability. Project Server 2003 can run on Windows 2000 Server or higher.

CAUTION

If you are running all Microsoft EPM solution components from a single server (perhaps it is the initial proof-of-concept evaluation server) and want to use WSS-based features—document libraries, issues, and risks—you need to install and run the EPM solution on Microsoft Windows 2003 Server. WSS components cannot be run on Microsoft Windows 2000 Server.

If you do not have a clear idea about anticipated future growth for your organization, consider deploying Project Server in a single-node cluster so that you can add additional Project Server nodes as the load on your front-end application server increases.

> **NOTE**
>
> It is recommended that you consider adding another Project Server node (*node* being another Project Server machine) when the total number of PWA users approaches 4,000. This is just a recommendation and not a hard-coded limit. Of course, this assumes that you have already done some performance tests to establish a need for an additional Project Server node.
>
> For more details on Windows 2003 Server load-balancing and a technical overview of Windows Server 2003 clustering services, download ClusteringOverview.doc at http://www.microsoft.com/windowsserver2003/techinfo/overview/clustering.mspx.

Windows SharePoint Services (WSS)

WSS is an optional component of the Microsoft EPM solution that provides project team collaboration features such as document libraries and risk and issue tracking.

> **NOTE**
>
> WSS is available as a free download from Microsoft at http://www.microsoft.com/downloads/details.aspx?FamilyID=e084d5cb-1161-46f2-a363-8e0c2250d990&DisplayLang=en.

WSS is supported only on computers running Windows Server 2003 and IIS 6.0, with ASP.NET enabled.

> **CAUTION**
>
> Microsoft SharePoint Team Services, shipped with Project Server 2002, is not supported for use with Project Server 2003.

WSS is a web-based application integrated with IIS and provides team collaboration features for PWA and Project Professional users. Depending on how heavily WSS-based collaboration features are planned to be used, WSS can be installed along with Project Server 2003 on a single server or a load-balanced cluster. It can also be installed on a separate server or its own load-balanced cluster.

Users generally use PWA to access the WSS features of Project Server, although it is also possible to connect to a standalone WSS site via Internet Explorer.

▶ **SEE** "Enterprise Project Management Customization," **PAGE 731**.

Project Data Service (PDS)

The PDS is the Project Server 2003 application programming interface (API). The PDS is implemented as a web service hosted within IIS.

The PDS is an important component of the Microsoft Project 2003 EPM solution. Clients such as Project Professional, PWA, or a custom client written by a solution-provider developer all access the PDS to obtain project and resource data.

The PDS also ensures that Project Server data stored in the database remains consistent and that data integrity is not compromised. In that respect, the PDS acts as an ultimate security gatekeeper for the Project Server database.

The PDS authenticates users first, checks for their permission set, and only then provides read-only or read/write access to the Project Server data that users are authorized to view or modify.

Client programs can also programmatically log on to Project Server and use Simple Object Access Protocol (SOAP) to call the PDS API methods. The PDS implements a SOAP listener, which receives method calls in Extensible Markup Language (XML) format and then returns an XML response to clients.

A client application queries the PDS for connection information to the Project Server database. Using this connection information, the application connects to the Project Server database and then queries database views to retrieve and update information for the projects and resources that the application is authorized to view.

In Figure 5.4, you can see the relationship between client applications and Project Server. The PDS is a middle-tier EPM solution component hosted within Microsoft IIS that acts as the security gateway for accessing Project Server data. The PDS receives XML client requests, maintains a connection on behalf of the clients to the Project Server database, queries the Project Server database, and returns XML responses to the client machines.

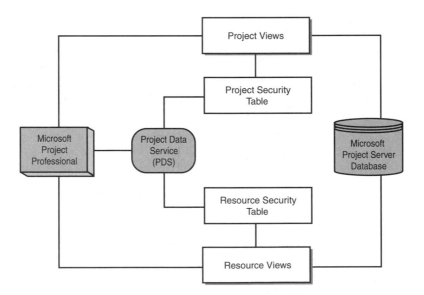

FIGURE 5.4   All requests from Project Professional clients to open or save project files first have to go through the PDS.

You can also query the Project Server database directly through SQL database views, which gives you access to project and resource information. After you have connected to the Project Server database, you can query the SQL database views to obtain required detailed information about your projects. The PDS provides programmatic methods to obtain the database connection information needed to connect to the Project Server database. You then can use views provided by the Project Server database to run queries against it—for example, to gather data for a customized cost or actual work report. These views ensure that client applications see only data that they have permission to see. As a matter of fact, client applications never access the actual Project Server database tables themselves.

Figure 5.5 documents the importance of PDS as a security gatekeeper during the process of project opening.

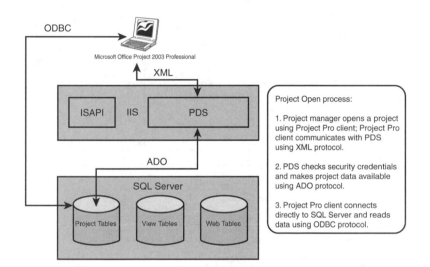

FIGURE 5.5   A request from a project manager using the Project Professional client to open a project file must go through security check-in PDS.

To maintain the data integrity of a Project Server database, any client application that needs to access Project Server data should operate within the Project Server 2003 security constraints as provided by the PDS, which here acts as a security gatekeeper for all Project Server data.

To access Project Server data, the client application has to do the following:

1. Log on to Project Server.

2. Call the PDS API to request the Project Server database connection information.

3. Make a connection to the Project Server database using that information and gather the SQL Process ID (SPID) for that connection.

4. Call the PDS to request access to the projects or resources that the client needs to access and provide the SPID from Step 3 to the PDS.

5. Make queries against the appropriate set of Microsoft SQL Server views to gather and/or update the required project or resource information.

6. Call the PDS when the access to Project Server database is no longer required to maintain the security of the data.

7. Disconnect from the Project Server database.

Figure 5.6 shows the process when a client application accesses the Project Server database.

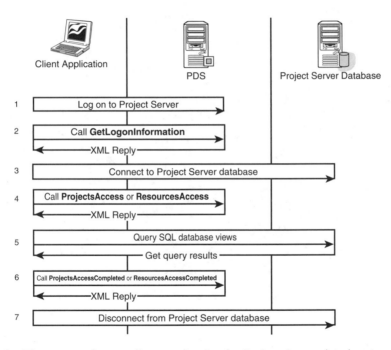

FIGURE 5.6   The request from a client application for Project Server data has to go through the PDS before the data is available for consumption in the client application.

The PDS manages access to the Project Server database views by tracking connections based on the SPID of the client connection.

The Project Server database has two tables for managing access to views: the MSP_PROJ_SECURITY table for project views and the MSP_RES_SECURITY table for global resource views. For each table, access is tracked separately for read and read/write views for a given SPID.

A client application cannot retrieve data from the Project Server database views without first logging on to Project Server and requesting access via the PDS to a view. This additional security check ensures that a client application sees only Project Server data accessible to the specified Project Server user logon ID.

> **NOTE**
>
> It may be a good idea that you configure IIS to use Secure Sockets Layer (SSL) for increased security. If you do not configure IIS to use SSL, potentially sensitive data will be sent in plain text between the clients and servers in your deployment.
>
> All information exposed through the PDS is transmitted in plain text, including the SQL Server 2000 username and password.
>
> For additional detailed information about the PDS, review the following Knowledge Base article: "Description of the Microsoft Project Data Service and the Microsoft Project Server security Architecture," located at http://support.microsoft.com/default.aspx?scid=kb;en-us;321377.

It is recommended that client-side applications perform only read operations on the Project Server database. If you need to create or update data, consider using a custom server-side PDS extension.

Project Server 2003 Services

The services layer of the application tier has two main components: the View Processing and the Session Manager services. These two services can be installed as part of a distributed Project Server 2003 architecture.

View Processing Service

The View Processing service processes requests to publish projects. The View Processing service also participates in building the SQL Server 2000 Analysis Services Online Analytical Processing (OLAP) cube.

The View Processing service is in charge of updating the View tables in the Project Server database each time a project or resource is added or modified.

By default, this service runs at below normal process and thread priority, which limits the system resources it uses. When the Project Server front-end application is installed in a load-balanced cluster, the View Processing service must be offloaded to a separate server machine. This offloading also allows the View Processing service to run at a normal thread priority on that server machine.

Even if you do not have the Project Server front-end deployed in a load-balanced cluster, you may consider offloading the View Processing service, if the average number of tasks per project reaches 800 to 1,000. Again, these numbers are for guidance only and require a careful interpretation. You need to consider not just the number of tasks per average project but also other project attributes such as number of resource assignments per task, number of custom task fields using formulas, and other project complexities.

> **CAUTION**
>
> The decision of whether to offload the View Processing service to a separate server machine depends on other factors such as the number of users in each role, the number of resource assignments per task, the length of the project, and the frequency of publishing based on the business rules identified.

The View Processing service only uses the resources from a single CPU, even if it is installed on a computer that has multiple CPUs. You may still want to use a multiple CPU computer to allow the View Processing service to use the maximum resources provided by one CPU while allowing other processes to access another CPU.

When a project manager saves a project, the entire project is saved to the Project tables and is available to other project managers, provided that they have permissions to open the project. After the project is saved in the Project Server database, it can—automatically or manually—be published.

The views of saved projects, however, are not always immediately available to other PWA users. The View Processing service reads the project data from the tables in the project database—Project tables—and then writes the project data in its fully expanded (time-phased) state to the View tables.

It is also important to understand that the View Processing service queues publish requests in serial and writes to views tables for only one project at a time. For this reason, depending on the sizes of the published projects—sizes in terms of tasks as well as overall project duration—project views may not be available to PWA users for a short time until all the required view data tables get populated.

Session Manager Service

The Session Manager service maintains session state information for PWA users. Each user is issued a session ID when she connects via a PWA client to a computer running Project Server. This session ID is used to save and retrieve user-specific information, such as the last used PWA view settings when the user connected to Project Server.

When the Project Server front-end is installed as a load-balanced cluster, the Session Manager service can be offloaded to a separate server computer. Depending on the identified business requirements and expected user load characteristics, the Session Manager service can be run from the same computer on which the View Processing service is installed, or it can be offloaded to a server computer separate from both the Project Server front-end load-balanced cluster and the server computer running the View Processing service.

Even if you do not deploy Project Server in a load-balanced cluster, consider offloading the Session Manager service to a separate server when the total number of EPM system users reaches 5,000 to 8,000.

Offloading the Session Manager service to its own server machine enables the service to maintain session state information for all users independently of the Project Server machine they access. Unlike the View Processing service, by default the Session Manager service runs at normal priority.

> **NOTE**
>
> When you install the Project Server front-end application in a load-balanced cluster, the Session Manager service can be installed on each computer running the Project Server front-end application. This is called *session affinity*, or *sticky sessions*. In this configuration, each instance of the Session Manager service maintains session state information only for the Project Server 2003 server it is installed on.

Project Server Email Layer

The optional email layer of the Microsoft EPM application tier may include an email server, such as Microsoft Exchange Server 2003, that is used to send task and assignment notification and reminder email messages to the appropriate users. All that is required to support email-based notification and reminder features is any Simple Mail Transport Protocol (SMTP)—or Post Office Protocol (POP)—compatible email server. Exchange Server may be a good choice because of the integration it provides, including Microsoft Outlook, a Windows-based email client, and Outlook Web Access, a web-based client.

Project Server Database Tier

The database tier in a Microsoft EPM solution is based on Microsoft SQL Server 2000. The database tier manages and stores all enterprise project and resource data and consists of several sets of database tables. These EPM solution data tables either can be stored on a single computer in the form of a single database running Microsoft SQL Server 2000 or can be partitioned in two or three separate databases across up to three separate database servers.

Organizations that require a centralized storage system of EPM solution data can take advantage of a storage area network (SAN).

Figure 5.7 represents the logical schema of a Microsoft EPM solution database comprised of four sets of database tables:

- MSP_* tables
- MSP_VIEW_* tables
- MSP_WEB_* tables
- MSP_CUBE_* tables

Project Database

The Project database is a set of Microsoft SQL Server 2000 tables that project managers and others who need to create, edit, or maintain enterprise projects or resources access by using the Project Professional client. When a project manager creates or updates a project, all related enterprise project data is stored in this set of tables, including data from all versions of each project. The project database consists of the MSP_* tables.

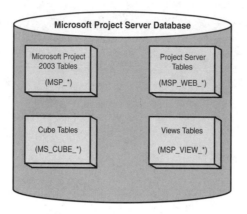

FIGURE 5.7   Project Server 2003 uses four table sets. All four sets of tables together constitute what is referred to as the Project Server database.

Views Database

The Views database is a set of Microsoft SQL Server 2000 tables that represent a fully expanded (time-phased) view of the project data stored in the Project database. When a project manager publishes or updates a project, the Project OLE DB Provider on the computer running the Project Server front-end application extracts the project and resource data and writes it to the Views tables. These read-only tables are used to generate a number of different views and reports used by PWA client users. The Views database consists of the MSP_VIEW_* tables.

Project Server Database

The Project Server database contains several sets of Microsoft SQL Server 2000 database tables primarily accessed by means of PWA. This database contains the MSP_WEB_*, MSP_VERSIONS, and MSP_CUBE_* tables, as well as views of tables in both the Project Server and Views databases.

OLAP Cube Staging Tables

MSP_CUBE_* tables are staging tables used for OLAP cube generation. These tables are populated from data in MSP_VIEWS_* tables and used to build the Project Server OLAP cube that is used by the Portfolio Analyzer feature.

Database Partitioning

A Project Server EPM database can be partitioned two or three ways. Partitioning enables you to place different project server sets of database tables on separate computers running Microsoft SQL Server 2000, thereby distributing data access by user role and activity type. For example, the project tables (MSP_* tables) can be accessed by project managers when opening or editing projects on one server running Microsoft SQL Server 2000, whereas the project views tables (MSP_VIEWS_* tables) can be accessed from a separate server running Microsoft SQL Server 2000 by users of PWA clients. This database partitioning improves overall response time for all clients and can provide means for greater solution scalability.

Analysis Services

SQL Server 2000 Analysis Services is a set of tools that provides access to data stored in OLAP databases. The main component of Analysis Services is the Microsoft SQL Analysis Services server. The Analysis Services server constructs multidimensional OLAP cubes of data to speed up and assist with multidimensional data analysis and reporting. This aggregate multidimensional data cube can be used for complex analytical reporting on projects and resources such as monthly project progress across the whole project portfolio or future resource skills capacity and allocation reporting.

In multidimensional analysis, you want to analyze and view your project and resource database from different points of views. That capability is provided by enterprise outline codes that function as dimensions in the OLAP cube.

The primary data resource for Analysis Services is the OLAP cube. A *cube* is a multidimensional representation of both detail and summary data. *Detail data* is specific row data, whereas *summary data* is aggregate data. Cubes are constructed based on the analytical requirements set by the enterprise project and resource data itself.

> **CAUTION**
>
> It is important to define your EPM solution enterprise outline codes correctly. They are the dimensions for your EPM solution OLAP cube and determine the quality of reporting you will be able to perform later on with Portfolio Analyzer.

▶ **SEE** "Portfolio Management Using Portfolio Analyzer and Portfolio Modeler," **PAGE 393**.

Each OLAP cube can represent a different business division or departmental project portfolio. You can think of the OLAP cube sides as different dimensions associated with your enterprise projects and resources.

Microsoft SQL Analysis Services is a required component if you want to use the Portfolio Analyzer feature available in Project Server 2003. The Portfolio Analyzer feature enables PWA users to view enterprise project and resource information efficiently, from different angles and in a variety of already well-known and familiar formats, such as a PivotTable or column chart.

To provide this functionality, Project Server uses Microsoft Office 2003 Web Components. These are a collection of ActiveX controls designed to let users view and publish fully interactive worksheets, charts, PivotTable reports, and databases to the web. If your users are familiar with Microsoft Excel PivotTable and Chart features, they will feel comfortable using Portfolio Analyzer in a PWA client.

Microsoft SQL Analysis Services can be installed on a server computer running Microsoft SQL Server 2000 (or—for small proof-of-concept or pilot projects—on a computer running both Microsoft SQL Server 2000 and Project Server 2003). For large deployments with many active projects, you can improve EPM system performance significantly by installing Microsoft Analysis Services on a separate server computer. At some point, the

OLAP cube generated for all your enterprise projects and resources may become fairly big, and the time required to generate the OLAP cube can exceed 10 hours. The OLAP generation process at that point may start to interfere with other system and Project Server processes because it consumes a significant portion of CPU cycles as well as available memory. If the Microsoft Analysis Services are run on the same server computer as your Microsoft SQL Server 2000, the access to Project Server database can be severely impacted for all EPM solution users until the process of OLAP generation is finished.

CAUTION

If the Microsoft SQL Analysis Services component is installed on its own server, or on a computer other than the computer running Project Server 2003, the Microsoft SQL Analysis Services Decision Support Objects (DSO) component of SQL Analysis Services must be installed on the computer or computers running Project Server 2003.

Microsoft EPM Solution Architecture

There are many different ways to architect a Microsoft EPM solution based on Project Server 2003. When architecting such a solution many factors will have a significant impact on your EPM system performance that you must consider, such as hardware and software, as well as user-related issues.

When considering the final hardware architecture for your EPM solution, you also need to address questions related to scalability and reliability. Based on the answers to your questions you can start designing your EPM system hardware architecture.

When designing your EPM solution architecture, consider the factors discussed in the following sections.

Number of Users and Their Roles in Your Organization

Per user, your project managers will place the greatest load on your EPM system and the team members the lowest. However, as the number of team members increases, the load and impact of this team members group increases as well.

The reasons for these different load characteristics are explained by different roles project managers and team members play in an organization. Project managers need to create, edit, and monitor their project plans. For that they use the Project Professional client. On the other hand, a typical role of a team member involves some team collaboration on issues, risks, and documents, as well as actual task assignment progress submissions. To do that, team members use the web-based PWA client.

A typical team member's EPM system usage tends to be concentrated within particular time periods, creating sometimes significant usage peaks. The example of such a peak created by team members is Friday afternoon timesheet submission. If your process for timesheet submission defines that all timesheets must be submitted between 2:00 p.m. and 4:00 p.m. and you have 8,000 timesheet users to process, the peak EPM system load during that time can be significant.

On the other hand, typical executives and resource managers place a relatively low load on your EPM system. The reason is because their activities are generally spread across different times. It would be highly unusual to see a large number of executives or resource managers trying to access the system at the same time to do the same things.

Also, you need to distinguish between the number of total system users and the number of concurrent users. When you need to deal with system usage peaks, you need to determine the number of "concurrent" users and design your system architecture to be able to handle the usage peaks and not the average load. After all, ultimately it will be your EPM system users from the whole organization—project managers, team members, resources managers, and executives—who will determine through their personal experience whether the system performance is acceptable.

> **NOTE**
>
> The *Microsoft Configuration Planning Guide*, Chapter 3, has a detailed discussion about identifying organizational requirements, including a discussion about estimating the number of concurrent users, project characteristics, and usage patterns. The *Microsoft Configuration Planning Guide* is available for download from http://www.microsoft.com/technet/prodtechnol/office/proj2003/ reskit/default.mspx.

> **CAUTION**
>
> The collective experience of many EPM system implementers shows that you definitely do not want to be too mistaken when it comes to assumptions made about usage patterns, average size of your projects, current number of EPM system users, and future growth of your organization when designing the architecture of your EPM system. The EPM solution is a complex and sophisticated system, and the last thing you need to be concerned about on top of this technological complexity is having to deal with unfulfilled user performance expectations.

Your Projects and Their Characteristics

It is important to also consider the impact of your projects. Think about not just the number of tasks in your projects but also, perhaps more importantly, the total number of resource task assignments in your projects.

Many big projects stored in your EPM database may increase the processor load of the EPM solution servers.

> **CAUTION**
>
> When defining what a large project is, do not think only in terms of total number of tasks per project. Also consider the number of resources assigned to all tasks, the number of custom fields with formulas, and other task attributes such as baselines used.

Many active enterprise projects also require many EPM system database user accesses as well as many and frequent views publishing requests. Publishing projects takes up processor time on the server where you run the View Processing service.

Usage Patterns

Business rules and processes you design may often cause traffic jams. A classic example is when timesheets are due by 5:00 p.m. Thursday afternoon for everybody in your organization. What is the result of this business process? Most of your resources who are required to submit their timesheets hit the EPM system servers between 2:00 p.m. and 5:00 p.m. on Thursday.

Another example might be all enterprise project updates are due by 1:00 p.m. on Monday. Again, think about the impact of that business requirement.

All your project managers will need to update and publish changes for their projects between 8:00 a.m. and 1:00 p.m. Monday morning.

The most sensible way to deal with these peaks created by your business processes is to design the system for peak loads created by these business requirements and not average loads.

Feature Usage Across Your Organization

Some features available for your EPM solution users create big loads on the EPM system servers.

For example, OLAP cube generation creates a large processing load on the server running SQL Server 2000 and Analysis Services. Also, many timesheet users may create big peak loads.

> **NOTE**
>
> Microsoft holds annual Project Technical Briefings. These technical briefings are usually held in Seattle during May or June each year. It is worth considering attending the next Project Technical Briefing for any IT professional or business analyst involved in designing, architecting, planning, or implementing a Microsoft EPM solution. Microsoft also produces a DVD from each Project Technical Briefing that is loaded with useful information, such as all presentations and keynotes from this three-day conference. It is strongly recommended that you get your hands on the DVD produced from the Project Technical Briefing 2004. You can review the last Project Technical Briefing agenda at http://www.projecttechnicalbriefing.com.

Scalability

This section defines system scalability and availability.

Scalability is the capability of a system or a component to accommodate greater demand while maintaining an acceptable response time for users. Scalability is an important factor for organizations that anticipate future growth. Although it is important for organizations to deploy a configuration that can accommodate current performance requirements, organizations also need to consider their plans for future growth when planning their configuration.

Because the EPM solution is a multitiered infrastructure, you can plan for and manage the performance of each EPM solution component within each tier. In this way, your EPM solution design is a highly scalable system that can handle from a few hundred users, up to several thousand users.

Availability is the capability of a system or system components to respond to user input regardless of the immediate status of the individual system component. A system or individual component that has a high degree of availability continues to be available to users during planned downtime or in the event of an unexpected system failure or disaster.

> **NOTE**
>
> Availability can be an important factor for organizations of any size. This means that high availability is not necessarily associated only with large enterprises but also can be an important consideration for some medium and small corporations.

Specifically, availability is important to organizations that have the following characteristics:

- **Users working in different time zones**—A high-availability configuration may be required if users in an organization are located across different time zones. When users are geographically dispersed, the definition of workday across the enterprise is much longer. This leaves much less time for regular maintenance.

- **Use of critical applications**—A high-availability configuration is required for organizations that cannot afford planned or unplanned downtime of any system components.

When you think about scalability metrics for your EPM system, here are the variables that you should consider:

- Users per hour:
    - Maximum number of times a specified set of user operations, based on your business workflows, can be completed per hour.
    - Focus on peak times such as weekly progress reporting as determined by your business processes.
    - Size and complexity of project and resource data will affect this metric.
- Cube building time
- Size of your projects
- Views publishing frequency and volume

Now that you understand what scalability and availability are, the following section looks at some key factors that impact the scalability of your EPM system.

Network Performance

Network performance is the most frequent bottleneck for most EPM solution installations. How do you know that you may have a problem with a network bottleneck? It may be typically indicated by poor performance or throughput with low CPU utilization on all tiers of the EPM solution.

In most cases, it is the result of latency rather than bandwidth, and the overhead associated with each network "round-trip."

Database Server Performance

A database server performance problem often presents itself as a bottleneck after resolving any problems with your network. To deal with these problems, use typical database server performance analysis and tuning tools. Solutions to these problems are well established and documented but can be costly in terms of software or hardware.

Project Server Security Usage

What enterprise project and resource data a given user has access to impacts the amount of data that needs to be retrieved from your Project Server database and transported throughout the other parts of your EPM system until it is ready for the consumption by your PWA or Project Professional client users.

You definitely want to consider use of restrictive permissions to limit the amount of data available to Project Professional users. Also, RBS-based security is a preferred way to leverage a role-based security system that is an integral part of a Microsoft EPM solution.

> **NOTE**
>
> For additional details about default security settings for a Project Server 2003 EPM solution, review the *Microsoft Office Project Server 2003 Security Group Guide* at the following location: http://www.microsoft.com/technet/ prodtechnol/office/proj2003/reskit/default.mspx.

Project Server Data Usage

Project Server data usage patterns are another key scalability metric. To understand what is meant by data usage patterns, you should follow a few basic guidelines when it comes to how you want to use your enterprise project and resource data:

- Depending on the portfolio management requirements of your organization, project management processes and standards can impact the way project data is grouped, filtered, and exposed for viewing in the EPM system.

- It is important to find a balance between the number and size of your enterprise projects. You may want to decide what constitutes the maximum size of "manageable" projects for your organization and when it may make sense to break a large project into smaller, more manageable subprojects.

- When your enterprise project average size exceeds about 1,500 to 2,000 tasks, consider segmenting these large projects into separate smaller ones. This can help to make projects more manageable and speed up the opening and saving of projects.

- Use the Open (opening projects in Project Professional) feature from Project Center and enterprise outline codes to work with "sorted and filtered" project subsets efficiently.

- Try to stay away from practices and business processes that require many project baseline saves.

- Consolidate nonproject or administrative tasks into a small number of administrative projects. It is a good practice to create separate administrative projects for all departments for each fiscal or calendar year. That way, you can control the size of the administrative projects effectively without creating a huge performance impact on your system when administrative projects need to be updated.

TIP

If you ever need to explore Microsoft EPM solution architecture further and need more details, download the *Microsoft Office Project Server 2003 Configuration Planning Guide* from the following location and review Chapter 2, "Identifying Availability and Scalability Solutions"; Chapter 4, "Identifying Environmental Factors"; and Appendix H, "Best Practices for Deploying an EPM Solution" at http://www.microsoft.com/technet/ prodtechnol/office/proj2003/reskit/default. mspx.

For further details also review the following Microsoft website titled Project Server Deployment Resources: http://office.microsoft.com/en-us/FX011442351033.aspx.

This Microsoft website provides an incredible wealth of information related to Microsoft EPM solution deployment with many useful links to other sources of information you may find beneficial when designing, planning, and implementing your EPM solution.

If you are still thirsty for more real-life, practical guidance from somebody "who's done it before," review the following Microsoft Technet webcast for additional ideas and concepts for your EPM solution deployment, titled "Planning the Project Server 2003 Infrastructure": http://msevents. microsoft.com/CUI/EventDetail.aspx?EventID=1032244736&Culture=en-US.

Network/System Security

When talking about EPM system security, you must consider several components of the overall EPM system related to the security.

User Authentication

Project Server 2003 can authenticate users who have a Windows user account, a Project Server user account, or both. It can be said that Windows authentication generally provides for better overall security than just Project Server authentication or mixed authentication methods.

By default, authentication for Project Server is set to Mixed, which means that both Windows and Project Server authentication methods are allowed. Users who need to access information stored on servers running WSS, Microsoft SQL Server 2000, or Analysis Service will still require Windows authentication.

You can consider the following general security guidelines when determining whether to choose Windows authentication only, Project Server authentication only, or Mixed authentication:

- If all users accessing Project Server already have (or can have) a Windows domain account, you should configure Project Server to accept only Windows authentication. Windows authentication is the most secure, and EPM solution users will not be prompted for their usernames and passwords after the initial network logon.

- If some users need to access Project Server from the Internet but do not have a Windows account, use Mixed authentication and consider setting up unique sets of roles, permissions, and categories to separate internal access users from external access users.

- Determine whether project managers will be allowed to create resources in Project Server as they publish projects and assignments to the Project Server database. If project managers are allowed to create their own resources, although this is not recommended, they should use Windows authentication for all resources that have a Windows user account.

- If your organization is using WSS, you should support Windows authentication for users who need to access the documents, risks, and issues features. Use of WSS-based features requires Windows accounts.

Implementing Secure Sockets Layer (SSL)

You can configure SSL security features on your web server to encrypt network transmissions between PWA clients and your Project Server 2003. The SSL encryption helps to ensure the integrity of your data transmission and to verify the identity of your PWA users.

Consider implementing SSL for your extranet users who access your Project Server 2003 from outside your corporate intranet. SSL may not be needed for your corporate intranet users.

NOTE

For more technical details about implementation of SSL, review information available at the following Microsoft website: http://www.microsoft.com/ resources/documentation/ WindowsServ/2003/all/deployguide/en-us/Default.asp?url=/resources/documentation/ windowsserv/2003/all/deployguide/en-us/ iisdg_sec_puzm.asp.

For more details on extranet scenarios, also review the *Microsoft Project Server 2003 Configuration Planning Guide*, Chapter 4, "Identifying Environmental Factors," available from http://www.microsoft.com/technet/prodtechnol/office/proj2003/reskit/servcfpl.mspx.

When you implement SSL as part of your EPM solution for your extranet users, you create a performance impact (10% to 15%) on the CPU of your Project Server computer. The Project Server machine CPU has to handle encrypting and decrypting of all communication traffic between your extranet users and Project Server machine. To alleviate this performance impact, you may consider using a special hardware accelerator card to offload intensive cryptographic operations from the host CPU to a dedicated processor on the card itself.

Project Server 2003 Security Model

The Project Server 2003 security is modeled on Microsoft Windows Active Directory security concepts, which is based on granting users and user groups access to objects and principals. There are similarities, but there are also differences in the way user groups are defined and used in Microsoft Windows Active Directory and Project Server 2003.

Security features in Project Server are designed to control and manage access to enterprise projects, resources, models, and reports and views stored in the Project Server database, as well as features available in Project Professional and PWA.

Project Server 2003 security architecture makes it easier to manage many EPM solution users and projects by allowing permissions to be assigned to groups of users and unique project and resource data categories, reducing the user and security permissions administrative load.

What a user can ultimately see in terms of enterprise data content and what he can do in terms of performing actions or manipulating that enterprise project and resource data are determined by the relationship between the user, the Project Server permissions at the organizational level, the individual permissions the user has or the groups to which he belongs, the data categories to which he is assigned, and the views of data defined within those data categories.

As you can imagine, based on the preceding short description of the Project Server security model, this security model can be complex.

Because the things a user needs to see and do usually depend on the role she plays within an organization, it makes sense to define groups, security permission templates, and data categories in terms of the job role she performs within the corporate environment.

Some users have implied roles; for example, users who publish project plans to Project Server are usually project managers. User groups should be defined in terms of the jobs or roles they carry out—for example, team members, project managers, executives, and those who have similar permissions assigned to them. These roles would then map to the different enterprise data categories, depending on the role's information and software features needs. For example, project team members usually need access only to their tasks, and, therefore, it makes sense to assign them to a My Tasks data category.

NOTE

This approach to security is reflected in the default predefined user groups, security templates, and data categories created when Project Server is installed.

The following are elements of the Project Server security model:

- A *group* is a collection of users who have similar information and functionality needs. These users are usually aligned with the type of roles played within an organization.

  Users can belong to multiple groups depending on the type of work they perform in your organization. Groups are security principals.

- *Permissions* are rules that determine the actions a user can perform while using Project Server. *Global permissions* provide rights over functionality within the instance of Project Server. *Object permissions* are associated with data categories. These permissions give users and groups rights to perform actions on objects associated with a data category. Permissions can be applied to a server (or organization), group, category, or an individual user. This means that the user's actual final permissions will consist of the combination of all permissions the server has, the groups the user belongs to, categories the user has access to, as well as permissions granted directly to the user.

- *Categories* are the collections of projects, resources, assignments, views, and models to which users and groups in Project Server are granted access. Categories define the scope of the information accessed, providing multiple types of access to data for groups of users.

- *Views* are sets of data fields that can be displayed for the collections of projects, assignments, and resources in a data category. Views also define the format of the display—for example, the columns displayed, a grouping style, or a filter.

The Project Server 2003 security model can be used effectively in many different ways. For example, it can

- Protect confidential data from other users

- Secure data from malicious or accidental damage

- Provide data depending on the information needs and functionality requirements of the user or user group

- Enforce project management processes discipline within the organization

    ▶ **SEE** "Establishing Security Model Settings," **PAGE 143**.

By now, you should have a good idea about what needs to be done to ensure a successful EPM solution implementation. You already went through an extensive planning phase, defined your EPM solution scope, identified your business processes, and developed your business requirements. You also should understand all the EPM solution architecture components, the way these components fit together, and the options you have when designing a comprehensive, reliable, and scalable EPM system.

Best Practices

- Before moving on to the physical design of EPM solution technology components architecture, it is a good idea to review your business requirements and establish a fundamental user profile.

- Choose the right approach to designing your EPM solution hardware infrastructure.

- Get the best possible hardware your budget can afford for your Microsoft SQL Server 2000.

5

CHAPTER 6

Designing the Enterprise Project Management Solution Architecture Details

IN THIS CHAPTER

- Reviewing the Business Requirements
- Server Hardware
- Network Topology and Architecture
- Hyperthreading
- Software Prerequisites
- Multiple Configurations
- Best Practices

As mentioned in Chapter 5, "Understanding Project Server Architecture," there are many different ways to architect your Microsoft EPM solution based on Microsoft Office Project Server 2003.

It was also suggested that when architecting such a solution many factors—hardware and software related as well as userrelated—will have a significant impact on the overall performance of your EPM system.

On top of all the previously mentioned requirements, you need to address the questions related to scalability and reliability of your EPM solution before deciding on the final EPM solution architecture.

Reviewing the Business Requirements

During your definition and planning phases, you developed a set of business requirements for your EPM solution. Before moving on to the physical design of the EPM solution technology components architecture, it is recommended that you review your business requirements again.

Perhaps there was a significant time delay between the planning and implementation phases, or maybe some assumptions related to the EPM solution usage and load characteristics you made previously might not be valid anymore, and you need to review and correct them.

A part of your business requirements collected for your EPM solution was also information about

- Number of users and their roles in your organization
- Your projects and their characteristics
- Usage patterns
- Feature usage across your organization

Based on the business requirements collected, you should be able to define some sort of fundamental user profile for your EPM solution that represents your fundamental assumptions about the EPM system usage and future load. This fundamental user profile can help you as guidance when you start designing your hardware architecture. Table 6.1 represents an example of such a fundamental user profile.

> **NOTE**
>
> Table 6.1 is just an example. You can add your own additional specific information and expand on what a fundamental user profile means for your organization. Examples of additional information you might want to collect can be information about whether you want to make your Project Server 2003 available via the Internet or whether you need to consider implementing SSL to make your EPM solution secure.

TABLE 6.1   Fundamental User Profile Example

Question	Answer
Number of Microsoft Project Professional 2003 users:	
Number of Microsoft Project Web Accessusers: (users in all roles)	
How many projects do you expect to have ongoing at any one time?	
What is the average duration of a project?	Small:
	Medium:
	Large:
What is the average size of a project (in number of tasks)?	Small:
	Medium:
	Large:
What is the largest project you expect to have? (tasks, duration, and number ofresources on the project team)	
Total number of enterprise resources (size of Enterprise Resource Pool):	
Average number of resources per project (size of the project teams):	Small:
	Medium:
	Large:
Average number of resource assignments per task:	
How will we track the projects?	
Backup requirements:	

TABLE 6.1 Continued

Question	Answer
OLAP cube generation schedule: Does your organization need to minimize apotential downtime for EPM solution components? Do you plan to use WSS-based features—issues, risks, and document libraries? If you plan to use WSS-based features, how many items per project would you need to createsand store?	

Server Hardware

At last, you have cleared all the hurdles and have enough information to sit down and design your EPM solution hardware infrastructure. You can choose from two basic approaches. The first approach assumes that you have all the required information to design your EPM solution hardware infrastructure, that the quality of that information is good, and that there are few doubts and uncertainties about the information provided—for example, information about use of WSS-based features such as issues, risks, and document libraries. Also, this approach assumes that you have a large enough budget to design a robust EPM solution hardware infrastructure that can handle all expected future load increases for the next few years.

> **NOTE**
>
> You do not want to find yourself in the situation where you need to deal with a large initial estimation error 18 months after the EPM solution is implemented and the solution hardware architecture you designed is not flexible enough to be scaled up or out further.

The second approach has a more humble beginning. Initially, you may recognize that you do not have enough good information about future growth needs or information about all usage patterns and feature use. Also, your budget is perhaps constrained at this point. If that is the situation you find yourself in, there are still ways you can design a flexible enough hardware architecture that will allow you to grow and scale up or out in the future without experiencing major pains of redesigning your whole EPM solution architecture from scratch.

The first approach will be discussed here first.

Based on the best practices of many EPM system implementers, you need to gather information about and have an understanding of the following:

- The network topology (bandwidth available and the network latency between client machines and servers)

- The range of complexity of your individual enterprise project plans

- Total numbers of Project Professional 2003 users and Project Web Access (PWA) users and combine this information with client peak usage scenarios determined by your business processes such as

  - Weekly Friday afternoon timesheet submission

  - Monday morning project plan review and updates with the actual work information submitted on the previous Friday

This information, especially the peak usage levels for various scenarios determined by business processes, is estimated based on a vision of the EPM system usage several years into the future.

Then, the collected information can be reviewed in relationship and compared with the six configuration profiles documented in *Microsoft's Project Server 2003 Planning Configuration Guide*. It is absolutely essential that the EPM system implementer's and her firm's personal experience with other EPM implementations is also considered and reviewed. Reliance on only the six configuration profiles documented by Microsoft is risky because EPM system performance is extremely sensitive to the data complexity of individual project plans in many ways.

This EPM solution architecture design process typically results in an order for machines, the definition of a specific EPM solution topology across those machines, and creates a scenario of the customer having an EPM system ready for future growth.

This is a necessary process you should go through when designing your EPM solution architecture and is the best practice of today. However, many clients cannot accurately predict the needs of tomorrow or the acceptance of the system within their companies and frequently either underestimate or overestimate the speed of the deployments.

NOTE

For large EPM solution implementations you probably want to start with hardware architecture based on three servers as an absolute minimum. The first server would run SQL Server 2000 and Analysis Services. The second server would be your Project Server 2003 front-end application and also run the Views Publishing and Session Manager services. The Project Server 2003 box should be configured as a single node web farm for possible future server node additions. The third server would be dedicated to WSS.

The second approach to designing your EPM solution hardware is an initially more humble approach and may be more acceptable for clients without large budgets.

Many clients cannot afford to invest in a system scoped and architected for forecasted/expected usage levels two or three years down the road. They require the ability to start small and grow and scale up or out their EPM solution architecture. For this scenario, some general guidance based on current best practice knowledge would be helpful, but, unfortunately, very little information is readily available. This section attempts to define some basic principles for the second "start small and grow" scenario.

The best practice to date is to get the best possible hardware your budget can afford for your Microsoft SQL Server 2000 and, if absolutely necessary, run all EPM solution components from this single server box for small deployments or pilot projects.

Optionally, you can consider starting with two servers, one running Project Server 2003 and the second, more powerful server, running your SQL Server 2000 and Analysis Services. The question in this case is where to install and run WSS. The answer depends on how heavily the EPM solution features based on WSS will be used and whether your SQL Server 2000 hardware provides enough capacity to handle additional load from WSS.

The next scale point would be to break out the Project Server 2003 front-end application to a separate server machine. If you want to keep your options open for scaling out your EPM solution architecture in the future, install and configure this Project Server front-end server as a single node web farm for possible future server node additions.

After this point, your options can become vague and are even more dependent on individual EPM solution implementation. Moving SQL 2000 Analysis Services or Views Publishing service off the SQL Server 2000 box are typically the next steps. In most cases, SQL 2000 Analysis Services is usually moved first. Moving the Views Publishing service to another server is a trade-off because it may run faster and reduce the amount of network traffic between EPM system servers when it is running on the SQL Server 2000 box. However, the SQL Server 2000 machine CPU is impacted, and you have to make sure that your SQL Server 2000 machine has enough capacity to handle additional load from the Views Publishing service.

Database segmentation techniques should be an option reserved for cases when you deal with extreme performance issues of your EPM system. Figure 6.1 presents detailed hardware architecture diagrams showing some of your scaling options.

Both of the previous scenarios (large initial EPM hardware architecture and "start small and grow") require life cycle monitoring of system performance. In general, the most critical measure of performance is the user perception of the EPM solution performance. Unfortunately, the user perceived performance is the end result of a complex system, and you also have to sometimes determine whether the user perception of the system performance is correct. You need to be able to make adjustments to your EPM system and react quickly to address your user concerns.

> **NOTE**
>
> For additional hardware configuration details and examples of six configuration profiles, review *Microsoft's Project Server 2003 Planning Configuration Guide,* Chapter 6, "Selecting a Project Server Configuration." The *Guide* is available for download from http://www.microsoft.com/ downloads/ details.aspx?FamilyID=5f467651-4f7c-4aa5-9243-a529b8b49015&DisplayLang=en.

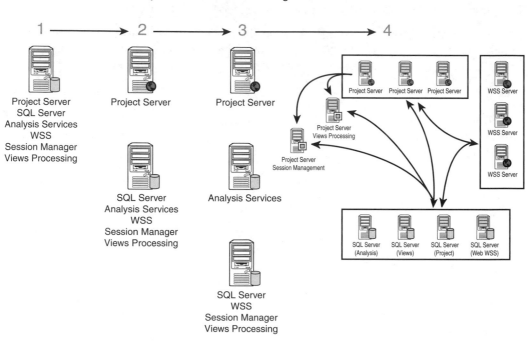

Project Server 2003 - Scaling Scenarios

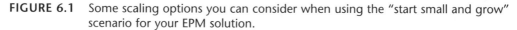

FIGURE 6.1   Some scaling options you can consider when using the "start small and grow" scenario for your EPM solution.

Network Topology and Architecture

In the previous sections some basic networking issues and their potential impact on EPM system performance were covered. It was mentioned that network performance is the most frequent bottleneck for most EPM solution installations and as such your network architecture and topology demands your attention and careful consideration.

Network Latency and Bandwidth

The network bottleneck may be typically indicated by poor performance or throughput with low CPU utilization on all tiers of the EPM solution, and, in most cases, it is the result of latency rather than bandwidth problems.

Bandwidth is defined as the maximum throughput of a network connection. The greater the network bandwidth, the greater the amount of network data that can be transmitted during a specific period of time. High-bandwidth connections between all server components of your EPM solution are important to the overall EPM system performance. However, if you have a high-bandwidth connection in place between all EPM solution components, but your users experience high network latency, the performance of your EPM system may still be unacceptable.

Latency is defined as the delay that occurs when network packets are transmitted from one network to another or from one segment of a network to another. The delay is measured in milliseconds (ms) and is typically caused by gateway devices such as routers and bridges, which process packets and perform network protocol conversion.

Unfortunately, you may have limited tools available to alleviate the problems related to latency, and that is because network latency is determined by your corporate network topology. Chances are you may be able to do something about inadequate bandwidth between the EPM solution components. You could move the EPM components closer to each other or place them at your corporate data center with a 1Gb Ethernet or fiber connection available between server components. But even then, you may be able to do little about your corporate network topology, the physical location of your network routers and bridges. Fifty milliseconds and higher latency can cause significant increases in project open and save times.

Network bandwidths of less than 10Mbps may indicate the need for Terminal Services server as part of your EPM solution.

> **NOTE**
>
> For additional suggestions on how to improve network performance, review the *Microsoft Project Server 2003 Planning Configuration Guide*, Appendix H, "Best Practices for Deploying an EPM Solution."

Using Multiple NIC Cards or NIC Teaming

One of the top 10 recommendations from the Microsoft Customer Architecture Review Team (CART) is to use multiple network interface cards (NICs) on the Project Server database server.

The CART program was initiated in December 2002 by Microsoft as a means of providing detailed recommendations to large customers preparing to deploy Microsoft Office Project Server 2002 and, later on, Microsoft Office Project Server 2003. CART also assists in providing a thorough review of the hardware architecture and configuration that the customer intended to deploy. After completing a number of customer reviews, Microsoft identified a set of technical recommendations that most routinely appeared during these reviews.

> **NOTE**
>
> The following information is based on recommendations from the CART team. Many of the CART recommendations are documented in the *Microsoft Office Project Server 2003 Configuration Planning Guide*, Appendix H, "Best Practices for Deploying an EPM Solution," available from http://www.microsoft.com/technet/prodtechnol/office/proj2003/reskit/default.mspx.

The recommendation to use multiple NICs or NIC teaming was frequently made to improve the scalability of the system where CPU and memory on the database server appear underutilized. In high use cases, you may notice a network bottleneck developed at the network interface on the database server machine. This bottleneck is caused by communication traffic from the PWA web server, Project Professional clients, and the Views Processing/Cube Generation system. In the end, all these EPM solution components and clients need to communicate with the Project Server database, and this can cause a high volume of traffic to be sent to a single NIC on the database server. There are multiple ways to mitigate this bottleneck.

Dual NIC Configuration

The most frequently recommended, least expensive, and most easily implemented solution is to add a second NIC to the database server and then configure the EPM solution components to selectively initiate communications with one of these two NIC interfaces. For example, by altering settings in the Project Server registry, you could force all communications from the PWA web server to go to NIC #1 on the database server, while all Views Processing and Cube Generation traffic goes through NIC #2. By doing this, you can successfully spread the network traffic across both NICs and reduce the bottleneck at this point of the EPM system.

Hardware Solution

Many hardware vendors sell systems generally referred to as *NIC teaming* or *NIC clustering* that support the use of multiple NIC interfaces to simulate a single logical NIC. This type of solution can reduce the network bottleneck if used with the database server.

> **NOTE**
>
> The following URL link is one of the sites that has some useful information and more details on NIC teaming solutions: http://h18004.www1.hp.com/ products/servers/networking/teaming.html#switch.

Multiple Network Segments Configuration

The final way to more effectively spread network traffic across various NIC interfaces on the database server is to install multiple network segments to carry different traffic. In this configuration, LAN segment 1 could support traffic between the IIS server(s) and the database server only, while LAN 2 supported traffic between Project Professional clients and the database server. This is an effective but more complex solution to the problem.

Wide Area Networks (WAN)

Latency and bandwidth issues have to be carefully considered in a WAN environment. Many large corporations deploy their EPM solution in a WAN environment. Although bandwidth is an important factor in a WAN environment, latency is usually a much bigger concern for a Project Server 2003–based EPM solution deployment.

Network bandwidth and network latency are separate terms. Networks with high bandwidth do not necessarily guarantee low latency. For example, a network path traversing a satellite link often has high latency, even though throughput is very high. It is not uncommon for a network round trip traversing a satellite link to have five or more seconds of latency.

It is important to understand the implication of such a delay. For example, an application designed to send a request, wait for a reply, send another request, wait for another reply, and so on, will wait at least 5 seconds for each packet exchange, regardless of how fast the server is.

Despite the increasing speed of computers, satellite transmissions and network media are based on the speed of light, which generally stays constant, at least as far as we humans can say. As such, improvements in latency for existing satellite networks are unlikely to occur.

The lower the latency delay, the better your WAN performance will be. Latency becomes an issue if you are transporting large amounts of data over the WAN connection—for example, when a Project Professional user opens or saves a project from or to the Project Server database.

For an EPM solution, WAN performance is generally acceptable if latency does not exceed 30 to 50ms. If your WAN users' connections experience a latency delay above 50ms, you may consider using Terminal Services as part of your EPM solution deployment.

As mentioned earlier in this chapter, network bandwidths of less than 10Mbps may also indicate the need for Terminal Services.

TIP

Several TCP/IP tools can be used to get a better idea of what latency your connection is experiencing. The following tools can be useful when troubleshooting your TCP/IP network and finding out what the latency of your WAN connection is:

- Pathping
- Ping
- Tracert

For more details about how to use these TCP/IP utilities, review the information available at the Microsoft Windows 2000 Resource Kit:

http://www.microsoft.com/resources/documentation/Windows/2000/server/reskit/en-us/Default.asp?url=/ resources/documentation/Windows/2000/server/reskit/en-us/cnet/cnbd_trb_ssis.asp.

EPM Solution for Users in Multiple Geographic Locations

The final EPM solution configuration also depends on the geographic distribution of your EPM system users.

If all EPM solution users in your organization are located at a single physical location and have low-latency, high-bandwidth connections to your corporate data center where all EPM solution server components are installed, geographical distribution of your users will probably not play a major role in determining your EPM solution hardware configuration.

On the other hand, if EPM solution users in your organization are spread across different geographic regions, you must take the multiple geographic locations and all their characteristics under consideration when planning your Project Server 2003 hardware configuration.

You also have to evaluate the impact of your users working in multiple time zones. It is highly probable that they will be accessing the Project Server corporate database around the clock and, therefore, leaving little or perhaps almost no time for regular IT maintenance tasks on the server components of your EPM solution. If this is the scenario you are faced with, consider a high-availability EPM system configuration to allow for needed IT maintenance.

If EPM solution users in your organization are spread across different geographic regions, you can consider the following scenario.

Deploy all your EPM solution servers in the same domain and ensure that all server components are connected with high-bandwidth, low-latency LAN connections. For all your EPM system users located wherever, deploy Terminal Services to provide access to the Project Server database through Microsoft Office Project Professional 2003 client.

EPM Solution Deployment in Trusted and Nontrusted Domain Environments and Extranets

To clarify, installing all Project Server 2003 EPM solution components on a single server, perhaps for an initial proof-of-concept project, is fairly simple, provided that you have reviewed the *Microsoft Office Project Server 2003 Installation Guide* and followed all the steps in the correct sequence. The *Microsoft Office Project Server 2003 Installation Guide* is available from http://www.microsoft.com/downloads/ details.aspx?FamileID=ca99b5e3-0478-4ac3-a230-c4f2d82096c1&DisplayLang=en.

As soon as you start to consider distributed hardware architecture for your EPM solution components, things get much more complex, and you need to be aware of some potential issues and problems. The main reason for this complexity is that Project Server architecture is flexible. In addition, Project Server relies on and integrates with other Microsoft products such as WSS, IIS, and SQL Server 2000.

Several key deployment options are available to you. First, you can deploy all the EPM solution components in a single domain on single or multiple servers. If that is the case, things usually work well, and issues such as user authentication and security are typically of less concern.

Second, you can deploy the EPM solution components across multiple domains. At that point, things become a lot more interesting because you have to start thinking about what accounts, domain or local, to create and use for what, as well as understand trust relationships between your multiple domains.

The ultimate "fun" is to deploy the EPM solution components in a multiple domain environment with corporate firewalls in place and requirements specifying extranet access for your users. Here you need to make sure that your hardware architecture provides safe and efficient access to both internal and external users. The question now is what TCP/IP ports you need to open to provide safe external and internal access for your users. Figure 6.2, for example, demonstrates hardware architecture for your EPM solution components deployed across single and multiple domains.

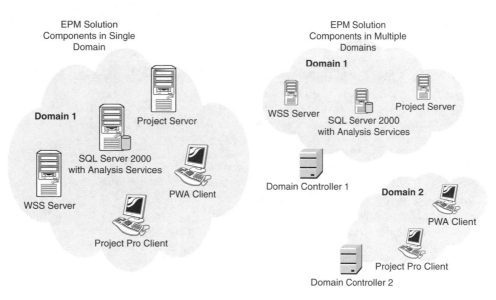

FIGURE 6.2   Example distributed architecture for your EPM solution components deployed across single and multiple domains where users are in different domains.

How you define your EPM solution external and internal users, as well as what is considered extranet and intranet, is based on the user's location relative to your corporate firewall.

EPM Deployment in Trusted Domains

You can deploy EPM solution components in a single domain, in multiple domains, or in a workgroup. Regardless of the domain configuration in which you deploy your EPM solution components, you must ensure that all your users can be authenticated when accessing all required resources. The nature of the trust relationships that exist between your domains, in which users and EPM solution components are deployed, affects the ability of all users in your organization to access corporate project data and the Project Server functionality.

In a single domain or a multiple domain configuration in which two-way trust relationships exist between multiple domains, your users are automatically authenticated access to Project Server components and resources, provided that you use Windows authentication. If two-way trust relationships do not exist between your multiple domains, you must create local accounts for each EPM component server in the domain in which the EPM component server requires access.

Maintaining corporate project and resource data in the same domain in which your users are located and defined or in a domain that exists in the same *forest* (a single domain tree or a group of domain trees grouped together to share resources) as the domain in which the users who need to access the corporate data are located is the easiest way to enable access to your Project Server data. Domains located in a single Active Directory forest also have automatic two-way trust relationships established. You can also manually establish two-way trusts between domains located in different Active Directory forests.

> **NOTE**
>
> To understand the concepts of Active Directory forests, trees, domains, and organizational units, refer to the following Microsoft TechNet page for more detailed information: http://www.microsoft.com/ technet/prodtechnol/windowsserver2003/technologies/directory/activedirectory/default.mspx.

Now you see an example of the EPM solution components distributed across three domains that exist in the same Active Directory forest. Project Server components are located in domains 1 and 3, and PWA and Project Professional users are located in domain 2. Figure 6.3 shows users in domain 2 accessing all distributed Project Server components in domains 1 and 3 automatically using Windows authentication because all domains in the same Active Directory forest have two-way trust relationships established.

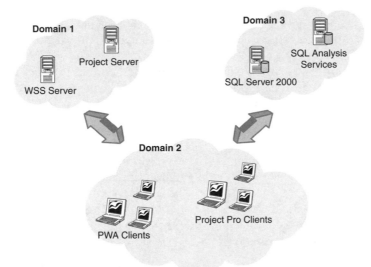

FIGURE 6.3   Distributed EPM solution components deployed across three domains in the same Active Directory forest.

> **NOTE**
>
> When you perform Active Directory synchronization across trusted domains in separate forests, you must reference the domains by using the Fully Qualified Domain Name (FQDN). This is because trusted domains located in different forests do not share the root of the global catalog.

One-Way Trust Relationships

If the domains in which your users and your EPM solution components are located are not in the same forest, the two-way trust relationships between domains are not automatically configured. Make sure that you account for this in your configuration planning.

To enable EPM solution users from a domain in one forest to have authenticated access to project and resource data residing in a domain in another forest, you can establish manually one-way trusts.

Figure 6.4 shows a one-way trust relationship in which domains 1 and 2 are in one forest and share a two-way transitive trust relationship, and domain 3 is in a separate forest. A one-way trust is established between domain 3 and domain 1. Because domain 2 trusts domain 3 by means of a transitive trust relationship with domain 2, users in domain 2 can access Project Server data in domain 3.

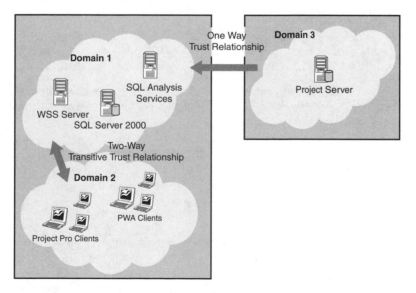

FIGURE 6.4   EPM solution components deployed across three domains in different Active Directory forests with a one-way trust relationship configured between domains in separate forests.

EPM Deployment in Nontrusted Domains

The Project Server 2003 architecture is flexible enough that you can deploy EPM solution components across nontrusted domains. You can also deploy an EPM solution in a Windows workgroup or in a Novell network environment.

Figure 6.5 shows an environment in which EPM solution components are deployed across four domains that do not have any trust relationships configured. In this scenario, EPM solution users do not have authenticated access to the domains in which the EPM solution components are located.

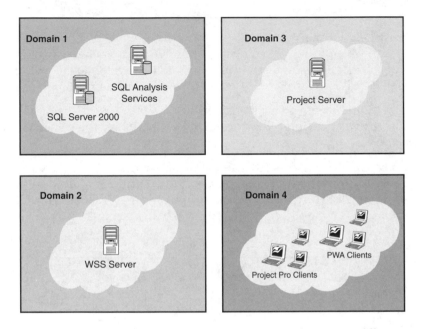

FIGURE 6.5   EPM solution components deployed across four domains in different Active Directory forests with no trust relationship configured between domains in separate forests.

You need to understand that in general this configuration provides limited Project Server functionality that can reduce the overall security of your EPM solution deployment, and increases administration effort significantly. Use of the Portfolio Analyzer feature is limited, and you have limited ability to publish projects and assignments to the Project Server database.

If you absolutely must deploy Project Server 2003 in a nontrusted domain environment, it is recommended that you create local user accounts on each EPM component server to which users require access. This definitely creates additional administrative overhead, but it allows users in nontrusted domains to access Project Server data. You may also need to give the default IIS anonymous user account (IUSR_*ComputerName*) permissions on the ViewDrop folder used by the Views Publishing service.

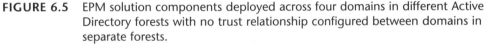

NOTE

Allowing users to access Project Server data from a nontrusted domain, regardless of the authentication method, is not as secure as requiring users to use Windows user accounts to access Project Server data from trusted domains.

Windows SharePoint Services in a Nontrusted Domain Environment

As was mentioned previously, you can enable users to use the PWA client to work with documents, issues, and risks in a nontrusted domain environment by creating local user accounts on the server running WSS. However, in this scenario, the Project Server database tables are not updated to reflect the additional site content.

SQL Analysis Services in a Nontrusted Domain Environment

Server computers running Project Server 2003, SQL Server 2000, and Analysis Services must all be in the same domain, or in trusted domains, for you to be able to have a full feature set of the Portfolio Analyzer available. Portfolio Analyzer is based on the OLAP cube built and managed by SQL Server 2000 Analysis Services. Because access to the OLAP cube requires Windows authentication, users who attempt to create Portfolio Analyzer views from a nontrusted domain are denied access to the OLAP cube. If you need to allow users from nontrusted domains to access Portfolio Analyzer features, you must explicitly grant them permission to access the computers running SQL Server and Analysis Services through a Windows user account.

If a user in a nontrusted domain attempts to access Portfolio Analyzer from PWA, the error message "Unable to access the Microsoft Portfolio Analyzer OLAP Cube" displays, unless the user can specify a Windows user account on the computer running Analysis Services.

You can enable the user to access the computer running Analysis Services in one of the following ways:

- Configure Portfolio Analyzer for access by means of HTTP (SQL Server 2000 Enterprise Edition is required) and then enable SSL. You can use one of the following methods to do this:

    - Allow a user to log on by using the username and password defined on the server running Analysis Services when the user is asked to enter a username and password.

    - Embed the username and password in the connection string when creating the Portfolio Analyzer view.

- Create a local Windows user account that is granted permission to view OLAP cube data.

Creating a local Windows user account is not recommended because it allows users from nontrusted domains to access computer servers running SQL Server and Analysis Services, and that creates potential security risks.

> **NOTE**
>
> For more details about configuring an EPM solution in an extranet and nontrusted domains environment, refer to the *Microsoft Project Server 2003 Installation Guide*, Chapter 9, "Extranet and Non-Trusted Domain Scenarios." The *Microsoft Project Server 2003 Installation Guide* is available for download from the Project Server 2003 Technical Library at http://www.microsoft.com/technet/prodtechnol/office/proj2003/reskit/default.mspx.

Extranet Configurations for EPM Solutions

Extranet configurations for EPM solutions enable users outside your corporate firewall to access Project Server data through component servers placed in your demilitarized zone (DMZ) or a computer running Terminal Services. Internal EPM solution users access Project Server data through your corporate intranet behind your corporate firewall.

When providing external access for your EPM solution users, you have two basic choices: provide access via the Internet or by means of a virtual private network (VPN).

It is recommended that you enable external users to access data on the intranet by deploying duplicate computers running Project Server 2003 and WSS, one for extranet users and one for internal users, as shown in Figure 6.6. For external EPM solution users who access corporate project data over a high-latency network connection, provide a Terminal Services in DMZ zone.

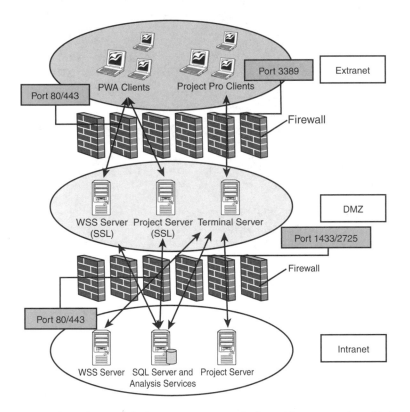

FIGURE 6.6   Distributed EPM solution components deployed for external and internal users.

Users who connect via the extranet access EPM corporate data on the external facing servers running Project Server 2003 and WSS. It is recommended that these servers are deployed with the SSL protocol. Internal users access data on intranet servers. Both external and internal servers use the same SQL Server databases. View Processing and Session Manager services are deployed on only the internal network and do not have to be duplicated in the DMZ. These two EPM solution components are not installed on the extranet computers.

If you decide to use WSS, you need to deploy a second WSS installation outside your corporate firewall and connect to the content database for your existing (intranet) deployment.

> **NOTE**
>
> For the detailed steps on Project Server and WSS in the extranet environment, review Chapter 9, "Extranet and Non-Trusted Domain Scenarios," in the *Microsoft Office Project Server 2003 Installation Guide*, available for download from the Project Server 2003 Technical Library at http://www. microsoft.com/technet/prodtechnol/office/proj2003/reskit/default.mspx.

Extranet users must be authenticated before they can connect to the external facing servers running Project Server 2003 and WSS. A VPN solution can be used to provide this connection using Internet Protocol Security (IPSec) with a public key infrastructure (PKI) to provide Internet Protocol–based authentication and encrypted communication.

Users in remote offices can be authenticated by means of user accounts or digital certificates mapped to user accounts. Encryption for Hypertext Transfer Protocol (HTTP) access is provided by means of the SSL protocol.

Project Professional clients require direct open database connectivity (ODBC) connection to the computer running SQL Server 2000 that hosts the Project Server 2003 database tables. A direct SQL Server connection for external users in an extranet scenario is not recommended for a couple of reasons. It requires deploying the computer running SQL Server in the DMZ and opening an inbound port (typically port 1433) to potentially dangerous Internet traffic. Exposing a computer running SQL Server to Internet traffic creates a risk of infection from database-related worms and viruses. The second reason is performance related. Project Professional client is very "chatty," and opening and saving even the average size project this way could take a few minutes. That may not go well with your project managers who are typically busy as well as impatient.

The Portfolio Analyzer feature of Project Server 2003 uses Microsoft Office Web Controls (OWC) to bind directly to the SQL Analysis Services server. To enable users to access OLAP over the extranet, you must do the following:

- Install the Enterprise version of SQL Analysis Services that is part of SQL Server 2000 Enterprise Edition.

- Install SQL Analysis Services on a computer running IIS. It is recommended that you do not install SQL Analysis Services on the same computer as Project Server 2003.

- Ensure that the client computers and the server running SQL Analysis Services both have the same version of MS XML installed.

- The client computers that are accessing SQL Analysis Services over the extranet must be running the correct version of OLE DB Provider for OLAP. The version must also match the version installed on the computer running SQL Server 2000.

NOTE

You can verify the version of the msolap80.dll file in the Program Files\Common Files\System\ Ole DB directory. To install OLE DB Provider for OLAP, run ptsfull.exe, located in the msolap\ install\PTS\ directory on the Microsoft SQL Server 2000 setup disc.

For more information, see Microsoft Knowledge Base article 279489, "How to Connect to Analysis Server 2000 By Using HTTP Connection," located at http://go.microsoft.com/fwlink/ ?linkid=20174.

Using Terminal Services As Part of an EPM Solution

Although it is technically possible for Project Professional 2003 users to access Project Server data directly from an extranet environment, this configuration is not recommended for reasons just stated in the previous section. Limitations to this configuration include performance degradation, some feature limitations, as well as potential security risks.

The Terminal Services configuration is an option for organizations that require tight security of their EPM system and do not want to compromise their network security by placing servers in their DMZ network. These organizations can deploy a computer running Terminal Services, or a load-balanced cluster of computers running Terminal Services, to provide connectivity for their external users of Project Web Access 2003 and Project Professional 2003 clients. Figure 6.7 illustrates the EPM solution hardware configuration that includes Terminal Services.

Using Terminal Services to accommodate access for your external users does not create any limitations for your EPM solution component configuration.

TIP

A lot of detailed technical information is available for Terminal Services at the Technology Center for Terminal Services: http://www.microsoft. com/windowsserver2003/technologies/ terminalservices/default.mspx.

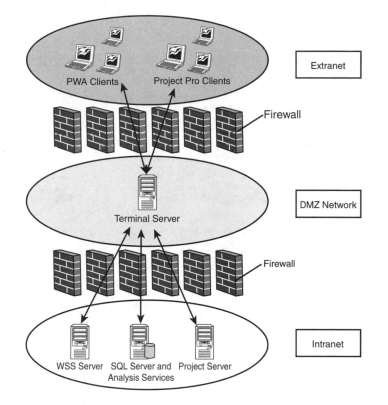

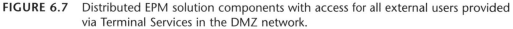

FIGURE 6.7   Distributed EPM solution components with access for all external users provided via Terminal Services in the DMZ network.

Hyperthreading

Hyperthreading is a BIOS level setting. Hyperthreading technology enables multithreaded software applications to execute threads in parallel. To improve performance in the past, threading was enabled in the software by splitting instructions into multiple streams so that multiple processors could act on them.

Hyperthreading technology is a form of simultaneous multithreading technology where multiple threads of software applications can be run concurrently on one processor. This technology essentially fools the operating system into thinking it's hooked up to two processors, allowing two threads to be run in parallel, both on separate "logical" processors within the same physical processor. The operating system sees double through a mix of shared, replicated, and partitioned chip resources, such as registers, math units, and cache memory.

This technology is largely invisible to the platform. In fact, many applications are already multithreaded and will automatically benefit from this technology.

Why is hyperthreading technology interesting in the context of the EPM solution? Hyperthreading is really advantageous for applications that are multiprocessor aware, and generally it is good to turn it on for IIS and SQL servers. The only time when you may consider disabling hyperthreading is when you have separate servers running Views Processing or Session Manager services. The reason is that both of these services can use only a single CPU and therefore cannot take any advantage of the hyperthreading feature. For all other scenarios leave hyperthreading enabled.

> **NOTE**
>
> If you want to read more about the hyperthreading technology, explore the following resources:
>
> Intel: http://www.intel.com/technology/hyperthread/
>
> Microsoft Windows-Based Servers and Intel Hyperthreading Technology: http://intel.com/ business/bss/ products/hyerthreading/server/demo/index.htm
>
> The Register: http://www.theregister.co.uk/2002/ 06/18/what_the_hell_is_hyperthreading

Software Prerequisites

Before you start looking at system requirements for all Microsoft Project 2003 EPM solution components, make sure that you understand the following:

- The information is based on detailed system requirements listed by Microsoft at the Microsoft Project 2003 system requirements website: http://www.microsoft.com/office/project/prodinfo/sysreq.mspx.

- The requirements listed are the "minimum" requirements and should be taken as such. If you use the minimum requirements for your EPM hardware components, your system will "walk" but definitely will not "run." You need to design significantly more powerful hardware architecture to use the Project Server 2003 EPM solution with any real-life enterprise project and resource data.

> **NOTE**
>
> The workgroup functions of Microsoft Project Standard 2003 will be no longer available in versions subsequent to Project 2003. Therefore, this section focuses on the enterprise configuration only; Microsoft Project Standard 2003 is not discussed.

Microsoft Office Project 2003 Software Product and Version Requirements

To plan the deployment of a Microsoft Project 2003 EPM system, you need to know the details of all associated EPM solution components. The next sections specify these software version requirements for each product required to run the Microsoft Project 2003 EPM solution.

> **NOTE**
>
> The Microsoft Project Professional 2003 client and server components can both be installed on the same computer.

Client-Side Requirements

The following products must be installed on a user's system for the full Microsoft Project 2003 Professional edition capabilities to be available to that user:

- **Operating system**—Microsoft Windows 2000 with Service Pack 3 (SP3), Microsoft Windows XP, or later.

- **Browser**—Internet Explorer 5.01 with SP3 or later, Internet Explorer 5.5 with SP2 or later, or Internet Explorer 6 with SP1 or later (Internet Explorer 6 recommended for best experience).

- **Applications**—Microsoft Project Professional 2003 (for project managers, administrators, and any other users requiring the ability to open, modify, and save project plans).

For more detailed Project Professional 2003 system requirements, review the following website: http://www.microsoft.com/office/ project/prodinfo/proreq.mspx.

> **NOTE**
>
> Each Project Professional 2003 client user automatically also has a PWA license to access the Project Server 2003 data repository.

Microsoft Project Web Access client system requirements are as follows:

- **Operating system**—Windows 98 Second Edition or higher; the latest service pack for your operating system is highly recommended.

- **Browser**—Internet Explorer 5.01 with SP3 or later, Internet Explorer 5.5 with SP2 or later, or Internet Explorer 6 with SP1 or later. (For full functionality, Internet Explorer 5.5 or greater is required.)

- **Applications**—For Portfolio Analyzer and Resource Availability views, the following are required:

  - For read-only mode, Microsoft Office Web Components (OWC) 2003 running on Windows 2000 with Service Pack 3 or later.

  - In addition, to use OWC in full interactive mode to create Portfolio Analyzer views, a valid end-user license for a Microsoft Office 2003 Edition, Project Professional 2003, or any Microsoft Office System program is needed.

For more detailed PWA client system requirements, review the following website: http://www.microsoft.com/office/project/ prodinfo/webreq.mspx.

Server-Side Requirements

Minimum requirements assume one server where all Project Server components and supporting technologies (that is, Microsoft SQL Server, Microsoft Windows SharePoint Services) are installed.

> **NOTE**
>
> Additional system requirement information about advanced Project Server configurations is available in the *Microsoft Office Project Server 2003 Installation Guide* at the following URL: http://www.microsoft.com/technet/prodtechnol/office/proj2003/default.mspx.

The following products must be installed on a system that contains Project Server 2003 for the full Microsoft Project 2003 edition capabilities to be available to that user:

- Microsoft Windows 2000 Server with Service Pack 3 (SP3) or later, Windows 2000 Advanced Server with SP3 or later, or Microsoft Windows Server 2003 Standard or Enterprise Edition

- Microsoft SQL Server 2000, SP3 or later

- Microsoft SQL Server 2000 Analysis Services, SP3 for OLAP reporting (Portfolio Analyzer functions)

- Microsoft Internet Information Server (IIS) 5.0 or above (IIS 6.0 is recommended for extended functions)

- Microsoft Project Server 2003

> **NOTE**
>
> You must use Microsoft Windows Server 2003 or later if you are using Windows SharePoint Services for document management, issues, or risks features.

For more detailed Microsoft Office Project Server 2003 system requirements, review the following website: http://www.microsoft.com/office/project/prodinfo/ serverreq.mspx.

Multiple Configurations

Your organization may have multiple divisions corresponding to multiple lines of business with different requirements for EPM solutions. Your IT department may also want to have a separate Project Server instance configured for testing and troubleshooting purposes. In these cases you need to set up and configure multiple Project Server sites.

Multiple Project Server Instances and Edit Site Utility

You can use the Edit Site utility to quickly create a Project Server–hosted deployment and to edit the properties for existing hosted sites. A hosted deployment is typically a large installation of Project Server 2003 that hosts Project Server site collections for different departments or divisions within the organization.

The host company can also be an application service provider (ASP) that hosts Project Server site collections for other external companies.

In a Project Server hosted deployment, a single installation of Project Server hosts multiple instances of PWA, each with its own SQL Server database. Typically, in a hosted deployment, multiple Project Server instances share a single Windows WSS content database but a separate WSS content database can be set up and configured for each Project Server instance.

When you install Project Server, only one site is available (by default called ProjectServer) and can be accessed by means of the URL http://computername/projectserver. When you use the Edit Site utility to add a Project Server site, a new URL (http://computername/site-name) is available, from which you can access a new instance of PWA.

To install the Edit Site utility, do the following:

1. Download and run the file EditSiteDownload.exe from the Microsoft Download Center: http://go.microsoft.com/fwlink/?LinkId=20891.

2. To start Edit Site, double-click EditSite.exe.

> **NOTE**
>
> You must have .NET Framework version 1.1 installed on the computer on which you want to run Edit Site.

Figure 6.8 shows the Edit Site utility interface. You must run the Edit Site utility on the computer on which Project Server 2003 is installed, and you must be the administrator or have equivalent permissions on the computers running Project Server, Views Notification Service, and Windows SharePoint Services, if applicable.

You can edit the site and database information for an existing Project Server site by clicking that site in the Virtual Directory list. You can also add a new Project Server site or test one of the existing Project Server sites.

> **TIP**
>
> Many other useful Project Server tools were released lately. Review the following Microsoft Knowledge Base article for information about additional Project Server tools available: http://support.microsoft.com/default. aspx?scid=kb;en-us;839457.

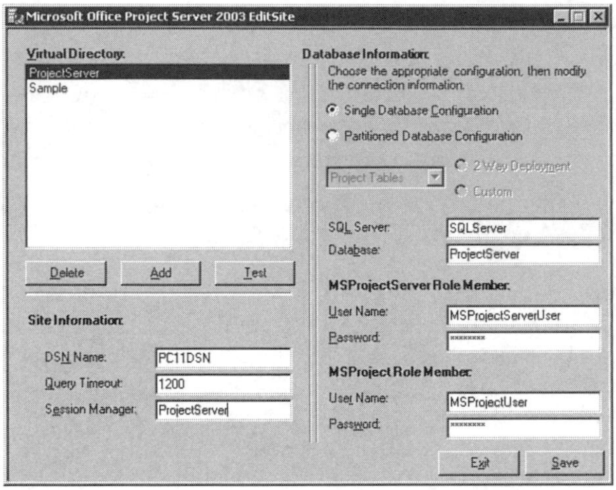

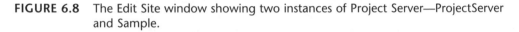

FIGURE 6.8   The Edit Site window showing two instances of Project Server—ProjectServer and Sample.

Virtualizing EPM Solution Infrastructure

You may also decide that it would be a good idea for your organization to virtualize the entire EPM solution infrastructure. A *virtual infrastructure* provides a layer of abstraction between the computing, storage, and networking hardware and the software that runs on it. A virtual infrastructure simplifies IT and enables companies to leverage their storage, network, and computing resources to control costs and respond faster.

Virtual machine (VM) technology applies to both server and client hardware. VM technology enables multiple operating systems to run concurrently on a single machine. In particular, the Microsoft virtual PC products enable one or more operating systems to run on the same computer system as the current Windows operating system.

Figure 6.9 illustrates the basic architecture of the Microsoft virtual machine technology.

VM technology serves a variety of purposes. It enables hardware consolidation because multiple operating systems can run on one computer. Key applications for VM technology include cross-platform integration as well as the following:

- **Consolidation for development and testing environments**—Each VM acts as a separate environment, which reduces risk and enables developers to quickly re-create different operating system configurations or compare versions of applications designed for different operating systems.

- **Legacy application re-hosting**—Legacy operating systems and applications can run on new hardware along with more recent operating systems and applications.

- **Server consolidation**—If several servers run applications that consume only a fraction of the available resources, VM technology can be used to enable them to run side by side on a single server, even if they require different versions of the operating system or middleware.

- **Software demonstrations**—With VM technology, users can re-create a clean operating system environment or system configuration quickly.

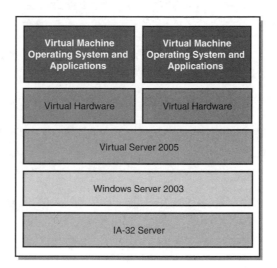

FIGURE 6.9   Basic architecture of the Microsoft virtual machine technology.

Managing a virtual infrastructure enables your IT department to address various business needs quickly. With virtual infrastructure, your data center can be treated as a single pool of processing, storage, and networking power.

You can choose from several vendors offering solutions for a virtual infrastructure. The two best known are VMware and Microsoft.

Figure 6.10 illustrates the basic architecture of the VMware virtual infrastructure technology.

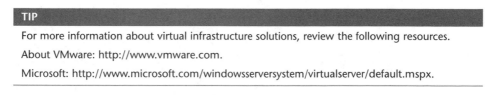

TIP

For more information about virtual infrastructure solutions, review the following resources.

About VMware: http://www.vmware.com.

Microsoft: http://www.microsoft.com/windowsserversystem/virtualserver/default.mspx.

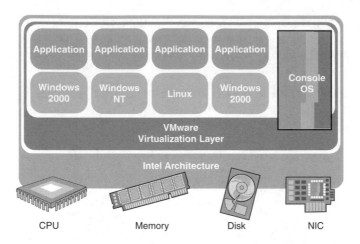

FIGURE 6.10   Basic architecture of the VMware virtual infrastructure technology.

Best Practices

- Review the *Microsoft Project Server 2003 Planning Configuration Guide*, Appendix H, "Best Practices for Deploying an EPM Solution."

- Understand fully the choices you have when deploying your EPM solution components across your corporate WAN and all issues related to domain trusts, security, use of Terminal Services, and impact of network latency on system performance.

- Review software requirements for EPM solution components.

- For additional information on an EPM solution based on Microsoft Project Server 2003, refer to the following website for a list of all available Project webcasts: http://office.microsoft.com/en-us/assistance/ HA010999531033.aspx.

PART III

Implementing Microsoft Office Project Server 2003

IN THIS PART

CHAPTER 7	Enterprise Project Management System Deployment Considerations	137
CHAPTER 8	Establishing Security Model Settings	143
CHAPTER 9	Enterprise Global Codes	163
CHAPTER 10	Creating Project Web Access Project and Resource Views	209
CHAPTER 11	Completing the Implementation and Configuration	239

Enterprise Project Management System Deployment Considerations

IN THIS CHAPTER

- Introduction to EPM Solution Deployment

- Installing Prerequisites

- Best Practices

Microsoft Office Project Server 2003 is a powerful and flexible project management tool. Many features and customizing options can produce a unique Enterprise Project Management (EPM) solution to integrate with unique business processes. This chapter contains an introduction to the Project Server configuration areas and the top 10 items to consider when undertaking a deployment of Project Server 2003.

Introduction to EPM Solution Deployment

Implementation of Project Server 2003 involves a number of actions to ensure that business goals and objectives are achieved. Each organization is unique in its project management methodology, infrastructure, processes, functional areas, and system objectives. Each component of the Project Server configuration requires analysis of the business environment and integration with organizational processes. Many internal processes may require changes, and new processes will need to be developed. Each area is critical to success, and any deficiencies reduce the effectiveness and benefits of the Project Server implementation.

Security Models

The Project Server security model is flexible and should reflect the organizational role responsibilities for each member. Project and resource data should be controlled and distributed on an as-needed basis. The security model provides the capability to assign functional permissions and data access to a specific role. The security model should be developed with maintainability in mind.

Enterprise Global Codes

The enterprise global codes are used to organize and enhance the project and resource data stored in the system. They provide data standards for the enterprise and can be enforced by specifying codes as a required field. Enterprise custom fields should be defined to support enterprise data requirements. As with any information system, each data requirement should have a purpose and be justified for the effort required to collect and maintain the information.

Views

Views are available to PWA users and present project and resource data in the web interface. A significant benefit of Project Server is the reduction of Microsoft Project users. Users can view project and resource data as needed without the desktop software. The views can be created to effectively present information clearly and concisely.

Calendars

Accurately reflecting project schedules requires that working days and holidays are specified for planning purposes. In the Project Server environment, enterprise calendars are used to standardize the scheduling of all projects and resources. Multiple calendars can be developed to support an organization's business environment.

Timesheet Setup

Timesheet functions in Project Server provide both efficiency and collaboration to project managers and team members. The method of tracking project progress is one key to achieving system objectives. The information collected on task status should support the organizational goals. Progressing projects also require the workflow to be established. There are many options in Project Server to route and approve task status, and they should integrate with the organization's processes.

Installing Prerequisites

Prior to installing Project Server 2003, an organization needs to develop the specific goals and objectives for the system. The installation and configuration of the software are supported by other system components. Training, processes, infrastructure, quality assurance, and other elements are critical to a successful implementation. Review the following considerations and put together a project team from all areas of the organization that will be affected by the implementation.

Get Professional Assistance

Acquiring professional EPM consultants reduces the time to deploy and effectively meet business objectives; the added value is well worth the one-time cost. Many organizations have not achieved the desired results of a Project Server 2003 implementation due to many reasons. One primary reason is due to the lack of experience with an EPM system. Project Server 2003 is only a part of the entire system. Other components include business processes, quality assurance, training, infrastructure, organizational model, and integration with other business systems.

Microsoft Project Premier Partners have the experience to effectively guide an organization through the implementation process. From architecture to business processes to training, Partners can customize the system to match your organizational needs.

At a minimum, provide the implementation team with training on EPM deployments from a certified Partner. This training should cover the full spectrum of requirements.

Establish a Program Management Office

A critical factor in successfully implementing the EPM solution is the effectiveness of a program office. This office should be the lead in defining the project management methodology and integrating processes into the EPM configuration. The following responsibilities should be assigned to the office:

- Project methodology

- Project management tools and templates

- Project management processes

- Application administrator

- Project training

- Quality assurance

- Create and enforce standards

- Configuration management (Project Server)

- Project management mentoring and support

The program office should continually monitor and audit compliance with process standards and ensure data accuracy in the system.

Training

Training is often underestimated in an EPM deployment. There is a considerable difference in working on project schedules on a local file system versus Project Server. Even the most experienced Microsoft Project users need to be trained on operating in an enterprise environment.

Training also needs to include the organization's specific project management processes—from the fundamental question of what constitutes a project to specific work flow and timing of required actions. Furthermore, organizations need to plan on recurring training, and training to support new users to the system.

Training should be customized for each user role in the system. This is important to focus the user group on its requirements and role in creating a successful EPM implementation.

Architecture

Performance and availability of the system influence the acceptance of the end users. A poorly architected infrastructure can have irreversible consequences. This does not mean that you have to purchase the most expensive equipment but rather build your infrastructure to support the user base. The highly scalable EPM solution provides flexibility in initial design and postimplementation options to expand scale.

Business requirements should drive the architecture designed to support the operational use. Build in a scalable infrastructure; set up the Project Server front-end web server in a Network Load Balanced (NLB) configuration. This allows you to easily expand the server farm if and when required. Dispersing the Project Server services also provides greater scale and performance.

An organization with a geographically dispersed resource base should consider a distributed application server. This can dramatically improve performance of Project Professional connections to the server. Maintainability and support of the application are also efficient.

Establish Standards

Establishing enterprise standards is typically an objective for all organizations. This is usually easier to talk about than to implement. Standards can be created for scheduling, reporting, training, custom fields, and views. The standards created in an EPM configuration should support the overall goals of the organization. Consider the effort to collect and maintain custom fields created as part of the enterprise data standards. The benefits should justify the collection and maintenance effort required. Each required data element should be justified so that the effort to collect and maintain the data supports an objective.

Standards are not isolated to the Project Server configuration but must also be created for project scheduling processes. Project schedule templates, task modeling, resource assignments, local resources, tracking procedures, and other interactions with the system should be fully documented.

Incremental Deployment

Understanding the Project Server 2003 features, processes, and techniques to achieve the organizational goals is critical to a successful project. Organizations differ in their project management methodologies, project management skill sets available, types of projects executed, and EPM solution implementation objectives. Project Server 2003 is designed to be flexible enough to support the project management needs of virtually any organization. The key to deploying an EPM solution is a thorough understanding of the goals and the solution components required to achieve the goals.

Goals can be categorized into four areas:

- Schedule management
- Resource management
- Cost management
- Portfolio management

Meeting specific objectives should be staged in the deployment schedule. Project management maturity should be achieved at one level before proceeding to the next maturity level. A roadmap with incremental achievements should be developed to move the organization from its current project management maturity to the desired maturity. This will not happen overnight, and expectations should be measured.

Moving from a standalone project management methodology to an enterprise environment can take months. Listing and prioritizing the objectives you are trying to achieve will assist in building a realistic implementation schedule.

Conduct a Pilot Deployment

Conducting a pilot deployment is essential to validate the Project Server configuration, performance, and internal processes, and to get the end users involved. The pilot should contain a representative sample of actual project activities. The team should be small enough to manage and exercise the system to collect feedback on processes and configuration.

The configuration and processes should be baselined prior to commencing the pilot. A post pilot review should be conducted to review issues and take action as necessary. Expect changes to the configuration and project management processes used and implement these changes prior to a production rollout.

Integrate with Business Systems

The EPM solution can easily integrate with current business systems used. This can be a critical area to explore. To achieve the efficiencies expected from the EPM solution, duplicated processes must be removed or integrated into a single contiguous process. Data sharing is an essential efficiency you can achieve by only keying in data once. This applies to adding users to the corporate network and automatically synchronizing Project Server users through the Active Directory integration built in to the EPM solution. Time recording is also an area that should be investigated for integration. Project Server is not a payroll system; however, common elements could be shared to present the user with one timesheet interface and pass data to the appropriate system. Project accounting systems, human resources systems, document management systems, and other lines of business applications can be integrated with significant operational efficiencies.

Integrate with Business Processes

Project Server 2003 has enormous flexibility in the configuration, which can help tailor the system to your business environment. The tool should not drive the processes. There are boundaries in the functionality of Project Server, and some areas may require business process changes. The efficiency of current project management business processes can be improved with the EPM solution. Be conscious of the amount of change you are introducing and phase in the changes.

Sell the Solution

Resistance to change is a human attribute that will not go away. You can mitigate reservations by highlighting the benefits of the change. Project Server 2003 is beneficial to all levels in the organization, and this should be communicated throughout the deployment. Reassure team members that the data is to be used for project decisions. Team members have access to assignment information and can collaborate on those tasks. Project managers gain efficiencies in updating project schedules through the use of timesheets. Executives have information on resource utilization and data to make informed decisions. The benefits are many but must be communicated to users to build enthusiasm and acceptance.

▶ **SEE** "Manage the Organizational Change," **PAGE 14**.

Best Practices

- Gain a thorough understanding of the capabilities of the Project Server 2003 software before attempting to install.

- Understand the organization's objectives and tailor the configuration to achieve these objectives.

- Identify an administrator to configure and maintain the system.

- Keep it simple; don't overcomplicate a system.

- Understand the organization's current project management capabilities and design the system to incrementally introduce change.

- Integrate the system to the unique organizational environment.

CHAPTER 8

Establishing Security Model Settings

IN THIS CHAPTER

- Server Configuration—Features
- Identifying Roles
- Security Templates
- Security Groups
- Creating Categories
- Associating Groups and Categories
- Assigning Resources to Proper Groups
- Best Practices

Security is separated into two distinct criteria: use permissions (functionality) and data permissions (data access). Use permissions define what a user can do in the system, and data permissions define what data will populate views visible by the user. Use permissions are maintained by the Group to which a user is assigned, and data permissions are maintained by the Category or Categories associated with the Group to which a user is assigned. Hence, the user's system security, what a user can do and what data a user can see, is defined through a Group and Category.

It is important to remember that the security model in Microsoft Office Project Server 2003 is a matrix that allows a user to be assigned to multiple Groups depending on her role in the system. Also, multiple Categories can be assigned to a Group to define specific conditional data requirements for users in the Group. These combinations provide a mix of functionality and data access appropriate for the roles the user will perform using Project Server.

Project Server security is complex. A thorough understanding of and adherence to best practices will guarantee a successful configuration and enhance your ability to easily maintain the complex criteria of Project Server system security as shown in Figure 8.1.

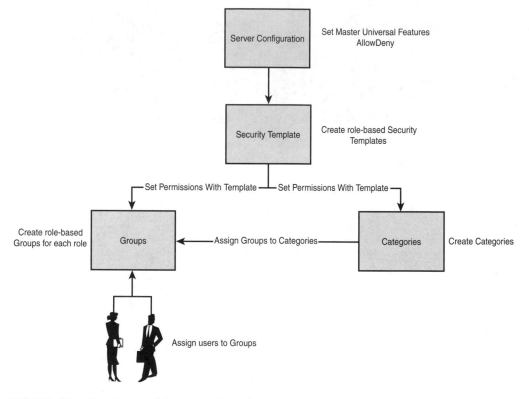

FIGURE 8.1   Security model process flow diagram.

Server Configuration—Features

To be robust for multiple organizational situations, Project Server user security is complex. Security settings can be affected by multiple conditions, and managing those conditions requires much time and documentation. The security model allows for many-to-many relationships in the association of Groups, Categories, and Users. Follow these steps to reduce administrative management and the possibility of hidden conditions causing troubleshooting frustration:

1. In the Project Web Access (PWA) window, select the Admin tab.

2. Select Server configuration.

3. Find the Select the Features That You Want to Make Available to Users in Project Web Access section (see Figure 8.2).

4. When all selections are complete, click Save Changes.

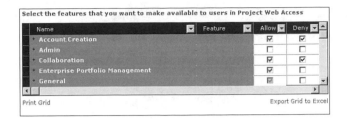

FIGURE 8.2   Select features for your system.

Allow/Deny

When at all possible, use universal settings. Under the Admin tab, Server Configuration, Features is a security template used for universal Allow/Deny. All features identified here must be either allowed or denied; no features should be left blank. The Allow/Deny selection is actually a three-state selection. Allow means that the feature is active. Any permission denied in this template is denied for all users of the system. A Deny anywhere is an absolute Deny everywhere. A blank, neither Allow nor Deny, means that the decision to provide the feature to a particular user is decided at another security level and is called a *soft deny*. Blank features are inappropriate on the Server Configuration Features template as universal features are being selected.

Selecting Features

The Server Configuration Features template is the correct place to Deny unwanted functions or permissions to all users. For instance, you want to disable the Delegate Task feature because you do not allow delegation of tasks as a matter of policy. The Delegate Task permission would be set to Deny thus denying Delegate Task to all users. Review "Project Server Permissions" in Appendix C of the *Microsoft Project Server 2003 Administrator's Guide* to determine whether a feature is appropriate for your installation.

All permissions are set to Allow by default with the exception of Connect to Project Server Using Microsoft Project 2002, Approve Timesheet for Resources, and Timesheet Approval. For a complete 2003 installation, including Microsoft Office Project Professional 2003, the Deny for Connect to Project Server Using Microsoft Project 2002 is appropriate. If the installation is a mixed environment of Server 2003 and Professional 2002, this use permission should be set to Allow. Be aware that several features of Project Server 2003 are not available in a mixed installation.

The features Approve Timesheet for Resources and Timesheet Approval are used with the managed timesheets functionality. If you do not intend to use managed timesheets, make sure that these features are set to Deny. If you choose to apply the managed timesheets feature, make sure that these features are set to Allow.

▶ **SEE** "Completing the Implementation and Configuration," **PAGE 239.**

TIP

It is strongly recommended that the Account Creation permissions be set to Deny, as shown in Figure 8.3.

These Deny permissions protect the creation of user accounts in the database to only those Groups that have Manage Users and Groups permissions, or Groups authorized to add resources to the Enterprise Resource Pool. Allowing the Account Creation permissions under any other conditions loosens authority over user account creation and jeopardizes resource pool and database user integrity.

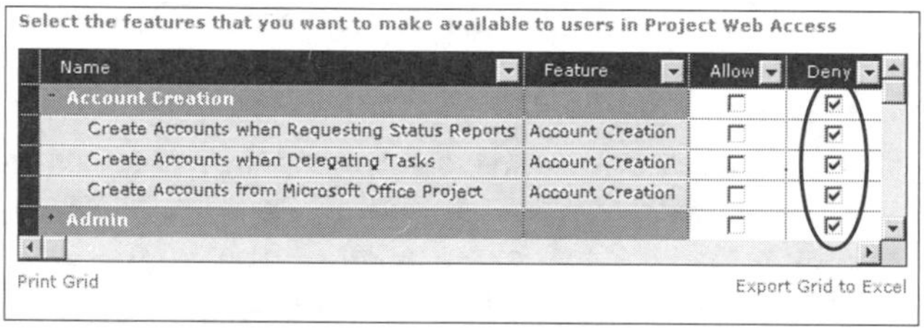

FIGURE 8.3   Account creation features should be set to Deny.

It is assumed that few defaults will be changed in features. Changes will be due to your identifying features not applicable to your particular operation. All changes should be documented to assist the administrator with future security troubleshooting. To document your initial settings, select Print Grid below the Features window, which exports the current grid to an Excel spreadsheet, as shown in Figure 8.4.

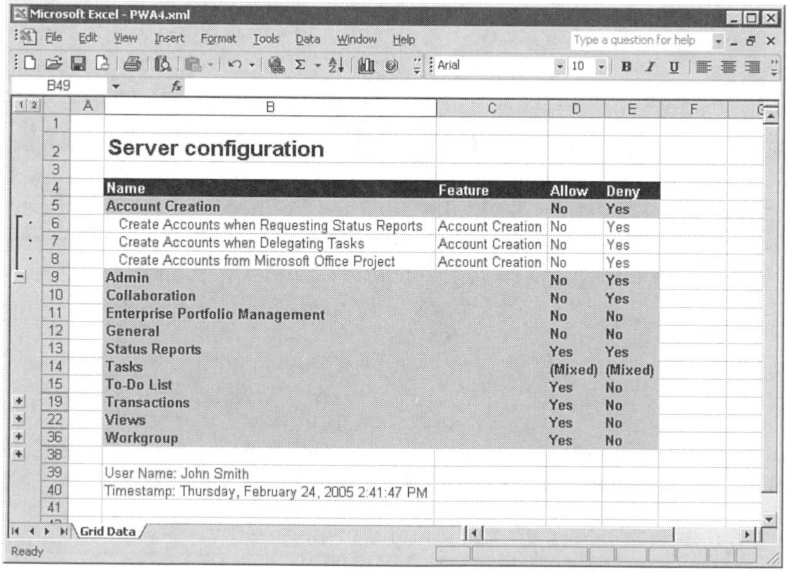

FIGURE 8.4   Print Grid documents your Features settings.

Identifying Roles

After the universal settings are determined, it is important to identify the Groups of users who will access the system. Groups are roles-based collections of users. Seven default Groups (roles) are identified by Microsoft Project:

- Administrator
- Executive
- Portfolio Manager
- Project Manager
- Resource Manager
- Team Lead
- Team Member

The default Groups are sufficient for most organizations. Remember, these are not necessarily the names that will be applied to the Groups but are the expected roles of users in your organization. Clarity around the roles users perform makes completing the security model easier and more successful.

Review these Groups to determine whether your user community fits into the defaults. Additional Groups can be identified as necessary. This collection of role-based information is used in the following sections to identify security templates and Groups as part of the security model.

Security Templates

Adjust or create security templates for each of the roles identified. It is important that there be a security template for each role. This eliminates the possibility of redundant permission entries at other stages of security design. There are several opportunities to affect permissions in different steps of the security process. By allowing one security template per role and only managing the security template for permissions, redundancy and hidden assignments are eliminated.

Security templates are the best place to manage roles-based security. Later in this chapter, you will see multiple places to select permissions for an individual user, Group, Category, or system feature. Applying permissions at any or all of these locations makes troubleshooting security impossible. Both Groups and Categories have a Set Permissions with Template button to copy permissions from the template to the Group or Category. By maintaining permissions at the security template, there is only one place to manage permissions and then distribute them to the correct Group or Category as necessary.

Creating Security Templates

Security templates are created by selecting Admin, Manage Security, Security Templates, and then Add Template. To create a security template, perform the following steps:

1. In the PWA window, select the Admin tab.
2. Select Manage Security.
3. Under Security Options select Security Templates.

4. Select Add Template or Modify Template as appropriate (see Figure 8.5).

5. When all selections are complete, click Save Changes.

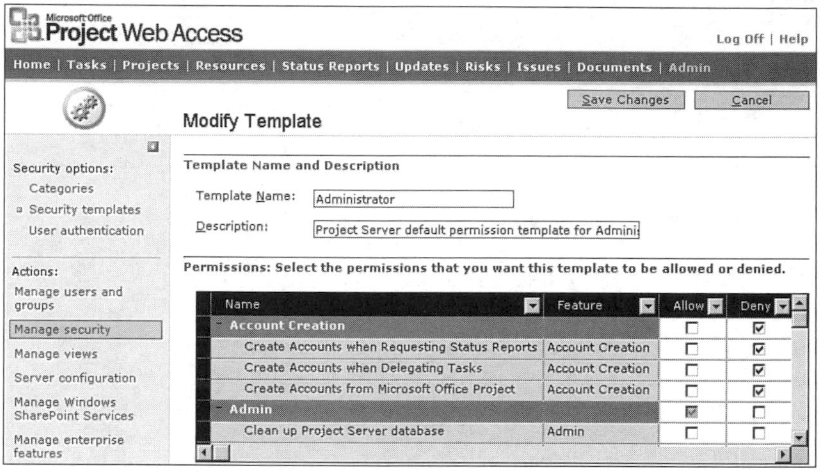

FIGURE 8.5   Add Template or Modify Template.

There is no harm in modifying the current templates or adding additional templates. Templates should be named with a unique name so that the distinction is obvious long after this exercise is complete—for example, Organization Project Manger, Project Manager See All Projects, Division Executive, and so on. These distinctions will come in handy later when you define the Groups. Templates and Groups should be named the same, and that name should identify the role you want a person to assume when assigned to a proper Group. This naming is not trivial because it will help you troubleshoot later why a Group or person has a particular security model.

After you have chosen the template names by adding or modifying templates, open each template and select the permissions that role possesses. In the template, select both use and data permissions. Review "Project Server Permissions" in Appendix C and "Default Settings" in Appendix D of the *Microsoft Project Server 2003 Administrator's Guide* to determine whether a feature is appropriate for this role.

Because some features have been turned off at the features level, you must decide how to note this in the templates. In the previous discussion of Allow/Deny, remember that a blank state means "not decided here." Therefore, it is suggested that you leave all template selections tuned off at the features level blank, signifying that the selection has been decided at a different security level. Because the only level above templates is features, a blank selection in a template tells you that the feature has been turned off at the system level. This is not a requirement, but it will help you troubleshoot security model problems well into the future.

Do not select Deny in the template. Because Deny is absolute, it is better to have the Allow/Deny selection blank, creating a soft Deny (see Figure 8.6). It is possible for a user to be placed in more than one Group. A Deny anywhere would be a Deny everywhere for that user causing troubleshhoting problems. Deny is best used only at the Select Features level turning off a permission for everyone.

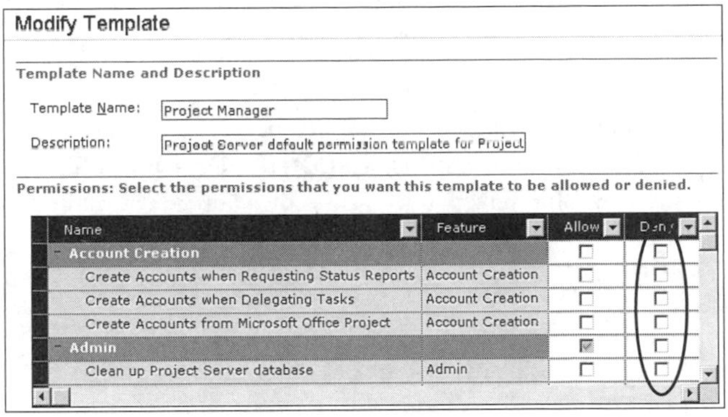

FIGURE 8.6   Template selection blanks used for denied features.

Because the templates contain both use and data permissions, take your time to analyze and discuss each selection in light of the role this template represents. Both the Group and Category selections have a Set Permissions with Template button that assigns the template permissions to the appropriate Group and/or Category. Because the Template permissions are transferred to the Group and Category, the template is the best place to define the permissions a role needs to be a successful user in Project Server. Because of this association between Templates, Groups, and Categories, Templates are the best place to manage role-based security.

Security Groups

Groups are "buckets" of permissions that have people assigned to them. After a person is assigned to a Group, that person assumes the use permissions defined by the Group. Groups are simply collections of permissions in the security model.

Creating Groups

After all the templates are defined and proper selections made, it is time to define the Groups. Perform the following steps to define Groups:

1. In the PWA window, select the Admin tab.

2. Select Manage Users and Groups.

3. Under Security Options select Groups.
4. Click Add Group or Modify Group as appropriate.
5. When all selections are complete, click Save Changes.

NOTE

The Groups are named the same as the default templates. You need to define the names of your Groups to be the same as your newly defined templates.

As you either add or modify a Group, pay close attention to the sections on the Group page: Users, Categories, Global Permissions, and Digital Dashboard Link. Each of these sections is distinguished by blue letters and a blue line across the page (see Figure 8.7).

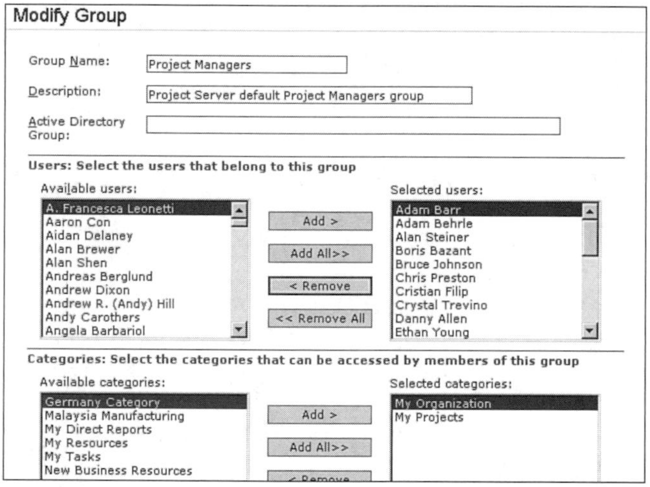

FIGURE 8.7 The Group page has defined sections.

In the User section you assign the appropriate people to the correct Group, which is the last step in the security model process. After a user is assigned to a Group, the permissions define what a user can do in the system and what general views a user can see in PWA. The data that populates the view is defined by Categories.

The Category section shows you the Category or Categories assigned to this Group. Categories are discussed in more detail in the "Creating Categories" section later in this chapter. The Digital Dashboard Link is a place to identify a URL, which is a digital dashboard or any other portal your organization wants to use. If one is selected, it shows up on the home page of each person assigned to this Group. In designing the security model, only the global permissions are considered now.

Setting Global Permissions for Members of This Group

With the Group page open and looking at the Global Permissions section, use the pull-down menu to select the proper template (see Figure 8.8). Assign permissions by selecting the Set Permissions with Template button. Having the same Group name and security template name reduces the confusion of what global permissions to set for each Group. Do the same for each Group until all defined Groups have their permissions set by a similarly named security template.

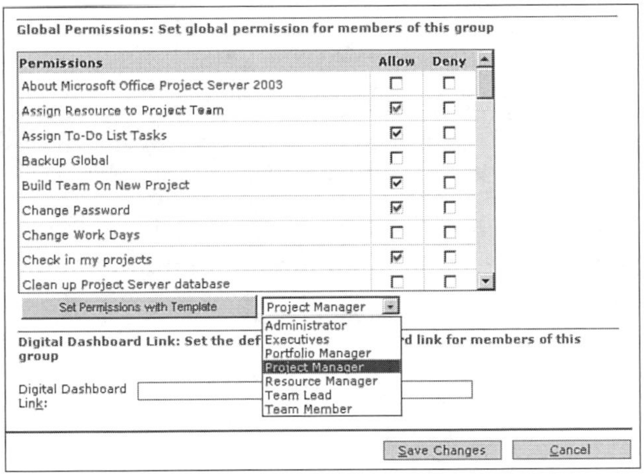

FIGURE 8.8   Select the proper template by choosing from the Set Permissions with Template drop-down menu.

Creating Categories

You use Categories to define data permissions. For example, data permissions include the See Projects in Project Center View permission. What projects will be visible in that view are described by the data restrictor also found in the Category. So, Categories allow data to be seen and managed and may restrict the data to be seen and managed by a user.

Like the Groups page, Categories also have sections, explained individually in the following sections. Also, there are Microsoft default Categories, which are not roles based. The defaults and an optional Category design are discussed in the "Optional Category Configuration" section later in this chapter.

Creating Categories

After all the Templates and Groups are defined and proper selections made, it is time to define the Categories. Perform the following steps:

1. In the PWA window, select the Admin tab.

2. Select Manage Security.

3. Under Security Options select Categories.

4. Select Add Category or Modify Category, as appropriate.

5. When all selections are complete, click Save Changes.

The default Category names are not like the Groups or Templates in that they describe what data permissions are necessary for a function in the organization. The default Category names are as follows:

- **My Direct Reports**—Intended for resource managers who approve timesheets.

- **My Organization**—Used to grant access to all information in the database or in an organization. It is usually used for a Project Management Office or executives, or key users needing to view all project and resource data. Resource Breakdown Structure may restrict information depending on the security model.

- **My Projects**—Intended for project managers and grants permission to create and edit project schedules that they have created. By default, project managers can view all enterprise resources.

- **My Resources**—Intended for resource managers and uses security rules based on Resource Breakdown Structure (RBS) and is useful only if RBS is defined.

- **My Tasks**—Intended for team members assigned to tasks in project schedules. By default, it grants access to all the collaborative features, such as timesheets, documents, issues, risks, and status reports.

When open, the Category page has sections distinguished by blue letters and a blue line across the page, as shown in Figure 8.9.

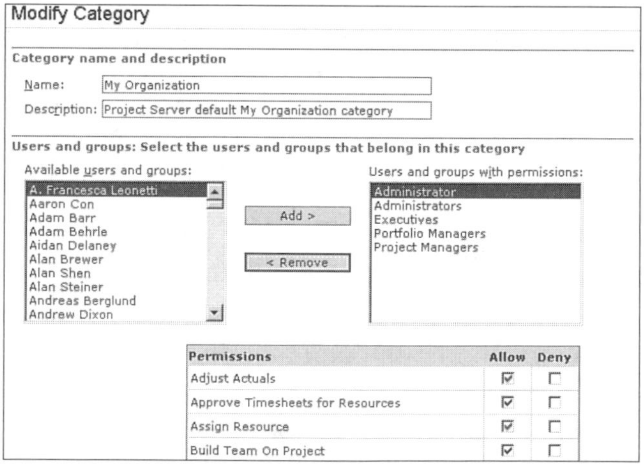

FIGURE 8.9   The Category page has defined sections.

Category Name and Description

To add or rename a Category, you must type in the name and description. It is suggested that you create a description that reminds you of the overall reason for this Category.

Users and Groups

In the Available Users and Groups list, select the Group(s) you want this Category to be assigned to and select the Add button to associate the Category and Group.

> **TIP**
>
> It is strongly recommended that only Groups be assigned to Categories and never individual users. To maintain the integrity of the security model, users should be assigned only to Groups. If you assign a user to a Category, assign a Category to a Group, and assign users to Groups, you will experience unexpected security behavior at the user level. Troubleshooting this condition is extremely difficult.

> **NOTE**
>
> A Group must be assigned in the Users and Groups with Permissions window for the permissions selection window to become active.

For each Group in the Users and Groups with Permissions window, set the permissions in one of two ways:

- To set Category permissions by using a security template, in the Users and Groups with Permissions window, select a Group. Select the template to apply from the drop-down list next to the Set Permissions with Template button and then select Set Permissions with Template.

- To set Category permissions manually, in the Users and Groups with Permissions window, select a Group. In the Permissions window, select Allow for each permission you want to grant.

> **TIP**
>
> Do not select Deny in the Category. Because Deny is absolute, it is better to have the Allow/Deny selection blank, creating a soft Deny. Deny is best used only at the Select Features level turning a permission off for everyone.

The 14 data permissions in the Permissions window are actually controlled by the Category. Setting the Category permissions in the Category is the right thing to do. The data permissions are as follows:

- Adjust Actuals

- Approve Timesheets for Resources

- Assign Resource

- Build Team on Project

- Create New Task or Assignment

- Delete Project

- Edit Enterprise Resource Data

- Open Project

- Save Project

- See Enterprise Resource Data

- See Projects in Project Center

- See Projects in Project Views

- See Resource Assignments in Assignment Views

- View Risks, Issues, and Documents

It is possible to set these 14 permissions in the Group. If these data permissions were defined by the Group, after the Group is assigned to the Category, the Category permissions defined in the Category will overwrite the Group-defined permissions. For each Group added to the Category, a unique set of data permissions will apply to specific Group/Category combinations. It cannot be overemphasized that these 14 data permissions are owned and managed by the Category regardless of your ability to change these settings elsewhere, such as in templates and in the Groups themselves.

Projects: Select the Projects That Users in This Category Can View

After the data permissions are set, the next sections of the Category page allow you to restrict the data according to radio buttons and security rules. The Projects section is the first of those areas of restriction (see Figure 8.10).

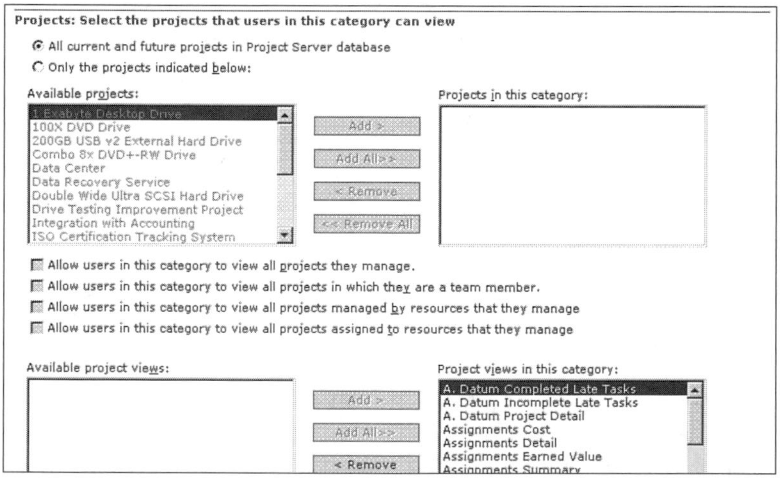

FIGURE 8.10   Restricting data for projects.

Under Projects: Select the Projects That Users in This Category Can View are two radio buttons—All Current and Future Projects in Project Server Database and Only the Projects Indicated Below.

All Current and Future Projects in Project Server Database Radio Button

The All Current and Future Projects selection means just that. If you allow the permission See Projects in Project Center, all current and future projects will populate the Project Center view for any Group with this Category assigned. This equates to no data restriction.

Only the Projects Indicated Below Radio Button

If you want to restrict the data in this Category, choose the Only the Projects Indicated Below radio button. This selection has two additional choices to determine the restriction.

The Available Projects window displays the current projects in the database. By selecting one or many of these projects and clicking the Add button you restrict this Category's projects to only those projects in the Projects in This Category window. Seldom, if ever, will you restrict a Category to a select set of projects.

On one occasion it was necessary to use this restrictor. A client had a very sensitive project that he wanted only two people in the company to see. An "eyes only" Category was created with only this sensitive project added. This Category was associated with a special Group with only two members and thus accomplished only two people in the company being able to view the sensitive project.

Leaving the Projects in This Category window blank is usually proper because a series of security rules follow, which assist you in restricting the data according to the rules you choose. These rules are

- Allow users in this Category to view all projects they manage.

- Allow users in this Category to view all projects in which they are a team member.

- Allow users in this Category to view all projects managed by resources that they manage.

- Allow users in this Category to view all projects assigned to resources that they manage.

The first two rules are based on who created the project and whether the user is a member of a project team. The second two rules are based on the RBS.

▶ SEE "Resource Breakdown Structure (RBS)," **PAGE 185**.

Under the security rules, the system decides how to populate the Project Center view, for example. If you select rule one, your view is populated with only those projects on which you are the creator, also known as the *owner* in Project Server. If rule two is selected, you see only those projects on which you are a team member. If you select both, the effect is additive. You see your projects as a creator and a team member.

The third rule assumes that you have people reporting to you. How the system knows about who reports to whom is through the RBS. If you have people reporting to you who are project creators, your view includes all the projects that are true for the first two rules and all the projects of your resources who are project creators. The fourth rule adds to your view all the projects on which any of your reporting resources is a team member. Using the rules allows the system to dynamically populate your views according to the restrictions you choose.

Available Project Views

The last project restrictor enables you to decide which project view users in this Category can see in the View a Project view, which gives the details of the individual projects visible in PWA.

▶ **SEE** "Creating Project Web Access Project and Resource Views," **PAGE 209**.

Your ability to restrict project data is highly customizable using Categories. Let's continue defining Categories by looking at the next section of the Category page.

Resources: Select the Resources Whose Information Can/Cannot Be Viewed by Users in This Category

Now that the project restrictions have been set, the next section of the Category page allows you to restrict resource data visible in the Project Web Access Assignment and Resource Center views (see Figure 8.11).

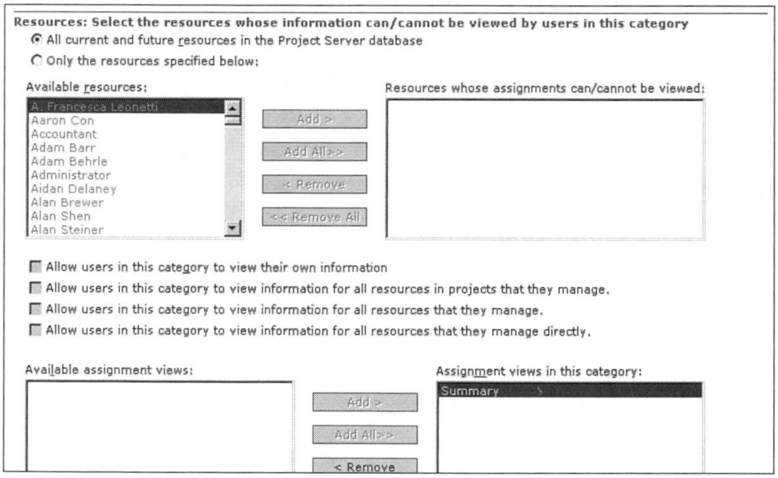

FIGURE 8.11   Restricting data for resources.

The section Resources: Select the Resources Whose Information Can/Cannot Be Viewed By Users in This Category contains two radio buttons—All Current and Future Resources in Project Server Database and Only the Resources Specified Below.

All Current and Future Resources in Project Server Database

The All Current and Future Resources selection means just that. If you allowed the permission See Enterprise Resource Data, all current and future resources in the Server Database will populate the Resource Center view for any Group with this Category assigned. This equates to no data restriction.

Only the Resources Specified Below

If you want to restrict the resource data in this Category, Only the Resources Specified Below is the appropriate choice. This selection has two additional choices to determine the restriction.

The Available Resources window displays the current resources saved in the database. By selecting one or many of these resources and clicking the Add button, you restrict this Category's resources to only those displayed in the Resources Whose Assignments Can/Cannot Be Viewed window. Seldom, if ever, will you restrict a Category to a select set of resources.

Leaving the Resources Whose Assignments Can/Cannot Be Viewed window blank is usually proper because a series of security rules follows, which will assist you in restricting the data according to the rules you choose. These rules are

- Allow users in this Category to view their own information.

- Allow users in this Category to view information for all resources in projects that they manage.

- Allow users in this Category to view information for all resources that they manage.

- Allow users in this Category to view information for all resources that they manage directly.

The first two rules are based on who created the resource and whether the user is a member of a project team. The second two rules are based on the RBS.

Under the security rules, the system decides how to populate the Resource Center and Assignment views, for example. Selecting rule one populates your view with only your own resource information. Selecting rule two shows you only those resources assigned to projects for which you are the creator. If you select both rules, the effect is additive.

The third rule assumes that you have people reporting to you. How the system knows about who reports to whom is through the RBS. If you have people reporting to you, your view includes all those resources. The fourth rule restricts your resource data to only your direct reports. For example, if you were a division manager, only those managers who report to you would be displayed, not every resource in your division. Using the rules allows the system to dynamically populate your views according to the restrictions you choose using the security rules.

Available Assignment Views

Continuing with resource restrictors, you need to decide which assignment views users in this Category can see in the View Assignments view, which shows the details of the individual resource assignments visible in PWA.

Available Resource Center Views

Next, you need to decide which Resource Center views users in this Category can see in the Resource Center in PWA.

Project Center Views

Under Project Center Views: Select Views for Displaying a Portfolio of Projects, the last set of Category data restrictors is the selection of Project Center views, Portfolio Analyzer views, and models you want a user to see (see Figure 8.12).

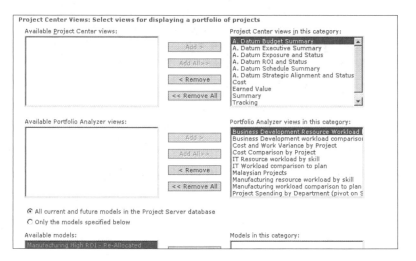

FIGURE 8.12   Restricting data using views.

The list of views in the Available Project Center Views window shows all the views currently created for the Project Center. By selecting the views that a Category manages, you restrict the data available to the users. For example, the best views for an Executive are usually less detailed than for a Project Manager. Select the appropriate views for this Category and click the Add or Add All button to apply the appropriate views.

▶ **SEE** "Creating Project Web Access Project and Resource Views," **PAGE 209**.

The list in the Available Portfolio Analyzer Views window shows all the views currently created for the Portfolio Analyzer. Select the appropriate views for this Category and click the Add or Add All button to apply the appropriate views.

> **NOTE**
>
> During the initial installation, no Portfolio Analyzer views will be available. No default Portfolio Analyzer views exist in Project Server. Portfolio Analyzer views must be created for each specific client. As Portfolio Analyzer views are created, they can be assigned to Categories during the view creation process.

▶ **SEE** "Portfolio Management Using Portfolio Analyzer and Portfolio Modeler," **PAGE 393**.

The last selection in the Category is Models. Select the All Current and Future Models in the Project Server Database radio button to allow users who have permissions to this Category to see all models. Select Only the Models Specified Below if you want to restrict the available models. Just like in Projects and Resources, you can restrict this Category to only a specific set of models visible in the Available Models window, or you can select security rules to manage what models are visible, such as the following:

- Allow users in this Category to view their own models.

- Allow users in this Category to view models created by resources that they manage.

The first rule is based on who created the model, and the second rule is based on RBS.

> **NOTE**
>
> If you do not want to display any models for a Category, choose Only the Models Specified Below and do not select any available models or either security rule. Under these conditions, nothing is selected below, and, therefore, nothing will be displayed.

Optional Category Configuration

The Project Server default Categories describe well how data permissions and restrictors manage the flow of data for Groups of users. However, the default Categories do not follow the roles-based convention displayed by templates and Groups. Because the security model is complex, it may be more advantageous to you to create Categories with the same names as Templates.

By changing the Categories to roles-based names, you can remember the reason for a set of user permissions, data permissions, and restrictors because all the permissions are kept in the template. Because the template is the master permissions library for a role, the Set with Template button transfers template permission knowledge to the Group and to the aptly named Category.

Under these conditions, the template is the master security model for each role's permissions and can be the place where all security changes are maintained. After a template is altered, the corresponding Group can be Set Permissions with Template, and repeating for the corresponding Category means that the permissions are always managed in only one place, the template.

As you have seen, there are at least five different places where a permission can be set. Remembering where you put all the check marks can be daunting. It is suggested that the check marks be maintained in the template and applied through the Set Permissions with Template button in both Groups and Categories. Both the default Categories and the optional naming of Categories work. Choose the one that helps you remember and maintain the security model for future expansion and more complex permissions as your system evolves.

Associating Groups and Categories

As mentioned earlier, it is necessary to assign or associate Categories and Groups as the Categories are being defined because a Group must be assigned to a Category for the Category Permissions window to be active. Normally, there is one Group per Category, but there is no maximum requirement, so many Categories could be assigned to a Group.

This association is important because, after a resource is assigned to a Group, the resource gets the use permissions assigned to the Group and the data permissions and restrictors assigned to the Category assigned to the Group. This association defines all that a user can do or see while operating in the system.

The Case for Multiple Categories

This section explores a complex data scenario. You want project managers to see all projects in the Project Center but only edit their own projects. Two Categories need to be defined so that the ability to save a project to the database is based on the data criteria of role and permission.

The Project Manager Group would have two associated Categories. One Category would not restrict the projects, so the All Current and Future Projects radio button would be selected. But the Category permissions would allow Open Projects, and the Save Projects permission would be blank. Open Projects and Save Projects are features that control the behavior between Project Professional and Project Server. Open allows the project manager to open all the projects in the database into Project Professional but not save them to the database.

The second Category would select the Only the Projects Indicated Below radio button and then select the security rule Allow Users in This Category to View All Projects They Manage. The permissions Open Projects and Save Projects would be allowed. This data structure would allow the project manager to open and save only those projects for which he was the creator (owner).

The total permissions for a project manager are now set so that the project manager can see all projects (defined by Category 1) but can only edit (open and save) the projects that he created (defined by Category 2). The system understands the association of the user to the Group and the association of the different Categories to the Group to control the users' conditional use of data.

Assigning Resources to Proper Groups

After all the Templates, Groups, and Categories have been defined and associated, it is time to assign the individual resources to the Groups. Open the individual Groups and assign the proper resources who have the role-based responsibility defined by the Group.

What if a resource is both a Project Manager and a Resource Manager? These roles require different use permissions and data permissions within the system. Any resource can be assigned to multiple Groups and thus take on the permissions of all Groups to which the resource is a member. To modify user Groups, follow these steps:

1. In the PWA window, select the Admin tab.

2. Select Manage Users and Groups.

3. Under Security Options select Groups.

4. Select the Group to be managed.

5. Click Modify Group.

6. When all selections are complete, click Save Changes.

In the Users: Select the Users That Belong to This Group window, select the appropriate users, and click the Add button to add them to the Group. You can hold down the Ctrl key and click and drag down to select multiple users together, or you can hold down the Ctrl key and click to select multiple users and then add the collection.

Managing Users

Under the Manage Users and Groups selection, you have the opportunity to add, modify, and delete users (see Figure 8.13). Never modify a user's permissions in this window. To maintain control over the security model, it is always better to manage user permissions within the Template, Group, or Categories collection.

CAUTION

Although possible, managing each individual user's security at the individual user level is not advised.

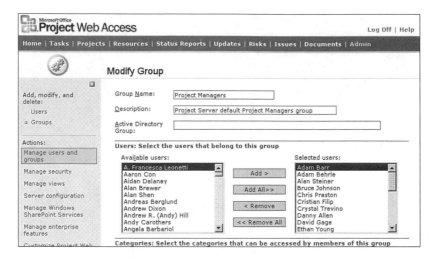

FIGURE 8.13   Assigning users to Groups.

Best Practices

- Read and understand the *Microsoft Project Server 2003 Administrator's Guide*.

- Security is most easily managed through security templates than any other method.

- Never assign a resource to a Category without a justifiable cause.

- Categories should only serve a single finite purpose.

Security Design Recommendations

Security should be established in the following order:

- Set universal Allow/Deny in Server Configuration, Features.

- Review the Microsoft Project security template defaults to determine the role-based name for each template.

- Determine necessary roles and permissions. Review "Project Server Permissions" in Appendix C of the *Microsoft Project Server 2003 Administrator's Guide*, if necessary.

- Define a security template for each role and assign permissions.

- Define Groups using Add/Modify Group and assign permissions from the Set Permissions with Template button by selecting from the security templates previously defined. Each Group should have a predefined security template of the same name.

- Assign the appropriate role-based Group to Category.

- Set permissions and data restrictors for each Category.

- Assign resources to Groups.

CHAPTER 9

Enterprise Global Codes

IN THIS CHAPTER

- Overview of the Enterprise Outline Codes and Fields
- Project Outline Codes
- Resource Outline Codes
- Resource Breakdown Structure
- Enterprise Resource Pool
- Enterprise Task Outline Codes
- Enterprise Custom Fields, Formulas, and Graphic Indicators
- Best Practices

In the enterprise environment, a Microsoft Office Project Server 2003 database is usually a large collection of project and resource-related data. You can use Enterprise Outline Codes to define an additional set of custom task, project, and resource-related attributes that reflect your unique business requirements and help you to organize and manipulate this large volume of project-related data.

Well-defined Enterprise Outline Codes can help you enforce project management process standardization in your organization and are an important part of the foundation for a comprehensive enterprise reporting system.

Overview of the Enterprise Outline Codes and Fields

Enterprise Outline Codes are custom hierarchical tags you can associate with projects, tasks, and resources. You can use them to filter and group your projects, tasks, and resources in many ways, as well as display summarized or rolled-up reports.

When you want to associate a descriptive attribute with a task, project, or resource, Enterprise Outline Codes are convenient.

With Project Server 2003, you have 90 Enterprise Outline Codes—30 Enterprise Task Outline Codes, 30 Enterprise Resource Outline Codes, and 30 Enterprise Project Outline Codes—at your disposal. Enterprise Outline Codes are defined as hierarchical sets of metadata that describe attributes of the tasks, resources, or projects in your portfolio.

You can define the basic structure of any Enterprise Outline Code by creating a code mask first. A code mask definition includes the following:

- The number of levels in the hierarchy

- The sequence (or type) of characters used by each level

- The number of characters used by each level

- The separator characters used by each level

An appropriate definition of your custom set of Enterprise Outline Codes is one of the most important steps in planning your Enterprise Project Management (EPM) solution based on the Project Server 2003 platform. Your custom Enterprise Outline Codes are used as part of many different custom views and reports as well as for filtering, sorting, and grouping of your enterprise project and resource data exposed as in your custom reports.

If you do not spend enough time defining and designing a comprehensive set of Enterprise Outline Codes based on your business requirements, your EPM system might not adequately meet the reporting and portfolio management needs of your organization.

A limited number of people should have permissions to define Enterprise Outline Codes in your organization. Only users who have permission to check out and edit the Enterprise Global template can create, modify, or delete Enterprise Outline Codes—this is typically a task handled by your EPM system administrator.

One special Enterprise Resource Outline Code (Enterprise Resource Outline Code number 30) is reserved for Resource Breakdown Structure (RBS) code. The RBS code can be used for any resource attribute, but it should be reserved for the RBS code value that is one of the most important and most often used in a typical large organization. The RBS outline code plays an important role in the overall system security and is also used by other features such as the Build Team from Enterprise, the Resource Substitution Wizard, and the Assign Resources dialog tools when filtering and selecting resources. The RBS code is covered in detail later in this chapter.

When you want to associate a custom, nonhierarchical attribute consistently with all the projects, resources, or tasks in your organization, you can use the enterprise custom fields. The difference between Enterprise Outline codes and Enterprise Custom Fields is that Enterprise Custom Fields are defined as a single level list of values and cannot be hierarchical. Also, custom fields cannot be used as dimensions in the Portfolio Analyzer.

Typically, the EPM system administrator together with your Project Management Office (PMO) defines and creates Enterprise Outline Codes and Custom Fields, making sure that their use is consistent across the whole organization.

To create and change Enterprise Outline Codes and Fields you need to open the Enterprise Global template first. By default, only the EPM system administrator can open and edit items in the Enterprise Global template.

To configure Enterprise Outline Codes and Fields, you need to log on to Project Server 2003 from Microsoft Project Professional client with administrator or equivalent privileges.

▸ **SEE** "Introduction to Microsoft Office Project Professional," **PAGE 537**.

NOTE

For your Enterprise Outline Codes to be permanently added to the Project Server 2003 repository, you must first open the Enterprise Global template. If you cannot add Enterprise Outline Codes because the data entry fields are grayed out, you most probably don't have the Enterprise Global template open.

To create a new custom Enterprise Outline Code or Field, follow these steps:

1. Select Tools, Enterprise Options, Open Enterprise Global from the menu.
2. Choose Tools, Customize, Enterprise Fields from the menu to display the dialog box shown in Figure 9.1.

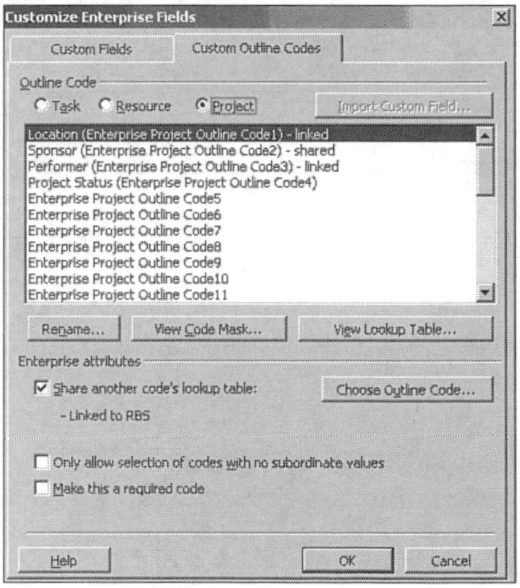

FIGURE 9.1 Location, Sponsor, Performer, and Project Status Enterprise Project Outline Codes are defined using the first four available Enterprise Project Outline Codes.

3. In the displayed dialog box, select the Custom Outline Codes tab.
4. Select the category of outline code you want to create—choose from Task, Resource, or Project.
5. Select the Enterprise Outline Code field that you want to use (1 through 30 for enterprise task or project outline codes, 1 through 29 plus reserved code for RBS for Enterprise Resource Outline Codes).

6. To specify a descriptive name for the Enterprise Outline Code, click the Rename button, and the dialog box shown in Figure 9.2 appears. Enter the desired code name and then click OK.

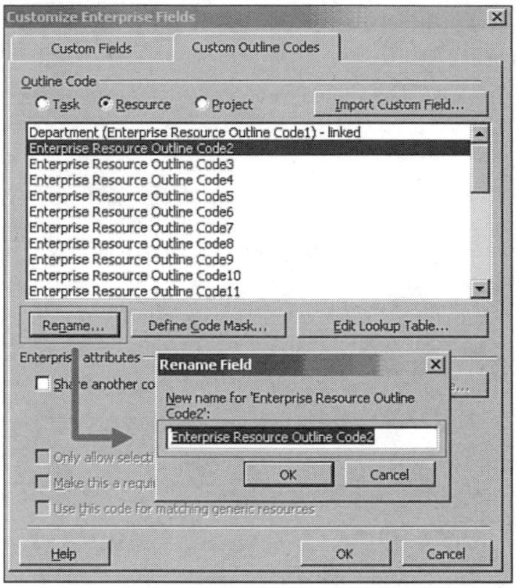

FIGURE 9.2   Use descriptive names for your Enterprise Resource Outline Codes.

7. To display the Outline Code Definition for "Enterprise Reso..." dialog box shown in Figure 9.3, click the Define Code Mask button. Make sure that you define a code mask for each level of outline code.

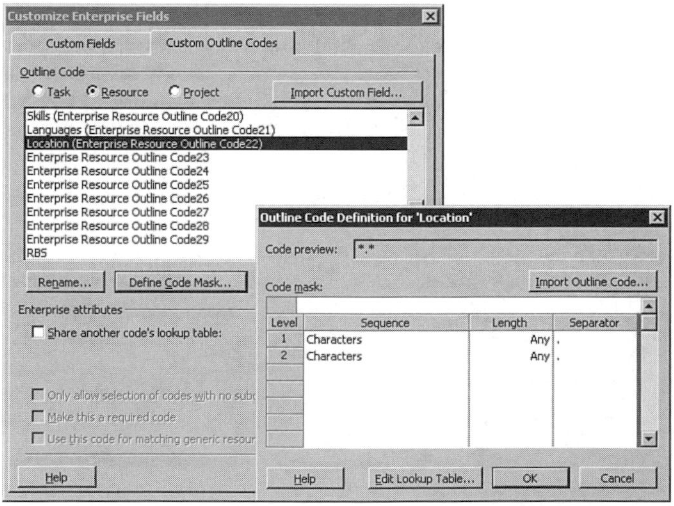

FIGURE 9.3   If you are defining the Enterprise Resource Outline Code to describe location with Level 1 as state and Level 2 as city, create code mask definitions for two levels, as shown.

8. To display the Edit Lookup Table dialog box shown in Figure 9.4, click the Edit Lookup Table button. Here, enter your outline code hierarchical list items. For example, if you are defining a location outline code for state and city, your Level 1 code might be Colorado, and your Level 2 list items underneath Colorado might be Boulder, Colorado Springs, and Denver. Use the Indent and Outdent buttons to create the proper hierarchy. Click Close to save the lookup table definition.

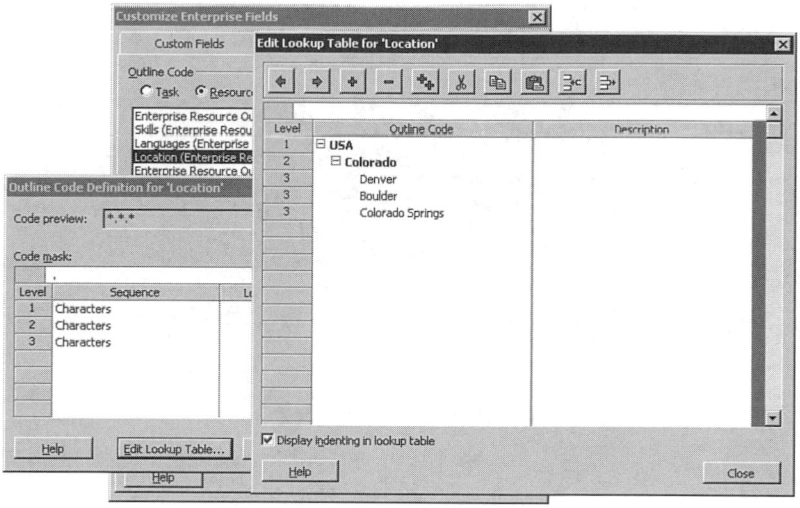

FIGURE 9.4 Use the icons at the top of the dialog box to create the proper lookup table list hierarchy; hover your mouse pointer over each icon to learn what it does.

9. If you want to share the same lookup table with another Enterprise Outline Code, as shown in Figure 9.5, select the Share Another Code's Lookup Table check box and click the Choose Outline Code button. Select the outline code's field type and field name from the pull-down lists. When outline code lookup tables are shared, changing the shared outline code's lookup table automatically changes the lookup table available for the second outline code that is linked. After you choose the outline code lookup table to share, click OK.

10. If you want your users to select entries only at the lowest level of detail in the outline code hierarchy, as shown in Figure 9.6, select the Only Allow Selection of Codes with No Subordinate Values check box. For example, if you entered location codes with cities of Denver and Boulder under the state of Colorado, selecting this check box requires users to always select one of the cities (the lowest level of the outline code, the city, has no subordinate values).

11. If you want to make a particular Enterprise Outline Code required before allowing any schedule or resource to be saved or published to the Microsoft Project Server, select the Make This a Required Code check box.

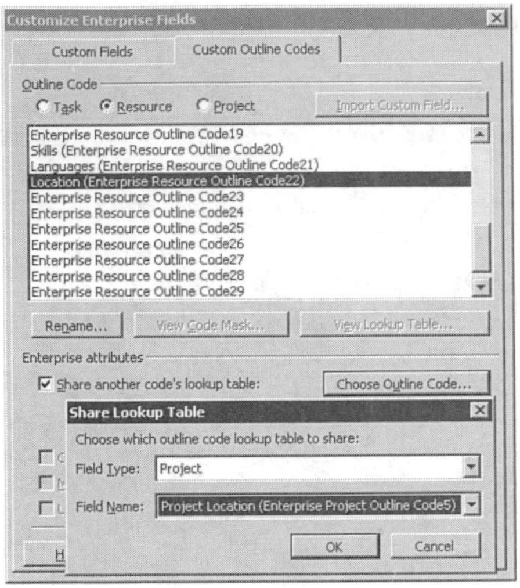

FIGURE 9.5   The Location Enterprise Resource Outline Code lookup table is shared with the Location Enterprise Project Outline Code.

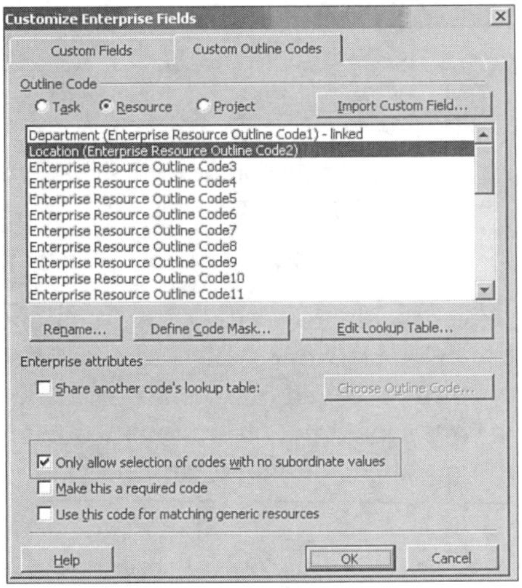

FIGURE 9.6   You can limit your users to select from the list items at the lowest level of the Enterprise Outline Code hierarchy.

12. To designate an Enterprise Outline Code as a code used for matching used by the Resource Substitution Wizard and Build Team from Enterprise feature, select the Use This Code for Matching Generic Resources check box.

> **NOTE**
>
> The Use This Code for Matching Generic Resources check box is available only for Enterprise Resource Outline Codes.

13. When you are finished defining your Enterprise Custom Outline Codes and Fields, click the Close button. You are now back at the Customize Enterprise Fields dialog box. Click OK to exit the dialog box.

14. Save and exit the Checked-Out Enterprise Global. Your new or newly edited Enterprise Outline Codes and Fields are now part of the Enterprise Global template and can be used with all projects and resources stored in the Project Server database.

> **NOTE**
>
> Before you can see and use the new Enterprise Outline Code entries, you need to exit, restart the Project Professional client, and reconnect to Project Server.

Project Outline Codes

Enterprise Project Outline Codes provide a set of customizable hierarchical fields that you can use to model your unique project data requirements. These hierarchical attributes can be later assigned to individual tasks, resources, or projects in your portfolio.

Planning Enterprise Project Outline Codes

This section discusses some planning considerations for Enterprise Project Outline Codes.

Organizational and project portfolio reporting requirements should be always on your mind when it comes to Enterprise Project Outline Codes.

You may start with a look at your reporting requirements first and then work your way back to define a set of outline codes and custom fields to support your organizational reporting requirements.

Begin with the planning and design of Enterprise Project Outline Codes. Organizations that have a small number of projects in their corporate project portfolio compared to the number of their enterprise resources might find them easier to relate to and define than Enterprise Resource Outline Codes.

If your organization has a sizable portfolio of projects, it is best to find an approach that minimizes the number of future changes needed to be made to the Enterprise Project Outline Codes. The following example will help you better understand why.

The Enterprise Resource Pool allows you to manage all your enterprise resources centrally. If you need to make changes to 3,000 resources in your resource pool, you can do this in a single place—the Enterprise Resource Pool. If you have 1,000 projects in your corporate project portfolio, it may take a long time to change a single required Enterprise Project Outline Code for all your projects. If your organization is experiencing problems with a particular required Enterprise Project Outline Code, change that Enterprise Outline Code to a nonrequired code first before removing it completely.

To establish a set of project attributes for your organization, you first need to determine all information that needs to be reported about projects.

Consider a short example of how you might establish the Enterprise Outline Code requirements. BBBpm Consulting has offices in Denver and Toronto. Some projects are located in Toronto, and some are in Denver. BBBpm Consulting also has many other clients and several project sponsors overseeing the projects. Based on this information, BBBpm Consulting can consider the following three Enterprise Project Outline Codes: location (includes country, state, and city), client (the clients), and project sponsor (the project sponsors). In addition, BBBpm Consulting wants to be able to group and filter its project portfolio by project priority and project status. For each task, BBBpm Consulting decided that project tasks will have billing code information attached.

The design of your Enterprise Project Outline Codes determines to a large degree your project portfolio reporting capabilities. Part of the EPM solution design is a design of custom reports and views. Views enable sophisticated and flexible project portfolio reporting. Enterprise Project Outline Codes enable you to use custom filtering, sorting, and grouping as part of your custom views used for project portfolio reporting.

Project Center views can use the Enterprise Project Outline Codes to filter, group, and sort projects by location, status, sponsor, or other information defined as Enterprise Project Outline Codes.

▶ **SEE** "Creating Project Web Access Project and Resource Views," **PAGE 209**.

You also need to think about how and where you develop and define your Enterprise Project Outline Codes. Your Enterprise Project Outline Codes may already be defined in other enterprise systems. Perhaps your accounting system already has project attributes, such as project location and status defined, and you can integrate your accounting system with Project Server 2003 and use the codes already defined in your accounting system. To integrate with other enterprise systems, Project Server 2003 provides the Project Data Service (PDS) interface.

▶ **SEE** "Extending Enterprise Project Management Through Customization," **PAGE 793**.

The other, more often used option is to define, develop, and maintain your Enterprise Project Outline Codes in the Enterprise Global template.

Defining Enterprise Project Outline Codes

The capability to perform effective resource assignments and enterprise reporting are the two primary features driven by the Enterprise Resource Outline Codes.

You are now ready to define your Enterprise Project Outline Codes based on the business requirements you previously identified.

Before you can define your Enterprise Project Outline Codes, make sure that the following actions are completed:

- Identify your company's business requirements.

- Plan the Enterprise Project Outline Code implementation.

- Establish the Enterprise Project Outline Code utilization guidelines.

- Define and develop the custom filters, views, and reports that will use the Enterprise Project Outline Codes.

- Review the project portfolio reporting requirements.

Enterprise Project Outline Codes have a major impact on your overall EPM solution usability. Proper definition and use of Enterprise Outline Codes make project portfolio management tasks easier and reduce the overall time required for EPM system administration.

Another benefit of well-designed Enterprise Project Outline Codes is that they can help you with standardization of your project portfolio management processes.

An Enterprise Project Outline Code should be defined as a required code only when there is a good reason to ask all project managers in your organization to use it. Consider the following scenario. Projects managed by your IT Infrastructure team may have different requirements than projects managed by your Marketing department. If any Enterprise Outline Code is defined as a required code, the Marketing department will need to specify a value for the outline code even if it is only relevant to the IT Infrastructure team.

Rules for Defining Enterprise Project Outline Codes
Consider the following general rules based on recommendations from the *Microsoft Project Server 2003 Application Configuration Guide* when defining your Enterprise Project Outline Codes:

- Use names that are clear, concise, and unambiguous to other members in your organization.

- Use names that match names used by related systems or systems that may be a source of data—for example, external Human Resources systems or Microsoft Active Directory.

- Avoid special characters such as / " ; : < > | [ ] , . ' ? ~ ` ! $ % ^ & * ( ) - + = { or } when naming Enterprise Outline Codes; these may cause errors when generating the OLAP cube used by the Microsoft Office Project Web Access 2003 View tables, Portfolio Modeler, and Portfolio Analyzer.

- If an Enterprise Outline Code data is located in some form of external data, it can be extracted and used to define a lookup table (only after the code mask is defined) by copying and pasting the data into the lookup table directly.

- You can also use the PDS application programming interface (API) to automatically populate Enterprise Outline Codes from other systems. The Service for Enterprise Data Maintenance in the PDS can simplify the maintenance of lookup tables associated with Enterprise Outline Codes.

6

> **NOTE**
>
> For more details about the rules for planning and defining Enterprise Outline Codes, review the *Microsoft Project Server 2003 Application Configuration Guide*, Chapter 5, "Working with Enterprise Outline Codes," available from http://www.microsoft.com/technet/prodtechnol/office/proj2003/reskit/default.mspx.

Additional Considerations for Enterprise Project Outline Codes

You should take into account several other considerations:

- Consider establishing an Other, NA, or Unspecified entry for each Enterprise Outline Code. Enterprise Outline Codes are defined in advance, and users should be allowed to select a "fallback" code lookup table entry if they do not find an appropriate code lookup table entry to use.

- Codes are alphabetized within each outline code level during selection of values. If you want to force a different, nonalphabetical order, prefix the code values with a number (01) or a series of letters (AA).

- Making an outline code a required code is the best way to ensure that project attributes are consistently applied to all your projects. A project manager cannot save a project without entering a value for a required Enterprise Project Outline Code.

Using Enterprise Project Outline Codes

After you define your project outline codes, it is time to take a closer look at their use. Table 9.1 provides an example of project attributes used for Enterprise Project Outline Codes.

TABLE 9.1   Project Attributes Example

Project Attribute	Value
Client	Internal
	IT
	Operations
	Finance
	Marketing
	Sales
	External
	Government
	Municipal
	State
	Federal
	Business
	Large
	Medium
	Small

TABLE 9.1   Continued

Project Attribute	Value
Location	USA
	Colorado
	Denver
	Texas
	Houston
	Dallas
	California
	Los Angeles
	San Francisco
	Canada
	Ontario
	Toronto
	British Columbia
	Vancouver
Project Sponsor	List of sponsor names

To create new Enterprise Project Outline Codes, follow these steps:

1. In the Project Professional client select Tools, Enterprise Options, Open Enterprise Global Template.

2. To display the Customize Enterprise Fields dialog box, choose Tools, Customize, Enterprise Fields from the menu.

> ▶ **SEE** "Overview of the Enterprise Outline Codes and Fields," **PAGE 163**.

To attach an Enterprise Project Outline Code representing a project attribute to projects themselves, the project manager specifies the outline codes upon saving the project schedule the first time.

TIP

If the Enterprise Outline Code was configured as a required code, and your users experience difficulties with the use of the code, remove the required flag first, making the outline code optional, before deleting the outline code completely.

If you define any Enterprise Outline Code with too many entries—thousands of entries and many hierarchy levels—it can negatively affect the performance of the Project Professional and Project Web Access (PWA) client when you view project data organized (filtered or grouped) by that Enterprise Outline Code. For more details, review the Microsoft knowledge base article 872819 available from http://support.microsoft.com/ default.aspx?scid=kb;en-us;872819.

Resource Outline Codes

After you define your Enterprise Project Outline Codes, continue with the Enterprise Resource Outline Codes definition.

The mechanics of creating Enterprise Resource Outline Codes are the same steps as when creating Enterprise Project Outline Codes. However, some unique properties of Enterprise Resource Outline Codes need to be discussed and understood.

Planning Enterprise Resource Outline Codes

Many organizations find it easier to define Enterprise Resource Outline Codes that are not related to their resource skills. You may consider separating nonskill Enterprise Resource Outline Codes from the skill-based ones. Experience from the field suggests that many companies, especially small and medium-sized ones, may not even want to do skill-based scheduling. The level of commitment and consensus required for meaningful enterprisewide skill-based resource assignment and capacity planning is fairly high. The skill-based resource assignment and capacity planning may be appropriate only for organizations with high project management maturity.

CAUTION

Before you decide to use the skill-based Enterprise Resource Outline Codes as part of your EPM system design outside the United States or where resources are included in an Enterprise Resource Pool physically located outside the United States, first determine whether it is legal to record skills. For all installations in organizations that have unions, you also need to make sure that there are no contractual restrictions on classifying union members by skill.

Before you can create skill-based Enterprise Resource Outline Codes for your organization, it is important to decide on an approach to the skill definition in your organization. It is usually a challenge to get agreement from all participants on what the skills outline codes should look like, what should and should not be included in each skills outline code definition, and whether your organization also needs skill levels defined.

In addition, you need to understand the differences between Enterprise Outline Codes, Local Outline Codes, and Enterprise Custom Fields, as well as the role of RBS code.

Finally, understand the potential impact of large Enterprise Resource Outline Codes on the functionality of your EPM solution.

Considerations for Planning Enterprise Resource Outline Codes

To establish a set of resource skills and attributes for your organization, you need to first determine all possible information that needs to be reported about your enterprise resources.

The following list shows some possible questions that may help you establish the Enterprise Resource Outline Codes requirements:

- What attributes do you want to use when reporting on your enterprise resources?

- How are your resources organized?

- Do you need to use resource skills and skill levels?

- Do you have existing RBS structures documented?

- When a project is conceptualized, how are resources allocated to it?

- What is the process used to forecast resource load?

- Are all your project managers and resources in one location?

The design of your Enterprise Resource Outline Codes determines to a large degree your resource management reporting capabilities. Part of the EPM solution design is a design of custom reports and views. Views enable sophisticated and flexible project portfolio reporting. Enterprise Resource Outline Codes enable you to use custom filtering, sorting, and grouping as part of your custom views used for resource management reporting.

Resource Center views can use Enterprise Resource Outline Codes to filter, group, and sort resources by location, department, skills, or other information defined as Enterprise Resource Outline Codes. The Resource Center also enables resource managers and executives to view resource availability and commitments.

▶ **SEE** "Project Web Access Project and Resource Views," **PAGE 209**.

You also need to think about how and where you develop and define your Enterprise Resource Outline Codes. Your Enterprise Resource Outline Codes may already be defined in other enterprise systems. Perhaps your HR system already has resource attributes such as resource location and skills defined, and you can integrate your HR system with Project Server 2003 and use the codes already defined in your HR system. To integrate with other enterprise systems, Project Server 2003 provides the PDS interface.

The other, more often used option is to define, develop, and maintain your Enterprise Resource Outline Codes in the Enterprise Global template.

Probably the most important Enterprise Resource Outline Code you need to define and create is the RBS. The RBS outline code affects the organizational security, access to project views, resource assignments, and reports.

▶ **SEE** "Resource Breakdown Structure," **PAGE 185**.

Another possible resource attribute might be the location of the resource. Consider the example discussed earlier in the chapter in which BBBpm Consulting has offices in Denver and Toronto. Some resources are located in Toronto, and some are in Denver. Assigning a location resource attribute for each enterprise resource may be useful. Your project and resource managers can then see the resource usage and capacity information by resource role and location.

Resource skills are another type of resource attribute you can define and can include skills such as project manager, technical writer, network administrator, programmer, and trainer. Start with planning your enterprise resource skills definitions by discussing what roles people play on your project teams. Look at past and current projects, and come up with a list of roles or skills being required on those projects.

After you determine the roles or skills available in your organization, break down the skills definitions even further. For example, instead of simply listing the skill *programmer*, define the skills in terms of development technology types, such as Web, Visual Basic, or C++ programmers. You can also define skill levels, such as junior, intermediate, and senior, for each skill. Consider as well skills that you might use in the future, not just the skills currently in use.

▶ **SEE** "Using Multiple Skills Per Resource," **PAGE 181**.

Defining Enterprise Resource Outline Codes

You are now ready to define your Enterprise Resource Outline Codes based on the business requirements identified previously.

Before you can define your Enterprise Resource Outline Codes, make sure that the following actions are performed:

- Identify the business requirements.

- Plan the Enterprise Resource Outline Codes implementation.

- Establish the Enterprise Resource Outline Codes utilization guidelines.

- Define and develop custom filters and views and define reports that will use the Enterprise Resource Outline Codes.

- Examine the resource management reporting requirements.

- Consider the security requirements and effects of the RBS code.

Defining Skills for Your Enterprise Resources

In general, you can choose from three approaches when defining skill codes for your organization:

- Use a single Enterprise Resource Outline Code to define all available skills when you have a small number of skills to choose from and only a single skill is used to define resource assignment skill requirements.

- Use multiple Enterprise Resource Outline Codes to define distinct skills when multiple skills are needed to define resource assignment skill requirements. This approach can significantly improve your understanding of resource load and capacity across your organization. However, it comes with a price. It also requires significantly more administrative effort to keep resource information in your Enterprise Resource Pool up-to-date.

- Use multivalue Enterprise Resource Outline Codes to define different levels of distinct skills when resource assignments require different skill levels. Enterprise resource multivalue outline codes can allow you to define skill levels. This approach also requires significantly more administrative effort to keep your Enterprise Resource Pool information up-to-date.

> **NOTE**
>
> Before you implement large multivalue Enterprise Resource Outline Codes for your enterprise resources to define all available skills in your organization, first consider potential performance effects.

> **CAUTION**
>
> Multivalue outline codes used to define skill levels have one limitation you need to be aware of. It is not possible to filter for values above or below a node in the multivalue outline code. For example, a project manager cannot filter for a VB programmer with intermediate or higher level of skills. They can filter only for intermediate levels. If they are looking for a higher level of skills, they must then filter resources again for a senior VB programmer.

After you define and create your skill codes, you can then assign the skill code values to the appropriate Enterprise Resource Outline Codes of your enterprise generic resources to be used in resource skill matching.

Your individual enterprise resources need to be assigned values for the skill code appropriate to the Enterprise Resource Outline codes. After that, you are ready to use the skill matching features such as the Build Team from Enterprise feature or the Resource Substitution Wizard. This is a required step for being able to perform skill-based resource capacity planning.

You have two options for resource matching. Resource matching based on a single Enterprise Resource Outline Code is relatively straightforward. A match is considered any resource with a matching value in the skill code. Resource matching based on multiple Enterprise Resource Outline Codes requires that the values for all relevant skill codes match for a resource to qualify as a match.

> **NOTE**
>
> Resource matching can be performed between individual as well as generic resources. An example can be a project manager needing to identify an alternative individual resource with the same skill set when the original resource assigned becomes unavailable.

Additional Considerations for Enterprise Resource Outline Codes

Before creating a new Enterprise Outline Code, consider the following:

- Consider establishing an Other, NA, or Unspecified entry for each Enterprise Outline Code. Enterprise Outline Codes are defined in advance, and users should be allowed to select a fallback code lookup table entry if they do not find an appropriate code lookup table entry to use.

- Codes are alphabetized within each outline code level during the selection of values. If you want to force a different, nonalphabetical order, prefix the code values with a number (01) or a series of letters (AA).

- Making an outline code a required code is the best way to ensure that resource attributes are consistently applied to all your resources. An administrator cannot save a new resource to your Enterprise Resource Pool without entering a value for a required Enterprise Resource Outline Code.

Using Enterprise Resource Outline Codes

After you create a list of resource attributes and determine their hierarchy and values, you need to configure them in the Project Professional client using the Enterprise Resource Outline Codes structures.

Here are some sample scenarios of Enterprise Resource Outline Code usage:

- Categorize resources to view usage and capacity information at different organizational levels.

- Resource skills search.

- Query your Enterprise Resource Pool for matching skills.

Based on careful analysis of business requirements, BBBpm Consulting from the previous example decided to use the resource attributes shown in Table 9.2.

TABLE 9.2   Resource Attributes Example

Resource Attribute	Value		
RBS	BBBpm		
		IT	
			Development Group
			Technical Support
			Networking Group
			Corporate Data Group
		Operations	
			HR
			R&D
			Finance
			Marketing
			Sales
		Consulting	
Location	USA		
		Colorado	
			Denver
		Texas	
			Houston
			Dallas
		California	
			Los Angeles
			San Francisco

TABLE 9.2 Continued

Resource Attribute	Value
	Canada
	Ontario
	Toronto
	British Columbia
	Vancouver
Skills	Director
	Manager
	Consultant
	Methodologies
	Technology
	Implementation
	Trainer
	Project Manager
	General Administration
	IT
	Developer
	C++
	Visual Basic
	Web
	.NET and SQL
	Database Administrator
	Network Administrator
	Technical Writer

To create new Enterprise Resource Outline Codes, follow these steps:

1. In the Project Professional client select Tools, Enterprise Options, Open Enterprise Template.

2. To display the Customize Enterprise Fields dialog box choose Tools, Customize, Enterprise Fields from the menu.

3. Use the Custom Outline Codes tab and select the Resource radio button.

> ▶ **SEE** "Overview of the Enterprise Outline Codes and Fields," **PAGE 163**.

You need to associate the Enterprise Resource Outline Codes values with each enterprise resource before you can manipulate your enterprise resources—filter, sort, or group—using these Enterprise Resource Outline Codes.

To report on your enterprise resources and their attributes, you need to use the Enterprise Resource Outline Codes as part of the custom view definition in the Resource Center or Portfolio Analyzer.

Using Skill Levels As Part of Your Skill Codes

The Microsoft EPM solution supports the concept of multivalue Enterprise Resource Outline Codes. You can use this feature to define skill proficiency levels—for example, for programming skills, design skills, languages, and so on. This feature may become handy if you need to distinguish between skill proficiency levels when performing initial resource assignment or when you need to perform resource substitution. For example, suppose that you get a project in Prague. Anybody able to speak at least some Czech would be preferred for this assignment. The Prague project goes well and the next thing you know, based on your excellent reputation, you get a large project to deliver for one of the Czech government ministries. This new project requires advanced project management as well as advanced Czech language skills.

To enable skill proficiency levels definition, you need to set up your skill codes with the proficiency levels defined at the lowest level of the code, as shown in Figure 9.7.

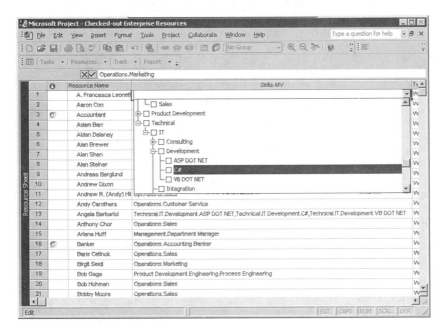

FIGURE 9.7   You can define your resource skill codes with proficiency levels included.

A review of how the matching process works with skill proficiency levels defined is in order. A resource is considered to have skills at the level of and all subordinate levels below the skill level assigned. The following example documents this behavior. If a generic resource is assigned the skill Developer.C#, the Build Team from Enterprise Match feature would find any individual resource with a skill that matches Developer.C#, Developer.C#.Senior, Developer.C#.Intermediate, or Developer.C#.Junior.

> **NOTE**
>
> If you want to be able to assign skill codes at any level, make sure that the Only Allow Selection of Codes with No Subordinate Values check box in the Customize Enterprise Fields dialog box is not selected.

Using Multiple Skills Per Resource

Many resources have multiple skills and, therefore, Project Professional client supports assigning multiple skill codes to resources. For example, a VB developer might also be a C# developer, and a technical writer might also be an excellent trainer. By associating a resource with just one skill code, you are limiting the Resource Substitution Wizard capabilities. The resource associated with only one defined skill will be matched only with that single skill, possibly overlooking other resources' capabilities.

For example, to enable enterprise resources to have up to three skills defined, you can define a total of three skill code Enterprise Resource Outline Codes. When you define three Enterprise Resource Skill Codes, you can associate up to three skills with all your enterprise resources, as required.

To enable assignment of multiple skills per resource, follow these steps:

1. Set up the first skill code using one of the Enterprise Resource Outline Codes. Figure 9.7 provides an example of the Enterprise Resource Skill Code. Notice that skill proficiencies have also been defined as part of this skill code.

2. After you define your initial skill code hierarchy, create one or more additional Enterprise Resource Skill Codes using other available Enterprise Resource Outline Codes and link each of them to the first skill code lookup table by using the Share Another Code's Lookup Table check box.

3. Make sure that you have each defined Enterprise Resource Skill Code's enterprise attributes set correctly. Figure 9.8 shows the attributes associated with the initial skill code, and Figure 9.9 shows the attributes associated with subsequent skill codes.

4. Assign skill codes to your resources, as appropriate.

> **NOTE**
>
> Multiple skills and skill levels are not mutually exclusive features. You can define Enterprise Resource Skill Codes with both features combined.

Working with Enterprise Resource Multivalue Skill Codes

Because a single resource can have more than one skill as well as different skill levels, Project Server 2003 supports multivalue resource skill codes that help project and resource managers to better match required resource skill sets with individual resources.

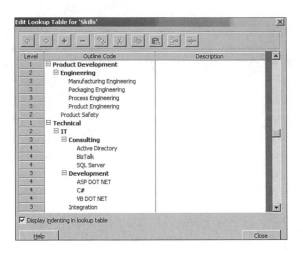

FIGURE 9.8   At least one Enterprise Resource Skill Code is required to enable the Resource Substitution Wizard, the Build Team from Enterprise, and the Team Assign dialog box skill matching features.

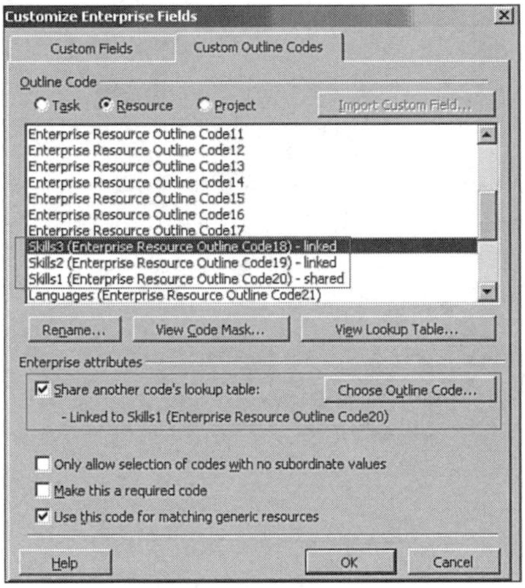

FIGURE 9.9   Subsequent Enterprise Resource Skill Codes add to the skill matching capabilities of the Resource Substitution Wizard, the Build Team from Enterprise feature, and the Team Assign dialog box.

In most cases, project and resource managers know what skill sets and qualifications are required for a project, but it may be difficult to match the skill set requirements with individual resources especially when the Enterprise Resource Pool is large, containing thousands of resources, and/or geographically distributed. This task may be easier to accomplish when the Enterprise Resource Pool is smaller and "everybody knows your name."

Matching Resource Skills

To match the required skills with individual or generic resources use the Build Team from Enterprise or Resource Substitution Wizard features available in Project Professional client.

▶ **SEE** "Building Project Team and Resource Substitution," **PAGE 563**.

You can also use the Build Team feature available in the Project Center of your PWA client. From the home page, go to the Project Center page. Select the project for which you want to perform a skill matching search and then click Build Team.

The project may already have individual resources assigned to tasks. In the example shown in Figure 9.10, a resource manager wants to substitute an individual resource that is already assigned to a task for another individual resource that has the same skill set because the originally assigned resource became suddenly unavailable.

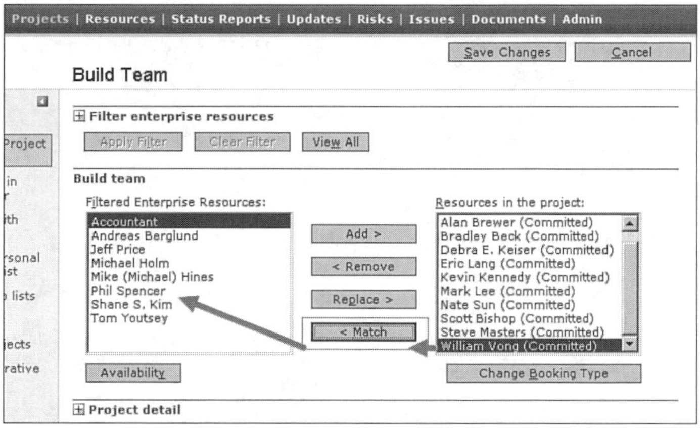

FIGURE 9.10   Resource managers don't need to have the Project Professional client installed on their machines to build project team or substitute resources.

▶ **SEE** "Using Project and Resource Centers," **PAGE 345**.

Assigning Enterprise Resource Outline Codes and Custom Fields to Resources

After you define and create your Enterprise Resource Outline Codes, custom fields are entered in the Enterprise Global template, and enterprise resources are created in your Enterprise Resource Pool. The resources in your Enterprise Resource Pool need to have the attributes represented by Enterprise Resource Outline Codes and custom fields assigned to them.

To assign attributes represented by Enterprise Resource Outline Codes to your enterprise resources, follow these steps:

1. Select Tools, Enterprise Options, Open Enterprise Resource Pool from the menu.

2. To choose all resources in your enterprise pool click the Select/Deselect All button, and then click the Open/Add button to open the selected enterprise resources in the Resource Sheet view (as shown in Figure 9.11).

3. Assign attributes represented by the Enterprise Resource Outline Codes to your enterprise resources.

TIP

An efficient way to maintain Enterprise Resource Outline Codes is to create a new Resource Outline Codes view and table in the Enterprise Global template, where the columns in your table include all Enterprise Resource Outline Codes. You can then use this view to assign or edit outline code information for the entire Enterprise Resource Pool.

---

4. When you are finished, save your work and exit the Enterprise Resource Pool.

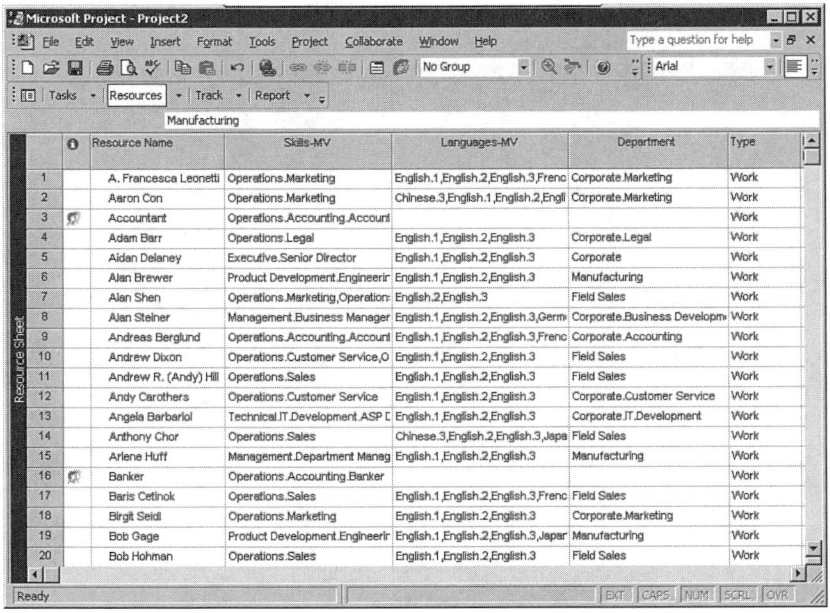

FIGURE 9.11   Customized Resource Sheet view includes resource skill codes for easier resource skill code management.

NOTE

If you cannot select enterprise resources to open from your Enterprise Resource Pool, those enterprise resources might already be checked out by somebody else. Provided that you have administrative permissions, choose Admin, Manage Enterprise Features from the menu in the PWA client and then select Check in Enterprise Resources. You see a list of currently checked-out enterprise resources and who checked them out.

After you define and create all Enterprise Resource Outline Codes and custom fields, you can edit these resource attributes by selecting a resource and clicking Edit Resource Details on the Resource Center page in the PWA client.

Resource Breakdown Structure

The Resource Breakdown Structure (RBS) is a hierarchical structure representing your enterprise resources that enables you to create project plans with detailed resource assignments and compare this workload with detailed resource availabilities. The RBS also enables roll-up of both resource assignments and availabilities data to a higher level.

Planning and Defining RBS Hierarchy

One specific reserved Enterprise Resource Outline Code is called RBS. RBS is represented by Enterprise Resource Outline Code 30, and its design can have a significant effect on the EPM solution security, views, reports, processes used for project team building, and resource assignments, as well as how you report on resource commitments. It is recommended that you organize your EPM solution security model around RBS by defining it in such a way that it reflects the hierarchical relationships of all your enterprise resources in your organization rather than your organizational structure itself.

Proper definition of RBS is important to the success of your EPM solution deployment. RBS impacts the way your organization manages EPM solution security, access to project and resource views, resource assignments, and other EPM solution features.

You can use the hierarchical relationships defined as part of RBS to simplify data access for your users and user groups. Use RBS to define five security rules when you later create the security categories in the PWA client.

RBS code functionality is also used in the following areas of the EPM solution:

- Resource Substitution Wizard
- Portfolio Modeler
- Portfolio Analyzer
- Build Team
- Two default security categories—My Direct Reports and My Resources

RBS code is a hierarchical structure. For executives to see information about the projects and resources they manage, they must be placed appropriately in the RBS hierarchy. If you are using an organizational RBS, make sure that you place your executives above the people they manage. If your executives want to see resource information for projects in their organization, make sure to place them in the RBS hierarchy above anyone who works on projects in their organization. Without that, they may not be able to see all the information about projects they "own."

Three primary factors to consider when you define the RBS code layout for your organization are as follows:

- Your process for assigning resources to projects and tasks
- Your organizational security design goals
- The method your organization uses to determine whether a particular resource is appropriate for a particular task assignment

Proper definition of RBS code is very important. RBS code plays the largest role in resource assignments when your resource managers make the staffing decisions. RBS code plays a lesser role when resource assignments are done in a more collaborative manner by a group of managers in your organization. RBS may play a relatively small role when your project managers make resource assignment decisions.

The next consideration is to determine what your organizational goals are for securing your Enterprise Project Management environment.

The questions you should be able to answer are the following:

- Do you want to minimize the EPM solution's administrative burden for your organization?

- Does your organization generally allow everybody to see and edit all enterprise project and resource data, or does your organization need to limit data access and system permissions?

- If you limit data access, should your users be able to view each other's project and resource data, provided that they are from the same area or department of your organization?

If your organization wants to implement a secure, easily administered EPM solution, RBS will play an integral role in the security design. If your organization's project management processes are generally less defined, RBS may play a less important role in your organization's security design.

Finally, review the processes that your organization uses to determine whether a resource is a good fit for a project:

- Do you assign resources to your projects and tasks based on departmental or organizational structure?

- When assigning resources to your projects, does the geographic location of a resource matter?

- Do you perform skill-based resource planning and scheduling?

- Which of the above three criteria is most important?

The answers to all these questions help you determine the most appropriate RBS structure for your organization.

Most organizations use one of the following:

- An organizational RBS

- A modified organizational RBS

- A geographic RBS

You can define only one RBS code for your organization. You can modify your RBS code structure over time. If you decide to make significant changes to your RBS code structure, be aware that implementing a new RBS code or significantly modifying your existing RBS code structure after you have been using your EPM solution for a few months may be a time-consuming and complex task requiring careful analysis of the impacts of all RBS changes.

> **NOTE**
>
> Use group names rather than individual names when you define your RBS structure entries. Group names change generally less often than individual names. This trick can help you minimize future changes to the RBS hierarchy.

You can choose from three methods when creating RBS:

- Manually define the lookup table hierarchical structure.

- Define RBS structure as part of the process of importing resources using the Import Resources Wizard. This method may be time consuming and prone to errors and omissions.

- Use the PDS to create RBS structure.

Organizational RBS Code

An *organizational RBS* is usually appropriate for most organizations. Resources perform roles based on the functions of their departments. Figure 9.12 shows an example of organizational RBS code.

Organizational Resource Breakdown Structure

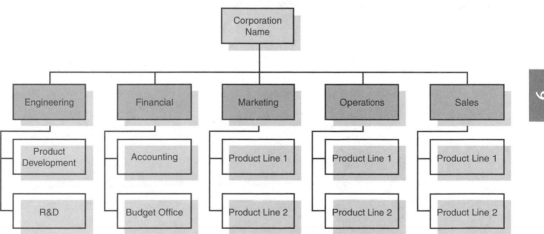

FIGURE 9.12   Use the organizational RBS code structure to associate your resources with their departments and groups.

The organizational RBS code structure closely mirrors the structure of your organization. You build the RBS code hierarchy that reflects all company levels, such as divisions, departments, groups, and resource levels. Resources are then tied to a particular resource level, and managers are tied to the workgroup, department, division, or company level based on their level of responsibility and influence. Most organizations find that an organizational RBS meets their overall needs best.

Modified Organizational RBS Code

A *modified organizational RBS* is generally appropriate when managers and resources require a higher and wider level of data access than their position in the organizational hierarchy might otherwise suggest. For example, many IT departments are organized into additional groups such as development, network administration, and technical support. A modified organizational RBS would stop at the IT department level so that all IT departmental resources would be able to view and access all project data related to the IT department.

Another example of when a modified organizational RBS might be required is when a strategic long-term resource allocation is determined by a team of people from various departments. Figure 9.13 shows an example of a modified organizational RBS hierarchy.

Modified Organizational Resource Breakdown Structure

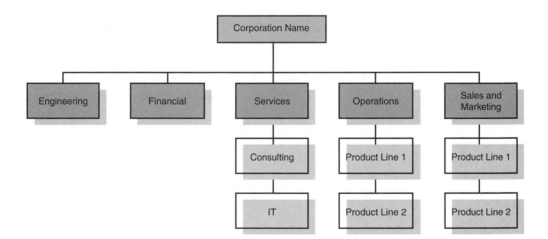

FIGURE 9.13   Use a modified organizational RBS code structure to widen the data access in your organization.

Geographical RBS Code

You use a *geographical RBS* code when the primary concern in defining your project team is where your resources are located. Your EPM solution users will also be able to use RBS code to see only the resources and projects in their geographic location.

To create a geographical RBS code, build a hierarchy of the geographical locations for your organization's offices. You can use continents, countries, regions, cities, and actual office locations to define the RBS code hierarchy. Each resource in your organization is assigned an RBS code identifying the resource location and hierarchical position. Figure 9.14 shows an example of a geographical RBS code.

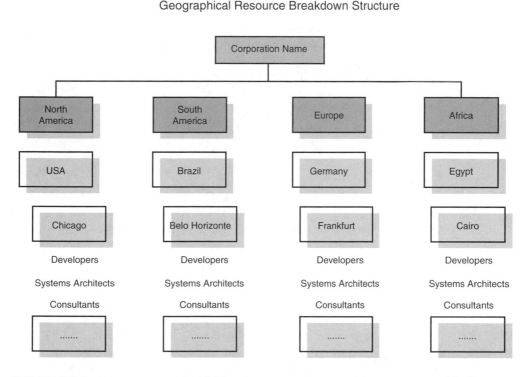

Geographical Resource Breakdown Structure

FIGURE 9.14   Use a geographical RBS code structure to assemble your geographically dispersed virtual project teams.

NOTE

For additional details on RBS definition and design, review the *Microsoft Office Project Server 2003 Application Configuration Guide,* Chapter 6, "Working with Resource Breakdown Structure," available from http://www.microsoft.com/technet/prodtechnol/office/proj2003/reskit/default.mspx.

Also review the Microsoft knowledge base article "Description of the Resource Breakdown Structure and How to Use It in Microsoft Project Server 2002" at http://support.microsoft.com/default.aspx?scid=kb;en-us;831611. Although this article was written for Project Server 2002, most of the information applies to Project Server 2003 as well.

Using RBS

The RBS code features include dynamic security features based on the Category security object. You can control which projects and resources any given group of users can see and access.

The Project Server 2003 security model uses RBS to determine enterprise resource hierarchy. This hierarchy is used by the category security settings that allow members of a category to view resources that they manage or to view projects managed by resources they manage. The managing versus managed relationship is based on relative position in the RBS hierarchy. Because this hierarchical relationship tends to follow an organizational structure, you can use your company organizational structure as a starting point when developing your RBS code structure. You can then modify the RBS structure, if needed, to accommodate your unique reporting and security needs.

RBS and Project Server Security

The RBS code structure is used to determine the enterprise resource hierarchy.

The standard security settings available after the initial setup and configuration of Project Server 2003 are the recommended starting point for using the five RBS-based dynamic security rules.

To understand the long-term effects of the RBS code structure on your EPM solution security, you should review two of the default security categories, My Resources and My Direct Reports.

The My Resources category determines which people a resource manager is allowed to view. It does make sense for resource managers to be able to see all the resources that they manage. You can configure this relationship using the Allow Users in This Category to View Information for All Resources That They Manage automatic security rule. Project Server uses the RBS code structure to find all resources with RBS code subordinate to the RBS code of the resource manager. A resource manager can be considered anybody in the RBS hierarchy that has at least one subordinate position defined.

The My Direct Reports category uses the Allow Users in This Category to View Information for All Resources That They Manage Directly automatic security rule to allow resource managers to view resource data for resources immediately subordinate (one level below) to them in the RBS hierarchy.

The common element in each of the five rules is the "resources that they manage" phrase. Figure 9.15 shows five RBS-based dynamic security rules that can be enabled in the Admin module of the PWA client.

RBS can be an important element of your overall Project Server data security strategy, but it is not the only element you should focus on.

▶ **SEE** "Establishing Security Model Settings," **PAGE 143**.

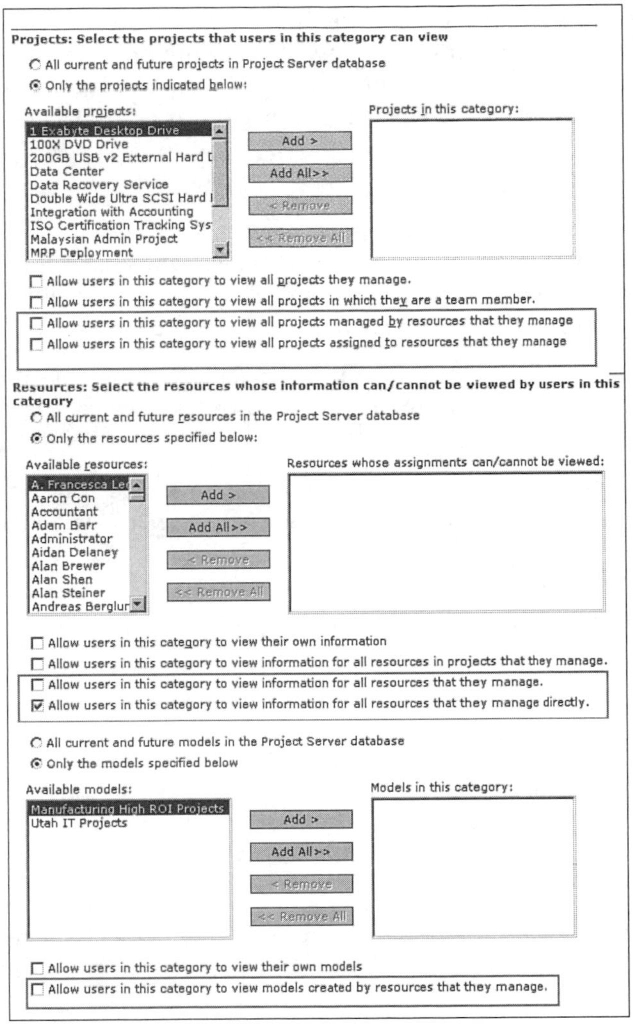

FIGURE 9.15   Five dynamic RBS code-based security rules can be used to streamline your Project Server data security management.

Enterprise Resource Pool

There are two basic types of resources that you can deploy within your project plans. *Enterprise resources* are resources defined by a Project Server 2003 administrator, resource manager, or member of your organization's Project Management Office (PMO) as resources that are part of your Enterprise Resource Pool. *Local resources* are defined and stored at the project level by a project manager and are used only for a specific project.

In addition, there is a third type of resource/user, the *Project Web Access (PWA) client user*. PWA client users are not necessarily members of your Enterprise Resource Pool and are not necessarily local resources; they simply have permission to log on to the PWA client and use the features available to them. An example of this user type can be an external stakeholder.

When Project Server is installed, only one Project Server account is created and stored in the Project Server database—the default Project Server Administrator account. All other users and resources must be added to the Project Server database. Proper creation and maintenance of the Enterprise Resource Pool requires that Enterprise Resource Outline Codes be carefully defined, documented, and created in the Enterprise Global template.

In addition, in a large organization, the initial population of the Enterprise Resource Pool is just as important as keeping the Enterprise Resource Pool always accurate and up-to-date.

For large organizations with many resources, keeping track of significant changes in resource information stored and managed in the Enterprise Resource Pool can be a full-time activity.

Building the Enterprise Resource Pool

Before you begin the task of building your Enterprise Resource Pool, first consider your options.

Creating the Enterprise Resource Pool Manually

In this scenario, you define and create your Enterprise Resource Pool in the Project Professional client 2003. Using the Project Professional client, connect to Project Server first and check out the Enterprise Resource Pool. Enter the resources and their attributes, and then save the information.

Later, you need to assign your new resources to the appropriate user groups using the PWA client. All users when they are created belong to the Team Member user group by default.

Using the Import Resources Wizard to Add Resources to the Enterprise Resource Pool

Select a project file that contains your resource data that you want to import and then follow the steps in the Import Resources Wizard. Your resource data file may require some "sanitization" before you attempt to import the resource data into your Enterprise Resource Pool.

TIP

It is recommended that you import your resource data and create your Enterprise Resource Pool first, before you start importing your existing projects into your Project Server database—for that you use the Import Projects Wizard. When you start importing projects, and you already have your Enterprise Resource Pool created, you can map local resources defined in each project you are importing to your enterprise resources as part of this project import process. If you do not have your enterprise resources ready prior to starting your existing project's import process, you end up with projects in your Project Server database that are using local resources. You will need to map these local resources to your enterprise resources sooner or later to do any meaningful resource allocation and capacity planning.

Make sure that you can map the custom field information defined in the imported resource data file to the custom field information available in the Enterprise Resource Pool.

> **NOTE**
>
> For a detailed description of the Import Resources Wizard steps, review the *Microsoft Office Project Server 2003 Application Configuration Guide*, Chapter 7, "Working with the Enterprise Resource Pool," page 146. The *Microsoft Office Project Server 2003 Application Configuration Guide* is available for download from http://www.microsoft.com/technet/ prodtechnol/ office/proj2003/reskit/default.mspx.

Migrating Active Projects

In this scenario, you manage multiple projects with Microsoft Project 98, Microsoft Project 2000, or Microsoft Project 2002, and projects are saved in the database. Each project may use different resources, rate schedules, or resource and project calendars. To simplify migration of these existing projects to Project Server, "sanitize" the existing projects first and then import them. All existing projects should use a consistent definition of resources, custom outline codes, fields, and calendars.

Again, as was the case in the previous scenario, you will need to assign your new resources to appropriate user groups using the PWA client.

Starting with New Projects

Less preparation and sanitization are required for this scenario. The process is even further simplified if you can centralize all your required resource information in a single document, be it either a project file or a Microsoft Excel file. You can then import the resulting spreadsheet or project file and save the information to your Project Server database.

As was the case in the previous scenario, you will need to assign your new resources to appropriate user groups using the PWA client.

Upgrading to Project Server 2003 from Project Server 2002

If you are upgrading from Microsoft Project Server 2002 to Project Server 2003, you will be able to upgrade your Enterprise Resource Pool. Project Server 2002 and Project Server 2003 share an almost identical architecture for the Enterprise Resource Pool.

Using Active Directory to Manage Your Enterprise Resource Pool

Project Server supports synchronizing a security group that exists in Active Directory with the Enterprise Resource Pool. Active Directory synchronization is managed from the PWA client. In this case, your Enterprise Resource Pool is dependent on a well-managed Active

Directory groups policy. It ties the Enterprise Resource Pool entries directly to all changes in the synchronized Active Directory group.

Creating Users in the PWA Client

Anyone with permission to log on to the PWA client and permission to manage users and groups in the Admin center can create users. This is the easiest way to create users who will not be part of your Enterprise Resource Pool.

Working with the Enterprise Resource Pool

Enterprise resources are stored in the Enterprise Resource Pool, which provides a single repository for all enterprise resources.

Although enterprise resource information such as names and rates is stored in the Enterprise Resource Pool, your standard project and resource attributes such as Enterprise Outline Codes, custom fields, and company calendars are stored in the Enterprise Global template.

After the Enterprise Outline Codes and custom fields have been defined and stored in the Enterprise Global template, you can associate them with your enterprise resources by opening the Enterprise Resource Pool and editing required information for each resource.

Using Generic and Individual Resources

A *generic resource* is a placeholder for a skill set or role on a project. It is not associated with any individual person. For example, if you need someone to support an application but you are not sure yet who that individual might be, you could assign an enterprise generic resource named Technical Support to tasks related to application support.

An *individual resource* is a person in the company who can actually be assigned to tasks to work on them. For example, in the Office XP Deployment Project, when Christina who is a project manager is assigned the role of a project manager, the individual resource Christina replaces the generic resource Project Manager.

Using Enterprise Generic Resources

Generic resources, like individual resources, can be either part of your Enterprise Resource Pool or locally defined resource pool for a particular project (they are available to that project only). Defining and storing generic resources in the Enterprise Resource Pool ensures that the generic resources assigned to all your enterprise projects always have consistent resource attributes and skills.

The Generic check box is available from the General tab of the Resource Information dialog box for each resource defined in the Enterprise Resource Pool. If the Generic check box is selected, the resource is generic, as shown in Figure 9.16.

Graphic icons in the Indicators field make it easier to distinguish whether a resource is local and/or generic, as shown in Figure 9.17. If no icon is displayed in the Indicators field, it means that it is an individual resource defined in your Enterprise Resource Pool.

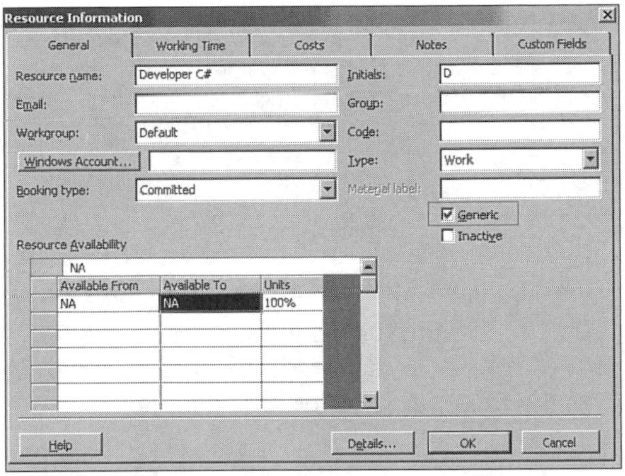

FIGURE 9.16 You can select the Generic check box to designate a resource as generic.

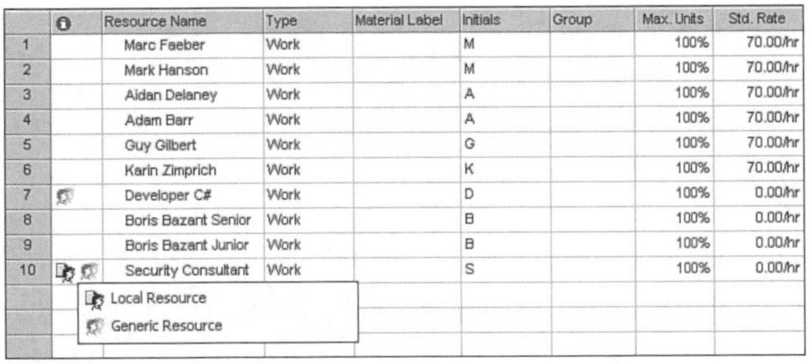

		Resource Name	Type	Material Label	Initials	Group	Max. Units	Std. Rate
1		Marc Faeber	Work		M		100%	70.00/hr
2		Mark Hanson	Work		M		100%	70.00/hr
3		Aidan Delaney	Work		A		100%	70.00/hr
4		Adam Barr	Work		A		100%	70.00/hr
5		Guy Gilbert	Work		G		100%	70.00/hr
6		Karin Zimprich	Work		K		100%	70.00/hr
7		Developer C#	Work		D		100%	0.00/hr
8		Boris Bazant Senior	Work		B		100%	0.00/hr
9		Boris Bazant Junior	Work		B		100%	0.00/hr
10		Security Consultant	Work		S		100%	0.00/hr

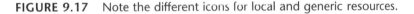

FIGURE 9.17 Note the different icons for local and generic resources.

▶ **SEE** "Building Project Team and Resource Substitution," **PAGE 563**.

Generic resources are often used in project templates to indicate required skills for tasks or in early phases of project planning before the individual resources that will be assigned to the project team are known.

Generic resources are treated similarly to individual resources, except that you cannot create Project Server accounts for generic resources or send them task assignments. If your Enterprise Resource Pool includes generic resources, you can add them to project teams and assign them to tasks as you would any other individual resources.

Using Local Generic Resources

Local generic resources are similar to enterprise generic resources, but they are available only to the project plan in which they are defined. Typically, local generic resources are used as placeholders until named resources are assigned. Also, you cannot use the Resource Substitution Wizard or the Build Team from Enterprise feature to perform skill matching for local generic resources.

> **NOTE**
>
> A local resource has a head icon with a page behind it in the Indicators column. A two-heads icon in the Indicator column indicates a generic resource.

Using Individual Enterprise Resources

Most of your enterprise individual resources should be defined and created during an initial enterprise resource pool building phase. After you define and populate your Enterprise Resource Pool, your enterprise resources are available for task assignments in all your enterprise projects. Defining and storing your individual resources in the Enterprise Resource Pool ensures that these individual resources assigned to all your enterprise projects always have consistent resource attributes and skills.

Using Individual Local Resources

Local individual resources are resources that represent individuals in your organization and that are defined and created in a single Microsoft Project schedule only. The local resources are available for task assignments in the project schedule in which they are defined and saved but cannot be used for other projects.

It is not recommended that a project manager use local individual resources widely unless absolutely necessary. Wide and often use of individual local resources defeats the purpose of implementing a companywide EPM solution. Your locally defined resources are not included in enterprise resource utilization and capacity information available through various Project Server views and reports. The only way to report on local individual resources capacity and workload would be through individual project plans using Project Professional custom views.

> **NOTE**
>
> Most organizations need a defined process for anybody requesting a new individual and/or generic enterprise resource. Adding new enterprise resources to the Enterprise Resource Pool or making changes to their attributes is an administrative task that should be performed by your Project Server administrator.

Creating a New Enterprise Resource

The mechanics of how to create both generic and individual resources are the same; the only difference is the selection of the Generic check box in the Resource Information dialog box.

You can create new resources or import them from a variety of external data sources, such as spreadsheets or Microsoft Outlook Contacts.

The following steps describe the process for adding a new resource to your Enterprise Resource Pool:

1. Start the Project Professional client. You need to have appropriate permissions. You need to have the New Resource global permission to add new resources to your Enterprise Resource Pool. Using Project Server 2003 default group permissions, only the administrator, portfolio manager, and resource manager can add new resources.

2. Choose Tools, Enterprise Options, Open Enterprise Resource Pool Resources dialog box, shown in Figure 9.18, appears. The dialog box shows all enterprise resources currently defined in your Project Server database. Select the resources that you want to edit and click the Open/Add button, or click the Open/Add button without selecting any resources to add new enterprise resources.

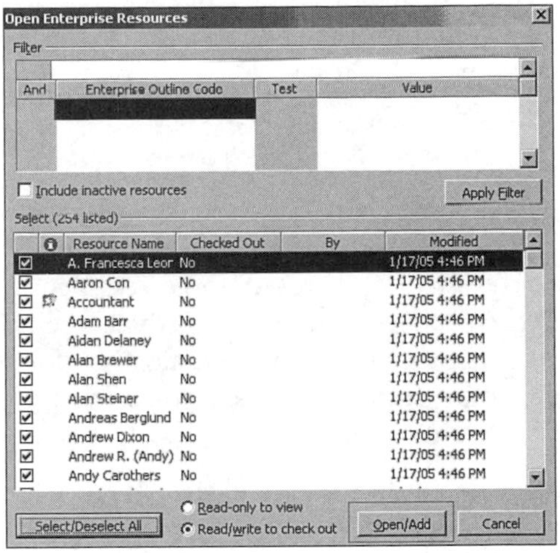

FIGURE 9.18   Open the Enterprise Resource Pool, select the enterprise resources you want to edit, and then click the Open/Add button.

3. To modify a resource, double-click the resource name to display the Resource Information dialog box. Use the Custom Fields tab in the dialog box to define resource attributes as shown in Figure 9.19.

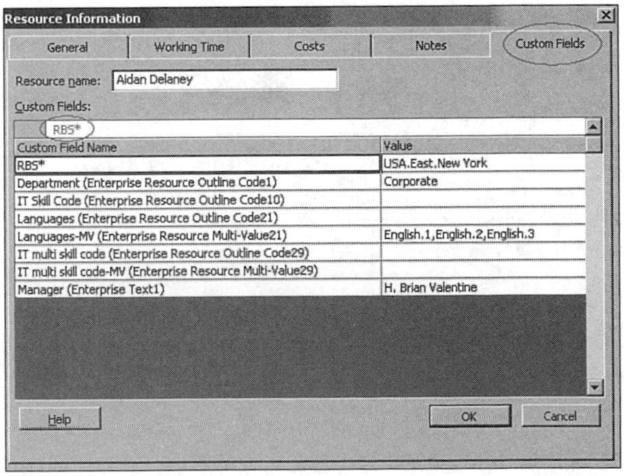

FIGURE 9.19   Enter or edit your enterprise resource attributes in the Resource Information dialog box.

4. To enter resource information such as name and email address, switch to the General tab in the Resource Information dialog box. If the enterprise resource is a generic resource, select the Generic check box.

5. Select a collaboration method you want to use from the Workgroup drop-down list. The Default selection allows you to collaborate with this resource using the default method that has been configured by your Project Server administrator. The Project Server selection allows collaboration using Project Server only. The None selection means no collaboration with this resource.

6. Save and close your Enterprise Resource Pool.

If you need to work with large numbers of enterprise resources that have many Enterprise Custom Outline Codes or Enterprise Custom Fields defined, use the Resource Sheet view and add the custom fields representing your enterprise resource attributes. You can then assign or edit these enterprise resource attributes directly in the Resource Sheet view without the need to use the Resource Information dialog box for each enterprise resource separately. This will help you to effectively manage your enterprise resource data and possibly save a significant amount of time.

To add your Enterprise Resource Outline Codes to the Resource Sheet view, follow these steps:

1. Open the Project Professional client and connect to your Project Server.

2. Select Tools, Enterprise Options, Open Enterprise Global from the menu.

3. Select View, Resource Sheet from the menu.

4. In the Resource Sheet view, right-click the column header to the right of where you want to add your Enterprise Resource Outline Code and then select Insert Column to open the Column Definition dialog box (see Figure 9.20).

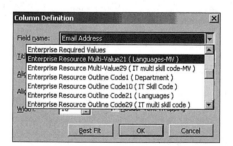

FIGURE 9.20   Edit the default Resource Sheet view and add your enterprise resource attributes to the view.

5. In the Column Definition dialog box, select the Enterprise Outline Code that you want to add to the Resource Sheet view definition from the Field name list. If you want to use a customized name for the resource outline code, type the custom name in the Title box and then specify the remaining field format-related information.

6. Click OK to add the resource outline code to the Resource Sheet view definition.

7. Repeat steps 4, 5, and 6 for each resource outline code that you want to add to the Resource Sheet view.

Enterprise Resource Pool and Active Directory Synchronization

Project Server supports synchronizing a security group that exists in Active Directory with the Enterprise Resource Pool. You manage Active Directory synchronization from the PWA client.

You can use two separate processes or features when adding and updating new users from Active Directory to the Project Server:

- The Enterprise Resource Pool is first updated with new users from Active Directory by using the Server Configuration pages of PWA. New members added this way are automatically added to the Team Members group.

- New and current users who have been added to other Active Directory groups are synchronized with their corresponding security groups configured in the Project Server admin module. These groups typically include project managers, portfolio managers, executives, resource managers, team leads, and administrators. Members of these groups are not automatically added to the Enterprise Resource Pool; you add them as Project Server users only if needed.

Figure 9.21 shows these two available separate AD synchronization features.

Active Directory Synchronization

Group Synchronization

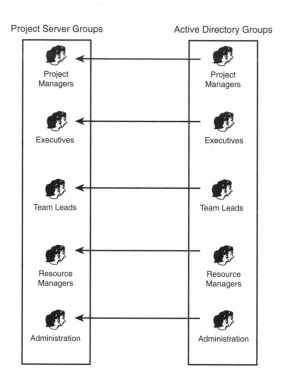

FIGURE 9.21   Synchronize your Enterprise Resource Pool with the Active Directory group.

> **NOTE**
>
> Users are added to PWA security groups. When new users are added to the Enterprise Resource Pool from the Active Directory, they are automatically placed in the Team Members group. If one of these team members is, for example, a resource manager, that person must be added manually to the appropriate Project Server group as well.

If the Active Directory connector for Project Server finds a user in the Active Directory who is absent from the Enterprise Resource Pool, Active Directory adds the user to the

Team Members security group in Project Server. If a user is found in the Enterprise Resource Pool who is not also in Active Directory, and the user has an Active Directory Globally Unique Identifier (GUID), the user account is deactivated in the Project Server database. A user who doesn't have an Active Directory GUID, such as a user who is added directly to Project Server through a project assignment, is not deactivated.

> **NOTE**
>
> Deactivating a user does not delete the user from the Project Server database. A record of that user's work on project tasks, including any actual work hours, is retained after deactivation.
>
> The synchronization steps can be automated to occur at specific intervals. Typically, the synchronization of Active Directory security groups happens after the initial synchronization of the Enterprise Resource Pool.

> **NOTE**
>
> For additional detailed information about synchronizing the Enterprise Resource Pool with Active Directory, see the topic "Synchronizing the Enterprise Resource Pool with Active Directory" in Chapter 5, "Configuring Project Server 2003" of the *Microsoft Office Project Server 2003 Administrator's Guide*.
>
> For more information about synchronizing Project Server security groups with security groups in Active Directory, see the topic "Security Group Synchronization with Active Directory" in Chapter 2, "Managing Users and Groups," of the *Microsoft Office Project Server 2003 Administrator's Guide*, available for download from http://www.microsoft.com/technet/ prodtechnol/office/proj2003/reskit/default.mspx.
>
> Microsoft knowledge base is another excellent source of updated information about AD synchronization. Review the articles (search for "Active Directory") available at http://support.microsoft. com/search/?adv=1&spid=2526.

▶ **SEE** "Server Maintenance and Configuration Management," **PAGE 651**.

Enterprise Task Outline Codes

This section examines in detail some planning considerations for Enterprise Task Outline Codes. You may start with a look at your task reporting requirements first and then work your way back to defining a set of task outline codes and custom fields to support your organizational reporting requirements.

The mechanics of creating Enterprise Task Outline Codes are the same as the steps used when creating Enterprise Project Outline Codes.

Generally, Enterprise Task Outline Codes allow creating hierarchical structures that are an alternative or addition to Work Breakdown Structure (WBS) outline code. These additional hierarchical structures can be used in task or resource assignment views to add additional filtering, grouping, and sorting capabilities.

Planning Enterprise Task Outline Codes

Enterprise Task Outline Codes have one, perhaps serious, limitation compared to Enterprise Project and Resource Outline Codes. It is not possible to include Enterprise Task Outline Codes in your Portfolio Analyzer views. Project Server 2003 does not support the use of tasks and associated Enterprise Task Outline Codes in Portfolio Modeler and Portfolio Analyzer. Enterprise Task Outline Codes can be used only for Project Server views available in PWA and Project Professional clients. Because Enterprise Task Outline Codes are not compiled as part of the OLAP cube, it is not possible to use Portfolio Analyzer to perform any analysis based on tasks unless you customize and extend your OLAP cube.

> **NOTE**
>
> See Portfolio Analyzer OLAP Extensions Solution Starter for more details on OLAP extensions available from http://msdn.microsoft.com/office/understanding/project/solution/default.aspx.

The only advantage that Enterprise Task Outline Codes have over standard task fields is the capability to handle hierarchical structure.

Defining Enterprise Task Outline Codes

Before you can define your Enterprise Task Outline Codes, make sure that the following actions are completed:

- Identify requirements for resource and task assignments reporting.

- Plan Enterprise Task Outline Codes implementation.

- Establish Enterprise Task Outline Codes utilization guidelines.

- Define and develop custom filters and views and define assignment and timesheet views that will use the Enterprise Task Outline Codes.

Enterprise Task Outline Codes can be used as part of two Project Server view types: Assignment views and Timesheet views.

Assignment views provide information about your enterprise resources' task assignments. The Resource Center enables resource managers and other users with appropriate permissions to look at the status of the individual task assignments for a particular resource or group of resources.

Assignment views can use Enterprise Task Outline Codes to filter, group, and sort the tasks that have resources assigned to them. Assignment views are different from other views in PWA and Project Professional clients. Assignment views show the task assignments for your enterprise resources published to your Project Server.

You need to customize or add to the default set of published task fields to be able to use Enterprise Task Outline Codes in the Assignments and Timesheet views first. If you want to make the set of Enterprise Task Outline Codes available for the Assignment or Timesheet views, perform the following steps:

1. Open the Enterprise Global template.

2. From the menu, select Tools, Customize, Published Fields.

3. In the Customize Published Fields dialog box, select required Enterprise Task Outline Codes and Fields listed under Available Fields, and then move them to the list under Fields in the Tasks view as shown in Figure 9.22.

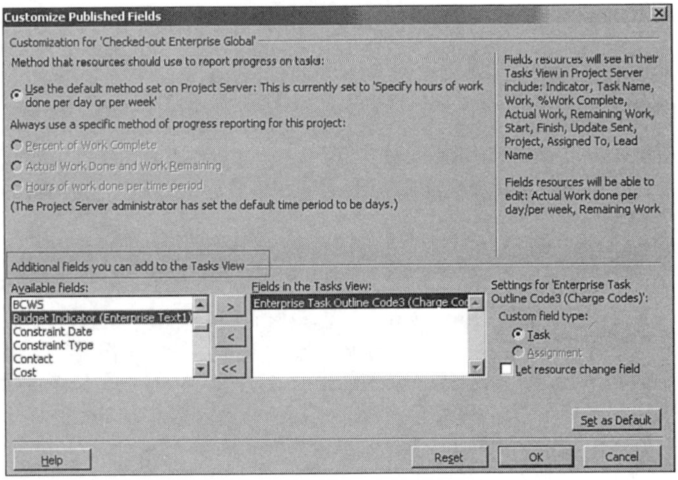

FIGURE 9.22   Use the Customize Published Fields dialog box to make additional Enterprise Task Outline Codes and Fields available for your Assignment and Timesheet views.

Timesheet view is used by your team members to track their actual task assignments progress and can be customized to accommodate your unique reporting requirements. Project managers can set up the custom Enterprise Task Outline Codes and Fields they want their team members to report on to make additional task information available.

Using additional custom Enterprise Task Outline Codes and fields as part of your Timesheet view, you can filter and rearrange the task list to make timesheet reporting faster and easier.

Using Enterprise Task Outline Codes

After you create a list of task attributes and determine their hierarchy and values, you need to configure them in Project Professional client using Enterprise Task Outline Codes structures.

Based on careful analysis of business requirements, the example BBBpm Consulting company decided to use attributes listed in Table 9.3.

TABLE 9.3   Task Attributes Example

Task Attributes	Values
Progress Status	Ahead of schedule
	On time
	Behind schedule less than 5 days
	Behind schedule more than 5 days
Task Type	Billable
Nonbillable	

To create new Enterprise Task Outline Codes, follow these steps:

1. In the Project Professional client, select Tools, Enterprise Options, Open Enterprise Global Template.

2. To display the Customize Enterprise Fields dialog box, choose Tools, Customize, Enterprise Fields from the menu. Use the Custom Outline Codes tab and select the Task radio button.

> ▶ **SEE** "Overview of the Enterprise Outline Codes and Fields," **PAGE 163.**

You need to associate Enterprise Task Outline Codes values with tasks in your enterprise projects before you can manipulate your task and resource assignments—filter, sort, or group—using these Enterprise Task Outline Codes.

CAUTION

Make sure that you understand the potential impact of having many Enterprise Task Outline Codes and Fields defined. If you also have large, unique project schedules with thousands of tasks in your project portfolio, you may spend a lot of time associating task attributes with all your tasks in all your projects.

Enterprise Custom Fields, Formulas, and Graphic Indicators

If you want to make sure that a custom field is associated consistently with all projects, resources, or tasks in the enterprise, you need to use enterprise custom fields. The difference between custom fields and enterprise custom fields is that enterprise custom fields are defined for the entire enterprise and stored in the Enterprise Global template, whereas custom fields are defined for a single project only.

It is typically a role of the Project Server administrator together with the PMO to define and create Enterprise Outline Codes and Custom Fields, making sure that their use is consistent across the whole organization.

Overview of Enterprise Custom Fields

Enterprise custom fields can contain information unique to your organization. The number of enterprise custom fields and their entries is driven by your corporate reporting needs.

For example, to report on project status, define an enterprise project number field linked to a formula that automatically calculates project status based on date fields such as current end date compared to planned end date.

Defining Enterprise Custom Fields

You can create and edit enterprise custom fields using the Customize Enterprise Fields dialog box in the Enterprise Global template. To create an enterprise custom field, follow these steps:

1. Select Tools, Enterprise Options, Open Enterprise Global from the menu.

2. To display the Customize Enterprise Fields dialog box shown in Figure 9.23, choose Tools, Customize, Enterprise Fields from the menu.

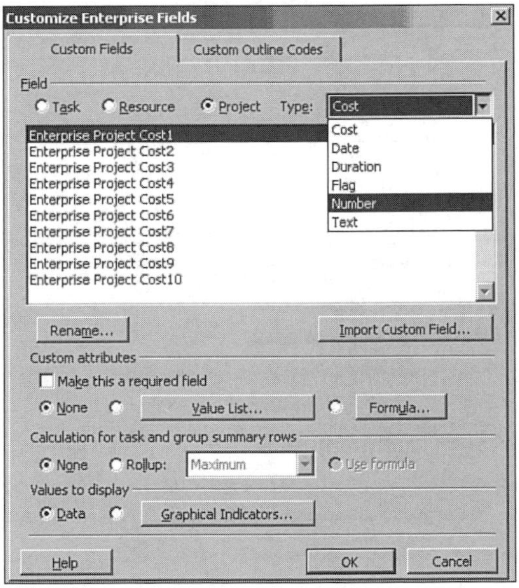

FIGURE 9.23 Log on as Project Server administrator to define or edit enterprise custom fields.

3. Select the Custom Fields tab.

4. Select the custom field category you want to create (task, resource, or project), and select the field type (such as Number).

5. From the list, select a generic custom field that you want to use.

6. Click the Rename button to establish a new name for the code, enter the new name for the custom field, and then click OK.

7. Select the custom attributes you want to associate with the field. You have a choice of None, Value List, or Formula.

8. To create a Value List linked with the custom field, click the Value List button. To create a formula for the custom field, click the Formula button to display the Formula for "<custom field name>" dialog box that you can see in Figure 9.24. Click OK twice when you are finished.

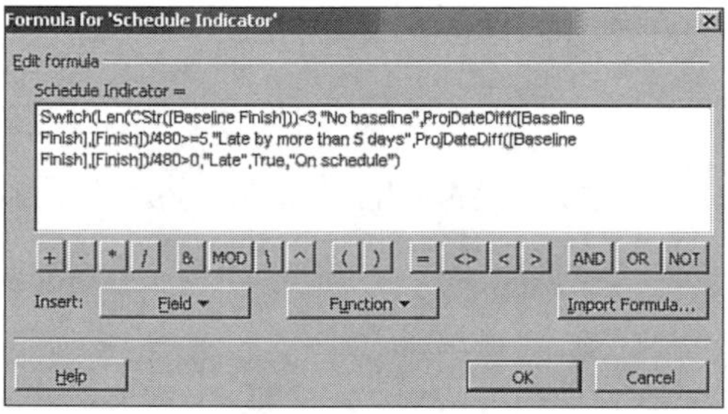

FIGURE 9.24   EPM solution users can see the results of the formula by adding the Enterprise Task Text2 (Schedule Indicator) field column to a custom view.

9. The Graphical Indicators feature enables use of visual indicators as part of custom views and reports instead of requiring your EPM solution users to understand and translate numeric or alphabetic code values. To define a graphical indicator for an Enterprise Custom Field, under the Values to Display section of the Customize Enterprise Field dialog box, click the Graphical Indicators button to open the Graphical Indicators dialog box, or select the Data radio button to display numerical or text entries as shown in Figure 9.25.

10. Save and close the Enterprise Global template. Your enterprise custom fields are now stored in the Enterprise Global template and can be used consistently for all projects, tasks, or resources that are part of your Project Server database.

NOTE

There is a lot more detailed information you need to review before you can start building your custom views and reports that use formulas, value lists, and graphical indicators. For this additional in-depth information about defining and using enterprise custom fields and various custom field options such as value lists, formulas, and graphic indicators, see the *Microsoft Office Project Server 2003 Application Configuration Guide*, Chapter 4, "Working with Enterprise Custom Fields."

Microsoft Office Project Server 2003 Application Configuration Guide is available for download from http://www.microsoft.com/technet/prodtechnol/office/proj2003/reskit/default.mspx.

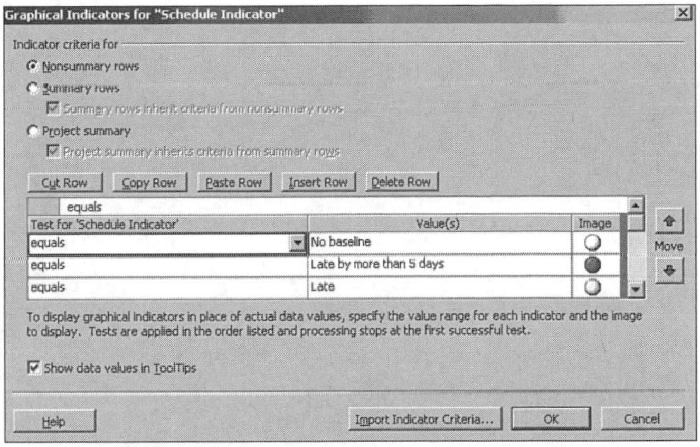

FIGURE 9.25   EPM solution users can see the graphical indicators by adding the Enterprise Task Text2 (Schedule Indicator) field column to a custom view.

Best Practices

- When creating Enterprise Outline Codes, keep it simple—start with a few important outline codes.

- Keep the bar high for new Enterprise Outline Codes.

- Keep the size of lookup tables manageable.

- Use the shared lookup tables wherever possible.

- Use the "required" flag carefully.

- Make sure that each outline code has a clear meaning for your EPM solution users. Keep the end product always in mind.

- If you want to delete an Enterprise Outline Code, clean up all projects that might have used it first.

- Minimize future changes to RBS. Many changes can create a significant administrative burden.

CHAPTER 10

Creating Project Web Access Project and Resource Views

IN THIS CHAPTER

- Project Web Access Project and Resource Views

- Portfolio Analyzer Views

- Managing Views Using Project Web Access Client

- Microsoft Project Professional Views

- Additional Recommended Readings

- Best Practices

You can think of views as interactive reports that include detailed or summary project, resource, and task information. The data used by reports is stored in the Microsoft Office Project Server 2003 database. Views allow your EPM solution users to see what is happening in your organization.

Views also play an important part in collaborating on and communicating critical information about your projects, resources, tasks, and other project-related artifacts to other individuals and groups in your organization.

Project Web Access Project and Resource Views

Views available through Microsoft Office Project Professional and Project Web Access (PWA) client interfaces deliver many default reports for EPM solution users. Enterprise Outline Codes and Fields are a core component of an efficient reporting system design and allow your organization to define filters, sorts, and groups based on the specific reporting needs of your organization.

Five view types are available through PWA client:

- Project Center views use Enterprise Project Outline Codes and Fields to help filter, group, sort, and define views.

- Project views use Enterprise Task Outline Codes and Fields to help filter, group, sort, and define views.

- Resource Center views use Enterprise Resource Outline Codes (including Enterprise Resource Multivalue Outline Codes) and Fields to help filter, group, sort, and define views.

- Assignment views use Enterprise Task Outline Codes and Fields to help filter, group, sort, and define views.

- Portfolio Analyzer views use Enterprise Project Outline Codes and Enterprise Resource Outline Codes to help filter, group, sort, and define views.

Project Center Views

Project Center views provide summary-level information about projects in your portfolio. You can use Enterprise Project Outline Codes and Fields to organize and manipulate data through your custom filters, groups, and sorts that are part of your Project Center view definitions.

> **NOTE**
>
> Before you can use information in the Project Center page, you must log on to Project Server. Also, the projects displayed in the Project Center include only your enterprise projects and not the projects that you saved as separate project files.

The Project Center also includes useful indicators for project-related information. For example, document or issue indicators are displayed in the Indicators column if you have linked documents or issues to a project.

Your role in the organization typically determines what you can see and do in the Project Center using PWA client—your security context. Depending on the permissions settings associated with your user role and account (your security context), you can perform different actions on your projects and resources or see different sets of project and resource data.

Creating and Modifying a Project Center View

To create a new Project Center view, select Admin, Manage Views, Add View, and then select the Project Center radio button.

To modify a Project Center view, select Admin, Manage Views, and then select the Project Center view that you want to modify and click Modify View.

Also, you have the ability to copy an existing view definition and use it as a starting point for a new view.

The menus and options you have available for creating and modifying a Project Center view are identical, except that when you are modifying any view, the current view definition information is displayed.

For example, if you want to add the Project Status Enterprise Project Outline Code to the Project Center Summary view, you need to perform the following steps:

1. In PWA select Admin, Manage Views from the menu.

2. Select the Summary view below the Project Center view type and then click Modify View. The screen to add or modify a Project Center view is divided into sections, as shown in Figure 10.1.

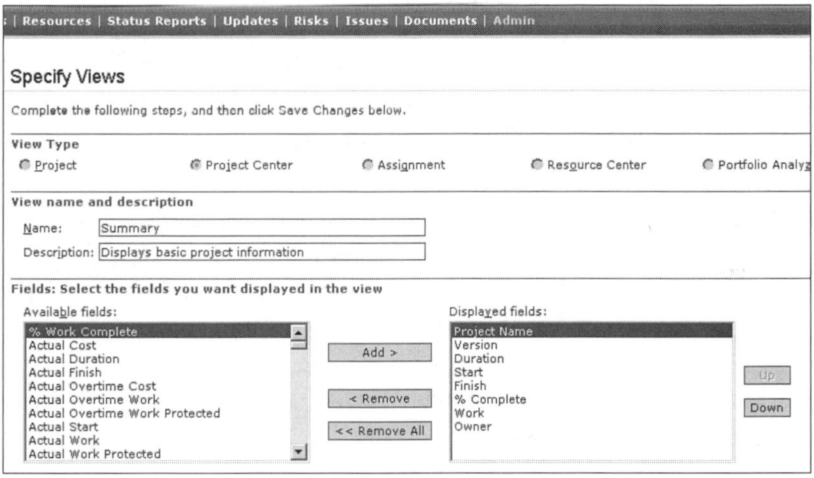

FIGURE 10.1   Enter the information required to define a new Project Center view.

In the Modify View section you can edit an existing view by changing its attributes. These attributes are as follows:

- **View Type**—The view type is already set to the Project Center view type when you choose to modify one of the Project Center views. Select a view type if you are defining a new view.

- **View Name and Description**—The view name must be unique. Choose a name that describes the purpose of the view or the view users. The Description field is available for editing only to the administrator, and it is used to describe the view purpose in more detail.

- **Fields**—This section has two panes. The pane on the right lists fields that are currently part of the view definition. The left pane displays the list of fields available for use in the view but have not yet been added to the view definition. You move fields between the left and right pane by selecting the appropriate fields and then clicking Add, Remove, or Remove All.

- **Field Width**—Defines the width in pixels you want to use for the field to display. The default is to allow PWA client to automatically adjust the column width for the field.

10

> **NOTE**
>
> Three fields—Project Name, Start, and Finish—are included as default fields set for all Project Center views and cannot be removed from the view definition.

- **Up and Down buttons**—Allow you to change the field display sequence in the view.

- The field listed at the top in the right pane appears on the far left in the Project Center view, the second field from the top in the right pane appears second from the left, and so on, when the view is displayed.

- **Splitter Bar**—Allows you to choose where you want the splitter bar to appear in the view. You can change the default number of pixels displaying in the field.

- **Gantt Chart Format**—In this section, choose the type of Gantt chart or custom Gantt chart you want to use to display information. The default Gantt chart format is Gantt Chart (Project Center). You change the format by selecting the drop-down list box and selecting an alternative Gantt chart format.

- **Grouping Format**—This section allows you to associate a unique grouping scheme with your views. Grouping format provides additional visual cues to users about the view being used. The default grouping format is Timesheet. You can change the grouping format by selecting the drop-down list box and choosing an alternative grouping scheme.

- **Default Group, Sort**—Select the default group schemes and/or sorting order you want to use with your view. Users can later change the group or sort when they use a particular Project Center view, and click the Revert button on the Filter, Group, Search section of the screen to return to the default settings.

- **Outline Levels**—Select default outline levels displayed as part of the view. The administrator can control the outline levels and therefore the details displayed as part of the view.

- **Filter**—Specify filters to be applied to a view to limit the number of items displayed. A filter is applied to the raw data before the view is displayed. For example, you could filter the view to display only active projects. Each filter has four components, as shown in Figure 10.2.

  If you want to define a view with preexisting filters, you need to understand the function of each field to make sure that the data displayed will be correct. A description of filter fields follows:

  - **Field**—Click the cell under the Field heading to see a drop-down list of all fields that can be used as part of a filter.

  - **Operator**—Click the cell under the Operator heading to see a drop-down list of all operators that can be used to define a filter test condition.

- **Value**—Specifies the value being tested by the operator.

- **And/Or**—Up to three separate fields can be tested as part of the filter definition, using logical And/Or operations. If you select And, the data must pass all tests to be included in the view. If you select Or, the data is excluded if any of the tests are passed. For example, if you specify a filter for Generic equals No And RBS equals USA.Seattle, all resources that are both individuals and have the location code USA.Seattle associated with them are displayed in the view. If you use Generic equals Yes Or RBS equals USA.Seattle, all resources that are either generic or have the location code USA.Seattle are included in the view.

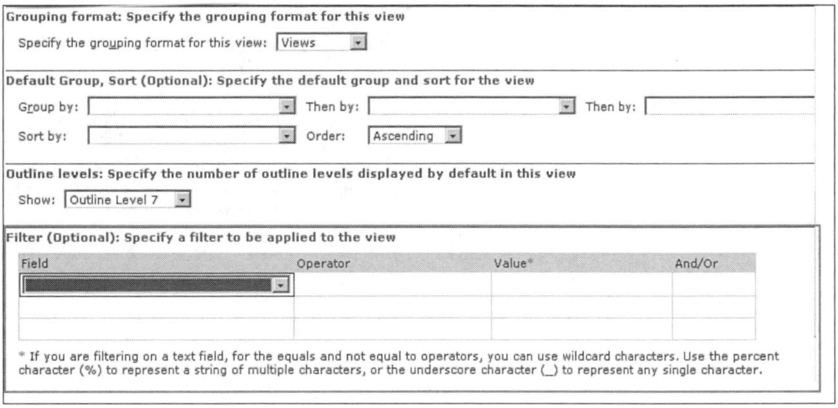

FIGURE 10.2   Define an optional filter as part of the view to limit the number of items displayed in the view.

- **Categories (Optional)**—Control users who can see and use the view. Users associated with categories that include this view can see the view in the Project Center.

  The Categories section has two panes. The pane on the right side defines the categories that the view is currently part of. The left pane contains the list of available categories. You can move categories between panes by selecting the category name and clicking Add, Add All, Remove, or Remove All.

3. Select Enterprise Project Outline Code4(Project Status) from the list of available fields and click Add.

4. Select Enterprise Project Outline Code4(Project Status) at the bottom of the list of displayed fields, and click the Up button as many times as necessary to move the selected Enterprise Outline Code to the position where you want it in the view.

5. Click Save Changes.

6. In PWA client, select Project Center and make sure that the Summary view is selected.

7. Select the Filter, Group, Search tab, and from the Group By pull-down list, select Project Status. Your projects are now grouped by Project Status value, as shown in Figure 10.3.

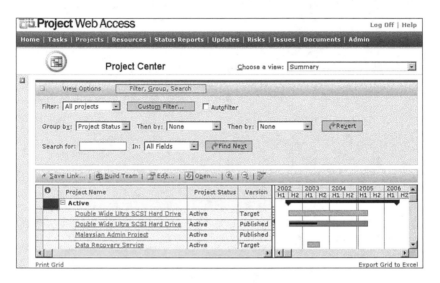

FIGURE 10.3   Organize your projects in Project Center Summary view showing your projects grouped based on their Project Status.

NOTE

Use the horizontal scrollbar at the bottom of the project list to review fields that do not appear on the screen. Remember that you can change the field placement by using the Up and Down buttons in the Modify Views page (where you add or modify fields within a view).

NOTE

You need to review more detailed information before you can start building custom views and reports. For additional in-depth information about defining, using, and managing custom views, see the *Microsoft Office Project Server 2003 Administrator's Guide*, Chapter 4, "Managing Views."

Project Views

Project views display task, assignment, or resource information specific to a single project.

Project views display detailed information about project tasks, including Enterprise Task Outline Codes and Fields. You can view, group, filter, and sort information in Project views based on the information defined in the Enterprise Task Outline Codes.

Creating and Modifying a Project View

To create a new Project view, select Admin, Manage Views, Add View, and then select the Project radio button.

To modify a Project view, select Admin, Manage Views, and then select the Project view that you want to modify and click Modify View.

In addition, you have the ability to copy an existing Project view definition and use it as a starting point for a new Project view.

The menus and options you have available for creating and modifying a Project view are identical, except that when you are modifying any view, the current view definition information is displayed.

You can choose from three types of Project views available:

- Task

- Resource

- Assignment

For example, if you want to add the Charge Codes Enterprise Task Outline Code to the Project Task Summary view, you need to perform the following steps:

1. In Project Web Access, select Admin, Manage Views from the menu.

2. Select the Task Summary view below Project view type and then click Modify View. The screen to add or modify a Project view is divided into sections, as shown in Figure 10.4.

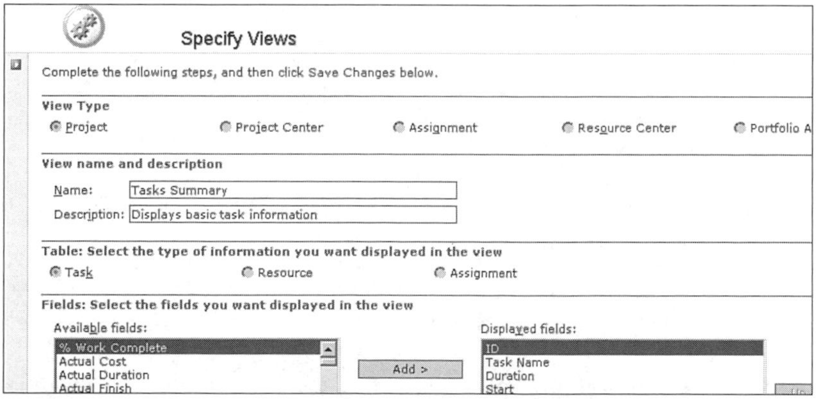

FIGURE 10.4   Enter the information required to modify the Task Summary view.

- **View Type**—This is already set to the Project view type when you choose to modify one of the Project views. Select a view type if you are defining a new view.

- **View Name and Description**—The view name must be unique. Choose a name that describes the purpose of the view or the view users. The Description field is available for editing only to the administrator, and it is used to describe the view purpose in more detail.

- **Table**—Select the appropriate information type based on what details (task, resource, or assignment) you want to see in the report.

- **Fields**—This section has two panes. The pane on the right lists fields currently part of the view definition. The left pane displays the list of fields that are available for use in the view but have not yet been added to the view definition. You move fields between the left and right pane by selecting appropriate fields and then clicking Add, Remove, or Remove All.

- **Field Width**—This field defines the width in pixels you want to use for the field to display. The default is to allow PWA client to automatically adjust the column width for the field.

> **NOTE**
>
> Three fields—Task Name (or Resource Name if the Resource table is selected for the view), Start, and Finish—are included as default fields set for all Project views and cannot be removed from the view definition.

- **Up and Down**—These buttons allow you to change the field display sequence in the view.

- The field listed at the top in the right pane appears on the far left in the Project Center view, the second field from the top in the right pane appears second from the left, and so on, when the view is displayed.

- **Splitter bar**—Allows you to choose where you want the splitter bar to appear in the view. You can change the default number of pixels displaying in the field.

- **Gantt Chart Format**—Using this section, choose the type of Gantt chart or custom Gantt chart you want to use to display information. The default Gantt chart format is Gantt Chart (Views). You change the format by selecting the drop-down list box and selecting an alternative Gantt chart format.

- **Grouping Format**—This allows you to associate a unique grouping scheme with your views. Grouping format provides additional visual cues to users about the view being used. The default grouping format is Timesheet. You can change the grouping format by selecting the drop-down list box and choosing an alternative grouping scheme. To prevent unauthorized access to project data, you can group only by fields displayed in the view.

- **Default Group, Sort**—Select the default group schemes and/or sorting order you want to use with your view. Users can later change the group or sort when they use a particular Project view and click the Revert button on the Filter, Group, Search section of the screen to return to the default settings.

- **Outline Levels**—Select default outline levels displayed as part of the view. The administrator can control the outline levels and therefore the details displayed as part of the view.

- **Filter**—Specify filters to be applied to a view to limit the number of items displayed. A filter is applied to the raw data before the view is displayed. For example, you could filter the view to display only tasks that have a particular charge code attached. Each filter has four components as shown previously in Figure 10.2 and as listed here:

  - **Field**—Click the cell under the Field heading to see a drop-down list of all fields that can be used as part of a filter.

  - **Operator**—Click the cell under the Operator heading to see a drop-down list of all operators that can be used to define a filter test condition.

  - **Value**—Specifies the value being tested by the operator.

  - **And/Or**—Up to three separate fields can be tested as part of a filter definition, using logical And/Or operations. If you select And, the data must pass all tests to be included in the view. If you select Or, the data is excluded if any of the tests are passed. For example, if you specify a filter for %complete equals 0 And Enterprise Task Outline Code3(Charge Codes) equals division1.001, all project tasks that have not started and have the Charge Code "division.001" associated with them are displayed in the view (see Figure 10.5).

Filter (Optional): Specify a filter to be applied to the view			
Field	Operator	Value*	And/Or
% Complete	Equals	0%	And
Enterprise Task Outline Code3 (Charge Codes)	Equals	division1.001	

FIGURE 10.5   Define optional filter as part of the view to limit the number of tasks displayed in the Project view.

- **Categories (Optional)**—Control users who can see and use the view. Users associated with categories that include this view are able to see the view when they select a project in the Project Center.

  The Categories section has two panes. The pane on the right side defines the categories that the view is currently part of. The left pane contains the list of available categories. You can move categories between panes by selecting the category name and clicking Add, Add All, Remove, or Remove All.

3. Select Enterprise Task Outline Code3(Charge Codes) from the list of available fields and click Add.

10

4. Select Enterprise Task Outline Code3(Charge Codes) at the bottom of the list of displayed fields, and click the Up button as many times as necessary to move the selected Enterprise Outline Code to the position where you want it in the view.

5. Click Save Changes.

6. In PWA client, go to Project Center. Select a project you want to view detailed task, resource, or assignment information for by clicking on the link representing the project. Select Task Summary view from the list.

7. Select the Filter, Group, Search tab, and from the Group By pull-down list, select Charge Codes. Your projects are now grouped by Charge Codes value, as shown in Figure 10.6.

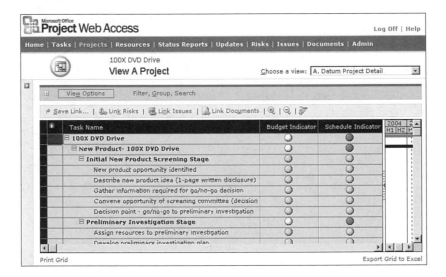

FIGURE 10.6   View task information for a single project using the Task Summary view showing your tasks grouped by their charge codes.

> **NOTE**
>
> For additional in-depth information about defining, using, and managing custom views, see *Microsoft Office Project Server 2003 Administrator's Guide*, Chapter 4, "Managing Views."

Resource Center Views

Resource Center views provide information about all your company resources. The Resource Center provides views for your resource managers and executives to analyze resource availability and commitments. You use your custom Enterprise Resource Outline Codes to filter, group, and sort views in the Resource Center by location, department, skills, or other information that you defined as Enterprise Resource Outline Codes and Fields.

The default Resource Center Resources Summary view contains a list of resources that are part of your Enterprise Resource Pool. The Resource Center can also include resource views that use views with grouped resources based on various Enterprise Resource Outline Codes, a view that allows a user to edit resource attributes such as Location, Department, or Skills and availability and usage views for any selected resource.

Creating and Modifying a Resource Center View

PWA has one Resource Center view defined, called Resources Summary, that is created by default during the installation. You can create another Resource Center view by selecting Admin, Manage Views, Add View from the menu and then selecting the Resource Center radio button. As with the Project Center views, you can copy an existing view to create a basis for a new view as well.

To modify a Resource Center view, select Admin, Manage Views from the menu; then select the Resource Center view that you want to modify and click Modify View.

The functionality and options associated with creating or modifying Resource Center views are identical, except that the currently selected view configuration information is displayed when you modify the view.

To create or modify a Resource Center view, follow these steps:

1. Using PWA client, log on as the administrator and select the Admin tab.

2. Select Manage Views from either the main menu or the side pane menu.

3. To add a new Resource Center view, select Add View, and then select the Resource Center radio button. To modify an existing Resource View, select the view from the list and click Modify. Figure 10.7 shows the partial view of the Specify Views screen to create/modify a Resource Center view.

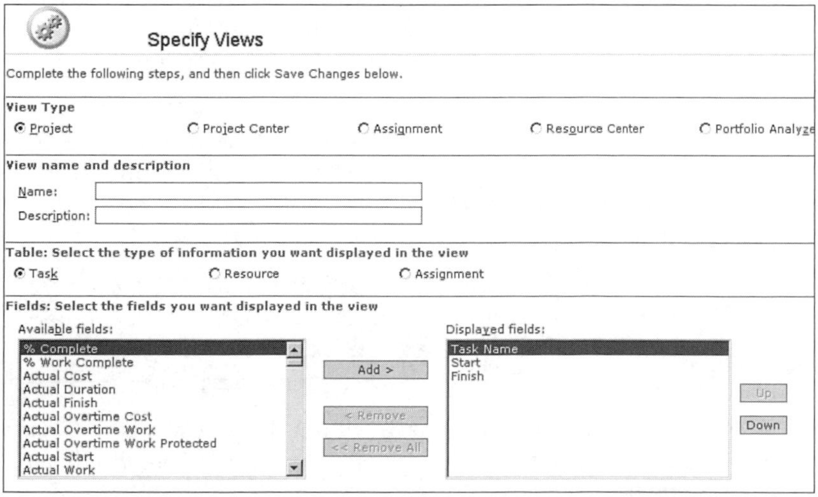

FIGURE 10.7   Provide the information required to create or modify a Resource Center view.

In the Modify View section you can create a new view, or you can edit an existing view by changing its attributes, described as follows:

- **View Type**—The view type is already preset to the Resource Center view if you are modifying a Resource Center view. However, you need to select the Resource Center view type if you are creating a new Resource Center view.

- **View Name and Description**—The view name must be unique. Choose a name that describes the purpose of the view or the view users. The Description field is available for editing only to the administrator, and it is used to describe the view purpose in more detail.

- **Fields**—This section has two panes. The pane on the right lists fields that are currently part of the view definition. The left pane displays the list of fields that are available for use in the view but have not yet been added to the view definition. You move fields between the left and right pane by selecting appropriate fields and then clicking Add, Remove, or Remove All.

- **Field Width**—This field defines the width in pixels you want to use for the field to display. The default is to allow PWA client to automatically adjust the column width for the field.

NOTE

Two fields—Unique ID and Resource Name—are included as default fields set for all Resource Center views and cannot be removed from the view.

- **Up and Down**—These buttons allow you to change the field display sequence in the view.

- The field listed at the top in the right pane appears on the far left in the Resource Center view, the second field from the top in the right pane appears second from the left, and so on, when the view is displayed.

- **Grouping Format**—This section allows you to associate a unique grouping scheme with your views. Grouping format provides additional visual cues to users about the view being used. The default grouping format is Timesheets. You can change the grouping format by selecting the drop-down list box and choosing an alternative grouping scheme.

- **Default Group, Sort**—Select the default group schemes and/or sorting order you want to use with your view. Users can later change the group or sort when they use a particular Resource Center view, and click the Revert button on the Filter, Group, Search section of the screen to return to the default settings.

- **Outline Levels**—Select default outline levels displayed as part of the view. The administrator can control the outline levels and therefore the details displayed as part of the view.

- **Filter (Optional)**—Specify filters to be applied to a view to limit the number of items displayed. A filter is applied to the raw data before the view is displayed. For example, you could filter the view to display only resources from a particular location or department. There are four components to each filter, as shown in Figure 10.8 and in the following list:

  - **Field**—Click the cell under the Field heading to see a drop-down list of all fields that can be used as part of a filter.

  - **Operator**—Click the cell under the Operator heading to see a drop-down list of all operators that can be used to define a filter test condition.

  - **Value**—Specifies the value being tested by the operator.

  - **And/Or**—Up to three separate fields can be tested as part of filter definition, using logical And/Or operations. If you select And, the data must pass all tests to be included in the view. If you select Or, the data is excluded if any of the tests are passed. For example, if you specify a filter for Enterprise Resource Code1 (Department) equals "Corporate.Accounting" And Generic equals "No", all individual resources from Accounting department are displayed in the view.

Filter (Optional): Specify a filter to be applied to the view

Field	Operator	Value*	And/Or
Enterprise Resource Outline Code1 (Department)	Equals	Corporate.Accounting	And
Generic	Equals	No	

* If you are filtering on a text field, for the equals and not equal to operators, you can use wildcard characters. Use the percent character (%) to represent a string of multiple characters, or the underscore character (_) to represent any single character.

FIGURE 10.8   Define optional filter as part of the view to limit the number of resources displayed in the Resource Center view.

- **Categories**—Control users who are able to see and use the view. Users associated with categories that include this view are able to select the view when they go to Resource Center.

  The Categories section has two panes. The pane on the right side defines the categories that the view is currently part of. The left pane contains the list of available categories. You can move categories between panes by selecting the category name and clicking Add, Add All, Remove, or Remove All.

- **RBS Filter**—When the administrator selects the RBS Filter box to implement this optional filter, the resources listed in a view will be restricted to the resources associated with the RBS hierarchy below the position of the user who is viewing the resource list.

4. Click OK to save the new or modified Resource Center view. Click Cancel to return to the Specify Views screen without making any changes.

NOTE

For additional in-depth information about defining, using, and managing custom views, see *Microsoft Office Project Server 2003 Administrator's Guide*, Chapter 4, "Managing Views."

Assignment Views

Assignment views provide information about the resource assignments in your organization. The Resource Center enables resource managers and executives to look at the status of the individual task assignments. Assignment views can include Enterprise Task Outline Codes to filter, group, and sort the tasks that have resources assigned to them. Before you can use Assignment views, task assignments in your projects must be published using Project Professional client.

Creating and Modifying an Assignment View

Assignment views display task assignments for your resources, including projects and tasks that resources are currently working on, nonproject time entered by resources, and other assignment-related data, including the time-phased information about resource work and actual work.

To create a new Assignment view, select Admin, Manage Views, Add View, and then select the Assignment radio button.

To modify existing Assignment view, select Admin, Manage Views, and then select the Assignment view that you want to modify and click Modify View.

Also, you have the ability to copy an existing view definition and use it as a starting point for a new view.

The menus and options you have available for creating and modifying Assignment views are identical, except that when you are modifying an existing view, the current view definition information is displayed.

For example, if you want to add the Task Type field to the Assignment Summary view, you need to perform the following steps:

1. In PWA select Admin, Manage Views from the menu.

2. Select the Summary view below Assignment view type and then click Modify View. The screen to add or modify an Assignment view is divided into sections, as shown in Figure 10.9.

   As discussed previously in this chapter, creation of new views, or editing an existing view for both projects and resources, can be customized to suit end users' requirements. Similarly, Assignment views can be customized to respond to end users' needs by entering information in the fields displayed, as discussed here:

   - **View Type**—The view type is already set to the Assignment view type when you choose to modify one of the Assignment views. Select a view type if you are defining a new view.

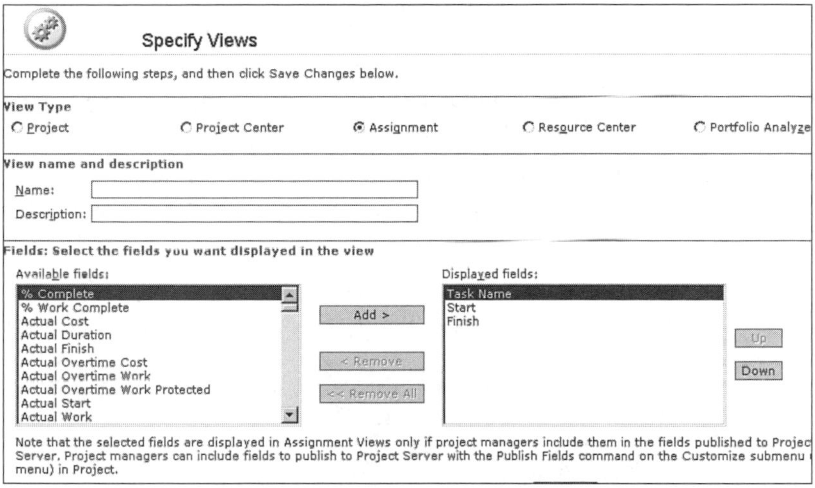

FIGURE 10.9   Enter the information required to define a new Assignment view.

- **View Name and Description**—The view name must be unique. Choose a name that describes the purpose of the view or the view users. The Description field is available for editing only to the administrator, and it is used to describe the view purpose in more detail.

- **Fields**—This section has two panes. The pane on the right lists fields that are currently part of the view definition. The left pane displays the list of fields that are available for use in the view but have not yet been added to the view definition. You move fields between the left and right pane by selecting appropriate fields and then clicking Add, Remove, or Remove All.

NOTE

The custom fields you select are displayed in Assignment views only if your project managers include them in the fields published to the Project Server database. Project managers can include fields to publish to the Project Server database by using the Publish Fields command on the Customize submenu of the Tools menu in Project Professional client. To use Publish Fields, select Tools, Customize, Published Fields. Project Professional client has to be connected to the Project Server database when you want to publish additional custom fields.

- **Field Width**—This field defines the width in pixels you want to use for the field to display. The default is to allow PWA client to automatically adjust the column width for the field.

NOTE

Three fields—Task Name, Start, and Finish—are included as default fields set for all Assignment views and cannot be removed from the view definition.

10

- **Up and Down**—These buttons allow you to display sequence in the view.

- The field listed at the top in the right pane appears on the far left in the Assignment view, the second field from the top in the right pane appears second from the left, and so on, when the view is displayed.

- **Splitter Bar**—Allows you to choose where you want the splitter bar to appear in the view. You can change the default number of pixels displaying in the field.

- **Gantt Chart Format**—Choose the type of Gantt chart or custom Gantt chart you want to use to display information. The default Gantt chart format is Personal Gantt (Tasks). You change the format by selecting the drop-down list box and selecting an alternative Gantt chart format.

- **Grouping Format**—This section allows you to associate a unique grouping scheme with your views. Grouping format provides additional visual cues to users about the view being used. The default grouping format is Timesheet. You can change the grouping format by selecting the drop-down list box and choosing an alternative grouping scheme.

- **Default Group, Sort**—Select the default group schemes and/or sorting order you want to use with your view. Users can later change the group or sort when they use a particular Assignment view, and click the Revert button on the Filter, Group, Search section of the screen to return to the default settings.

- **Outline Levels**—Select default outline levels displayed as part of the view. The administrator can control the outline levels and therefore the details displayed as part of the view.

- **Categories (Optional)**—Control users who will be able to see and use the view. Users associated with categories that include this view are able to see the view in the Project Center.

  The Categories section has two panes. The pane on the right side defines the categories that the view is currently part of. The left pane contains the list of available categories. You can move categories between panes by selecting category name and clicking Add, Add All, Remove, or Remove All.

3. Select Enterprise Task Flag1(Billable) and Enterprise Task Text3 (Task Type) from the list of available fields and click Add.

4. Select Enterprise Task Flag1(Billable) and Enterprise Task Text3 (Task Type) at the bottom of the list of displayed fields, and click the Up button as many times as necessary to move the selected Enterprise Outline Code to position where you want it in the view.

5. Click Save Changes.

6. In PWA client select Resource Center; then select View Resource Assignments and make sure that the Summary view is selected.

7. Select the Filter, Group, Search tab, and from the Group By pull-down list, select Project and set the field Then By to Task Type. Your tasks are now grouped by Project Name and then Task Type value, as shown in Figure 10.10.

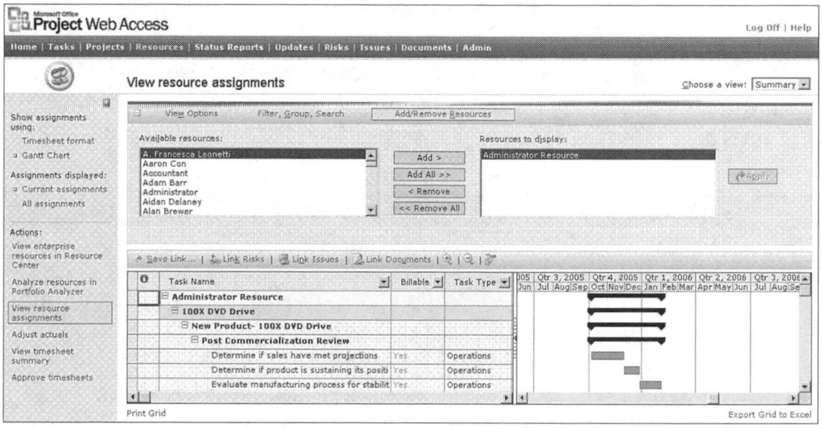

FIGURE 10.10   Organize your projects in the Project Center Summary view showing your projects grouped based on their project status.

NOTE

Use the horizontal scrollbar at the bottom of the project list to review fields that do not fit on the screen. Remember that you can change the field placement by using the Up and Down buttons in the Modify Views page (where you add or modify fields within a view).

NOTE

For additional in-depth information about defining, using, and managing custom views, see *Microsoft Office Project Server 2003 Administrator's Guide*, Chapter 4, "Managing Views."

Portfolio Analyzer Views

Portfolio Analyzer views are different in many ways from other Project Server views available, such as Project, Project Center, Resource Center, and Assignment views.

Before you can start defining your custom Portfolio Analyzer views, you must build an Online Analytical Processing (OLAP) multidimensional cube that contains resource availability and work data. You first configure OLAP services in PWA client, and then you can configure custom Portfolio Analyzer views. Whoever wants to define a new Portfolio Analyzer view must have a permission to manage views. Users who will be Portfolio Analyzer view consumers must also have permission to access the projects and resources through PWA client to access existing Portfolio Analyzer views.

10

> **NOTE**
>
> Portfolio Analyzer requires that Project Server have the Enterprise Features enabled to view the data. Portfolio Analyzer displays only enterprise projects (non-enterprise projects are not part of the OLAP cube).

Portfolio Analyzer views provide powerful data analysis tools. It is beyond the scope of this chapter and this book to exploit all possible features, customizations, extensions, and nuances of OLAP cubes and Portfolio Analyzer use.

> **NOTE**
>
> Portfolio Analyzer features are based on OLAP and Microsoft SQL Server Analysis Services. If you want to learn more about the fundamentals of OLAP and Microsoft SQL Server Analysis Services, consider reviewing the following book available from Sams Publishing: *Microsoft SQL Server 2000 Unleashed, Second Edition*, by Ray Rakins, Paul Bertucci, and Paul Jensen, ISBN: 0672324679.

▶ **SEE** "Portfolio Management Using Portfolio Analyzer and Portfolio Modeler,"
PAGE 393.

The Enterprise Outline Codes that you define for your organization determine the dimensions (such as Location, Department, Project Status, and so on) available to you in Portfolio Analyzer views for reporting. These Enterprise Outline Codes enable you to analyze workload from many different perspectives: by skill, location, department, project, and more.

> **TIP**
>
> By design, task information is not included in the Analysis Services database. Therefore, you cannot use task information in Portfolio Analyzer views.
>
> If your organization wants to include task data in Portfolio Analyzer views, you need to extend the OLAP cube (manually or programmatically) to include task and other custom data required for your organization.

▶ **SEE** "Extending the Cube," **PAGE 800**.

In addition to using Enterprise Outline Codes for focused, executive style reporting, Portfolio Analyzer views can be used to filter, group, or search for data values, including data in your Enterprise Outline Codes. Portfolio Analyzer is based on a reporting interface that uses the PivotChart and PivotTable features. By using these two features, you can manipulate and interact with your project and resource data and drill into specific dimensions of data based on hierarchical structures defined by your Enterprise Outline Codes.

To use and/or define the Portfolio Analyzer views, users must be assigned the following related permissions:

- **Manage Enterprise Features**—A global permission that allows a user to access the Manage Enterprise Features page from the Admin page in PWA client. Users who have permission to access the Manage Enterprise Features page can create the OLAP cube for Portfolio Analyzer.

- **Manage Views**—A global permission that allows a user to access the Manage Views page from the Admin page in PWA Access. Users who have permission to access this page can add, modify, or delete Portfolio Analyzer views.

- **View Portfolio Analyzer**—A global permission that allows a user to view the Portfolio Analyzer by using PWA or Project Professional client.

- **View Project Center**—A global permission that allows a user to access the Project Center from PWA or Project Professional client.

Creating and Modifying Portfolio Analyzer Views

Project Server uses OLAP technology to generate multidimensional OLAP cubes and then stores the information in Extensible Markup Language (XML) for presentation and loading into the Project Center pages for the Portfolio Analyzer views. Also, Project Server updates the resource tables for viewing and reporting based on parameters you specify.

Views store definitions of the fields and formats available in a report. Views do not determine the resources or projects visible through the report. After you define a Portfolio Analyzer view, you add the view to one or more categories to allow the PWA client users assigned to that category to access it. If you omit this step, the view will not be available for any data analysis. Categories define the specific projects and resources that a particular user or group of users can see. By adding views to categories, you define the objects (projects and resources) and the properties of the objects (views) available to any user or group of users.

> **NOTE**
>
> OLAP databases are called *cubes* because they include several dimensions, such as project, resources, and time, with summarized data, such as work, cost, and availability.

OLAP cubes are designed for ad hoc data reporting. It is often used to organize large business databases. OLAP cubes are built based on your reporting requirements as defined by Enterprise Outline Codes. If you define your Enterprise Outline Codes carefully, you can easily create the reports you need for multiple user groups in many different roles.

> **NOTE**
>
> OLAP cubes generated by Microsoft Project Server 2003 can be accessed by other tools such as Microsoft Office Excel 2003.

10

All new projects saved to a Project Server are saved with the version Published first. Other project versions can be created and saved later, but the Published version has to be created first. For example, if you want to save a Baseline version of a project schedule to the server, you must first save a Published version.

In addition, there is no way to exclude a Published version of any project when generating an OLAP cube. Therefore, Baseline and other project versions published to a Project Server are included when OLAP cubes are generated. You can control which project versions you want to include and analyze using filters. You can also use the project and resource "dimensions" in the OLAP cube data to manually include or remove the specific projects or resources in the view that you're interested in using for your analysis.

Portfolio Analyzer uses the following Microsoft Office Web Components features:

- **PivotTable**—Provides dynamic views that allow users to analyze Project Server data by sorting, grouping, filtering, and pivoting. The data is extracted from the Project Server database view tables and is displayed in a familiar Microsoft Excel PivotTable format.

- **Chart**—provides graphical representation of data in PivotTable. Chart is linked directly to the PivotTable component, so it is updated instantly in response to user actions in the PivotTable.

When you define a Portfolio Analyzer view, you can choose whether to display data in the form of a PivotTable, chart, or combination of both.

When you create a Portfolio Analyzer view, you have the option to link the view to a Project Server OLAP cube on the current or a different server. You can also bind the Portfolio Analyzer view to one of several possible Project Server OLAP cubes—multiple OLAP cubes are supported. However, each single Portfolio Analyzer view can be connected only to a single Analysis Services database (OLAP cube). Although you can create multiple OLAP cubes, no utilities are available to help you manage them or the Portfolio Analyzer views that bind to them. If you want to create multiple Project Server data cubes within a single Project Server instance, the system administrator must manage OLAP cube refresh using manual techniques.

Portfolio Analyzer view data is as up-to-date as the OLAP cube it is bound to. Typically, the Project Server administrator schedules Project Server OLAP server cube updates.

> **TIP**
>
> You can use the Portfolio Analyzer view PivotTable Commands and Options dialog box (Data Source tab) to change the OLAP cube that the view is currently bound to.

To create a new Portfolio Analyzer view, select Admin, Manage Views, Add View, and then select the Assignment radio button.

To modify an existing Portfolio Analyzer view, select Admin, Manage Views; then select the Portfolio Analyzer view that you want to modify and click Modify View.

Also, you have the ability to copy an existing view definition and use it as a starting point for a new view.

The menus and options you have available for creating and modifying Portfolio Analyzer views are identical, except that when you are modifying an existing view, the current view definition information is displayed.

For example, if you want to create a new Portfolio Analyzer view, you need to perform the following steps:

1. In PWA select Admin, Manage Views from the menu.

2. Click the Add View button and select Portfolio Analyzer in the View Type section. Figure 10.11 shows the Portfolio Analyzer screen.

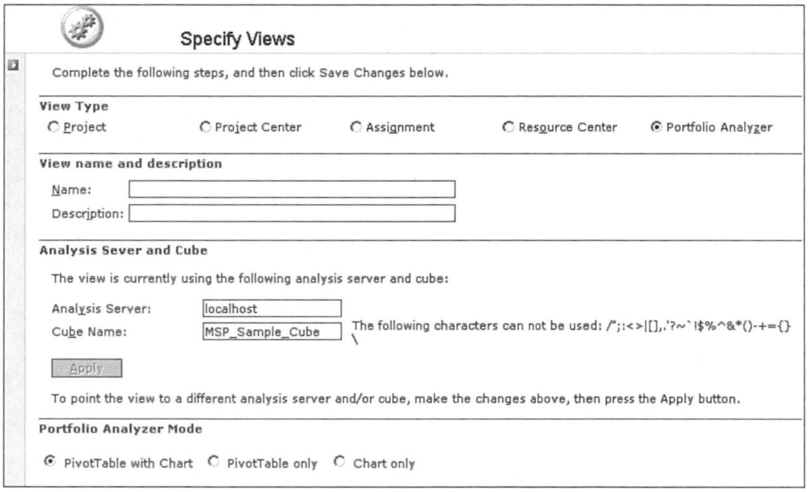

FIGURE 10.11   Enter the information required to define a new Portfolio Analyzer view.

Following is the description of fields that can be customized to create a new view or used to edit an existing one:

- **View Type**—The view type is already set to the Portfolio Analyzer view type when you choose to modify one of the Portfolio Analyzer views. Select a view type if you are defining a new view.

- **View Name and Description**—The view name must be unique. Choose a name that describes the purpose of the view or the view users. The Description field is available for editing only to the administrator, and it is used to describe the view purpose in more detail.

- **Analysis Server and Cube**—Specify the name of the Analysis Services server and the OLAP cube name.

10

- **Portfolio Analyzer Mode**—Select one of the following options:

  - **PivotTable with Chart**—Displays both the PivotTable and Chart workspaces.

  - **PivotTable Only**—Displays only the PivotTable workspace.

  - **Chart Only**—Displays only the Chart workspace.

- **Customize the PivotTable and Chart**—Allows you to add fields to your custom Portfolio Analyzer view. Right-click the Chart or PivotTable workspace and select Field List from the shortcut menu to open the Field List dialog box as shown in Figure 10.12.

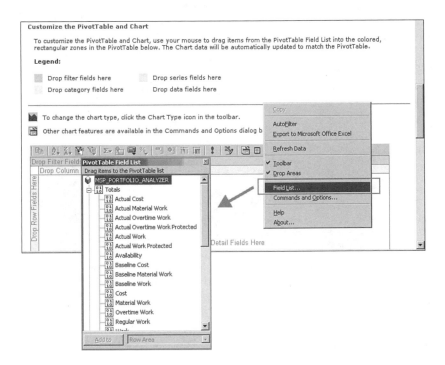

FIGURE 10.12   Choose and lay out the information you want to display as part of a new Portfolio Analyzer view.

Creating a new Portfolio Analyzer view, or editing an existing one, is different from creating views for projects, resources, and assignments. The steps involved in creation or modification of a view for Portfolio Analyzer are as follows:

1. Select Versions, Resource Department, and Resource Status from the PivotTable Field List and drag them to the Drop Filter Fields Here area of the PivotTable workspace. Resource Department and Resource Status are example Enterprise Outline Codes that you may have defined in your Enterprise Global Template, as shown in Figure 10.13.

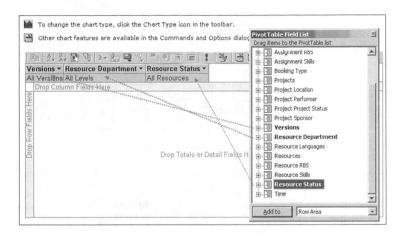

FIGURE 10.13   Choose and lay out the Enterprise Outline Codes you want to use as filters in your new Portfolio Analyzer view.

2. Consider adding the Time dimension to your custom views to organize your view data by years, quarters, months, or days. Expand the Time set of fields in the PivotTable Field List, select Years, and add it to the Drop Column Fields Here PivotTable area, as shown in Figure 10.14.

NOTE

You may prefer to add the Time dimension to Column fields rather than Row fields. The Time dimension creates generally fewer columns in the PivotTable than, for example, adding Projects or Resources. This arrangement makes PivotTable reports more memory efficient, and you can stay away from PivotTable limits.

For more details on the limits of PivotTable reports, see article 820742 in Microsoft Knowledge Base, available from http://search.support.micrsoft.com/search/?adv=1.

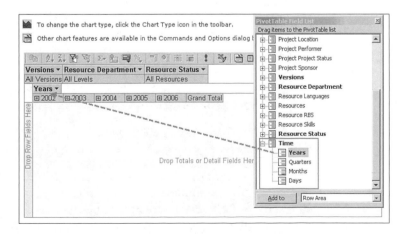

FIGURE 10.14   Add the Time dimension to your new Portfolio Analyzer view.

3. Add the required fields to the Drop Row Fields Here PivotTable area—select the Resources field for the Row fields display as shown in Figure 10.15.

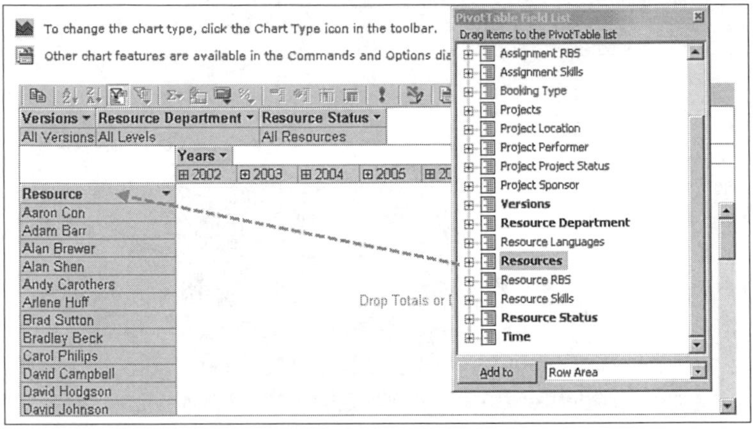

FIGURE 10.15   Add Resources to your new Portfolio Analyzer view.

4. Expand the Totals set of fields in the PivotTable Field List, select Work and Availability, and then add them to the Drop Totals or Detail Fields Here PivotTable area. Review the resulting Portfolio Analyzer view shown in Figure 10.16.

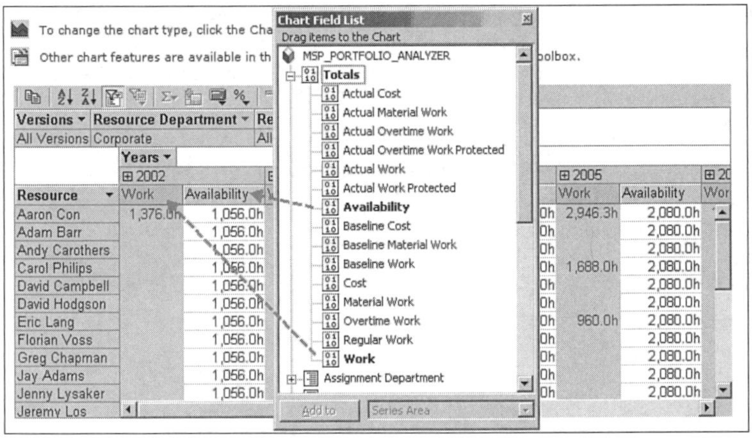

FIGURE 10.16   Add Resource Work and Availability to finish your new Portfolio Analyzer view.

5. Now all your resources are displayed as part of the view, making the view, especially the chart part, too cluttered. Use the Resource Department filter to restrict the data displayed to a group of resources. Expand the Resource Department field, clear the All box, and then select the Corporate department. Also, you may want to filter

only the Published versions of projects. Use the Versions filter and ensure that only the Published version is selected. For the Resource Status filter, select Enterprise Active only. Figure 10.17 shows the resulting view.

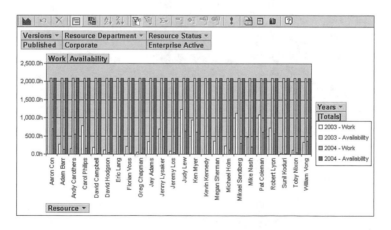

FIGURE 10.17   Use filters to limit the amount of data displayed in your new Portfolio Analyzer view.

6. You can also control the graph type you want to use with your Portfolio Analyzer views. Review the default chart (Clustered Column type) further filtered for years 2003 and 2004 in Figure 10.18.

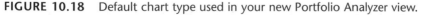

FIGURE 10.18   Default chart type used in your new Portfolio Analyzer view.

7. Change to a different chart type by selecting the Chart Type button (first icon from the left in the toolbar) to display the Commands and Options dialog box. You can choose from 12 predefined chart types as seen in Figure 10.19. Be careful to select an appropriate chart type for your data—not all chart types are created equal, and some of them are not that useful when displaying project and/or resource data.

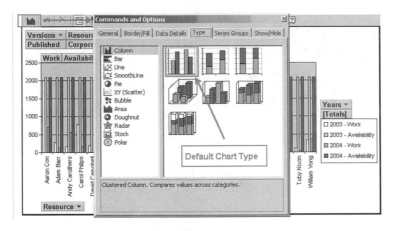

FIGURE 10.19   Twelve chart types are available for your Portfolio Analyzer views.

8. When you further filter currently displayed Portfolio Analyzer view data, the chart is updated immediately to reflect your changes as shown in Figure 10.20. Resources were further filtered to show only the IT department resources.

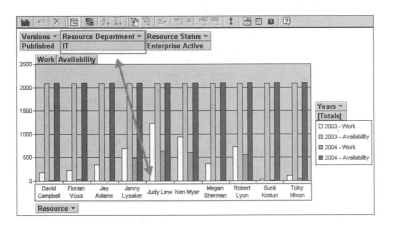

FIGURE 10.20   Your Portfolio Analyzer views are updated as soon as you make any changes in the definition of the view.

When defining the Portfolio Analyzer views, a couple more sections on the Specify Views page can be edited. These two sections are described here:

- **Default View Settings**—Select the Show Field List or Show toolbar options to make the Portfolio Analyzer Field List and Toolbar available to Portfolio Analyzer view users. Users will be able to temporarily modify and manipulate (add or remove fields) the view.

- **Categories (Optional)**—Control users who will be able to see and use the view. Users associated with categories that include this view can see the view in the Project Center.

  The Categories section has two panes. The pane on the right side defines the categories that the view is currently part of. The left pane contains the list of available categories. You can move categories between panes by selecting a category name and clicking Add, Add All, Remove, or Remove All.

After you save your changes, this Portfolio Analyzer view becomes available to all users in your organization who belong to the security categories that this view belongs to. On the Portfolio Analyzer page, users need to select the Portfolio Analyzer view from the Choose a View drop-down list.

> **NOTE**
>
> For additional in-depth information about defining, using, and managing Portfolio Analyzer views, see *Microsoft Office Project Server 2003 Administrator's Guide*, Chapter 10, "Working with Portfolio Analyzer."

Managing Views Using Project Web Access Client

As the Project Server administrator, you are responsible for creating and modifying the Project Center, Resource Center, Project, Timesheet, Assignment, and Portfolio Analyzer views and setting permissions for your users to use these views.

After you install and configure Project Server 2003 and add users to your Enterprise Resource Pool, users are ready to view and analyze Project Server data using the Project Professional and/or PWA client. However, you must also grant the appropriate permissions to your users who will create or access views. Users who are allowed to create and modify views must have permission to manage views.

You can use the Specify Views page in PWA client available under the Admin, Manage Views menu, to manage all Project, Project Center, Assignment, Resource Center, Portfolio Analyzer, and Timesheet views that are currently available and displayed. Figure 10.21 displays a list of all available view types in PWA client.

View management goes hand-in-hand with management of other security components such as security templates, users, user groups, and categories. To successfully and effectively manage your EPM solution environment, you need to think of all system components and technologies and come up with a comprehensive system management strategy.

10

> **NOTE**
>
> For in-depth information about using and managing custom views, see *Microsoft Office Project Server 2003 Administrator's Guide*, Chapter 4, "Managing Views."

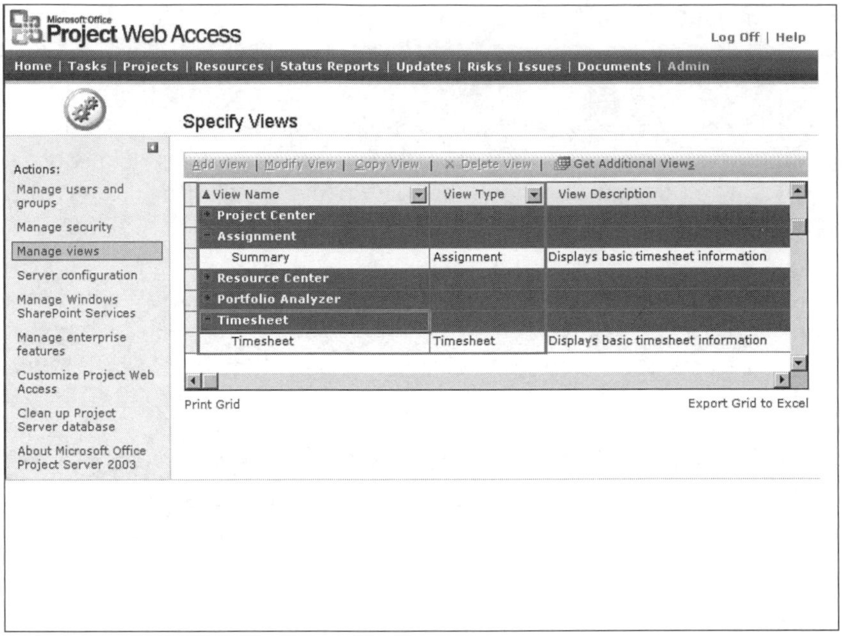

FIGURE 10.21   Expand the view type and review the existing views.

Microsoft Project Professional Views

In addition to managing PWA client interface views, it is also important to understand the views available within Project Professional client.

> **NOTE**
>
> The views and features available in Project Professional are not the focus of this book; other books are available that focus on Project Professional client features and its capabilities, including views and reports available from within Project Professional client.
>
> Consider reviewing the following book available from Sams Publishing for more in-depth information on Project Professional views: *Show Me Microsoft Office Project 2003* by Brian Kennemer, ISBN 0789730693.

Views in Project Professional display a subset of your project, resource, or assignment data using a predefined format.

Project Professional client provides many predefined task, resource, and combination views. A combination view is a split view containing two panes. For example, the bottom pane view can show additional detailed information about the tasks or resources selected in the top pane view. Views may use different formats, including the Gantt chart, graph, form, sheet, table, or network diagram that shows dependencies between project tasks.

Creating and Modifying Views in Project Professional Client

All views have a predefined set of components. Also, all views have at least one filter specified as part of the view definition that defines or limits the data displayed. Sheet views and some Chart views start out using a predefined table to determine what data to display.

The table or filter that is part of the view definition can be replaced with any of the predefined tables and filters, or other custom tables and filters can be created and applied to the view. The tables can also be customized on-the-fly by inserting or hiding columns (fields). Autofilters, filters, grouping, and formatting also can be applied to a view.

To help create standards for Project Professional clients, project managers may want to define common views and their formats. Typically, this is a collaborative effort between project managers and your Project Server administrator. To define a common set of Project Professional views, the administrator opens the Enterprise Global template and defines or changes any views using the following steps:

1. Start Project Professional client, and first connect to your Project Server. Select Tools, Enterprise Options, Open Enterprise Global from the menu.

2. To review/change the settings under the View dialog tab, select Tools, Options. You might want to change items such as Currency, Symbol, and other attributes.

3. Select Format, Text Styles from the menu and adjust the color or format of how task items such as milestones, summary tasks, or critical path tasks are displayed in project views.

4. Create required views that are standard and appropriate for your project managers in your organization. You may also modify tables used in views by adding fields, such as Work, Actual Work, or other custom fields to any tables already defined while the Enterprise Global is open.

Managing Views in Microsoft Project Professional

In Project Professional client, you do your view management in three locations:

- **Tools**—Organizer
- **Tools**—Options dialog box
- **View**—More Views dialog box

Remember that before you can start managing standard corporate views for Project Professional clients, you need to open your Enterprise Global template first.

10

Additional Recommended Readings

This section presents a number of reference materials specific to views in Project Professional and Project Server. These materials are available also on Microsoft's website for download.

- *Microsoft Office Project Server 2003 Administrator's Guide*
  http://go.microsoft.com/fwlink/?linkid=20236

- *Microsoft Office Project Server 2003 Configuration Planning Guide*
  http://go.microsoft.com/fwlink/?linkid=20235

- *Microsoft Office Project Server 2003 Disaster Recovery Guide*
  http://go.microsoft.com/fwlink/?LinkID=20234

- *Microsoft Office Project Server 2003 Installation Guide*
  http://go.microsoft.com/fwlink/?linkid=20233

- *Microsoft Office Project Server 2003 Application Configuration Guide*
  http://go.microsoft.com/fwlink/?linkid=20237

> **NOTE**
>
> The preceding URLs were valid at the time of printing.

Microsoft created a DVD titled "Microsoft Office Enterprise Project Management Solution End User Training Kit (DVD)." This DVD also contains a manual with a section "Communicating Results with Microsoft Project Professional, Working with Views," page 428, which contains extensive coverage of Project Professional views.

Best Practices

- Create Enterprise Project Outline Code Summary view for Project Center and add all Enterprise Project Outline Codes to it. Also, add the Version field to this view.

- Create Enterprise Resource Outline Code Summary view for Resource Center and add all Enterprise Resource Outline Codes to it.

- Portfolio Analyzer views should provide focused executive style information. Create more views with fewer fields to provide this focus rather than fewer views with many fields.

CHAPTER 11

Completing the Implementation and Configuration

IN THIS CHAPTER

- Using Administrative Projects
- Managing Enterprise Project and Resource Calendars
- Performing Enterprise Global Backup and Restore
- Timesheet Setup
- Best Practices

Several features of Microsoft Project Server need discussion to complete the implementation. Some of these features directly affect the current project management culture and need close scrutiny to ensure that the implementation will be positively perceived by the collective users. The use and configuration of administrative projects is one of these features. Administrative projects allow the organization to capture nonproject and nonwork activities. These projects may be new to the organization, so a thorough understanding is necessary.

How calendars are created and managed is another of the project management culture features. How calendar issues are currently managed needs to be weighed against the functionality of Project Server. An in-depth understanding is helpful to grasp the impact to your organization.

The capture of actual project work is a key function of Project Server and directly affects the accuracy of reports generated out of the database. How actuals are currently captured and reported needs to be discussed as part of the timesheet setup configuration decisions. Timesheet setup is an important feature, and understanding the various options is essential to a successful EPM implementation.

The Backup Global and Restore Global features are essential in your ability to capture and reuse created standards in the Enterprise Global template. How to use these features is discussed in this chapter.

Using Administrative Projects

Project Server allows you to create and manage administrative projects that are used to assign and track nonproject activities outside the normal bounds of particular projects. Administrative projects are visible through the Project Center view and managed through the Manage Administrative Projects button.

Goal of Administrative Projects

Administrative projects, or nonproject work, are used to capture work activities outside the scope of normal project work. Most nonproject-specific tasks fall into two main categories: HR benefits and departmental overhead. HR benefit tasks may include vacation, sick time, flex days, bereavement time, jury duty, leaves of absence, and other benefits offered by your organization. Departmental overhead tasks include maintenance and operations tasks, nonproject-specific training, company meetings, and other nonproject-specific work defined by your company, an example of which is shown in Figure 11.1.

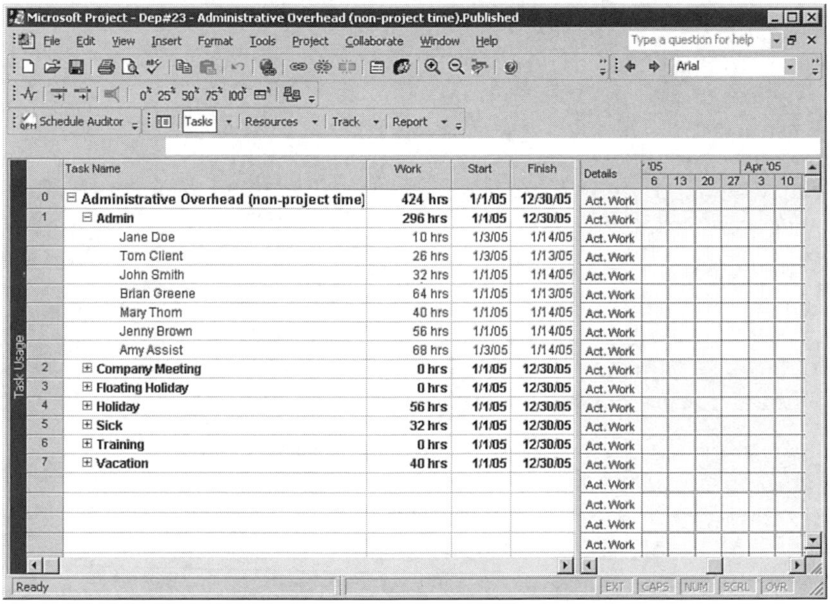

FIGURE 11.1 This example of an administrative project depicts some overhead tasks you may consider for your organization.

The administrative project provides a consistent mechanism to allow team members to enter and track their individual nonproject hours, notify the organization of planned extended absences, and track their overhead time. Time monitored at an organizational or departmental level can lead to a more accurate understanding of how benefit and overhead time is used in an ongoing basis, can show the impact of nonproject time on resource availability for project work, and can help predict trends for future planning.

There are several advantages to using administrative projects:

- Resources can use a common approach to report nonproject time.

- Individual working projects can eliminate the need to include these types of activities.

- Administrative project resource assignment information is used during the calculation of OLAP cube data displayed within the Project Center and Resource Center Portfolio Analyzer views.

> **NOTE**
>
> Displaying administrative project resource assignment information in the OLAP cube allows for a complete view of the resource's time assignments and availability. It also allows you to manipulate information across time.

▶ **SEE** "Analyzing Portfolio Data in the Portfolio Analyzer," **PAGE 394**.

Company Policy

The type of information tracked in the administrative project is determined by company policy, how the organization is run, and more specifically how each administrator wants to track time. Additionally, company policy determines the specific nonproject tasks that should be reported as well as how the administrative projects will be set up. Separate projects can be established for each type of nonproject work; however, it is recommended that both types of work be tracked in the same project. Company policy should also dictate the frequency that team members are required to provide updates and the approvals required.

You have the ability to track time at an organizational, departmental, or resource group level. Administrative projects work well for tight-knit groups of 30 or fewer team members with one centralized supervising executive. Organizations that have more than 30 people, and whose daily work does not correlate to others in the department on a regular basis, are advised to separate down to the departmental level. If necessary, departments can be broken down into smaller, more manageable resource groups, each group with its own supervisor.

Administrative Project Considerations

You need to take into account several considerations while implementing administrative projects. This section discusses the goal of administrative projects, their creation procedure, the effects of company policy, and other things you should keep in mind while implementing administrative projects.

Creating Administrative Projects

The most effective way to create administrative projects is using the Manage Administrative Projects button on the Project Center page. To create an administrative project, follow these steps:

1. In the Project Center, select the Manage Administrative Projects button at the bottom of the Actions list. The Manage Administrative Projects page is displayed, as shown in Figure 11.2.

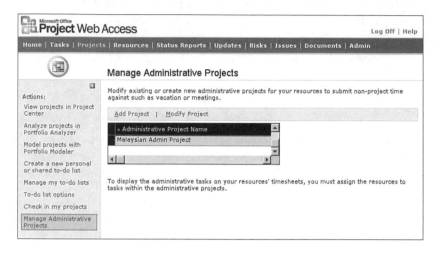

FIGURE 11.2   After you add a new project, you need to refresh the Manage Administrative Projects page to see it.

2. Click Add Project or Modify a Project.

Adding a project opens the default Administrative template and allows you to create your administrative project.

Choosing the Administrator

Administrative projects should be managed by someone directly involved with the resources assigned to the project. This person should also be familiar with company policy and have the authority to approve hours as updated. It is not recommended to give this administrative project to the general HR person or a general administrative person because he may not be closely associated with the reporting resources and may not have sufficient knowledge of the resource to evaluate project assignments and availability.

> **CAUTION**
>
> For smaller organizations it is recommended that the director of HR, or person with similar responsibilities, be appointed the administrator of the administrative project. In larger organizations it is recommended that one administrative project for each department be created. Generally, the number of team members within the administrative project should not exceed 30. Managing more than 30 people within a single administrative project can become burdensome.

Project Setup

Administrative projects can be created using any of the following three strategies:

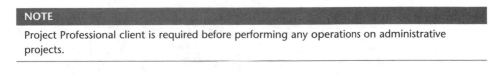

> **NOTE**
>
> Project Professional client is required before performing any operations on administrative projects.

- Use the Project Web Access Project Center Manage Administrative Projects menu (see Figure 11.3).

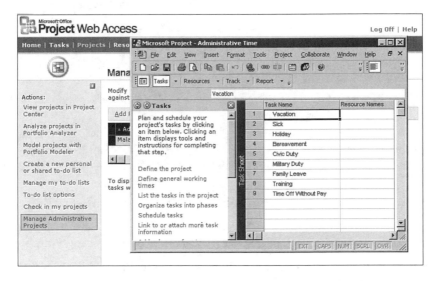

FIGURE 11.3   Selecting Add on the Manage Administrative Projects page launches a predefined administrative project template in Project Professional.

- Use the Microsoft Project Professional 2003 menu sequence File, Save As, Administrative Project check box, as shown in Figure 11.4.

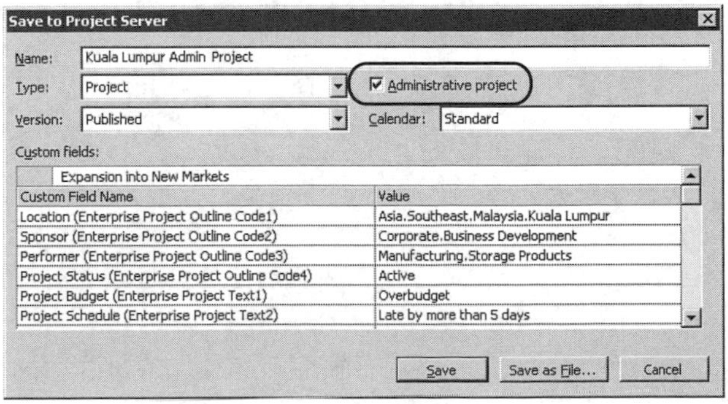

FIGURE 11.4   Selecting the Administrative Project option when saving a project displays this project on the Manage Administrative Projects page in PWA.

- Load a predefined Administrative Project template (see Figure 11.5).

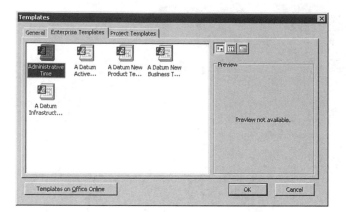

FIGURE 11.5   You can define the enterprise project templates, including the administrative projects, for use in the future.

Each technique creates a special type of project schedule designed to use particular administrative project scheduling and time tracking methods. These special features can be summarized as follows:

- Tasks are defined as Fixed Duration, not Effort Driven, for scheduling.

- Project Web Access Tasks timesheet data always uses direct time entry, Hours of Work Done Per Time Period, rather than %Complete or Remaining Work methods.

- Administrative projects appear at the bottom of the team member Timesheet view, as shown in Figure 11.6.

Task Name	Work		Sun 30	Mon 31	Tue 1	Wed 2	Th
☐ **Administrative Overhead (non-project time)**	805.4h	Act. Work	2h	1.2h	0.6h	2h	
Holiday	48h	Act. Work					
Training	0h	Act. Work					
Company Meeting	16h	Act. Work					
Admin	535h	Act. Work	2h	1.2h	0.6h	2h	
Sick	144h	Act. Work					
Floating Holiday	0h	Act. Work					
Vacation	62.4h	Act. Work					
Total:	66.88h	Act. Work	5.5h	7.5h	6.8h	3h	2.

View my tasks — Update All | Update Selected Rows | Save Changes

View Options | Filter, Group, Search | Delegation

Hide | Reject | Insert Notes | Link Risks | Link Issues | Link Documents | ← 1/30/2005-2/5/2005 →

Print Grid   Export Grid to Excel

FIGURE 11.6   Resources use the administrative project tasks to report their overhead time as they would on any other project.

- Administrative project tasks appear as categories selectable within the Notify Your Manager of Time You Will Not Be Available for Project Work option. This option is located in PWA on the Tasks page under the Actions menu (see Figure 11.7).

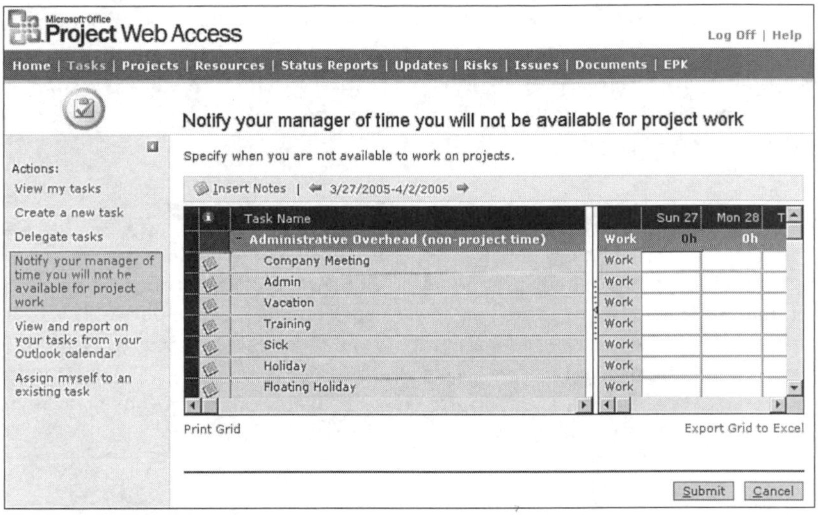

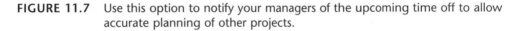

FIGURE 11.7 Use this option to notify your managers of the upcoming time off to allow accurate planning of other projects.

Except for these special conditions, administrative projects are developed and maintained like any other project schedule.

When creating an administrative project, individual tasks should be set up for each type of benefit offered by the organization and for each general overhead area. Because most benefits are established and managed annually, based on the organization's fiscal year, the administrative project should be set up to follow this same time frame. However, the administrative project will extend across several years. The project administrator can keep track of the benefit hours used for the established time period by accessing details in the OLAP cube. Additionally, the project administrator can view a specific time period while managing the administrative project using Project Professional.

TIP

It is not recommended that hours allowed for a particular type of benefit or overhead task (for example, vacation—80 hours/year) be entered in an administrative project due to the way Project allocates planned work.

Nonproject Tasks

HR benefit tasks include vacation, sick leave, flex days, bereavement time, jury duty, leaves of absence, and other benefits offered by your organization.

Overhead tasks are defined as tasks that each team member is required to perform but that do not affect company revenue. Each organization may choose a different level of detail. For example, some companies might choose to track time spent preparing for a meeting, monthly attendance at local professional society meetings, time spent preparing expense reports, time spent reading daily emails, and so on. Overhead tasks also encompass the majority of tasks given to office personnel, such as receptionists, office managers, network administrators, and other overhead personnel. Overhead tasks also include tasks necessary to maintain the organization, such as preventive maintenance or data backups. The ability to track this time and predict team member availability is crucial to corporate and project health.

CAUTION
The tracking of overhead time is not intended to become a burden to employees. However, the ability to monitor and track time spent on overhead tasks is important to some organizations. It is important that your company take time to evaluate your current time-tracking processes and the type of information you want to track in the future. It may be beneficial to plan this change in phases to promote the desired time-keeping behavior for your organization. It is worth noting that the more detailed your time tracking, the more accurate your understanding of resource assignments and availability.

Another task we recommend be included in your administrative project is that of company meetings. Each week team members spend time in meetings. Tracking this time is important for judging the overall health and efficiency of your company. Additionally, being able to consistently predict a meeting gives you an accurate reading on resource availability. For example, if your team has a weekly Tuesday meeting from 10:00 a.m. to 12:00 p.m., you know that your resources' project work availability on Tuesdays is a maximum of 6 hours (based on an 8-hour work day).

Training is another overhead task that may be tracked, whether team members are taking a two-day course or are enrolled in a semester-long class for growth within their position. If training impacts a team member's availability to a project, it should be tracked in the administrative project.

All these different benefit and overhead tasks within your administrative project give you a more accurate view of resource availability and help to identify trends within your department or resource group. An example of a trend would be that 90% of your team members take off the day prior to and following the Fourth of July. Another trend might be that certain team members' true availability is less than 50% because they are constantly consumed by meetings or maintenance tasks. Both of these examples can give you a good look into overall corporate health and the workings of your organization.

Choosing the Reporting Cycle

Guidelines should be established for the reporting of used benefit and overhead hours as well as for approvals and notification required for extended absences. It is recommended that benefit and overhead hours be reported by team members as they are used and not less frequently than weekly.

Company policy should determine the appropriate timing for reporting extended absences to minimize the impact to projects. Extended absences of more than five days will significantly impact project work. Thus, it is important that proper and timely notification be provided to managers and project managers when a team member will be unavailable for an extended period of time.

Ongoing Maintenance

The frequency of maintenance for the administrative project is determined based on company guidelines and expectations. If your team members are required to report time on a weekly basis, weekly maintenance would correlate to this procedure. After hours are entered against the administrative project, notification is provided to the project administrator. The project administrator should review each task submitted, make sure that the hours entered satisfy the company policy for each particular type of task (for example, vacation cannot be taken in fewer than 4-hour increments), and then either accept or reject the request using the standard timesheet approval functionality.

We recommend that time entered against the administrative project be reviewed prior to each payroll period. Data from this project can then be used to report benefit time taken to the payroll department.

Annual Cleanup   It is recommended that the time frame for administrative projects be ongoing. However, it is also recommended that the administrative project receive a detailed review and cleanup annually, whether the organization follows a calendar year or a fiscal year. An annual cleanup of the administrative project is a good way to track trends as well as benefit time while still keeping overhead time and other tasks at a manageable size. Cleanup tasks should include the following:

- Removal of inactive resources
- Verification of paid leave time usage

To remove inactive resources, someone with administrative privileges needs to do the following:

1. Navigate to the Admin tab.
2. Select Cleanup Project Server Database.
3. Click the Resource button.
4. Find the name of the inactive resource under Delete the Selected Resource.
5. Click the Delete button.

The inactive resource now becomes a local resource within the administrative project, yet the actual hours remain. Finally, when viewing the administrative project through Project Web Access (PWA), the view can be filtered so that only enterprise resources show.

Managing Enterprise Project and Resource Calendars

In Microsoft Project, calendars are used by the scheduling engine to understand how unique calendar items—for example, holidays, part-time employees, and so on—affect the plan for accomplishing work. Out of the box, only one calendar, Standard, is the base calendar for building all other calendars. Standard identifies every day as a work day from

8:00 a.m. to 5:00 p.m. except Saturday and Sunday. The Standard calendar is the default for all calendars until you define and assign additional, more useful calendars.

Normally, at least one additional calendar is created that contains the installing company's holidays and is given a name such as Company calendar. When assigned to a project, resource, or task, the Company calendar becomes the base calendar for most scheduling calculations. When assigned to a project, the Company calendar becomes the base project calendar. When assigned to a resource, the Company calendar becomes the base resource calendar. This base project or resource calendar can then be further refined for the calendar events that may be unique to that project or resource.

Enterprise calendars are managed through the Enterprise Global template. If a specific resource calendar is required, it is managed through the Enterprise Resource Pool in association with the resource.

Enterprise project calendars can be created only by users who have read/write access to Enterprise Global. Enterprise resource calendars can be managed only by users who have read/write authority to the Resource Pool. These permissions are granted through the security model.

▶ **SEE** "Establishing Security Model Settings," **PAGE 143**.

Review "Project Server Permissions" in Appendix C of the *Microsoft Project Server 2003 Administrator's Guide* to gain a thorough understanding of the necessary security setting to manage calendars.

Enterprise project calendars can be created by the administrator for use throughout an organization.

Managing Enterprise Project Calendars

When Project Server is first installed, it has one base calendar named Standard, and it is the default project calendar and resource calendar.

Every project saved to Project Server must specify which enterprise base calendar it is using. Any new enterprise calendar created in the Enterprise Global template is available to become the enterprise calendar for projects stored on the Project Server. Therefore, if a company operated in several countries, it may have several base calendars describing the unique calendar items for each country. Each of these base country calendars is available to be applied to the specific project or resources assigned to the project.

To create a new calendar, follow these steps:

1. Open Project Professional.

2. Select Tools, Enterprise Options, Open Enterprise Global.

3. Select Tools, Change Working Time.

4. Click the New button.

5. Name the calendar and make sure that the Copy of Standard is selected.

6. Adjust the calendar as necessary.

7. Click the Close button.

It is often necessary to create several base calendars for operations that have offices around the world. For example, you have workers in the United States and Germany working on the same project. The German resources will have different bank holidays that need to be considered when scheduling those resources on your project. Because all resources are assigned a resource calendar from the list of base calendars, it is necessary to create calendars for all holiday or working time variances on your project.

TIP

You cannot delete or rename the Standard enterprise project calendar.

To delete a calendar, follow these steps:

1. Open Project Professional.

2. Select Tools, Enterprise Options, Open Enterprise Global.

3. Select Tools, Organizer.

4. Select the Calendars tab.

5. Select the project calendar on the right side to be deleted or renamed.

6. Delete or Rename as necessary.

Managing Resource Calendars

When a new enterprise resource is created in the Enterprise Resource Pool, it is automatically assigned to the Standard calendar, and a resource calendar named for the resource is created from the base calendar for the resource. To assign an enterprise resource to a different base calendar, you must manually select a different calendar for the resource. In this way, you can account for the world resources mentioned previously, and their unique work schedules will be available to the scheduling engine.

Task scheduling is calculated for a resource by combining the information from the assigned base calendar for the project and the resource's assigned base calendar. If either calendar changes, the enterprise resource's assignments might change. For example, you have an 8-hour task on a Wednesday in your schedule. This Wednesday is not special; it is just another workday. Under normal conditions, the scheduling engine sees no project calendar exceptions for the workday and schedules a resource to work 8 hours that day.

Assume also that you need to assign a resource who only works part-time, 8:00 a.m. to noon. The resource calendar for this person has been adjusted to his specific workday. If he is assigned to this task, the scheduling engine uses the resource calendar information to schedule the 8 hours work for two 4-hour days, 8:00 a.m. to noon Wednesday and Thursday, unique to this particular resource.

The project manager cannot permanently alter a resource calendar from within a project schedule because resource calendars are maintained in the Resource Pool and are read into the schedule on opening. Calendar changes for planning purposes are allowed, but the project cannot write calendar changes back to the Resource Pool. If the project manager attempts to make resource calendar changes in the schedule, he receives a warning that all changes to enterprise resources will be lost, as shown in Figure 11.8.

This means that as long as the project manager has the schedule open, the changes he makes in the resource calendar apply. On closing and reopening the project, the resource calendar changes revert back to the resource's enterprise resource calendar held and managed in the Resource Pool, and the project-specific calendar changes are lost. Resource calendar information is cached in the schedule from the Resource Pool each time the schedule is opened in Project Professional. The benefit to this control is that no individual project manager can permanently alter a resource calendar. Only the user responsible for resource information can alter a resource calendar. Because resource calendars are held and maintained through the central Resource Pool the system guarantees that all project managers receive the same information about calendar data for any individual resource that may be assigned to multiple projects.

When a resource needs unique scheduling information added to his calendar, it must be performed in the Resource Pool.

To alter a resource calendar, follow these steps:

1. Open Project Professional.

2. Select Tools, Enterprise Options, Open Enterprise Resource Pool.

3. Select the resource or resources needing calendar changes.

4. Select the individual resource in the pool.

5. Select Tools, Change Working Time.

6. Make the necessary changes to the individual resource calendar.

7. Repeat for each resource as necessary.

8. Save and close the Enterprise Resource Pool.

The changes will be available to all project managers the next time they open their projects.

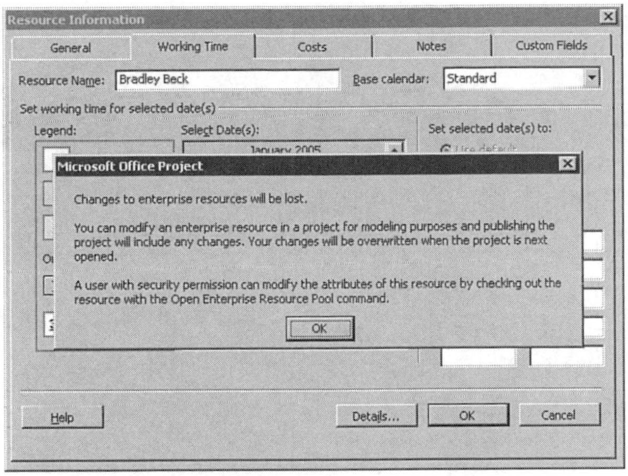

FIGURE 11.8   Resource calendar change warning.

Performing Enterprise Global Backup and Restore

Like any other data, the Enterprise Global template can become corrupted, or it can be changed in error and then fail to recover. For these reasons, you need to back up your Enterprise Global template(s) regularly. Another good use for the Backup Restore Enterprise Global template feature is to share the Enterprise Global settings across several Project Server databases. Some users will create both a production and training database. The training database is used for user training and configuration experimentation. After a configuration of Enterprise Outline Codes or Options is tested and accepted, the Backup Enterprise Global and Restore Enterprise Global can be used to move the tested Enterprise Global to the production environment.

Backing Up Enterprise Global Template Data

To back up an Enterprise Global template, you need to be logged in to Project Professional with sufficient privileges to perform the backups. Follow these steps to back up the Enterprise Global template data:

1. Open Project Professional.

2. Select Tools, Enterprise Options, Backup Enterprise Global.

A browse window prompts you to save the Enterprise Global template data to an external file. You also have the option to save this backup through an ODBC connection to a database. This method allows you to store several Enterprise Global templates in a central repository.

The default name for the backup file is EntGlobalBackup, but you may want to change the filename.

> **TIP**
>
> Consider using a filenaming convention that helps you easily identify the server name and last-used date of a particular Enterprise Global template. That way, you can use those files as starting points for changes to future global settings, and you have a historical record of backup timing.

Restoring Enterprise Global Template Data

To restore the Enterprise Global Template data, perform the following steps:

1. Open Project Professional.

2. Select Tools, Enterprise Options, Restore Enterprise Global.

3. Select Tools, Change Working Time.

A dialog box asks you to select a server account user profile to use when performing the restore, and the user profile must have the correct privileges.

> **CAUTION**
>
> Restoring the Enterprise Global template to a Microsoft Project Server cannot be reversed. Before clicking the Restore button, make a backup copy of the active Enterprise Global template so that you can recover the previous Enterprise Global settings, if necessary.

Timesheet Setup

Select the method of time reporting your organization wants to use and configure it for your organization's specific needs. Timesheet setup can be performed as follows:

1. In PWA, select the Admin tab.

2. Select Customize Project Web Access.

3. Select Tracking Settings under Customization Options.

Specify the Default Method for Reporting Progress on Tasks

Three choices are available under the heading Specify the Default Method for Reporting Progress on Tasks: Percent Complete, Actual Work Done and Remaining Work, and Hours of Work Done Per Day or Per Week.

- **Percent Complete**—Resources report the percent of work complete per task between 0% and 100%.

- **Actual Work Done and Remaining Work**—Resources report the actual work done and the work remaining to be done on each task.

- **Hours of Work Done Per Day or Per Week**—Resources report the hours worked on each task during each time period.

> **NOTE**
>
> If you choose Managed Periods, only Hours of Work Done Per Day or Per Week can be selected.

Lock Down Defaults

Lock Down Defaults allows the systems administrator to choose whether project managers can change the default method for reporting progress or must comply with the default method. To ensure timephased data accuracy across all projects, it is recommended that the Force Project Managers to Use the Progress Reporting Method Specified Above for All Projects radio button be selected. Data integrity is an important aspect of an Enterprise Project Management (EPM) system and should not be compromised for the sake of project management comfort.

Time Period Settings

Select the start day for your reporting week in the Week Starts On window. Next, determine whether you want to use managed periods:

- **Non-Managed Periods**—Allow Project and PWA users to update actuals.

- **Managed Periods**—Allow only PWA users to update actuals during open periods.

Non-managed periods allow for the input of actuals in both the schedule in Project Professional and through the timesheet feature of PWA. Managed periods restrict actuals to come only from the PWA timesheets. If actuals are altered directly in the schedule, a warning appears that the actuals are not in sync with the database. If you choose to sync the actuals, the timesheet data overwrites the altered actuals in the schedule. An out-of-sync condition can exist, but the message appears each time the project is written to the database. To maintain an out-of-sync condition, the project manager must deny the sync request for the life of the project.

If Managed Periods is selected, the administrator must manually open the Customize Project Web Access, Tracking Settings each timesheet period, create a new period, and then close the previous period. Usually several periods are open, which means that a user can alter the timesheet. After a period is closed, the timesheet is locked from changes with the exception of users who have Adjust Actuals permissions. The Open period is a floating window of alterable timesheets usually about four to six weeks. As a new period is created and an older one closed, the four to six week window floats through the calendar turning on and off timesheets available for entering actuals.

Select the Weekly or Monthly radio button and specify the number of weeks spanned to set the Display on Resources timesheets. This setting should be set to the standard for time reporting in your company—that is, each week, every two weeks, and so on.

Next, select the radio button for how you want the time entered on the timesheet:

• Resources Should Report Their Hours Worked Every Day.

• Resources Should Report Their Total Hours Worked for a Week.

• Resources Should Report Their Total Hours Worked During the Period Set Above.

Each of these settings selects a different behavior for the resource timesheet. Usually, the Resources Should Report Their Hours Worked Every Day is the most accurate. In this state of accuracy, daily actuals are placed directly into the timephased data in the Project Professional schedules as reported. Under the other two conditions, Project Professional contours the time entry across the defined period, and the daily timephased data is calculated and may be inaccurate. Let's assume that you have an 8-hour task to report this time period, and you worked all day Tuesday to accomplish it. On a daily reporting timesheet, you would put 8 hours on Tuesday and, when the timesheet was processed, there would be 8 hours on Tuesday in the timephased data in the project schedule.

If you reported the 8 hours in the other two methods, the 8 hours worked on Tuesday could only be reported as a lump sum for the task and would not reference Tuesday. Under this condition, Project Professional would average (or flat line contour) the 8 hours across the period of a five-day work week and put 1.66 hours worked for each day. The information is still true but less accurate than daily reporting.

Now select the maximum number of hours that can be entered per day for a single task. A zero is used for no limit. If your organization has a limit, it can be imposed here.

Time Period Considerations

How your organization currently captures project actuals needs to be considered when selecting the time period settings in Project Server 2003. How you capture actuals today and how you want to capture them in the future will become part of your project management culture. Remember, you may be trying to change the project management culture in your organization, and you will be affecting human behavior. The speed of adaptation will be directly proportional to the magnitude of the changes for each individual user.

Although the most accurate actuals capture method is hours per day, your organization may not be ready for the behaviors necessary to capture information at this level of accuracy. It may be necessary to plan a gradual movement toward actuals by day. You may first require % complete reporting for some period of time because this may be the least intrusive to the current culture. As the need for more accurate data drives organizational behavior, you may want to progress to the hours per period reporting. And finally, after careful consideration, move to hours per day reporting.

These methods must be carefully weighed against your current culture before deciding how much change your project management culture can manage. The success of an Enterprise Project Management installation may well depend on the thoughtful consideration of human behavior and culture change necessary to move your organization forward.

Define Current Tasks

This selection is sometimes called the "look ahead" for tasks. That means that a timesheet set to view current tasks sees all active assignments for this period plus the future tasks defined by the look ahead number. So, for instance, if the value is set to 10 days, the resource would see all tasks that should be done this week plus any incomplete tasks plus tasks 10 working days into the future. Choose the look ahead number correctly for your organization. The default is correct for most organizations.

Select Save Changes, and the Tracking settings are complete.

If you choose not to use timesheets, follow these steps:

1. In PWA, select Server Configuration.

2. Select Deny for all task-related permissions. The timesheet will not display at all for your organization.

You decide how your organization wants to reflect task completion directly in your Project Professional schedules.

Best Practices

- All nonproject-specific tasks should be tracked in one administrative project per department or resource group, depending on the size of the overall organization.

- Organizations should track benefit and overhead time at the departmental level to provide a more accurate view of resource availability as well as better control over how resources use this time.

- Administrative projects are best created using the PWA Project Center, Manage Administrative Projects menu.

- Ongoing time approval and maintenance should occur frequently, per pay cycle at a minimum.

- Administrative projects should receive a detailed review and cleanup annually whether the organization follows a calendar year or a fiscal year.

- Careful consideration needs to be given to the number and complexity of project and resource calendars.

- Companies with multinational work forces need to have multinational calendars.

- The choice for Managed Periods needs to be carefully weighed against the time required for manual management of periods.

- If projects are created against specific tracking settings and those settings are changed universally, the projects need to be opened and saved under the new tracking settings.

PART IV

Validating the Microsoft Office Project Server 2003 Implementation

IN THIS PART

CHAPTER 12   Microsoft Office Project Server 2003
Validation   259

CHAPTER 13   Troubleshooting Business Process
Implementation in the Application   277

Microsoft Office Project Server 2003 Validation

IN THIS CHAPTER

- Introduction to Validation
- Level 1—Technology Validation
- Level 2—Basic Project Server Configuration
- Level 3—Business Process Validation
- Best Practices

This chapter is divided into three main levels of validation that you as system administrator need to take time to perform to validate the implementation. Implementation validation is just as important as any other phase of planning an Enterprise Project Management (EPM) solution deployment and should be carefully planned and executed.

Introduction to Validation

Installation and implementation of Microsoft Office Project Server 2003 should be tested and validated to ensure that the system is performing and acting the way you intend it to. These validations are performed at various times during the server installation process and during the database configuration or implementation process.

Validating the system is broken down into three levels:

- Level 1—Technology
- Level 2—Basic Project Server configuration
- Level 3—Business process validation

Level 1—Technology

Technology validation is performed to ensure that the back-end infrastructure of servers, network systems, and application services is operating properly to support Project Server 2003.

Breakdown of Technology Validations

Technology validation is divided into three categories. Each category addresses a specific technical installation requirement for Project Server to function properly. The categories are

- Server operating system validation

- Network systems validation

- Application installation validation

Level 2—Basic Project Server Configuration

Configuration validation enables you to confirm that Project Server is configured to view project data in the form and content you need to support your project management processes.

Breakdown of Basic Configuration Validation

Validating basic configuration is divided into three areas. They are

- User role validation

- Security setup validation

- Data access and functionality validation

Level 3—Business Process Validation

It is beneficial for you to verify that the setup of Project Server supports your project management business process. This validation is performed using process *roles* to confirm that each user has the proper functionality for the roles they play in the business process.

Breakdown of Business Process Validation

The steps for validating business process are

- Establish role-based test users

- Validate roles-based test case scenarios

- Database cleanup after validation

Conclusion

The combination of all three validations ensures that Project Server 2003, Project Web Access (PWA), and Project 2003 are properly installed and configured to work with your EPM process.

Level 1—Technology Validation

As noted in the introduction, technology validation is divided into three separate categories. Each category focuses on the specific technology infrastructure being used by Project Server to support the application functionality. Because Project Server relies on several other applications and network services, it is crucial to confirm that all supporting technical facilities are working together. The three categories are, as follows:

- Server operating systems validation

- Network systems validation

- Application installation validation

Server Operating Systems Validation

Project Server 2003, Windows SharePoint Services, and SQL Server 2000 have similar server operating system requirements that need to be verified and validated before these applications can be installed on the servers. The validation sequence is the same whether the system architecture is a single server or multiple servers. Project Server View Processor, Session Manager, and SQL Server require Windows 2000 Server. PWA and Windows SharePoint Services require Windows 2003 Server.

Certain settings in Windows 2003 Server need to be verified and validated to ensure that Project Server works properly. These settings include setting the system as an application server, enabling Internet Information Services and ASP.NET, and deselecting Enhanced Internet Explorer Security.

Internet Information Services/Enhanced Internet Explorer Security Verification

Windows 2003 does not install and start Internet Information Services if the operating system was installed using the default settings.

Checking and installing Internet Information Services is accomplished by performing the following steps:

1. Log on to the server. (It is preferable to log on as the domain service account.) Go to the Control Panel and select Add or Remove Programs.

2. Select Add/Remove Windows Components on the left side of the dialog box.

3. Select applications and click on Details.

4. Verify that Internet Information Services and ASP Applications are selected, as shown in Figure 12.1.

5. Click OK.

6. Scroll down the list and verify that Enhanced Internet Explorer Security is not selected.

7. Click OK.

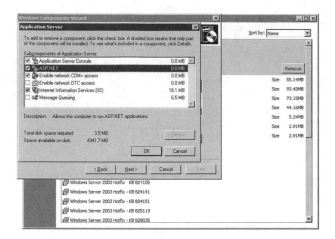

FIGURE 12.1   IIS and ASP.NET services must be active for proper Project Server installation.

If any changes were made as a result of the preceding steps, Windows begins installing the configuration.

Network Systems Validation

Project Server, Windows SharePoint Services, and SQL Server work most efficiently when the servers are members of the same domain. User authentication can be managed as a group from the primary domain controller or Active Directory group.

The installation of Project Server 2003 calls for the use of *service accounts*. The application references these accounts to perform processing and data access during normal operation.

Verifying the network system involves confirming that these accounts are properly defined and are members of the appropriate user groups on the servers running Project Server, Windows SharePoint Services, and SQL Server.

Verifying Local Administrators/OLAP Administrators on All Servers

Conduct the following steps on each server to verify that the Windows service account created on the domain or active directory server is a member of the local Administrators group:

1. Log on as a local administrator.

2. Go to Control Panel, Administrative Tools, Computer Management, as shown in Figure 12.2.

3. Select Local Users and Groups.

4. Select Groups and double-click the Administrators Group (see Figure 12.3).

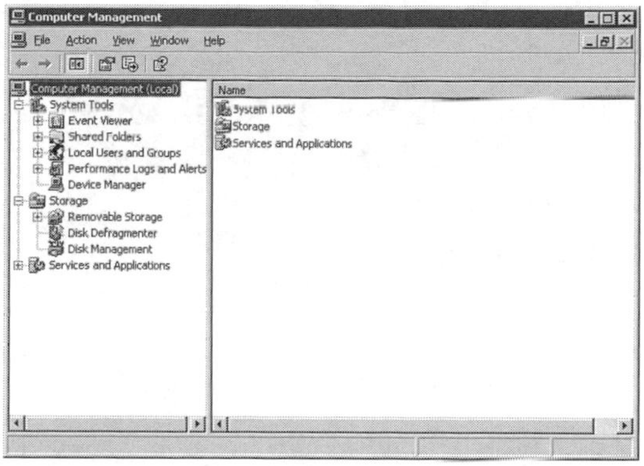

FIGURE 12.2   Verify that the domain service accounts are members of the appropriate local user groups.

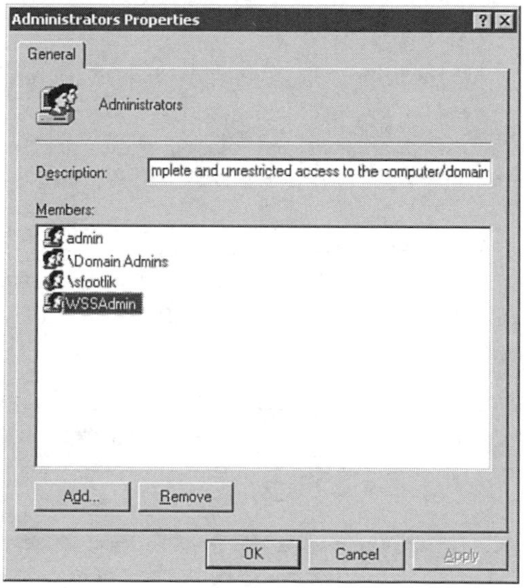

FIGURE 12.3   The service account must be a member of the Administrators group on the server running Project Server.

5. Double-click the OLAP Administrators Group. Verify that the OLAP service account is a member of this group (see Figure 12.4) .

6. Repeat Steps 1 through 5 for each server in the architecture.

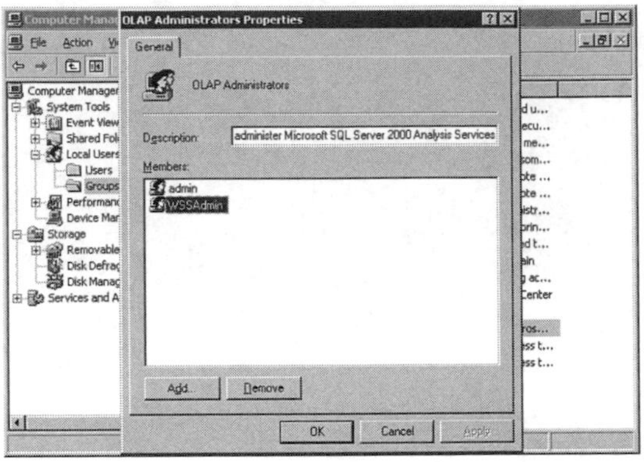

FIGURE 12.4   The service account must be a member of the OLAP Administrators group on the server running Project Server and SQL Analysis Services.

Application Installation Validation

Validating the installation of the various applications is conducted in three phases. Phase 1 validates the SQL Server installation including SQL Analysis Services. Phase 2 validates the Windows SharePoint Services installation. Phase 3 validates the installation of Project Server 2003 and connectivity through Project Professional 2003.

SQL Server/Analysis Services Installation Validation

Perform the following steps to validate that SQL Server 2000 is properly installed and configured for use with Project Server 2003. This validation includes both SQL Server and SQL Analysis Services.

1. Log on to the SQL Server using the service account logon and password, as shown in Figure 12.5. This account should have local administrator and OLAP administrator privileges.

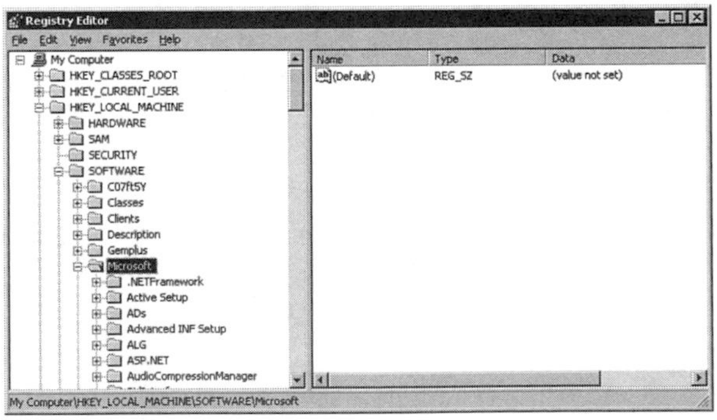

FIGURE 12.5   Navigate to the SQL Server registry key.

2. Verify that the version of SQL Server with Service Pack 3a has been installed by opening registry editor (Regedit). Navigate to the registry key for SQL Server and click on the Current Version registry, as shown in Figure 12.6.

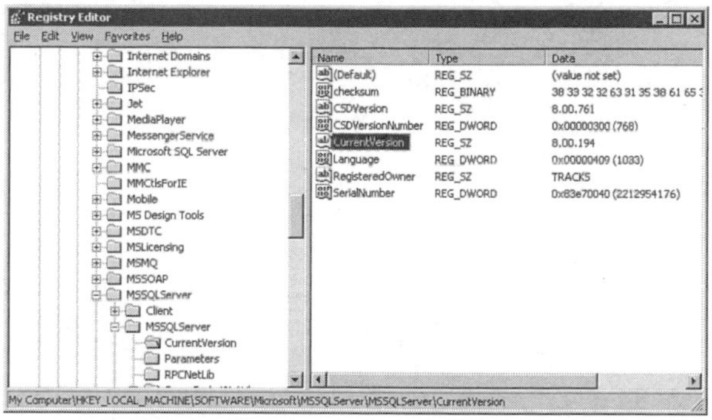

FIGURE 12.6   The Current Version registry should be 8.00.194 for SQL Server 2000 SP3a.

3. Launch SQL Analysis Manager, as shown in Figure 12.7.

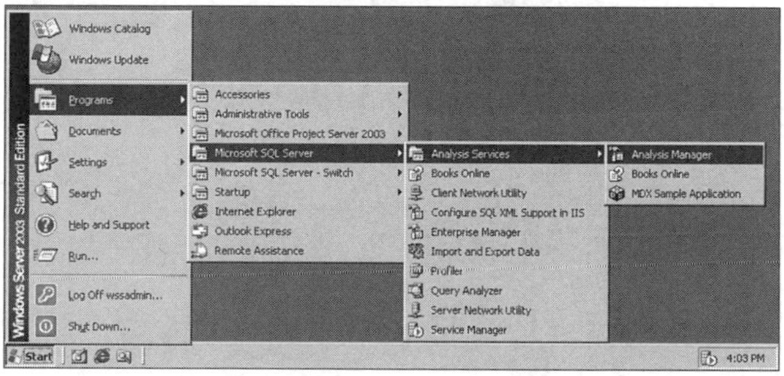

FIGURE 12.7   Use the SQL Server Analysis Manager client interface to manage the OLAP repository.

4. Right-click the server and select Edit Repository Connection String, as shown in Figure 12.8.

5. Verify that the repository has been migrated to a SQL database, as shown in Figure 12.9.

6. Close Analysis Manager. Log off SQL Server after completing the validation.

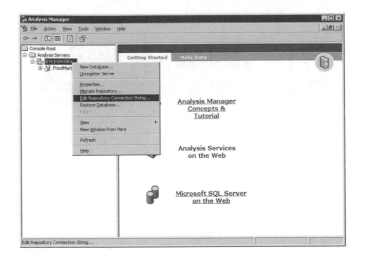

FIGURE 12.8   View the connection string for the OLAP repository.

FIGURE 12.9   The connection string should begin with `Provider=SQLOLEDB`.

Windows SharePoint Services Installation Validation

Validation of Windows SharePoint Services consists of three tests that verify proper installation. The first test verifies that the Windows SharePoint Services installation is valid. This is accomplished by performing the following steps:

1. Log on to the server running Project Server using the account identified as the Windows SharePoint Administrator.

2. Navigate to the Admin page and Manage Windows SharePoint Services.

3. Click Test URL next to the SharePoint Central Administration URL, as shown in Figure 12.10.

FIGURE 12.10   Proper access to the Windows SharePoint Central Administration will be granted only to a member of the local administrators group on the Windows SharePoint Server.

4. Proper installation is verified by the Central Administration website page opening on the desktop, as shown in Figure 12.11.

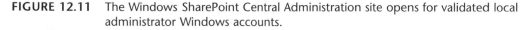

FIGURE 12.11   The Windows SharePoint Central Administration site opens for validated local administrator Windows accounts.

The second verification test verifies access to Windows SharePoint Central Administration using the Domain service account set up to administer Windows SharePoint. Follow these steps to perform the test:

1. Click on the Start menu and select Administrative Tools.

2. Select Windows SharePoint Central Administration, as shown in Figure 12.12.

3. Having the ability to access the SharePoint Central Administration website confirms that the service account has the proper permissions and that Windows SharePoint Services is installed correctly.

The third verification test confirms that the WSS site for Public Documents was properly created during the Windows SharePoint configuration process in Project Server. Follow these steps to perform the test:

1. Log on to PWA as an administrator.

2. Navigate to the Admin page and select Manage Windows SharePoint Services.

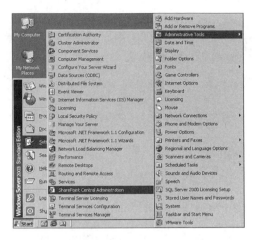

FIGURE 12.12   The service account should have access to the Windows SharePoint Services Central Administration menu item when logged on to the Windows SharePoint Server.

3. Click on the hyperlink to the Public Documents site, as shown in Figure 12.13.

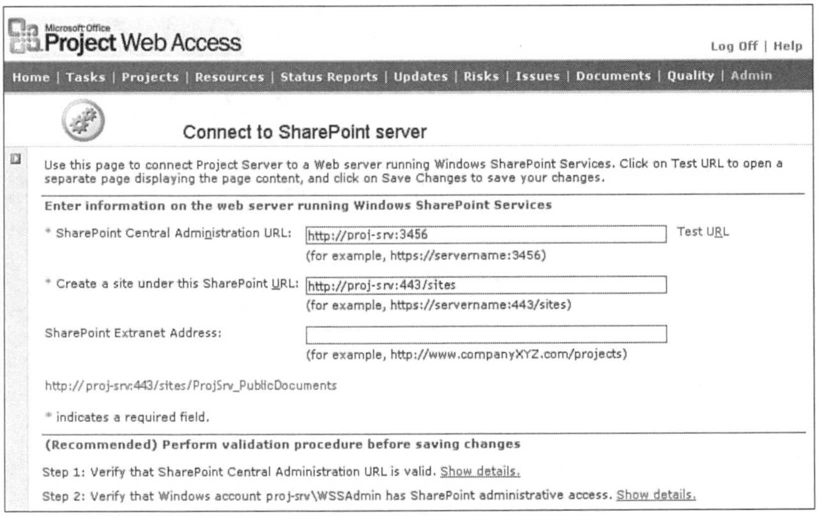

FIGURE 12.13   Access the Public Documents WSS site from PWA.

4. The Public Documents website opening up confirms proper configuration of Windows SharePoint Services with Project Server, as shown in Figure 12.14.

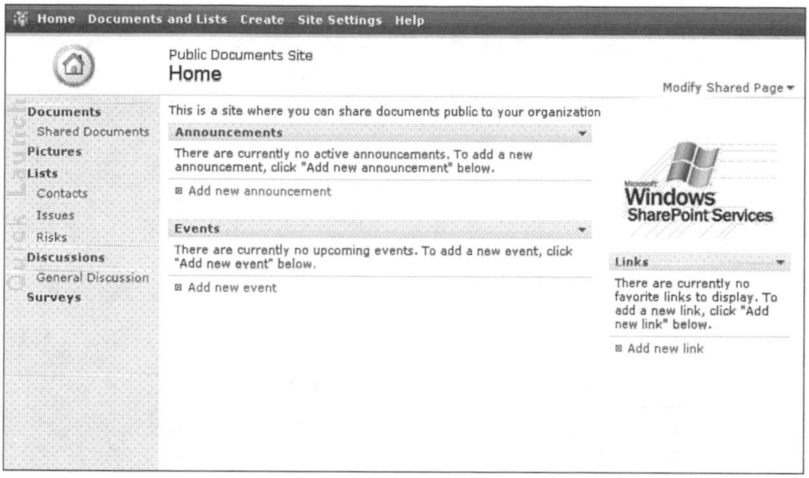

FIGURE 12.14   Accessing the Public Documents WSS site confirms proper configuration of WSS with Project Server.

Project Server Installation Validation

Project Server installation validation begins with the simple test of logging on to Project Server as an administrator. Several other verifications are performed by navigating to each main menu page including Task, Projects, Resources, Status Reports, Updates, Risks, Issues, and Documents. Navigate to all the action and option items on each page to confirm proper installation. A message indicating no data to view appears on any data view.

Additional tests are performed from the Admin page to verify proper installation of SharePoint Services and SQL Analysis Services. The SharePoint verification tests were discussed in the preceding section. Validation of the OLAP service is accomplished by performing the following steps from the Admin page:

1. Select Manage Enterprise Features.

2. On the Update Resource Tables and OLAP Cube page, scroll down to the Update Frequency section of the page and select the option Update Only When Specified.

3. Click on Update Now. This initiates the building of a new OLAP cube (see Figure 12.15).

4. Refresh the page until the Current Cube Status indicates that the cube was successfully built, verifying proper installation and configuration of the OLAP Service in Project Server.

5. A role needs to be defined on the Analysis Server and access granted to all users on the network so that the OLAP cube is accessible for view creation in Project Server. Log on to the Analysis Server as the OLAP administrator.

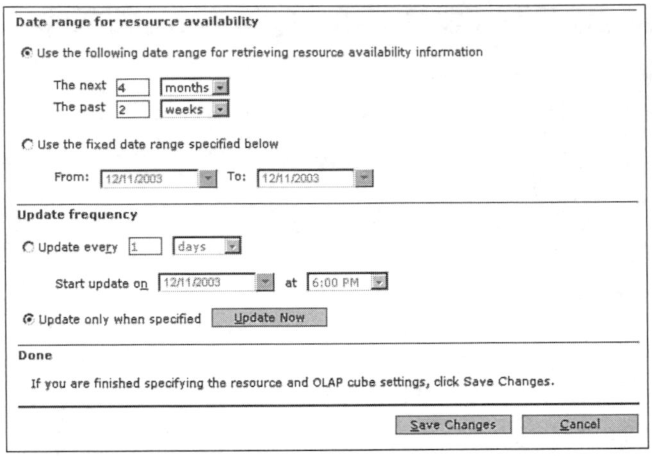

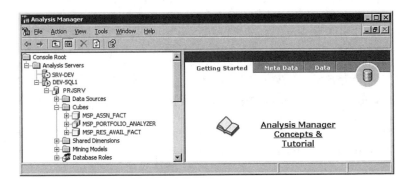

Date range for resource availability
Use the following date range for retrieving resource availability information
The next 4 months
The past 2 weeks
Use the fixed date range specified below
From: 12/11/2003 To: 12/11/2003
Update frequency
Update every 1 days
Start update on 12/11/2003 at 6:00 PM
Update only when specified
Update Now
Done
If you are finished specifying the resource and OLAP cube settings, click Save Changes.
Save Changes
Cancel

FIGURE 12.15 Selecting the Update Now button verifies the connection to OLAP server.

6. Start Analysis Manager. Expand the tree on the left until the cube created by Project Server is visible, as shown in Figure 12.16.

Analysis Manager
File Action View Tools Window Help
Console Root
Analysis Servers
SRV-DEV
DEV-SQL1
PRJSRV
Data Sources
Cubes
MSP_ASSN_FACT
MSP_PORTFOLIO_ANALYZER
MSP_RES_AVAIL_FACT
Shared Dimensions
Mining Models
Database Roles
Getting Started
Meta Data
Data
Analysis Manager Concepts & Tutorial

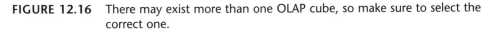

FIGURE 12.16 There may exist more than one OLAP cube, so make sure to select the correct one.

7. Right-click the mouse on the cube name and select Manage Roles.
8. Click the New button in the dialog and create a role such as "CubeViewers," as shown in Figure 12.17.
9. Click on the Options tab and select all three items in the list.

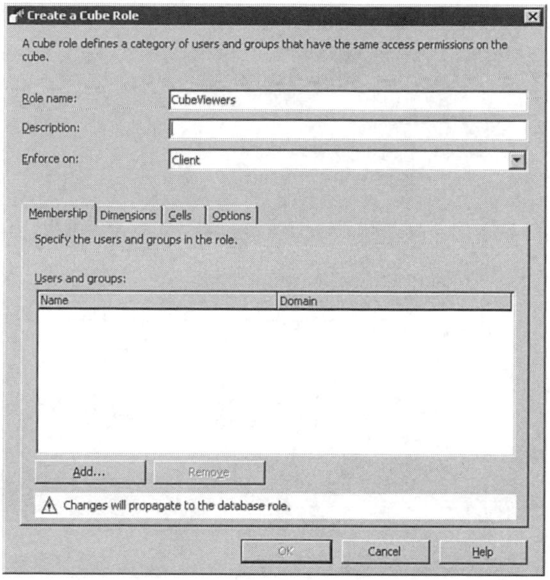

FIGURE 12.17   Creating a new user group to allow specific domain users to have access to the OLAP cube.

10. Add the group Domain Users or Everyone as members to the role. Specific domain users can be added to the role if the cube is to be limited to specific users. Make sure that you include the Project Server administrator if limited access is preferred.

At this point, the OLAP cube is available for view creation in PWA. The next test confirms that a Portfolio Analyzer view can be created using the OLAP server and the cube. Make sure that you perform this test from a workstation that has Microsoft Office Professional 2003 to fully verify this functionality. To perform the test, follow these steps:

1. Open PWA as the administrator. Navigate to the Admin page.

2. Select Manage Views. Click on Add View at the top of the list.

3. Select Portfolio Analyzer on the View Creation page, as shown in Figure 12.18.

4. Verify that the cube was accessed by viewing the field list and scrolling down the page to confirm that the Office Web Component PivotTable control and Chart control are visible and active.

5. Confirm that all items on the toolbar over each control are active by clicking on them, as shown in Figure 12.19.

6. Select Cancel at the bottom of the page after validation is complete.

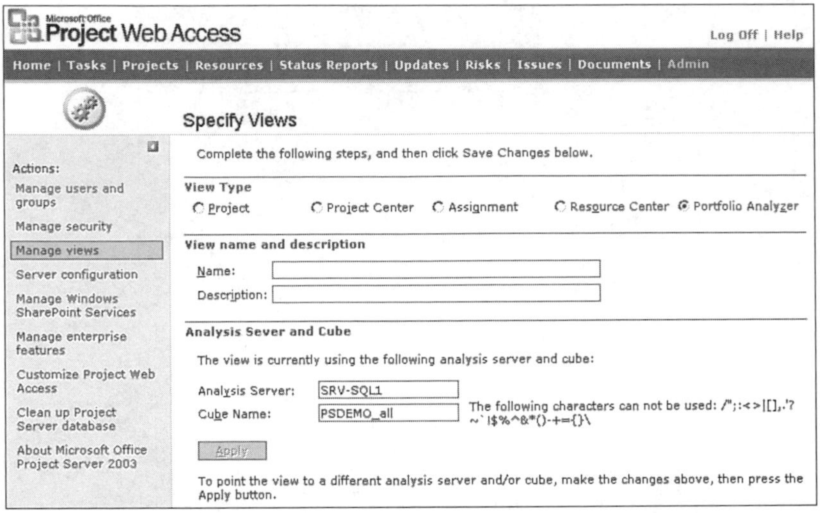

FIGURE 12.18 Selecting Portfolio Analyzer on the view creation page should connect to the OLAP server.

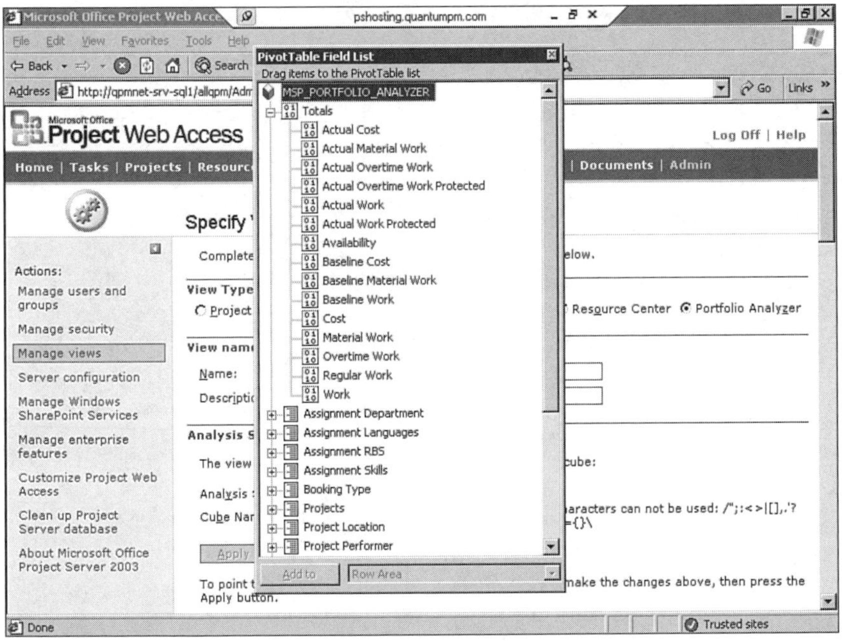

FIGURE 12.19 Check that the field list appears if you are able to connect to the OLAP server.

Level 2—Basic Project Server Configuration

Basic Project Server configuration validation consists of defining roles and representative users for these group definitions in Project Server 2003 and conducting *role test cases*. The tests verify that the role has the proper access to the features and functions in Project Server for the role they are performing in the business process. These roles include portfolio managers, project managers, resource managers, executives, team leads, and team members. Each user is created with Project Server authentication and assigned to the corresponding role group.

User Role Validation

Start the validation process by defining the roles in Project Server. Create multiple users for each of the default groups predefined in PWA, as shown in Figure 12.20. Having more than one user for each group is used in the next section for validating data access requirements from the configuration.

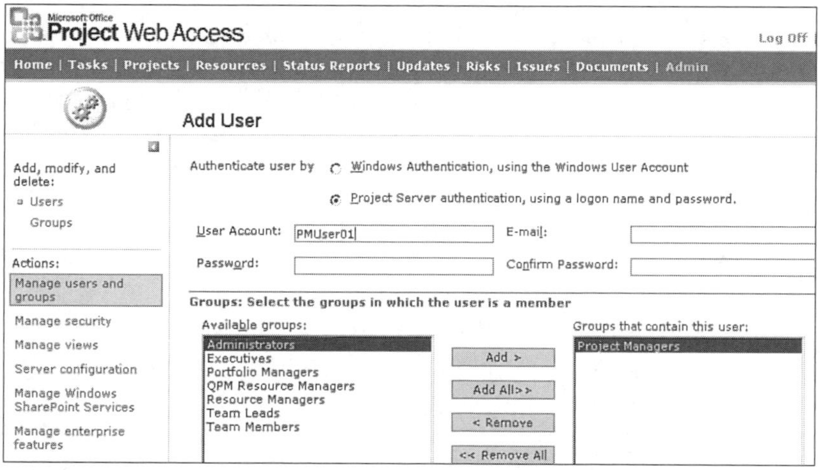

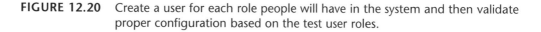

FIGURE 12.20   Create a user for each role people will have in the system and then validate proper configuration based on the test user roles.

Security Setup Validation

Run test case scenarios for each user or group of users. Start with the roles that create and manage project and resource data first. Then continue with project team roles and the decision support roles such as executives and portfolio managers. Each scenario should confirm proper feature and function capabilities required by each role.

Data Access Validation

Verify that each user or group has the correct data access for the role the user or group represents.

> **NOTE**
>
> Note what data is available to see and edit during the test case scenarios.

Keep the users created for this validation to use in the business process validation. Delete any project test data created to validate functionality.

Level 3—Business Process Validation

Business process validation is similar to server configuration validation with one exception. Now that the configuration has been validated for functionality, it can be validated for the business process it is intended to support.

This validation involves setting up representative test project and resource data to verify the business process flow using the toolset.

User Role Configuration

Configure the test users created previously to represent specific roles in the business process. Examples of this would be project managers for a particular set of projects or resource managers defined for specific resource pools. Configure each test user with the appropriate outline code assignments, such as RBS, location, or other codes defined for the configuration. The RBS is used extensively during this validation. A resource pool of test resources (including the roles being validated) needs to be configured as well. Finally, prepare representative project data to import into the database for all the test case scenarios.

Validate Business Process Test Scenarios

Run the test scenarios for each role. These scenarios should follow the basic process flow and life cycle of activities the user role will perform during those processes. Examples of test scenarios include project initiation—all roles, project planning—all roles, project execution and tracking—all roles, change control—all roles, and project closure—all roles.

Database Cleanup

Clean up the database of all test scenario data after validation is complete, as shown in Figures 12.21 and 12.22. Be careful to remove data in the following order to avoid leaving orphaned data records in the database:

1. Project data with accompanying Windows SharePoint Site

2. Resource data

3. Views

4. Categories

5. Users

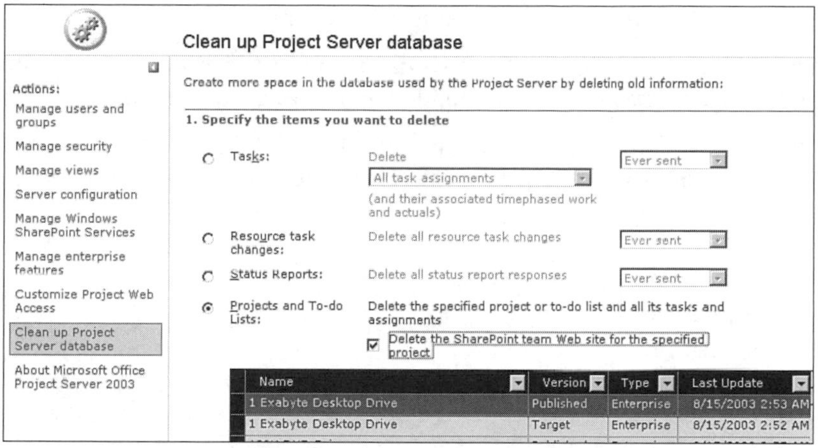

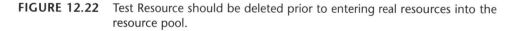

FIGURE 12.21   Select both the Projects and To-Do Lists radio button and the associated SharePoint site option when deleting test projects.

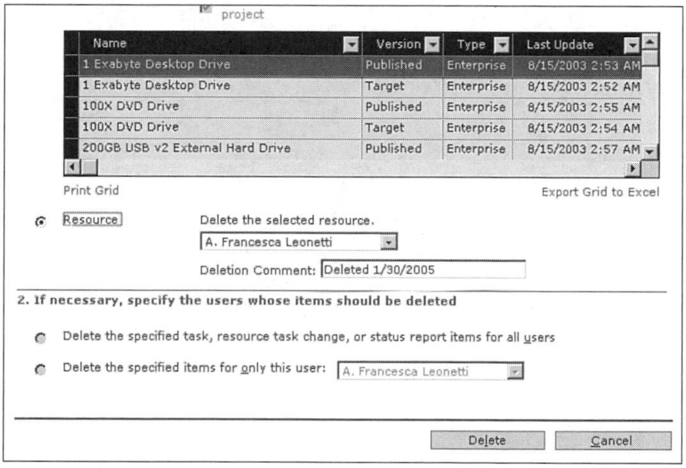

FIGURE 12.22   Test Resource should be deleted prior to entering real resources into the resource pool.

Best Practices

Given the complexity of the project management business process and the versatility of Project Server, it is always important to do a systematic validation of the application setup and configuration. Following these best practices ensures a smooth deployment and transition to the organization adapting this toolset:

- Run a technical validation of the servers and network architecture.

- Validate installation of all applications involved in the EPM system.

- Verify network authentication for Project Server and Windows SharePoint Services.

- Validate the basic configuration of the database to confirm use, functionality, and proper data access based on the intended user roles of the application.

- Verify that the application is configured to support the standard business processes of the organization intending to use Project Server, PWA, and Windows SharePoint Services.

Troubleshooting Business Process Implementation in the Application

IN THIS CHAPTER

- Common Implementation Issues, Causes, and Suggested Remedies

- Issues with Mapping of Business Process in the Project Server 2003

- Best Practices

This chapter presents suggestions for troubleshooting the Microsoft Office Project 2003 configuration from the application point of view. It also addresses issues related to configuration rather than issues related to troubleshooting the installation.

Sometimes the application may not respond as intended, and that may be due to installation, technical, or network issues. Project 2003 is a complex Enterprise Project Management (EPM) solution, and the cause of certain unexpected behavior may have multiple reasons. This chapter summarizes the most common problems encountered when deploying Project 2003.

Common Implementation Issues, Causes, and Suggested Remedies

Some of the most common problems that arise in the Project 2003 implementation are related to security, accessibility, and data errors. This section outlines some of the most common scenarios and the appropriate fixes for the problems.

Project Web Access Administrator Account Does Not Work As Expected

Possible causes:

- Improper IIS and Windows Server security.

- Improper IIS integration with Project Server.

- SQL Server database for Project Server is not operational.
- Core Project Server ASPs are not installed and are not functioning.
- Connection Manager Service is not operational.
- Project Server does not recognize user machine configuration details.
- User account on local machine cannot download and install ActiveX components.
- ActiveX downloads were not installed as expected.

Suggested remedy is to check the installation and make sure that the user has enough security permissions on IIS and Windows Server.

▶ **SEE** "Designing the Enterprise Project Management Solution Architecture Details," **PAGE 109**.

Cannot Create Project Web Access Windows-Authenticated Accounts

Possible causes:

- Improper Project Server and Windows Server security integration.
- Improper IIS integration with Project Server.
- Project Server accounts: `MSProjectServerUser` is not functioning.

Suggested remedies:

- Check domain names and usernames.
- Make sure that users have proper security permission on Project Server and Windows Server.
- Check the Project Server and Windows Server installation.

    ▶ **SEE** "Designing the Enterprise Project Management Solution Architecture Details," **PAGE 109**.

Timesheets Do Not Show Expected Data Entry Mode

A possible cause for this is that Project Web Access (PWA) Tracking Settings were not configured properly.

Suggested remedies:

- Make sure that the appropriate method of time tracking has been selected.
- Make sure that proper views have been defined for the timesheets.

Project Managers Cannot Open a Schedule in Project Professional 2003 When Clicking on the Project in Line in Project Web Access

Possible causes:

- Microsoft Project Server account has not been properly set up.

- User does not have sufficient permission to open a project schedule in PWA.

Suggested remedies:

- User belongs to a group that has permission to open the schedule.

- User is assigned to a category that allows users to open a project.

- Project Professional is installed and that it connects to Project Server.

  ▶ **SEE** "Designing the Enterprise Project Management Solution Architecture Details," **PAGE 109**.

Resource Managers Cannot See Any Resource Information

Possible causes:

- User does not have sufficient permission to see resource information.

- No views have been defined for Resource Center.

Suggested remedies:

- Check permissions and make sure that the user belongs to a group that has permission to see the resource information.

- Make sure that the user is assigned to a category that allows users to see the resource information and that the user is assigned to the appropriate branch of the RBS.

Some Users Can Access Project Portfolio Feature Although They Are Not Supposed to See It

A possible cause of this problem is that the user belongs to a group that has permission to access Portfolio Analyzer.

Suggested remedies:

- Check permissions on security template for the group and the categories that the user can access.

- Make sure that the user does not have access to Portfolio Analyzer through a combination of groups and categories permissions.

  ▶ **SEE** "Establishing Security Model Settings," **PAGE 143**.

13

Project Portfolio Security Issue

It is possible that project managers can access Project Portfolio, and they can see all projects and resources, although they are not supposed to see them according to the categories that they can access. A possible cause for this problem is that categories do not control individual settings for Portfolio Analyzer.

A suggested remedy for this is when a user is granted access to Portfolio Analyzer, she can view all projects and resources in the enterprise and their respective metrics.

User Cannot See the Projects and Resources According to His Group Security Permissions

Possible causes:

- User belongs to groups that cannot access categories that allow him to see certain projects and/or resources.

- No appropriate views have been defined for the categories that the user may access.

Suggested remedies:

- Check the groups' permissions and make sure that the groups can access the right categories.

    ▶ **SEE** "Creating Project Web Access Project and Resource Views," **PAGE 209**.

TIP

If a set of resources has special data permission needs, create a new group and assign the new category to it before assigning the special resources to the group. This method makes security management significantly easier than maintaining the security system based on a mix of group and individual user permissions.

- Make sure that the appropriate views have been defined and that the user groups can access these views.

User Cannot Save a Project Schedule As a Template

A possible cause is that the user does not have sufficient permission to save a project template in the groups to which she belongs.

Suggested remedies:

- Check the security templates of the relevant groups for the user.

- Check the security permission (Save Project Template) for the groups relevant to the user. This permission allows users to create and save a project as an Enterprise Project Template from Project Professional to the Project Server database.

User Does Not Receive Email Notification When She Has Been Assigned a New Task

Possible causes:

- Project Server is not properly processing the alerts.

- Project Server connections to SMTP email are not functioning correctly.

- The user cleared the check boxes in the Notification section that allow the system to send email notifications.

Suggested remedies:

- Check the installation notes and make sure that the email notification is working properly.

- Check the settings in the Notification page.

User Cannot See Documents, Risks, and Issues

Possible causes:

- Windows SharePoint Services site links are not created, and WSS is not functioning as expected.

- User does not have access to view Documents, Risks, and Issues.

Suggested remedies:

- Check to make sure that Project Server and Windows SharePoint Services integration is functioning correctly.

- Verify that the Windows SharePoint Services SQL Server configuration database is working properly.

- Make sure that Windows SharePoint Services SQL Server database repository for documents is enabled.

- Check to make sure that the COM+ subsystem is functioning properly.

- Ensure that the Project Server and Windows SharePoint Services database table cross-references are updated as expected.

- Check the security permissions (View Documents, View Issues) assigned to user.

- Make sure that the user is granted permission to View Risks, Issues, and Documents in the categories that he or she can access.

  ▶ SEE "Establishing Security Model Settings," PAGE 143.

User Cannot Delegate Tasks

Possible causes:

- User does not have sufficient security permissions to delegate tasks.

- Delegation of tasks is a permission that has been denied at the enterprise level.

Suggested remedies:

- Check the security permissions (Delegate Task) for the groups relevant to the user.

- Check with the system administrator to make sure that denying delegation at the server level is an appropriate setting.

- Ensure that the user is not a member of a category that allows users to Assign Resources.

User Cannot Create a New Task and Insert It Into Any Available Project

A possible cause for this problem is that the user does not have sufficient security permissions to create a new project task.

Suggested remedies:

- Check with the system administrator to make sure that the user is allowed by the business process to create a new task.

- Check the security permissions (New Project Task) for the groups relevant to the user. This is a global permission that allows users to access the Create a New Task page in the Tasks center of PWA.

- Check the security permissions to make sure that the user has access to the projects to which he wants to create and insert the task.

Users Cannot Assign Themselves to an Existing Task in Projects That Have Been Published to Project Server

A possible cause for this problem is that users do not have sufficient security permissions to assign themselves to an existing project task.

Suggested remedies:

- Check with the system administrator to make sure that users are allowed by the business process to assign themselves to a project task.

- Check the security permissions (New Task Assignment) for the groups relevant to the user. This is a global permission that allows users to access the Assign Myself to an Existing Task page in the Tasks center of PWA.

- Check the security permissions to make sure that the user has access to the projects to which he wants to create and insert the task.

- Users must also have the category permission Create New Tasks or Assignment, and they must also have access to the projects to which they want to assign themselves.

  ▶ SEE "Establishing Security Model Settings," **PAGE 143**.

Users Cannot Manage Status Report Requests

A possible cause for this problem is that the user does not have sufficient security permissions to manage Status Report requests.

Suggested remedies:

- Check with the system administrator to make sure that the user is allowed by the business process to manage status report requests.

- Check the security permission (Manage Status Report Requests) for the groups relevant to the user. This is global permission that allows users to access the Request a Status Report feature and to view team reports.

- Check the security permission (View Status Report List) to make sure that the user can view the list of status reports.

MERGING STATUS REPORTS

The Merge check box shown in the Resources Who Should Respond box defines whether the response from each individual automatically is included in the consolidated status report group. If you want to review the responses before adding them to a consolidated report, leave the check box unchecked.

User Cannot Create and Manage To-Do Lists

A possible cause for this problem is that users do not have sufficient security permissions to create and manage To-Do lists.

Suggested remedies:

- Check with the system administrator to make sure that the user is allowed by the business process to create and manage To-Do lists.

- Check the security permissions (Create and Manage To-Do List) for the groups relevant to the user. This is a global permission that allows users to access the Manage My To-Do Lists and Create a New Personal or Shared To-Do List pages in Project.

- If the user needs to assign activities on her To-Do list to other members of the team, they need to be granted the Assign To-Do List Tasks global permission. This is necessary to make available to the user a list of individuals that she can assign the To-Do list activities.

13

User Cannot Find a Specific Task That He Was Working on in His Timesheet

A possible cause for this problem is that the user hid, intentionally or by mistake, the specified task.

A task that has been deleted using the Hide Task method removes the item from the Project Server database, but it will not be deleted from the actual project schedule. To make it visible again, the project manager must republish the project schedule to the Project Server database.

User Cannot Add a New Resource to His Project/Organization

A possible cause for this problem is that the user has insufficient security rights to add new resources.

Suggested remedies:

- Check with the system administrator to make sure that users are allowed by the business process to add new resources.

- Check the security permissions (New Resource) for the groups relevant to the user. This permission allows users to add new resources to the Enterprise Resource Pool using Project Professional or the Project Data Service (PDS).

- If your organization is using the Active Directory synchronization feature, it is better to deny this permission and grant it only to IT administrators in your organization.

Team Member Did Not Get His Task Assignment on the Timesheet Page, Although the Project Manager Saved the Project Schedule

A possible cause of this problem is that new task assignments have not been published to Project Server.

To remedy this situation, the project manager must publish the task assignments for the team members to be able to see these assignments on their timesheet.

Project Managers Cannot Change the Method for Reporting Progress on Projects

A possible cause of this problem is that business processes have been defined to "not allow" project managers to change the default method for reporting progress.

Suggested remedies:

- Make sure that Tracking Settings have not been set to Force Project Managers to Use the Progress Reporting Method Specified Above for All Projects. If this is the case, project managers cannot change the progress reporting method.

- Select the Allow Project Managers to Change the Default Method for Reporting Progress If a Different Method Is Appropriate for a Specific Project option in the Tracking Settings page.

Project Managers Cannot Save the Baseline

Possible causes:

- The user has insufficient permission to save or clear the baseline.

- Business processes identify only certain individuals who can save or clear the baseline.

Suggested remedies:

- Check with the system administrator to make sure that users are allowed by the business process to save the baseline for the project.

- Check the security permissions (Save Baseline) for the groups relevant to the user. This permission allows users to save a baseline or clear a baseline associated with an enterprise project published to the Project Server database.

- Make sure that users have the category permission Save Project, and they must also have access to the projects to which they want to save the baseline.

Issues with Mapping of Business Process in the Project Server 2003

When implementing the EPM solution, you must keep in mind that the solution itself is a combination of Project Server 2003 configuration and business process adjustment. Some business processes that were in place before implementation of the EPM solution may need to be reviewed and analyzed to make sure that they do not contradict the process flow in Project Server.

Although the majority of business processes can be mapped against the Project Server solution, there are cases where the software does not support certain functions. In the absence of these features, it is important that you have documented the business processes in place.

For instance, if a team member rejects an assignment, it is advisable to insert a note informing the project manager about the reason why she is declining the task.

Troubleshooting the Resource Allocation Process

It is important for the deploying organization to set up the proper resource allocation process to be followed by project and resource managers.

Although each deploying organization has its own specific methodology and policies for allocating resources, it is important that participants in the resource allocation process understand their specific role. For example, project managers are responsible for project schedules and for allocation of generic resources, whereas resource managers are responsible for substitution of generic resources with specific individuals.

In this case, the process flow could be represented by the following steps:

1. The project manager and the management team members develop the project schedule and assign generic resources to tasks in the schedule.

2. Resource managers review the project schedule relevant to their area of expertise and make suggestions to project managers on the best individual candidate for each task.

3. The project manager and resource managers agree on the specific individuals who will work on each task. They also agree on the constraints of the task, such as duration and level of effort.

4. The project manager and/or resource manager communicate the assignment to specific individuals designated for the tasks.

5. Individual team members receive the assignment and accept or reject it.

6. If a team member rejects an assignment, she must inform the project manager and resource manager about this decision. In this case, the project manager, resource manager, and team member try to resolve the conflict. If after discussions it becomes apparent that the individual selected first is not the best choice, the resource manager allocates another individual to the task, and the process comes back to Step 5. But if the team member accepts the assignment, the process moves to the next step—performing the task.

7. When the task is completed, the team member informs the project and resource managers that the task is 100% complete and that she is available to work on the next assignment.

8. The project manager and the resource manager agree that the task has been indeed fully completed, and the project manager marks the task 100% complete.

The preceding process can be easily mapped in Project Server 2003. But it is also important to remember that certain decisions have to be made by the project or resource managers.

It is important to remember that a task is marked 100% complete only when the project manager agrees that the task is indeed finished.

Troubleshooting Data Accuracy: Data Presented in the Database Is Inconsistent with Reality

One of the biggest challenges is to make sure that the information contained in the system is accurate and representative of the reality.

It is worth mentioning here that the deploying organization must set standards for maintaining the accuracy of data. As such, the deploying organization may set as a rule that all team members update their timesheets by a certain day of the week, and that project managers update and reconcile the data received from team members within 24 or 48 hours. In doing so, the deploying organization makes sure that all projects have been properly progressed and that the data is reliable. This in turn ensures that decisions based on the existent information in the database have a strong foundation.

Troubleshooting Portfolio Analyzer: Data Is Not in Sync with the Information from Project or Resource Center

Portfolio Analyzer is a powerful feature in Project 2003 based on OLAP cube generation and compiles data about every resource in every project for every assignment. As such, generation of a new cube is server intensive, and it is only generated when scheduled or when initiated by the system administrator.

Therefore, the Portfolio Analyzer may be updated only once a day, or once a week, at a certain time. Any changes made to project schedules and assignments after the OLAP cube processing is initiated are not reflected immediately. They will be reflected only when the OLAP cube is run again or at the next scheduled update. So, it is possible that between two updates, the data in the Project Center and the Resource Center will be different from the data that exists in Portfolio Analyzer.

> **TIP**
>
> It is recommended that the deploying organization establish a schedule for updating the OLAP cube and make that schedule available and known to anyone who has access to Portfolio Analyzer. This ensures consistency of data analysis and ensures that comparisons of various project and resource metrics are relevant.

Troubleshooting Incorrect Results for Projects in Progress When You Use the Portfolio Modeler or the Resource Substitution Wizard

Portfolio Modeler and the Resource Substitution Wizard are two useful features that can help project and resource managers understand what resources can work on a particular project. The two features were designed to help managers consider the appropriate trade-offs in cases where projects are competing for the same resources.

Most organizations only have a limited number of resources available to work on projects, and project and resource managers are often faced with questions on how to best deploy their resources so that the use of resources is maximized.

Essentially, Portfolio Modeler is a great feature to understand whether there are enough resources to cover the work needed for all projects, and, if not, how to best redistribute projects in such a way that the impact on schedule is minimized.

Given those constraints and the underlying technology, it is important to understand that if you want to use these tools on projects with actual data posted, you must schedule any remaining work after the status date. This ensures that you will receive the correct results.

Troubleshooting Adjust Actuals: Cannot Change the Remaining Work Field When Adjusting Actuals

If your organization has chosen to use the Managed Time Period feature of Project 2003, at times you may need to adjust the actual work entered by your resources after a time period is closed. You can also use this feature if a resource is absent and you need to enter actual work for the resource.

It is important to understand that you cannot change the Remaining Work field. This feature is only for changing the actuals reported by the resource. The adjustment is sent to the project manager who follows the usual procedures for reviewing and updating the change into the project schedule through the Updates page.

Troubleshooting the Updates: Cannot View All Past Task Updates

Project Server stores an archive of past task updates that the project manager has received. This allows the project manager to review the history of task updates received for all their projects and resources.

The administrator can specify the number of days for which the history is kept up to 60 days. Any task updates older than 60 days cannot be displayed.

Troubleshooting the Application of Rules: Setting the Rule Produces Unexpected Results

In some cases where you have many resources working for you, you might want to create a set of rules that automatically accept changes and updates from resources based on various parameters. For instance, maybe you will automatically accept updates when "% Complete" = "100".

To process the task updates using the rules, you must click the Run Rules Now button on the Apply Rules tab. This applies each time resource updates are to be processed. The drop-down box allows you to apply the rules to selected projects or to those specified in the rules. You can limit the rules by the types of tasks, certain projects, or certain resources.

Only those names of resources with permissions to send updates and delegate tasks are available when creating rules. Rules take precedence.

> **CAUTION**
>
> A rule may override the Accept setting in the updates grid if the rule is applied to updated project progress.

Troubleshooting Duplicate Global.mpt Files

When you use the Standard edition of Microsoft Project, or work offline using Project Professional, Microsoft Project loads not only your project schedule file but also another file called Global.mpt. This global file holds basic default configuration information about your project environment. This is a local Global.mpt. It is similar to a user profile that defines the way you want to view and use your project files. This global file was used in previous editions of Microsoft Project to allow people to share custom fields, views, filters, tables, reports, and calendars by using the Organizer.

With the Enterprise edition of Project, you now have an enterprise global file that is launched and merged with your local global file and project files when you connect to Project Server. The enterprise global, which is configured by the Project 2003 administrator, loads into memory and caches all enterprise calendar, views, tables, and field settings for your projects. Toolbars and menus are then added from the local global template file— in particular, localized toolbars and menus—nonduplicate custom items from the local global are added to the cached enterprise global file.

Enterprise global items are copied into the project on demand. The Project Professional user sees both the enterprise items and the local items, as long as the names are not duplicated. If duplicates are found, the user is given a chance to rename the local items. When the project is saved back to the Project Server, enterprise items are not saved in the project plan. However, if there is a need to work offline, the enterprise items can be copied into the project plan.

If you have a local view named the same as a view in the enterprise global, you get messages saying that you need to rename the local file. This often happens when you import files. To remove the local view and this message, close the project, make sure that you are not in the view you want to remove, and select Tools, Organizer. Select the View tab and remove the view using the Organizer for the project.

Troubleshooting Versions: I Cannot Delete the Published Version

A *version* is a complete copy of the plan when it was published in Project Server and all the versions are stored on EP.

The published version is always the version for any project plan created within EP. It is the authorized copy of the project plan, and the published version name cannot be renamed or deleted.

> **TIP**
>
> Data from timesheets is generated only from the published version.
>
> Saving of a project plan to a new version is not related to the process of saving a new baseline within the project plan.
>
> The saving of a new version does not affect enterprise resources.

Troubleshooting Resource Calendars: Tasks Extend Their Duration Unexpectedly

Each resource has her own calendar. By default, the resource calendar is based on the standard calendar, which defines only weekends as nonworking time. You may edit the standard calendar to define a companywide enterprise calendar. The resource calendar then will reflect your organization's holidays but not a particular resource's vacations or other individual exceptions. Some resources may be on a different work schedule (consider equipment or part-time resources) and need to be assigned a unique calendar customized to match the actual availability of the resource. Usually, in the enterprise environment, the administrator manages the resource work calendars, and the project manager may not change them. If no custom resource calendar has been defined for a resource, the standard calendar is the default for each resource.

The advantage of a resource calendar is that the Project Professional scheduling engine will not schedule the resource during the time period indicated as nonworking for the resource. If a task is scheduled during the time period a resource is shown as unavailable, the Professional scheduling engine moves the task's end date out to account for that time off.

> **NOTE**
>
> Resource calendars take precedence over other types of calendars. However, if you are also using a Task calendar, you can specify on the Advanced tab in Task Information to ignore resource calendars and schedule a task to ignore the resource's nonworking time.

Best Practices

In cases when users cannot perform certain functions, make sure that

- Business processes prohibit users from accessing these functions. For example, if a project manager cannot access Project Portfolio, make sure that the business process does not allow them to view Portfolio Analyzer. If the business process does not allow project managers to access this feature, it means that the system has been properly configured.

- Users have sufficient permissions at the group level and that they can access categories with sufficient security permissions.

- Certain functions have not been denied at the server level.

In cases where users cannot access certain pages, make sure that views have been defined for the data categories and that they are accessible by users.

Always document changes made to the security model or to views, and make sure that these changes are in line with the organization's business rules.

PART V

Using Microsoft Office Project Web Access 2003

IN THIS PART

CHAPTER 14 Project Web Access Collaboration 293

CHAPTER 15 Time Tracking in Project Web Access 317

CHAPTER 16 Using Project and Resource Centers 345

CHAPTER 17 Portfolio Management Using Portfolio Analyzer and Portfolio Modeler 393

CHAPTER 18 Risks, Issues, and Documents Using Windows SharePoint Services (WSS) 441

CHAPTER 19 Using the Project Web Access Admin Menu Tab 477

Project Web Access Collaboration

IN THIS CHAPTER

- Using PWA
- Using the Home Page
- Managing Alerts
- Exchanging Textual Information Using Status Reports
- Best Practices

Project Web Access (PWA) is the main face of Microsoft Office Project Server 2003 because everyone uses it. It is the web application that allows all Project Server 2003 users to easily access project information, which is stored and managed through the set of functions found within PWA as illustrated in Figure 14.1. Everyone in your organization needs to understand it.

Using PWA

Although only the project manager (and maybe a resource manager and a portfolio manager) uses Microsoft Office Project Professional, all resources needing access to project information use PWA to some extent. Team members use PWA to see the tasks they have been assigned, and project managers and resource managers use it to approve actual work reported on the assigned tasks. Team members and project managers communicate about a project's issues and risks and use it to store, review, and revise project documents.

Perhaps more importantly, PWA provides executives and other managers views into the organization's overall performance through executive dashboards on project portfolios and resource utilization. The Project Center and Resource Center provide the visibility to the entire organization's project status and progress.

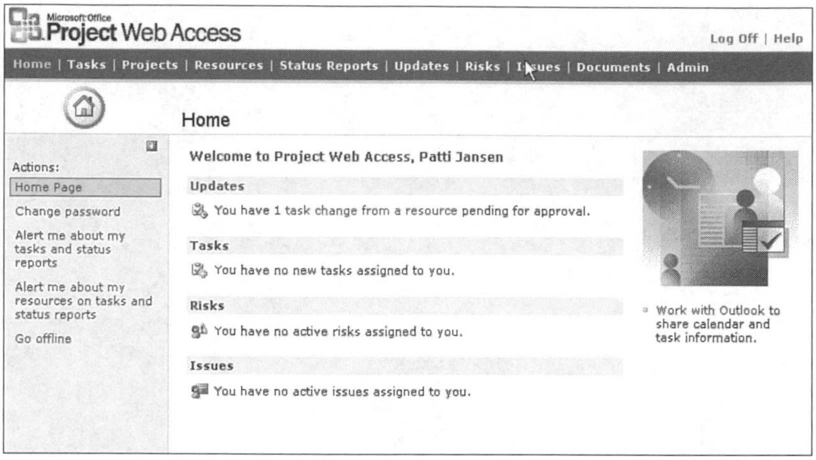

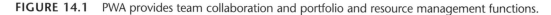

FIGURE 14.1   PWA provides team collaboration and portfolio and resource management functions.

Using PWA Functions

Your organization may employ PWA in a variety of ways. Table 14.1 explains the default functions set for some of the roles for the Project Server 2003 in PWA (this does not discuss permissions for Project Professional). You may want your organization to allow more or fewer features or functions. For instance, by default, team members cannot see their own availability in the Resource Center. You might want to change the default setting and allow them to use the View Availability function. Use this table as a basis to develop your own organization's understanding of how your roles will use PWA.

Make sure that you think about how people might play dual roles in your organization. For example, your functional managers may or may not enter time in a timesheet. If they do, you need to make those individuals in your organization both resource managers and team members. If not, just assign them as resource managers.

▶ **SEE** "Establishing Security Model Settings," **PAGE 143**.

TABLE 14.1   Default Features Available in PWA for Some Project Server Roles

Screen	Team Members	Project Managers	Resource Managers	Portfolio Managers	Executives
Home	View Home page to see their tasks, issues, risks, and document status. • Change password. • Set personal email notifications. • Go offline with PWA. • Use Outlook add-in to allow timesheet reporting in Outlook.	Same as team member with the following addition: • Set email notifications for project resources.	Same as project manager settings.	Same as project manager settings.	Same as project manager settings.

TABLE 14.1   Continued

Screen	Team Members	Project Managers	Resource Managers	Portfolio Managers	Executives
Tasks	View Tasks page to update and submit actual work. • Can create a new task in a project they have already been assigned to. • Can assign themselves to an existing task in a project they have already been assigned to. • Change work days (notify manager of days you're not available for project work). • Hide task. • Use Outlook add-in to allow timesheet reporting in Outlook.	Same as team member with following addition: • Delegate tasks.	Tasks tab does not appear. Note: This assumes resource managers will not be entering time in timesheets.	Tasks tab does not appear. Note: This assumes portfolio managers will not be entering time in timesheets.	Tasks tab does not appear. Note: This assumes executives will not be entering time in timesheets.
Project Center	View projects and details for projects they are assigned to. • Create and update to-do lists and assign to-do tasks.	View projects and details for projects they are assigned to and manage. Same as team member with the following additions: • Use Build Team. • Open projects in Project Professional from the Project Center. • Check in their own projects. • Edit project attributes.	Same as project manager with the following change: • Create and manage administrative projects.	Views all projects and details for projects. Same as project manager with the following changes: • View Resource Modeler. • View Portfolio Analyzer.	View all projects and details for projects. Also includes • View Resource Modeler. • View Portfolio Analyzer.

14

TABLE 14.1 Continued

Screen	Team Members	Project Managers	Resource Managers	Portfolio Managers	Executives
Resource Center	Resource tab does not appear.	See resource data and assignment detail for resources assigned to their projects. Includes • Adjust Actuals.	Same as project manager with the following additions: • View availability. • Edit resource attributes. For managed timesheets: • View and approve timesheets.	View all resources and their assignment and utilization data for their projects. Also includes • View Portfolio Analyzer.	View all resources and their assignment and utilization data Also includes • View Portfolio Analyzer.
Updates	Updates tab does not appear.	Has all update functions available including manage rules and view archived transactions.	Updates tab does not appear. If the resource manager needs to manage administrative projects, the resource manager should be given project manager permissions.	Updates tab does not appear. If the portfolio portfolio manager is to manage projects, should be given project manager permissions.	Updates tab does not appear.
Status Reports	Submit status reports.	May create and submit status.	Same as project manager.	Status report tab does not appear.	Same as project manager.
Issues	View, create, and edit issues for project they are assigned to.	View, create, and edit issues for projects they are assigned to or manage.	View, create, and edit. issues for projects they are assigned to or manage.	View, create, and edit. issues for projects they are assigned to.	View, create, and edit issues for projects they are assigned to.

TABLE 14.1   Continued

Screen	Team Members	Project Managers	Resource Managers	Portfolio Managers	Executives
Risks	View, create, and edit risks for projects they they are assigned to.	View, create, and edit risks for projects they are assigned to or manage.	View, create, and edit risks for projects they are assigned to or manage.	View, create, and edit risks for projects they are assigned to.	View, create, and edit risks for projects they are assigned to.
Documents	View, create, and edit documents for projects they are assigned to.	View, create, and edit documents for projects they are assigned to or manage.	View, create, and edit documents for projects they are assigned to or manage.	View, create, and edit documents for projects they are assigned to.	View, create, and edit documents for projects they are assigned to.
Workspace	View workspace for projects they are assigned to.	Create and edit events, announcements, links, issues, risks, and docs for projects they manage or are assigned to.	View workspace for projects they are assigned to.	View workspace for projects they are assigned to.	View workspace for projects they are assigned to.
Admin	No access.	No access.	No access.	Allows managing of Project Center and Resource Center views.	No access.

14

PWA Data Creation

Data updates to PWA essentially occur in three ways:

- Project Professional schedules are created and updated. Project managers use Microsoft Office Project Professional 2003 to develop work breakdown structures, assign team members to working tasks, save project schedules into the Project Server database repository, and update project progress. Each time the project manager publishes a project schedule, Project Server automatically manages information storage locations and transmits messages to team members and others who need to review updated project schedule and resource information.

  Team members, project managers, and other PWA users see the project information and can interact with the data using Project Server electronic collaboration techniques. As team members update project collaboration data, automatic messages (if email alerts are turned on in the system) are transmitted to the team members so that they can review the changes and stay informed about key project status and content.

▶ **SEE** "Managing Alerts" in this chapter, **PAGE 305**.

Data from Project Professional goes to the Tasks page (if the project manager chooses to publish information to update assignments), the Project Center, and the Resource Center (again, depending on how the project manager chooses to update the schedule information). Ultimately, it is also used by Portfolio Analyzer to create static reports for management analysis.

- When a schedule is created, if automatic updates are set for site creation, a Windows SharePoint Services (WSS) subsite is created, and documents, issues, and risks may then be created and updated for the project. All this data is updated in the WSS repository.

    ▶ **SEE** "Risks, Issues, and Documents Using Windows SharePoint Services (WSS)," **PAGE 441**.

After the WSS subsites are created, PWA users are given access to that information based on their individual Project Server security permissions to a project. If the PWA administrator changes user permissions, Project Server automatically directs WSS to update permissions accordingly.

The flow diagram in Figure 14.2 illustrates the WSS subsite creation.

After the project schedule collaboration infrastructure is established, PWA users can view project data and use the collaboration features to share information.

- Status reports are not connected to WSS or a particular schedule being created in Project Professional. The status reports are created and updated in PWA tables.

Using PWA to Its Full Advantage

Although team members will use PWA to communicate status and provide important actual work data, it is the domain of two major groups: the project manager for project communication and management for overall portfolio and resource management, analysis, and reporting. In assessing PWA, you will want to think about the processes and standards for these two domains.

Because communication is the major function of a project manager, the wise project manager will have a communications plan. She will use the collaboration features in PWA to help achieve the goals of the plan. Because decision-making is the major function of management, the organization must identify the key indicators that management needs to analyze and respond to project status and resource utilization.

As nice as the features are to have, if they are not used properly, the organization ends up with a great tool but doesn't have accurate or robust data because the organization didn't put processes and standards around the use of PWA. As you think about how you use the features, make sure that you design the processes around their use and communicate them often and effectively to the organization as a whole. If a project manager knows that the executive is looking at the status of his project in the Project Center each week and hears feedback about it, the project manager is more likely to update his project. If the team members understand when and why they are updating actual work on their task, perhaps the project will stay more up-to-date.

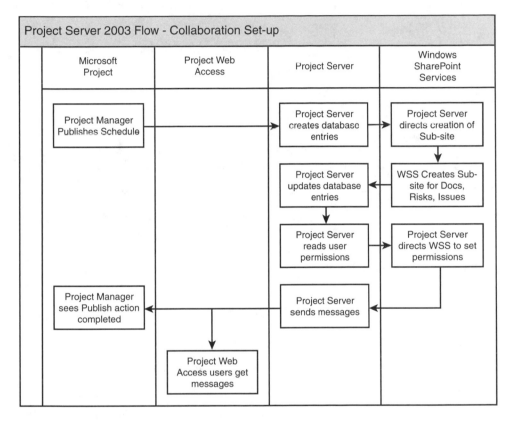

FIGURE 14.2   Project Server manages WSS information stores.

Accessing PWA

When the administrator adds you to the resource pool or authorizes you to use PWA, you are, by default, given access to log on and view the Home page in PWA as part of the team member group. The permissions of the tabs and functions you can use are set by the group you are associated with. So, after you are added to Project Server within a group role, you will log on to PWA by entering the URL address in Internet Explorer. If you are set for Windows Authentication logon, you immediately see the PWA Home page. If you are set for Project Server authentication, you see the following page and need to provide your username and password as shown in Figure 14.3.

> **NOTE**
>
> If you use Project Server authentication, you limit your use of the WSS issues, risks, and documents features.

FIGURE 14.3   Logon screen for PWA.

The screen shown in Figure 14.3 also appears after you log off PWA. If you are set as being Windows Authenticated and you want to enter PWA again from this screen, you must select Log On Using Your Microsoft Windows User Account on the left-side pane. If you try to type in your user ID and password, you get an error message.

First-Time Access to PWA

The first time you log on to PWA on your personal desktop or laptop you must accept a licensing agreement, and you must download the ActiveX controls. Also, you need to add the Project Server URL as a trusted site. To accomplish this, follow these steps:

1. Open Internet Explorer.

2. Choose Tools, Internet Options.

3. In the Internet Properties dialog box, choose the Security tab and then choose the Trusted sites zone. Click Sites.

4. In the Add This Web Site to the Zone text box, enter the name of the Project Server site. Use the following format http://computername.

5. Make sure that the Require Server Verification check box is not selected.

6. Click OK two times.

7. After you have updated the security settings, log on to the server by entering the Project Server name in Internet Explorer's URL Address text box and click Go. Accept the license agreement and click Next.

8. Click Yes to reply to the security warnings dialog boxes. You will see the PWA Home page.

In the Custom Level section of the same area in Internet Properties, make sure that all selections for ActiveX controls are enabled according to your organization's policies.

> **TIP**
>
> The administrator or implementer of Project Server should consider developing an instruction set to lead users through the first-time installation of PWA. You may also use Group Policies or System Management Server to help deploy the application for easier user setup.

Navigating PWA

The PWA interface screen is divided into four main areas as shown in Figure 14.4:

- **Menu tabs**—Use to navigate to the main functional areas of PWA. Refer to Figure 14.1 earlier in this chapter to see the full set of default menu tabs available. It is possible to add more functional menu tabs via customization of PWA as described in Chapter 17, "Portfolio Management Using Portfolio Analyzer and Portfolio Modeler." The tabs that appear depend on your permissions.

- **Side pane**—Use to select particular actions specific to the page displaying. You can open and shut the side pane using the button in the upper-right corner of the side pane. This is especially useful for seeing more on the Tasks page or a Portfolio Analyzer view. What actions appear depend on your permissions.

- **Content area**—Displays the content for the item selected via the menu and the side pane. By default, when you initially log on, this shows the Home page that displays an overview of items that have changed since the last time the user accessed PWA, and also items that require action.

- **Action bar**—On some main function pages, such as the Tasks page or Projects page, there is an action bar, which you use to take actions specific to the page displaying. You may not be able to perform some of the functions based on your permissions.

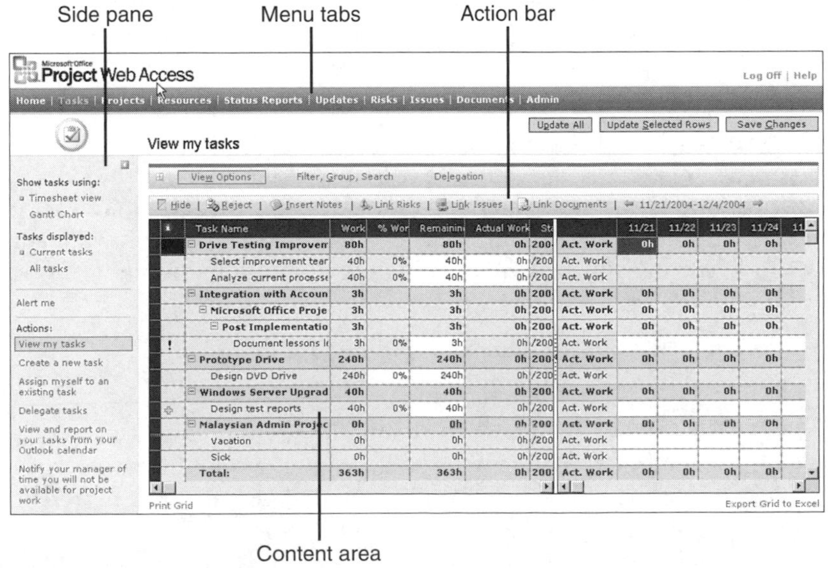

FIGURE 14.4   Navigation in PWA.

Using the Home Page

The Home page is the first screen you see when you successfully log on to PWA. You can access all your permitted PWA functions, and it displays status of tasks, risks, issues, and other items managed in PWA. For instance, if the project manager has assigned you a task, you will see that you have one new task assigned to you. After you view the task on your Tasks page, you will not see the note again. Refer to Figure 14.1 earlier in this chapter for an example of the Home page.

Status items in the Home content area show up only if they are new or if there is a change. The following may show in the content pane:

- **Updates**—Lets you know how many new task updates have been sent to you by your resources. This appears only for the project managers or others who can create and accept task updates for project schedules.

- **Timesheet**—If you are using the Managed Time Periods feature, this section provides the status of timesheets for manager approval. Otherwise, this does not appear. It describes what timesheets are still due for a particular open time period and, if they have been submitted, how many you still need to approve. This status is for organizations that have chosen to implement manager approvals. Project manager task approvals are performed under Updates.

- **Tasks**—Displays the number of your new task assignments and reminds you if you still need to submit your timesheet. The timesheet reminder shows only if your organization has chosen to use Managed Time Periods.

- **Risks**—Displays the number of active risks assigned to you.

- **Issues**—Displays the number of active issues assigned to you.

- **Status Reports**—Displays outstanding status reports you need to submit to your project manager or someone else who has requested status reports from you.

Changing Your Password

You can change your password via the Change Password selection on the side pane if you are given permission and you have a Project Server account for authentication. If users of the system are using a Windows account exclusively for authentication, your administrator might want to remove this feature for your organization. The administrator can do this via global permissions.

▶ **SEE** "Establishing Security Model Settings," **PAGE 143**.

Alert Me on the Home Page (Email Reminders)

Email reminders may be set to alert you about upcoming task due dates and to remind your resources of the same. This can be handy to remind you about status reports and other upcoming or late items in PWA.

▶ **SEE** "Managing Alerts," **PAGE 305**.

Working with PWA Offline

You can update tasks and status reports in PWA when you are not connected to your organization's network. When you go offline, you essentially have a snapshot of your timesheet and status report data to view, edit, and change on your local computer for the time frame you select. When you reconnect to the Project Server, the offline changes are synchronized with the current Project Server data.

TIP

You may want to consider removing the Go Offline function from the Home page by removing it from your organization's allowed permissions. This is because it usually takes only a few moments for resources to update task data, and if you are not using the Status Reports function, it may not be worth using this feature. Also, Internet options need to be changed and then reset on the local machine to make this feature work, which may be difficult for your PWA users to manage.

To start the offline process, set Internet options first and follow these steps:

1. In Internet Explorer, choose Tools, Internet Options. See Figure 14.5 for an example of the Internet Options dialog.

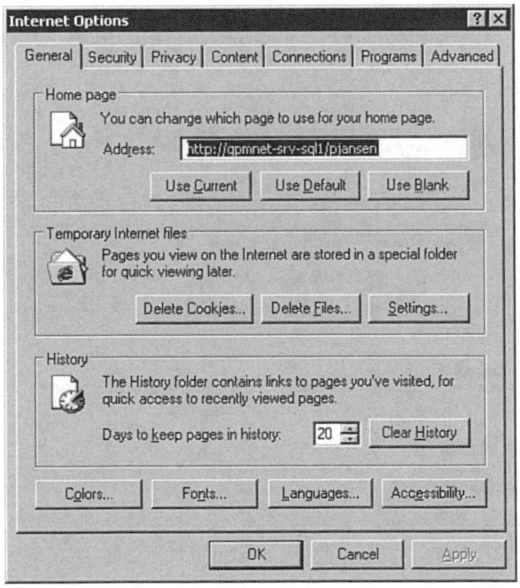

FIGURE 14.5 Before going offline, make sure that Internet Options are set properly.

2. Choose Security, click Local Intranet, and then click Custom Level.

3. In the Security Settings dialog box, under the Miscellaneous section, select Prompt for the Access Data Sources Across Domains.

4. Click OK and click Yes to indicate that you want to change the security settings.

5. In the same Internet Options dialog box, choose General.

6. In the Temporary Internet files section, click Settings.

7. In the Settings dialog box, choose Every Visit to the Page and click OK twice to close the Internet Options dialog box completely.

NOTE

Also make sure that you set all ActiveX settings to either Enable or Prompt in the Security tab of the local workstation's Internet Options. If any are disabled, you may not be able to go offline.

You may want to reset to your original Internet Options settings after you have completed working offline because other websites may run slower.

To go offline, follow these steps:

1. In the Home page side pane of PWA choose the Go Offline link.

2. Choose the dates for the information that you want to take offline. This is the time frame for the information you want to view, edit, or update.

3. Click Go Offline. You may receive messages related to ActiveX controls, and you should click Yes to allow them.

To access the offline information, do the following:

1. Choose File in Internet Explorer and make sure that the Work Offline option is checked.

2. Still in Internet Explorer, choose Favorites, Project Web Access.

Microsoft Project Web Access is added to the Favorites menu automatically. A copy of the Home page displays only the Home, Tasks, Status Reports, and Help menu tabs.

To go back online, complete these tasks:

1. Log on to PWA.

2. In the side pane of the Home page choose Go Online.

3. Click Connect to synchronize your offline changes, and then within the Offline Mode page, click Go Online.

If you choose Reset at this point, any changes made offline will not be saved. You can also choose to Stay Offline or Log Off. If you Log Off, you can choose to go online next time.

Microsoft Outlook and PWA Integration

If your organization uses Microsoft Outlook heavily and some of your users prefer working from Outlook, you can download some PWA functions to work within PWA. You can select to download the Outlook add-in from the Home page (and also the Tasks page) to update Tasks and view PWA dashboards or links from Outlook instead of using PWA. Figure 14.6 shows where you start the download process for the PWA add-in to Outlook.

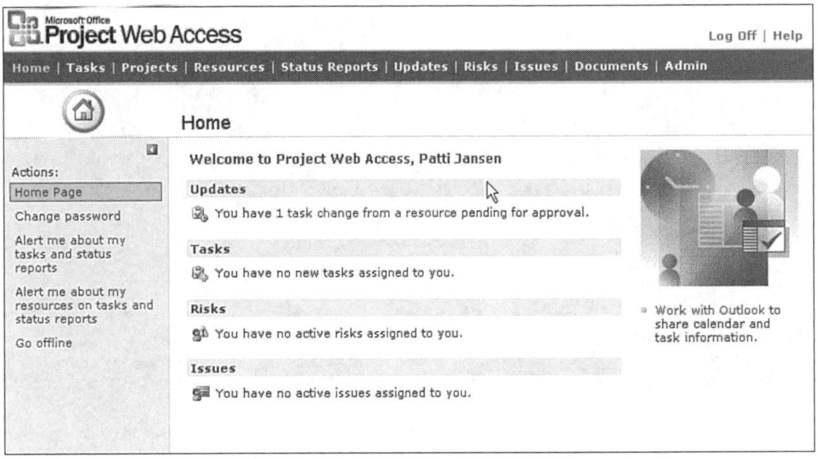

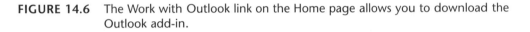

FIGURE 14.6   The Work with Outlook link on the Home page allows you to download the Outlook add-in.

Before this add-in will work, the PWA administrator must allow the Integration with External Timesheet System permission. When you use the Outlook download, make sure that you have permission as the local administrator or that your Windows policies allow you to perform this installation.

▶ **SEE** "Project Web Access and Project Professional Integration with Office," **PAGE 615**.

Managing Alerts

Alerts is the term that Project Server uses for sending email messages to team members and managers to let them know that tasks or status reports are coming due or are past due. You and your project resources can set how many and when alerts can be sent. Although this sounds like a great idea, because the alerts come from the "system" and not actually from a person and sometimes can be so numerous, team members may end up ignoring them. Some organizations actually have chosen to turn off the email alerts so that they don't clog the email system. However, if used wisely and sparingly, they could be useful. These are especially useful if you do not access PWA daily. Email reminders about existing and recurring events are generated by a daily scan of the Project Server and are sent in one email reminder. They are then sent out at a specified time (often overnight).

You may also initiate recurring email messages when project managers send a new assignment or make changes to an existing one. These notifications occur almost instantaneously, unless you choose to turn off the notification. These emails are sent when you publish the project schedule through the Publish function.

The two kinds of alerts are

- Alert Me About My Tasks and Status Reports

- Alert Me About My Resources on Tasks and Status Reports

Click on Alert Me About My Tasks and Status Reports to set email notifications for yourself. The defaults from the system are that you will receive notifications when a new task is assigned, an existing task is modified, or you are requested to submit a status report. This can be especially handy to set reminders for yourself just before you are supposed to start a task. Figure 14.7 shows how you can click on and off your email reminders and set them according to your preferences.

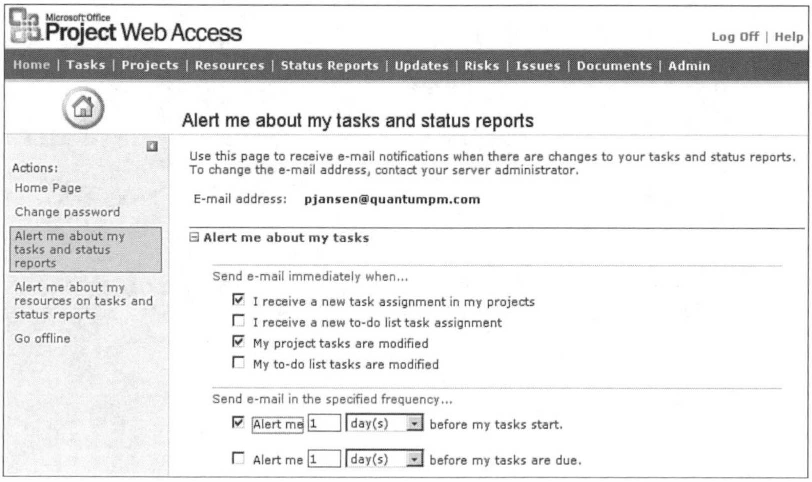

FIGURE 14.7   Select which reminders you want and when.

Click on Alert Me About My Resources on Tasks and Status Reports to set email notifications to remind your team members of task updates or about items your team members update. The system defaults are that you will receive reminders when your team members add or update a task, delegate a task, or submit a status report. You can select to send the email to yourself only, to your team members only, or to you and your team members. This function displays only for project managers. If you set a reminder for your team members, they cannot turn off the email alert. Figure 14.8 shows what kind of reminders you can select for your team.

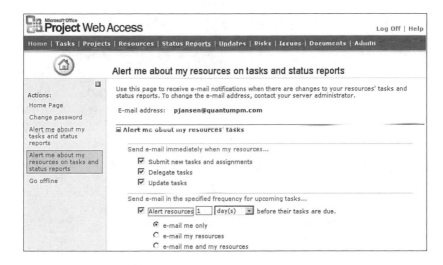

FIGURE 14.8   Select which reminders you want for your resources and when you want them sent.

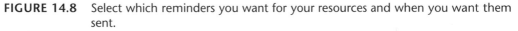

NOTE

These alerts are not the same as the Alert Me function set by team members using issues, risks, and documents. Those alerts are set by the team member only and are more specific about what changes the user wants to be notified about and when the user is notified.

The Alert Me function appears on several screens throughout PWA. It appears on the Tasks page, Status Report page, and the Updates page.

Exchanging Textual Information Using Status Reports

Status reports in PWA are a handy way to exchange textual information with your team members about the status of a project or items in addition to task progress, which you update on the Tasks page. The reports can be scheduled and assigned to team members for regular communication. However, in most organizations, this status report feature is not what you would use to inform executives, management, or others about project status if you need special formats, dashboards, or other special status communication methods. Many organizations use this status report feature to cut and paste into their more formal status report formats. Resource managers may also find this feature useful to request status from their functional or direct reports.

PWA provides a web form that the project manager can customize so that the team member can provide textual information in predetermined sections. One of the handiest features is that a project manager can request status reports from each team member and then use a merge feature to see all the status reports in one consolidated document. This feature allows the project manager to set up a regularly requested (such as weekly or monthly) status report that automatically shows up in each team member's Home page to remind her to complete and submit a status report to her project manager.

Anyone who has team member permissions can also use the status report feature to create and submit independent, ad hoc, or non-project-related status reports. All submitted status reports are archived, and team members can submit a previously sent status report to override what has already been sent.

> **NOTE**
>
> As with all functions in PWA, after reviewing what this function does and how it works, you might consider removing the Status Reports function, if it does not suit your organization. Some organizations leave many functions in place and tell their employees they can use them, but unless given express instructions, most people won't, and it just clutters the screen. Status Reports might be one of those functions you remove.

Alert Me for Status Reports

The Alert Me feature on the Status Report Overview page takes you to the page that allows you to set your preferences for email notifications about status reports you need to submit to project managers, email notifications about status report updates from your resources, and email notifications you want sent to your resources about upcoming status updates.

> ▶ SEE "Managing Alerts," **PAGE 305**.

Status Reports Based on Role/Permissions

What you can do with status reports is based on the role. Default settings allow only executives, project managers, and resource managers to request and view group responses to status reports. If you are a team member, you can only respond to a status report or create an ad hoc report so that you can send information to others.

After you select Status Reports on the menu tab of PWA, you might see a list of the status reports you need to send off next, miscellaneous status reports, or status reports you have requested for your own projects. See Figure 14.9 for the different sections of the Status Reports Overview page that might appear if you use the functions. If you do not use some of these features for status reports, you do not see them listed on the screen.

Requesting Status Reports

If you have resource, project manager, or executive default permissions, you can request status reports from anyone in the resource pool.

The Report request takes you through a wizard that has the steps listed in the left-side pane of the Request a Status Report page as shown in Figure 14.10.

FIGURE 14.9 Various selections on the Status Reports Overview page for someone with manager permission.

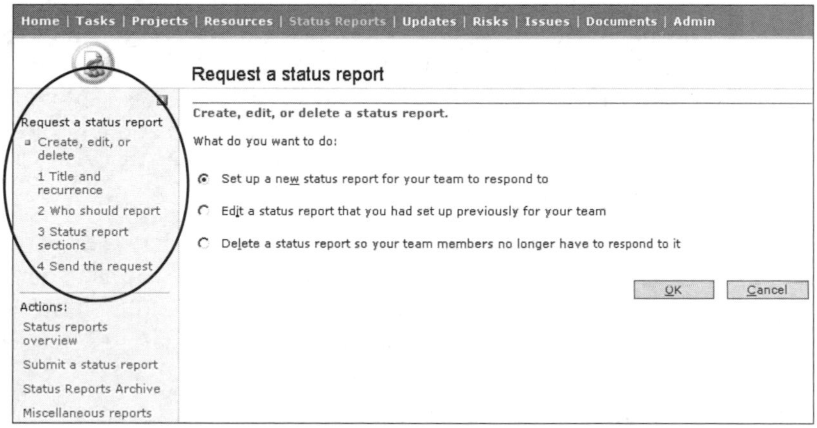

FIGURE 14.10 Create a new status report.

Use the following steps to create a new status report:

1. From the Status Reports Overview page, select Request a Status Report.

2. Select Set Up a New Status Report for Your Team to Respond To and click OK. This starts a wizard to set up a reporting format.

3. Fill in the title of the report. Indicate whether you want it weekly, monthly, or yearly and the specific recurrence days. Also include the initial date for the reporting period to begin. Select Next to continue with the report creation.

> **NOTE**
>
> The status report is not associated directly with a project in PWA. If you want to use it for projects, the project manager might name the status report the same as the project kept in PWA.

4. Select the resources who you want to submit status. The available resources from the resource pool appear on the left. Select a resource and click the Add button between the lists. You can use the Ctrl key to make multiple resource selections. After you have added all resources, click Next.

> **NOTE**
>
> The Merge check box shown in the Resources Who Should Respond box defines whether the response from each individual will automatically be included in a consolidated status report group. If you want to review the responses before adding them to a consolidated report, leave the check box not selected.

5. Use the dialog box to format the major subsections of the report. First, for each named topic, define subsections for the team members, so that they understand how they should fill out information for the topic. By default, Major Accomplishments, Objectives for the Next Period, and Hot Issues are the predefined topics. You can change these by selecting those heading rows and entering a new topic. You can specify additional topics by adding more rows. Click Next when you are finished.

6. You can send a notice that lets the resources know that they have a new status report by clicking Send, which automatically saves the report as well. You can click Save to make the report available for further editing before sending it off. If you select Cancel, you will lose all work on the status report.

After you request your first status report, you see a new section on your Status Report Overview page called Group Status Reports. This is where you can access the reports submitted by your team.

Scheduled status reports for the team members appear on their PWA Home page and Status Report Overview page under the Upcoming Status Reports section.

Submitting Status Reports

There are two ways to submit a status report:

- Respond to a scheduled status report request.

- Submit an unsolicited status report.

Respond to a Scheduled Status Report Request

You will respond to a scheduled status report when a manager sends you a template to fill out on a regular basis. You see the status report request on your Home page and on the Status Report Overview page whenever you select the Status Reports menu tab in PWA.

To complete the requested status report, perform the following steps:

1. Click on the report's link and start entering text for each heading you see on the report. You can format the text using the menu bar you see when you click in each section. Along with formatting options, such as bullets, numbering, and bolding, you can insert task names as text directly from your timesheet.

2. To provide status on tasks from your timesheet, select Insert Tasks from Timesheet from the formatting menu bar. Tasks from your timesheet appear in the Insert Tasks from Timesheet form that displays. Check the Insert? check box on the left column for each task you want to insert, select the section in the status report you want the tasks to go into, and then click on the Insert Tasks button at the bottom of the page. Repeat this process for each section and remember to unselect the tasks after each insert.

3. When you have completed inserting tasks, click the Done button in the Insert Tasks from Timesheet form.

4. When you are finished completing all sections of the status report, you can add more sections by clicking on the Click Here to Add Section button and complete the status for that section.

5. Click Send to submit the status report to your manager. If you want to save the work you've done and submit it later, click Save. Otherwise, you may Cancel your work by clicking Cancel.

You can access the saved or sent status report in the Status Reports Archive.

▶ SEE "Using the Status Reports Archive," **PAGE 314**.

Figure 14.11 illustrates an example of a status report that a team member is editing.

> **NOTE**
>
> Note that at the top of the status report, you can send copies to others using the Cc: field and may change the dates of the status report in the Covers Period from Field, if necessary.

Submit an Unsolicited Status Report

When you want to submit an ad hoc status report regarding any topic, select Submit a Status Report in the side pane on the Status Reports Overview page. Then, in the upper-left corner of the side pane on the screen that displays, you can select Submit an Unrequested Status Report.

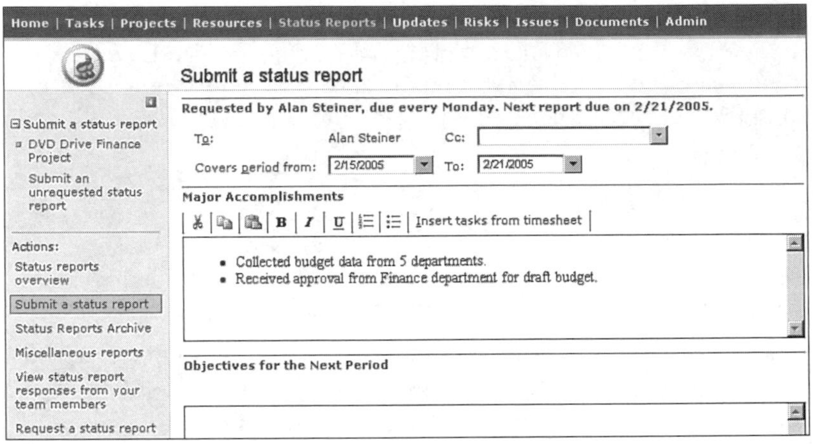

FIGURE 14.11 Team members provide status reports to project managers.

NOTE

If any status reports have been requested from you, the first status report form will appear. Don't be confused by this. The selection is in the side pane that will take you to the unrequested status report form.

You can also directly select to submit an unrequested status report by clicking on the Create and Submit an Unrequested Status Report hyperlink on the Status Reports Overview page as shown in Figure 14.12.

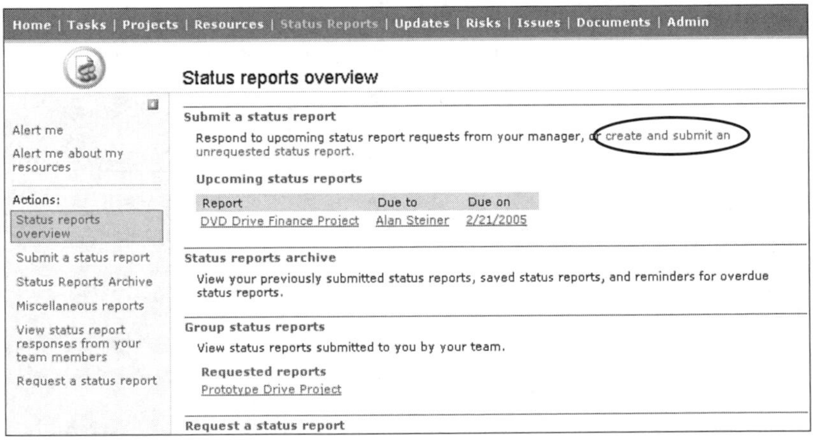

FIGURE 14.12 Hyperlink for selecting and requesting an ad hoc status report.

This displays a page where you can define a new status report format, enter text, and then submit a status report to anyone in the enterprise resource pool.

▶ **SEE** "Submitting Status Reports," **PAGE 310**.

Viewing and Compiling Submitted Status Reports

You can access your team's completed project status reports by clicking on the status report in the Group Status Report section on the Status Reports Overview page or by selecting View Status Report Submitted to You By Your Team in the status reports side pane.

The View Status Report Submitted to You By Your Team page shows a table displaying the status reports from each team member. Each report period column indicates who has submitted a report by displaying a report icon for that team member row. A Team Report icon appears at the top of each column.

The table allows you to look at past reports and keeps history going back to the original date when you created the request. Icons show whether the report has been submitted and whether it has been merged into the consolidated report. Selecting any of the icons for an individual or entire team report takes you to the associated report.

When you select a particular status report, you can merge, open, or delete the status report.

> **NOTE**
>
> You cannot edit the reports sent to you, nor can you send the consolidated status report to anyone else after you receive it. If you need to edit the status to send on to someone else, you might cut and paste into another status report format in MS Word.

Figure 14.13 shows how the project manager can view a composite report from the team members.

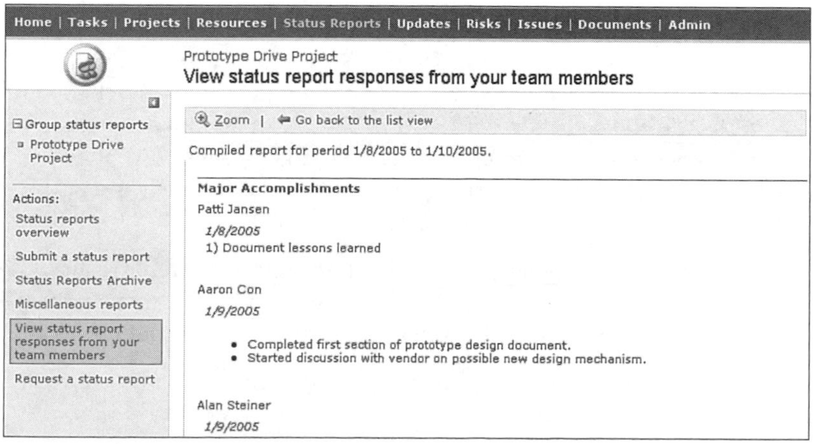

FIGURE 14.13   Managers can review composite team status reports.

Edit or Delete an Existing Status Report

You can edit or delete a status report by selecting Request a Status Report on the side pane. You see three selections on the subsequent page that allow you to edit or delete an existing report. If you have more than one status report, you see a drop-down list where you can select the report you want to edit or delete.

Miscellaneous Reports

The Miscellaneous Reports selection appears in the side pane only if you have sent an unrequested status report to someone. This lists all the miscellaneous status reports you have, and you may view or delete the reports. You cannot update the status reports using this feature. To update a report, you must go to the Status Reports Archive.

Using the Status Reports Archive

The Status Reports Archive selection appears in the side pane only after you have saved or submitted a status report. The archive contains all the status reports you have submitted to a manager or saved for later editing. It allows you to access these reports and view, update, or forward them on to other users. As this list gets larger, you can use filters and groups to help you organize your lists.

Several icons indicate the status of your report in the Report column. You can hover over the icon to see one of the following statuses:

- Your status report is past due.

- Your report was saved but not submitted.

- Your status report has been submitted.

- You have an update to the original report.

Sending Status Updates, Forwarding, and Deleting

You can perform various actions on archived status reports:

- **Update**—If you need to update a previously saved or sent report, you can do so by clicking on the report directly or by selecting the report row and clicking the Update button in the List menu. This allows additional text to be added to each topic section specifying any update to the original comments. When you send the update to your project manager, it automatically overlays the old report with the updated report (if it was for the same time reporting period).

- **Forward**—If you want to forward a status report, select the report row and click the Forward button in the List menu. A list of people you can forward it to appears, and you can use the Ctrl key and select rows to select nonsequential names.

- **Delete**—If you want to delete a status report, select the report row and click the Delete button in the List menu.

Filter and Group Reports

The Filter and Group Reports tab allows you to filter and group the archived status reports list to help you find old status reports. Click on the drop-down boxes to see the numerous selections you have.

Best Practices

In general, the Home page is not used much more than as a quick view of PWA tasks and an entry point for all the other functions in PWA. As such, you can think of it as your Project Web Access portal.

You may want to consider the following for PWA:

- Add hyperlinks to the Home page, such as to your Project Management Office link.

- Customize the headers on all PWA screens to add your organization's logo. You can change the Branding.gif file in the folder C:\Program Files\Microsoft Office Project Server 2003\IIS Virtual Root\IMAGES to do this.

- Remove the items on the side pane that your organization will not use (such as Change Password) via permissions in Admin, Server Configuration. In general, think about making sure that all PWA screens have only the functions you will really use in your organization.

- If your organization does not use the Status Reports function, you might consider setting the permissions so that people cannot use it. This removes the Status Reports tab from the PWA menu tabs set.

- Consider turning off the Alert Me function or make sure that you train your project managers to use it sparingly and wisely.

14

CHAPTER 15

Time Tracking in Project Web Access

IN THIS CHAPTER

- Using the Tasks Page to Record Actual Work
- Using the Updates Page
- Best Practices

Tracking project time in Project Web Access (PWA) is composed of two functions on the menu tab: Tasks and Updates. Anyone recording time enters his time on the Tasks page. Only the project manager uses the Updates page to approve the time. It's important to understand that everything you enter in the Tasks page must be approved by the project manager in the Updates page. So even though it sounds like it might be a bad idea to allow team members to create a new task or delegate a task, the project manager has final authority over whether the change is accepted into the schedule.

Using the Tasks Page to Record Actual Work

The Tasks page allows team members to report time spent on project tasks and nonproject tasks (such as vacation or training). The project manager then approves the time on the Updates page, and, when approved, the time is automatically entered in the project schedule. The timesheet on the Tasks page also allows team members to enter estimated remaining time so that they can indicate to the project manager how much time is left on the task to complete it (also known as *estimate to complete*). This ability of the team member to indicate changes in original task estimates is one of the most powerful features in Project Server. However, it creates a profound challenge because most team members are not used to the concept, and many project managers are worried about how changes will affect the project schedule. You can also implement the tool without having team members use this function and capture actual work information accurately, but allowing team members to change estimated remaining time can empower them to start thinking about their time spent on tasks.

To access the Tasks page from your Home page (or any other location in PWA), click Tasks in the menu bar. You see the View My Tasks screen as shown in Figure 15.1 with the tasks you have been assigned to.

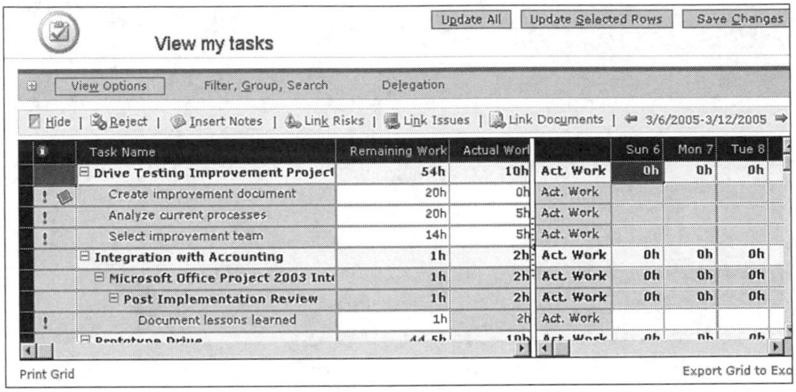

FIGURE 15.1   PWA Tasks page for reporting time spent on tasks.

Make sure that you have a strong vision for training in the use of timesheets in Project Server. Team members not used to providing actual work information on tasks will need reassurance and a good understanding of how the information they provide helps the organization understand what it takes to complete a project.

You also have some choices about how you want to implement Project Server 2003 for time tracking:

- **Managed Time Periods**—This allows you to open and close time frames in which people can enter their time. Some organizations choose this option because of the critical need for auditability, timesheet control, and integration with accounting systems. It also helps with more effective earned value performance reporting.

- **Non-Managed Time Periods**—This allows team members to enter time during any time frame for a task assigned to them. This system is not as auditable but provides flexibility and easier administration for organizations that simply want to capture and analyze actual time for project schedules.

Before making a decision on which method to use, make sure that you understand the entire process needed and the implications of each option. The administrator sets which option you choose, and the way timesheets look and act will be slightly different based on this choice.

▶ **SEE** "Time Period Settings," **PAGE 253**.

You also need to make a decision about who reports time to tasks. Generally, people doing the work will report time, including the project manager, but will resource managers ever report time or any other role using Project Server? You will want to assign the Team Member group role to anyone who will report time. Note that the project manager role already has team member settings. Project managers also need to understand several things about the timesheet update cycle:

- What they enter on the project schedule when they assign tasks to team members affects the accuracy and integrity of the data, which will ultimately show in reports.

- Maintaining the update cycle keeps the data current. This is not an easy task, but it is a critical habit to create.

- Team members see the results of a project manager's schedule in the timesheet. Poorly named tasks and too many tasks can be overwhelming and can negatively affect consistent use of the Tasks page.

One more decision your organization needs to make is to choose what features the team members can use on the Tasks page. Do you want them to be able to create new tasks or add themselves to existing ones? Some organizations do not like the idea of allowing team members to perform these actions. Remember, the project manager has full authority over accepting new tasks or a team member's addition to a task into a schedule. Some organizations also do not want to allow team members to delegate tasks to others.

The Timesheet Update Cycle

The Timesheet Update cycle defines how actual work and task progress are reflected in PWA and Project Professional. Processes need to be implemented to ensure that this cycle is completed to reflect current information.

The flow for updating a timesheet and actual work into the project schedule is as follows:

- In Project Professional, the project manager publishes a project schedule with tasks and resource assignments.

- The Project Server creates PWA timesheet and assignment views and sends email messages (if activated) about the assignments to team members.

- In PWA, the team member enters actual work (usually once a week) and submits the time to the project manager.

- The project manager receives an email message about the update (if the email message is activated), and the update displays in the Updates page in PWA.

- In PWA, the project manager approves or rejects the update from the team member. If the actual work is approved and updated, Project Professional opens, and the project manager saves the actual work into the project schedule.

- The project manager should review the changes in the project schedule, make adjustments as appropriate, and publish the changes in the schedule to initiate the update cycle once again.

▶ SEE "Updating Project Progress," PAGE 605.

Timesheet Format and Setup

The first thing you need to consider is setting up the standards for how you want the timesheet to display for the team members initially. You can set some of the formatting organizationally via a view in Admin called the Timesheet view. You may also want to recommend a few settings that the team member needs to set manually, such as adding Scheduled Work in the View Options tab.

▶ **SEE** "Creating Project Web Access Project and Resource Views," **PAGE 209**.

Different Tracking Methods for Timesheets

Your organization may select one of three time tracking methods for your projects in the enterprise environment: percent work complete, actual work, and day-by-day. The following list describes each method in more detail:

- **Percent work complete**—For this selection, the team member enters a percent complete and, if applicable, remaining work. This selection tracks how much work is completed based on the team member entering a percentage of the work assigned to the task. This assumes that the start date planned is the actual date the work started because the team member cannot enter the actual day the task started. Microsoft Office Project 2003 calculates the actual work and remaining work as Actual Work = Work * Percent Work Complete and Remaining Work = Work – Actual Work.

- **Actual work**—For this selection, the team member enters a total amount of work for a particular period and, if applicable, remaining work. This selection tracks how much work is completed compared with how much work remains, based on the total work planned for the task. This assumes that the start date planned is the actual date the work started because the team member cannot enter the actual day the task started. Project 2003 calculates the percentage of work complete and remaining work fields as Percent Work Complete = Actual Work / Work. Remaining Work = Work – Actual Work.

- **Day-by-day**—For this selection, the team member enters time worked on the task each day of the week. This selection tracks work completed by showing actual work day-by-day and uses the first day a team member enters actual work on a task as the start date for the task. Upon saving the actual work into the project schedule, the project manager may at times see a message saying that the task has started earlier than planned if the project team member starts working on the task earlier than what the project manager originally entered on the task. Project 2003 calculates the percentage of work complete and remaining work fields as Percent Work Complete = Actual Work / Work. Remaining Work = Work – Actual Work. This is the most accurate form of project time entry.

Your organization may have a circumstance where you need to support several tracking methods at the same time—for example, percent work complete and day-by-day for different departments within your organization. Although this isn't recommended for creating a true enterprise environment that standard processes encourage, sometimes you may need this choice until you can transition all your departments to one timesheet tracking method. To do this, the administrator needs to allow multiple tracking methods, and each project manager needs to publish her project schedules to indicate the tracking method she wants.

▶ SEE "Completing the Implementation and Configuration," PAGE 239.

> **NOTE**
>
> If the team member has been assigned tasks from different projects with different tracking methods, if even one task is using Hours of Work done per time period as its tracking method, the Timesheet view is displayed by default.

Viewing Data on the Timesheet

The main section of the timesheet is divided into two parts as shown in Figure 15.2.

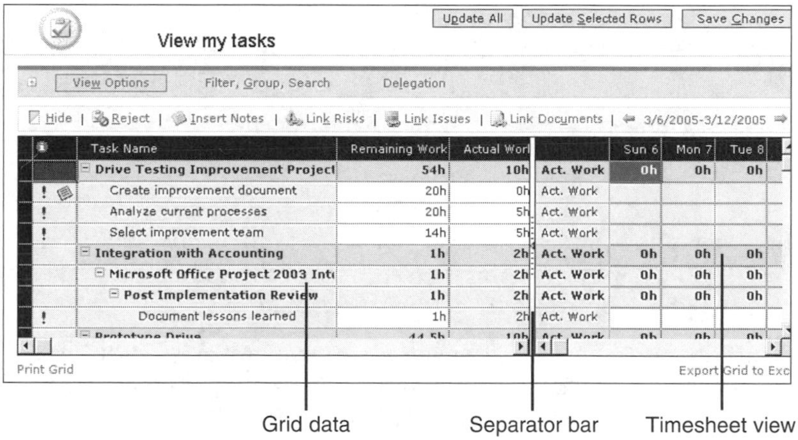

FIGURE 15.2   Grid and Timesheet entry view on the Tasks page.

Grid Data

On the left side of the separator bar is the grid data. It shows information from the task such as name, work, start and finish dates, and so on. These fields are set by default in the Timesheet view via the Admin tab, Manage Views. You may want to add or remove some of the fields that are shown here by modifying that view.

> **TIP**
>
> The administrator may want to move the Baseline Work field into the Timesheet view. Because the Work field can change due to updates to Remaining Work and Actual Work, it is useful for the team members to see the original estimate. You also may want to move the Remaining Work column to the left, just after the Task Name field to allow for easy data entry.

One of the most important fields in the grid data is the indicator field, the column on the far left. The field displays a number of indicators that identify the status of tasks or associated information. Placing the cursor over the icon displays a ToolTip with information relevant to each task. A large "X" in this field indicates that the task has been deleted from the project schedule.

Timesheet View/Gantt Chart

On the right side of the separator bar is where either the Gantt chart or the Timesheet view (not to be confused with the Timesheet view that the administrator sets in the Admin tab) can display. The Timesheet view is used for viewing assigned work and updating actual hours when entering time day-by-day. The Gantt chart is useful for understanding the relative timing, length, and order of the tasks to be performed.

The Timesheet view shows either day-by-day or actual work per week. Team members can enter time only in the day-by-day Timesheet view. Otherwise, they enter % complete or actual work in the grid data area to the left of the separator bar.

The Gantt chart does not allow any data entry. This will probably not be used very often by team members, but it may be used to understand overall task timelines. You can use the Go to Task icon to bring the Gantt bar for a particular task into view. To do so, highlight the task, and then click the Go to Task icon. The Zoom In/Zoom Out icons allow you to easily change the timeline scale, from day-by-day to week-by-week or month-by-month. Figure 15.3 shows the Zoom In/Zoom Out and Go to Task icons on the Gantt Chart view.

The team member can choose either display by selecting Timesheet View or Gantt Chart in the upper-left corner of the side pane as shown in Figure 15.4.

Indicator column   Zoom In/Zoom Out icon

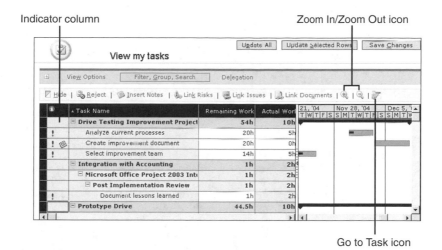

Go to Task icon

FIGURE 15.3   The Gantt Chart view with the Zoom In/Zoom Out and Go to Task icons.

15

Current Tasks/All Tasks

By default, only current tasks are displayed when you first enter the Tasks page. *Current tasks* are those currently in progress or scheduled to start in the near future. The administrator specifies the number of days from the current date that the current tasks view will show (10 days is a default setting). You can also choose to view all tasks, which displays every task assigned to you. Figure 15.4 shows where the team member can choose to view Current Tasks or All Tasks.

TIP

Sometimes team members say they do not have tasks in their timesheet, when the project managers know they have assigned the task. This could be due to a task not scheduled for the current time period. Make sure that the team members choose All Tasks, to confirm that the task shows in the tasks list.

View Options

You can manually set up what displays on the Tasks page via the View Options tab. Figure 15.4 shows some of the selections you have in the View Options tab when you are in the Timesheet view. What shows in this tab changes based on whether you are in the Timesheet view or the Gantt Chart view. Usually, the defaults set are sufficient, but you might be interested in instructing your team members about a few of them:

- **Show Summary Tasks**—Turning off this selection helps reduce rows on the timesheet and especially helps with long task lists. However, if some of the detailed task names are similar or the same in different project phases (summary tasks), it is useful to see the summary task to better identify the detailed task.

- **Show Scheduled Work**—Selecting this box shows you the work you have been originally scheduled to perform. This way, you can compare original work assignments against the actual task work. If you clear this check box, you will only see an Actual Work row, which is the default.

- **Show Overtime Work**—If you need to record overtime work, select this option to display this row on your timesheet.

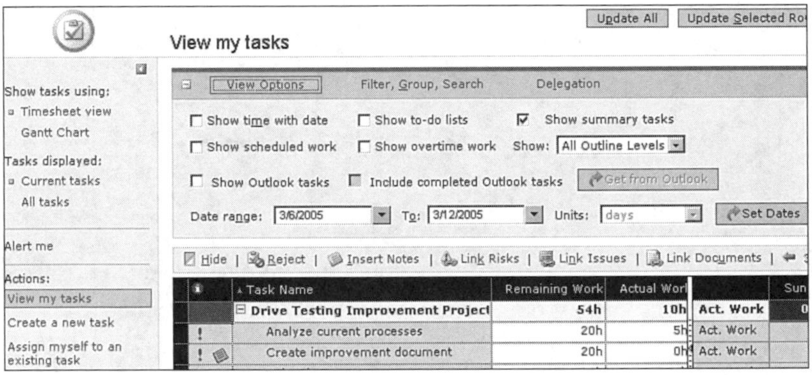

FIGURE 15.4   View Options for the Timesheet view.

You can also set the date range to see a different range of dates in your timesheet. You can change it to just a day, a few days, a week, two weeks, or whatever time period is most useful for you to see and then record actual work.

To change the currently displayed options or dates, you can click on the View Options tab. To hide the options, click on the tab again.

Filter, Group, Search

The Filter, Group, Search tab can help you view your task list from different perspectives. One of the most useful options on this tab is Filter. You may filter out task subsets you want to see as shown in Figure 15.5. For example, you could look at just recently assigned tasks by selecting Newly Assigned Tasks, or you might use Completed Tasks to view and then remove tasks you have completed work on (using the Hide function). You may want to use the Group field to group the tasks list by whatever fields shown in the grid, such as Project, Project Manager, or Work. However, the Project grouping is the default, and you usually will not need to change the grouping. The Search For selection finds characters or words you might need to find in the grid data.

Sizing/Moving Columns Around on the Timesheet

You also have several options to customize the look and feel for your timesheet as described in the following list:

- Column widths can be adjusted by hovering over the column dividers and dragging the divider icon while holding down the left mouse button.

- Column position can be changed by selecting the middle of the column header and dragging the column while holding down the left mouse key.

- Sort order can be adjusted by clicking on a column header. The arrow indicates ascending or descending order.

- The separator bar between the grid data and view pane can also be moved by dragging the bar while holding down the left mouse button.

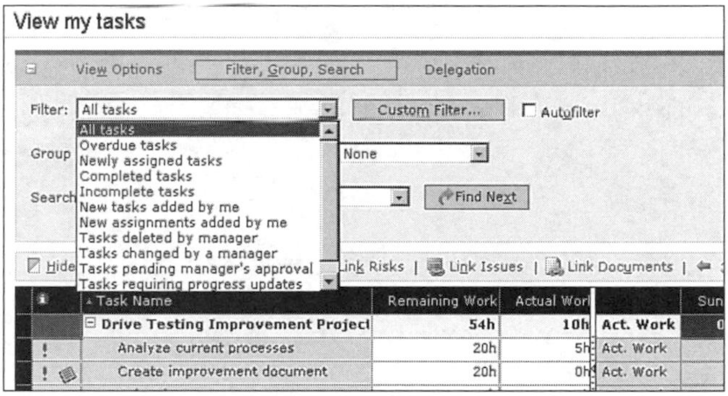

FIGURE 15.5   Filters for viewing tasks in the timesheet.

After you choose these settings, they will persist, so that when you log off and then log on to a new session, the task list will look the same as when you last saw it.

Entering Time on Tasks

You can enter actual work or day-by-day work for a given time period. In all cases, the Tasks page contains a Remaining Work field for the team member to provide a complete picture of the progress being made on the assignment. Your organization will have decided on one of three choices for entering time:

- **%Work Complete and remaining effort**—You enter the % Work Complete value, from zero through 100%, and also enter any remaining work effort needed for specific tasks. Figure 15.6 shows how the timesheet looks for this kind of selection.

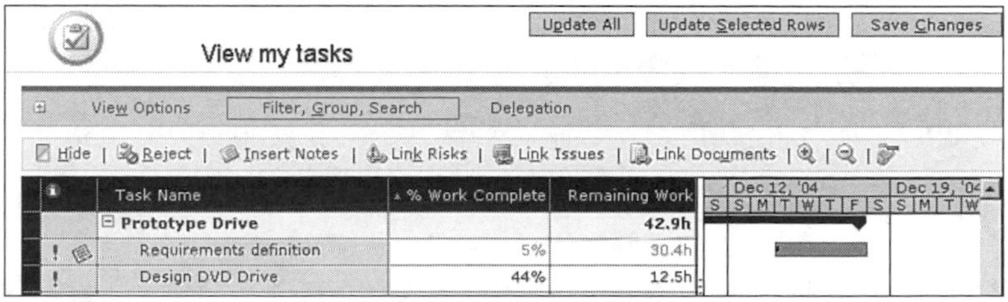

FIGURE 15.6   Tasks page with percent complete timesheet view.

- **Hours worked for the time reporting period and remaining effort**—You enter the summarized actual work and any remaining work for the entire report period. Time reporting periods can be for an entire week or longer periods, as established by the system administrator. Figure 15.7 shows how the timesheet looks for this kind of selection.

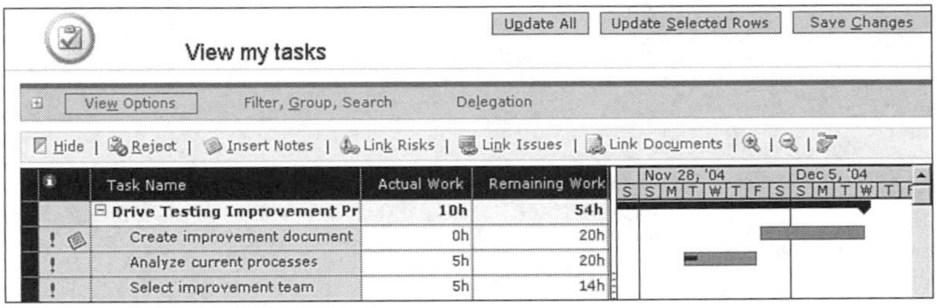

FIGURE 15.7   Tasks page with actual work timesheet view.

- **Hours worked per day and remaining effort for the time reporting period**—You can enter time for specific daily periods so that the actual work is reported at a detailed level. This is the only choice if your organization has selected Managed Time Periods, but you can use this with Non-Managed Time Periods. Figure 15.8 shows what the timesheet looks like with this view.

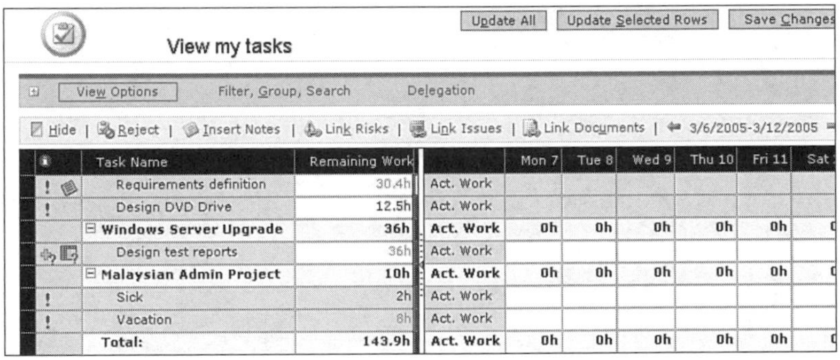

FIGURE 15.8   Tasks page with day-by-day timesheet view.

To enter time for a day-by-day timesheet, follow these steps:

1. Enter your actual work for each day for the current time reporting period. You cannot enter more than 24 hours per day, and the administrator can set a maximum limit for each day.

> **NOTE**
>
> It is easy to enter time for the wrong time period (the time period always defaults to the current week). Make sure that you check the time period and click on the right or left arrow to confirm that the correct time frame is displaying for the time entry.

2. After you enter your time, review the totals at the end of the task row for each task on the right side by scrolling to the last column. Review how many hours you have entered for each day by scrolling to the bottom of the Task view. You will see totals for each day and for the total time period. Make corrections if necessary. When you want to remove time entered in a field, delete it; do not type in a zero.

3. Review the Remaining Work field for each task and adjust as necessary to reflect the updated estimate to complete for that task. If you have completed a task, make sure that you set the Remaining Work field to zero.

4. If Remaining Work increases significantly from the original estimate, it is a good idea to communicate the change to your project manager, even though it will be reflected automatically in the Updates page. The schedule for the project may change, and the project manager needs to be aware of these changes.

After you are finished entering actual task work for the current reporting period, click on one of the following buttons in the upper-right corner of the Tasks page:

- **Update All**—Sends an update to all project managers of all projects you worked on, notifying them that the actual work was submitted for their projects.

- **Update Selected Rows**—Sends an update to the project managers for only the selected rows. You can use the Ctrl key and select the nonsequential tasks.

- **Save Changes**—This saves your task assignment actual work to the Project Server database but will not send the updates to the project manager.

When you enter actual work in the timesheet, the entry turns red to indicate that the actual task assignment work has been entered but not approved and saved. This remains red until the project manager approves the update, saves the project plan, and publishes the changes. If you see black in the timesheet, the project manager has accepted the time into the schedule.

Editable fields are shown in white. Time entry fields that appear in gray are closed due to your organization using the Managed Time Period feature. Tasks that have been delegated to others are highlighted in yellow.

> **NOTE**
>
> If a project manager rejects a task update, you will receive an email notification and an indicator icon will display in the indicator field.

Action Bar Actions

The Tasks page action bar allows you to perform the following actions on tasks, where each of the actions is performed by selecting a task in the task sheet and then clicking on the appropriate button in the menu:

- **Hide**—You can hide rows of tasks on the Tasks page. This does not actually delete the task from the schedule, just from the timesheet. Use this feature with caution because this permanently hides the tasks. However, this may be useful to remove completed tasks from your tasks list. If you hide a task prematurely, the project manager can republish the task, and it will reappear in the timesheet.

- **Reject**—This allows you to reject a task assigned to you that you may not be able to fulfill. You might want to insert a note to explain to the project manager why you are rejecting a task. Also note that your project manager can reject your rejection, and the task will show up in your list again. If you want to add a note to explain the rejection, you must insert a note prior to clicking Reject to send a note to the project manager. If you forget to do so, send an email to the project manager explaining why you cannot perform the task.

- **Insert Notes**—This allows you to insert a note for the project. Multiple notes can be added. Notes can be modified and added as the assignment progresses, giving you a place to record ongoing communication regarding the task updates. The comments in the notes can be viewed by everyone.

- **Link Risks**—You can link a risk to a task. You are taken to the Risks page to add a risk.

- **Link Issues**—You can link an issue to a task. You are taken to the Issues page to add an issue.

- **Link Documents**—You can link particular documents with a task as well. By selecting this, you are taken to the Documents page.

    ▶ **SEE** "Risks, Issues, and Documents Using Windows SharePoint Services (WSS)," **PAGE 441**.

Alert Me

The Alert Me function in the side pane takes you to the same email notification settings page you find on the home page. You can configure task-related events you want to be notified about.

▶ **SEE** "Managing Alerts," **PAGE 305**.

Creating a New Task

This feature is useful for team members to communicate about tasks that have been forgotten or that were unplanned. As you start working on a project, you may realize that the project manager has not created a task that you need. This may be because you have better knowledge about the tasks required to accomplish the project goal or the scope of the project changes requiring additional tasks. Some organizations also create project schedules that contain unplanned tasks, such as trouble tickets. This allows team members to add a task and then report actual work, without the project manager having to add them first in the project schedule.

When you create a new task you need to

1. Choose Create a New Task on the Tasks page side pane. The Create a New Task page appears, as shown in Figure 15.9.

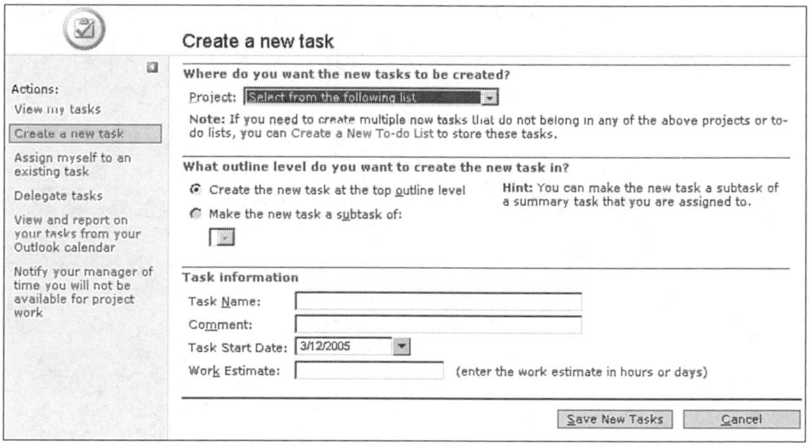

FIGURE 15.9   Create a New Task page.

2. Choose the project to which you want to add the new task in the Project field. Note that you only see a list of projects to which you have already been assigned.

3. Choose the summary task (if appropriate); otherwise, use the default and create the new task at the top outline level. You might always use the top outline level and let the project manager decide where she wants to put the task in the project schedule.

4. In the Task Name, enter the task description.

5. In the Comment field, enter a comment to describe the task more fully or the reason why you created the new task.

6. In the Task Start Date field, enter the date you will begin working on the task.

7. In Work Estimate, enter the number of hours you estimate the task will take, such as "40h" or "5d." If you do not include "h" or "d" after the selection, it defaults to hours.

8. Click Save New Tasks.

9. The task displays in your timesheet, and you can start recording actual work immediately against the task. Don't forget to submit the new task to the project manager for approval.

> **NOTE**
>
> The project manager needs to carefully review new tasks. He may need to reject the new task, change the work hours planned for the new task, or move it to a different place in a task hierarchy of the project schedule. The project manager still needs to review how it affects the work breakdown structure, linking, and the critical path and end date for the project.

Assigning Myself to a New Task

At times, you need to add yourself to an existing task because you have been asked to do some work that was not originally planned, you need to take the work over from someone else, or perhaps you need to replace a generic resource skill that was assigned to a task by the project manager. To add yourself to an existing task, perform the following:

1. On the side pane of the Tasks page, select Assign Myself to an Existing Task. The Assign Myself to an Existing Task page appears, as shown in Figure 15.10.

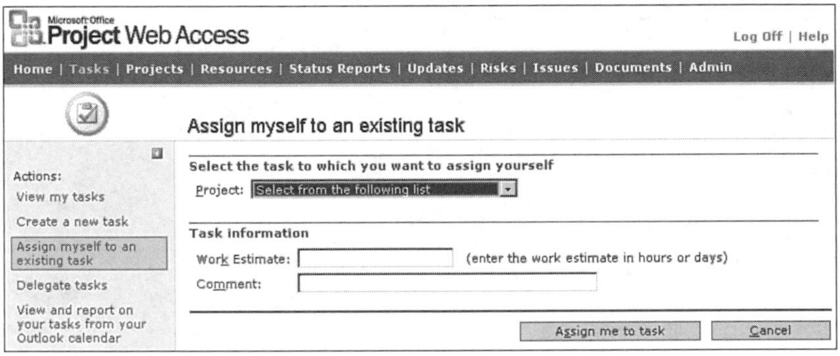

FIGURE 15.10   Assign Myself to an Existing Task page.

2. Choose the project you want to assign yourself to. Note that only those projects you have already been assigned to will appear. If you do not see the project you need to be assigned to, contact the project manager.

3. After you select the project, a task list appears. Only those tasks you have *not* already been assigned to will appear. Choose the appropriate task by clicking on it. (Make sure that you do not select a summary task row—you must pick the lowest level task.)

4. In the Work Estimate field, enter the number of hours you believe the task will take (example: "20h" or "2.5d"). Use "h" for hours or "d" for days. If you do not include "h" or "d" after the selection, it defaults to days.

5. In the Comment field, explain why you are adding yourself to the assignment.

6. Click Assign Me to Task, and the task displays in your timesheet.

7. Click OK when you see the message asking whether you want to be assigned to the task. You can start entering time immediately on the task. Don't forget to submit the task assignment to the project manager for approval when you are ready.

NOTE

The project manager needs to review the new task assignments resulting from resources adding themselves to existing tasks. She may need to adjust the hours in another resource assignment if this resource is taking over the task assignment. If this resource is helping another resource, the project manager may need to check to make sure that it will not increase the duration of the task.

Delegating Tasks

Sometimes it may be useful to transfer a task assignment to another resource using the Delegate Tasks function as shown in Figure 15.11. Some organizations use this feature when a project manager assigns tasks to a team lead, and then the team lead delegates the task to someone specific on his team. Some organizations send tasks to the resource manager, expecting him to then delegate the task to resources available in his department. When tracking delegated tasks, the actual values are reflected in your timesheet but do not require updating.

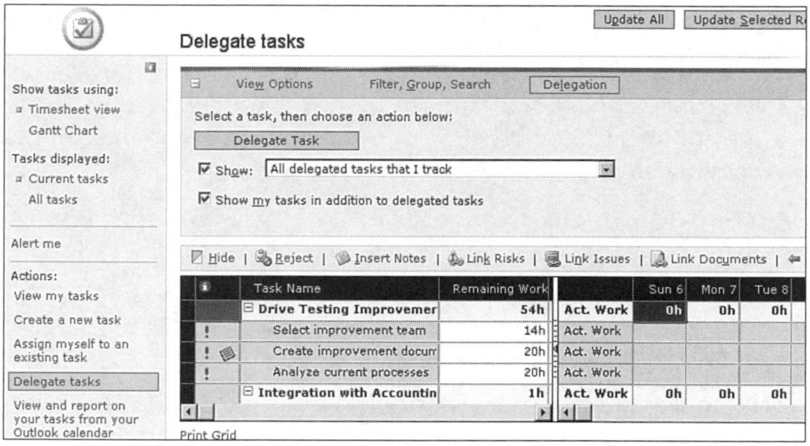

FIGURE 15.11   Delegating a task to another resource.

Delegate a task by selecting the task or tasks to delegate and then clicking the Delegation tab on the Tasks page, or select Delegate Task from the side pane. You need to select Delegate Tasks on the pane that then appears to see the Delegate Tasks Wizard to start the delegation process.

You may choose a summary task to select all the subtasks for delegation. If any tasks you select cannot be delegated, you see a message informing you that some of the tasks cannot be delegated. Choose the Show Details button in this dialog box to see which tasks cannot be delegated and why. You may not be able to delegate a task for one of several reasons:

- The project manager won't allow the tasks in this project to be delegated.

- Actual work has been entered on the task, and the project manager still needs to approve it.

- The team member just created the task, and the project manager still needs to approve it.

- The task is a nonproject (administrative) task.

- The task is already a delegated task.

- The project manager has deleted the task from the project schedule.

When you are ready to delegate the task, you see a wizard that lets you select what you want to do, as follows:

1. Decide who you want to delegate the task to in the Who Do You Want to Delegate This Task To? field. Choose a resource name from a drop-down list.

2. Decide on how you want to manage the delegated task. This allows three options:

   • **Assume the lead role**—Choose Yes to indicate that after the task has been updated by the resource you delegated it to, you want to see the update and then submit it to the project manager. Use this if you want to maintain responsibility for the task even though you are not performing the work.

   • **Track this task**—Choose Yes to indicate that the person you delegate the task to will update and submit the time to the project manager; however, you want a copy of the updates. Use this when you want to be informed of task progress without taking responsibility for the task update.

   • **No further role**—Choose No on both of the preceding options to remove the task from your timesheet and remove complete responsibility for the task from you.

3. Add a note about the task in the Notes field if you need to.

4. Click Next to see your delegation selection. You can once more decide how you want to manage the delegation by selecting to assume the lead role, only track the task, or delegate the task completely using the check boxes next to the task. When you are ready, choose Send to delegate the task.

Email notifications inform everyone about what has happened to a task that is being delegated. When you delegate a task, an email notification goes to whom you have delegated the task and to the project manager of the task. If the project manager rejects the delegation, you and the delegated resource will be notified, and you retain responsibility for the task. If the delegated resource rejects the delegated task, you and the project manager will be notified.

Requesting the Status of a Delegated Task
If you have the lead role in tracking a delegated task, you can request an update from the resource that's been delegated the task. To do so, select the task and click the Request Task Status button on the Delegation tab.

Viewing and Reporting on Your Tasks from Your Outlook Calendar
If your organization uses Outlook heavily and some of your users prefer working from Outlook, you can download the timesheet update function to work within Outlook. You can select to download the Outlook add-in from here or from the home page to update Tasks and view PWA dashboards or links from Outlook instead of using PWA.

Before this add-in will work, the PWA administrator must allow the Integration with External Timesheet System permission. When you use the Outlook download, make sure that you have permission as the local administrator, or that your Windows policies allow you to perform this installation.

Notifying Your Manager of Nonproject Time

If your organization chooses to use administrative projects to record nonproject time, you will be assigned to tasks such as administration, vacation, training, and so on, in a special project. These tasks display at the bottom of your timesheet.

▶ **SEE** "Using Administrative Projects," **PAGE 240**.

This feature allows you to notify your manager of upcoming time you will not be available via this special administrative project. Then, you will be shown as not available to work during that time in the future, just like any other project in the enterprise environment. When you in fact need to report the actual time, you will just enter the time into the Actual Work field of the timesheet for the task. To notify your manager of time you are taking off in the future, follow these steps:

1. Select Notify Your Manager of Time You Will Not Be Available for Project Work in the Tasks page side pane. The Notify Your Manager of Time You Will Not Be Available for Project Work page appears, where you request your time off (see Figure 15.12).

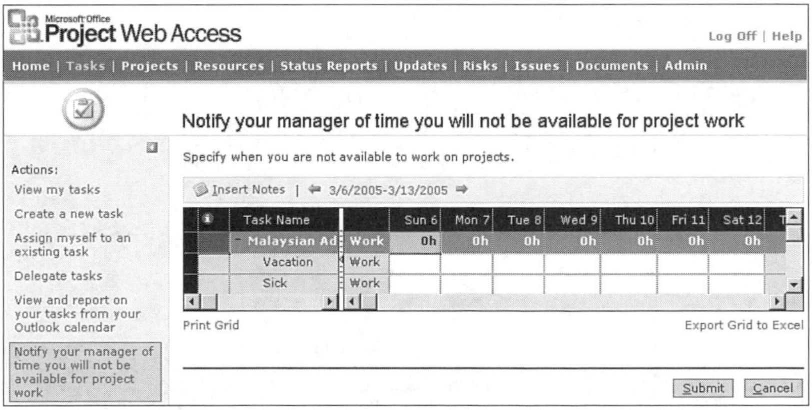

FIGURE 15.12   Notify your manager of time you will not be available page.

2. Make sure that you set the correct time period you need to record using the arrows in the time period control on the action bar. Record the future time you will be unavailable for project time for the appropriate administrative tasks.

3. When you are finished, click Submit. You may need to click it twice—make sure that you see the message, Administrative Time Updated Successfully and click OK.

4. To return to your Tasks page, select View My Tasks on the side pane or Tasks on the menu bar.

This request is submitted to your resource manager for approval and saved into a special project that records your request for future time off, training, or other nonproject activity. The time you have requested shows as Scheduled Work for that task in the Timesheet view if you checked Show Scheduled Work on the View Options tab.

When you actually take the time off, you enter the actual work as usual in your timesheet to reflect the actual hours you spent on the nonproject time.

Printing the Timesheet/Using Excel

You can use the Print Grid function to print the timesheet or export it to Excel. In some cases, you may have so many tasks—the size limit of characters or data may be exceeded if you choose to print the grid—that you need to export the data to Excel. Whichever you use, the Print Grid or the Excel spreadsheet, you might like to use this function to print your timesheet for the week, keep it by your desk, and then enter your time for each day. Subsequently, at the end of the week, you can easily transfer your time to the timesheet in Project Server. Some organizations use this function for managerial signature approval or other kinds of record-keeping the organization may require.

To select the Print Grid or Export Grid to Excel, follow these steps:

1. Click on Print Grid at the left bottom of the timesheet or Export Grid to Excel at the bottom right of the timesheet as shown in Figure 15.13.

2. To return to the Tasks page, click on the "X" in the upper-right corner of this window.

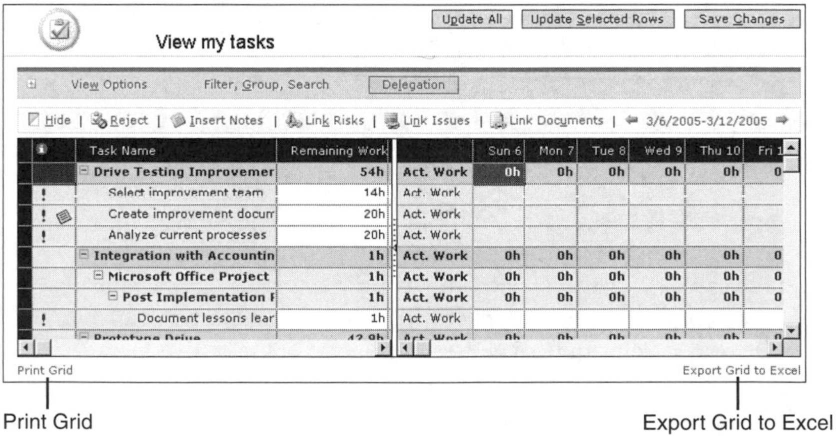

FIGURE 15.13   The Print Grid or Export Grid to Excel links on the Tasks page.

Timesheet or Grid Data Worksheet

When you choose Print Grid, a separate window displays. You can change the Worksheet format to Timesheet (which shows only the task list and actuals for the time period showing) or a Grid Data (which shows fields for the tasks, such as scheduled work, % complete, start/finish dates, and other task-related data). For each of these selections, you can choose to Arrange Columns and/or Format Columns as shown in Figure 15.13.

When you choose to arrange columns, follow these steps:

1. Select a column or columns in the Available Columns list.

2. Move the column Up or Down to move it to the left or the right in the view.

3. If you want to move a column, select it in the Available Columns list and then click Remove to move it to the Excluded Columns list. You can restore a column you have removed by clicking Restore. You can remove or restore all columns in the Available Columns list.

4. After you have completed the formatting, click Reformat Grid to make the change (see Figure 15.14).

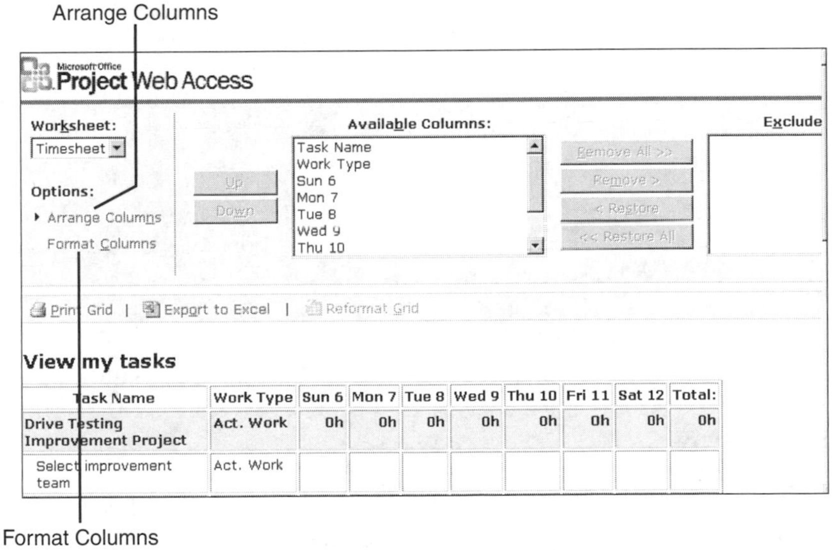

FIGURE 15.14 The Print Grid window with its various selections.

When you choose to format columns, select a column and then choose to allow or disallow column wrapping, allow or customize the column width, and/or set the column alignment.

Exporting the Timesheet to Excel

You can also export your timesheet to Excel. This allows you to show the Grid Data and Timesheet data in an Excel spreadsheet. Some organizations use this to add comments to the timesheet that might not be appropriate as task comments that would stay in the schedule. It allows you to print large collections of task data, whereas the Print Grid function has limitations.

Customizing the Timesheet

Your organization may need to add fields to timesheets so that team members can add custom data for your organization. For example, perhaps the project manager needs to record the task's billing code, and you need to record the information when you are entering time. You can do so through a series of steps to set up the timesheet to allow this customized reporting.

▶ **SEE** "Timesheet Setup," **PAGE 252**.

Using the Updates Page

The Updates page is used exclusively by the project manager to approve the time submitted by team members on their Tasks page. You then have the option to accept or reject the task updates from your resources before committing or saving the task changes to the appropriate project.

This process ensures that you are the ultimate approver for updates to the project schedule and gives you control over your resources' activities. Part of this approval process is making sure that the resources have entered the time correctly. For example, if someone enters eight hours on a week you know he was on vacation, you might need to ask him to fix his timesheet.

When you accept the time and click Update, Project Professional opens, and the time is saved into the project schedule in the exact quantities and on the exact days as recorded by the team member if she is entering time day-by-day.

▶ **SEE** "Updating Project Progress," **PAGE 605**.

This function also allows project managers to set rules for accepting time and to look at transaction history of their approvals and rejections. It's important to understand that this is different from timesheet approval accessed in the Resource Center. That approval allows functional or other managers to show that they have reviewed their resources' time, and they approve it from a functional standpoint. The Updates function is the domain of the project manager to accept time into her project schedules.

▶ **SEE** "Adjusting Actuals," **PAGE 391**.

Figure 15.15 shows the sections of the Updates page the project manager uses to approve the team members' time submittals.

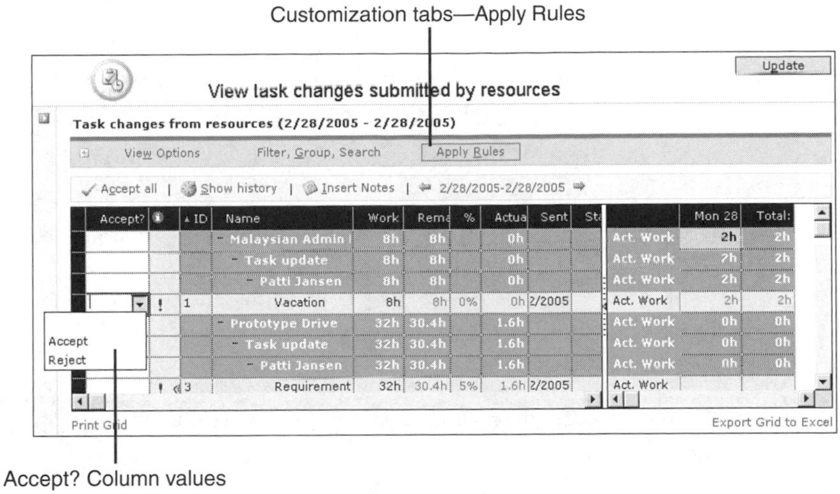

Customization tabs—Apply Rules

Accept? Column values

FIGURE 15.15   Sections on the Updates page you will use to approve time.

To use the Updates function to approve time, follow these steps:

1. In PWA, select the Updates page menu tab. If you are on the Updates page, you can select View Task Changes Submitted By Resources in the side pane to see where you will approve your project's time.

2. Review submitted actual work. The changes submitted by the resources display in red in the fields they changed. For example, if the resource submitted %complete, you see the number in the % Work Complete field and the change in the Remaining Work. All tasks display by project, resource, and task type.

3. Select values in the Accept Column to specify which updates you are rejecting or accepting. You may use the following options to select Accept or Reject for each task you want to update:

   - Click in the cell to the left of each task and select Accept or Reject from the drop-down box.

   - If you select a summary task, the Accept or Reject option will apply to all its subtasks.

   - You can accept all tasks submitted by clicking the Accept All button in the action bar.

TIP

If you are accepting all tasks except for a few rejections or blanks, it might be easier to click Accept All and then go to only those tasks you are rejecting or leaving blank and change them.

- If you reject time, it is a good idea to click on Insert Note and let the team member know exactly why you rejected the task. If you reject time submitted by a team member, an email is sent to the team member, and an indicator shows up on his Tasks page letting him know that the submittal was rejected.

- If you accept the time, an icon appears letting the team member know the time has been updated.

- If you have accidentally selected to reject or accept a line you are not ready to update into the time sheet, click in the cell to the left of the task, and you will also see a blank as a value you can select. This allows you to submit all tasks to update into the schedule except for this task.

CAUTION

When the schedule opens, you can either save the changes or cancel saving the updates into your project schedule. It is better to reject the changes up-front on the Updates page instead of clicking the Cancel button when the project opens in Project Professional. The task remains in your Updates page, and a red flag shows in the Indicators column, signifying that you need to update the task. In addition, you can no longer reject the task.

---

4. Click Update, and Project Professional opens where you can save the changes into the project schedule.

   ▶ **SEE** "Updating Project Progress," **PAGE 605**.

NOTE

If the project has been checked out by another project manager, you cannot update the project until the project is checked back in.

After all tasks' actual work entries have been saved into the project schedules, you see a screen similar to Figure 15.16 (this also shows if no one has submitted time to you). Also, the team member's time displays as black rather than red in his timesheet.

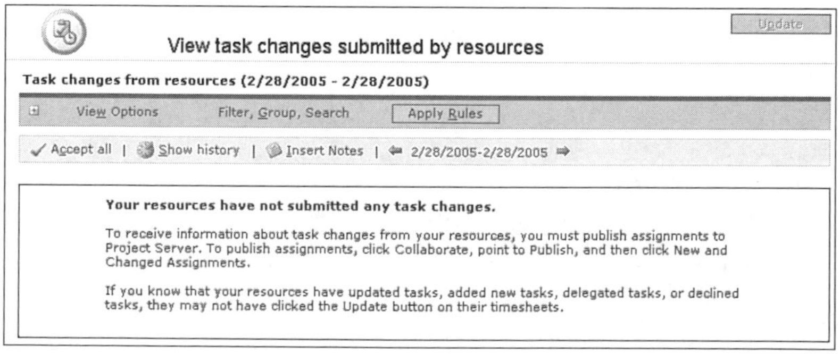

FIGURE 15.16   The Updates page indicates that you have accepted and saved all time, or no team members have submitted time.

> **TIP**
>
> In the Updates page, a project manager cannot see whether the team member has increased the Remaining Work (the estimate to complete) for the task from the original baseline. If she did, the project manager would have early warning that the submittal from the team member would possibly jeopardize an on-time completion of the task or even the project. At this time, there is no way to include Baseline Work into this Updates view. You have two alternatives: Bring up the project schedule in a separate window and review the baseline work for the assignment, or go ahead and accept the time, update your schedule, and then see what effect it has, adjusting the work in the schedule later.

General Information About Using the Updates Page

The Updates grid lists all the updates submitted by resources working on all your projects. The list shows the assignment fields with the task and a timesheet view of actual work hours, percent complete, and remaining work.

Column widths, positions, sort orders, and the pane divider position can all be changed. You can use the View Options and Filter, Group, Search functions as on the other PWA pages. You can change the view from Timesheet view to Gantt Chart view.

▶ **SEE** "Viewing Data on the Timesheet," **PAGE 321**.

The Updates page contains the following main areas:

- **Customization tabs**—Allows you to customize the way tasks are displayed in the Update sheet, allowing you to show summary tasks; show different outline levels, filters, and groups; and to apply rules (refer to Figure 15.14 for the customization tabs). You might want to use the filters shown in Figure 15.17 to help you approve time.

> **TIP**
>
> If you are using Managed Time Periods and you have a process where the resource or functional manager needs to approve time before the project manager updates the schedule, you may want to use the following feature: In View Options, select Show Timesheet Status. Nonapproved time displays an asterisk in the Act. Work field after the work total. The project manager may decide to call the resource manager to find out why the time was not approved and reject the hours for the team member.

- **Updates action bar**—Drives various actions in the update sheet such as accepting all tasks, showing history, inserting notes, and changing the time reporting period scale.
- **Accept/Reject Task Column and Updates list**—Displays all the tasks and associated update fields such as Work, Remaining Work, % complete, Start, and Finish dates. This also includes the Accept/Reject Task column where you select the value to indicate whether you are accepting or rejecting the resource's updates.

15

- **The Indicators column**—Displays icons that identify the status of the task updates or other associated information. You may see a red flag occasionally, which means that a task has been updated into the plan, but the project plan has not been saved. Click the Updates button again and open the project schedule to make sure that the information is saved.

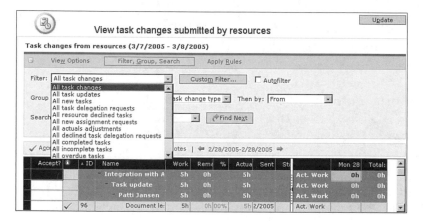

FIGURE 15.17   Filters available to help you approve time submitted.

Alert Me

As with the Tasks page, you can set email reminders based on the updates your resources make. You may want to be alerted via email whenever your resources create a new task or assignment.

▶ **SEE** "Managing Alerts," **PAGE 305**.

General Rules for the Updates Page

Here are some general rules for what can be expected in the Updates page:

- If a resource sends multiple updates on a single task, only the latest displays. Also, if the update is saved into the project schedule and the resource submits a correction, the change will be corrected into the schedule when you save the new update.

- If a resource delegates a task, one row will be displayed in the update list. If the resource rejects the delegation, it will be on a separate row, and the Accept field will not be editable because the two updates negate each other.

- The tracking mode of the pending updates determines whether to display a timesheet or a Gantt Chart view. If specific hours are used for any update, the timesheet displays—otherwise, a Gantt Chart view displays.

- Project Professional must be installed on the machine to accept the updates.

You may see the following kinds of task update transactions for each resource in the Updates page grid:

- Request for their task to be delegated to someone else.

- Declining task delegation and assignments.

- Update of a task such as changes to remaining work and/or actuals being submitted.

- Request for new tasks to be created or new task assignments.

After an update is completed successfully, the record is moved to a transaction history you can access by choosing View History of Past Task changes. Any updates left blank are pending and will remain on the Updates page until they are either accepted or rejected.

Setting Rules

In some cases, you might want to create a set of rules that automatically accept changes and updates from resources based on various parameters. For example, maybe you want to automatically accept any task updates on a project containing support work for ensuring that computers are up and operational. This work is routine, and you have many resources who are simply reporting their time. You are not concerned with how it affects the project schedule. You can set these rules by selecting Set Rules for Automatically Accepting Changes or by clicking on the Rules link, which is contained in the instruction text on the Apply Rules tab on the Updates page.

CAUTION

Use this feature with caution. It reduces oversight of the timesheet process. It means that if someone enters 12 instead of 1 (or 1 instead of 12), the project manager will not see it until it is already in the schedule.

The Set Rules function presents a wizard that allows you to select the criteria for the rule. Step 1 asks you the criteria for task updates you want to automatically accept. Figure 15.18 shows the criteria you can select in the first step. Step 2 asks you to select the projects you want the tasks to apply to. Step 3 allows you to name the resources you want the rules to apply to and allows you to set the name of the rule. The drop-down box allows you to apply the rules to selected projects or to those specified in the rules. You can limit the rules by the types of tasks, certain projects, or certain resources.

After you set up the rules you want, click the Apply Rules tab when the tasks that qualify show up in the Updates page. Then click the Run Rules Now button as shown in Figure 15.19.

The rule is applied each time the resource sends an update matching the rule, and the project schedule opens automatically when the Run Rules Now button is clicked. When you return to PWA, you see a message that the rules have been applied. Because this is automatic, it is easy to forget that you need to publish the schedule again to make sure that the changes are reflected to the team members, but you will need to do so.

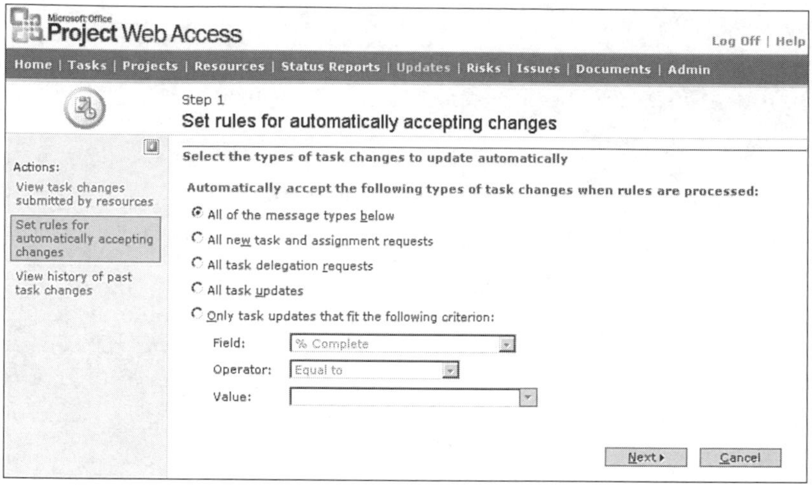

FIGURE 15.18   The first step in setting rules.

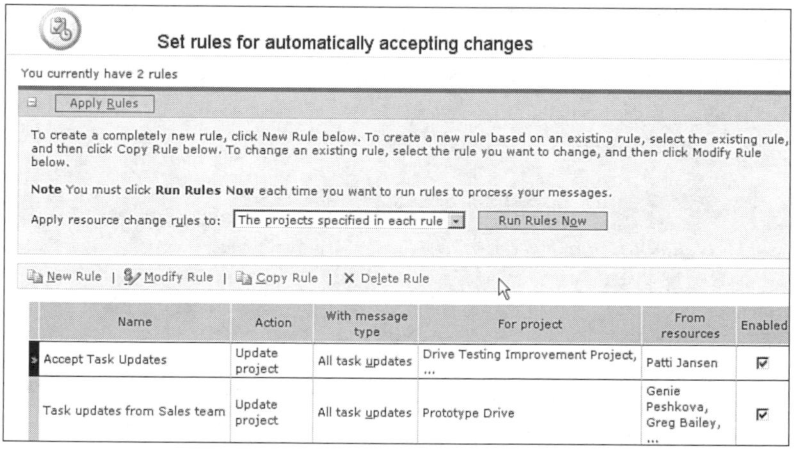

FIGURE 15.19   Use the Run Rules Now button to run the rules.

Only those names of resources with permissions to send updates and delegate tasks will be available when creating rules. Rules take precedence; a rule may override the Accept setting in the updates grid if the rule is satisfied.

Viewing History

Project Server archives past task updates that you have received and accepted or rejected. This allows you to review the history of task updates received for all your projects and resources. You may want to check this if you are not sure whether you approved a task or if you have a dispute with a team member about a particular task approval, but you usually will not use this information in day-to-day use of the system.

To see the transaction history for your task approval on the Updates page, click on View History of Past Task Changes on the side pane or click on the Show History button in the action bar. The major data you see depends on whether the tasks were accepted or rejected when the task was updated, the resource to whom the task was assigned, and actual work on the task.

You see the task approval history in a grid similar to the example shown in Figure 15.20. This grid can become large if you have numerous projects and assignments to manage.

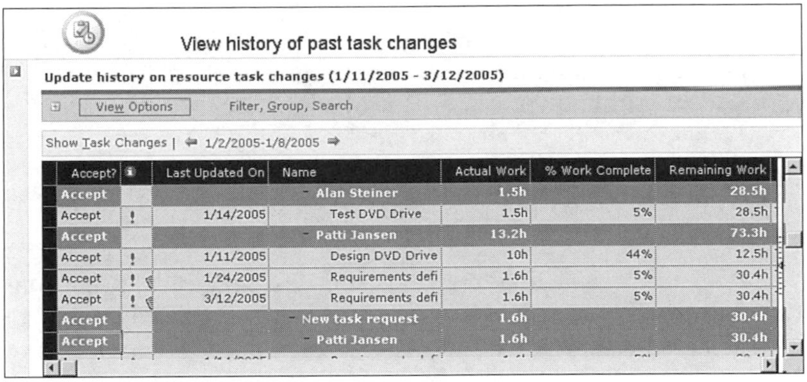

Accept?		Last Updated On	Name	Actual Work	% Work Complete	Remaining Work
Accept			– Alan Steiner	1.5h		28.5h
Accept	!	1/14/2005	Test DVD Drive	1.5h	5%	28.5h
Accept			– Patti Jansen	13.2h		73.3h
Accept	!	1/11/2005	Design DVD Drive	10h	44%	12.5h
Accept	!	1/24/2005	Requirements defi	1.6h	5%	30.4h
Accept	!	3/12/2005	Requirements defi	1.6h	5%	30.4h
Accept			– New task request	1.6h		30.4h
Accept			– Patti Jansen	1.6h		30.4h

FIGURE 15.20   Task changes transaction history.

NOTE

Do not use the View History feature as a way to see totals applied to each task for an assignment. This view shows each transaction. The totals for a task are not the total actual work applied to the task—it is an accumulation for the multiple transactions on each task.

The default number of days this transaction history is viewable is 60 days, and the administrator may change this setting.

Adjusting Time and Managerial Timesheet Review and Approval

Three other functions for managing time and timesheets exist in Project Server if you use Managed Time Periods.

Adjust Actuals in the Resource Center allows managers to enter or change time for a resource. This is especially useful when a time period is closed and the resource cannot enter time, or if a resource cannot get access to the Project Server but still needs to record time.

View Timesheet Summary in the Resource Center allows a manager to review the time entered by resources. At a glance, you can see whether the project manager has approved the time entered by the resource and whether the functional manager has approved the time via the process described next.

Approve Timesheets in the Resource Center allows a manager other than the project manager to approve the time. This is used when the functional manager needs to approve time before the project manager accepts actual work into the project schedule.

▶ **SEE** "Adjusting Actuals," **PAGE 391**.

Best Practices

It is important that your organization thinks through why it needs to record time and what is required to do so. Some organizations see the Tasks page and think that this can be the way to record all time for the organization for both project and accounting purposes. The main focus of the timesheet in Project Server is to record actual work for project reporting. Your organization can use the Managed Time Periods, the Timesheet API, or perhaps other Project Server add-ins from Microsoft partner companies to integrate with accounting systems and to help create one-stop time entry. To do so takes a great deal of design, programming, and testing before you will be able to deploy a robust and accurate accounting timesheet function for your organization.

If project management is new to your organization, you might want to first consider using the timesheet for only recording project actual work and transition to an accounting timesheet after your organization has time to hone the timesheet update cycle process.

Take the time to train your project managers and team members to understand how entering actual work and remaining work affects estimates. The Work field increases if more time than what was actually estimated is entered in the Actual Work or Remaining Work fields. This is why it is so important to baseline your projects or project tasks before publishing your task data to the Tasks page. The Work field on the Tasks page is equal to Remaining Work plus Actual Work. To see the original estimate, you might want to add the Baseline Work field to that Tasks page.

Do not use the Manage Rules feature until your organization has some experience with using the Updates page manually. It helps the project managers to understand the process of task updates, the errors that can be made in time entry, and how the time is recorded in the schedule, before you create rules that automatically process this.

CHAPTER 16

Using Project and Resource Centers

IN THIS CHAPTER

- Understanding the Project Center
- Understanding the Resource Center
- Best Practices

This chapter presents information about using the Project and Resource Centers in the context of analysis and prioritization of projects and resources to align with your corporate strategy.

To use the functionality of Microsoft Office Project 2003 to its full extent, it is important for you to understand the roles of project and resource information. The Project Center is designed to provide project information to several roles, such as executives, project managers, resource managers, and so on. The Resource Center is more specific to those managing a collection of resources such as executives and resources managers.

Views are created for these centers to help you understand your collection of projects and resources. You may especially want to build views in Project Center to see status, budget, return on investment, and prioritization data for projects that can roll up to a particular category of your project portfolio.

This chapter also discusses in detail the various features available to you in the Project and Resource Centers and how you can leverage them to complete numerous tasks.

Understanding the Project Center

The Project Center is a core part of the EPM solution because it truly reflects the concept of visualizing all aspects of projects. Project Center provides access to all projects, including project data, robust reports, views, modeling, and analytical tools.

Project Center displays project information defined by your administrator; this includes data columns, views, and the Enterprise Outline Codes created during configuration.

▶ **SEE** "Enterprise Global Codes," **PAGE 163**.

You can access Project Center through PWA (by selecting Projects in the top navigation menu), as shown in Figure 16.1.

TIP

Project Professional has collaboration functionality built in that allows you to see PWA Project Center (and other PWA screens) within the Project Professional frame. To view PWA Project Center within PWA, select Tools, Collaborate, and then Project Center.

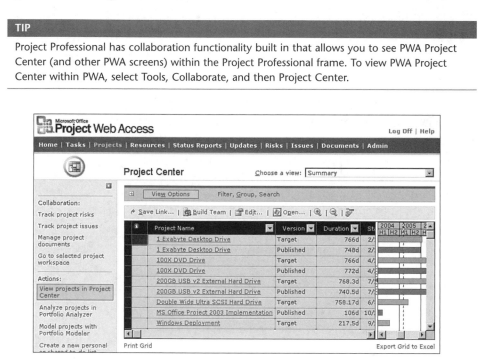

FIGURE 16.1   Project Center provides a comprehensive view of a portfolio of projects.

Project Center performs six main functions:

- **View Project in Project Center**—Provides high-level dashboard analysis of all projects in the Project Server database and allows you to review, compare, and analyze project progress, cost, variance, and other defined information. This option also provides you with the ability to view details of a specific project, various views, filters, and grouping and sorting options, and to change the type of data displayed in the columns of the view.

- **Analyze Projects in Portfolio Analyzer**—Allows you to analyze project data stored in the OLAP cube for better understanding of your entire portfolio. The OLAP cube contains all the information available from the published projects and is created on an impromptu basis or on a scheduled basis by your administrator.

- **Model Projects with Portfolio Modeler**—Allows you to model your future implementations or proposed changes to observe the effect they may have on your Project Server implementation. This option allows for execution of what-if scenarios without having an impact on the real data in the system.

- **Manage To-Do Lists**—Allows you to create, modify, and maintain personal to-do lists. To-do lists can be used for smaller personal tasks that do not require formal scheduling.

- **Check-in My Projects**—Allows you to release database locks on checked-out projects left open due to network or other technological problems. You need to have proper permissions to use this function.

- **Managing Administrative Projects**—Allows you to manage special projects created to track time spent on tasks that do not belong to projects that deliver goods and services. The administrative projects require different scheduling, actual time reporting, and resource usage.

The Project Center allows everyone with the appropriate permissions to drill into project data without having Project Professional installed on their desktop. Your project's status may be displayed here based on selected reports and fields. Your executives may use an Executive Summary Report, where they can see each project's budget and schedule status at a glance. A financial manager may have a Financial Report, where she may view each project's financial health in relation to strategic initiatives within the organization.

As a project manager, it is important that you understand that the Project Center brings visibility to your project. You need to keep your project's status and data up-to-date and as accurate as possible according to the processes set up in your organization.

The following sections discuss these and other functions of Project Center in more detail.

Using Project Center Views

The Project Center lists all the existing projects in the database that you have permission to view. From this view, you can select a project to work with in several ways. Project Center contains various prebuilt views that you can use to display the specific data you are looking for. Views can be a powerful tool when used for an at-a-glance look or a high-level summary perspective. Views can also provide the detailed information for more in-depth analysis.

▶ **SEE** "Project Web Access Project and Resource Views," **PAGE 209**.

Project Center views are displayed in the Choose a View list in the top-right corner of PWA, which allows you to view information about your project in various ways. You can select any view you want to apply, and the page reloads displaying the requested data.

Many organizations allow their project managers to view only their own projects or those they are assigned to as a team member, whereas other organizations allow the project managers to view all corporate projects. Team members see only the projects to which they are assigned unless additional permissions are provided.

16

Your organization may create a custom view for you or others in the organization that can be used to analyze data in relevant ways for the organization, an example of which is shown in Figure 16.2.

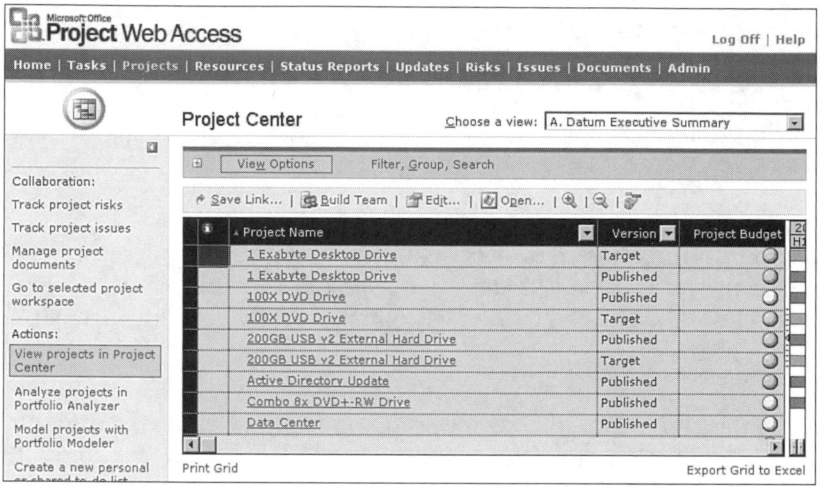

FIGURE 16.2   Project Center displaying a custom view called A. Datum Executive Summary of all projects (A.Datum is the prefix used in this database example for naming views).

This could be a useful view for portfolio managers and executives who need to have a complete view of the organizational portfolio of projects.

View Options

The View Options tab is located above the content window with the list of projects (or tasks if you are in the detailed project view) in Project Center. View Options allows you to specify the level of detail you want to apply to the current view. View Options changes slightly depending on whether you are looking at the project portfolio or project detail view.

From the Portfolio view of Project Center, View Options provides the following selections as shown in Figure 16.3:

- **Show Time with Date**—Displays the date and time for the Finish and Start dates of each project.

- **Show To-Do Lists**—Displays any existing to-do lists for all listed projects.

- **Show Outline Level**—Allows you to select the level of detail you want to see. For the Portfolio view, the outline level does not serve much purpose; it is a lot more useful when the project displayed contains levels (for example, the Detail view with the list of summary and regular tasks).

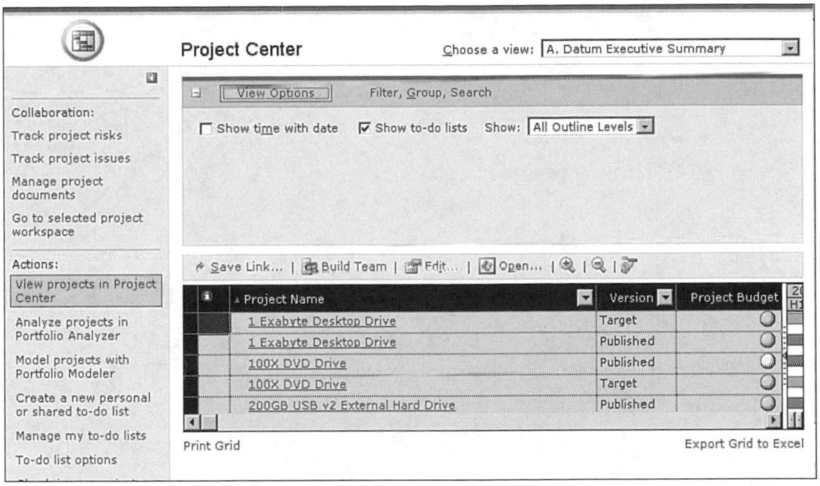

FIGURE 16.3 The View Options tab allows you to customize the current view even further.

From the Project view of Project Center, View Options provides the following selections, as shown in Figure 16.4:

- **Show Time with Date**—Displays the date and time for the Finish and Start dates of each project.

- **Show Summary Tasks**—When selected, this displays all summary tasks in the project schedule. You may want to remove the summary tasks to see just the actual tasks without the "tree" structure.

- **Summary Rollup**—Rolls up the summary data for the displayed project.

- **Show Outline Level**—Allows you to select the outline level to which you want the task list compressed/expanded. For example, all outline levels display the expanded list of all tasks. Outline level 1 reduces the list of tasks to the top summary task (generally the same as the project name). Outline level 2 displays the next level down from outline level 1, so it shows the summary task level below the main summary task. This expansion continues until all the tasks in the list are displayed.

Filter, Group, Search

The Filter, Group, Search tab is a powerful tool for presenting projects in different sorts and groupings. You can use this feature based on the parameters (columns) present only in the grid, as shown in Figure 16.5.

Using Filters You can use the Filter options provided in Project Center for filtering the displayed list of projects by various criteria. Project Center provides three types of filters:

- **Filter**—The drop-down box provides two options: All Projects and Custom Filter. If you select the Custom Filter option from the drop-down list (or by clicking the Custom Filter button), the More-Filters pull-down is displayed at the top of each column.

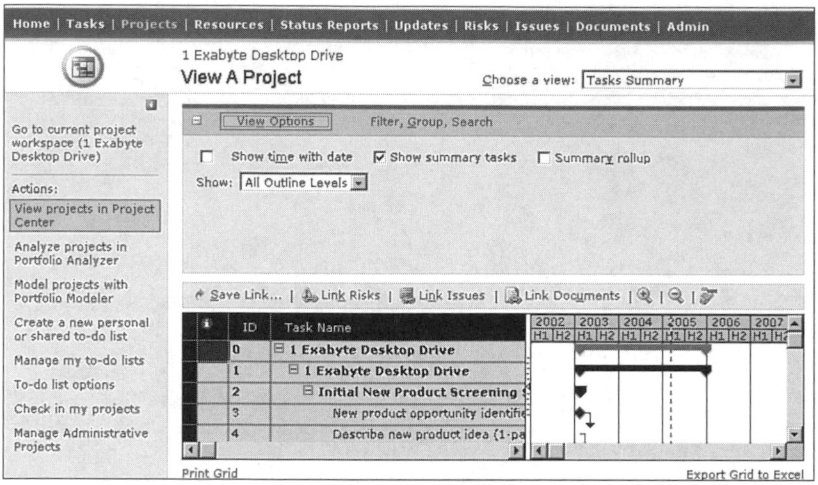

FIGURE 16.4   View Options allows you to customize the detailed Project view.

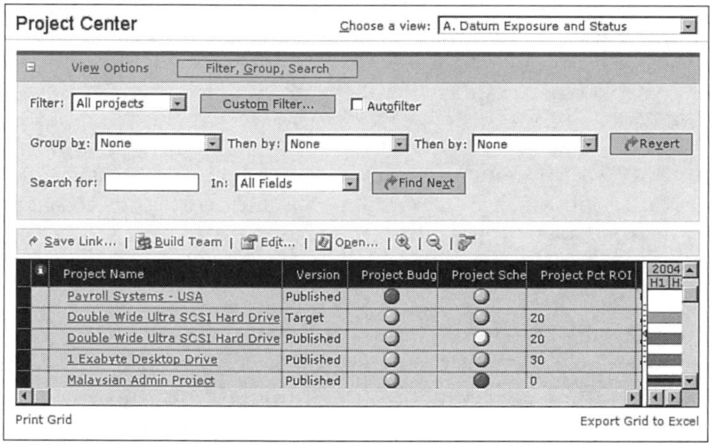

FIGURE 16.5   You cannot filter, group, or search for projects based on attributes not present in the Project Center grid.

- **Custom Filter**—Provides three criteria to filter the projects by. This allows for further customization and limiting of the data displayed, as shown in Figure 16.6.

- **Autofilter**—Displays drop-down arrows at the top of each column in the current view. When Autofilter is selected, it allows you to filter by a specific field within that column.

Using the Group Functionality   The Group By function in Project Center allows you to organize the displayed projects into groups. The Group By function in Filter, Group, Search is useful for showing the rollup for projects based on different conditions. In the example shown in Figure 16.7, the Group By function displays projects by location. You can change this grouping quickly and see a new report in seconds.

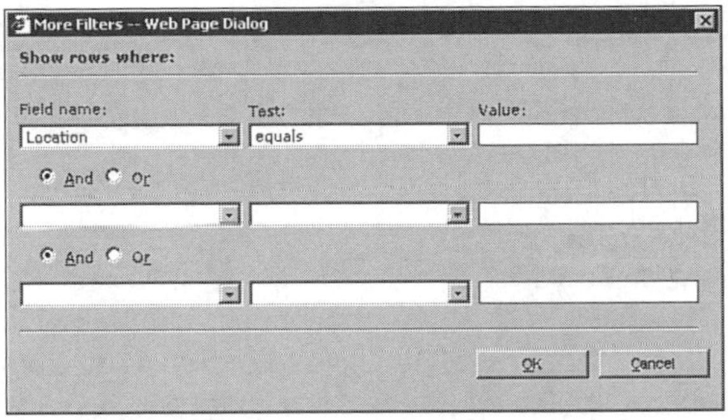

FIGURE 16.6   To apply the filter, select the field, condition, and value to filter by. You can filter by more than value by selecting the And or Or option.

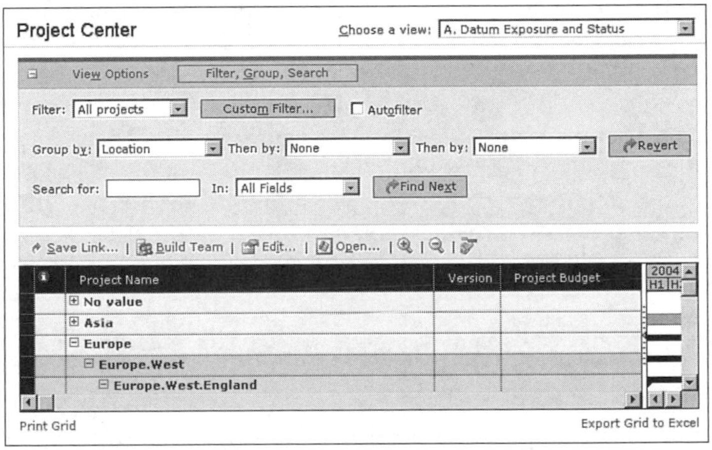

FIGURE 16.7   Project Center displaying projects grouped by location.

The administrator may set a special default grouping for your projects. You can change the grouping for the view. If you want to return to the default grouping, click Revert. Using Revert causes Project Center to display projects using the predefined view chosen.

> **NOTE**
>
> It is not possible to group on any field not currently defined for the view in the Project Center grid. If you want to group, filter, or do a search in a view with fields that aren't currently defined for the view, ask your Project Server administrator to modify or create a view for you.

Using Search   The Search function in Project Center provides you with the ability to quickly and efficiently locate the desired projects. Search allows you to search by all fields currently displayed in the view. You can use the Find Next button to move to the next item in the list that meets your search criteria.

TIP

If the field that you want to search by does not appear in the Field Name drop-down list of the Search function, make sure that this field is available in the current view. If the field is not available, find a view that contains the appropriate fields.

The Magic of Portfolio Management

Now that you've seen the functionality of views, options, and Filter/Group/Search in Project Center, portfolio management is more easily achieved. Portfolio management is viewing projects in collections aligned to your business processes. First, you need to choose a view that contains the columns of information you want to group on, such as A Datum Budget Summary. It is usually correct to include the Enterprise Outline Codes created during configuration because these are directly related to business processes.

Next, select the Filter/Group/Search button and select the business process to group on, such as Location. If you are the manager of the San Jose office, you now have a collection of projects for your office with the rollup cost and budget data you want in the columns, as shown in Figure 16.8. In this way, you can begin to analyze the importance, variance, and status of the collection of project making up your portfolio. There are many ways to analyze collections of projects against your business processes; this is just one example. Attention to detail is important when initially creating the Enterprise Outline Codes that describe the business processes for which you choose to capture data.

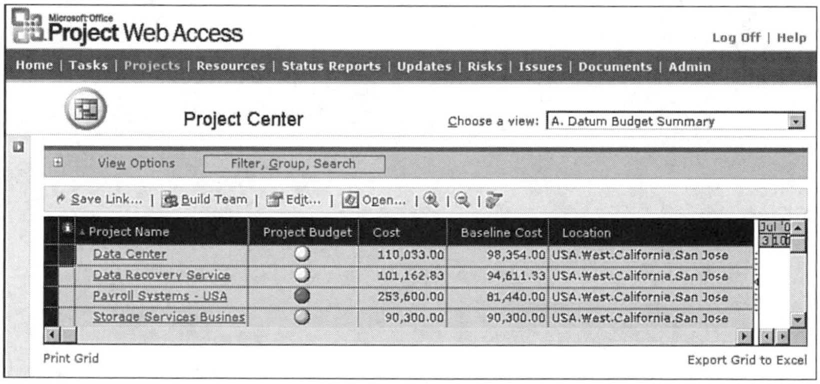

FIGURE 16.8   An example of a portfolio based on budgets and location.

Using Save Link to Create Custom Personal Views

The Save Link button allows viewing, filtering, sorting, and grouping formatting options to be saved as a customized view. As you find desired views in your day-to-day work, you can save these links as your own personal view.

CAUTION

Saved links are specific to your Project Server profile. They are not visible as enterprise views to the rest of the organization.

To save a link associated with your profile, select all desired view options and click Save Link. A dialog box displays, and you are prompted to enter the name of the view you want to save; then click OK.

You see a link created in the upper left of the side pane under Saved Links, as shown in Figure 16.9.

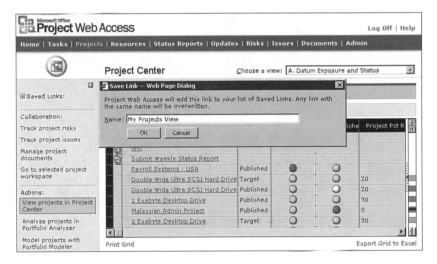

FIGURE 16.9   Create a unique and descriptive name for the view you are creating.

The Saved Links link does not display if you have not saved any links. To access any of your saved custom format views, click on this link. From here you can delete or rename your links as well. To do this, click on Organize Your Saved Links under Actions in the side pane. The Organize Your Saved Links page displays only if you have saved links, as shown in Figure 16.10. Select the link and either click Delete or Rename depending on the function you want to perform.

Using the Build Team Function

Assigning resources to tasks allows the project manager to track the resources' progress in completing the task. However, to assign the resources, the project and/or resource manager needs to build the project team first and look into Proposed versus Committed resources. The Build Team feature is a web-based version of the Build Team from Enterprise feature in Project Professional.

▶ **SEE** "Building Project Team and Resource Substitution," **PAGE 563**.

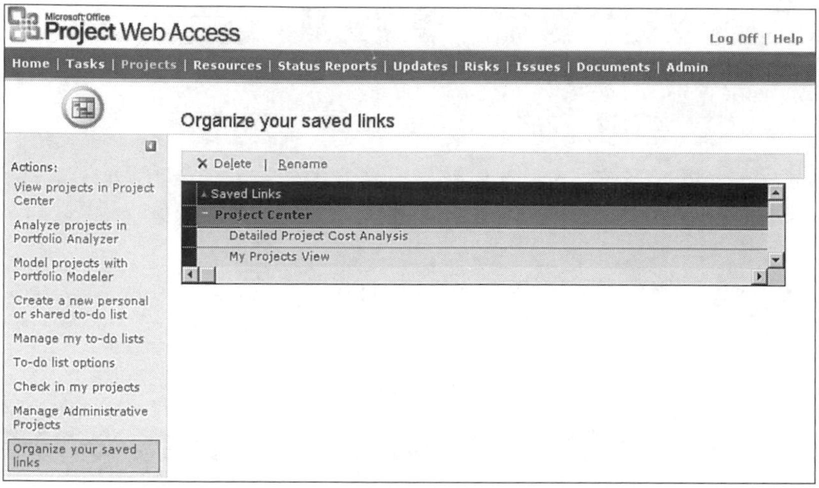

FIGURE 16.10   Select the link you want to change and click Rename to change its name, or click Delete to completely delete the link.

NOTE

Build Team in PWA does provide handy matching, searching, and analytical features, but it is recommended that you use the Project Professional full-featured Build Team from Enterprise to perform any advanced additions, matching, and assignments. Build Team in PWA is a light feature for quickly adding resources to your project. Build Team can also be handy for resource managers, who can still manage resources on different projects without having Project Professional installed on their desktops.

If you have appropriate permissions, you can build the project team from the Enterprise Resource Pool by adding enterprise resources to your project team in PWA. From the action bar in the Project Center, select the project you want to build the team for and move resources from the Enterprise Resource Pool to the project team.

You can also indicate whether a resource is committed to the project, or still is in a proposed state. You can view availability information for the proposed team members to help you decide whether they should be changed to Committed status for the project.

BOOKING TYPE: PROPOSED VERSUS COMMITTED

Project 2003 Professional allows you to change the booking condition of project resources.

All resources, by default, are assigned using the Committed status. This indicates that the individual resource has been confirmed as a working resource to the project.

If the project manager did not receive authorization yet to assign that resource to a particular task in his project, the project manager changes the status of booking to Proposed.

The main difference between the two types of bookings is that Committed resources receive task timesheet notices and can submit timesheet updates to the project manager, whereas Proposed resources do not receive task timesheet notices, so they cannot submit actual work to the project manager.

The primary benefit of this Proposed, *soft booking*, type is to allow project managers to simulate the resource loading and cost impact of selecting specific resources as part of the project team.

For example, if you are a project manager who is negotiating with resource managers to use certain resources for your project, you can use the Proposed type of booking for the resources to simulate the effects on your project and the workload on those resources. You then use the simulated soft booking analysis as a basis during your negotiations with appropriate resource managers. After the resources are confirmed to work on the project, you can change the resource booking type to Committed.

In organizations with both resource and project managers, the project managers use Project Professional to build the project schedule and assign generic resources to the specific tasks. An example of a generic resource may be a senior C++ developer, or an IT specialist. In this case, the resource manager uses the Build Team function in PWA to replace the generic resources with real people, based on resource availability and other characteristics. This allows for smooth resource allocation process and also does not require resource managers to have Project Professional installed on their desktops.

To build a team for a specific project, follow these steps:

1. Highlight the row containing the project.

2. In the top navigation menu, click Build Team.

3. The Build Team page is displayed.

> **CAUTION**
>
> The Project Center Build Team function attaches resources to a project but does not generally assign those resources to individual working tasks.

The Build Team page consists of three main areas:

- **Filter Enterprise Resources**—Allows you to apply a custom filter in searching for appropriate enterprise resources that meet your criteria to be added to the project, as shown in Figure 16.11.

- **Build Team**—Allows you to add, remove, replace, and match the resources for your project, as shown in Figure 16.12.

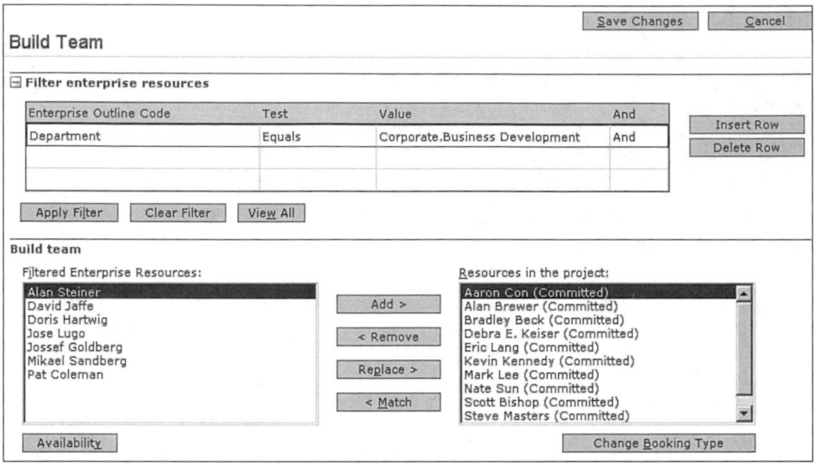

FIGURE 16.11 The filtered resources are displayed in the Filter Enterprise Resources box under Build Team.

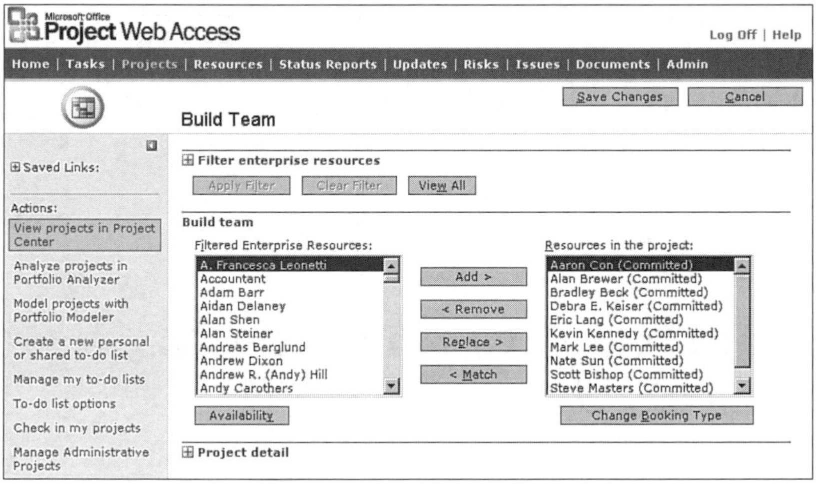

FIGURE 16.12 The Build Team displays both enterprise resources available in the Enterprise Resource Pool and already assigned project resources.

- **Project Detail**—Provides a detailed project schedule with the list of all tasks and other important project information, as shown in Figure 16.13.

The Build Team feature is used to find, match, and acquire the appropriate resources for your project. The main functionality included in Build Team is add, remove, replace, match, view availability, and change the booking type of resources.

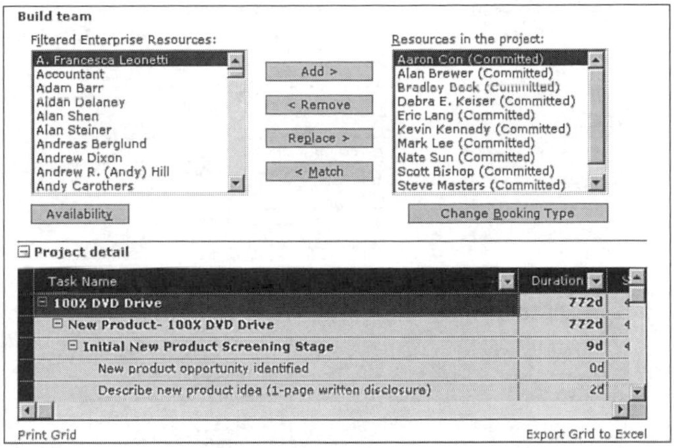

FIGURE 16.13 Scroll down to see each level of tasks available in the selected project.

Filter Enterprise Resources

To view all resources available from the Resource Pool, select View All. All resources display on the left side of the screen.

> **TIP**
>
> If you cannot see any resources available for assignment to a project, make sure that the Filter Resources box is cleared.

You can also use the filter to bring up all resources in the Resource Pool matching custom filter conditions defined. For example, you might filter resources for a particular skill or department. Filter conditions are based on Resource Outline Codes available. The Filter Enterprise Resources feature provides four selections: Enterprise Outline Code, Test, Value, and And, as shown in Figure 16.14.

Enterprise Outline Code is a drop-down list that retrieves all resource outline codes available in Project Server—for example, department, skill, RBS, and so on. The Test field is automatically filled in, depending on the Enterprise Outline Code you have selected. For example, if you select Department, the test is "equals," if you select Skills, the test value is "contains," and so on. The Value field retrieves available values for the selected Enterprise Outline Codes. The And field is used as a connective to combine more than one search criteria, if applicable.

You can also use the Match function under Build Team to achieve similar results, which is discussed in the next section.

> **CAUTION**
>
> The resource must meet the exact criteria set selected for Project Center to return the appropriate results.

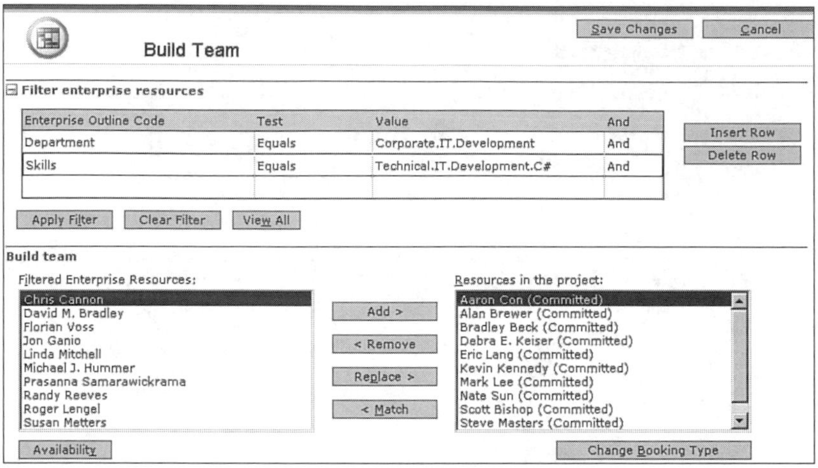

FIGURE 16.14   Enterprise Resources displays filtered resources that belong to the Development Department with C++ Developer skill set.

You may insert additional rows by clicking the Insert Row button. You can also delete rows by clicking the Delete Row button.

Adding Resources to a Project

The Add button adds the selected resource in the Filtered Enterprise Resources box to the Resources in the Project box with a Committed booking type. You may change the booking type of the resource by selecting the resource name and clicking the Change Booking Type button.

Removing Resources from Project

The Remove button allows you to remove a resource from the Resources in the Project box.

> **NOTE**
>
> The Remove button permanently removes resources from your project, but it does not delete them from the Enterprise Resource Pool. If you accidentally remove a resource, you can add it back using the Add button.

> **CAUTION**
>
> The PWA Build Team function does not allow you to remove resources that have actuals associated with them. When you attempt to save your changes on the Build Team page, it will display an error message. To properly remove the resource from your project, use Project Professional.

Replacing Resources

The Replace function allows you to select a resource in your project and replace it with a selected resource in the Filtered Enterprise Resources box. This function is especially handy because it performs the removal/addition of resources in one step.

> **CAUTION**
>
> The PWA Build Team function does not allow you to replace resources that have actuals associated with them. To replace a resource with existing actuals, use the Assign Resources feature in Project Professional. This retains the original resource's actuals and assigns the remaining work to the replacement resource.

Matching Resources

The Match function allows you to find a matching resource to your current project resource. To match a primary skill, make sure that the appropriate generic resource is selected in the Resources in the Project box, click on the Match button, and the individual resources with the matching primary skill will display.

To look for a match based on a skill of an individual resource who is already a member of the project team, select the individual resource in the Resources in the Project box on the right side, click Match, and all other enterprise resources with the same skill will be displayed on the left side in the Filtered Enterprise Resources box. This function is especially useful when you need to replace a resource on your team, but you may not have a specific person in mind who is able to perform the task. The Match function matches up the resource skills, languages, and any other attributes your resources may have and provides a list of people who match the resource who requires replacement.

The Match and Replace features of both PWA and Project Professional support the resource change problem by allowing quick resource matching and substitution. For example, one of the current resources on the project team has a family emergency and has to take a month off. The Match and Replace features can be used to substitute that resource for someone else with a matching skill set who can fulfill the task commitments.

Changing Resource Booking Type

You may change the booking type of a resource in your project by selecting the resource name and clicking the Change Booking Type button. When the resources are first added to the project using the Build Team function, their booking type is set to Committed. If you are a resource manager and the resource added to the project needs to be approved by the project manager, you may choose the Proposed booking type. The Proposed booking type does not "assign" the resource to the project but rather suggests that this particular resource should be used. To assign a resource to tasks within the project, the booking type must be set to Committed.

Viewing Resource Availability When Building a Team

In many cases, you may want to view the resource's availability before making the resource part of the project team. You can do this with the Build Team feature in both PWA and Project Professional.

The Project Center Build Team function provides a quick link to view resource availability from where you can select one or more resources from the Filtered Enterprise Resources and Resources in the Project boxes, and then click the Availability button to see a forecast of time the resources can work.

The Availability page displays all selected resources, allowing you to view them all together or separately by selecting or clearing check boxes next to their names. The Availability page also provides multiple views such as Assignment Work by Resource, Assignment Work by Project, Remaining Availability, and Work. These four views provide the flexibility to view and analyze specific resource availability information whether you are looking at a certain project, work in general, or remaining availability. The View Options button is also available that has the same functionality as the View Options button on the Project Center page.

Edit Projects in Project Center

The Edit function in PWA allows you to edit Enterprise Project Outline Codes assigned for the project. The fields not displayed in the PWA Edit Project Detail view can be modified by using the Project Professional, Project, Project Information menu. To edit a project, highlight the cell (do not click the project name hyperlink) of the project you want to edit and select Edit from the top menu. The Project Details screen is displayed and allows you to edit and save the available project information, as shown in Figure 16.15. Click Save and Close to save your changes, or select Go Back to Project Center to return to the Project Center View Projects page.

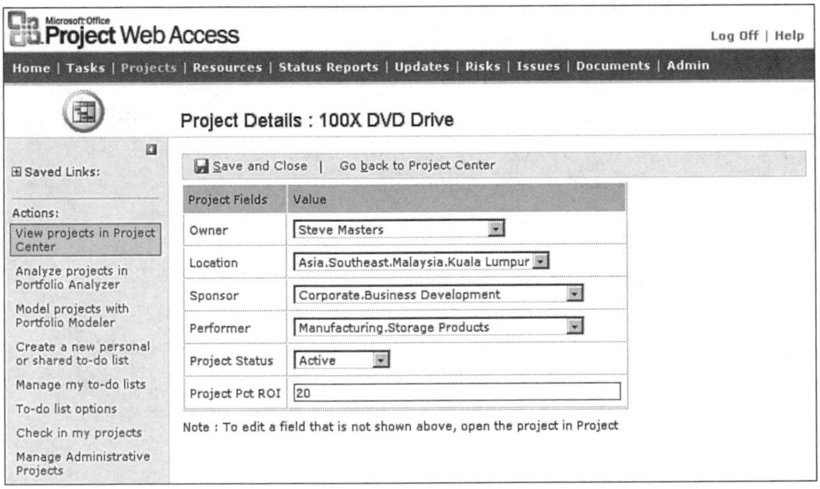

FIGURE 16.15   The changes you save using the Project Details screen in PWA are saved to the database and are reflected in the Project Information window within Project Professional.

Open Projects from Project Center

Project Center also has a functionality built in that allows you to open project plans in Project Professional from PWA. This feature allows for easy access to the desired project without having to look for it in a Project Professional list. For example, if you are using PWA to filter for projects that are behind schedule, you can select the specific project and open it in Project Professional to further analyze the reason for the project being late. To open a project in Project Professional, highlight the row containing the project you want to open and click Open in the top menu. This opens the project plan of the selected project in Project Professional, as shown in Figure 16.16.

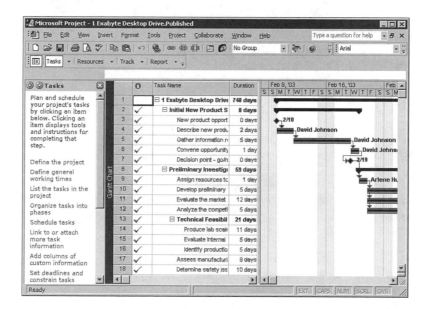

FIGURE 16.16   Project WBS in Project Professional.

You may also use this function to open multiple projects at once, as discussed in the next section on master projects.

Master Projects

Project Center allows you to open several projects at one time for analysis and reporting purposes. You can see several projects in one *master project* (also known as a *consolidated project*). To open such a project, highlight all the projects in the Project Center that you want to see and click the Open button in the action bar. A project opens in Project Professional containing all the projects that you selected, as shown in Figure 16.17. You can click on the plus sign next to the project name to display each of the project's details.

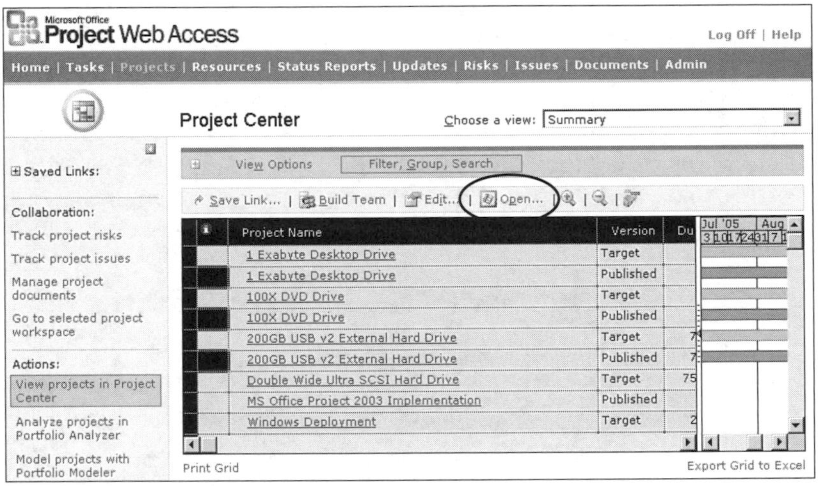

FIGURE 16.17 Selecting multiple projects in PWA.

TIP

If you want to pick multiple projects, hold down the Ctrl key on the keyboard while selecting the project row with the mouse. Each mouse click selects or clears an item from the project list.

You can also select multiple projects by using the PWA Group and Filter functions to cluster projects within a header group. If you select the header group, all projects within that group are selected, as shown in Figure 16.18.

NOTE

You need to close Project Professional before you can open a master project.

OPENING MORE THAN 10 PROJECTS AT A TIME

When you try to open more than 10 projects at a time you get a caution message that allows you to control how the projects are opened for Read/Write editing or just Read-Only review. If you open many projects for Read/Write, processing may take several minutes to check out each project from the Project Server repository and deliver it to your Microsoft Project 2003 Professional session. Use the Read-Only mode if you are reviewing multiple projects and you do not want to save changes. If you select Cancel, the projects are not opened, and you are returned to the PWA Project Center.

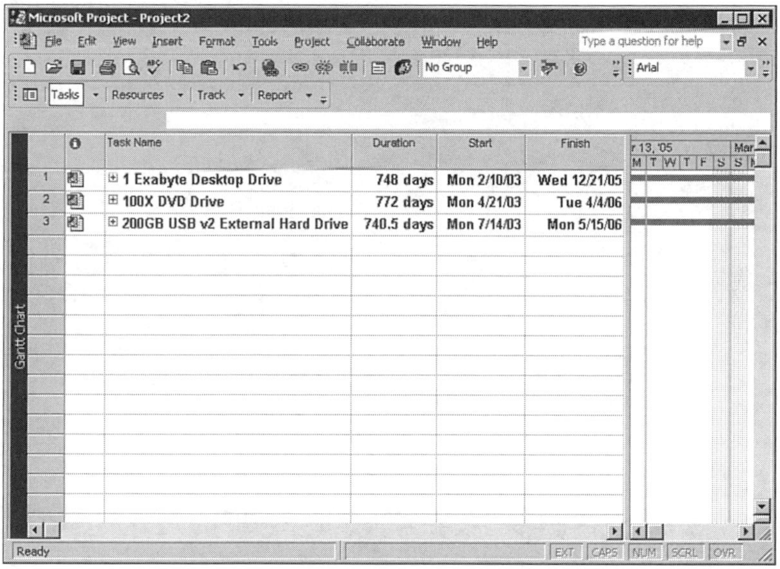

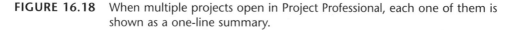

FIGURE 16.18   When multiple projects open in Project Professional, each one of them is shown as a one-line summary.

Gantt Chart Zoom Icon

Zoom In and Zoom Out is a feature that allows you to increase or decrease the time periods shown in the Gantt Chart view. This can be useful for viewing graphical details of a project schedule, as shown in Figure 16.19.

Gantt Chart Go to Task Icon

The Gantt Chart view in Project Center also contains the Go to Task icon, which allows you to move the focus of the chart to the specified task. Use the Go to Task icon to bring the beginning of the Gantt bar for a specific project into view. To do so, highlight the project (do not click the project name hyperlink because that will bring you to the project detail screen) and click the Go To Task button, as shown in Figure 16.20.

16

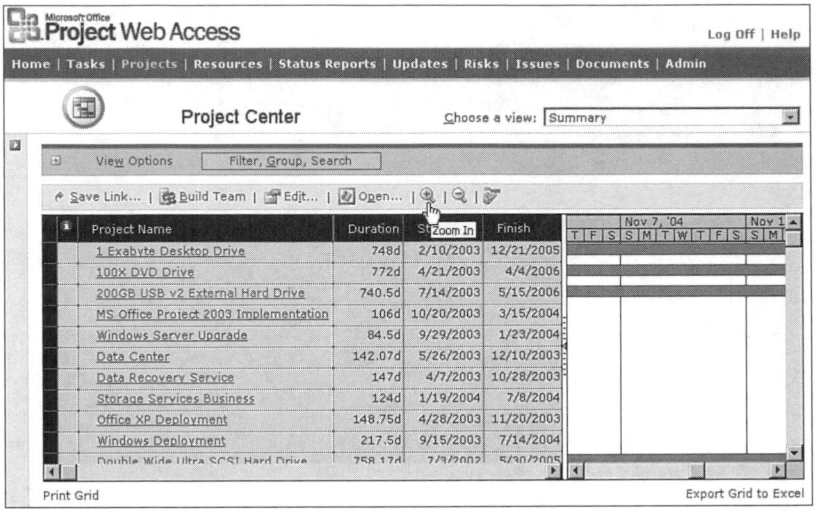

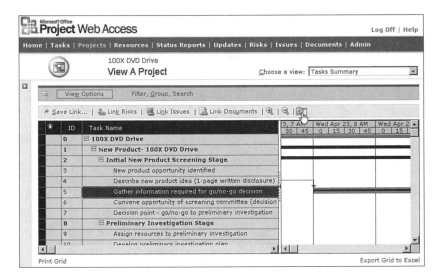

FIGURE 16.19   The Zoom Out feature allows you to view the high-level Gantt Chart view for the summary information, and Zoom In allows you to see the more intricate project schedule details.

FIGURE 16.20   Concentrating on a specific area of the Gantt chart allows you to better analyze the graphical representation of the project schedule in respect to other projects in your portfolio.

Project Center Printing

The Print Grid feature allows you to view a printer-friendly version of the current view. This option eases the printing process by removing unnecessary objects that are hard to print, such as the PWA frame, as shown in Figure 16.21.

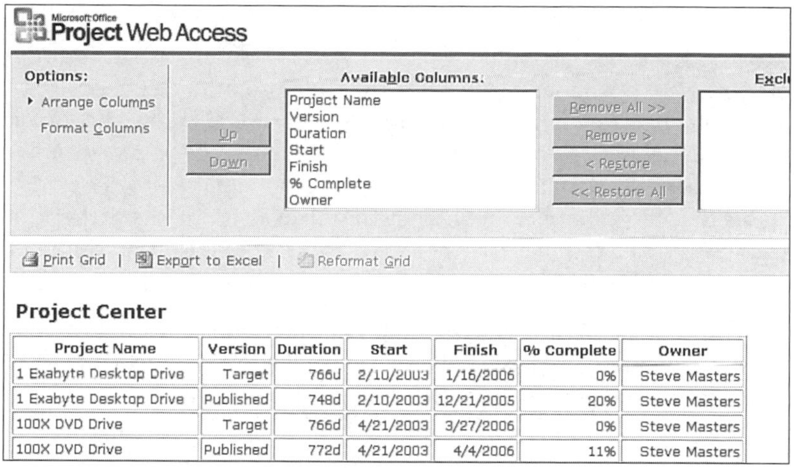

FIGURE 16.21   All project data is displayed in an easy-to-read format.

Project Center Export to Excel

Project Center also allows you export the detailed data into a Microsoft Excel worksheet. When you click the Export to Excel link, Microsoft Excel launches, and the data details are automatically exported to a new Excel worksheet, as shown in Figure 16.22. This feature may be especially useful if you want to take a snapshot of the current portfolio status, manipulate data using Excel functions, or take the snapshot offline for further analysis.

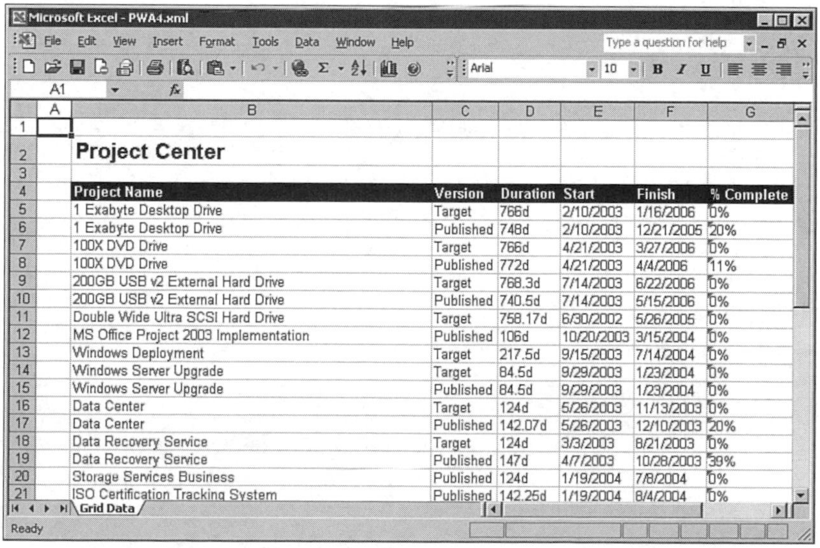

16

FIGURE 16.22   Excel preserves the data format of the Project Center and adds a user and date and time stamp for historic purposes.

Viewing Project Details

In addition to being able to select different views to consider all displayed projects, Project Center provides a detailed view of each specific project you choose. From the Project Center, you can select a project to work with in several ways. The Project Detail area contains the detailed work breakdown structure that allows you to see all project tasks. This option is particularly handy because you can view the project plan and look up specific tasks that, for example, require new resource assignments without having to open Project Professional. You may use the Print Grid and Export to Excel functions directly on the Project Detail.

Each project name listed is an active hyperlink that opens a page listing that project's data, as shown in Figure 16.23. This detailed view displays project schedule detail, related tasks, important task indicators, and other detailed information.

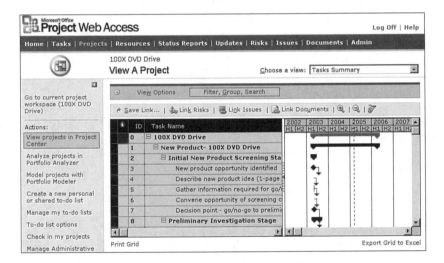

FIGURE 16.23   Project Center allows you to view a specific project's schedule.

The View a Project page also contains the Choose a View selection, which allows you to view specific reports matching the ones on the Project Center project portfolio page.

The detailed project view allows you to perform other activities, such as linking risks, issues, and documents to a specific task.

To link a risk to a project task, follow these steps:

1. Select the task you want linked by clicking on its name in the cell.

2. To link a risk specifically created for that task, you need to create it. To do so, click the New Risk button and follow the instructions. Click the Link Project Risks button to link a risk submitted for the entire project and not a specific task.

3. If you are linking a project risk, select the desired risk from the list of risks associated with the project.

4. Identify the relationship description between the linked items, as shown in Figure 16.24.

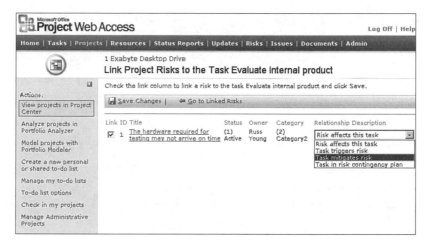

FIGURE 16.24   The Relationship Description specifies the effect the risk and the task will have on one another—for example, if the risk is going to affect the task or if the task is going to trigger the risk.

5. To create this link, click the Save Changes button.

To link documents and issues to a specific task, follow the steps described for risks and substitute Link Project Risks with Link Project Documents or Link Project Issues, respectively. Collaboration using the Project Center is also discussed in more detail later in this chapter.

▶ **SEE** "Risks, Issues, and Documents Using Windows SharePoint Services (WSS)," **PAGE 441**.

Collaboration Using Project Center

Project Center supports the powerful collaboration functionality of Project Server using risks, issues, and documents. Project Center collaboration allows you to

- **Track project risks**—Links you to the Risks page for the selected project

- **Track project issues**—Links you to the Issues page for the selected project

- **Manage project documents**—Links you to the Documents page for the selected project

- **Go to selected project workspace**—Opens the Windows SharePoint Services site for the selected project, which allows you to manage risks, issues, documents, and other project artifacts that support team collaboration

> **NOTE**
>
> If you receive the message "The documents, risks, and issues features in Project Web Access use Windows SharePoint Services. A Windows SharePoint Services site needs to be created for your project before you can share project documents or track project risks and issues. Site creation takes a few minutes, so if the project was just published, wait a few minutes and then visit the page again. Otherwise, contact your server administrator." while trying to access risks, issues, documents, or the project workspace, that means that the project you selected does not have a Windows SharePoint Services site associated with it. Contact your Project Server administrator and request a new site to be created for that project.

▶ **SEE** "Collaboration Using Windows SharePoint Services," **PAGE 442**.

Track Project Risks

The Track Project Risks function is located in the left pane under Collaboration. To track project risks, follow these steps:

1. Highlight the project row for which you want to track risks.

2. Click the Track Project Risks link under Collaboration in the left pane.

3. The Risks page for the selected project is displayed, providing you with a summary view of all risks currently entered for the project, as shown in Figure 16.25.

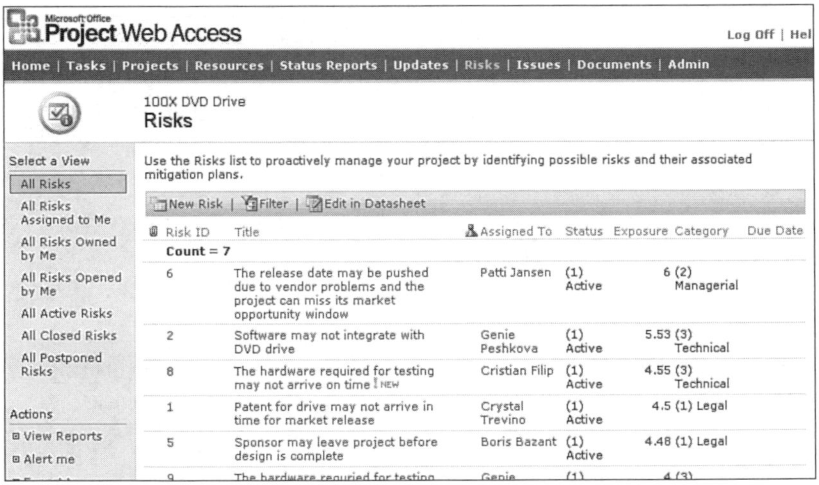

FIGURE 16.25   The Risks page allows you to create, modify, delete, and edit risks for the project.

▶ **SEE** "Risks," **PAGE 454**.

Track Project Issues

The Track Project Issues link is available in the left side pane under Collaboration and allows you to view, modify, and create issues for a particular project. To track issues

1. Highlight the project row for which you want to track issues.

2. Click the Track Project Issues link under Collaboration in the left pane.

3. The Issues page for the selected project is displayed, providing you with a summary view of all issues currently entered for the project, as shown in Figure 16.26.

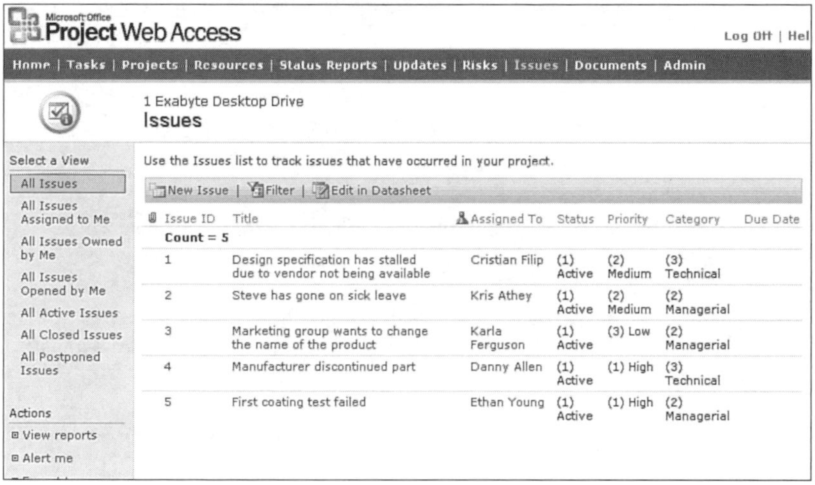

FIGURE 16.26   The Issues page allows you to create, modify, delete, and edit issues for the project.

▶ **SEE** "Issues," **PAGE 462**.

Manage Project Documents

The Manage Project Documents function is available in the left side pane under the Collaboration menu and allows you to control the document libraries and document artifacts for your project.

To manage documents, perform the following steps:

1. Highlight the project row for which you want to manage documents.

2. Click the Manage Project Documents link under Collaboration in the left pane.

3. The View and Upload Documents page for the selected project is displayed, providing you with a list of all document libraries available for the selected project, as shown in Figure 16.27.

▶ **SEE** "Documents," **PAGE 468**.

Go to Selected Project Workspace

Go to Selected Project Workspace is a feature that takes you to the Windows SharePoint Services (WSS) home page for the project. The project manager may list announcements and events here; you may store your project's directory; and you can also go to issues, risks, and documents for the project from that workspace. The project team may use this workspace for many functions to store information and communicate about the project. Figure 16.28 shows a snapshot of the project home page.

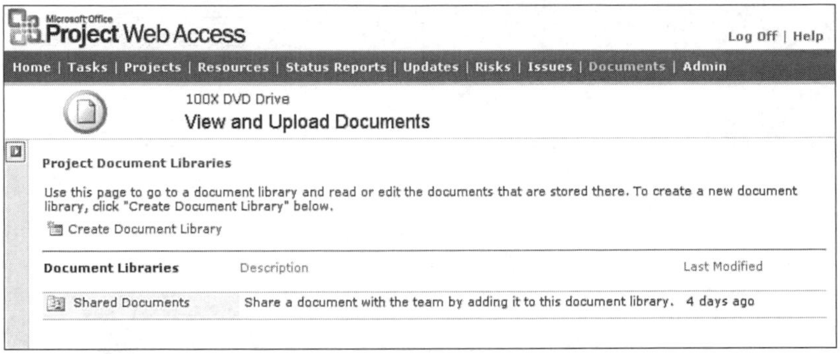

FIGURE 16.27   The View and Upload Documents page allows you to create, upload, organize, and edit documents in existing or new document libraries for the selected project.

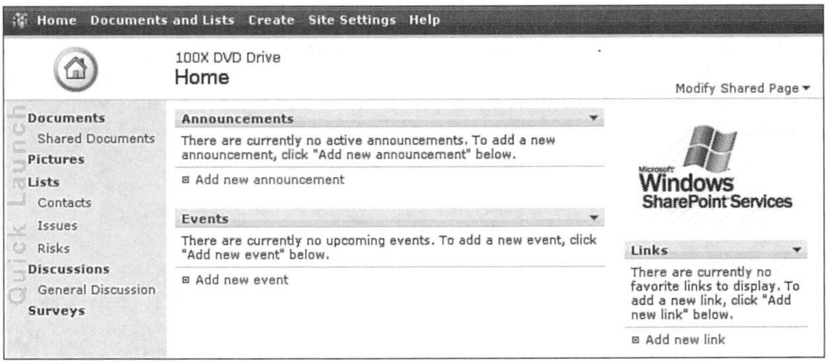

FIGURE 16.28   Each project has its own project workspace created.

A useful feature available on this WSS home page is that the project manager may insert additional web parts. You can insert standard web parts from PWA or from other areas. You can also insert links and pictures as needed, and you can add announcements and events. Included in the Events section is the capability to establish attendees and objectives, and to use templates to create a meeting agenda. There are many more features similar to this Events feature, which you and your project team will want to explore.

▶ **SEE** "Risks, Issues, and Documents Using Windows SharePoint Services (WSS)," **PAGE 441**.

▶ **SEE** "Windows SharePoint Services Customizing the Project Workspace," **PAGE 732**.

Analyze Projects in Portfolio Analyzer

The Analyze Projects in Portfolio Analyzer feature allows you to analyze the project schedule, resources, work, costs, and other variables that affect a project during its life. Portfolio Analyzer is a useful tool that provides project and resource managers valuable insight into project details, allows them to examine unfavorable situations, and helps them determine the potential problems early in the project life cycle. You can access Portfolio Analyzer by clicking the Analyze Projects in Portfolio Analyzer link under Actions in the left side pane.

▶ **SEE** "Analyzing Portfolio Data in Portfolio Analyzer," **PAGE 394**.

Model Projects with Portfolio Modeler

The Model Projects with Portfolio Modeler feature allows you to exemplify specific scenarios for your projects. This feature can be used for modeling situations such as resource assignments to see their effects on project cost, schedule, resource availability, and other project variables. Portfolio Modeler can be accessed by clicking the Model Projects with Portfolio Modeler link under Actions in the left side pane. The Portfolio Modeler page displays all the models currently available as well as allows you to create new models for your specific scenarios.

▶ **SEE** "Using Portfolio Modeler to Analyze Projects," **PAGE 424**.

Working with To-Do Lists

To-do lists are an easy and informal way for Project Server users to manage their responsibilities by creating electronic lists of tasks. From these lists, the list owner can assign tasks to others, and progress can be tracked. You can keep the to-do list to yourself, or you can share it with other resources using the Project Server. Project Center provides the following functions when working with to-do lists:

- **Create a New Personal or Shared To-Do List**—Allows you to create a personal or public to-do list by supplying a name, resources associated with it, and specific tasks for it. The actions provided on the Create a New Personal or Shared To-Do List page are the same actions you see on your PWA Tasks page.

- **Manage My To-Do Lists**—Allows you to view the existing to-do lists, manage tasks, and view the schedule details.

- **To-Do List Options**—Allows you to administer options for a specific to-do list, such as transfer list ownership to a different resource, promoting it to Project Professional, and so on.

Create a New Personal or Shared To-Do List

The Create a New Personal or Shared To-Do List option allows you to create a new to-do list; create new tasks; and assign resources responsible, dates, notes, and other features similar to project tasks.

To create a new to-do list, follow these steps:

1. Highlight the project row of the project for which to create the to-do list.

2. In the left side pane under Actions click the Create a New Personal or Shared To-Do List link.

3. Enter the to-do list name and select the list visibility, as shown in Figure 16.29. The to-do list visibility includes the following:

   - **Anyone**—Any resource with access to PWA has permission to view this to-do list.

   - **All Resources Who Are Assigned Tasks from This To-Do List**—Allows only the resources that you assign to tasks within the to-do list to see it.

   - **Me (only)**—Creates a completely personal to-do list, not visible to any other resources in Project Server.

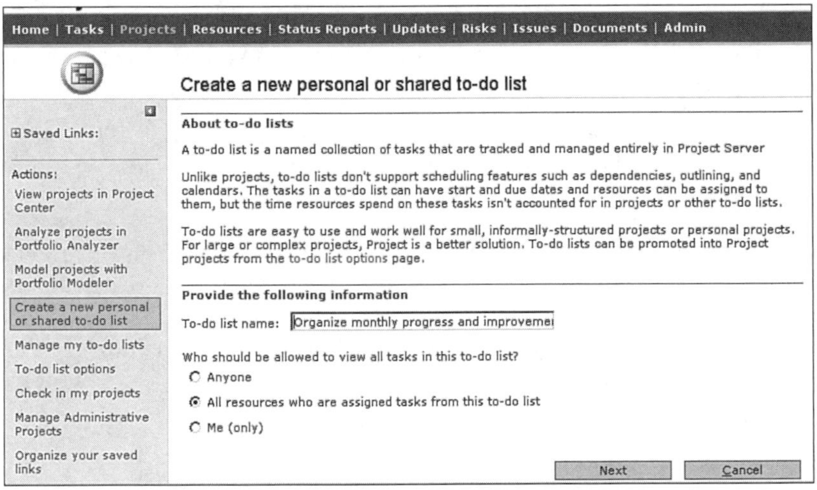

FIGURE 16.29   To-do lists can be used for small tasks such as organizing larger meetings to ensure that all needed information is available for the meeting.

4. After you select the visibility options, click Next. On the Create a New Task page, enter the tasks that you want to include in the to-do list. For each task specify task name, assigned to, priority, start and finish dates, % complete, and any additional notes.

5. When you finish entering all desired tasks, click the Save Tasks button.

6. The Manage My To-Do Lists page is displayed showing you the details of the to-do list you just created, as shown in Figure 16.30.

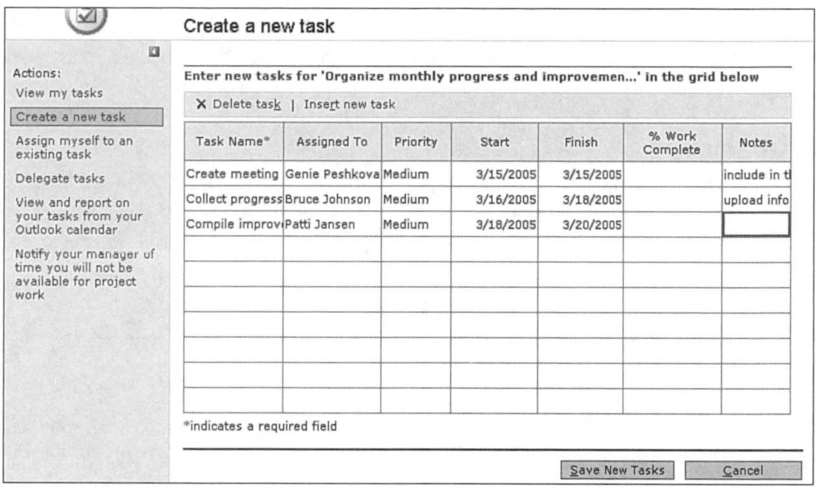

FIGURE 16.30   The Manage My To-Do Lists function provides similar functions to those available for projects in Project Center, such as creating a new task.

Notice that only core fields are available for each to-do task. There are two main reasons for this:

- To-do lists cannot support fields with calculated entries.
- A to-do list is specifically designed to be simple to use.

To-do lists are identified in the Project Center by a clipboard icon located in the Indicators column of the project grid.

Manage My To-Do Lists

To-do lists can also be viewed in the Manage My To-Do Lists page. To edit your to-do lists choose Manage My To-Do Lists on the navigator pane to the left of the task list. From here, you can view and manage those lists. The page is available only to the to-do list owner, not to-do list resources. If the Assigned To field is left empty, the task is assigned to the creator by default. The owner of a to-do list task can view his tasks from the Tasks page. You can perform various functions on a to-do list:

- **Delete**—Allows only one task to be deleted at a time. The summary task representing the to-do list cannot be deleted here.

- **Insert Notes**—Clicking the Insert Notes button launches a dialog box for typing a text message. The name of the user adding the note is appended to the beginning of the text message.

- **Adding New Tasks**—Clicking the New Tasks button takes you to the Tasks page for entering new to-do list task information.

16

The Manage My To-Do Lists page also provides the functionality available on the Project Center Home page, such as View Options; Filter, Group, Search; Zoom; Go to task; Print Grid; and Export to Excel.

To-Do List Options

The To-Do List Options page allows you to set some general options for individual to-do lists. To access the Options page, select To-Do List Options in the left side pane under Actions. The To-Do List Options page provides the following options, as shown in Figure 16.31:

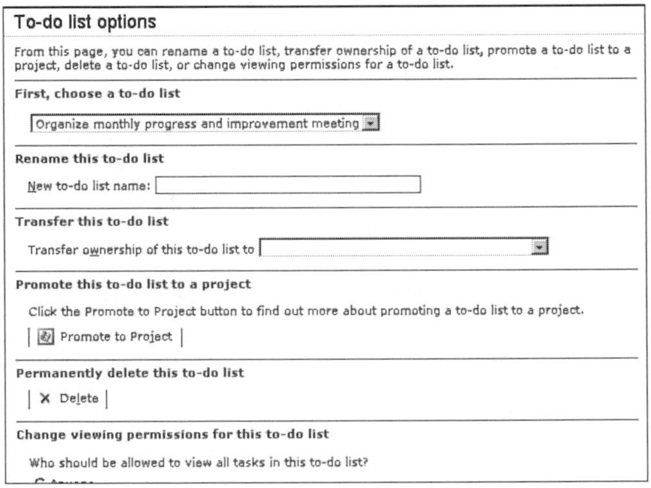

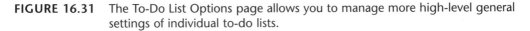

To-do list options

From this page, you can rename a to-do list, transfer ownership of a to-do list, promote a to-do list to a project, delete a to-do list, or change viewing permissions for a to-do list.

First, choose a to-do list

[Organize monthly progress and improvement meeting ▾]

Rename this to-do list

New to-do list name: [   ]

Transfer this to-do list

Transfer ownership of this to-do list to [▾]

Promote this to-do list to a project

Click the Promote to Project button to find out more about promoting a to-do list to a project.

| 🔲 Promote to Project |

Permanently delete this to-do list

| ✕ Delete |

Change viewing permissions for this to-do list

Who should be allowed to view all tasks in this to-do list?

FIGURE 16.31   The To-Do List Options page allows you to manage more high-level general settings of individual to-do lists.

- **Choose a To-Do List**—Provides the drop-down containing all existing to-do lists, where you are the owner.

- **Rename This To-Do List**—Allows you to rename the to-do list.

- **Transfer This To-Do List**—Allows you to "delegate" the to-do list to a different owner.

- **Promote This To-Do List to a Project**—Allows you to convert a to-do list into a project schedule within Project Professional.

- **Permanently Delete This To-Do List**—Deletes the to-do list.

- **Change Viewing Permissions for This To-Do List**—Allows you to modify the visibility of your to-do list.

Check in My Projects

Sometimes, a project you checked out for editing in Project Professional gets stuck in a checked-out state due to technical problems or network outages. If you checked it out, you can check it in yourself using the PWA Project Center Check in My Projects feature. To check in a project, you must be the project manager of that project or have equivalent permissions.

▶ **SEE** "Establishing Security Model Settings," **PAGE 143**.

> **NOTE**
>
> You may not use the Check in My Projects feature if the project you need checked back in was checked out by another project manager. In this case, you need to contact your Project Server administrator and request her assistance. Even if the project is checked out, you can still open the file by clicking on the Read-only option, which does not allow you to save any changes.

To check in a project, select Check in My Projects in the left side pane under Actions. The Check in My Projects page displays, as shown in Figure 16.32.

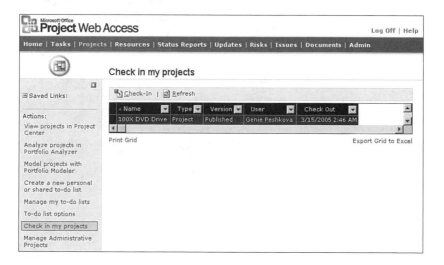

FIGURE 16.32   You can check in only your own projects.

> **NOTE**
>
> The Check Out? and Checked Out By fields in the Open dialog box within Project Professional help you determine whether the project has been checked out. If it is checked out, you cannot update the project unless you save it to a new file, or until it is checked in.

> **CAUTION**
>
> Checking in a project causes all changes since the last Save operation was performed to be lost.

Managing Administrative Projects

Administrative projects are a special kind of project that allows a resource manager or administrator to create a schedule that gathers data for future time off for team members and records actual work hours spent against administrative or other types of nonproject tasks.

Many organizations use administrative projects to account for nonproject time instead of using resource calendars for that purpose, as shown in Figure 16.33. These projects are usually created based on consensus and managed by resource managers and/or administrators to allow resources to enter their own vacation or other nonproject time. The project manager reviewing allocations for a resource can see whether the resource has planned to take time off for this administrative project.

> **CAUTION**
>
> Unlike a resource calendar, however, Project Professional may schedule a resource during the time off creating overallocation of a resource.

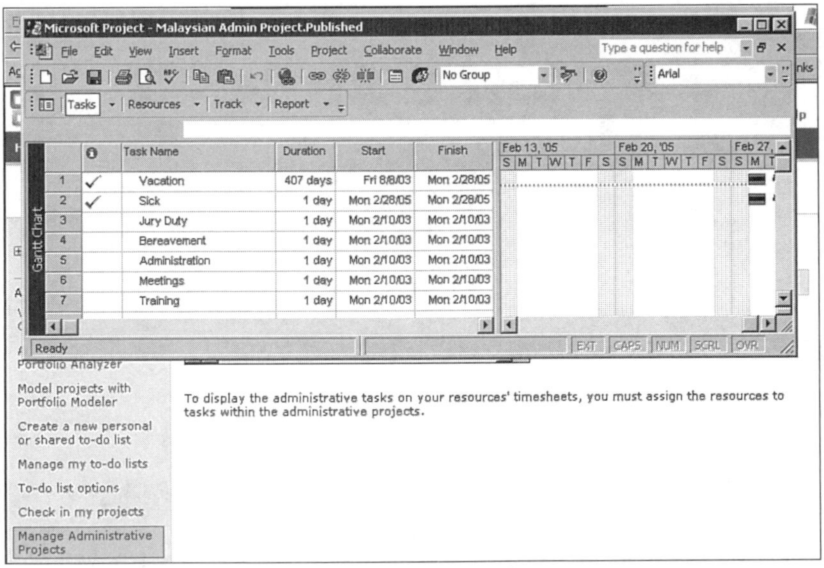

FIGURE 16.33   Administrative projects are an easy way to account for nonproject time.

After the resource has proposed future time off, managers and/or administrators can view availability information in PWA and Project Professional to see that the resource is not available during the proposed time off.

Team members enter requests for time off first and then use tasks defined in the administrative project to record actual work in the Tasks page.

Many organizations choose also to plan and capture time for any work-related activity in the organization. As such, an organization may face the situation where work activities can be divided into following categories:

- Pure project work

- Administrative type of activities, such as vacation, sick time, and so on

- Planned maintenance type of activities, such as scheduled system updates, planned routine system checkups, and so on

- Unplanned activities, such as emergency shutdowns for unplanned system upgrades in response to the emergence of an Internet virus

If your organization wants to capture all time spent by its employees for different activities, make sure that you create appropriate types of projects.

The Manage Administrative Projects link in Project Center allows you to add new or modify existing administrative projects, using Project Professional, as shown in Figure 16.34.

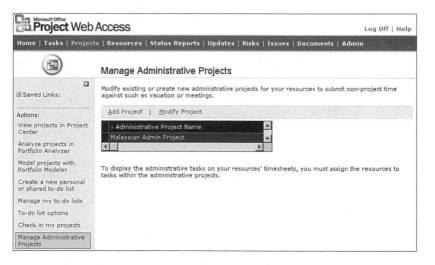

FIGURE 16.34   Click Add Project to create a new administrative project or click Modify Project to modify the existing selected project using Project Professional.

▶ **SEE** "Using Administrative Projects," **PAGE 240**.

Understanding the Resource Center

Project and resource managers in your organization have different needs when they access the Resource Center, each of them performing different actions. Resource managers need to view requests for generic resources, analyze resource loading, and identify and allocate specific resources based on specific criteria. These criteria are usually outlined in the project management methodology, or they are set by the project governance rules, such as project priority, skill-set requested, level of proficiency, and so on.

With the help of Project Center and Resource Center, project and resource managers have an opportunity to consider trade-offs, such as schedule priority versus budget or resource constraints.

Depending on specific security permission within Project Server and the business role you have in the organization, Resource Center enables you to perform up to six actions:

- View enterprise resources in Resource Center
- Analyze resources in Portfolio Analyzer
- View resource assignments
- View timesheet summary
- Approve timesheets
- Adjust actuals

> **NOTE**
>
> The View Timesheet Summary and Approve Timesheets options are available within the Resource Center only if your organization chooses to implement managed timesheets. The Managed Timesheets option allows both project and resource managers to approve timesheets submitted by their resources. The Managed Timesheets option also provides more control over the time-frame when the timesheets are submitted (are open).

▶ **SEE**, "Timesheet Setup, **PAGE 252**.

By default, the first action is common and can be performed by both project and resource managers, whereas the rest can be performed only by resource managers.

Using Resource Center Views

One of the most important aspects of Project 2003 is that it provides enterprisewide visibility of projects and resources. Resource Center provides detailed information about enterprise resources stored in the Enterprise Resource Pool, allowing managers to quickly view and analyze resource attributes, assignments, utilization, and availability, as shown in Figure 16.35.

One of the best methods to work with resources is using the features in Resource Center in PWA. Some project managers like to have both Project Professional and PWA open at the same time and switch between the two applications as they build their project team and analyze resource allocation. This next section introduces you to the features of the Resource Center.

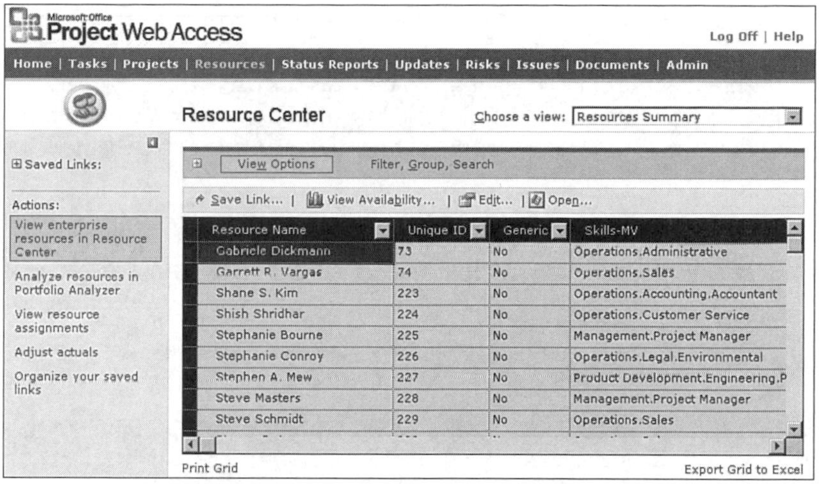

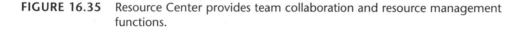

FIGURE 16.35   Resource Center provides team collaboration and resource management functions.

The Resource Center allows you to view information from the Enterprise Resource Pool. You can examine the details about resources according to permissions given to you by your Project Server administrator.

> **NOTE**
>
> When accessing the Resource Center from Project Professional, you can see only the View Enterprise Resource in the Resource Center displayed. To use all features and functionality in Resource Center you must access the Resource Center from PWA.

By default, you can access detailed information about resources only for project plans you own and manage. Unless you have permissions to add resources to the Enterprise Resource Pool, you may only "use" these resources. This page also contains many functions needed to manage resources and time reporting, such as viewing actual resource assignments (the team member's timesheet), reviewing timesheets, approving timesheets, and making adjustments after a time period has been locked down.

> **NOTE**
>
> Resource Center displays only enterprise resources. Resources local to any of the project schedules in the Project Server database will not be displayed in the Resource Center, but they are visible in the Resource Sheet of each individual project.

By default, project managers can see only the View Resource Assignments option and then display only those resources that have been assigned to projects they manage. Permissions to see additional resource assignments must be set up by the administrator for other resource information to display.

Resource Center provides many useful views that you can use to analyze the specific aspects of the enterprise resources. The default view, Resources Summary, lists basic data about the resources, most notably the Checked Out By column, as shown in Figure 16.36. This field lets you know what resources are currently available for editing. If a resource is checked out, this view lets you know the individual currently editing the information for that specific resource.

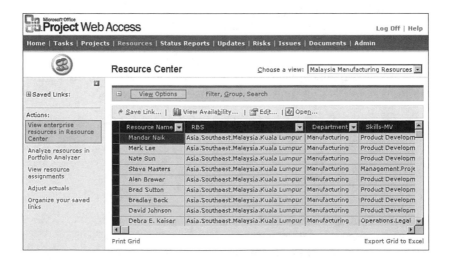

FIGURE 16.36   The Resource Summary view Checked Out column displays which resources are available for editing.

Your organization may create a custom view for you or others in the organization that can be used to analyze data in relevant ways for the organization, an example of which is shown in Figure 16.37.

FIGURE 16.37   Malaysia Manufacturing Resources custom resource view.

View Options

The View Options tab is located above the content window with the list of resources in Resource Center. View Options allows you to specify the level of detail you want to apply to the current view.

The View Options tab provides the following selections as shown in Figure 16.38:

- **Show Multi-Valued Fields At**—Allows you to specify the multivalued field enterprise outline level to apply to the current resource view.

- **Show**—Allows you to select the outline level to view.

- **Show Time and Date**—Displays the time and date when the resource is available from and to.

FIGURE 16.38   The View Options tab allows you to customize the current view even further.

Filter, Group, Search

The Filter, Group, Search tab is a powerful tool for presenting resources in different sorts and groupings. You can use this feature based on the parameters (columns) present only in the grid, as shown in Figure 16.39.

Using Filters   You can use the Filter options provided in Resource Center for filtering the displayed list of resources by various criteria. Resource Center provides three types of filters:

- **Filter**—The drop-down box provides two options: All Resources and Custom Filter. If you select the Custom Filter option from the drop-down list (or by clicking the Custom Filter button), the More-Filters pull-down is displayed at the top of each column.

- **Custom Filter**—Provides three criteria to filter the resources by. This allows for further customization and limiting of the data displayed, as shown in Figure 16.40.

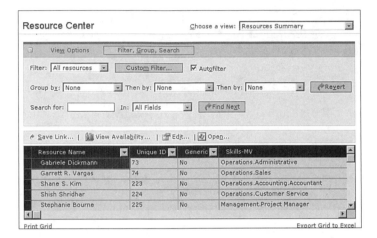

FIGURE 16.39   You cannot filter, group, or search for resources based on attributes that are not present in the Resource Center grid.

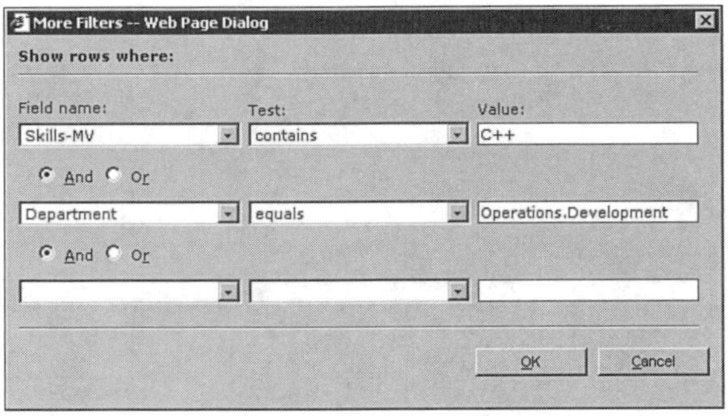

FIGURE 16.40   To apply the filter, select the field, condition, and value to filter by. You can filter by more than value by selecting the And or Or option.

- **Autofilter**—Displays drop-down arrows at the top of each column in the current view. When the Autofilter is selected, it allows you to filter by a specific field within that column.

Using the Group Functionality   The Group By function in Resource Center allows you to organize the displayed resource into groups. The Group By function in Filter, Group, Search is useful for showing the rollup for resources based on different conditions. In the example shown in Figure 16.41, the Group By function displays resources by multivalued skill set. You can change this grouping quickly and see a new report in seconds.

The administrator may set a special default grouping for your resources. You can change the grouping for the view. If you want to return to the default grouping, click Revert. Using the Revert function causes Resource Center to display resources using the predefined view chosen.

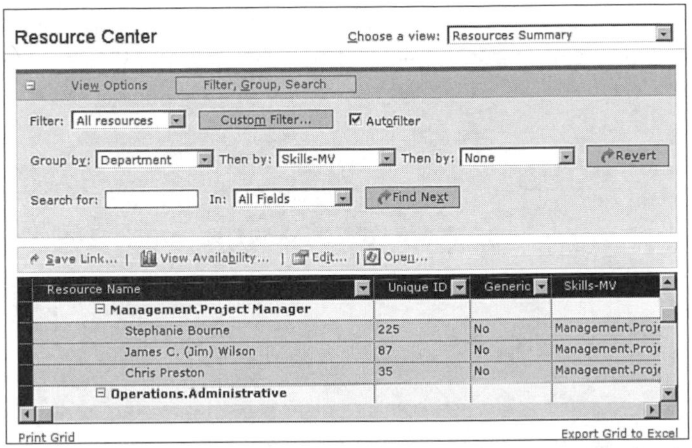

FIGURE 16.41   Project Center displaying projects grouped by location.

NOTE

It is not possible to group on any field that is not currently defined for the view in the Resource Center grid. If you want to group, filter, or do a search in a view with fields that aren't currently defined for the view, you need to ask your Project Server administrator to modify the view or create a new view for you.

Using Search   The Search function in Resource Center provides you with the ability to quickly and efficiently locate the desired resources. Search allows you to search by all fields currently displayed in the view. You can use the Find Next button to move to the next item in the list that meets your search criteria.

TIP

If the field that you want to search by does not appear in the Field Name drop-down list of the Search function, make sure that this field is available in the current view. If the field is not available, find a view that contains the appropriate fields.

Printing from the Resource Center

The Print Grid features allow you to view a printer-friendly version of the current view. This option was provided to ease the printing process by removing unnecessary objects that are difficult to print, such as the PWA frame, as shown in Figure 16.42.

Export to Excel from Resource Center

Resource Center also allows you to export the detailed resource data into Microsoft Excel worksheet. When you click the Export to Excel link, Microsoft Excel launches, and the data details are automatically exported to a new Excel worksheet, as shown in Figure

16.43. This feature may be especially useful if you want to take a snapshot of the current resource status, manipulate data using Excel functions, or take the snapshot offline for further analysis.

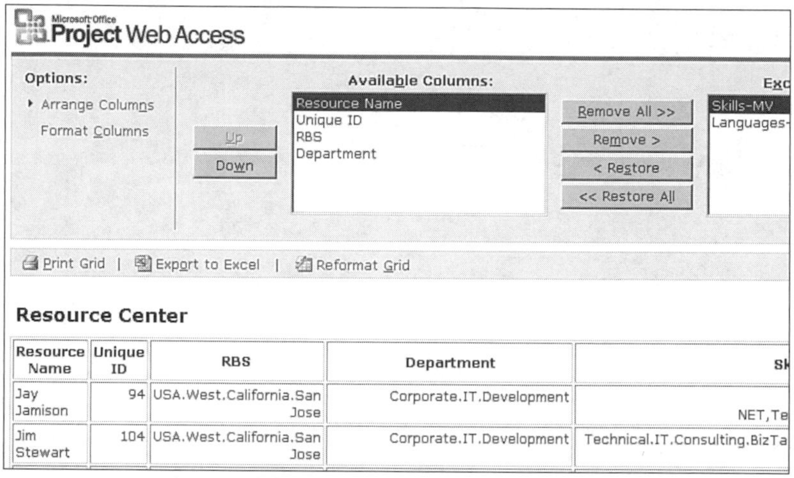

FIGURE 16.42   All resource data is displayed in an easy-to-read one-page format.

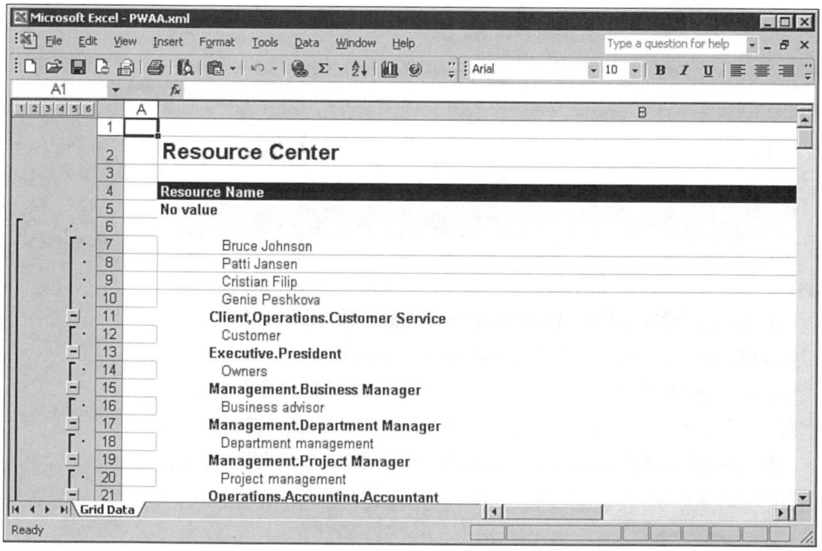

FIGURE 16.43   Excel preserves the data format of the Resource Center and adds a user and date and time stamp for historic purposes.

Using the Save Link to Create Custom and Personal Views

The Save Link button allows particular viewing, filtering, sorting, and grouping options to be saved as a customized view. As you configure desired view layouts in your day-to-day work, clicking the Save Link button preserves the view settings. A link is created in the navigation pane to the left of the project grid.

CAUTION

Saved links are specific to your Project Server profile. They are not visible as Enterprise views to the rest of the organization.

To save a link associated with your profile, select all desired view options and click Save Link. A dialog box is then displayed, and you are prompted to enter the name of the view you want to save; then click OK.

You see a link created in the upper left of the side pane under Saved Links, as shown in Figure 16.44.

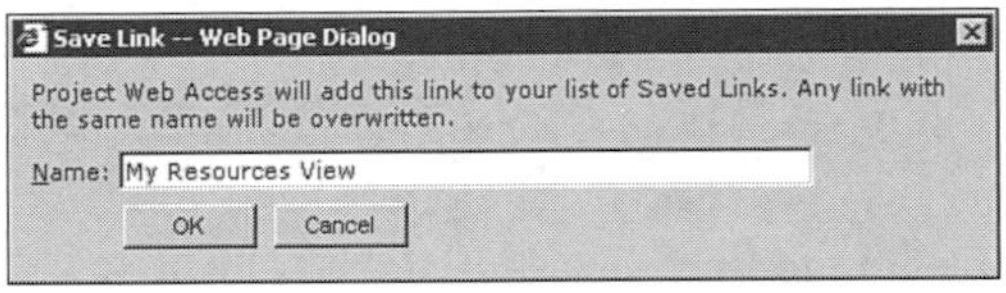

FIGURE 16.44   Create a unique and descriptive name for the view you are creating.

Organize Your Saved Links

The Saved Links link does not display if you have not saved any links. To access any of your saved custom format views, click on this link. From here you can delete or rename your links as well. To do this, click on Organize Your Saved Links under Actions in the side pane. The Organize Your Saved Links page displays only if you have saved links, as shown in Figure 16.45. Select the link and either click Delete or Rename depending on the function you want to perform.

View Availability

View Availability is a function that allows you to select an individual resource or group of resources to view the resource availability. To view availability, highlight the resource or resource group you want to view availability for, and click View Availability. You can also highlight the summary row in the list to view everyone within a particular resource category, such as all C++ programmers, or everyone in the Denver office.

After the availability screen appears, you can clear the names of the resources to remove their availability information from the displayed graph.

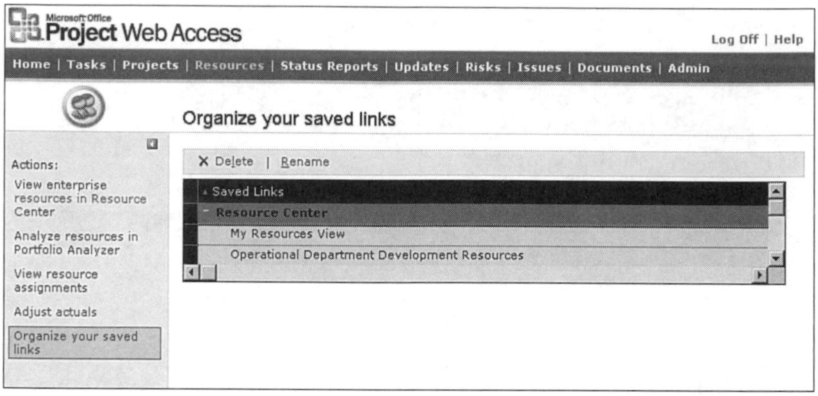

FIGURE 16.45   Select the link you want to change and click Rename to change its name, or click Delete to completely delete the link.

Choose a View

Choose a View allows you to choose from the views available to analyze resource availability. Resource Center provides four views:

- **Assignment Work by Resource**—Displays the amount of work assigned for each resource during the specified time frame. This view is useful if you are trying to compare the overall workload between different resources.

- **Assignment Work by Project**—Displays the amount of work used by each project the selected resources belong to in the specified time frame. This view is useful for analyzing which projects use up the most resources.

- **Remaining Availability**—Displays the remaining availability of each selected resource in the specified time frame. Use this view to see the resource availability and to avoid overloading the resources.

- **Work**—Displays the amount of work hours each selected resource is committed to in the specified time frame. This view can be used to gain better understanding of the current resource workload.

View Options

The View Options feature allows you to set options for the View Availability page, as shown in Figure 16.46.

The options include

- **Include Proposed Bookings**—This view lets you show availability based on just committed assignments, or both proposed and committed assignments when you check Include Proposed Bookings. If this box is checked the view displays all resources, committed and proposed.

- **Date range**—You can change the date range and see resource capacity versus utilization for days and weeks based on a date range you select.

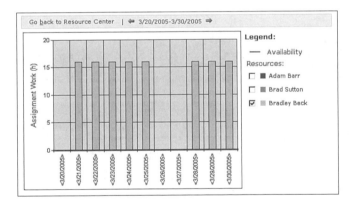

FIGURE 16.46   Specify the booking type and the date range options to apply to the Resource Availability view.

Availability Graph

The Availability graph and chart allows you to view the various reports using a graph and chart view. A graph with assignment work on the Y-axis and the time period on the X-axis displays by default, as shown in Figure 16.47. This view contains an availability line that represents the total availability for the resources selected. The bars on the graph represent the total work that the selected resources are assigned to do in the same time period form. The total work is calculated from the published versions of project files to which the resource is assigned.

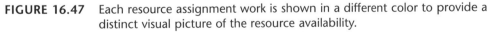

FIGURE 16.47   Each resource assignment work is shown in a different color to provide a distinct visual picture of the resource availability.

Resource Details

The Resource Details portion of the View Resource Availability page provides a timesheet view of each resource, allowing you to see hourly work commitments for the selected time frame, as shown in Figure 16.48.

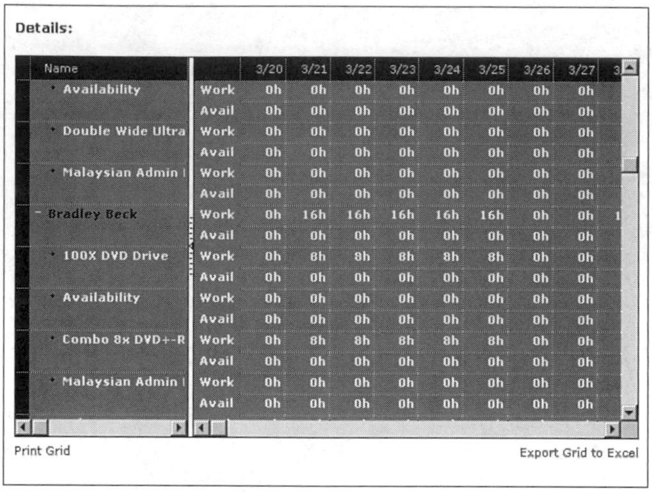

FIGURE 16.48   Scroll down to see the details of each resource.

Edit Resources

When you select a resource from the initial Resource Center view and click on the Edit Resource Details button, you can see and edit (if you have the appropriate permissions) the resource's Enterprise Resource Outline Codes, as shown in Figure 16.49.

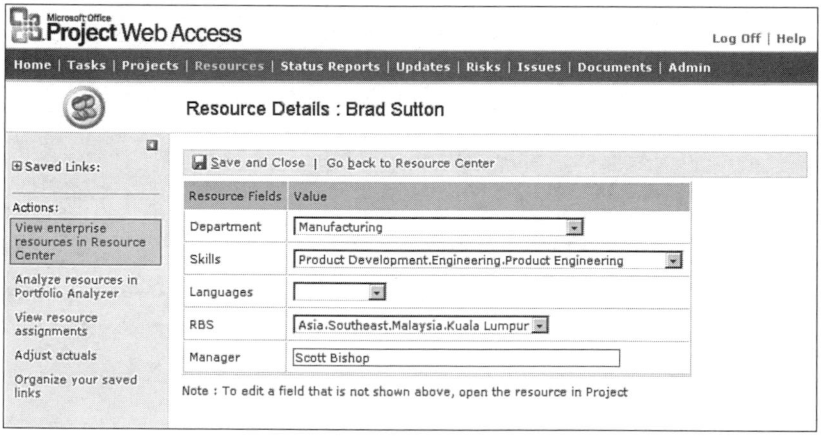

FIGURE 16.49   Use the Resource Details screen to view and edit Enterprise Resource Outline Codes.

Enterprise resources have one predefined outline code called the Resource Breakdown Structure (RBS) code. The RBS code can be any code that differentiates resources, but it should be reserved for the code value that is the most important, or most often used, throughout an organization. This is because the RBS code is built in to the Team Builder, the Resource Substitution Wizard, and the Assign Resources dialog tools when filtering and selecting resources. It also plays an important role in the Security model of the system.

Generally, the RBS should reflect at any given time the organizational breakdown structure of an enterprise. If proper values are not stored, resource managers cannot allocate resources to the proper RBS value.

▶ **SEE** "Resource Breakdown Structure (RBS)," **PAGE 185**.

Any other outline code values can be changed and saved for an individual resource by a user with sufficient permission.

The Edit button allows enterprise resource information to be edited. You can, for example, change outline codes associated with a resource previously defined in your Enterprise Resource Pool, or you may add a secondary skill of database administrator to someone who has a primary skill of programmer assigned. When Edit is selected, a Resource Details page displays for the selected resources. You can edit only Enterprise Resource Fields defined in the Enterprise Global template.

▶ **SEE** "Resource Outline Codes," **PAGE 173**.

Opening the Enterprise Resource Pool

The Open button in Resource Center allows users to open the Enterprise Resource Pool.

To open the Enterprise Resource Pool, select the desired resources using the Ctrl key on your keyboard and click the Open button. This launches Project Professional and opens the Enterprise Resource Pool, as shown in Figure 16.50.

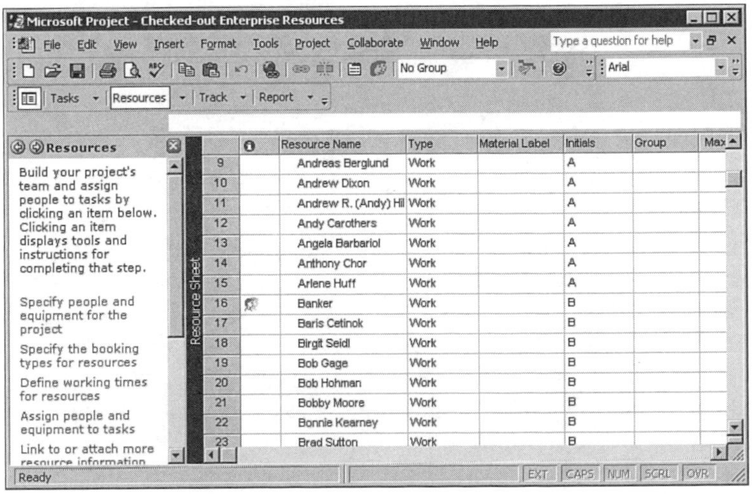

FIGURE 16.50 The Enterprise Resource Pool allows you to globally modify enterprise resources.

> **NOTE**
>
> Typically, only the Project Server administrator has permission to use this feature.

Analyzing Resources in Portfolio Analyzer

If you navigate to Projects, Analyze Projects in Portfolio Analyzer, you get exactly the same view and tools as if you were in PWA and selected Resources, Analyze Resources in Portfolio Analyzer.

Viewing Resource Assignments

Viewing resource assignments allows you to review the timesheet or Gantt Chart view for multiple resources. The resources available may be limited to resources assigned to any project you own or have permission to view.

This page works just like the Tasks page in a view mode only, as shown in Figure 16.51.

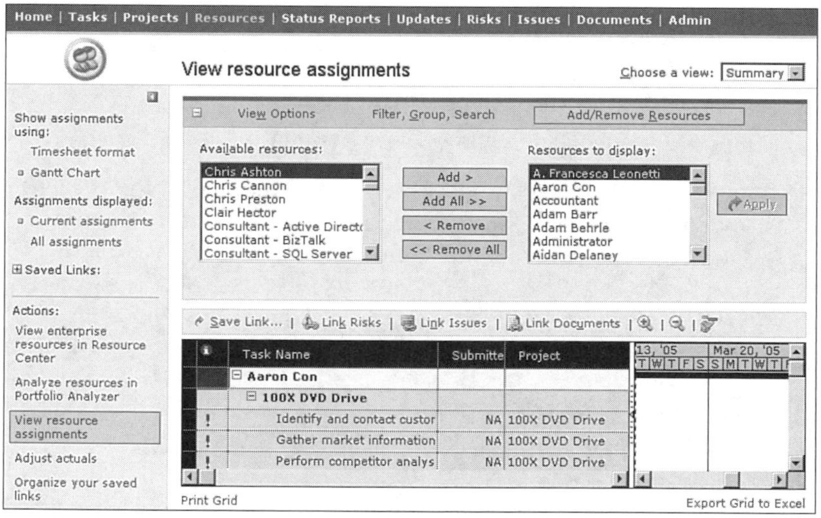

FIGURE 16.51   Use the View Resource Assignments page to display details for each assignment.

As shown in Figure 16.51, you may use the Add/Remove Resources feature to move resources you want to view assignments for in and out of your view. After you have the list of resources you want to view, you may use the Save Link function to save and easily bring up that view of all the resources specified.

This feature may come in especially handy if one of your project team members calls you with a question about a task displayed on her Tasks page. You can easily reproduce what the team member sees on her Tasks page.

Also, resource managers can get rolled-up timesheet data to see actuals per week for each resource they manage. If you collapse the projects and subtasks for a resource, you see the total actual work on one line for the resource for the current time period.

The View Options and Filter, Group, Search features can be helpful in viewing the timesheets according to your needs. For example, the View Options function allows you to show scheduled work as well, so that you can compare scheduled to actual work. The Filter function allows you to specify criteria for items you want to see such as only approved or rejected timesheet tasks.

Adjusting Actuals

If your organization has chosen to use the Managed Time Period feature of Project 2003, you will find times you may need to adjust actual work entered by your resources after a time period has been closed, as shown in Figure 16.52. You can also use this feature if a resource is absent and you need to enter actual work for the resource.

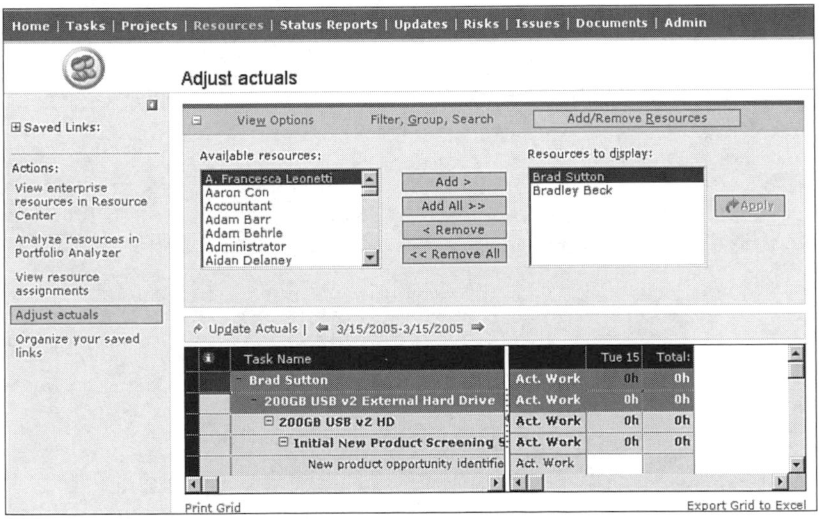

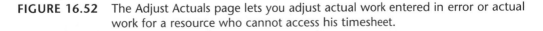

FIGURE 16.52   The Adjust Actuals page lets you adjust actual work entered in error or actual work for a resource who cannot access his timesheet.

To use this feature you must choose the resource(s) whose actual work you need to adjust by using the Add/Remove Resources feature.

Click Apply to display the timesheets you selected and then use the time period scale in the action bar to move to the appropriate period to change the time for the resource in question. After you enter the time, click Update Actuals in the action bar.

Note that you cannot change the Remaining Work field. This feature is only for changing the actuals reported by the resource. The adjustment is sent to the project manager who follows the usual procedures for reviewing and updating the change into the project schedule through the Updates page.

When updated, the changes are reflected in the resource's timesheet.

Best Practices

- Build Team in PWA does provide handy matching, searching, and analytical features, but it is recommended that you use the Project Professional full-featured Build Team from Enterprise to perform any advanced additions, matching, and assignments. Build Team in PWA is a light feature for quickly adding resources to your project. Build Team can also be handy to use by resource managers, who can still manage resources on different projects without having Project Professional installed on their desktops.

- When you check in projects other than yours, make sure that you have communicated to the owner of the project your intent to check in the project. It is also a good idea to wait for the project owner to confirm that it is okay to check the project back in. That is because all changes to the project schedule since the last save operation will be lost.

- When viewing resource availability, make sure that you account for both committed and proposed bookings. This is the only way you can ensure that you have a true picture of resource allocation forecast.

- Using administrative projects helps project and resource managers to identify all tasks and activities that resources are required to perform. It allows managers to have a true and accurate picture of resource allocation and better forecast the workload.

Portfolio Management Using Portfolio Analyzer and Portfolio Modeler

IN THIS CHAPTER

- Analyzing Portfolio Data in the Portfolio Analyzer

- Using Portfolio Modeler to Analyze Projects

- Best Practices

This chapter discusses the Portfolio Analyzer and Portfolio Modeler tools within Microsoft Project Web Access. Each of these tools provides valuable information about projects, resources, work, costs, and so forth. When you configure PWA views, your organization can use these tools for general analysis. These tools provide a starting point for the project managers, resource managers, staff managers, and others to determine conditions for each project and the resources within those projects.

> **NOTE**
>
> The Portfolio Analyzer and Portfolio Modeler tools can provide a lot of information, but you should consider each one part of the entire PWA suite of functions. Use all the PWA tools to gain a complete understanding of your Enterprise Project Management information.

Figure 17.1 depicts a typical view within the Portfolio Analyzer tool. Notice how Portfolio Analyzer views can display a combination of graph and pivot table information. You can learn more about the details within this chapter.

The Portfolio Modeler uses a display technique that allows you to combine information about several projects and see work load conditions for resources within those projects. Figure 17.2 shows a typical Portfolio Modeler view.

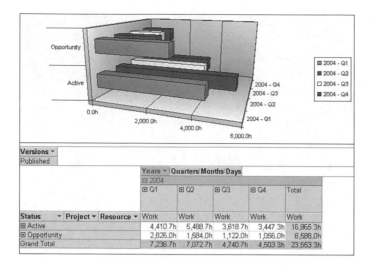

FIGURE 17.1   Typical Portfolio Analyzer views.

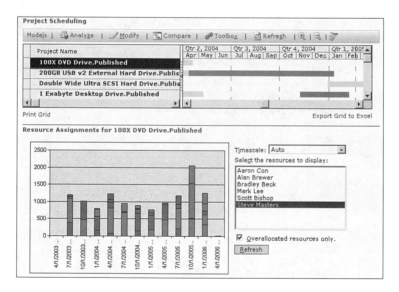

FIGURE 17.2   Typical Portfolio Modeler views.

This chapter describes how to use each of these important PWA analysis tools.

Analyzing Portfolio Data in the Portfolio Analyzer

The Portfolio Analyzer can be a powerful tool that provides people with a lot of combined information about projects and resources. Portfolio Analyzer views are typically used by managers who need to see a mix of project and resource data that are part of a family of information such as programs or portfolios of projects.

The settings you design and configure within the Enterprise Global and PWA views allow managers to see information about projects that are logically part of a grouping of projects based on Enterprise Global Project Outline Codes that you define. Enterprise Global Resource Outline Codes are also used to group and filter information about resources within each Portfolio Analyzer view. The combination of Enterprise Global definitions is therefore an important factor for people who use Portfolio Analyzer functions.

Portfolio managers typically need to see a mixture of project and resource information so that they can begin to answer questions such as the following:

- How much work is scheduled for projects within a certain portfolio of projects related to sponsors, billing centers, or other key business attributes?

- How many hours are scheduled for generic and named resources that have certain skills and other attributes within a particular time span?

- How much actual work has been accumulated for projects within particular portfolios of projects?

- What are the accumulated costs compared to baseline predictions across multiple projects?

These and other questions can be answered using Portfolio Analyzer views that you create and grant user permissions for people in the organization.

Each view can display various formats of chart data driven from the details of a pivot table that you define for specific views. The chart data can be exported to GIF graphic files to be included within Microsoft Word or other documents such as portfolio status reports. The pivot table data can be exported to Microsoft Excel for additional analysis or discussion with people who do not have PWA access.

The permissions that you grant to PWA users allow them to see and interact with specific Portfolio Analyzer views. These permissions also enable or disable the use of certain viewing details to protect sensitive business data such as project or resource costs. You can also set viewing conditions to enable or disable users from temporarily altering the view details. Portfolio Analyzer provides advanced viewing and analysis functionality, so you need to understand how this tool functions. The choices you make provide managers throughout the organization with information they need to make decisions about portfolios of projects and resources.

Building and Changing Portfolio Analyzer Views

Prior to creating new Portfolio Analyzer views, it is important for you to understand some of the technology parts. This section introduces you to these technology parts, building your base knowledge and instincts before creating Portfolio Analyzer views.

The Portfolio Analyzer Uses SQL Analysis Services OLAP Cube Data

SQL Analysis Services is one of several core technologies behind views within the Portfolio Analyzer views. SQL Analysis Services is connected to Project Server during the software installation process, so PWA views can use Online Analytical Processing (OLAP) data stored within a separate SQL database.

Figure 17.3 shows a simple flow diagram that depicts how Project Server and SQL Analysis Services are connected. The left side of the diagram shows the basic steps that Project Server takes during the OLAP rebuild process. Project Server generates instructions.

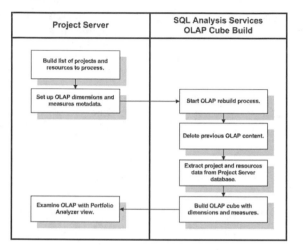

FIGURE 17.3   Overview of OLAP cube rebuild flow.

The OLAP cube build process uses a staging technique whereby Project Server creates the instructions used by SQL Analysis Services to regenerate OLAP cube data that includes Dimensions based on Enterprise Global Codes and resource assignment data, with Measures based on details such as work, actual work, costs, and so on. When the OLAP cube is regenerated, it contains project and resource information as of the OLAP rebuild time. Therefore, the data within the OLAP cube is a snapshot of Project Server content and is updated only when that OLAP data is regenerated.

> **CAUTION**
>
> Figure 17.3 also shows how the previous OLAP cube is completely cleared of previous data, so any edits or customizations you added to the OLAP cube data are lost during the rebuild process.

The OLAP regeneration process also updates other Project Server information, such as resource availability measurements, viewable within the Resource Center functions such as View Availability. This availability information is stored within other Project Server database tables that are not part of the OLAP cube data.

▶ **SEE** "Creating Project Web Access Project and Resource Views," **PAGE 209**.

> **NOTE**
>
> If you want to learn more about the fundamentals of OLAP and Microsoft SQL Server Analysis Services, consider reviewing the following book available from Sams publishing:
>
> *Microsoft SQL Server 2000 Unleashed, Second Edition*, by Ray Rakins, Paul Bertucci, and Paul Jensen, ISBN: 0672324679.

Office Web Components Are Needed for Portfolio Analyzer Views

Office Web Components (OWC) are used within Internet Explorer pages to show information in the Portfolio Analyzer views. These ActiveX components provide nice display functions within the pivot table and related graph that show data within each Portfolio Analyzer view.

> **CAUTION**
>
> The first time a user accesses the Portfolio Analyzer views, Project Server automatically downloads the ActiveX OWC components so that the pivot table and chart can be displayed. This download is a transparent activity that is generally hidden from the user. The download process also requires that some files be stored within the user's desktop computer Windows file system and a software registration function is performed to create Windows Registry entries. These actions require the user to have Administrator rights on the desktop machine.

Microsoft ActiveX components and other software upgrades to user desktops can be done interactively or by scheduled software changes using technology such as Systems Management Server (SMS). SMS allows Windows system administrators to automatically send software and updates to user desktop systems.

> **TIP**
>
> If your users do not have personal settings that grant them Administrator rights on their desktop machines, consider doing a Windows SMS file push. Alternatively, you can have a person with Administrator rights log on to the user's desktop machine and access the Portfolio Analyzer views within PWA. The OWC ActiveX functions will be stored within the Windows file system for any user on that machine.

> **NOTE**
>
> To find more information on SMS, see the Microsoft website at http://www.microsoft.com/smserver/default.asp

After the OWC functions are downloaded, Project Server directs Internet Explorer to use these ActiveX functions to show pivot table and/or graphs within the Portfolio Analyzer views. This enables users to see the data dimensions and measures you designed for Portfolio Analyzer views without having a licensed Office 2003 product.

17

The OWC pivot table functions behave much like Excel, so you can interact with the data and export the data to Excel. The internal formula values are not accessible, so you cannot modify those formulas within Portfolio Analyzer pivot table sections. You can, however, add your own custom calculated formulas as described later in this chapter.

The OWC graphic chart functions also behave much like Excel and are directly linked to the data Dimension columns, rows, and measures values within the pivot table of each Portfolio Analyzer view. When the user interacts with the Drop Area drop-down lists, the pivot table and chart displays are simultaneously updated.

> **NOTE**
>
> Even though the OWC functions are installed on the user's computer, this does not allow the user to modify Portfolio Analyzer views. The computer must have one Microsoft Office 2003 product to modify Portfolio Analyzer views.

End Users Need Permission to View Data Within the OLAP Cube

Each Portfolio Analyzer view connects to a specific OLAP cube for the data displayed within the view. People in the organization need to have two permission settings to use these views:

- **Project Web Access Category**—Permissions are needed with appropriate settings that include the name of the Portfolio Analyzer view. This is typically done by assigning each user to appropriate PWA Groups with associated Category permissions.

- **SQL Analysis Services OLAP cube**—Permissions must be set to enable read access to the data within the cube. The SQL Analysis Services manager must use the Manage Roles function to establish permission roles. Figure 17.4 shows examples of OLAP cube Manage Roles functions where several role groups are defined with individual authenticated user identifiers specified.

After you add users to the OLAP cube roles you have defined, use the Cubes tab to mark which items within the cube should be accessed (see Figure 17.5). Make sure that you check each of the cube names because those are used within the Portfolio Analyzer views.

> **TIP**
>
> Consider using the Windows Everyone security group to allow everyone to use the OLAP cube data. This reduces the overall management of the SQL Analysis Services roles because you will not need to maintain specific groups of usernames.

> **CAUTION**
>
> If your PWA Admin settings and processes use more than one OLAP cube for Portfolio Analyzer views, you need to use the SQL Analysis Services Manage Roles function to grant read permissions for each defined OLAP cube. If individual users receive a permissions error while attempting to display a Portfolio Analyzer view, you should inspect the settings of the OLAP permissions.

▶ SEE "Establishing Security Model Settings," **PAGE 143**.

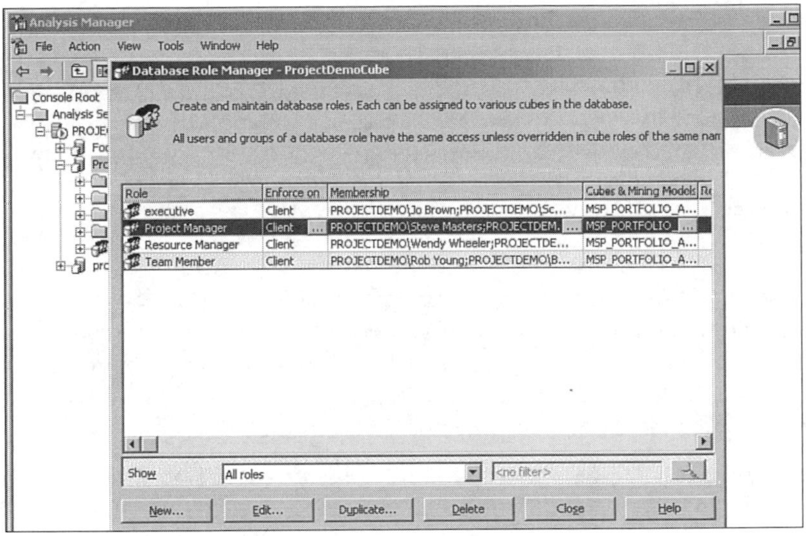

FIGURE 17.4   Example of SQL Analysis Services OLAP Cube Manage Roles definition.

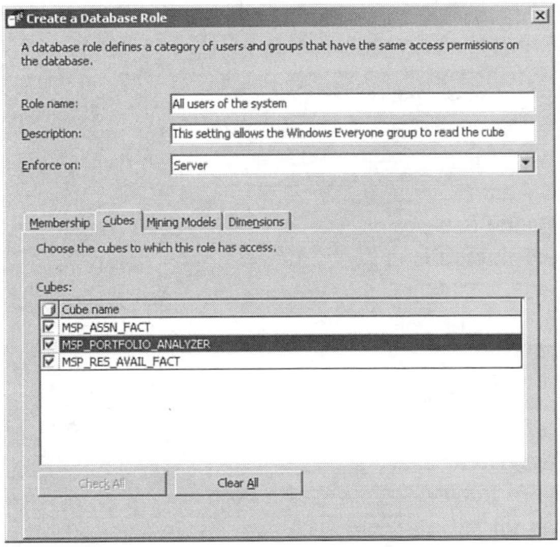

FIGURE 17.5   Example of SQL Analysis Services OLAP cube settings.

Overview of OLAP Cube Dimensions and Measures

SQL Analysis Services creates and manages the OLAP cube used within the Portfolio Analyzer views that are part of PWA. During the installation of Project Server 2003, the OLAP cube data is set to be stored within regular SQL Server databases that are later filled with project and resource data from the Project Server database. Each time the OLAP cube is regenerated from within PWA, the data becomes the core for each Portfolio Analyzer view.

> **NOTE**
>
> Enterprise Global Project Outline Codes are automatically included within the OLAP cube rebuild process after at least one project is published using those codes. If you later add a new outline code to the Enterprise Global, you must publish at least one project schedule with a value from the new code items before that outline code is included within the OLAP cube.

The Project Server OLAP cube contains certain information that has been compiled from data about projects, resources, resource assignments, and values, such as work and cost. These data also include cross-references to attributes about projects and resources such as Enterprise Global Outline Codes that your configuration has defined. The attributes about projects and resources are known as *Dimensions* within the OLAP cube.

Dimensions serve as the primary method to filter and group information about projects and resources when you create a Portfolio Analyzer view. Figure 17.6 shows the Field List box that contains typical Dimensions available for use within a Portfolio Analyzer view. These Dimensions can include attributes such as Projects (names of each project), Time (Years, Quarters, Months, and Days), Resources (names of each resource), and other attributes you define within the Enterprise Global Project and Resource Outline Codes.

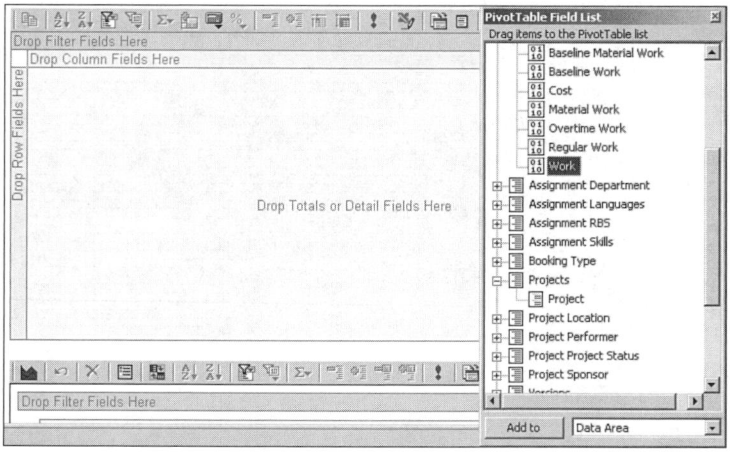

FIGURE 17.6   Portfolio Analyzer Field List box example.

As you drag and drop the Dimensions from the Field List box to the row, column, or filter areas of the pivot table, those Dimensions become part of the cross-references to the Measures of data in the OLAP cube.

> **CAUTION**
>
> As of Project Server 2003 SP1, the OLAP cube data does not include information about tasks within project schedules. This means that task-level attributes and details are not available to see within Portfolio Analyzer views.

Measures are values that can be accumulated down columns and across row totals within the pivot table. These values include predefined values such as Work, Baseline Work, Actual Work, Cost, Availability, and so on. Figure 17.6 also shows some of these values within the Field List box. These values can be dragged into the Totals and Fields data area of the pivot table where the accumulated values show as column and row totals.

Dimensions also include the Enterprise Global Custom Outline Codes you have defined for projects and resources. These Dimensions allow you to create Portfolio Analyzer views that can be grouped and filtered based on the outline code definitions you create.

When Project Server spawns the processes to rebuild the OLAP cube, it prepares the type of data to be included within the OLAP cube data. This includes instructions to SQL Analysis Services about which parts of Project Server database content should be assembled within the OLAP cube database.

Table 17.1 shows values that are not included within the OLAP cube as of Project Server 2003 SP1.

TABLE 17.1   Dimension and Measure Type Limitations

Dimension or Measure Type	Limits and Notes
Time.Weeks	The Time dimension does not automatically include Weeks, as desired by most organizations.
Task data	Task names and details are not part of the default OLAP Dimensions or Measures. If you need task data, you should extend the OLAP cube with .NET custom functions.
Enterprise Global Custom Fields	Custom fields such as text, numbers, flags, and so on are not included within the OLAP cube content.
Enterprise Global Task Outline Codes	Task outline code data is not included within the OLAP cube. If you need this data within the cube, you need to use .NET techniques to extend the OLAP cube content.
Dimension counters	There are no automatic count functions to enable you to just count the number of occurrences of a given Dimension. You can include customized column formulas, but row and column totals or subtotals may not accumulate as desired.
Percentage values	Default Measures do not automatically include percentages such as %Complete, %Work Complete, and so on. You need to create custom formulas for this type of data.
Rule-based formatting	There are no built-in pivot table format controls that change font, color, and so on based on some numeric condition or threshold value.

17

> **NOTE**
>
> If you need to include the types of data in Table 17.1, consider customized Portfolio Analyzer view formulas or extending the OLAP cube data using .NET technology.

▶ **SEE** "Extending Enterprise Project Management Through Customization Overview," **PAGE 793**.

Designing Project Web Access Portfolio Analyzer Views

Portfolio Analyzer views are much like any other PWA view except that each Portfolio Analyzer view connects to an OLAP cube as the source of the data. Each Portfolio Analyzer view is therefore connected to the OLAP cube that contains a complex mix of project, resource, and other attribute data.

You need at least three conditions if you want to create or modify a Portfolio Analyzer view:

- PWA permission is necessary to allow the view author to use the Admin tab, which also contains the Views functions. This means that each view author must belong to a PWA user Group with Category permissions that enable the Manage Views function.

- An Office 2003 software license is needed because the PWA Views edit function checks for this license before enabling view authoring or modification functions.

- SQL Analysis Services permission to the OLAP cube is also needed before the Portfolio Analyzer view author can connect to and use the OLAP cube data.

> **TIP**
>
> If you start a Portfolio Analyzer view with a workstation that does not have an Office 2003 product license, you will not be able to edit that view on a workstation that does have an appropriate Office 2003 product license. You need to delete the invalid view and re-create it on an appropriate workstation with an Office 2003 license.

A blank Project Server 2003 installation has no predefined Portfolio Analyzer views, so you must create and modify these views to suit your business needs. The business requirements from groups across the organization should specify how the Portfolio Analyzer view data will be used during the normal business cycles. These requirements then allow you to design each Portfolio Analyzer view and organize the format of those views.

Chapter 10, "Creating Project Web Access Project and Resource Views," describes the basic mechanics to paint a Portfolio Analyzer view, but it does not go into a lot of detail about what type of data is beneficial to show within these views.

▶ **SEE** "Portfolio Analyzer Views," **PAGE 225**.

As you define each Portfolio Analyzer view, consider the audience who will use the view(s) to get information about projects, resources, work, and so on. When you design these views, consider that each Portfolio Analyzer view may be defined with the following general data themes:

- *Project-centric views* allow the end users to see the data with the primary focus on portfolios of projects. These views use Dimensions that have strong reference to projects and attributes about projects. Typical project-centric views might have Dimensions such as business programs or portfolios, sponsoring organizations, life cycle phases, and so forth. Each project-centric view is usually enabled for viewing by people who belong to PWA security groups with permissions to see and use Project Center functions.

- *Resource-centric views* provide end users the ability to see resources and attributes that are important about resources. These views typically show resources grouped by attributes such as Resource Breakdown Structure (RBS), skills, system knowledge, working location, and so on. Each resource-centric view is usually enabled for people who belong to PWA security groups with permissions to see and use Resource Center functions.

- *Assignment-centric views* enable the end users to see attributes about resource assignments within projects. Although these views cannot show tasks or task details, these views can show resources' work within projects over a span of time.

- *Mixed views* allow the end users to see attributes about projects, resources, and assignments over a span of time. These views often mix several different kinds of information that include projects, resources, and assignments. This type of view can be confusing to novice users of Portfolio Analyzer views, so carefully consider the audience for this type of view.

> **TIP**
>
> If you load the sample database that Microsoft provides on the Project Server 2003 installation media, you can see several Portfolio Analyzer view examples. This gives you a starting point for designing your own views.

Figure 17.7 shows a simple example of a project-centric Portfolio Analyzer view that uses project portfolio attributes on the far left side as the primary grouping filter. Notice how each filter Dimension can be expanded to show the numeric data, such as work, along a time Dimension across the top of the pivot table. The graph also shows how the projected work increases and decreases over time.

Project-centric views such as Figure 17.7 allow Project Center users to easily filter data by project attributes so that they can visualize project data such as work, baseline work, cost, and so forth. A view like this also allows the project and portfolio managers to predict the anticipated cost and, therefore, cash flow across time periods in the future.

17

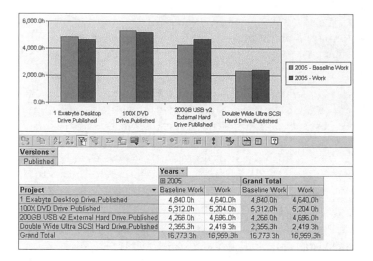

FIGURE 17.7   Project-centric view showing anticipated work for time periods.

Figure 17.8 shows an example of a resource-centric Portfolio Analyzer view. On the left side, you can see how resource names form the primary filtering criteria about resources in the Enterprise Global Resource Pool. Resource and staff managers can use this type of view to understand the work load demand for each resource they manage. This forms a good starting point for managers to use Resource Center views for more details about which tasks resources are assigned to complete.

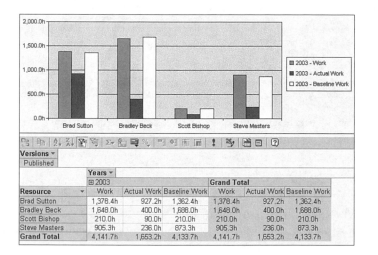

FIGURE 17.8   Resource-centric view showing work or actual work compared to baseline work.

Notice how a view like this allows the end user to also compare Measures such as actual work compared to baseline work for a time period.

Assignment-centric views, as shown in Figure 17.9, provide special information about resource assignments on tasks within projects included within the OLAP cube. Although assignment data does not show task-level details, this assignment data can be useful while analyzing the work load demand for certain resource characteristics such as technology skills, knowledge of manufacturing systems, or other attributes, such as the ability to lift weight while performing work activities.

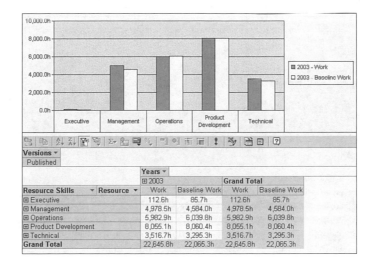

FIGURE 17.9   Assignment-centric views can show demand for skills.

Portfolio Analyzer views that show assignment information also use attributes from Enterprise Global Resource Outline Codes that you define within the Enterprise Global configuration settings. The specific outline code data attached to a resource assignment within each Project schedule is used to group OLAP assignment data.

> **CAUTION**
>
> Some assignment attributes such as multivalue Enterprise Global Resource Outline Codes do not automatically show up within Portfolio Analyzer views. Project managers must use special Microsoft Project Professional usage views to assign which specific attribute is being used for each task assignment.

▶ **SEE** "How the Resource Matching Feature Works," **PAGE 574**.

Figure 17.10 shows a mixed mode view that shows project, resource, and assignment data. A view such as this allows the end user to expand or contract attributes about projects and resources. Mixed mode views such as this enable project and resource managers to see which resources are working on projects throughout programs or projects.

Mixed mode views also provide valuable information about individual projects or resources. The end user can use a variety of filters to focus attention on specific data.

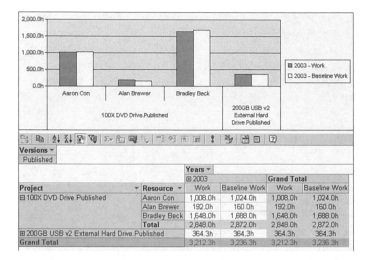

FIGURE 17.10   Mixed mode views show project and resource data.

TIP

If you create a mixed mode view, consider setting the column width and headers to narrow display so that people with smaller display monitors can start with a simple display of information. If you make the columns wide, users must scroll right and left to see the information on the view.

Formatting Portfolio Analyzer Pivot Tables

Portfolio Analyzer views can be formatted to make them more appealing and more productive for the people throughout your organization. You should design certain format schemes for each view and save those formats within the views.

You can set color and text font formats when you create a Portfolio Analyzer view by using the Commands and Options functionwithin the view as described in Chapter 10. This section expands on those concepts to provide more details on formatting functions within Portfolio Analyzer views.

The Commands and Options function uses an object-oriented approach summarized by the phrase "Pick an object and then take an action."

After the Command and Options function is visible, you can select different object areas within the pivot table or chart. As you select each object, the Commands and Options function changes to match the context of the object you select. Each Commands and Options display enables a set of control tabs that allow you to manipulate the selected object.

Figure 17.11 shows how you can use the Commands and Options function to format Totals rows and columns.

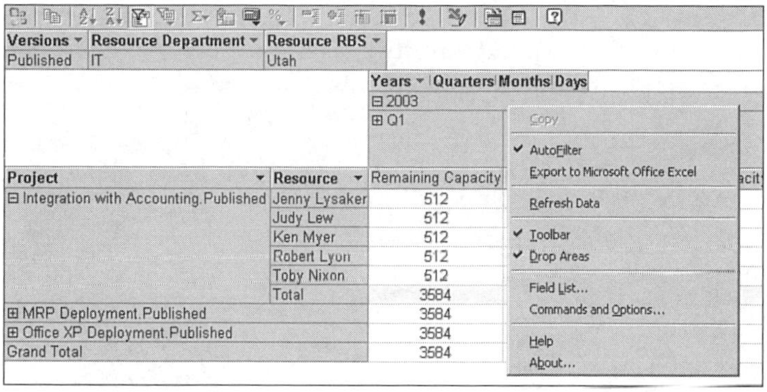

FIGURE 17.11 Use the Commands and Options function to change formats.

To access the Commands and Options function within a Portfolio Analyzer view, follow these steps:

1. Right-click on a pivot table column or row items and select the Commands and Options menu item near the end of the list as shown in Figure 17.11.

2. Select the Format tab and then the Background Color as shown in Figure 17.12. You can also use the Format tab to set the font style, size, and so on.

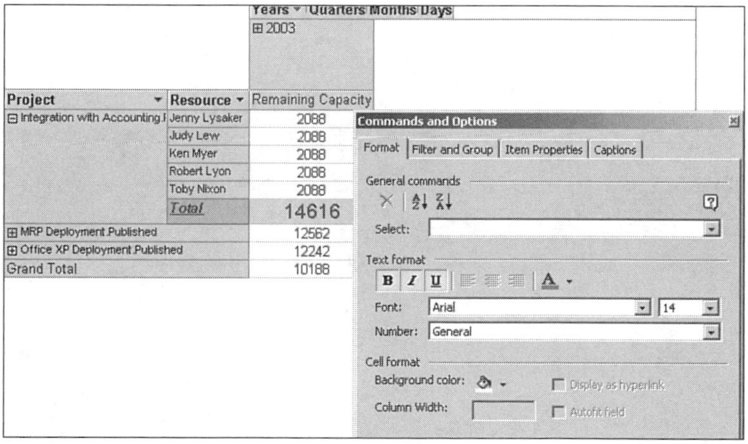

FIGURE 17.12 Set the Background color, font, and style for rows and column Totals.

3. Use the Filter and Group tab to filter out data to include the Top, Bottom, or percentage of the values in the cube, as shown in Figure 17.13. Notice how a funnel icon appears (next to Resource) for Dimensions that have a filter applied.

4. When you select another object within the pivot table, you can then control the format for that item, as shown in Figure 17.14 where the Remaining Capacity column is selected. Notice how you also can use a numeric format template such as

###,###.0 to indicate the format of numeric values. In this case, the format template indicates that the values should have two fields of three characters with a separating comma and a single trailing decimal fraction value appended to the right end of the values.

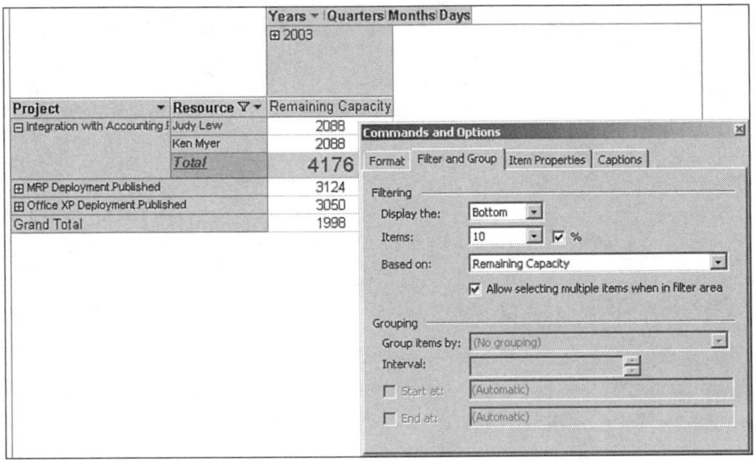

FIGURE 17.13   Set a filter to show part of the cube data in the view.

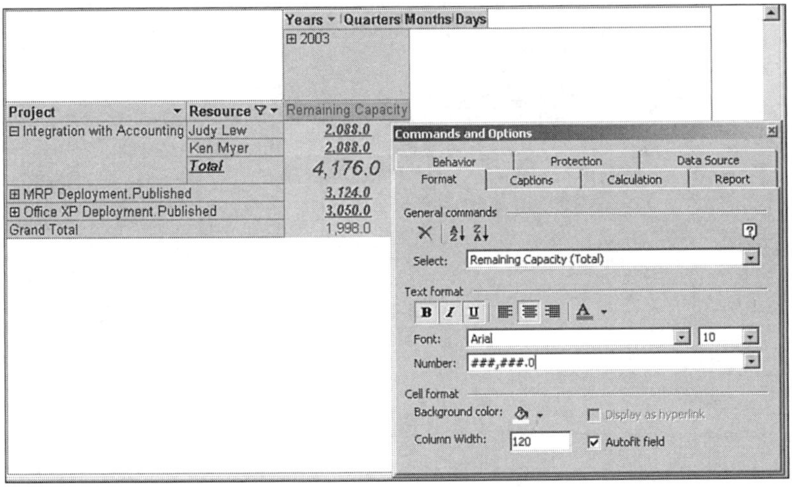

FIGURE 17.14   Select other objects to control those formats.

CAUTION

The Commands and Options function enables you to control other aspects about the data, more than just formats. Do not change the Data Source tab options unless you know how to connect to other OLAP cube data sources. Save your intermediate views before manipulating these settings; otherwise, you may lose your work.

Formatting Portfolio Analyzer Charts

The Commands and Options function can also be used to control the formats of Portfolio Analyzer charts. You can control conditions such as the following:

- **Change the Chart type**—Enables you to see different chart configurations and show mixed graphic styles within the same chart—for example, bars and lines.

- **Add or Change Axes and Titles**—Allows you to alter the appearance and scale of the vertical axis or even add another axis to reflect a dual-scale chart. You can also add major and minor grid tick marks as an aid to viewing data across the chart.

- **Change the Colors and Patterns**—Provides controls that offer a variety of colors and fill patterns—for example, adding color gradient fill for bar charts.

- **Alter Font Types and Formats**—Using various character styles, colors, and formats such as bold, italics, and underlines.

Figure 17.15 shows an example chart that has several modifications. Note the use of features such as the chart title "Cost Variance as a % of Cost to Baseline Cost," the "Cost" label on the left-vertical axis, the "Cost Var % of BL Cost" label on the right-side axis, the "Projects" label along the bottom axis, major vertical-grid tick marks, the use of a curved line superimposed on the bar chart, and so on.

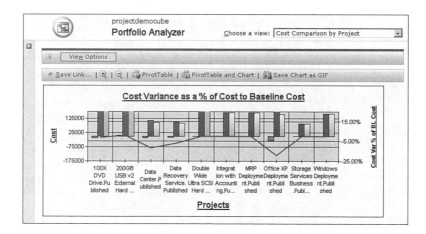

FIGURE 17.15   Portfolio Analyzer view chart example.

Figure 17.16 shows how a right-click on a blank area within the chart provides a menu where you can select the Commands and Options function.

TIP

The Chart and pivot table functions use an object-oriented technique for Commands and Options. First you pick an object and then take an action. For example: Click on different sections of a chart and watch the Commands and Options window change as the selected object gains focus.

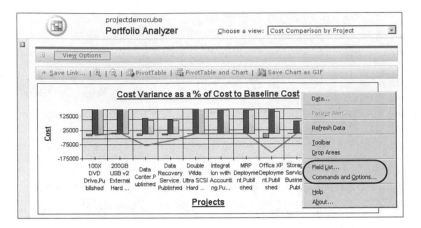

FIGURE 17.16   Right-click in the chart to see Commands and Options.

After you select the Commands and Options menu item, you can navigate to various areas of the chart by selecting an object or using the drop-down menu item as shown in Figure 17.17. Notice how the list shows all the active chart areas that can be modified.

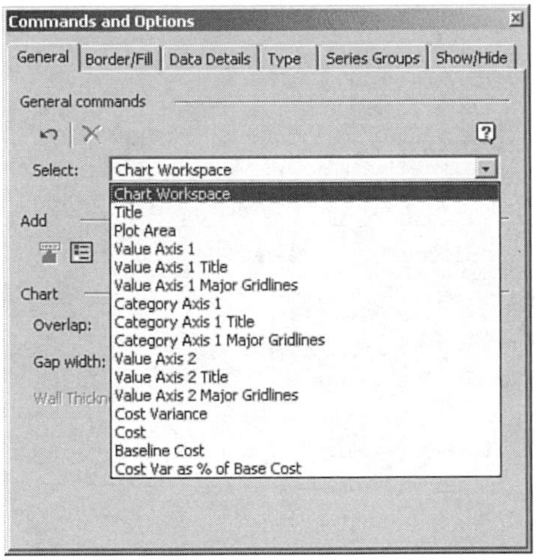

FIGURE 17.17   Chart area sections available from the drop-down list.

Suppose that you are creating a Portfolio Analyzer view with a chart and you want to add a chart title like that shown within Figure 17.15. When you select a blank area in the background of the chart, you can select the icon to Add a Title as shown in Figure 17.18.

When you use the Add a Title icon, you can select that title and change the chart title caption text as shown in Figure 17.19. You can also use text formatting functions to control font style, font size, bold, italics, underline, and color.

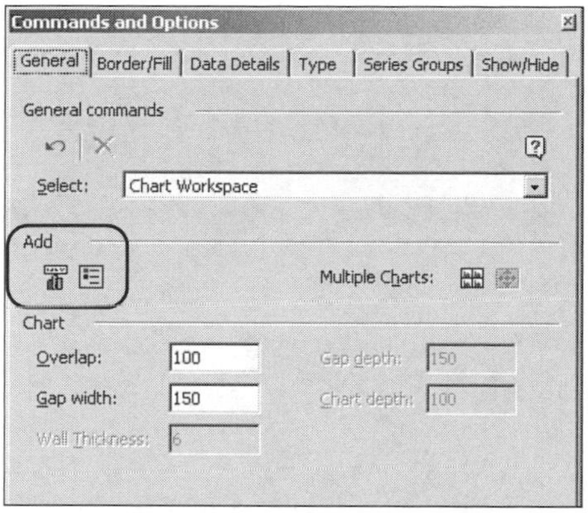

FIGURE 17.18   Look for icons like Add a Title on the chart.

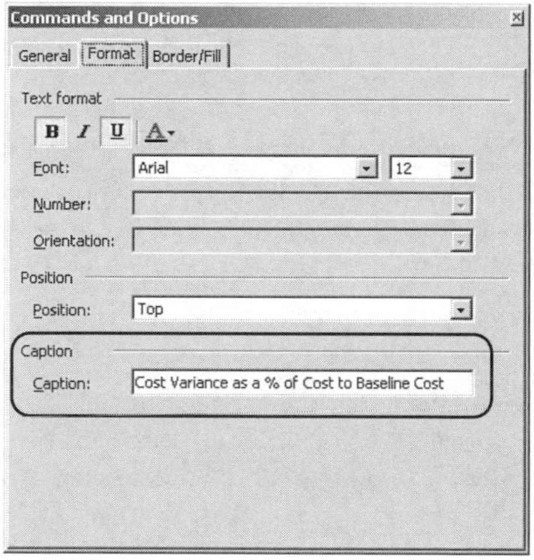

FIGURE 17.19   Enter the Caption text for the chart title.

TIP

When using the Commands and Options function to edit text, as in a chart title, make sure that you press the Enter key to complete the action within the text entry data field.

The Commands and Options function also provides controls for the overall chart type or individual data measures within the chart. Figure 17.17 shows how you can select an item such as "Cost Var as % of Base Cost" and then control how that item is plotted within the chart area. Figure 17.20 shows how the chart Type can be set to use different line, bar, curve, or other display modes for a specific measure. Notice how a Smooth Line style can also show individual data item markers along the curve. If you hover over those data items, a pop-up item appears showing the value of the specific data marker.

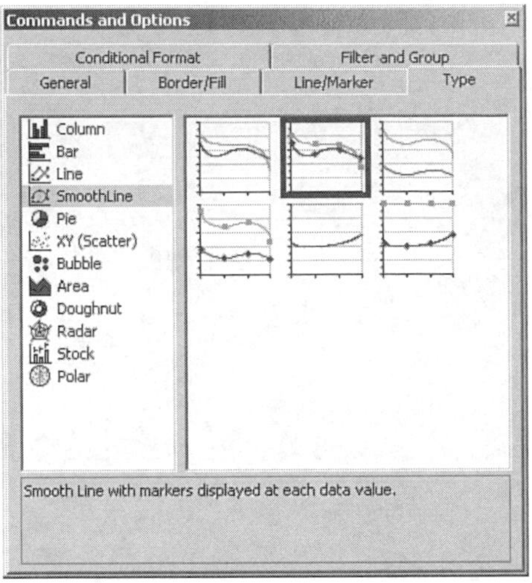

FIGURE 17.20   Change the chart graph display for individual measures.

> **TIP**
>
> Try changing the Miter, Marker Shape, Fill Type, and other controls when you select chart items such as curves, markers, and so on. These allow you to make the chart items stand out or make them easier to find as the end users view the chart or export charts to GIF graphic formats.

The Commands and Options function also allows you to place additional measurement axes on the chart like the one on the right side of Figure 17.15, shown previously. Say that you want to add this type of axis to your chart, and you want the new axis to have a different scale than the original axis on the left. You can use the simple steps as follows:

1. Right-click on the chart background and select the Commands and Options menu item.

2. Make sure that Chart Workspace is selected from the pull-down menu as shown in Figure 17.21.

3. Select the Series Groups tab and select the Series Item, such as Cost Var as % of. Then click OK to create a logical data measures group that will use the new axis. When you click the Add button, a new axis is automatically created that is associated with the selected data measure grouping, as shown in Figure 17.22.

> **TIP**
>
> If you make a mistake while creating a new series grouping, use the Operation drop-down list and select the Merge with Group 1 function. Then click OK to rejoin the series into a single logical group.

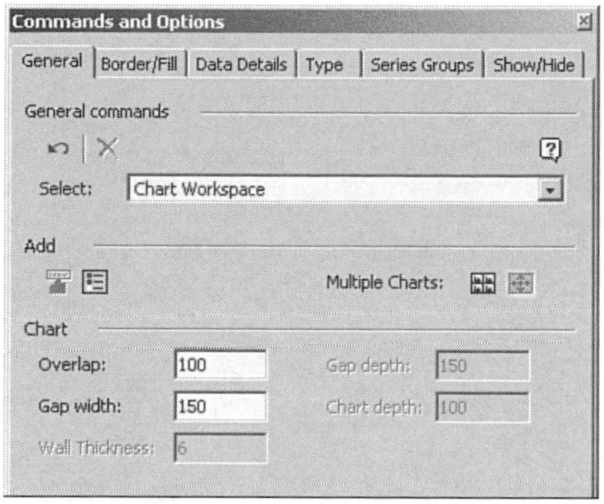

FIGURE 17.21   Select the Chart Workspace to add an axis.

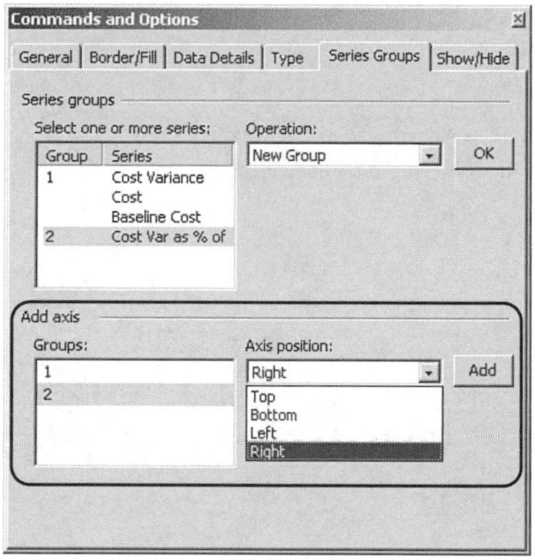

FIGURE 17.22   Select the data series to establish a chart "group."

4. Adjust the scale of this new axis to suit the criteria of the data measures. In this case, the scale is percentage values, so the maximum and minimum values are set to decimal fractions, as shown in Figure 17.23.

5. The last step you may want to take is to add axis titles so that people will understand the difference between an axis on the left versus the new one on the right side of the chart. Select the Add a Title icon, as shown previously in Figure 17.18. Then select the Format tab and enter the new title in the Caption entry area as shown in Figure 17.24.

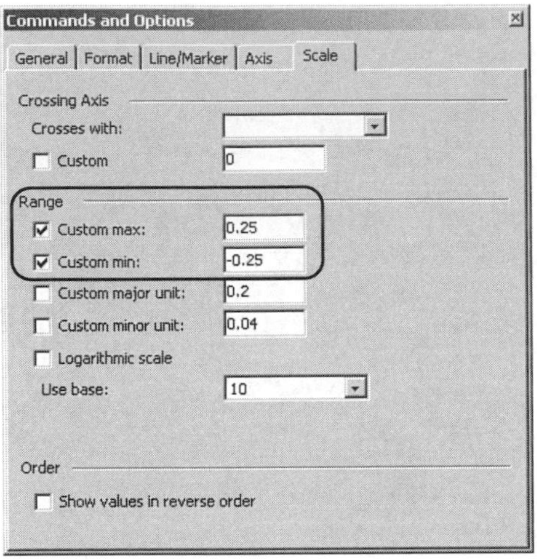

FIGURE 17.23   Adjust the scale of a chart Axis.

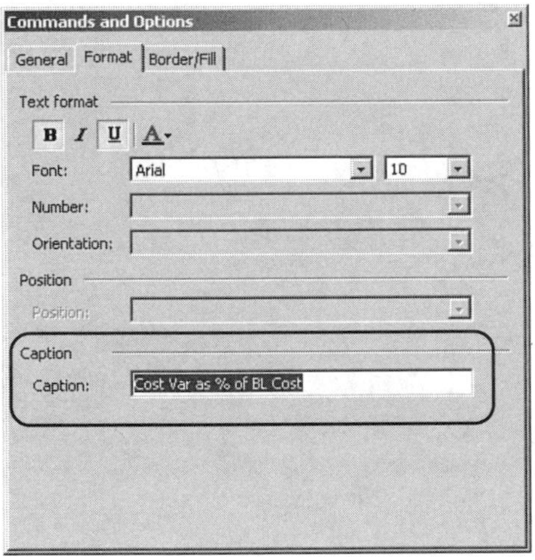

FIGURE 17.24   Give the chart axis a title.

Building Custom Formulas Within Portfolio Analyzer Views

Portfolio Analyzer views can contain customized formulas whereby you insert additional calculated data columns within the measures section of the pivot table. This section introduces custom calculated data values so that you can understand some possibilities to show special data conditions not part of the default OLAP cube data.

The calculated data measures allow you to use certain formula functions, but you must first understand some of the principles behind these functions:

- Calculated measures use SQL Analysis Services MDX language functions to display customized column data. These functions are listed within the Multidimensional Expressions (MDX) function list within the compiled help files for SQL Analysis Services documentation.

- Default OLAP measures can be used as variables within custom formulas, so you can reference measures such as work, baseline work, availability, actual work, and so forth.

- Some customized formulas may not total as expected for subtotal or grand total columns or rows. This is especially true when using MDX functions, such as DistinctCount, that return the number of items within a referenced return set.

- Debugging formulas can be difficult because the formula parsing functions return basic error codes that do not always provide clear descriptions of the error.

- Custom formulas are calculated on the end user computer, so the performance of Portfolio Analyzer views may be slow for users with slow computers.

> **TIP**
>
> Designing and coding customized calculated formulas can be frustrating. Consider engaging the help of a software developer who has experience using the SQL Analysis Services MDX language functions.

You can easily add custom formulas while creating or modifying a Portfolio Analyzer view. Suppose that you want to create a customized data measure column called Remaining Availability that shows the difference between assigned work versus the calendar availability for resources within the Enterprise Global Resource Pool. Furthermore, you want to graphically display a chart that shows any condition where a resource is overloaded, as shown in Figure 17.25 where the bars for overloaded resources display below the horizontal zero axis.

The following steps illustrate how to create this type of view with a customized formula:

1. Click on the Calculated Totals and Fields icon within the pivot table as shown in Figure 17.26.

2. Select the Calculation tab to enter a formula and enter the Calculation Name, also known as the Caption text, within the Captions tab.

3. From the Insert Reference To list, select an appropriate Measures field such as Availability, as shown in Figure 17.27. You can also type in the formula if you are comfortable with writing formulas by hand.

4. Enter an arithmetic operator such as "-" (minus sign) followed by another field such as Work Total.

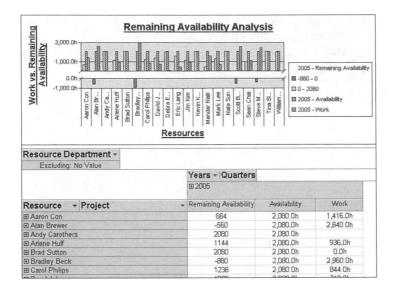

FIGURE 17.25   Example Portfolio Analyzer view showing remaining availability for resources.

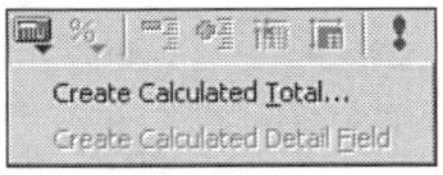

FIGURE 17.26   Use the Calculated Totals and Fields to create a custom formula.

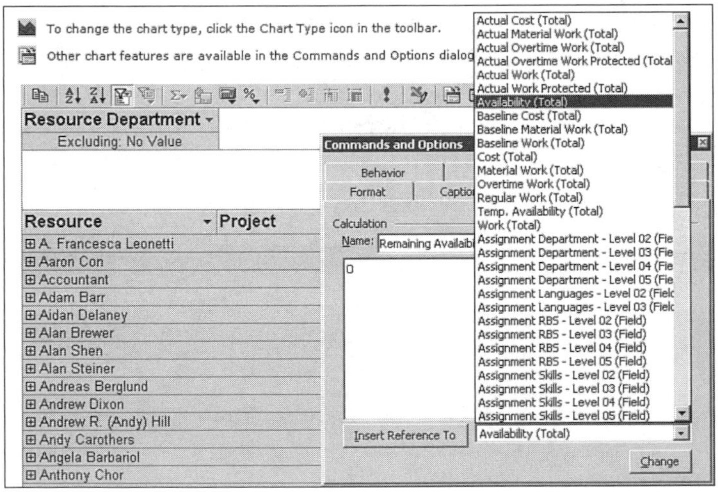

FIGURE 17.27   Use the Insert Reference To list to build formulas.

5. Click the Change button, and the formula is entered within the new column as shown in Figure 17.28.

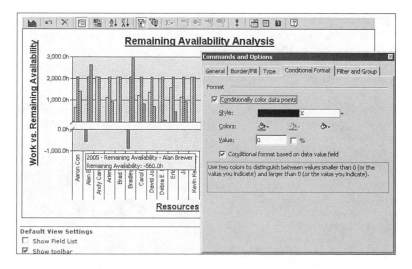

FIGURE 17.28   Custom formula result.

> **TIP**
>
> Use embedded newline characters (Enter key) placed within the formula to make the formula easier to read.

The results of calculated formulas can also be displayed within the graphic charts associated with the pivot table. Figure 17.29 shows how the Remaining Availability can be displayed using a split vertical axis and conditional formatting to display negative values that stand out compared to other data.

17

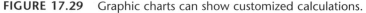

FIGURE 17.29   Graphic charts can show customized calculations.

CAUTION

Make sure that you understand how end users interpret the meaning of customized formula results. Figure 17.29 shows an example of how information such as Availability is displayed when the user opens subvalues within the pivot table. Notice how the rows show 2,080 hours of availability for each row. Also notice how the Remaining Availability rows may also show unexpected values as in Figure 17.30. This is a general condition of data fields such as Availability that is derived from each resource personal calendar within the Enterprise Global Resource Pool. But that value does not consider the assignments within each project schedule, so use caution when designing Portfolio Analyzer views that show this type of data.

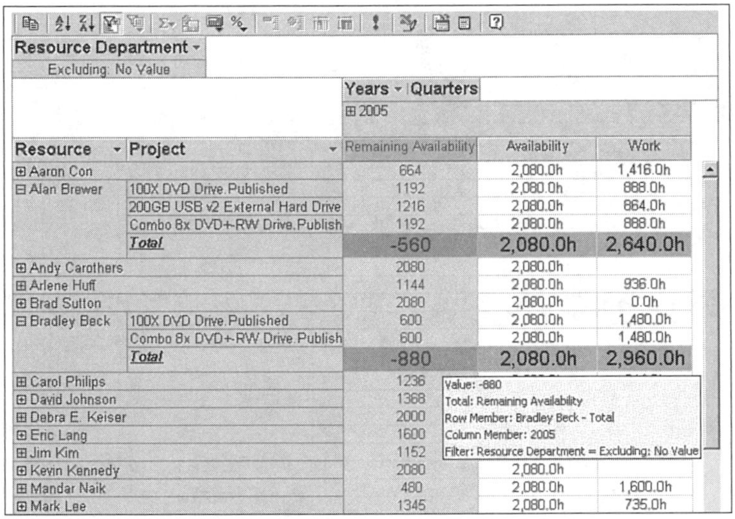

Resource ▾	Project ▾	Remaining Availability	Availability	Work
⊞ Aaron Con		664	2,080.0h	1,416.0h
⊟ Alan Brewer	100X DVD Drive.Published	1192	2,080.0h	888.0h
	200GB USB v2 External Hard Drive	1216	2,080.0h	864.0h
	Combo 8x DVD+-RW Drive.Publish	1192	2,080.0h	888.0h
	Total	-560	2,080.0h	2,640.0h
⊞ Andy Carothers		2080	2,080.0h	
⊞ Arlene Huff		1144	2,080.0h	936.0h
⊞ Brad Sutton		2080	2,080.0h	0.0h
⊟ Bradley Beck	100X DVD Drive.Published	600	2,080.0h	1,480.0h
	Combo 8x DVD+-RW Drive.Publish	600	2,080.0h	1,480.0h
	Total	-880	2,080.0h	2,960.0h
⊞ Carol Philips		1236	Value: -880	
⊞ David Johnson		1368	Total: Remaining Availability	
⊞ Debra E. Keiser		2000	Row Member: Bradley Beck - Total	
⊞ Eric Lang		1600	Column Member: 2005	
⊞ Jim Kim		1152	Filter: Resource Department = Excluding: No Value	
⊞ Kevin Kennedy		2080	2,080.0h	
⊞ Mandar Naik		480	2,080.0h	1,600.0h
⊞ Mark Lee		1345	2,080.0h	735.0h

FIGURE 17.30   Use caution when designing views with calculated data columns.

If you make a mistake while building a calculated formula, the MDX language formula parser issues cryptic errors like that shown in Figure 17.31. You must correct the offending error before any of the pivot table values are displayed. This error is a result of a missing closing brace "]" to the right of the Work.

TIP

Save the general view changes *before* you create a customized calculated formula. If you cannot correct a formula syntax error, you may have to use the view Cancel button to abandon the view edits and recover a previous working view design.

NOTE

For more information about SQL Analysis Services MDX functions, look on the SQL Analysis Services machine for compiled help files such as C:\Program Files\Microsoft SQL Server\80\Tools\Books\olapdmad.chm.

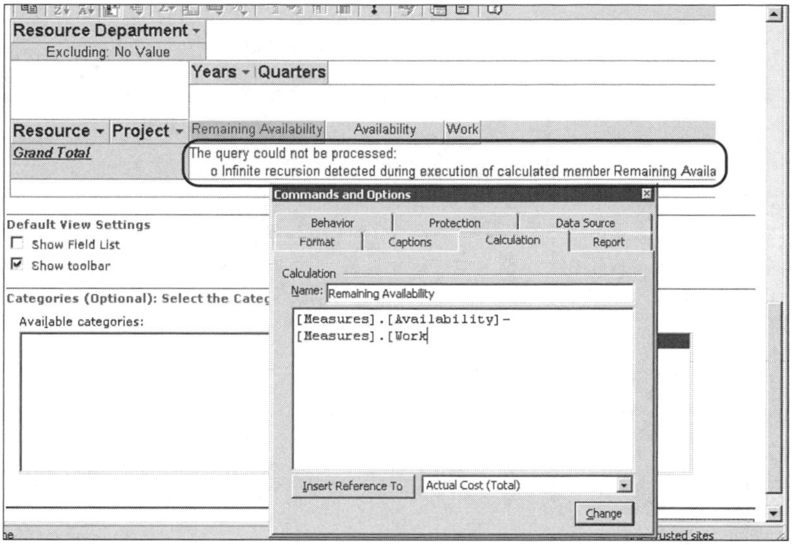

FIGURE 17.31   Formula errors may be difficult to resolve.

Enterprise Global Resource Single-Value Versus Multivalue Outline Codes

All the Enterprise Global Project Outline Codes and Enterprise Global Resource Outline Codes 1 through 19 are considered single-value codes because you can select a single value from the defined list. Single-value codes are used as dimension attributes when the OLAP cube is regenerated.

Enterprise Global Resource Outline Codes 20 through 29 are considered multivalue codes because you can select multiple values from the same list. This condition is perfect for representing resource attributes such as skills that project managers and resource managers can use to search for resources with these kinds of attributes. These attributes can be helpful when using the Match function within PWA and Project Professional Build Team functions because the query filter uses the "Contains" clause to search for substring matches within the composite items selected for each resource.

Multivalue resource codes are not used when the OLAP cube is generated because the OLAP build process cannot uniquely identify which specific codes are used when a resource is assigned to tasks within a project schedule.

Consider the following example and questions. Your Project Server 2003 Enterprise Global configuration includes the definition of three multivalue resource codes: Computer Language Skills, Software Applications, and Manufacturing Machine Tools. Becky Young is a resource within the Enterprise Global Resource Pool, and she has a number of attributes established from each of these three multivalue codes. Becky has been added to the project team for several projects and has been assigned to several working tasks.

Resource and staff managers may need to answer the following questions:

- Are all of Becky's skills used within each project?

- Which of Becky's specific skills are being used for each task she is assigned to work?

- How can Portfolio Analyzer views be used to determine how much work is predicted for each of Becky's skills used within projects?

Each of the Enterprise Global Resource Outline Codes 20 through 29 also has an associated single-value code item identified with the same code number as the multivalue counterpart. These single-value codes can be used when making a resource assignment to a task within the project schedule, within the Usage views. So when Becky is assigned to each working task, the project manager can select which of the specific multivalue codes is being used for each task.

When the single-value codes are established for each task assignment, the OLAP cube automatically contains Measures such as work, cost, actual work, and so forth. These Measures then have a direct relationship to the single-value outline code settings as OLAP Dimensions. Therefore, the pivot table contains the appropriate direct relationship to the defined multivalue codes.

Figure 17.32 shows an example of setting single-value codes for each resource assignment within a project schedule. The Develop Preliminary Investigation Plan task has Steve Masters and Bradley Beck assigned to complete the work activity. The project manager used the Task Usage view to set which of the multivalue Skills codes is used for each resource on that particular task.

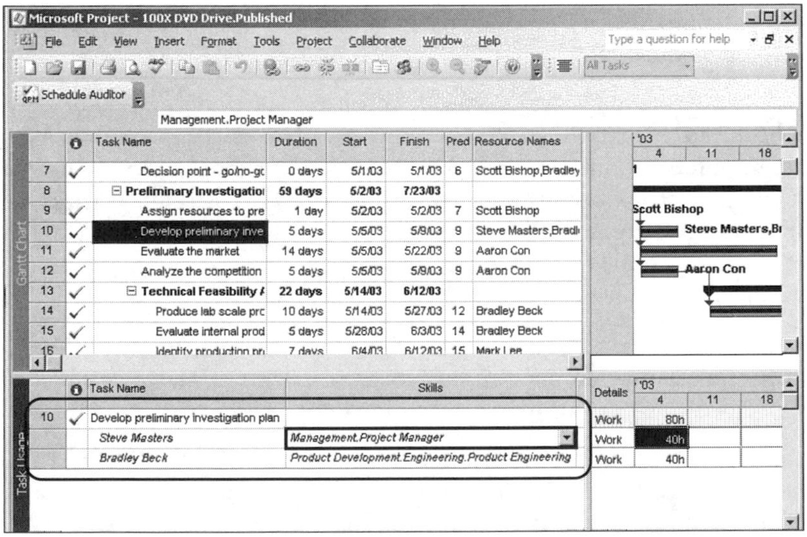

FIGURE 17.32   Single-valued codes set for each resource assignment in a project schedule.

The end result of using the multivalue and associated single-value code is that the Portfolio Analyzer views can show Resource Assignment Measures in the pivot table as shown in Figure 17.33. This allows resource managers and others to see if the work distribution is based on worker skills used within all project schedules.

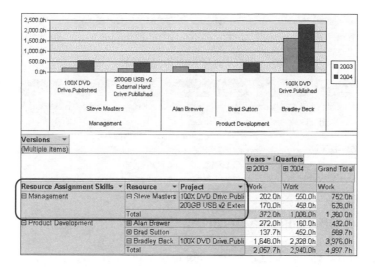

FIGURE 17.33 Multivalue code settings can be displayed within the pivot tables and graphs.

▶ **SEE** "Skill-Based Scheduling Overview," **PAGE 577**.

The specific details used within the Enterprise Global Resource Outline Codes depend on your business requirements. You need to carefully consider how these attribute codes are used within Portfolio Analyzer views and other PWA functions.

Figure 17.34 shows a variation of a mixed mode view whereby resource managers can look for local resources in projects. This is a common situation whereby project or resource managers do not use entities from the Enterprise Global Resource Pool, or they may accidentally create local resources by typing in the names of resources instead of using the Build Team functions in PWA or Project Professional.

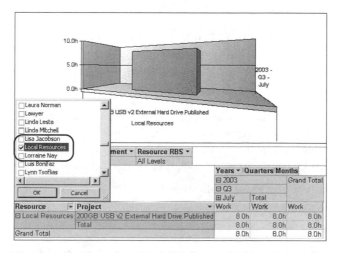

FIGURE 17.34 Mixed mode view showing local resources in projects.

17

A Portfolio Analyzer view like this is a valuable starting point to inform project managers that they need to exchange local resources for those found within the Enterprise Global Resource Pool.

> **TIP**
>
> If project schedules have resources that are not part of the Enterprise Global Resource Pool, those resources will show up as local resources within the schedules. Use the resource name filter to uncheck all resources except the resource called local. You can then see which projects have work assigned to those non-Enterprise Global resource entities. Use the Grand Total rows and columns to quickly find this data.

Manipulating Portfolio Analyzer Views

The PWA view administrators can create Portfolio Analyzer views and also allow end users to manipulate those views to suit their individual analysis needs. If the View toolbar is turned on and the user's desktop has an Office 2003 product installed, the user can use the toolbar features to temporarily alter a view.

Pivot Table Toolbars

When you create Portfolio Analyzer views, you can optionally allow the users to temporarily alter the view by using the available Office Web Components (OWC) toolbars above the graph or pivot table sections of the view. Figure 17.35 shows an example of these pivot table toolbar functions, which are explained as follows:

- **Logo**—If you click on the Microsoft Office logo symbol a pop-up window shows the current version of OWC.

- **Copy**—Allows you to place the selected range of rows or columns into your computer copy/paste buffer. You can then paste the copied data into another application, such as Excel.

- **Sort Ascending and Sort Descending**—Enable you to invert the order of data within a selected Dimension item.

- **Auto Filter**—Provides a quick toggle method to clear or reapply all individual filtered Dimensions.

- **Show Top/Bottom Items**—Enables you to remove all data except those Measures that meet the selected criteria range. This is a useful tool to find the top or bottom percentage of items that meet a specified Measures range entered within the Commands and Options window that appears when you select this toolbar icon.

- **Autocalc**—This OWC option is disabled for Portfolio Analyzer views.

- **Subtotal**—This function toggles subtotal and grand total value displays for the selected Dimension item.

- **Calculated Totals and Fields**—Provides an option to create a new calculated total field formula with the Commands and Options control window.

- **Show As %**—This icon provides a method to change a Measures column data format to a percentage value.

- **Collapse and Expand**—Provides a simple way to collapse or expand the selected Dimension.

- **Hide Details and Show Details**—These OWC options are disabled for Portfolio Analyzer views.

- **Refresh Data**—Reconnects to the OLAP cube and refreshes the information in the view.

- **Export to Excel**—This icon starts Microsoft Excel and sends the pivot table information to Excel for more analysis.

- **Commands and Options**—Opens the Commands and Options window to allow formatting and other customization functions.

- **Field List**—Click on this icon to show the Measures and Dimensions field list so that items can be added to the pivot table display.

- **Help**—This icon opens a general OWC help window that allows you to better understand features and functions of the OWC pivot table.

FIGURE 17.35   Toolbar functions allow users to manipulate a Portfolio Analyzer view.

> **NOTE**
>
> If the toolbar is not displayed or is grayed out, you may not have permission to alter the view, or your desktop does not have an Office 2003 component installed. Expand the View Options tab at the top of the Portfolio Analyzer view page to see whether the Show Toolbar item can be selected.

Using the Data Field List to Modify Views

The data Field List contains a mix of data types including Dimensions and Measures held within the OLAP cube. The author of Portfolio Analyzer views uses the Field List to load the Measures and Dimensions into the pivot table areas as depicted previously in Figure 17.6. When the view is saved, it contains the structure and format the author intended.

Portfolio Analyzer view users can be given the permission to temporarily modify a default view by adding or removing Dimensions and Measures within the pivot table. They can select the Field List icon on the pivot table toolbar and then move the data to different locations within the view or drag additional items from the Field List into the pivot table areas.

The Field List manipulation functions provide each user a lot of flexibility to show the data they need to make decisions about projects, resources, and assignments. The Portfolio Analyzer views therefore become a powerful decision support analysis tool.

Saving Personal Links to Retain View Modifications

Users of Portfolio Analyzer views may be given the permission to temporarily alter the view content. After a user modifies a view, she may want to retain those modifications to be used at a future time.

The user can use the Save Link view function, at the top of each view, to specify a personalized name for the view. A saved link allows you select this link to restore the view with personalized modifications. These links retain the original view in addition to the personal changes, but this action does not affect the original default view for other users.

Using Portfolio Modeler to Analyze Projects

The Portfolio Modeler allows you to simulate proposed changes to projects or resource assignments and view the impact of the changes, without affecting the actual project schedules. The Portfolio Modeler does not make changes to the project schedules, so this tool is therefore useful for performing what-if analysis on projects and project teams.

A common use of the Portfolio Modeler is to show which resources are overloaded and how that condition creates schedule delivery risks to one or more projects. The Portfolio Modeler also allows you to simulate what the project delivery dates might be if the overloaded resource conditions are reduced.

The Portfolio Modeler provides a starting point to understand overall risk to project delivery if resources are overloaded. You can then use Project Center, Resource Center, and Portfolio Analyzer to get a comprehensive understanding of project delivery conditions.

> **CAUTION**
>
> The software algorithms within the Portfolio Modeler are generally the same as those used within the Microsoft Project Professional Tools Substitute Resources menu. Therefore, you can use the Portfolio Modeler analysis settings to simulate the substitution of resources within single or multiple project schedules that do not yet have actual work reported. Be aware of potential faulty results when modeling projects that have actual work reported. Refer to the Microsoft TechNet Knowledge Base article number 828826 for more information.

> **NOTE**
>
> For more information about the Portfolio Modeler, you may want to acquire the Que book *Using Microsoft Office Project Professional 2003*.

Creating a Model

You need to understand some of the concepts within the Portfolio Modeler before you get started with this tool. You can access the Portfolio Modeler features by using the PWA Project Center and then selecting the Model Projects with Portfolio Modeler link. Figure 17.36 shows an example of a simple model and the control menu functions.

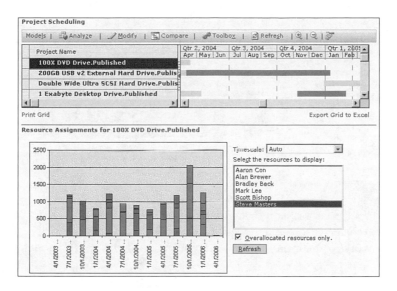

FIGURE 17.36   Simple Portfolio Modeler example.

Figure 17.37 shows the main menu within the Portfolio Modeler; each of those functions is briefly described:

- **New**—Starts the new model creation process.

- **Modify**—Provides functions to alter the previously defined model conditions.

- **Open**—Allows users to view and interact with the model results.

- **Analyze**—Shows the conditions of a selected model with a resource Demand/Capacity/Utilization Chart. Use this information as a starting point for additional research into project and resource conditions. The analysis can also be used within the Project Professional Substitute Resources functions.

- **Delete**—Allows you to permanently remove a model.

- **Unlock**—Provides a mechanism to release a read/write lock on a model so that model can be modified.

Follow these steps to create a model:

1. Click the New button to start the process as shown in Figure 17.37.

2. Give the model a name and description that indicates the purpose of the particular model. Figure 17.38 shows a name that contains the phrase "as-is" to indicate that this model shows the default conditions of project schedules and resource work loads without modification.

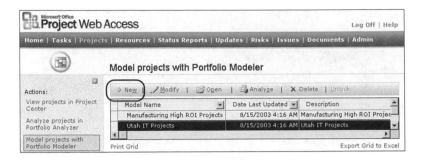

FIGURE 17.37   Start a new model.

3. Select which project schedules are included within this specific model. These projects are used within the model to show the overall schedule deliveries and resource work load conditions. Projects not included within the model are not shown in the analysis.

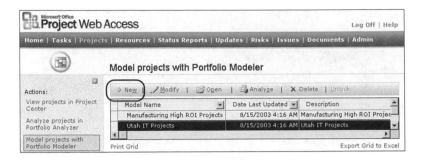

FIGURE 17.38   Start a new model with a name, description, and selected projects.

TIP

Develop a portfolio model naming scheme that indicates the purpose of each model. The term "as-is" in the name can indicate that the model shows the default current conditions of projects within the model. A term such as "what-if" might indicate the schedule delivery when resource overload conditions are reduced. A term such as "replace-resources" might indicate conditions where overloaded resources are replaced with others that have less work within a time span.

---

4. Select the resources that should be used within the model, as shown in Figure 17.39 and in the following list:

- **Include Resources in the Model's Projects**—Uses the resources within the projects selected for this model. External resources are not considered.

- **Include Resources at or Below RBS Level**—Can be used to limit the resource substitution algorithm to resources within a specified Resource Breakdown Structure (RBS) branch.

- **Include Resources Specified Below**—Allows you to select specific resources to be used for substitution within the model.

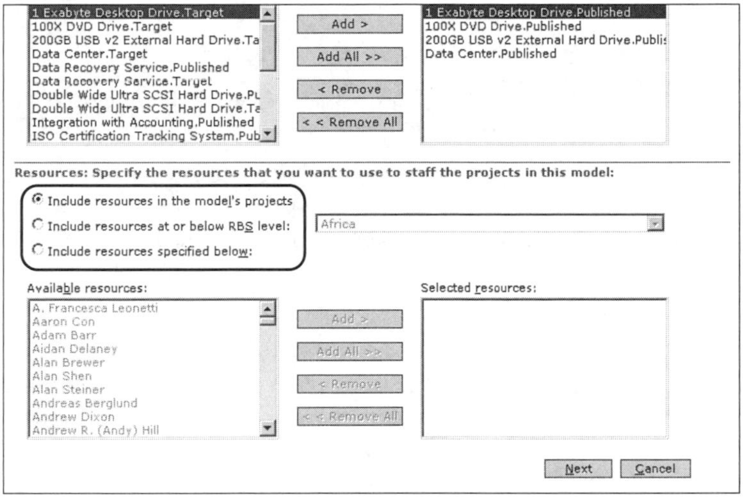

FIGURE 17.39   Set the resource substitution options.

NOTE

Resource substitution algorithms have a strong reliance on the logical design of the Enterprise Global Resource Outline Codes for your Project Server 2003 implementation. The substitution algorithms also use the special setting Use This Code for Matching Generic Resources. The automatic matching functions will therefore use any resource outline codes with this setting, so the combinations of these settings affect the resource substitution results.

---

5. Click Next to continue creating a new model.

6. Figure 17.40 shows a list of projects that are somehow related to the specific schedules you selected within the model. You see additional projects that are using the resources used within the schedules you have selected for the model. If you check additional projects, those projects will become part of the Portfolio Modeler analysis for resource work load display and potential resource substitution. The Relationship column typically shows that other projects use the same resources as used within the projects in the model. The Related To column shows which project(s) in the model are related to the other projects not in the model.

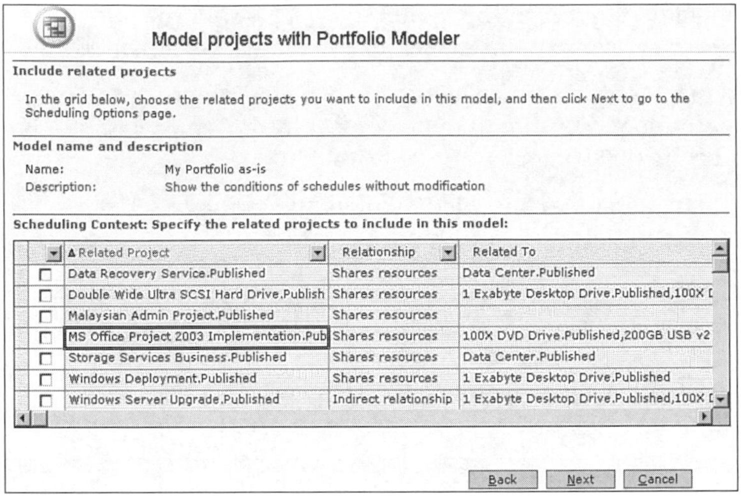

FIGURE 17.40   Include other projects within the Portfolio Model analysis.

7. Click Next to continue the model.

8. Figure 17.41 shows the functions that allow you to see the priority number given to each project as it is stored within the Project Server 2003 database. You can also choose how the resources should be considered for substitution within each project. You can optionally declare that each project should be delayed to a specified date. The Scheduling Options are briefly described as follows:

   - **Keep Dates and Assignments**—The default condition that uses the current conditions of the project resources. The substitution algorithms do not simulate the effects of modifying the date ranges or resource assignments.

   - **Use Current Assignments**—The model analyzer functions use the current resource assignments but alter the date ranges based on work load conditions.

   - **Reassign Resources in Project**—The substitute resources algorithm simulates the replacement of resources within the specified project.

   - **Reassign Resources in Model's**—The substitute resources algorithm simulates the replacement of resources by using any matching resource within any project within the model, including the related projects.

9. Click Next to continue the model.

NOTE

Each model created can be viewed by PWA users with appropriate permissions. Use the Admin Manage Security Categories functions to set these permissions.

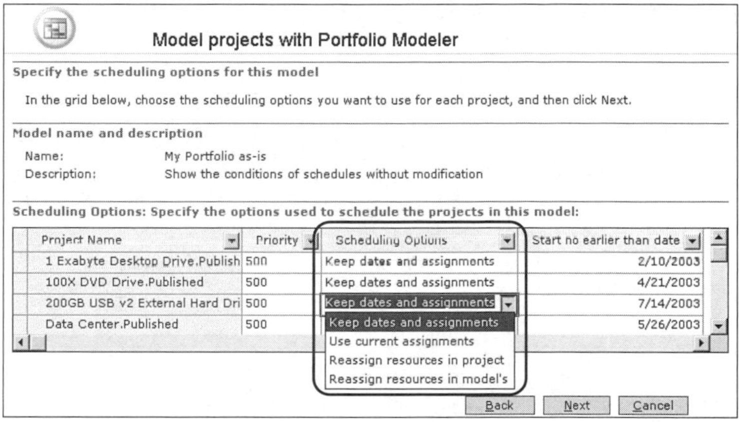

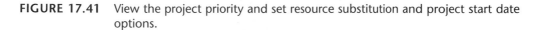

FIGURE 17.41   View the project priority and set resource substitution and project start date options.

Viewing and Analyzing Data in a Model

Each portfolio model consists of a relationship between project and resources within the model. Those relationships are captured within the Project Server 2003 database by using a series of complex data queries to extract data about each project and resource within the model.

The Open model function enables users to see the information within a selected model, as shown in Figure 17.42.

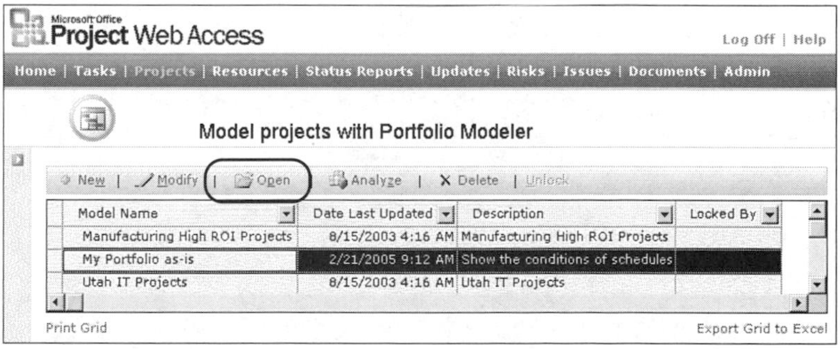

FIGURE 17.42   Use the Open function to see model results.

When the model opens, users can view data results and move the columns to meet their needs, as shown in Figure 17.43.

The vertical split bar can be repositioned between the data on the left and the Gantt chart on the right. You can also Zoom In and Out to see more details within time spans. Figure 17.44 shows how the Gantt chart information can display periods of time when resources are overloaded. Each Gantt chart row can show a mix of Green, Yellow, and Red bar sections:

- **Green**—If the resource work load demand is less than the resource capacity, the bar is set to green.

- **Yellow**—When the work load exceeds the resource capacity by less than 10%, the bar is set to yellow.

- **Red**—If the resource work load demand exceeds capacity by greater than 10%, the bar section shows red.

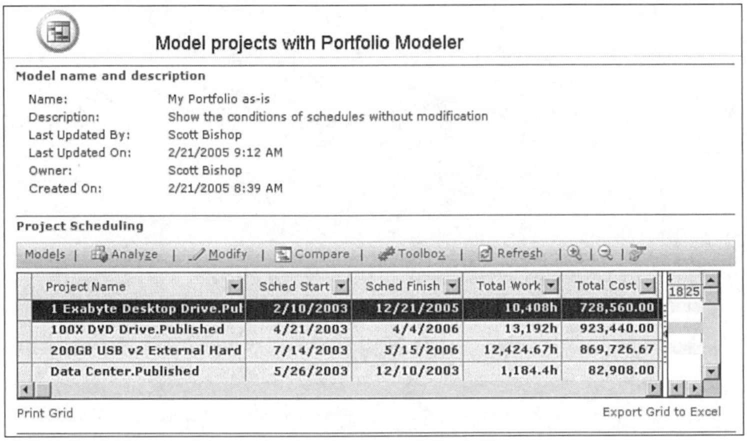

FIGURE 17.43   Manipulate columns and view model results.

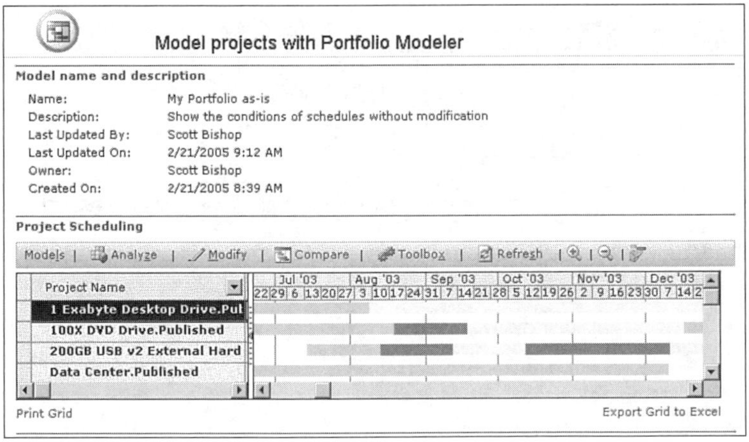

FIGURE 17.44   Use the Gantt chart to display time spans when resources are overloaded.

TIP

The Gantt chart bar colors are an average of resource work load through a span of time. Use the Zoom In and Out functions to examine resource work load in more detail. When you Zoom In on a green area, you may see sections of time where the Gantt section shows yellow or red.

The area below the project list and Gantt chart shows individual resource work loads throughout a span of time. Figure 17.45 shows several function controls that allow you to examine the work for resources within each project.

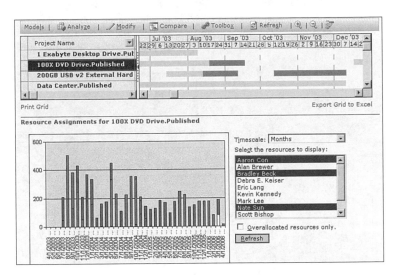

FIGURE 17.45   Select a project and view the resource work loads in the bar graph.

When you select a single project schedule, the resources within that project are displayed in the vertical bar chart. You can then use several functions to examine more details about each resource:

- **Timescale**—Allows you to set the detail, ranging from days, weeks, months, quarters, years, or auto. As you select a timescale, the bar chart is redisplayed to include data at that resolution of detail.

- **Select the Resources to Display**—Enables you to select individual or all resources from the list. If you hold down the Ctrl key while clicking on the resource names, you can select individual resources for analysis.

- **Refresh**—Redisplays the bar chart with the data from individual resources selected from the list.

- **Overallocated Resources Only**—Allows you to quickly determine those resources that have work load demands beyond their individual capacity, which is controlled by individual resource calendars.

- **Display Chart in Monochrome**—Allows you to reduce the chart color to shades of gray.

- **Hover Mouse over Bar Chart**—When you pause the mouse cursor over particular bar chart items, a small pop-up appears that shows the metrics for a resource within the bar chart section. Each vertical bar may show multiple sections, one for each resource within the time span for that bar.

TIP*

Move your mouse cursor over the bar chart and then right-click to select Commands and Options. You can then select the Type tab and change the chart format to other formats as shown in Figure 17.46. The chart type you select is temporary, returning to the default display when the page refeshes.

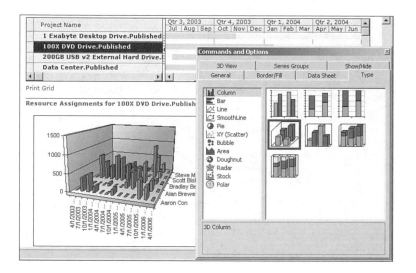

FIGURE 17.46   Right-click and then select Commands and Options to change the chart format.

TIP

Right-click on the chart to select the Data menu item from the option list. You can then use the Data Sheet tab to see the numeric values that drive the graphic display as shown in Figure 17.47. If you select the upper-left corner cell, you can copy and paste the numeric data into Excel.

Manipulating Models and What-If Analysis

The Portfolio Modeler functions include special features that can be used to do what-if analysis by comparing models that use different definition settings.

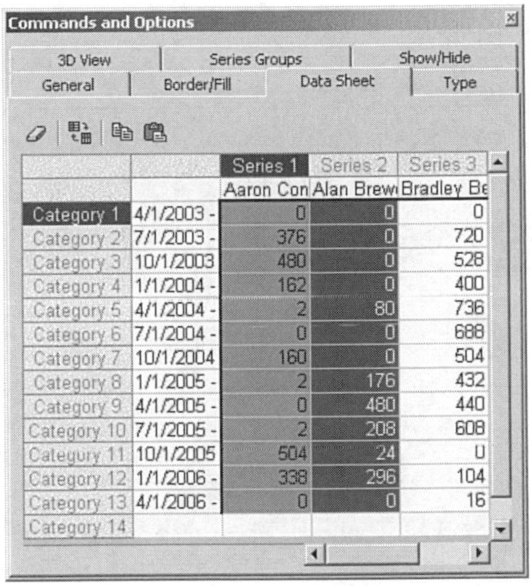

		Series 1	Series 2	Series 3
		Aaron Con	Alan Brew	Bradley Be
Category 1	4/1/2003 -	0	0	0
Category 2	7/1/2003 -	376	0	720
Category 3	10/1/2003	480	0	528
Category 4	1/1/2004 -	162	0	400
Category 5	4/1/2004 -	2	80	736
Category 6	7/1/2004 -	0	0	688
Category 7	10/1/2004	160	0	504
Category 8	1/1/2005 -	2	176	432
Category 9	4/1/2005 -	0	480	440
Category 10	7/1/2005 -	2	208	608
Category 11	10/1/2005	504	24	0
Category 12	1/1/2006 -	338	296	104
Category 13	4/1/2006 -	0	0	16
Category 14				

FIGURE 17.47 View and copy the numeric data behind the chart.

The what-if analysis process is based on simple definitions of named models that have differences within the resource conditions using settings as shown previously in Figure 17.41. Different models can be opened by using the Portfolio Modeler Compare function to view two models within the same display. You can then compare and contrast the schedule delivery and resource work load conditions of the models. This type of model comparison allows you to do what-if analysis to determine what could happen if project managers modified project schedules to resolve resource work load conditions.

17

NOTE

Some model settings may result in accelerated schedule delivery because resource work load can be increased within the individual resource capacity for the defined model. If you allow the Portfolio Modeler to simulate substitution of resources, an overloaded resource may be replaced by those with less work load. Be careful to model the conditions of all projects that share resources so that you have a complete understanding of the what-if conditions.

You may want to use two models to do what-if analysis. The following steps assume that two models have been defined using the same four project schedules. The "as-is" project keeps the original schedule and resources; the "what-if" model allows the resource work load conditions to delay the schedule finish dates. When both models are compared, you can see the differences in delivery dates and resource work load conditions. The following steps generally describe the comparison process:

1. Open one model.
2. Use the Compare function to select a second model, use the Add function to include that model, and then click OK as shown in Figure 17.48.
3. Adjust the display to show appropriate details of the Gantt chart as shown in Figure 17.49.

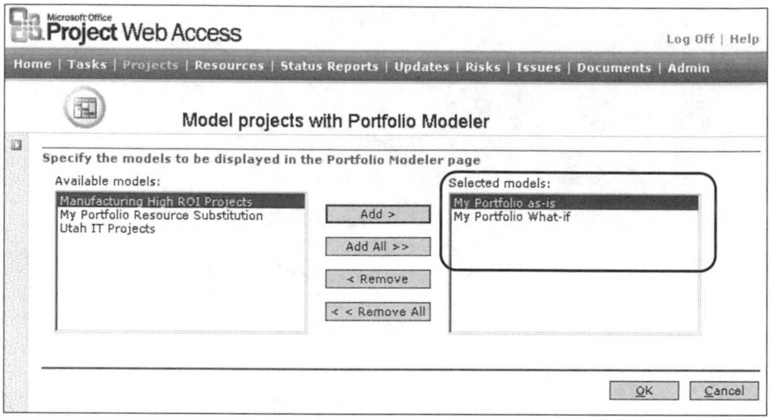

FIGURE 17.48   Use the Compare function to open a second model.

Notice how the "what-if" schedule delivery dates have been significantly delayed because the model simulation removes resource overload conditions. This simulation therefore delays the schedule finish dates as in Figure 17.49.

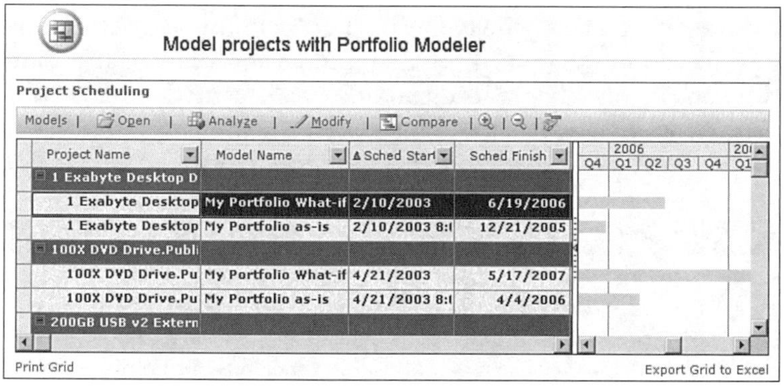

FIGURE 17.49   View two models within the same display.

> **CAUTION**
>
> Model simulations do not optimize all resources within the model context. The software algorithms simulate what could happen when overloaded resource conditions are removed. These simulations may also result in other resources having less work load than the original "as-is" model conditions.

This type of what-if analysis can be extended by including another model that has resource control settings like those shown in Figure 17.50. These settings allow the software to use Enterprise Global Resource Outline Codes and work load analysis to simulate changing resources across projects within the model.

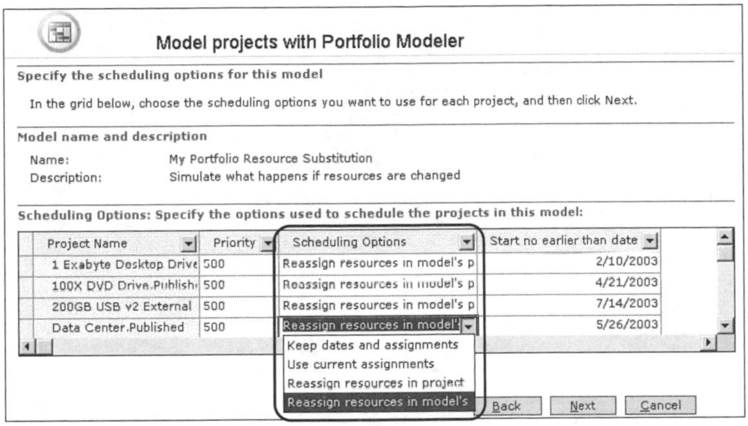

FIGURE 17.50   Create a model that allows resource substitution across projects.

When the three models are compared, you can see what might happen if overloaded resources are replaced by those resource with less work load. Figure 17.51 shows this condition and illustrates how the My Portfolio Resource Substitution model comes close to the original delivery dates without resource overload conditions from the original "as-is" model.

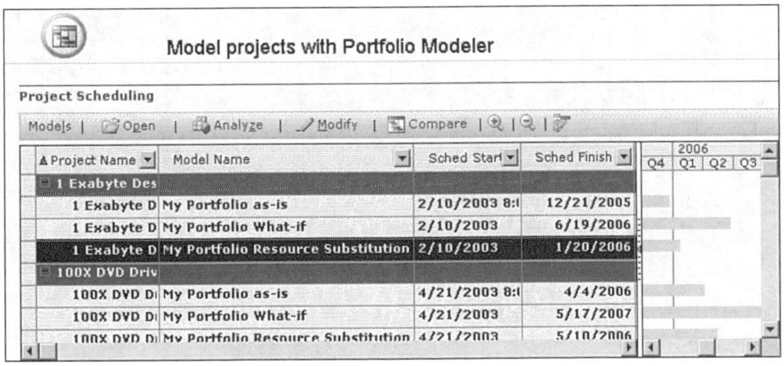

FIGURE 17.51   Create a model that allows resource substitution.

Using the Analyze and Toolbox Functions

Suppose that you like the overall impact of the My Portfolio Resource Substitution model and you want to know what actions the software algorithms recommend. Select a project and then use the Analyze function button to see the model details such as those shown in Figure 17.52.

> **NOTE**
>
> The Portfolio Modeler Analyze function does not provide automatic comparison between two or more models. You must use manual methods to compare which factors or resources are changed.

Models | ⟋ Modify | ☐ Open

Model name and description

Name:	My Portfolio Resource Substitution
Description:	Simulate what happens if resources are changed
Last Updated By:	Scott Bishop
Last Updated On:	2/22/2005 10:04 PM
Owner:	Scott Bishop
Created On:	2/22/2005 10:03 PM

Summary Statistics

	Shortest Schedule	Modeled Schedule
Start Date	2/10/2003 12:00 AM	2/10/2003 12:00 AM
Finish Date	5/15/2006 12:00 PM	5/15/2006 12:00 PM
Resource Utilization	19%	19%
Total Work	4,651.13d	4,651.13d
Resource Overhead	19,215.87d	19,215.87d
Total Cost	$2,604,634.67	$2,604,634.67

FIGURE 17.52   Use the Analyze function to see the model summary.

If you scroll down the screen, you can see more information about the resource conditions within the model. Figure 17.53 shows a Demand/Capacity/Utilization Chart with the capability to list Skill Profiles. The default Skill Profiles is All, but you can select specific items from the list to determine measurements for a selected skill attribute.

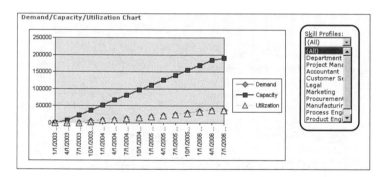

FIGURE 17.53   The Analyze function Demand/Capacity/Utilization Chart.

The lower section of the Analyze page shows the details of each project within the model, as shown in Figure 17.54.

The Portfolio Modeler also includes a Toolbox function that allows you to quickly modify the modeling conditions for individual projects within a model. Figure 17.55 shows how you can also modify conditions such as project Priority, elevated to 750 for the selected project schedule.

The model is recomputed when you click the Apply button. The changes you make affect the model simulation, so you can see what happens if you change conditions such as Priority. For example, you can reduce the priority of one project relative to the other in the model so that the project with higher priority has resource work distribution favoring it.

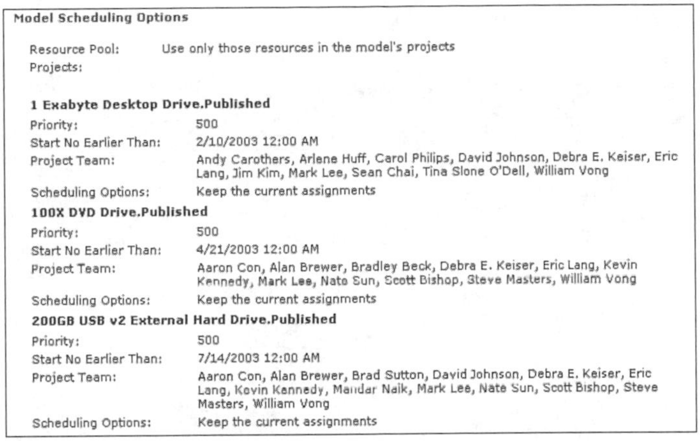

Model Scheduling Options

Resource Pool: Use only those resources in the model's projects
Projects:

1 Exabyte Desktop Drive.Published
Priority: 500
Start No Earlier Than: 2/10/2003 12:00 AM
Project Team: Andy Carothers, Arlene Huff, Carol Philips, David Johnson, Debra E. Keiser, Eric
                      Lang, Jim Kim, Mark Lee, Sean Chai, Tina Slone O'Dell, William Vong
Scheduling Options: Keep the current assignments

100X DVD Drive.Published
Priority: 500
Start No Earlier Than: 4/21/2003 12:00 AM
Project Team: Aaron Con, Alan Brewer, Bradley Beck, Debra E. Keiser, Eric Lang, Kevin
                      Kennedy, Mark Lee, Nate Sun, Scott Bishop, Steve Masters, William Vong
Scheduling Options: Keep the current assignments

200GB USB v2 External Hard Drive.Published
Priority: 500
Start No Earlier Than: 7/14/2003 12:00 AM
Project Team: Aaron Con, Alan Brewer, Brad Sutton, David Johnson, Debra E. Keiser, Eric
                      Lang, Kevin Kennedy, Mandar Naik, Mark Lee, Nate Sun, Scott Bishop, Steve
                      Masters, William Vong
Scheduling Options: Keep the current assignments

FIGURE 17.54   Use the Analyze function to see the model details.

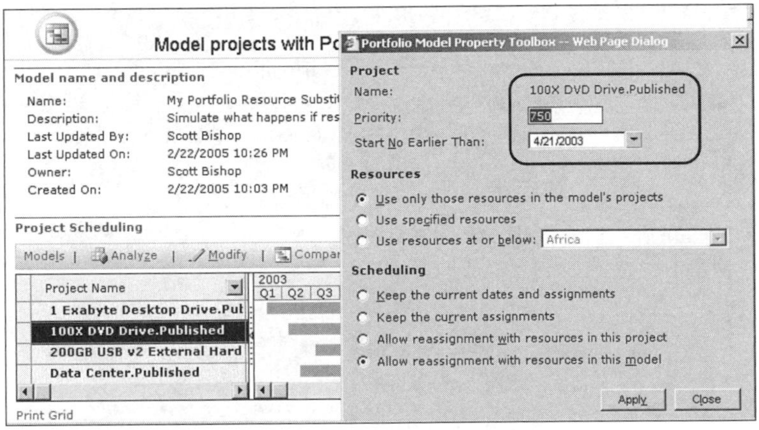

FIGURE 17.55   Use the Toolbox function to change project modeling conditions such as
               Priority.

Understanding the Portfolio Modeler and the Microsoft Project Professional Substitute Resources Function

The Project Professional Tools menu contains the Substitute Resources function that uses the same general algorithms as used within the PWA Portfolio Modeler. When you choose this function, a wizard leads you through similar functions as those used in Portfolio Modeler.

> **TIP**
>
> The Project Professional Substitute Resources menu contains advanced functions and may create results that are difficult to understand. Experiment with simple schedules so that you can understand the complexity of this advanced feature.

Figure 17.56 illustrates the starting screen for the substitution wizard.

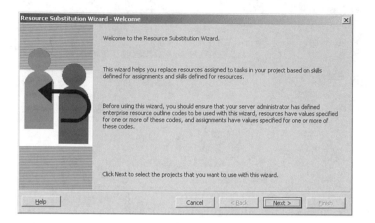

FIGURE 17.56   Microsoft Project Professional Resource Substitution Wizard startup screen.

You can use the Portfolio Modeler analysis conditions as settings within the substitution wizard to actually change the resource assignments within the projects of the model. Figure 17.57 shows how you can select the same projects from the model within the Resource Substitution Wizard.

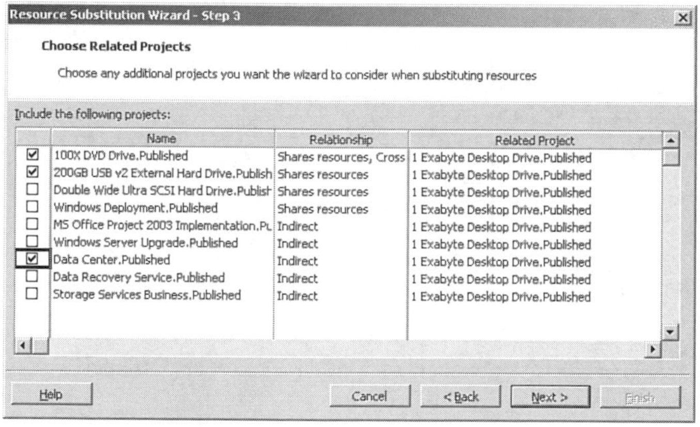

FIGURE 17.57   Use the Portfolio Modeler analysis as the guide to select the same projects for the substitution wizard.

When choosing the Next button, Project Professional opens each of the project schedules so that changes can be made to those schedules. Figure 17.58 shows how you can set resource substitution controls and project priority settings for each of the opened projects.

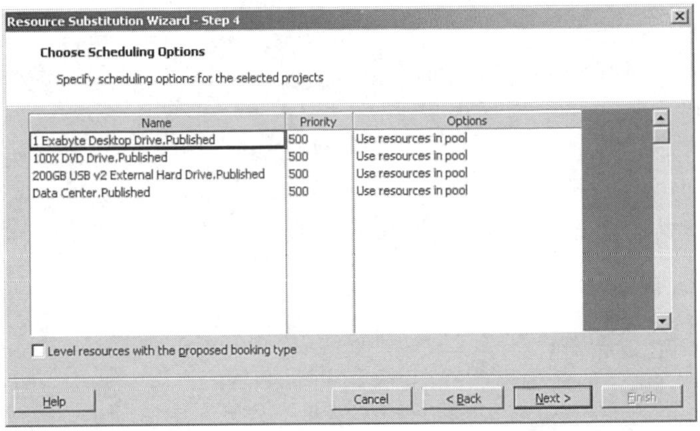

FIGURE 17.58   The Resource Substitution Wizard sets resource controls and project priorities.

After you allow the wizard to run the analysis, you see a summary screen like that shown in Figure 17.59. Notice how the wizard uses the Skill Profile settings to replace the Requested Resource with the Assigned Resource. You can scroll down the project and task list to see the changes made for each project schedule you selected within the wizard.

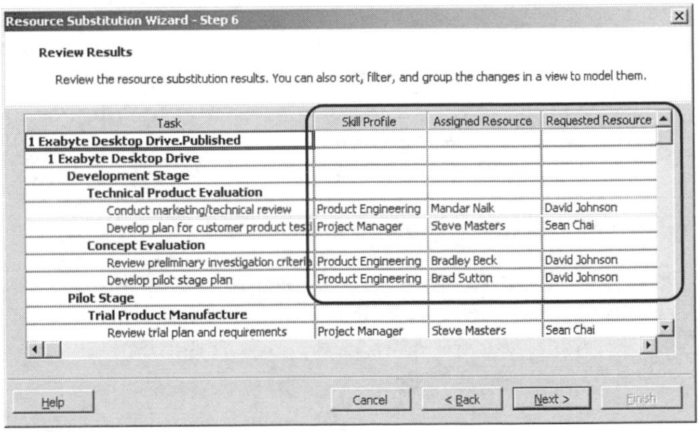

FIGURE 17.59   Substitution wizard results summary screen.

CAUTION

Carefully review the Microsoft Project Professional Resource Substitution Wizard summary with the Portfolio Modeler Analyze results to ensure that the software algorithms used the same resources for substitution.

Best Practices

Portfolio Analyzer and Portfolio Modeler functions provide a wide variety of data display functions so that you can understand project and resource data such as work, cost, and so forth. Consider the following recommendations:

- Make sure that the business processes guide people to create project and resource data that contains consistent levels of detail. Portfolio Analyzer and Portfolio Modeler data may be flawed if the data is not similar across the spectrum of projects and resources.

- Some Portfolio Analyzer Measures fields contain data about resource assignments. That data is derived from the task assignment details within the Project Professional Usage views. The associated Dimensions for resource assignment Measures comes from the single-value Enterprise Global Resource Outline Codes that may be related to multivalue paired codes. Consider assigning generic resources to project tasks before replacing those generic resources with named resources. The single-value Enterprise Global Resource Outline Code settings from the generic resources are retained when those resources are replaced by named resources.

- Develop a simple view-naming scheme when you create Portfolio Analyzer and Portfolio Modeler views. Choose view names that clearly depict the intent of the data displayed within those views so that end users can select the views they need.

- Portfolio Analyzer customized formulas are processed on the end user desktop machine; therefore, these formulas can directly impact the overall end user CPU performance. Consider using the OLAP cube extension techniques to embed customized formula results within the OLAP cube data so that end users can see the results without have to wait for the computer to process customized formulas.

  ▶ **SEE** "Extending the Cube," **PAGE 800**.

- If you grant end users permission to use the Portfolio Analyzer Show Toolbar or Show Field List functions, those users can temporarily manipulate data columns to meet their needs. End users can use the Save Link function to name a personal link that contains the conditions they set.

- Some Portfolio Analyzer views can display data that may not have clear meaning to end users. You should preview the range of display functions for each view to determine the value and logic of the data displayed within each view.

- Consider using color format controls as you create each Portfolio Analyzer view. Background color on Totals rows and columns can provide easy visual aids to people using those views.

CHAPTER 18

Risks, Issues, and Documents Using Windows SharePoint Services (WSS)

IN THIS CHAPTER

- Collaboration Using Windows SharePoint Services
- Risks
- Issues
- Documents
- Best Practices

Microsoft Office Project Server 2003 provides the ability to collaborate with your project team through managing risks, issues, documents, and a project workspace provided by the integration with Windows SharePoint Services (WSS). You can download WSS free from Microsoft and then use the default application settings and capabilities as designed to integrate with Project Server.

▶ **SEE** the "Windows SharePoint Services" section, **PAGE 35**.

> **NOTE**
>
> You can download WSS from the Microsoft website at http://www.microsoft.com/windowsserver2003/techinfo/sharepoint/wss.mspx.
>
> The Microsoft website also contains the Windows SharePoint Services Administrator Guide that can be found at http://www.microsoft.com/downloads/details.aspx?FamilyID=a637eff6-8224-4b19-a6a4-3e33fa13d230&DisplayLang=en.

Each project you publish to the project server can have an associated project website, called a *workspace*, provided that Project Server is connected to a valid Windows SharePoint Services web server and the site is provisioned either automatically or manually. The project website format is created from the project workspace template when WSS is installed, which contains a picture library, discussion boards, surveys, announcements, events, links, and contact lists in addition to the risks and issues lists and a document library for a project. Access security to the project workspace and the associated lists and documents is controlled by Windows SharePoint Services. This chapter describes general WSS functions, risks, issues, and documents, and provides some advice on how you can quickly customize the risks, issues, and documents lists to better suit your organization's existing standards.

▶ **SEE** the "WSS Project Workspace Customization" section, **PAGE 732**.

Collaboration Using Windows SharePoint Services

Project Server alone allows people to easily see project schedules and update task progress. It also allows you to create and update team status reports. But it does not have a place for your team to communicate about and manage issues, risks, and documents without WSS. With WSS, you can use issues to discuss and prioritize current problems on the project. You can use the risks feature to discuss and plan for future problems or opportunities, to help you build mitigation and contingency into your project plan, and you have one place that everyone can access to see and update the project documents. If you choose to be a forward-thinking project manager, you can use the project workspace (something like a project website) to create a place for team members and other stakeholders to go to get the latest project information. In fact, in some organizations, team members may use WSS more than Project Server. The team may simply click on the URL for the project's workspace to see the current project information and work on documents, issues, and risks frequently. They may only access the Project Web Access (PWA) Tasks page to update tasks just once a week.

To understand a bit more how you can think about using WSS, let's look at the two places you can get to WSS and its features. Figure 18.1 shows the Risks, Issues, and Documents tabs in Project Server. If you select any one of these tabs, you can get to a list of projects you are allowed to see. Clicking on a particular project takes you to the specific issues, risks, or documents list for the project.

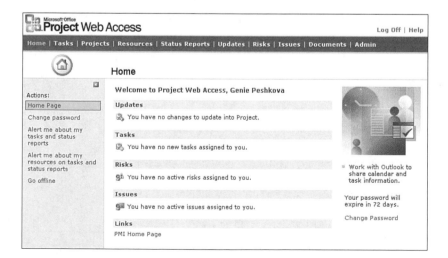

FIGURE 18.1   Risks, issues, and documents in PWA.

You can also get to the risks, issues, and documents for a particular project via the workspace in the Project Center. Figure 18.2 shows how you can select a project in the Project Center and then click on Go to Selected Project Workspace in the left side pane to access a project's workspace.

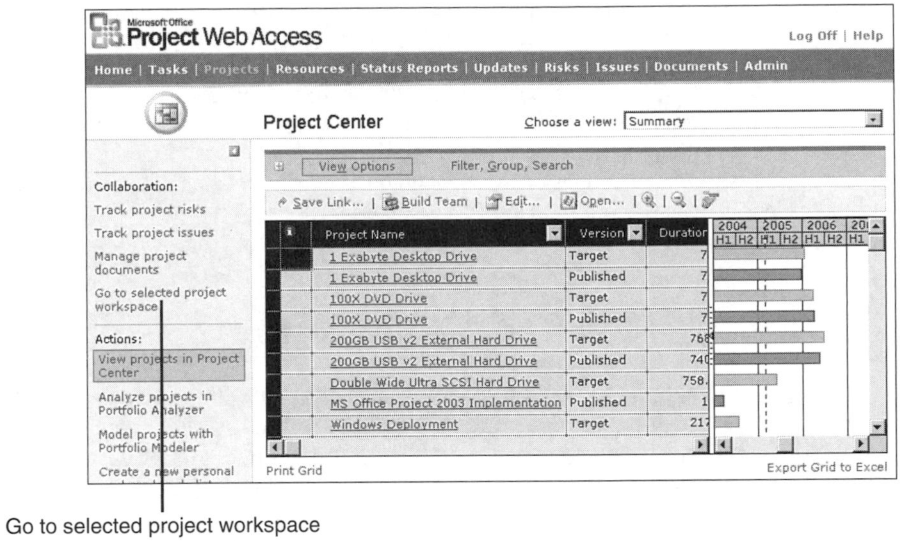

Go to selected project workspace

FIGURE 18.2   Selecting the workspace for a particular project.

When you do this, you go to a screen similar to the workspace shown in Figure 18.3.

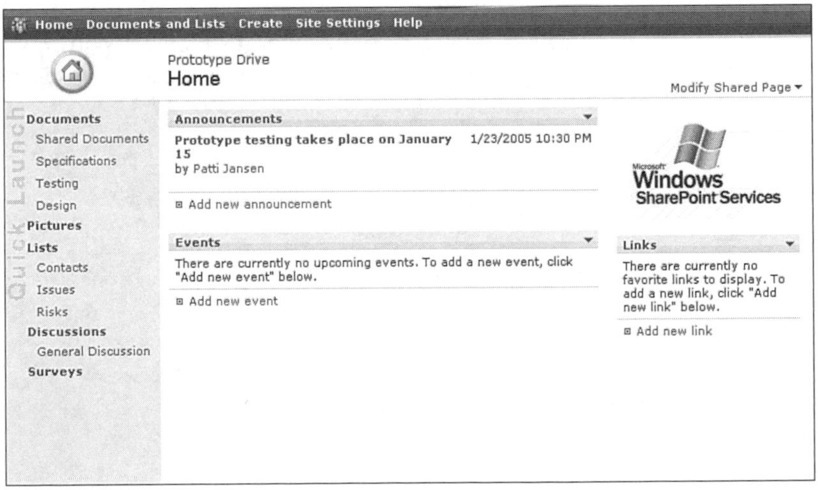

FIGURE 18.3   The WSS project workspace.

Notice the items here called Shared Documents, Issues, and Risks in the left side pane. These are exactly the same items you had in Project Server under the Risks, Issues, and

Documents tab. Also note the URL in Figure 18.3. Team members may choose to just save the URL as a favorite and then click on it whenever they want to access the project workspace directly. Note also that you can use features such as discussions, announcements, events, and surveys to promote different kinds of communication about your project. You can also add links to other locations on the intranet or extranet. This website may become the main communication forum for the project team.

> **TIP**
>
> Many organizations deploy Project Server with a plan on how they will build project schedules, but many do little with risks, issues, documents, and the project workspace. Consider adding a bit more time to the design of the system for your organization by creating a standard for using each of the WSS functions and have some of your most effective project managers lead the charge in using them.

Permissions in WSS

Permissions for using the WSS functions are set up based on the Project Server group permissions. However, they are tied to WSS site group permissions, and it is important to understand how the permission schema works. You will need to know how to update permissions in WSS because you may want stakeholders who do not have permission to PWA to be able to use the project workspace, or you may want to change some of the default permissions settings (such as team members being allowed to delete documents). To do so, you must understand how WSS site groups and permissions work.

Project Server creates four site groups within the workspace environment to control an individual's rights to the workspace: Project Managers, Readers, Team Members, and Web Administrators. If you are using WSS, Project Server places individuals into the site groups based on their Project Server security permissions and their assignments on the project schedule. Each time the project is published to the server, users are synchronized to the project workspace and placed in the appropriate site group. Table 18.1 describes the four site groups.

TABLE 18.1   Site Group Permissions in WSS

WSS Site Group	Description
Project Managers (PM)—Microsoft Office Project Server	Users who have published this project or who have Save Project permission in Microsoft Office Project Server
Readers (Rdr)—Microsoft Office Project Server	Users who have View Project Documents, Issues, and Risks permission in Microsoft Office Project Server
Team Members (TM)—Microsoft Office Project Server	Users who have assignments in this project in Microsoft Office Project Server
Web Administrators (Web)—Microsoft Office Project Server	Users who have Manage Windows SharePoint Team Services permission in Microsoft Office Project Server

Individual List Security

WSS also defines the functions you can perform on the lists that exist in WSS. That is, you have access to an issues list, risks list, and documents list. You can also create other kinds of lists, such as a change management list, which you would want to set up list security for. In addition to the Project Workspace permissions established by Project Server, each individual list has customizable security permissions that can be modified. By default, a new list inherits the permissions from the parent workspace. Table 18.2 describes what those default permissions are per site group. Notice that a team member can delete a document. You may want to change this for your particular project.

TABLE 18.2   Site List Permissions in WSS

List Rights	PM	TM	Rdr	Web
Manage List Permissions. Grant, deny, or change user permissions to a list.	No	No	No	Yes
Manage Lists. Approve content in lists, add or remove columns in a list, and add or remove public views of a list.	Yes	No	No	Yes
Cancel Check-Out. Check in a document without saving the current changes.	Yes	No	No	Yes
Add Items. Add items to lists, add documents to document libraries, add web discussion comments.	Yes	Yes	No	Yes
Edit Items. Edit items in lists, edit documents in document libraries, edit web discussion comments indocuments, and customize web part pages in document libraries.	Yes	Yes	No	Yes
Delete Items. Delete items from a list, documents from a document library, and web discussion comments in documents.	Yes	Yes	No	Yes
View Items. View items in lists, view documents in document libraries, view web discussion comments, and set up email alerts for lists.	Yes	Yes	Yes	Yes

NOTE

The Project Workspace template modifies the permissions for the Team Member site group on the issues and risks lists to remove the Delete permission. This prohibits team members from deleting items within these lists. However, the Project Workspace template does not modify the permissions on the document library, which allows team members to delete documents in the library.

Rights to Changing the Website

The administrator and project manager also have rights to change the project website itself. That is, they can define the permissions on the website and also change the look and feel of the project website itself. Table 18.3 describes some of the major website design and management functions that each site group can perform. For instance, in

18

Table 18.3, the project manager cannot change site groups as shown in Table 18.1 for his project workspaces. Perhaps he needs that control, and the administrator should change this permission to allow the project manager to manage site groups. Review Table 18.3 to understand what rights each site group has for functions on a project website.

TABLE 18.3 Site Rights in WSS

Site Rights	PM	TM	Rdr	Web
Manage Site Groups. Create, change, and delete site groups, including adding users to the site groups andspecifying which rights are assigned to a site group.	No	No	No	Yes
View Usage Data. View reports on website usage.	Yes	No	No	Yes
Create Subsites. Create subsites such as team sites, meeting workspace sites, and document workspace sites.	Yes	No	No	Yes
Manage Web Site. Grant the ability to perform all administration tasks for the website as well as manage content and permissions.	No	No	No	Yes
Add and Customize Pages. Add, change, or delete HTML pages or web part pages, and edit the website using a Windows SharePoint Services–compatible editor.	Yes	No	No	Yes
Apply Themes and Borders. Apply a theme or borders to the entire website.	Yes	No	No	Yes
Apply Style Sheets. Apply a style sheet (.CSS file) to the website.	Yes	No	No	Yes
Browse Directories. Browse directories in a website.	Yes	Yes	No	Yes
View Pages. View pages in a website.	Yes	Yes	Yes	Yes

Personal Rights to WSS

Individuals also have some rights in WSS. For instance, they can create their own views and web parts that no one else can see but that they can use to analyze or view things they want individually. For instance, a team member might want to set up a personal link or web part on his view of the project workspace so that he can look up an Internet address quickly on the site. Table 18.4 describes the personal WSS rights for each site group.

TABLE 18.4 Personal Rights in WSS

Personal Rights	PM	TM	Rdr	Web
Manage Personal Views. Create, change, and delete personal views of lists.	Yes	Yes	No	Yes
Add/Remove Private Web Parts. Add or remove private web parts on a web part page.	Yes	Yes	No	Yes
Update Personal Web Parts. Update web parts to display personalized information.	Yes	Yes	No	Yes
Create Cross-Site Groups. Create a group of users who can be granted access to any site within the site collection.	Yes	No	No	Yes

Building Templates

A workspace template is created when you first install WSS. This template is set up with specific functions such as discussions, surveys, events, and announcements, and allowing for issues, risks, and documents. You can change the template so that all project websites have the same settings and functions. The risks, issues, and documents templates may be changed per project worksite. However, your organization may want to create overall standards that are different from the out-of-the-box configuration of those lists. To do so, you need to modify the Project Server WSS template, which may be changed by an administrator.

▶ **SEE** the "WSS Project Workspace Customization" section, **PAGE 732**.

Modifying Settings

On all the default lists in WSS—Risks, Issues, and Documents—you have the capability to add to and change the fields that display for the lists. Figure 18.4 shows the default settings for the issues list.

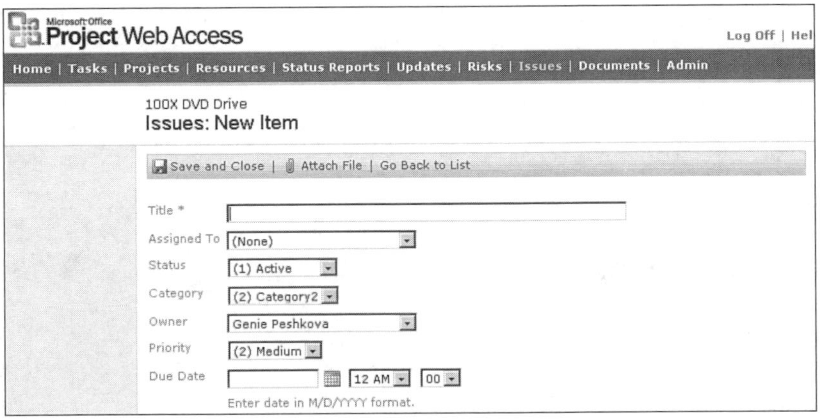

FIGURE 18.4   Default fields and settings for the issues list.

For example, the Category column may be set to Category 1, 2, or 3, which are values provided out-of-the-box. You may actually have values you want to enter in this column so that you can sort by those categories (such as technical, managerial, legal, or operational). Also, maybe you want to add another column you want to track called "Actions Taken." You can change columns and settings on the main list for each project under Modify Settings and Columns as shown in Figure 18.5.

When you select Modify Settings and Columns, you see a screen as shown in Figure 18.6.

The screen is divided into three sections:

- **General Settings**—You can set general rules about navigation and email as well as permissions for this particular list.

- **Columns**—You can add new columns, change their order, or add or change values and formats to the current columns showing.

- **Views**—You can create new kinds of sorting for the kinds of reports (views) you can see about the issues list.

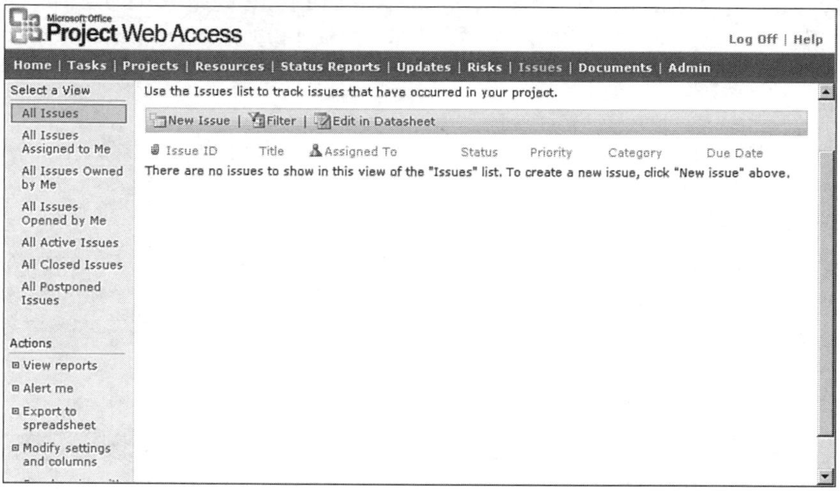

FIGURE 18.5 Modify settings and columns.

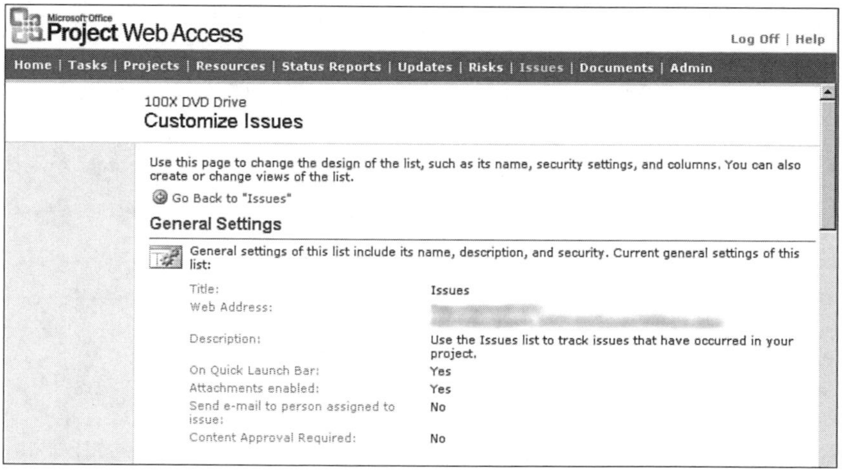

FIGURE 18.6 Screen to customize your list settings.

General Settings

You can change the settings you see in gray on the first page. Use the following fields to change general settings:

- **Name and Description**—Allows you to change the name of the list. The default value describes the list as Issues, Risks, or Documents. If you have another word that describes the list, you could change the name here. Also, describe what the list is for so that your team members understand how to use the list.

- **Navigation**—The default Yes indicates that the list name will show on the project workspace Quick Launch bar, which is the left side pane area of the project workspace. Select No if you do not want the list name to show in the project workspace Quick Launch bar. This affects only the list on the project website workspace, not the way issues are seen in Project Server.

- **Attachments**—The default Enabled indicates that you want to attach documents to the list item. Select Disabled if you do not want to see attachments on the list items. You might select Disabled if you are trying to save disk space.

- **Email Notification**—The default No indicates that you do not want an email sent if someone is assigned to the list item or something has changed. Select Yes if you want emails sent when the list item is assigned or changed.

When you make a change, click OK at the bottom of the screen to set the change.

Change Permissions for This List

When you click on Change Permissions for This List, a screen similar to the one shown in Figure 18.7 displays.

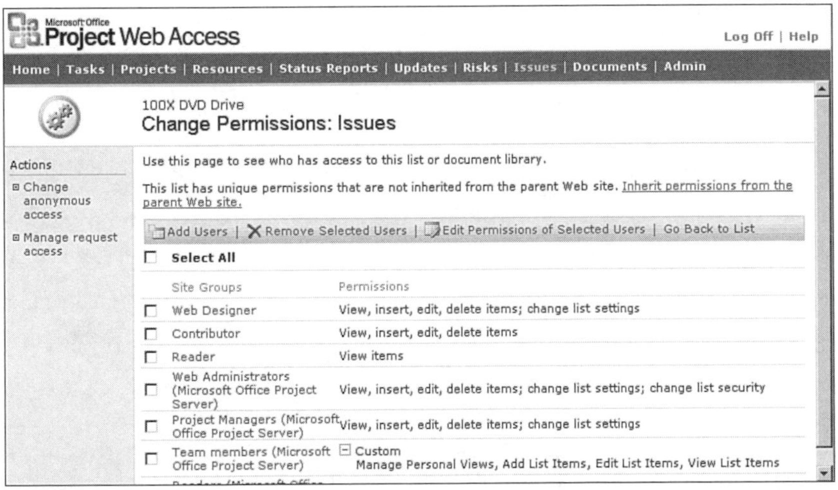

FIGURE 18.7 Use the Change Permissions screen to add users and change permissions.

Note that you can inherit the permissions of the parent website. The parent website is the settings set up for the project workspace. For instance, in some lists, team members can delete the list items, but for issues and risks, team members cannot delete risk or issue items.

If you want to add a user to the list, follow these steps:

1. Click on Add Users on the action bar. You are taken to the Add Users Wizard for the kind of list you are in.

2. The first step allows you to add the email address, username, or group names for stakeholders you want to add to the site (other than those people who have permission via Project Server permissions).

3. The second step allows you to choose the specific permissions, such as the View, Insert, Edit, Delete, and Change Settings permissions.

4. Click Next.

5. In Step 3, Confirm Users, you confirm the information for each user you added.

6. In Step 4, Send E-mail, you decide whether you want to send the user an invitation email.

7. Click Finish, and you return to the Change Permissions screen where you see the new users at the end of the list.

To remove a selected user or site group, click on the item in the list and click Remove Selected Users on the action bar. You will receive a message, and if you click OK, you will remove the user or site group.

To edit the permissions listed next to the site group or user, follow these steps:

1. Click on Edit Permissions of Selected Users in the action bar.

2. A screen opens where you can change the permissions of View, Insert, Delete, and so on.

On the Change Permissions screen, you also see two actions on the left side pane:

- **Change Anonymous Access**—Specifies the options for people who are not the actual users of the list to have anonymous access to the site.

- **Manage Request**—Provides a setting so that a nonuser of a list can ask the administrator for access to the site.

Columns

When you want to change the default columns that show in the risks, issues, or documents lists, you update information in the Columns section.

To change a column name, format, or values go to the specific field to change what you want. Click on the column you want to change. A screen similar to Figure 18.8 appears. For more about completing the fields, see the following discussion on how to add a column.

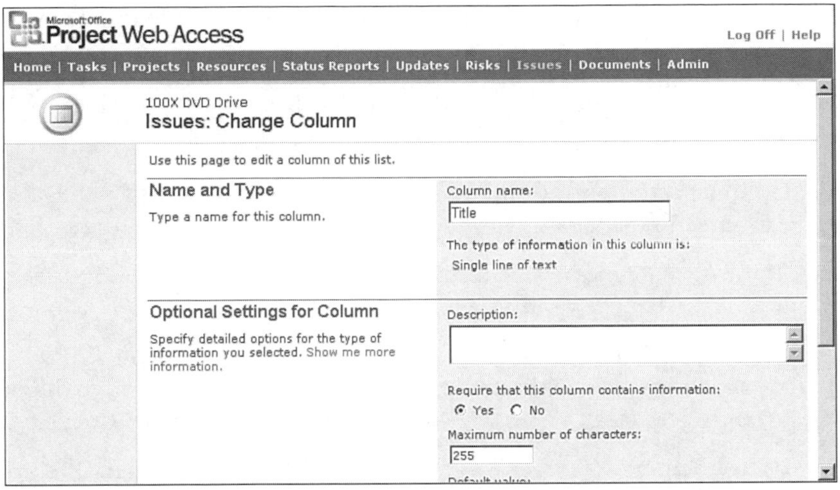

FIGURE 18.8 Customize WSS list items on the Change Column screen.

> **NOTE**
>
> You cannot change the type of information in the column (choice or calculation field). If you want to change the type, you need to delete the column and create a new one with the new type.

To add a new column, follow these steps:

1. Click on Add a New Column under the Column section. A screen similar to Figure 18.8 appears.

2. Enter the column name and select the type of information you want to designate that this column should have. Click on the radio button for the type of field you want to create. Your selections are listed below the Column name.

> **NOTE**
>
> The section called Optional Settings for Column changes based on which type you select, although the following Steps 3 through 6 are constant.

3. Under Optional Settings for Column, for each type you can enter a Description to help users understand how they should use the column.

4. Under Optional Settings for Column, select whether an entry is required in the field. Select Yes or No in the Require That This Column Contains Information field.

5. Under Optional Settings for Column, enter information into Default Value if you want a like value to show up in the column. Users can change the field if necessary, but you can use this to prepopulate the field. If you have chosen a text field, make sure that you keep the Text radio button selected. For a calculation field, you can select the Calculated Value radio button.

6. Under Optional Settings for Column, select Add to Default View if you want the column to show in the default view of the list; otherwise, remove the selection.

7. Based on the format type of a field, also enter the following under Optional Settings for Column for each type of information you choose:

   - **Single Line of Text**—Allows you to format the field to permit entry of one line of text up to a maximum of 255 characters. You can change the number of characters to fewer than 255 in the Maximum Number of Characters field.

   - **Multiple Lines of Text**—Allows you to format the field to permit entry of large strings of text. You can change the Number of Lines to Display field to more than 500 lines, but make sure that you make this usable for people who would actually enter text into this field. Also, select Yes in the Allow Rich HTML Text field if you want to allow text formatting in the field, or select No if you want simple text only in the field.

   - **Choice**—Allows you to enter values that your users can choose from. You have several selections for designating the format for the values. Under Type Each Choice on a Separate Line, enter all the values you want users to have. Select one of three options for displaying the values: Drop-down Menu, Radio Buttons, or Checkboxes. Checkboxes allow for multiple value selections, not just one value. Select Yes under Allow "Fill-in" Choices if you want users to be able to enter other values than what is displayed, and select No if you want them to use only the values provided.

   - **Number**—Allows you to enter parameters for the format of the Number field. Under Optional Settings for Column, you can specify a minimum and maximum allowed value (such as 1 for Min and 100 for Max). Also you can set the Number of Decimal Places, with the values of Automatic and 0–5. Set the Default value as a Number or Calculated Value. You can also select Show As Percentage.

   - **Currency**—Allows you to enter parameters for the format of the Currency field. You can specify a minimum and maximum allowed value (such as 1 for Min and 100 for Max). You also can set the Number of Decimal Places, with the values of Automatic and 0–5. Set the Default value as Currency or Calculated Value. You can also select the currency format (such as U.S. dollars, Mexican pesos, and so on).

   - **Date and Time**—Allows you to enter the date format. You can specify a Date Only and Date & Time format. You can also set a default value, Today's Date, or enter a specific date you choose. You can also select the value to be a Calculated Value.

- **Lookup**—Allows you to select data from a list or library from the project site to include in the column. You can select where you will Get Information From to show the Display Name, ID, Email, or User Name from the list or library you select. By selecting Include Presence Information you can also show online status of the people using the list.

- **Yes/No (check box)**—Allows you to select Yes or No in a check box to indicate the status of the column. For example, you might have a column saying "Required project document?" to indicate whether the document you are saving is required or an optional document for project work.

- **Hyperlink or Picture**—Allows you to set a column where you can enter a URL as a hyperlink or a picture.

- **Calculated**—Allows you to set a formula to indicate the result of a calculation on two or more columns. The Help function for this selection has a great deal of information to describe the use of formulas for calculated fields.

NOTE

The Help section for Optional Settings for Column is extensive. Click on Show Me More Information under Optional Settings for Column to learn more about how to use types and their options.

---

8. When you are finished creating the new column, click OK.

To delete a column, click on the column you want to delete. Scroll to the bottom of the Change Column screen that appears, and click Delete. Any data that has been entered into that field will be lost, so use this with caution.

To change the order the columns appear in, click on Change the Order of the Fields in the Columns section of the Customize list screen. The Change Field Order screen appears including all columns of the list. You can type the order of the column by selecting a value in the Position from Top field. Click OK to have the changes take effect.

Views

Views allow you to filter and group your WSS lists according to how you want to see them. It can be important to have various viewing options when lists become long. You can select one of the current views by clicking on the Views hyperlink in the Views section and change some of the selections. You can also add a new view and select one of the views as shown in Figure 18.9.

To create a Standard view, click on Standard view on the Create View screen. You see a screen that allows you to name the view; select whether it is a public or personal view; select the columns you want to display in the view; specify the sorting, filtering, and grouping forms; specify the columns you want to see in the totals; select the style (table formatting of the view); and set the limit for the number of items in the list that will be returned in the view.

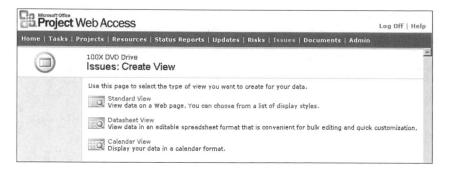

FIGURE 18.9   Types of views you can select.

To create a Datasheet view, click on Datasheet View on the Create View screen. You see a screen that allows you to name the view, select whether it is a public or personal view, select the columns you want to display in the view, specify the sorting and filtering, specify the columns you want to see in the totals, and set the limit for the number of items in the list that will be returned in the view.

To create a Calendar view, click on Calendar View on the Create View screen. You see a screen that allows you to name the view; select whether it is a public or personal view; select the columns based on the date the column was Modified, Created, or its Due Date; choose the calendar setting of month, week, or day; and specify the filtering that will be returned in the view.

Risks

Risk management is a common process used by project teams to help analyze the probability and impact of challenges and opportunities to a project, which are called risks. After understanding the risks, the project team can then put in place plans to deal with the risks, if they should occur. PWA provides a tool for capturing and managing risks associated with projects. This tool includes the capability to describe the potential risk areas of the project, the probability that a risk will impact the project, any mitigation plan to minimize the potential risk, and the definition and triggering of the contingencies if the mitigation is not successful. This feature provides all the basic elements of a risk management repository including risk probability and impact, risk category, responsible team member, risk manager, critical dates, and descriptive elements.

Selecting the Risks tab reveals a list of projects you have permissions to view as shown in Figure 18.10.

NOTE

You must have Windows SharePoint Services to use the Risks feature in PWA.

▶ **SEE** the "Windows SharePoint Services" section, **PAGE 35**.

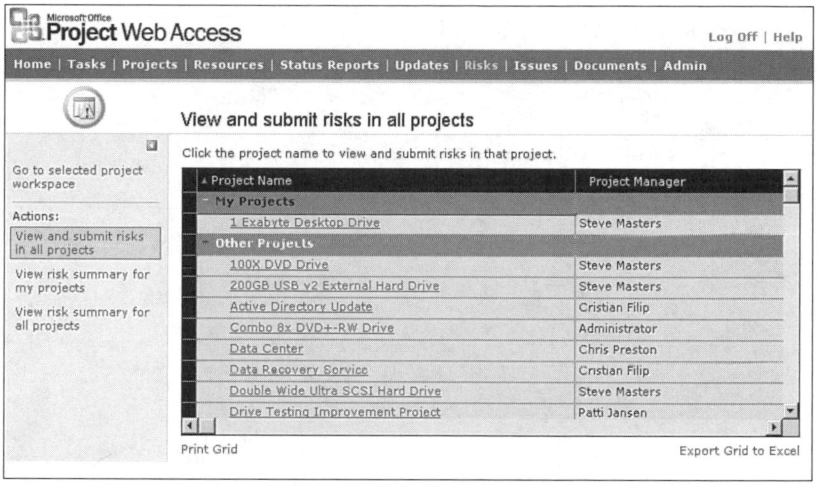

FIGURE 18.10   View and submit risks in all projects.

Risk Summaries

On the initial projects Risks page, you may choose to select summaries of risk statistics for all projects you can view. This allows you to see the number of active, postponed, or closed risks for your projects. This grid can then be printed or exported to Excel using the links at the bottom of the grid.

> **NOTE**
>
> The Go to Selected Project Workspace selection, as shown in Figure 18.2, allows you to go to the workspace for the selected project if you want to view documents, risks, and issues related to a project you select. For details on the project workspace, see the "Collaboration Using Windows SharePoint Services" section earlier in this chapter.

When you select a project name link, the risk list for that project is presented, and you can view, update, and report on risks for the project as shown in Figure 18.11. Features on this screen are described later in the chapter in "Creating Risks." Note that in Figure 18.11, the first risk listed is risk 6, which is the highest on the list. This is because, based on the probability and impact, it has the highest exposure. In other words, it has the highest risk factor of all risks rated. Notice how you can quickly view who is responsible for the risk, and when action on the risk is due. This screen allows you to quickly view all your risks based on the criteria you select (filtering and views are also described in the sections "Viewing and Reporting Risk Items" and "Filtering Risks" later in this chapter.

Creating Risks

To be able to add a risk to the project you must be a member of the Team Members site group, meaning that you have an assignment within the project schedule. The project manager of a project has full permissions to change the risks for the project.

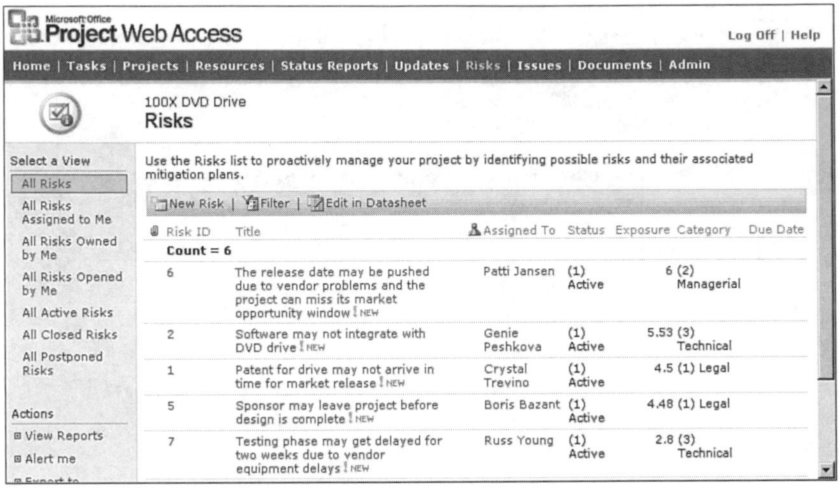

FIGURE 18.11   Risk list for a project in PWA.

To add a risk, perform the following steps:

1. Click on New Risk in the toolbar above the risk list. An edit form displays, as shown in Figure 18.12, where you can fill in the risk data.

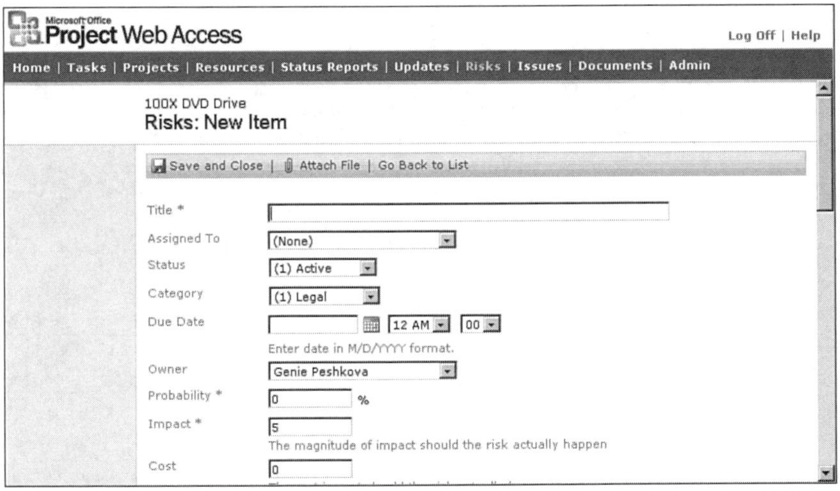

FIGURE 18.12   Information you can add for a risk.

2. Complete the relevant fields as discussed in the following list. Note that these are the default fields. You can change and customize these fields to match your organization's particular risk management repository.

▶ **SEE** "Collaboration Using Windows SharePoint Services," **PAGE 442**.

The fields that appear for a risk are as follows:

- **Title**—Enter the title of the risk item (this is required). Make sure that this briefly, yet clearly describes the risk.

- **Assigned To**—Click on the arrow on the drop-down box, and select the person responsible for managing this risk item.

- **Status**—Enter the status of the risk item as Active, Postponed, or Closed.

- **Category**—Enter the category associated with the risk. By default, the values are Category 1, 2, or 3. This is a field you should consider for customization. For instance, you might create categories such as legal, managerial, technical, and so on, to categorize risk types.

- **Due Date**—Enter the expected or required resolution date for the risk item.

- **Owner**—Click the arrow on the drop-down list, and select the person responsible for creating or performing the mitigation and contingency for the risk.

> **NOTE**
>
> The Assigned To and Owner drop-down lists contain only those users who have permission to access the risks for the project.

- **Probability**—Enter the probability (from 1% to 100%) that this risk item will occur. (This is a required field.)

- **Impact**—Enter a value (from 1 to 10) to indicate the severity of the effect this risk item will have on the project if it occurs.(This is a required field.)

- **Cost**—Enter the dollar amount to indicate how much this risk would financially affect the cost of the project if it occurred.

- **Description**—Enter a full description of the risk.

- **Mitigation Plan**—Enter a description of how you plan to handle the risk, prevent it from occurring, or lower the impact if it occurs. This is usually written by the owner of the risk.

- **Contingency Plan**—Enter the fallback plan if the risk occurs. This is used if the mitigation plan does not succeed to prevent or lower the impact of the risk.

- **Trigger Description**—Enter a description of the condition that would result in the Contingency Plan being implemented. This can be a date, a cost value exceeded, or other quantifiable measure within the project data.

- **Trigger**—Enter the value to indicate the condition that would trigger the contingency plan.

18

Linking List Items to Tasks

Based on what is happening on your project, you often need to show a dependency between a task in a project and a risk (or issue, or document), or perhaps to other risks, issues, or documents. PWA 2003 allows you to link individual risks or other list items in WSS to specific tasks within a project schedule. These links are visible as a document icon in the indicator column when you view the schedule details within the Project Center and on the Tasks page next to the task. When you create a new list item (risk, issue, or document), you have the option of clicking on the link that allows you to select a task the item is related to. Figure 18.13 shows you the fields where you can select the link. This is similar on all lists.

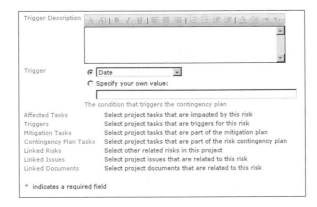

FIGURE 18.13   Selecting to link to tasks.

1. Click on a link such as Select Project Tasks That Are Impacted By This Risk, shown in Figure 18.13. A dialog box appears with a list of tasks filtered for My Tasks, similar to Figure 18.14.

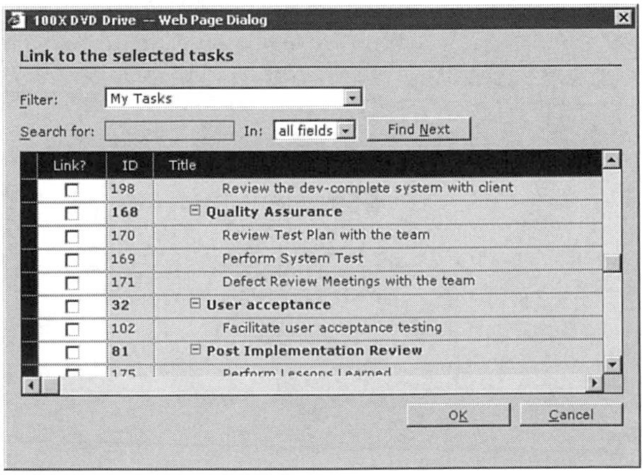

FIGURE 18.14   Link to selected tasks.

2. Select the related tasks by clicking the check box on the left side of the list adjacent to the task name. Click OK after you select the tasks.

The selected task names then appear in the edit form below the final field in the list form.

> **NOTE**
>
> When a risk is defined for a project, a graphical icon is displayed adjacent to the project within the Project Center Summary view. If a risk is attached to a specific working task, a graphical icon appears within the Project Center detail views. If you select a risk graphic icon, PWA opens the appropriate project risk group for review and updates.

Editing, Deleting, and Alert Me Actions on Risks

From the project's risk list, the Risk ID and Title are hyperlinks that take you to the detailed view of an existing risk. From this view, you can edit, delete, or create an alert for the risk so that you can be notified about changes to that risk. Select Edit Risk, Delete Risk, or Alert Me from the toolbar.

You can also click to the right of the risk description and, in the drop-down list that displays, select Edit Risk, Delete Risk, or Alert Me as shown in Figure 18.15.

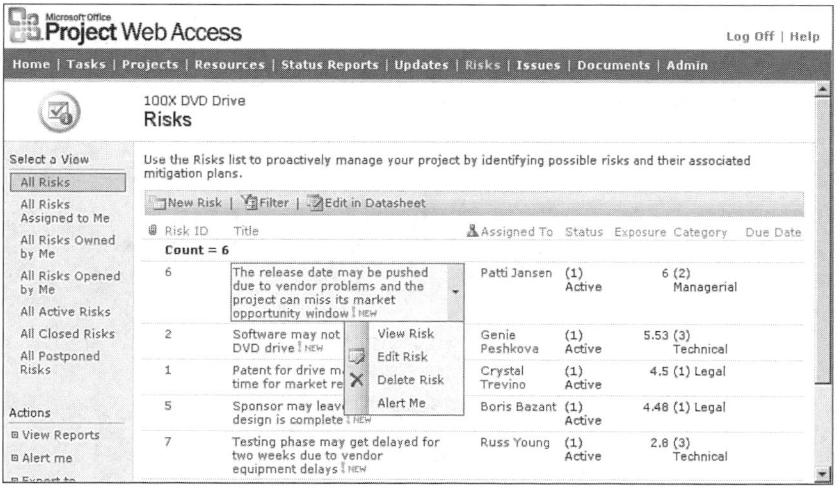

FIGURE 18.15   Drop-down list to select action on risk.

Viewing and Reporting Risk Items

You have several options for viewing and reporting on the risks for a project. These especially come in handy for sorting through long risk lists, or analyzing the risks that could affect your project.

Filtering Risks

To view the risks on your project in different ways, you can select one of numerous filters under Select a View in the side pane as shown in Figure 18.15. You can also select Filter on the toolbar above the risk list and use the filters from the drop-down lists that appear above each field on the list. For example, you could view only those risks assigned to a particular team member on your project. After enabling the filtering function, the Filter button changes the Change Filter or Hide Filter choices to change or remove the filtering you have applied.

View Reports

Under Actions in the side pane, you can select View Reports. On the Report Types screen, select the type of report you want to view. You can analyze risks by category, owner, or dates. Figure 18.16 shows a category report.

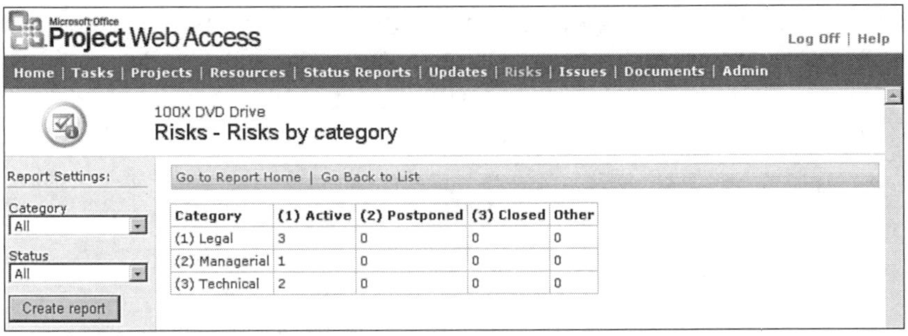

FIGURE 18.16   A category risk report.

Alert Me

You can use the Alert Me option at the risk list level to receive an email to notify you of any changes for all risks in the project. You can choose to be notified when risks are added, changed, or deleted, or for all changes. You can also choose to be notified immediately or in a daily or weekly summary. Figure 18.17 shows the options for how you want the emails to be sent to you when the risks for this project are updated.

> **NOTE**
>
> This is different from the Alert Me function described previously for individual risks. You can select to be emailed about individual risks and all risks on a project.

Export to Spreadsheet

You can export the risks list to an Excel spreadsheet as shown in Figure 18.18. To do so, click on Export to Spreadsheet in the Actions side pane on the risk list for the project. This is especially handy for taking the list of risks to meetings to discuss and update them within the meeting itself, or for sharing the risk list with others who may not have access to Project Server. Then, after you have made changes in Excel, you can use the

Synchronize with Project Server selection on the side pane to bring the changes you made in Excel back into Project Server.

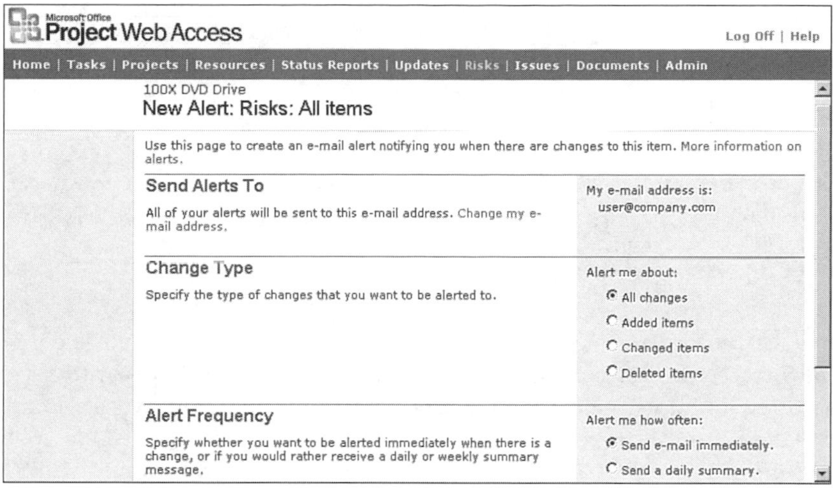

FIGURE 18.17   Alert selections for a list item.

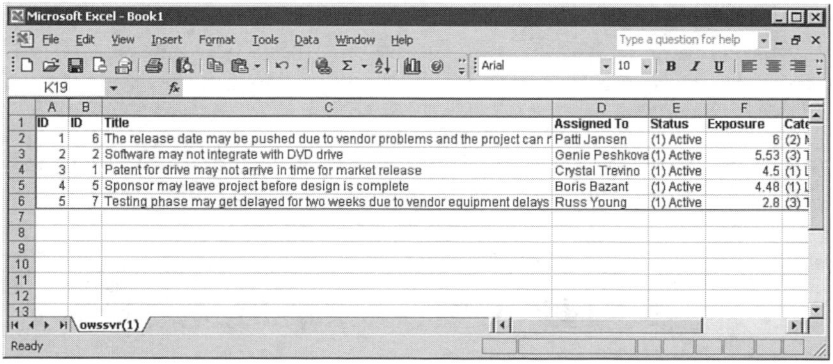

FIGURE 18.18   The risks list exported to an Excel spreadsheet.

Edit in Datasheet

The risk list can also be mass edited by using the Edit in Datasheet option on the toolbar. This presents the data elements from the view in a datasheet form. You can edit the risks more easily and more quickly than in the Standard view.

> **TIP**
>
> In the Datasheet view, select the Task pane and explore the various Microsoft Office tools you can use to analyze and report on risks. For example, you can use Create an Excel PivotTable Report to chart your risk trends.

Modify Settings and Columns

The Modify Settings and Columns feature allows you to make changes to the risk columns and values to customize the risks repository to match your risk management standards.

▶ **SEE** "Modifying Settings," **PAGE 447**.

Synchronize with Project Server

Use this function to synchronize data you might have changed in Excel or Access, if you exported the risks to an Excel spreadsheet or an Access database. When you select this feature, it updates the data changed in those applications within Project Server.

Issues

Project managers use issues management to help organize and prioritize the current challenges that threaten project success. Issues are different from risks, in that they have already occurred and usually need some immediate attention, whereas risks are issues that *may* occur. Often, team members approach project managers with issues that are impeding their assignment progress. By documenting, analyzing, and assigning them to be resolved, issues are often taken care of quickly and with thought toward project priorities instead of languishing in inaction. All projects should use issues management to help resolve what's important versus what's not important in the issues that come up for a project. PWA provides a feature for defining and managing issues on each project in the repository. This facility includes the ability to describe the issue, categorize the impact of the issue, assign resolution to a resource, establish a due date, and set the status of the issue.

Selecting the Issues tab reveals a list of projects you have permissions to view as shown in Figure 18.19.

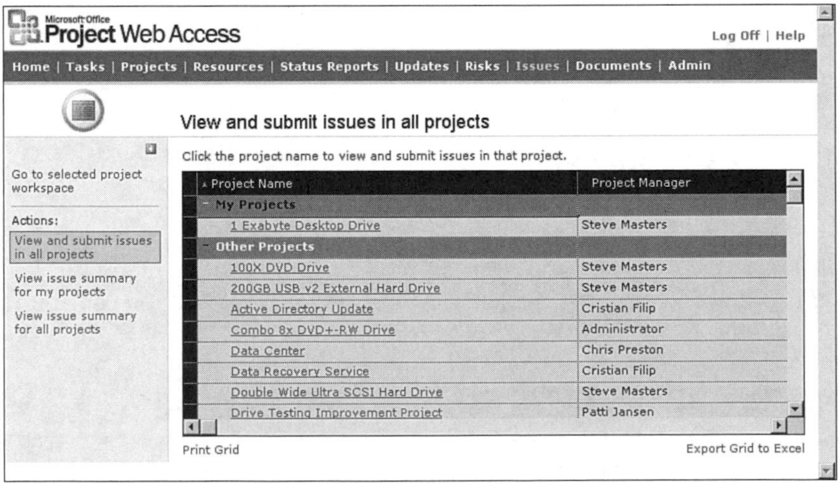

FIGURE 18.19 View and submit issues in all projects.

> **NOTE**
>
> You must have Windows SharePoint Services to use issues in PWA.

▶ **SEE** the "Windows SharePoint Services" section, **PAGE 35**.

Issues Summaries

On the initial projects Issues page, you may choose to select summaries of issue statistics for all projects you can view. This allows you to see the number of active, postponed, or closed issues for your projects. This grid can then be printed or exported to Excel using the links at the bottom of the grid.

> **NOTE**
>
> The Go to Selected Project Workspace selection as shown previously in Figure 18.2 allows you to go to the workspace for the selected project if you want to view documents, risks, and issues related to a project you select. For details on the project workspace, see "Collaboration Using Windows SharePoint Services" earlier in this chapter.

When you select a project name link, the issues list for that project is presented, and you can view, update, and report on issues for the project as shown in Figure 18.20.

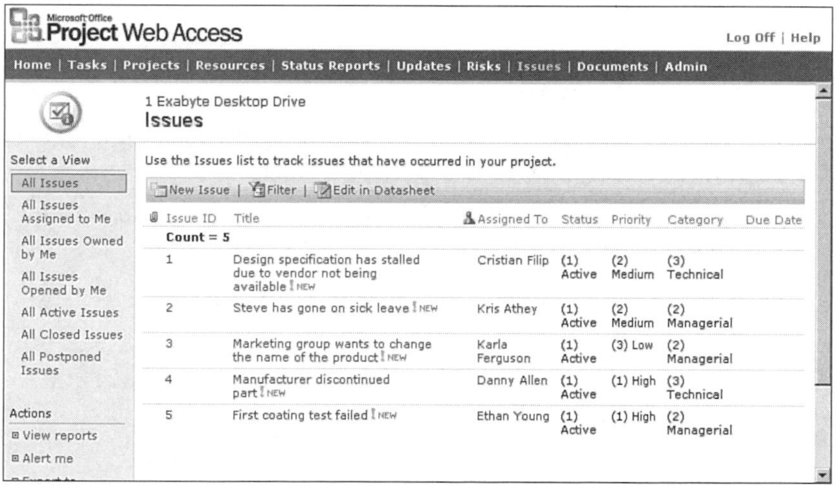

FIGURE 18.20   Issues list for a project in PWA.

Creating Issues

To be able to add an issue to the project you must be a member of the Team Members site group, meaning that you have an assignment within the project schedule. The project manager of a project has full permissions to add and change the issues for the project.

To add an issue, perform the following steps:

1. Click on New Issue in the toolbar above the issues list. An edit form displays where you will fill in the issue data.

2. Next, complete the relevant fields as described in the following list. Figure 18.21 shows part of the New Issues screen. Note that these are the default fields. You can change and customize these fields to match your organization's particular issues management process. The fields are as follows:

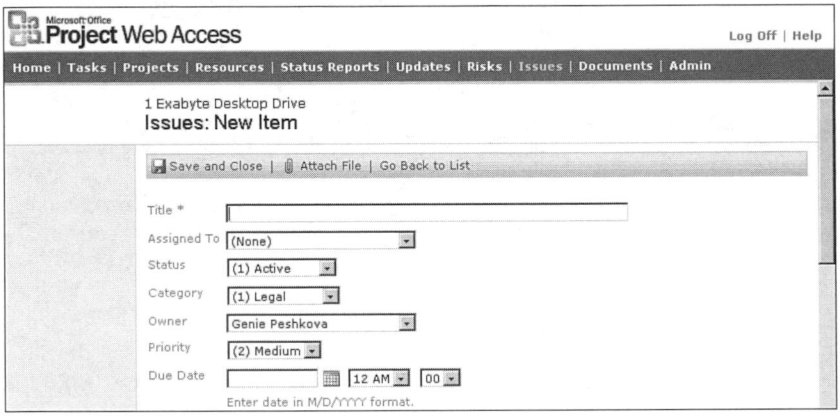

FIGURE 18.21   Adding an Issues item.

▶ **SEE** "Modifying Settings," **PAGE 447**.

- **Title**—Enter the title of the issue. (This is required.) Make sure that this briefly yet clearly describes the issue.

- **Assigned To**—Click on the arrow on the drop-down box, and select the person responsible for managing this issue.

- **Status**—Using the default values, the issue can be either Active, Postponed, or Closed.

- **Category**—Enter the category associated with the issue. By default, the values are Category 1, 2, or 3. This is a field you should consider for customization. For example, you might create categories such as managerial, technical, and so on to categorize issues.

- **Owner**—Click the arrow on the drop-down box, and select the person responsible for determining the resolution for the issue.

NOTE

The Assigned To and Owner drop-down lists contain only those users who have permission to access the issues for the project.

- **Priority**—Enter the value for importance of the issue. The default values are High, Medium, and Low.

- **Due Date**—Enter the expected or required resolution date for the issue.

- **Discussion**—Enter a description of the issue in more detail. Sometimes this is a running thread as team members discuss and analyze the issue to help resolve it. If you use Discussion as a running thread, make sure that each team member dates and signs his comments.

- **Resolution**—Enter a description of how the issue was resolved.

- **Linking to Tasks, Risks, Other Issues, or Documents**—You can associate an issue to tasks, other issues, risks, or documents contained within the project workspace by using the links at the bottom of the Issues form. Clicking on any of these selections brings up a task dialog box with the project tasks. Multiple tasks can be selected by checking the box to the left of the task name. You must be a team member in the project to access the tasks within the project. For instance, you could link the issue to a task that was delayed because of the issue.

3. You can attach file(s) to the issue by clicking on the Attach File button in the toolbar at the top of the form.

4. Select Save and Close from the toolbar at the top of the form after you enter all required information.

> **NOTE**
>
> When an issue is defined for a project, a graphical icon is displayed adjacent to the project within the Project Center Summary view. If an issue is attached to a specific working task, a graphical icon appears within the Project Center detail views. If you select an issue graphical icon, PWA opens the appropriate project issue group for review and updates.

18

Editing, Deleting, and Alert Me Actions on Issues

From the project's issues list, the Issue ID and Title are hyperlinks that take you to the detailed view of an existing issue. From this view, you can edit, delete, or create an alert for the issue so that you can be notified about changes to that issue. Select Edit Issue, Delete Issue, or Alert Me from the toolbar.

You can also click to the right of the issue title and, in the drop-down list that displays, select Edit Issue, Delete Issue, or Alert Me as shown in Figure 18.22.

Viewing and Reporting Issue Items

You have several options for viewing and reporting on the issues for a project. These especially come in handy for sorting through long issues lists or analyzing the issues.

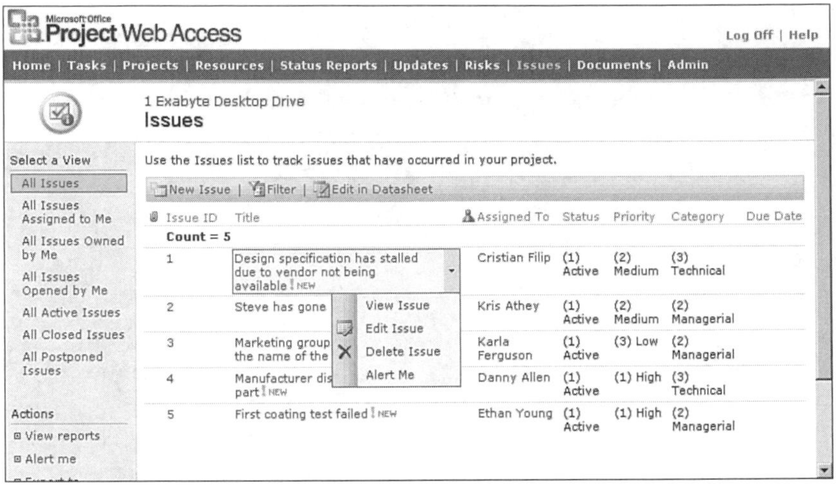

FIGURE 18.22   Drop-down list to select action on an issue.

Filtering Issues

To view the issues on your project in different ways, you can select one of numerous filters under Select a View in the side pane as shown in Figure 18.22. You can also select Filter on the toolbar above the issues list and use the filters from the drop-down lists that appear above each field on the list. For example, you could view only those issues assigned to a particular team member on your project. After enabling the filtering function, the Filter button alters the Change Filter or Hide Filter choices to change or remove the filtering you have applied.

View Reports

Under Actions in the side pane, you can select View Reports. On the Report Types screen, select the kind of report you want to view. You can analyze issues by category, issue assignee, or dates. Figure 18.23 shows a report by person (the person assigned to the issue).

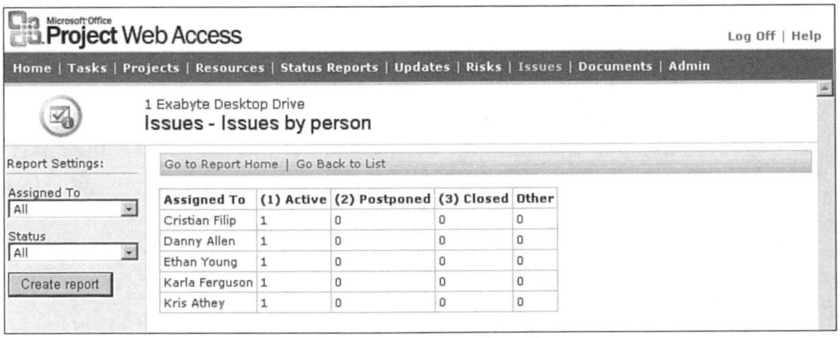

FIGURE 18.23   A category issues report.

Alert Me

You can use the Alert Me option at the issue list level to receive an email to notify you of any changes for all issues in the project. You can choose to be notified when issues are added, changed, or deleted, or for all changes. You can also choose to be notified immediately or in a daily or weekly summary.

> **NOTE**
>
> This is different from the Alert Me function described previously for individual issues. You can select to be emailed about individual issues and all issues on a project.

Export to Spreadsheet

You can export the issues list to an Excel spreadsheet as shown in Figure 18.24. To do so, click on Export to Spreadsheet in the Actions side pane on the issues list for the project. This is especially handy for taking the list of issues to meetings to discuss and update them within the meeting itself, or for sharing the issues list with others who may not have access to Project Server. Then, after you make changes in Excel, you can use the Synchronize with Project Server selection on the side pane to bring the changes you made in Excel into Project Server.

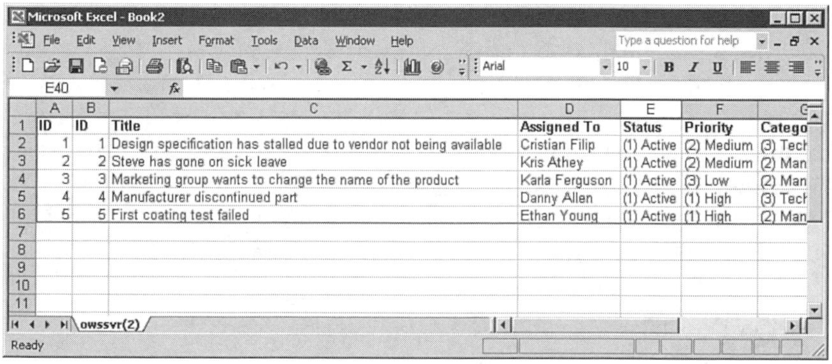

FIGURE 18.24   The issues list exported to an Excel spreadsheet.

Edit in Datasheet

The issues list can also be mass edited by using the Edit in Datasheet option on the toolbar. This presents the data elements from the view in a datasheet form. You can edit the issues more easily and more quickly than in the Standard view.

> **TIP**
>
> In the Datasheet view, select the Task pane and explore the various Microsoft Office tools you can use to analyze and report on issues. For example, you can use Create an Excel PivotTable Report to chart your issues trends.

Modify Settings and Columns

This feature allows you to make changes to the issues columns and values to customize the issues repository to match your issues management standards.

▶ **SEE** "Collaboration Using Windows SharePoint Services," **PAGE 442**.

Synchronize with Project Server

Use this function to synchronize data you might have changed in Excel or Access, if you exported the issues to an Excel spreadsheet or an Access database. When you select this feature, it updates the data changed in those applications within Project Server.

Documents

Documents can be an important part of your use of Project Server. The document library provides your project team one easy place to find all documents associated with your project. You also have the ability to check out and version the documents to help control document changes. You can attach documents to particular tasks, too. For example, suppose that one of your tasks is Complete Business Feasibility Study, and it will take Russ 20 hours to perform this activity. When Russ is finished, he could attach the document itself to the task he is assigned.

The documents management function is designed so that only those assigned to the project can work on the documents for that project. No other people can access the documents unless the project manager gives express permission to a user to use the site. See "Permissions in WSS" earlier in this chapter for more information about how permissions are established for a WSS site. This requires some administrative overhead for the project manager to grant permissions, but this level of security may be exactly what an organization needs. Some organizations, however, want a completely open site for documents, so that team members and other people from across the organization can look at and share documents. If your organization needs this capability, consider using SharePoint Portal Services (SPS).

When you select Documents from the top menu bar in PWA, you see a list of project libraries. The document libraries are grouped by My Projects, which are projects that have task assignments for you; Other Projects, which you have permission to access; and Public Documents, which all Project Server users may access. The Go to Selected Project Workspace selection on the side pane allows you to go to the workspace for the selected project if you want to view all the documents, risks, and issues related to a project you select.

TIP

You may also want to store the typical forms your organization uses for project management activities, such as the Project Charter template or a Communications Plan template, in the Public Documents library. You could also store your documents for your Project Server deployment project, such as the Project Server configuration requirements, in the Public library.

You can open a project document library by selecting a project link from the list. Graphical folder icons are displayed with the name and description of each folder. By default, each project library has a Shared Documents folder created for it. You can also add new folders to contain various documents related to a project as shown in Figure 18.25.

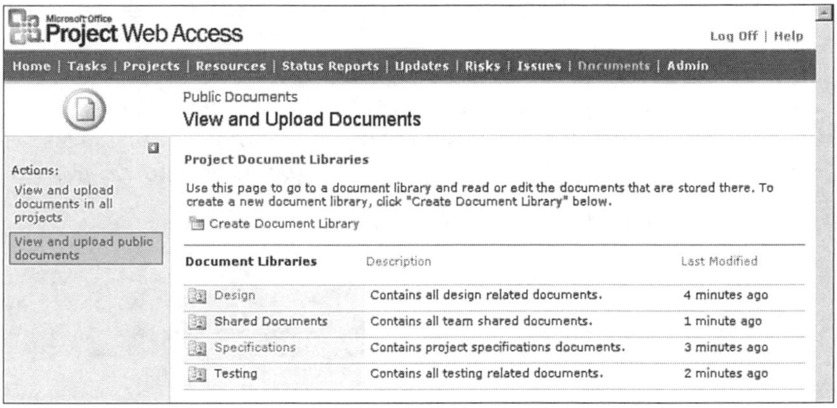

FIGURE 18.25   Document libraries for a project.

For example, you might create folders for project management documents, specifications, business requirements, project planning, testing, or any other categories that would help your team members easily find documents pertaining to the project.

To create a folder for a project library, on the Project Document Libraries page, click on Create Document Library as shown previously in Figure 18.25.

You then see a page called New Document Library where you can set some general properties for the folder:

- **Name and Description**—Name the folder and provide a description of the folder so that team members know what kinds of documents they can find in the folder.

- **Navigation**—Select Yes if you want the library to show on the Quick Launch bar, which is the left side pane of the project workspace (this does not display when you are in Project Web Access itself), or select No if you do not want the library to show in the Quick Launch bar.

- **Document Versions**—Select Yes if you want document versions to be created each time you edit a document in the library, or select No if you do not want versions for the documents in the folder.

- **Document Template**—Indicate the document template (such as Word, Excel, or PowerPoint) based on the drop-down list. Note that the kinds of documents you store in the folder are not limited to the applications in the drop-down list, and you can have several kinds of documents in the same folder.

18

When you are finished setting up the folder properties, click Create.

> **NOTE**
>
> If you need to change any of the settings for the folder, select the folder and then click on Modify Settings and Columns in the side pane. Select Change General Settings at the end of the General Settings section to make the changes.

To view the list of documents stored in a folder, click on the folder or folder name. The displayed list includes document names and other important information about each document as shown in Figure 18.26. You can change the columns available and the values in them based on the kind of information you want to have for your document.

▶ **SEE** "Modifying Settings," **PAGE 447**.

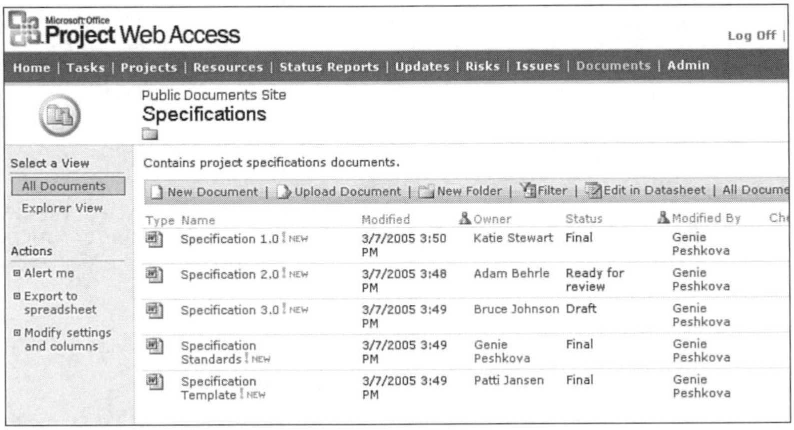

FIGURE 18.26 Documents listed in a folder. Note the status and other information for the document.

Uploading or Creating a Document

To create or upload a document for the project, you must be a member of the Team Members site group, meaning that you have an assignment within the project schedule. The project manager of a project has full permissions to add and modify documents for the project.

To create a document, perform the following steps:

1. Click on New Document in the toolbar above the document list.
2. Word opens (or the default document application as defined for the library if available on the client machine), and you may start creating a document. When you are finished, click Save.
3. You are asked to save the document to a particular location (do not change the location for the document to be saved from the location showing). Name the document and click Save.

4. An edit form appears where you can fill in the Owner from a drop-down list (if other than the default showing, which is "None") and Status from a drop-down list (Draft, Ready for Review, or Final).

5. Click OK. When you close the application, the document appears in the document library list with a New indicator next to it.

To upload a document, click on Upload Document in the toolbar above the document list. An edit form displays where you can fill in the document data, as follows:

- **Overwrite Existing File(s)?**—Leave the default check mark if you want to overwrite any previous file when you are saving a document with the same name to WSS.

- **Name**—Enter the name of the document. (This is required.) Make sure that this briefly yet clearly describes the document.

- **Upload Multiple Files**—If you have more than one file to upload at one time, click on this hyperlink. A screen appears that lets you find the document folder you want to select files from. You can check each file you want to upload.

- **Owner**—Click on the arrow on the drop-down box and select the person who is the manager or owner of the document.

- **Status**—Using the default values, the document can be Draft, Ready for Review, or Final. When the document is uploaded, it defaults to Ready for Review status.

- **Linking**—You can associate a document to tasks, other issues, or risks contained within the project workspace by using the links at the bottom of the Upload Document form.

  ▶ SEE "Creating Risks," **PAGE 455**.

When a document is defined for a project, a graphical icon is displayed adjacent to the project within the Project Center Summary view. If a document is attached to a specific working task, a graphical icon appears within the Project Center detail views. If you select a document graphical icon, PWA opens the appropriate project document library for review and updates.

New Folder, Filter, and Other Actions in a Document List

You can create subfolders within a document library. To do so, click on New Folder in the action bar. A new screen appears where you may name the folder.

To view the document lists on your project in different ways, you can select Filter on the toolbar above the documents list and use the filters from the drop-down lists that appear above each field on the list. For example, you could view only those documents in a Draft status. After enabling the filtering function, the Filter button changes the Change Filter or Hide Filter choices to change or remove the filtering you have applied.

18

Edit in Datasheet

The documents list can also be mass edited by using the Edit in Datasheet option on the action bar. This presents the data elements from the view in a datasheet form. You can edit the documents list more easily and more quickly than in the Standard view.

TIP

In the Datasheet view, select the Task pane and explore the various Microsoft Office tools you can use to analyze and report on issues. For example, you can use Create an Excel PivotTable Report to chart your documents' trends.

All Document Libraries

When you select All Document Libraries, you are returned to the main project document library page.

Actions on Documents

Hovering the mouse pointer over the document name without clicking on the hyperlink displays a pull-down list of options. You can view or edit the properties of the document, check out the document, edit the document using Microsoft Office Word, view the document version history, set email alerts, and start a discussion about the document, as shown in Figure 18.27. These same selections can be seen in a different format if you select the View Properties or Edit Properties selections for the document, as shown in Figure 18.28.

Clicking on the document name hyperlink opens the document for viewing in a web-based facility. If you want to edit the document, always choose the Edit function from the drop-down list.

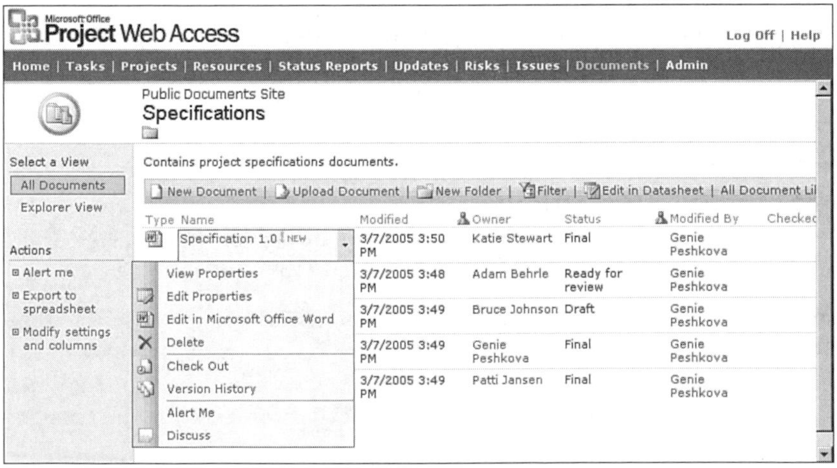

FIGURE 18.27   Drop-down list to select action on a document.

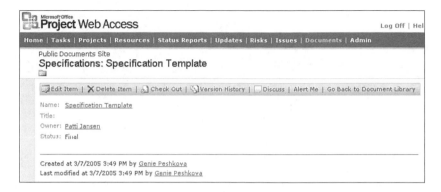

FIGURE 18.28   Functions available after selecting View Properties or Edit Properties.

The following list describes the actions you can take on documents:

- **View Properties and Edit Properties**—You can view and change the information about a document via properties. If you choose to Edit Properties, you change the same information you created when you uploaded the document as described previously. You can also select actions on documents as shown in Figure 18.28.

- **Edit in the Document Application**—Use this function to open and edit the document in the application it was created in. The particular application displays, such as Edit in Microsoft Office Word.

- **Delete**—Allows you to delete the document. You may want to change the permissions for this library if you do not want team members to delete documents.

- **Check Out**—Select this to work on the document so that you are the only one who can modify the document, although others can still read it. When the document is checked out, you can see who the document is checked out to in the document list as shown in Figure 18.29. After you select this option, you still need to select Edit in whatever application is appropriate. Also, if the document is checked out, this option on the drop-down list changes to Check In. If for some reason a document is checked out, but not checked in as expected, the administrator can check the document back in.

> **NOTE**
>
> You can edit a document without checking it out. You will have a short-term lock on the document, but the lock will expire, and if someone else checks it out in the meantime, that person's check-out lock will take precedence, and you will not be able to save your changes under the same document name.

- **Version History**—This selection shows you the various versions of the document. You can select each to view dates and times, see who modified the document, and delete versions, as shown in Figure 18.30.

18

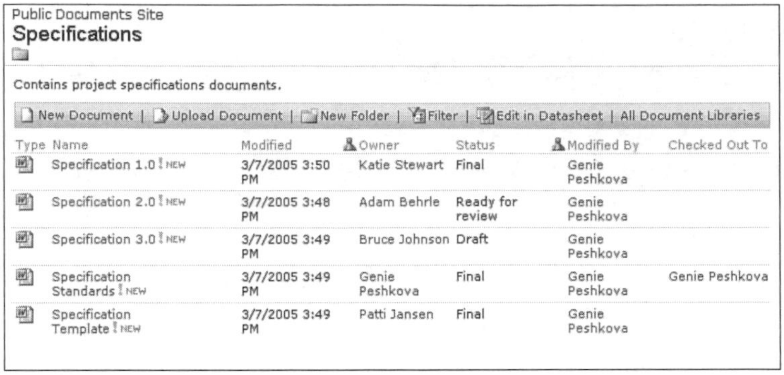

FIGURE 18.29   A document checked out in the document list.

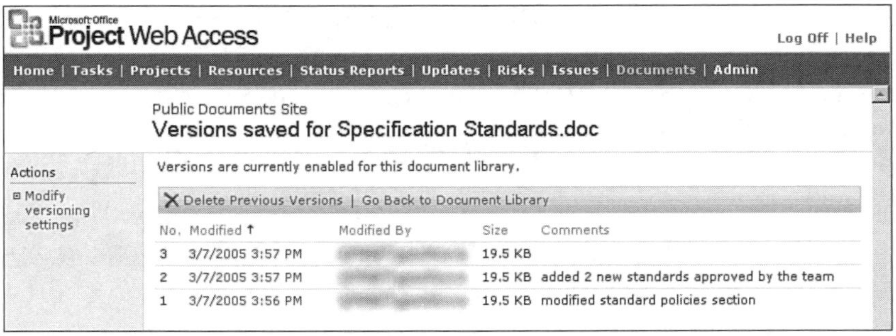

FIGURE 18.30   Version history for a document.

- **Alert Me**—Select this to get email notifications about changes to the document. You can receive these emails on a daily, weekly, or monthly schedule.

  ▶ **SEE** "Creating Risks," **PAGE 455**.

- **Discuss**—Select this to use the discussion feature in Internet Explorer.

Actions on the Document Library from the Side Pane

You can perform some common actions on a document library as described in the following sections.

Select a View

You can choose to view the document in a list via All Documents or via an Explorer view. The Explorer view provides more flexible navigation in moving, copying, and renaming the documents in the library, which is not allowed in the normal documents lists.

Alert Me

You can use the Alert Me option at the folder level to receive an email notifying you of any changes for all documents in the particular document folder. You can choose to be notified when documents are added, changed, or deleted, or for all changes. You can also choose to be notified immediately or in a daily or weekly summary.

> **NOTE**
>
> This is different from the Alert Me function described previously for individual documents. You can select to be emailed about individual documents and all documents on a project.

Export to Spreadsheet

You can export the documents list to an Excel spreadsheet as shown in Figure 18.31. This is especially handy for taking the list of documents to meetings to discuss and check status within the meeting itself, or for sharing the documents list with others who may not have access to Project Server. If you make changes to any of the data items in Excel, click the Synchronize with Project Server selection on the side pane to bring the changes you made in Excel into Project Server.

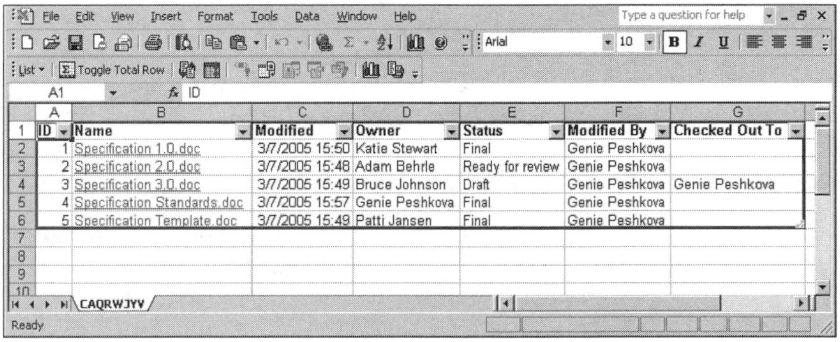

FIGURE 18.31   The documents list exported to an Excel spreadsheet.

Modify Settings and Columns

This feature allows you to make changes to the documents columns and values to customize the documents repository to match your documents management standards.

▶ **SEE** "Modifying Settings," **PAGE 447**.

Synchronize with Project Server

Use this function to synchronize data you might have changed in Excel or Access, if you exported the documents list to an Excel spreadsheet or an Access database. When you select this feature, it updates the data changed in those applications within Project Server.

Best Practices

Many organizations are interested in building project schedules in Project Server but fail to use all the benefits of what the WSS features provide. Use the project workspace as much as possible for important projects to draw team members and all stakeholders into the website for status and other project information. Learn how to use the WSS site permissions to allow others besides Project Server users to use the workspace.

One item to consider is that if you use the Public Documents library as the main area for your Project Management Office templates, you might want to remove the permission for project managers and team members to be able to delete documents. As a project manager, you might want to change the permissions for team members so that they can't delete a document.

Instead of using the default risk fields when you implement, you should analyze your own issues and risk management processes and customize the default issues and risks fields. At the very least, you should remove values from or add meaningful values to the Category field, which does not contain meaningful default values.

Also, you may want to consider changing the Issues and Risks templates to enhance the fields that show in the lists. This is because when you export to an Excel spreadsheet, you export only those fields that show on the list (refer to the example earlier in Figure 18.31 to understand the fields that would be exported).

Many organizations implement the Issues and Risk functions as an optional feature for project managers to use. Chances are it won't be used if it is optional. Yet all projects have issues and risks that should be managed. Consider implementing these features with processes and standards to start helping your project managers manage their issues.

Unless you have an existing documents management system, your organization should seriously consider setting standards for using the Documents function.

CHAPTER 19

Using the Project Web Access Admin Menu Tab

T he Admin tab in Project Web Access (PWA) is used by the administrator or Project Management Office (PMO) lead to set overall PWA screen settings, configurations, and security settings, and to perform general database maintenance such as deleting projects. To complete full configuration for the system, the PMO also sets up Enterprise Outline Codes in Project Professional as well. This chapter describes each function that displays in the side pane under the Admin tab. Other chapters in this book may include full instructions for using a particular feature, whereas this chapter provides overview information. When you select the Admin tab you see a screen listing all the Admin functions, as shown in Figure 19.1.

CAUTION

Most changes (for instance, permissions to view functions or see data, timesheets, and updates to PWA views) you make using the Admin tab are effective immediately after you save the change. Make sure that you take that into consideration prior to making a change. Also, several functions that change the PWA page (such as adding ToolTips) do not take effect until the administrator logs off and logs on again.

IN THIS CHAPTER

- Admin Overview
- Using the Manage Users and Groups Function
- Using the Manage Security Function
- Using the Manage Views Page
- Using the Server Configuration Function
- Using the Manage Windows SharePoint Services (WSS) Function
- Using the Manage Enterprise Features Function
- Using the Customize Project Web Access Function
- Using the Clean Up the Project Server Database Function
- The About Microsoft Office Project Server 2003 Page
- Best Practices

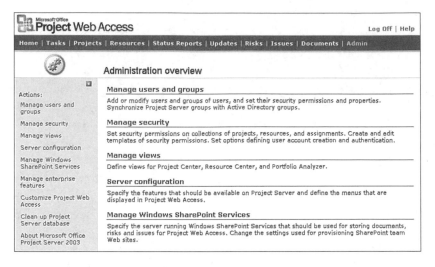

FIGURE 19.1   The Admin tab functions.

Admin Overview

The Admin tab in PWA allows you to manage all the settings for permissions and data views in PWA. It does not control any items for configuration in Project Professional. The Admin tab contains the following configuration and maintenance functions:

> **TIP**
>
> You may want to print out a list of the Admin subfunctions as described in the following list to make it easier to remember what you want to do because some of the names of these functions are not intuitive as to what specific functions they allow.

- Manage Users and Groups:
  - Add, modify, and delete users to allow access to PWA and Project Pro.
  - Set up, change, and delete groups (for permissions). You also set up the Active Directory group synchronization options here.
- Manage Security:
  - Add, modify, and delete categories used for data views.
  - Add, modify, and delete security templates, which are the basis for group permissions.
  - User authentication to set up general server authentication as Windows authentication, Project Server, or both modes.

- Manage Views:

  - Add, modify, and delete views for Project Center and Project Detail views from projects in the Project Center, Resource Center, Portfolio Analyzer, and Timesheet.

- Server Configuration:

  - **Features**—Allows you to set up what you allow around master projects, local calendars, and other enterprise features. It also allows you to set up your Active Directory synchronization with the Enterprise Resource Pool. Features are additionally used to set up the overall enterprise permissions.

  - **Menus**—Allows you to change the order of options on all the PWA screens and to create ToolTips.

- **Manage Windows SharePoint Services**—You can see more detail about what specific functions you will perform in the section about WSS in this chapter. The functions available are

  - Connect to SharePoint Server

  - Site provisioning settings

  - Manage SharePoint sites

  - Synchronize administrator accounts

  - Connect to SharePoint Portal Server

- Manage Enterprise Features:

  - Update resource tables and OLAP cube. This allows you to update Portfolio Analyzer views with the latest information and to set availability.

  - Check in enterprise projects.

  - Check in enterprise resources.

  - Add or delete versions.

- Customize Project Web Access:

  - **Tracking settings**—Allows you to set the timesheet options and whether you want to use Managed or Non-Managed Time Periods.

  - **Gantt Chart formats**—Change the colors, shadings, and patterns for the bars on the Gantt chart in PWA views.

  - **Grouping formats**—Change the colors, shadings, and patterns for the bars on the Gantt chart in PWA views.

  - **Home Page format**—Add links or other content to the PWA home page.

  - **Notifications and reminders**—Set up the email servers for Project Server.

- **Clean Up Project Server Database**—This feature allows you to Delete projects and resources. You can also delete tasks assignments, status reports, to-do lists, and other specific items as shown on the page.

- **About Microsoft Office Project Server 2003**—This feature provides licensing information so that you can see how many people are active PWA users.

NOTE

Make sure that you understand there are two places to complete Active Directory synchronization. One is to synchronize the Project Server Security Groups and is under the group function in Managing Users and Groups. The other Active Directory function synchronizes an Active Directory group with the Enterprise Resource Pool. This is performed under Server Configuration. You do not have to use both synchronization functions. For example, many organizations just use Active Directory to add and synchronize users into their proper security group in Project Server.

Using the Manage Users and Groups Function

The Manage Users and Groups function is one of the most commonly accessed administrative functions. PWA users can be added, modified, or deleted, and users can be placed in security groups to set the features and data an individual user has access to. From this interface, groups can also be added, modified, or deleted, and user accounts can be merged to create a single user account with all the attributes of the current user but with data from both user accounts.

Before using any of the Manage User and Groups functions under Admin, make sure that you understand the Project Server security model.

▶ **SEE** "Establishing Security Model Settings," **PAGE 143**.

Managing Users

All PWA users are accessible through the administrative function Manage Users and Groups. You need to access this function when users change Project Server roles or when account information changes, as shown in Figure 19.2.

Adding a User

In the Project Server environment, there are three ways to add users to PWA:

- **Active Directory**—Use Active Directory synchronization.

- **Enterprise Resource Pool**—Add a user as a resource in the Enterprise Resource Pool. This is the most efficient way to add a user if you are not using Active Directory synchronization. When you do add a resource to the pool, Project Server automatically adds the resource as a user in the Team Member role in PWA. When you do this, make sure that you also include at least the Domain\User ID in the Windows Account and the email address in the Email data fields for the resource(s). Then, all you need to do is change the role of the resource if it is different from the default Team Member.

- **Manage Users and Groups of the Admin tab**—You can add users directly via this function. This may be used to add a user who will not be a resource on a project schedule, such as a client, executive, or someone who needs to use only the collaborative features of PWA.

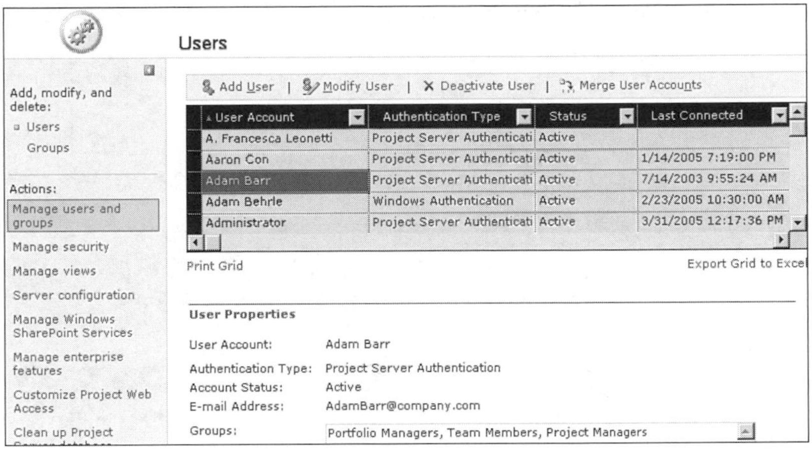

FIGURE 19.2   The Users page contains all functions to add, delete, or change users.

> **NOTE**
>
> If you add a user or resource via the Add User function in PWA and run Active Directory synchronization, Active Directory actually removes the user if it does not find the username in Active Directory.

To add a user, follow these steps:

1. Under the Admin tab select Manage Users and Groups.

2. Under Add, Modify, and Delete in the side pane select Users.

3. Click Add User from the menu. The Add User page appears, as shown in Figure 19.3.

4. Select an authentication method for this user and add the information as required.

> **NOTE**
>
> Users added directly in the Add Users page are not automatically added to the Enterprise Resource Pool.

5. Select the groups that the user should belong to and click Add. Users can be in one or multiple groups.

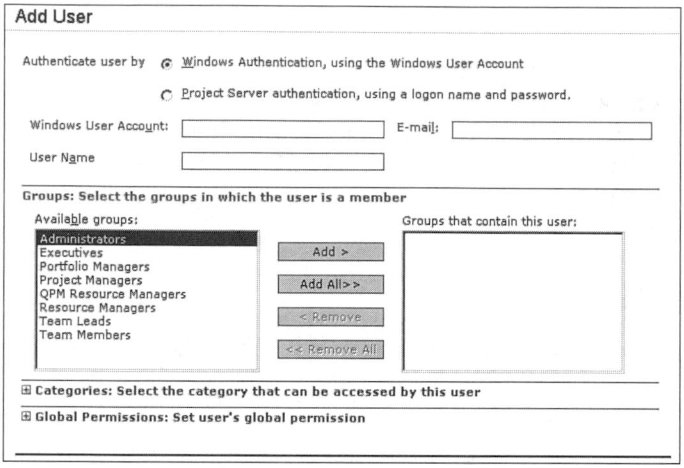

Add User

Authenticate user by   ◉ Windows Authentication, using the Windows User Account

                              ○ Project Server authentication, using a logon name and password.

Windows User Account: [   ]   E-mail: [   ]

User Name [   ]

Groups: Select the groups in which the user is a member

Available groups: Groups that contain this user:

Administrators	
Executives	[Add >]
Portfolio Managers	
Project Managers	[Add All>>]
QPM Resource Managers	
Resource Managers	[< Remove]
Team Leads	
Team Members	[<< Remove All]

⊞ **Categories: Select the category that can be accessed by this user**

⊞ **Global Permissions: Set user's global permission**

FIGURE 19.3   The Add User page allows you to configure new system users.

NOTE

The user will be a member of the groups selected and inherit the permissions in the group(s).

Categories should be associated with security groups and should not be assigned directly to users.

---

6. Click Save Changes.

Modifying Existing Users

At times, you need to change information about a user, such as the user's email address, domain, or account status. To do so, you use the Modify User function:

1. Under the Admin tab, select Manage Users and Groups.

2. In the side pane under Add, Modify, and Delete, select Users. The Users page, which consists of a drop-down list with all PWA users and user properties, appears. To filter and sort by user, authentication type, and status, you can view users in a grid, as shown previously in Figure 19.2.

NOTE

The grid may require several minutes to load if you have many users.

NOTE

The grid can be sorted by last connected to view PWA access, providing useful information on which users are actively using the system.

3. Highlight the user in the grid or select the user from the drop-down list and click Modify User from the menu.

4. On the Modify User page, as shown in Figure 19.4, make the necessary changes and click Save Changes.

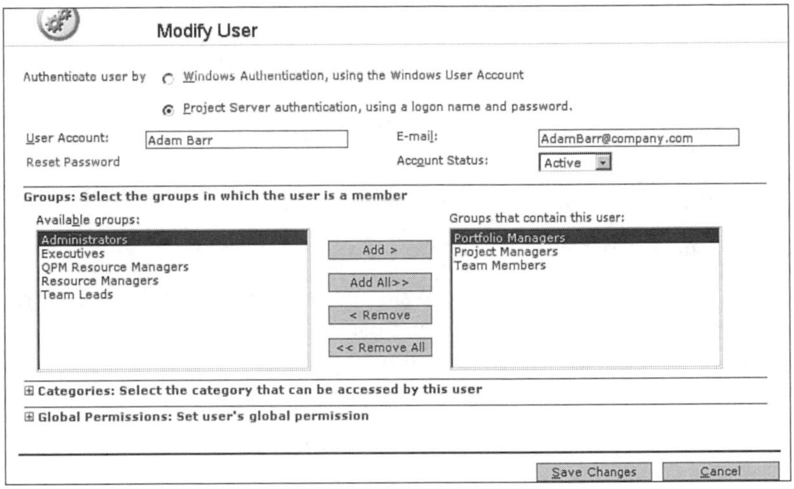

FIGURE 19.4   The Modify User page allows you to configure settings for the selected user.

NOTE

If the PWA user is also in the Enterprise Resource Pool, changes to the user or resource are reflected in both PWA and the Enterprise Resource Pool data.

NOTE

The Clear User AD GUID check box is enabled only on the Modify User page for Project Server users who use Windows authentication and only when the user has an associated Active Directory Globally Unique Identifier (GUID). Clearing the Active Directory GUID prevents any further updates for the particular user from Active Directory.

TIP

Do not set global permissions on an individual user or add users directly to categories through this page.

Deactivating Existing Users

There are several ways to deactivate a user in PWA:

- **Active Directory**—use Active Directory synchronization. If the user is removed in Active Directory, it marks the user as Inactive.

- **Enterprise Resource Pool**—Mark the user as Inactive.

- **Manage Users and Groups of the Admin tab**—Under Modify User, select Inactive in the Account Status field.

- **Manage Users and Groups of the Admin tab**—Use the Deactivate User function.

To use the Deactivate function, follow these steps:

1. Under the Admin tab, select Manage Users and Groups.

2. Under Add, Modify, and Delete in the side pane, select Users. This displays the Users page, which consists of a drop-down list with all PWA users and user properties. To filter and sort by user, authentication type, and status, you can view users in a grid, as shown previously in Figure 19.2.

3. Highlight the user in the grid or select the user from the drop-down list.

4. Click Deactivate User from the menu.

> **NOTE**
>
> Deactivating a user inactivates the user's account so that it can no longer be used to log on to the computer running Project Server 2003. User accounts, when deactivated, are not actually deleted from the Project Server database. If the user is an enterprise resource, he will no longer be available in Build Team.

Merging Two User Accounts

It is possible that two accounts can be created for the same person. This often happens when an organization first starts using Project Server and does not yet have good processes or standards to ensure unique account creation. You can merge two such accounts to create one account for a user.

> **NOTE**
>
> To minimize the possibility of two accounts being created for a user, create a standard to allow only the administrator to create new accounts.

To merge two user accounts, follow these steps:

1. Under the Admin tab, select Manage Users and Groups.

2. Under Add, Modify, and Delete in the side pane, select Users.

3. Highlight the user account that you want to merge another user into from the grid or select the user from the drop-down list and click Merge User Accounts from the menu.

4. On the Merge User Accounts page, select the user you want to be merged.

> **NOTE**
>
> You should merge user accounts only if they refer to the same person. If you try to merge user accounts that have been assigned the same tasks or status reports, you could have data conflicts.

5. Click Save Changes.

> **NOTE**
>
> This creates a single user account with all the attributes of one user but with data from both user accounts.

Managing Groups

Groups contain security rules defined for a particular role. Users are added to groups to simplify the maintenance of user permissions. The Groups page allows you to create, modify, and delete groups, as shown in Figure 19.5.

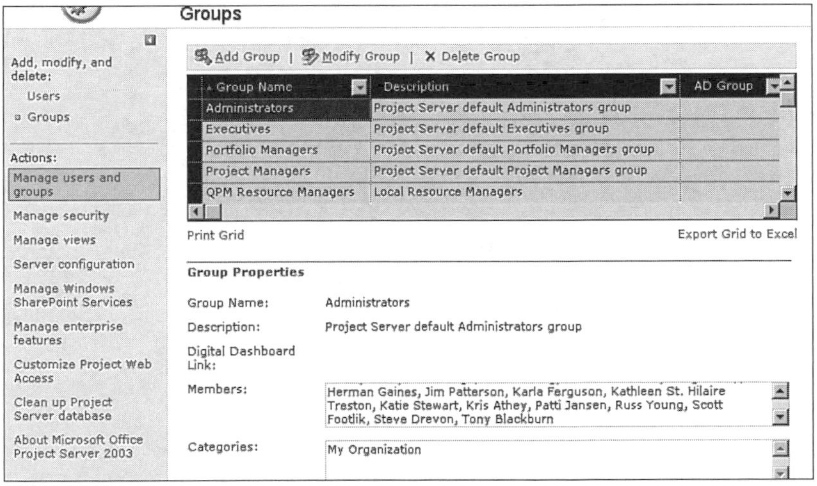

FIGURE 19.5   The Groups page contains all functions to add, delete, or modify groups.

Creating a Group

You will want to create groups when you have a customized role you want to use in your organization, or if you want to have your organization's own group roles, based on the default groups established in Project Server. Before creating a group, make sure that you define and document the functions and data you want the group to use and see to decide what permissions the group should have and what category should be attached to the group.

> **NOTE**
>
> As described in Chapter 8, "Establishing Security Model Settings," you might create a security template for the role prior to creating the group.

When you are ready to create a new group, follow these steps:

1. Under Admin tab, select Manage Users and Groups.

2. Under Add, Modify, and Delete in the side pane, select Groups. This displays the Groups page, which consists of a grid containing all groups, as shown in Figure 19.5.

3. Click Add Group from the menu. The Add Group page appears, as shown in Figure 19.6.

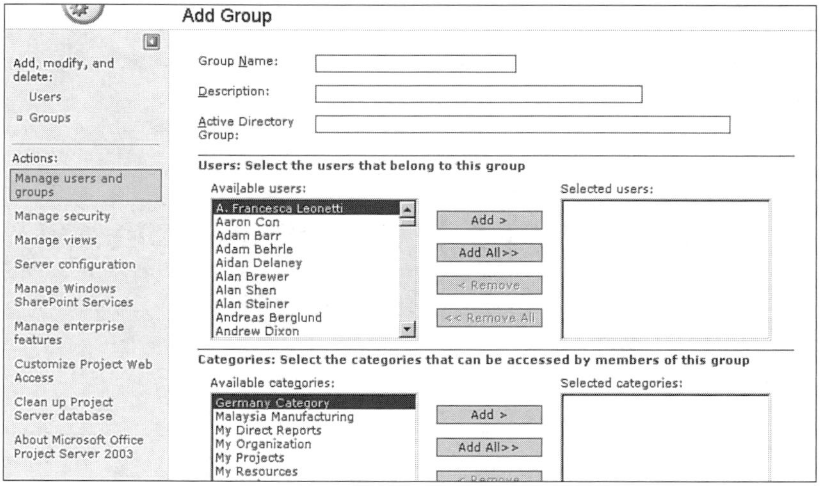

FIGURE 19.6   The Add Group page.

4. Enter the name and description for the new group in the fields provided. Enter the Active Directory group in the provided box if using Active Directory synchronization.

5. Select users to add to the group by highlighting the username in the list of available users and clicking Add.

> **NOTE**
>
> Users can be added at any time using the Modify Group or Modify User option.

6. Select the categories from the available categories and click Add.

> **NOTE**
>
> As described in Chapter 8, the best method for creating a new group is to develop the custom category the group will use prior to actually creating the group via the Admin function. That way, after you create the group, you can attach the proper category (which indicates what data the group can see) to the group.

7. For each category added in Step 6, highlight the category name in the Selected Categories list and set the permissions this group will have by checking the Allow box or applying a group security template.

> **NOTE**
>
> Review and set category permissions for proper settings. Each category may require different security permissions.

8. Set the Global permissions by selecting the security template from the drop-down list and clicking Set Permissions with Template.

9. If you want to use a digital dashboard, Under Digital Dashboard Link: Set the Default Digital Dashboard Link for Members of This Group, and enter the path to the portal site URL for this group.

10. Click Save Changes.

> **NOTE**
>
> If changing permissions on a group, first modify the security template for the role prior to applying the permissions to the group.

Modifying an Existing Group

You may need to change the permissions, categories, or users for a group. Be careful making any changes. It's best to test the change for the group to make sure that you did not inadvertently take away or give a permission you did not intend. To modify a group, follow these steps:

1. Under Admin tab, select Manage Users and Groups.

2. Under Add, Modify, and Delete in the side pane, select Groups. The Groups page, which consists of a grid containing all groups, appears, as shown previously in Figure 19.5.

3. Select the group to modify.

4. Click Modify Group from the menu, and the Modify Group page appears.

5. Make the required changes to the group and Click Save Changes.

Deleting an Existing Group

At times, you may need to delete a group that you created. If you do, make sure that you add the users who are in the group to be deleted to another group before deleting it. Those users will not be able to use PWA if they are not associated with another group. Follow these steps to delete a group:

1. Under Admin tab, select Manage Users and Groups.

2. Under Add, Modify, and Delete in the side pane, select Groups. The Groups page, which consists of a grid containing all groups, appears, as shown previously in Figure 19.5.

3. Select the group to delete.

4. Click Delete Group from the menu. In the confirmation dialog click Yes.

> **NOTE**
>
> The default groups created at installation cannot be deleted.

Using the Manage Security Function

The Manage Security function in PWA allows you to modify Category information (which is the data a group can see), change templates (which group permissions are based on), and set the authentication option for users who log on to PWA.

Managing Categories

Categories define what data permissions a user has as defined for a user based on the group to which the user is assigned. Data permissions include what projects, resources, and views will be visible to the user. The Categories page allows you to create, modify, and delete categories as shown in Figure 19.7.

Before setting up or using Categories, make sure that you understand the Project Server security model.

▶ **SEE** "Establishing Security Model Settings," **PAGE 143**.

Adding a Category

You will want to create new categories when you have a customized category for data viewing that you want to use in your organization, or if you want to create your organization's own categories, based on the default groups established in Project Server. Before creating a category, make sure that you define and document the category permissions and data you want the category to use and see to decide what permissions the category should have and what data any users assigned to the category will need to see.

▶ **SEE** "Creating Categories," **PAGE 151**.

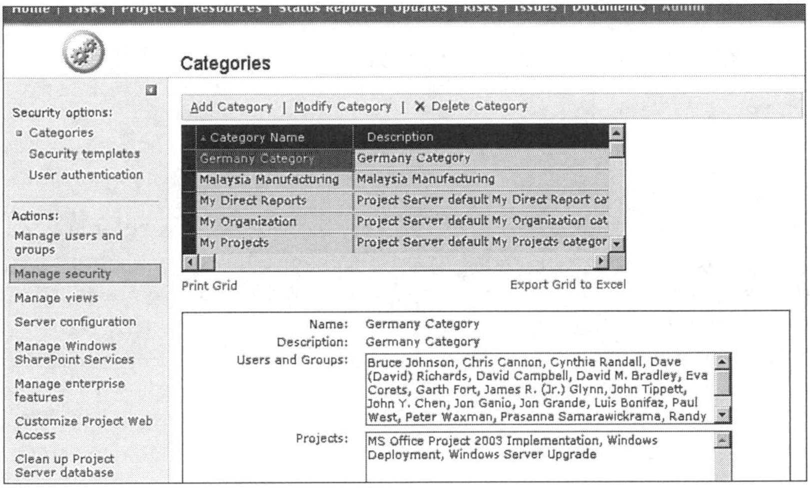

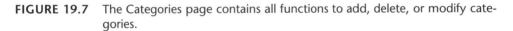

FIGURE 19.7   The Categories page contains all functions to add, delete, or modify categories.

When you are ready to create a new category, perform the following steps:

1. Under the Admin tab, select Manage Security.

2. Under Security Options in the side pane, select Categories. The Categories page, which consists of a grid containing all existing categories, appears, as shown previously in Figure 19.7.

3. Click Add Category from the menu, and the Add Category page opens.

4. Enter the name and description for the new category. Make the name as descriptive as possible so that you understand what kind of data it represents, such as "All projects viewable."

5. Select available users and groups to add to the category by highlighting the username or group in the list of available users and clicking Add. To help make management of categories easier, add only groups to the category.

> **NOTE**
>
> Users or groups can be added at any time using the Modify Category or Modify Group option.

6. If you have assigned a group to the category, under Permissions, select the kinds of activities the users of this data category will need to perform. Instead of checking the permissions individually, you can also set the permissions by using a security template for a group. To do so, select the group in the drop-down menu and click Set Permissions with Template.

7. For the rest of the areas about projects, resources, and views on the screen, select the specified data you want for the category.

   ▶ **SEE** "Creating Categories," **PAGE 151**.

8. When you are finished making the changes, click Save Changes.

Modifying an Existing Category

You may need to change the settings for a category at times. Be careful making any changes. It's best to test the change for the groups assigned to the categories to make sure that you did not inadvertently take away or give a data permission you did not intend. To modify a category, follow these steps:

1. Under the Admin tab, select Manage Security.

2. Under Security Options in the side pane, select Categories. This displays the Categories page, which consists of a grid containing all categories, as shown previously in Figure 19.7.

3. Select the category to modify.

4. Click Modify Category from the menu, and the Modify Category page appears.

5. Make the required changes to the category and Click Save Changes.

Deleting an Existing Category

At times, you may need to delete a category that you created. If you do, make sure that you add the groups assigned to that category to another category before deleting it. These groups will not be able to use PWA if they are not associated with another group. Follow these steps to delete a category:

> **NOTE**
>
> The default categories created at installation cannot be deleted.

1. Under the Admin tab, select Manage Security.

2. Under Security Options in the side pane, select Categories. The Categories page displays, which consists of a grid containing all categories, as shown previously in Figure 19.7.

3. Select the Category to delete.

4. Click Delete Category from the menu. In the confirmation dialog, click Yes.

Managing Security Templates

Security templates are the basis of the permissions set up for groups. The default group permissions are based on the default security template permissions you see when you first install Project Server. There is a one-for-one match for security templates and groups.

NOTE

You might want to keep the default templates as is out-of-the-box. You might want to create a new template for each of the groups you will use and then set permissions from the template for each of your groups.

▶ **SEE** "Security Templates," **PAGE 147**.

Adding a Security Template

You might want to create a new security template to match the groups your organization will use, or when you set up a customized group. To create a new security template, follow these steps:

1. Under the Admin tab, select Manage Security.

2. Under Security Options in the side pane, select Security Templates. This displays the Security Templates page, which consists of a grid containing all existing templates, as shown in Figure 19.8.

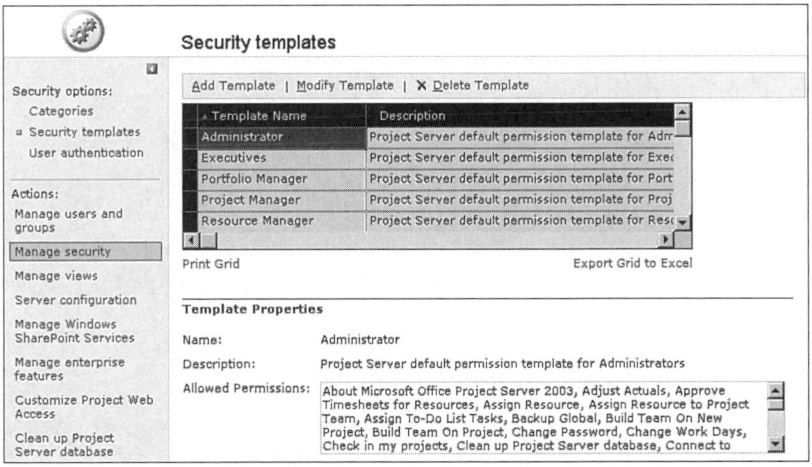

FIGURE 19.8   The security templates grid on the page.

3. Click Add Template from the menu, and the Add New Template dialog box appears, as shown in Figure 19.9.

4. Enter the name of the custom group you will be creating in the Template Name text box, enter a description in the Description text box, and select the name of the default template you will be using as a base from the Copy Template drop-down list; then click OK.

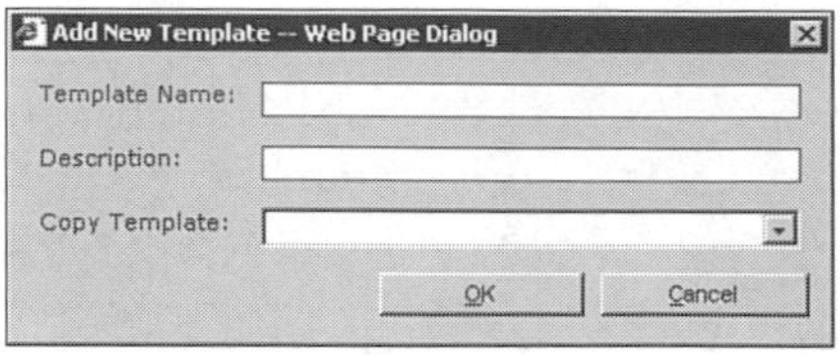

FIGURE 19.9   The Add New Template dialog box.

5. The new template name appears in the grid. Select the template and select Modify Template in the menu. Change the permissions for the new custom group according to your documented requirements. Do not check the Deny option for any permissions at this level.

6. Click Save Changes in the upper-right corner of the page.

Modifying a Security Template

You may need to modify an existing security template now and then.

> **NOTE**
>
> Because the main purpose of creating or modifying a template is to set permissions for a group, if you should ever modify a security group template, don't forget that you will need to apply that template again to the group it is associated with.

To modify an existing security template, follow these steps:

1. Under the Admin tab, select Manage Security.

2. Under Security Options in the side pane, select Security Templates. The Security Templates page displays, which consists of a grid containing all existing templates, as shown previously in Figure 19.8.

3. Click Modify Template from the menu, and the Modify Template page appears, as shown in Figure 19.10.

4. Select or deselect the permissions for this template.

> **NOTE**
>
> Review "Project Server Permissions" in Appendix C and "Default Settings" in Appendix D of the *Microsoft Project Server 2003 Administrator's Guide* to determine whether a feature is appropriate for this role.

5. Click Save Changes.

FIGURE 19.10 The Modify Template page.

Deleting an Existing Security Template

At times, you may need to delete a template that you created. If you do, make sure that you consider any group permissions set with this template. To delete a template, perform the following steps:

1. Under the Admin tab, select Manage Security.

2. Under Security Options in the side pane, select Security Templates. This displays the Security Templates page, which consists of a grid containing all templates, as shown previously in Figure 19.8.

3. Select the security template to delete.

4. Click Delete Template from the menu. In the confirmation dialog, click Yes.

Setting Project Server Authentication Mode

Your organization's preference of how Project Server authenticates users trying to log on to the system will be set during installation (usually defaulting to the Mixed choice). You may change the authentication choice in PWA. You have the following choices:

- **Microsoft Project Server authentication**—Users are required to have a Project Server user ID and password to access Project Server. Users see a dialog box to get into Project Professional or PWA in which they must enter their User ID/password.

- **Windows Server authentication**—Users are logged on automatically using their Windows user ID and password when they access Project Professional or PWA.

- **Mixed authentication**—Allows either of the preceding two modes. This is recommended when you might have some users who are not on your internal network but who still need access via Project Server authentication.

> **NOTE**
>
> Windows SharePoint Services (which allows you to use the Documentation, Risks, and Issues functions) requires the use of Windows authentication.

To change your authentication option, follow these steps:

1. Under the Admin tab, select Manage Security.

2. Under Security Options in the side pane, select User Authentication. The User Authentication page displays, as shown in Figure 19.11.

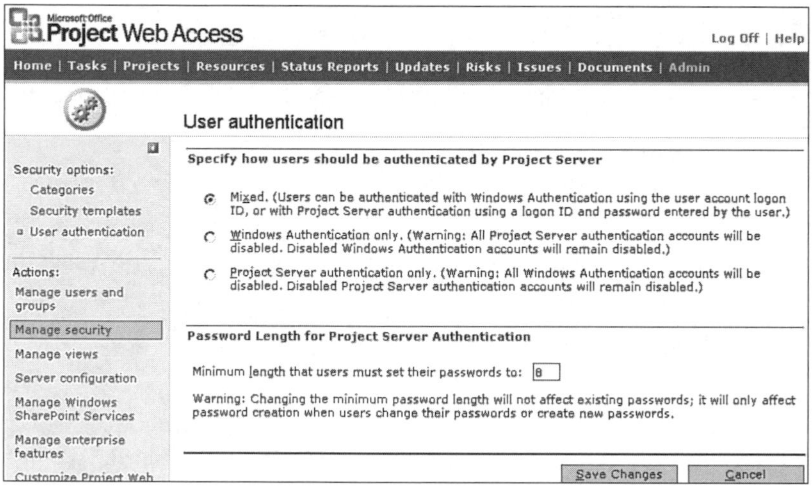

FIGURE 19.11   Changing options on the User Authentication page.

3. Select the radio button for the mode you want. If you select Mixed or Project Server Authentication Only, you can change the length of the password for a Project Server authentication logon. You can enter any number from 0 to 99.

4. Click Save Changes.

Using the Manage Views Page

The Manage Views page allows the user to modify, create, or delete a view for Projects, Project Center, Resource Center, Resource Assignment, Portfolio Analyzer, and the Timesheet. Views are part of the security model: PWA views can be added and modified and then are placed in categories to set the data an individual PWA user has access to. To change the fields and formatting of a view in PWA, the user must have Manage Views permission. Often, this permission is given to portfolio managers, the PMO, and the administrator, so that they can create new reporting views for the organization. Most organizations move their particular Enterprise Outline Codes into the view to create meaningful reports based on their project or resource information.

▶ **SEE** "Creating Project Web Access Project and Resource Views," **PAGE 209**.

To access the page where you can manipulate views, under the Admin tab select Manage Views. The Specify Views page displays, as shown in Figure 19.12.

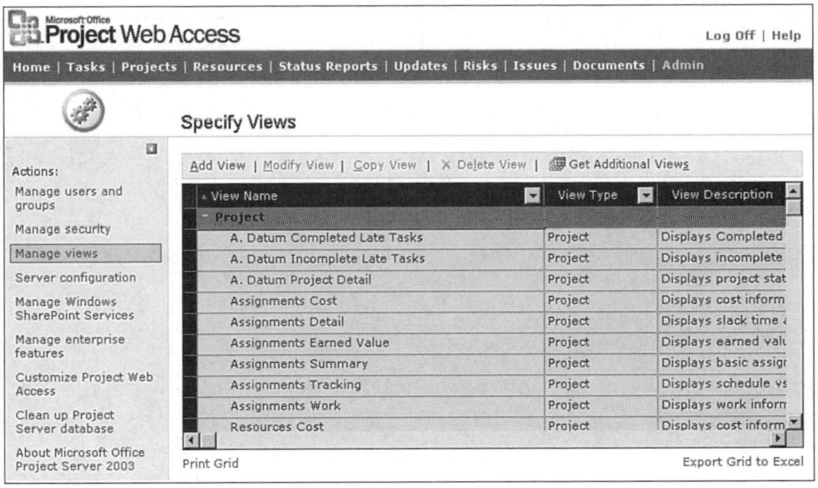

FIGURE 19.12   The Specify Views page.

A list of the default detailed views appears under the specific group heading of Project, Project Center, Resource Center, Assignment, Portfolio Analyzer, and Timesheet. The following describes where you see the views in PWA:

- **Project views**—The views listed under the Project grouping are detailed views you see when you click on a project hyperlink in Project Center. When you click the hyperlink, the View a Project page displays, and you can select a detailed Project view in the Choose a View drop-down list. Nineteen default Project views are available.

> **TIP**
>
> So many Project views are available that the sheer number of selections may be confusing for first-time users. You might want to consider removing some of the Project views for users and leaving only the most-used views.

- **Project Center**—The views listed under the Project Center grouping are summary views of projects you will see when you select a view in the Choose a View drop-down list. Five default Project Center views are available. Most organizations create some custom views so that they can see specific status reports to help management understand program or portfolio status.

- **Assignment**—The view listed under the Assignment grouping is the view you see when you click on View Resource Assignments in the side pane on the Resource Center screen. The default view is similar to the Timesheet view and helps project or resource managers view actual time entered by team members.

- **Resource Center**—The view listed under the Resource Center grouping is a summary view of resources. One default view lists everyone in the Enterprise Resource Pool, if the user has been given permission to view all resources. Many organizations create many more views for their resource management reporting.

- **Portfolio Analyzer**—There are no default views for the Portfolio Analyzer. The views you create for this group display when you select Analyze Projects in Portfolio Analyzer in the side pane of the Project Center page, or when you select Analyze Resources in the Resource Center in the side pane of the Resource Center.

  ▶ **SEE** "Portfolio Management Using Portfolio Analyzer and Portfolio Modeler," **PAGE 393**.

- **Timesheet**—This view can only be modified. You can add new fields to the Timesheet view, which can include a field that a team member can use to perform data entry (for example, to include an account code). However, the project manager also has to physically publish the project itself with the additional field to add new fields to the view.

Adding a Project View

When you want to add a Project view, which provides the detail for a particular project, perform the following steps. (You can use the same instructions to understand the fields you need to change for modifying a view.)

1. From the Specify Views page shown in Figure 19.12, click Add View from the top menu to create a new view, as shown in Figure 19.13.

2. Under View Type, select Project.

3. Under View Name and Description, type the name of the view and a description in the text boxes provided.

4. Under Table, select the type of information you want displayed in the view. Each view type provides a different set of fields to use. You can multiselect fields by pressing the Shift or Ctrl key when selecting fields.

5. In the Available Fields list, select the fields that you want included in the view and then click Add to add them to the Displayed Fields list.

NOTE

The fields can be ordered by selecting the field in the Displayed Fields list and using the Up or Down buttons.

By default, all fields are added to the Displayed Fields list as Automatically Fit This Field to Width. You can specify a width for a field by selecting the Field Width option and entering a width.

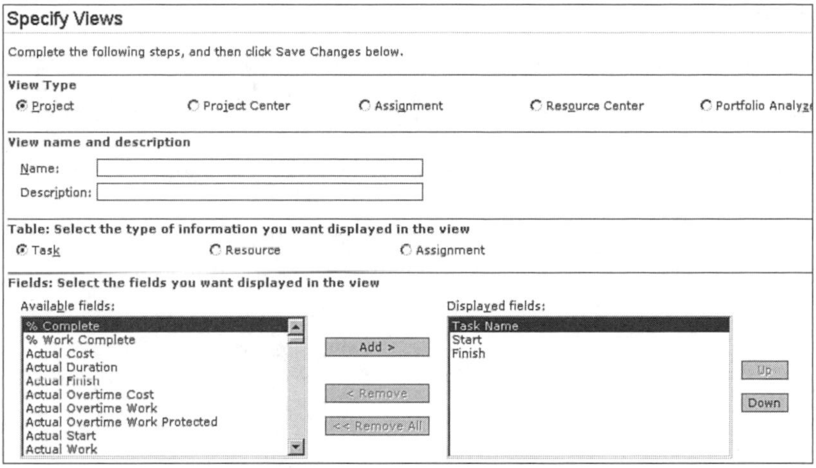

FIGURE 19.13   The Specify Views page (Add Project view).

6. Specify the offset (from 1 to 1,000 pixels) of the splitter bar in the view. Enter the number of pixels from the left of the view display that you want the Gantt chart splitter bar to be displayed. Project views using the resource table do not display a Gantt chart, and the splitter bar offset and Gantt chart format options are not available.

7. Specify the Gantt chart format by selecting from the provided drop-down list. To properly render the Gantt chart, all required fields must be in the Displayed Fields list. For example, the tracking Gantt format requires Baseline Start, Baseline Finish, Actual Start, and Actual Finish.

8. Specify the grouping format by selecting from the provided drop-down list. Views can be grouped and sorted by only those fields displayed in the view.

9. Under the Default Group, Sort heading, specify the grouping for the view and sort order.

10. Specify the outline levels to show in the view by selecting all levels or level 1 to 10.

11. Filter the data displayed in the view by entering the field, operator, and value in the Filters table. You can use the percent character (%) to represent a string of multiple characters, or the underscore character (_) to represent any single character when the operator is set to equals or not equal to.

> **NOTE**
>
> Filtering a view presents the data that meets the conditions of the filter. All data elements in the table are available to filter the view. A user cannot remove the filter in the PWA interface.

12. Specify the categories you want the view to apply to. The view will be listed in the Available Views list on the PWA pages.

13. Click Save Changes.

Adding a Project Center View

When you want to add a Project Center view, which provides the summary information about projects, perform the following steps. (You can use the same instructions to understand the fields you need to change for modifying a view.)

1. From the Specify Views page shown in Figure 19.12, click Add View from the top menu to create a new view.

2. Under View Type, select Project Center, as shown in Figure 19.14.

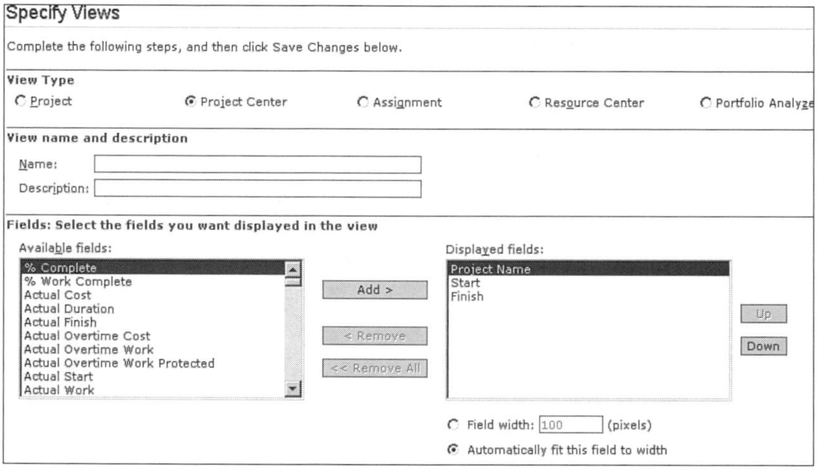

FIGURE 19.14   The Specify Views page (Add Project Center view).

3. Under View Name and Description, type the name of the view and a description in the text boxes provided. Project Center views contain summary task data only. You can multiselect fields by pressing the Shift or Ctrl key when selecting fields.

4. In the Available Fields list, select the fields that you want included in the view and then click Add to add them to the Displayed Fields list.

> **NOTE**
>
> The fields can be ordered by selecting the field in the Displayed Fields list and using the Up or Down buttons.
>
> By default, all fields are added to the Displayed Fields list as Automatically Fit This Field to Width. You can specify a width for a field by selecting the Field Width option and entering a width.

5. Specify the offset (from 1 to 1,000 pixels) of the splitter bar in the view. Enter the number of pixels from the left of the view display that you want the Gantt chart splitter bar to be displayed.

6. Specify the Gantt chart format by selecting from the provided drop-down list. To properly render the Gantt chart, all required fields must be in the Displayed Fields list. For example, the tracking Gantt format requires Baseline Start, Baseline Finish, Actual Start, and Actual Finish.

7. Specify the grouping format by selecting from the provided drop-down list. Views can be grouped and sorted by only those fields displayed in the view.

8. Under Default Group, Sort heading, specify the grouping for the view and sort order.

9. Specify the outline levels to show in the view by selecting all levels or level 1 to 10.

10. Filter the data displayed in the view by entering the field, operator, and value in the Filters table. You can use the percent character (%) to represent a string of multiple characters, or the underscore character (_) to represent any single character when the operator is set to equals or not equal to.

NOTE

Project Center views can be filtered only by Enterprise Project Outline Codes. Filtering a view presents the data meeting the conditions of the filter. A user cannot remove the filter in the PWA interface.

11. Specify the categories you want the view to apply to. The view will be listed in the Available Views list on the Project Center page.

12. Click Save Changes.

Adding an Assignment View

When you want to add an Assignment view, which provides the specific information about the task work a resource is assigned to, perform the following steps. (You can use the same instructions to understand the fields you need to change for modifying a view.)

1. From the Specify Views page shown in Figure 19.12, click Add View from the top menu to create a new view.

2. Under View Type, select Assignment, as shown in Figure 19.15.

3. Under View Name and Description, type the name of the view and a description in the text boxes provided. Assignment views contain resource assignment data and are accessed in the Resource Center by selecting the View Resource Assignments option. You can multiselect fields by pressing the Shift or Ctrl key when selecting fields.

4. In the Available Fields list, select the fields that you want included in the view and then click Add to add them to the Displayed Fields list.

19

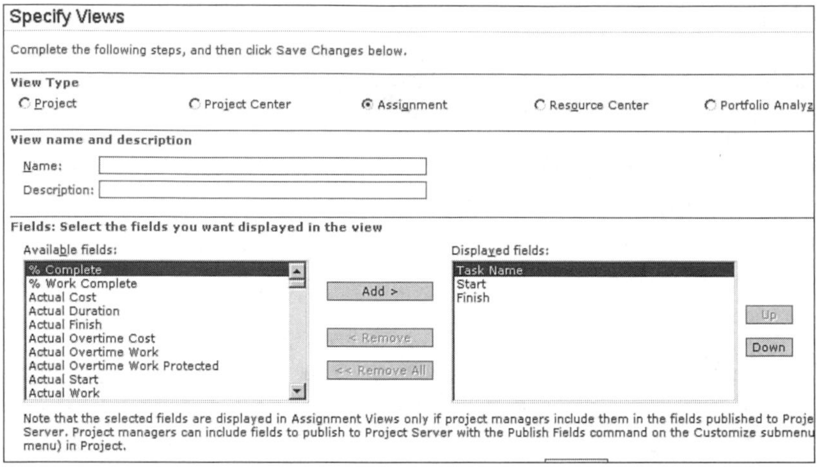

FIGURE 19.15   The Specify Views page (Add Assignment view).

NOTE

The fields can be ordered by selecting the field in the Displayed Fields list and using the Up or Down buttons.

By default, all fields are added to the Displayed Fields list as Automatically Fit This Field to Width. You can specify a width for a field by selecting the Field Width option, and entering a width.

---

5. Specify the offset (from 1 to 1,000 pixels) of the splitter bar in the view. Enter the number of pixels from the left of the view display that you want the Gantt chart splitter bar to be displayed.

6. Specify the Gantt chart format by selecting from the provided drop-down list. To properly render the Gantt chart, all required fields must be in the Displayed Fields list. For example, the tracking Gantt format requires Baseline Start, Baseline Finish, Actual Start, and Actual Finish.

7. Specify the grouping format by selecting from the provided drop-down list. Views can be grouped and sorted by only those fields displayed in the view.

8. Under the Default Group, Sort heading, specify the grouping for the view and sort order.

9. Specify the outline levels to show in the view by selecting all levels or level 1 to 10. Assignment views cannot be filtered when defining the view.

10. Specify the categories you want the view to apply to. The view will be listed in the Available Views list on the View Resource Assignments page.

11. Click Save Changes.

Adding a Resource Center View

When you want to add a Resource Center view, which provides the specific information about a particular resource's attributes (such as skill type), perform the following steps. (You can use the same instructions to understand the fields you need to change for modifying a view.)

1. From the Specify Views page shown in Figure 19.12, click Add View from the top menu to create a new view.

2. Under View Type, select Resource Center, as shown in Figure 19.16.

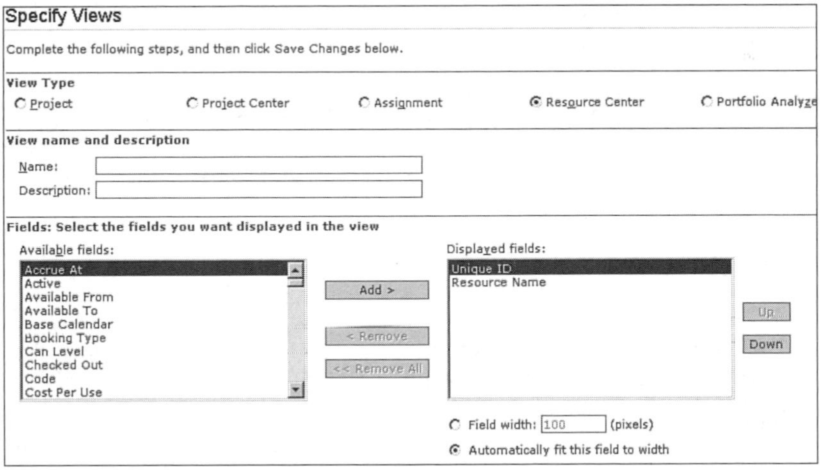

Specify Views

Complete the following steps, and then click Save Changes below.

View Type

○ Project   ○ Project Center   ○ Assignment   ⦿ Resource Center   ○ Portfolio Analyze

View name and description

Name:

Description:

Fields: Select the fields you want displayed in the view

Available fields:

Accrue At
Active
Available From
Available To
Base Calendar
Booking Type
Can Level
Checked Out
Code
Cost Per Use

Add >

< Remove

<< Remove All

Displayed fields:

Unique ID
Resource Name

Up

Down

○ Field width: 100   (pixels)

⦿ Automatically fit this field to width

FIGURE 19.16   The Specify Views page (Add Resource Center view).

3. Under View Name and Description, type the name of the view and a description in the text boxes provided.

> **NOTE**
>
> Resource Center views contain resource data only. No task or assignment data is available. You can multiselect fields by pressing the Shift or Ctrl key when selecting fields.

4. In the Available Fields list, select the fields you want included in the view and then click Add to add them to the Displayed Fields list.

> **NOTE**
>
> The fields can be ordered by selecting the field in the Displayed Fields list and using the Up or Down buttons.
>
> By default, all fields are added to the Displayed Fields list as Automatically Fit This Field to Width. You can specify a width for a field by selecting the Field Width option and entering a width.

5. Specify the grouping format by selecting from the provided drop-down list. Views can be grouped and sorted by only those fields displayed in the view.

6. Under the Default Group, Sort heading, specify the grouping for the view and sort order.

7. Specify the outline levels to show in the view by selecting all levels or level 1 to 10.

8. Filter the data displayed in the view by entering the field, operator, and value in the Filters table. You can use the percent character (%) to represent a string of multiple characters, or the underscore character (_) to represent any single character when the operator is set to equals or not equal to.

> **NOTE**
>
> Resource Center views can be filtered by any resource field. Filtering a view presents the data that meets the conditions of the filter. A user cannot remove the filter in the PWA interface.

9. Specify the categories you want the view to apply to. The view will be listed in the Available Views list on the Project Center page.

10. Specify whether the view should be filtered for each user based on the resource breakdown structure by selecting the RBS Filter check box.

11. Click Save Changes.

Adding a Portfolio Analyzer View

A Portfolio Analyzer view provides a PivotTable or Chart view of information in your Project Server database, often based on the Enterprise Outline Codes you choose to group by. Building a Portfolio Analyzer view is complex. Building a view is thoroughly described in this book in Chapter 17, "Portfolio Management Using Portfolio Analyzer and Portfolio Modeler." The following steps describe the process for building the view, but Chapter 17 provides the complete set of information you need to truly manipulate a Portfolio Analyzer view:

1. From the Specify Views page shown previously in Figure 19.12, click Add View from the top menu to create a new view.

2. Under View Type, select Portfolio Analyzer. The Specify Views screen displays for the Portfolio Analyzer view.

3. Under View Name and Description, type the name of the view and a description in the text boxes provided.

> **NOTE**
>
> A user must be a member of the OLAP Administrators group to create Portfolio Analyzer views.

4. Enter the Analysis Server and Cube Name in the provided text boxes.

5. Select the Portfolio Analyzer Mode by checking the radio button for PivotTable with Chart, PivotTable Only, or Chart Only. To display the field list, right-click in the view area and select the Field List option (see Figure 19.17).

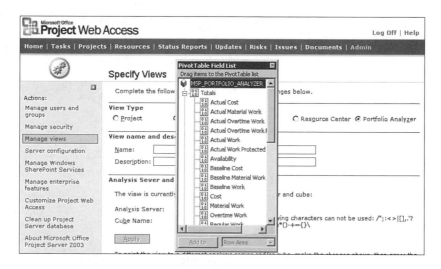

FIGURE 19.17   The Specify Views page (Add Portfolio Analyzer view with PivotTable Field List).

6. Create the view by adding fields to the view.

7. Set the Default View Settings by checking the boxes to Show Field List and/or Show Toolbar.

8. Specify the categories you want the view to apply to.

9. Click Save Changes.

Managing the Timesheet View

The Timesheet view is unique in PWA. You cannot add a new Timesheet view, copy, or delete it. You can only modify the Timesheet view. When you modify it by adding a new field for the timesheet, to show or allow data entry in the field, the project manager has to Republish the project schedule. The following describes the steps for modifying a Timesheet view:

19

1. By scrolling to the bottom of the views listed on the Specify Views page shown previously in Figure 19.12, select Timesheet. Only the Modify View function is available.

2. Click Modify View, and the Modify Timesheet View page for the Timesheet displays as shown in Figure 19.18.

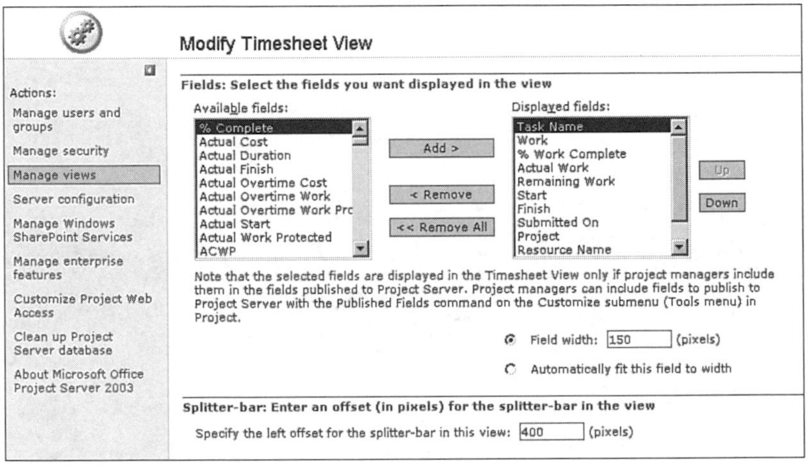

FIGURE 19.18   The Modify Timesheet View page.

3. In the Available Fields list, select the fields that you want included in the view and then click Add to add them to the Displayed Fields list. If you want to remove a field, highlight the field in Displayed Fields and click Remove.

NOTE

The fields can be ordered by selecting the field in the Displayed Fields list and using the Up or Down buttons.

By default, all fields are added to the Displayed Fields list as Automatically Fit This Field to Width. You can specify a width for a field by selecting the Field Width option and entering a width.

---

4. Specify the offset (from 1 to 1,000 pixels) of the splitter bar in the view. Enter the number of pixels from the left of the view display that you want the Gantt chart splitter bar to be displayed.

5. Click Save Changes when you are finished.

Although any fields added appear in the Timesheet view on the Tasks page, project managers must perform some steps in their project schedule for data to be displayed or entered into the field. In Project Professional, project managers need to perform the following steps:

1. Select Tools, Customize, Published Fields.

2. The Customize Published Fields dialog box appears. Select the field from the Available Fields list and click the right arrow to move it to the Fields in the Task View area.

3. Make sure that the Assignment radio button is selected. If the field should allow data entry, check the Let Resource Change field.

4. Click OK.

5. Select Collaborate, Publish, Republish Assignments.

Copying, Deleting, and Modifying a View

The procedure for copying, deleting, and modifying views is the same for each of the views groups described previously. The following procedures can be applied to each view.

Modifying a View

You can modify any view to change the fields or viewing interface as described in the preceding sections on adding views. To use the Modify View function, perform the following steps:

1. From the Specify Views page shown previously in Figure 19.12, highlight the specific view you want to modify.

2. Click Modify View from the top menu. The Specify Views page for the view you chose appears, and you can make changes as needed.

3. Click Save Changes when finished with the changes.

Copying a View

Think of the Copy View function as a way to add a new view without having to start from scratch. You may have an existing view that is similar to a view you want to create, so do the following:

1. From the Specify Views page shown previously in Figure 19.12, highlight the view you want to copy.

2. Click Copy View from the top menu. A dialog box similar to the one shown in Figure 19.19 appears.

3. Enter a new name in the Name field and click OK. The new screen appears in the list for the group view. To change the view, highlight it and select the Modify View function from the Specify Views page.

Deleting a View

You can delete any view to remove it from your list of available views. To use the Delete View function, perform the following steps:

19

1. From the Specify Views page shown previously in Figure 19.12, highlight the view you want to delete.

2. Click Delete View from the top menu. A dialog box appears asking you to confirm whether you want to remove the view.

3. Click OK.

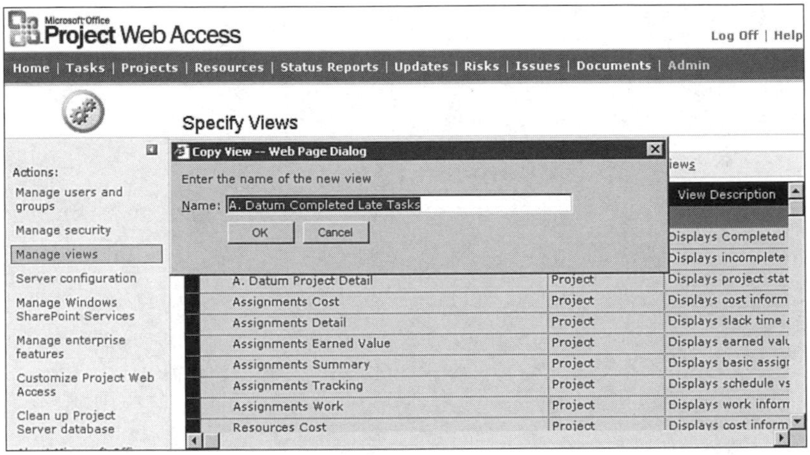

FIGURE 19.19 The Copy View dialog box.

Using the Additional Views Function

You may create some custom views using data access pages, ASP pages, or hypertext markup language. Those views can be used in the Project Server by placing them in the Project Server 2003 root directory called C:\Program Files\Microsoft Office Project Server 2003\IIS Virtual Root\Views. The custom view needs to be placed under the folder named after the particular view group, such as Project, Project Center, Assignment, Resource Center, or Portfolio Analyzer. Then, when you click Get Additional Views on the Specify Views page, the view will be brought into the proper view group to be used in this Project Server.

Using the Server Configuration Function

The Server Configuration function allows you to globally set the enterprise features available to PWA users with the proper permissions, as well as modify the PWA menu system. The server configuration should be initially set up during the installation process. Modifications will be required when enabling features initially disabled or when removing features from the EPM system. The PWA menu system can be modified or enhanced at any time.

Setting Enterprise Features

Project Server can operate in two modes: Enable Enterprise Features or Enable Only Non-Enterprise Features. If you select non-enterprise features, your users will not be able to use enterprise templates, the Enterprise Global template, or the Enterprise Resource Pool, and several functions in PWA will not be available, such as the Resource Center.

To modify the mode and associated features, follow these steps:

1. Under the Admin tab, select Server Configuration. Under Configuration Options in the side pane, select Features.

2. Set the mode by selecting the appropriate radio button. The feature set for the mode is presented and allows the administrator to enable or disable features, as shown in Figure 19.20.

3. Enable the features by selecting the check boxes as follows:

   - Check Allow Master Projects to Be Saved to Microsoft Project Server Database if you want to save projects with inserted projects to the Project Server. This creates a project file for the master project, and you can open it easily in Project Professional or PWA.

   - Check Allow Master Projects to Be Published to Microsoft Project Server Database if you want to report on information from the OLAP cube or other reporting functions in Project Server.

> **NOTE**
>
> It is recommended that you do not publish master projects in the enterprise environment. Resource assignments will be counted twice, and the Project Server will have inaccurate data.

   - Check Allow Projects to Use Local Base Calendars if you want project managers to be able to create their own project, resource, and task calendars. If you are using the Enterprise mode and do not allow this selection, the organization would want to select to use enterprise calendars when project managers attach calendars to projects or tasks in Project Professional. However, this means that project managers cannot create or modify calendars for the special circumstances of their projects, nor can they create or modify calendars for resources.

   - Check Enforce Single Currency as Specified in the Enterprise Global Template to ensure that only one monetary currency is used for the rates assigned to resources and other monetary calculations.

   - Check Allow Only Enterprise Projects to Be Published to This Server if you want projects to be validated against the enterprise settings in your Project Server. If you do not use this, projects can be saved to the Project Server that would have non-enterprise information in them.

19

4. Enable Active Directory synchronization by entering the Active Directory Enterprise Resource Pool group name and setting the frequency that Active Directory should be run. This adds resources to the Enterprise Resource Pool or removes them based on the Active Directory group. This function can be performed manually by selecting the Update Now button.

> **NOTE**
>
> Review "Synchronizing the Enterprise Resource Pool with Active Directory" in the *Microsoft Project Server 2003 Administrator's Guide* for more information about Active Directory synchronization.

> **NOTE**
>
> A user can select Update Now only when she is logged on locally to the computer running Project Server and has permission to read from Active Directory.

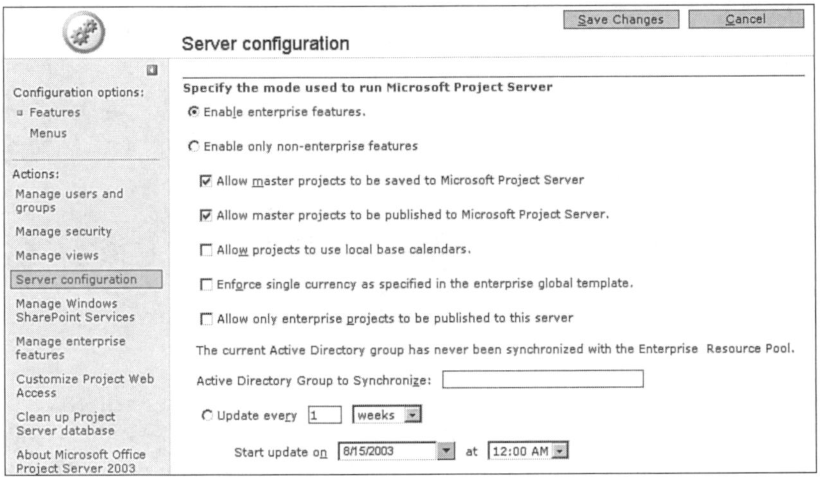

FIGURE 19.20 Server Configuration—enterprise features.

You can also modify the overall features available to all users of Project Server. To modify the available features, do the following:

1. Navigate to the PWA feature table, as shown in Figure 19.21.

2. Enable a feature by selecting the Allow check box; disable a feature by selecting the Deny check box.

> **NOTE**
>
> All PWA features should be set to either Allow or Deny at the server configuration level. Enabling a feature makes it available to PWA users with the proper permissions; selecting Deny for a permission makes it unavailable to all users regardless of group permissions.

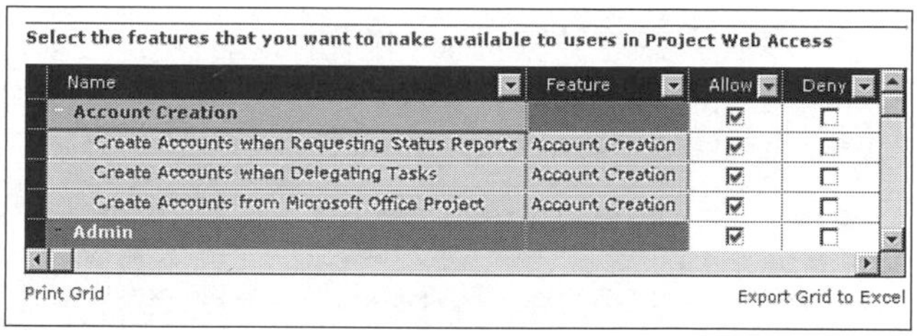

FIGURE 19.21   Select the features that you want to make available to users in Project Web Access.

▶ **SEE** "Server Configuration—Features," **PAGE 144**.

You also set the server address that will be displayed in Project Server email notifications and reminders. The intranet address must be consistent with the WSS site configuration. To set the intranet/extranet address in notifications, follow these steps:

1. Navigate to the bottom of the Server Configuration page, as shown in Figure 19.22.

2. Enter the URL for the intranet/extranet in the text boxes provided.

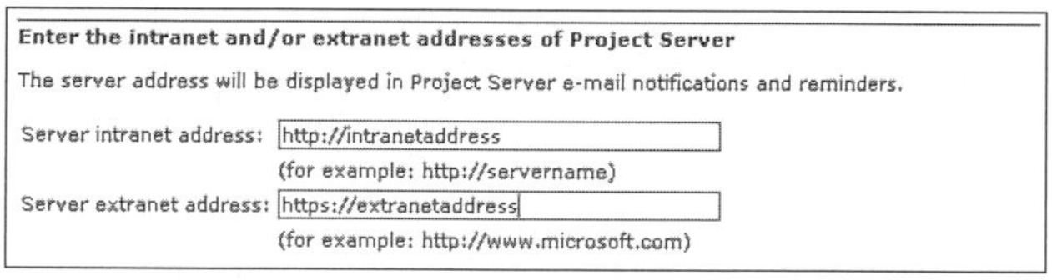

FIGURE 19.22   Intranet/extranet address.

Defining PWA Menus

You can add a new page to PWA and change the default information on the side panes for each of the screens in PWA. You might want to add a new menu called Change Management, for example. If you wanted to change an item on a side pane (called a *submenu* on this page), you may do so. For example, on the home page, you might want to change the name of the default selection called Change Password to say Change Project Server Password, and add a ToolTip that says "Use this only if you have Project Server authentication, not Windows Authentication" when you hover over the selection. You can also create new selections in the side pane and add a URL to take users to that page. To change or define the menus displayed in the PWA client, perform the following steps:

> **NOTE**
>
> Default submenus in PWA are associated with the security permission of the user. Moving a submenu does not prevent it from being displayed.

1. Under the Admin tab, select Server Configuration.

2. Under Configuration Options in the side pane, select Menus. The menus page appears, as shown in Figure 19.23.

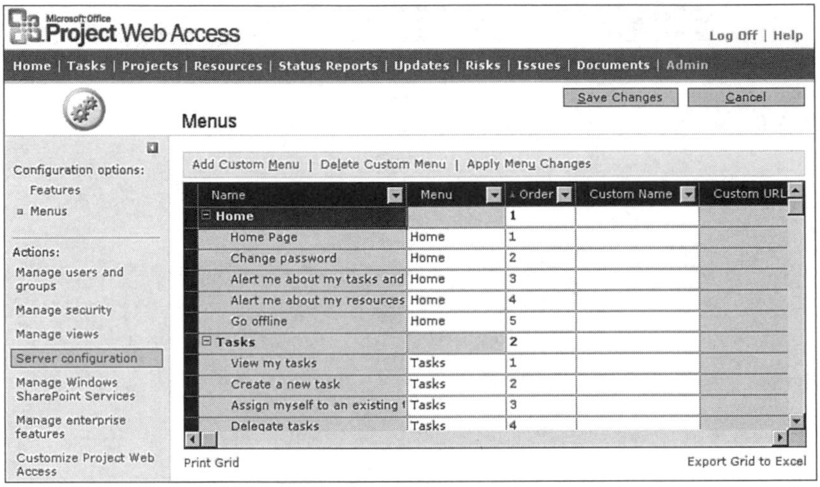

FIGURE 19.23   The Menus page allows you to add, delete, and apply menu changes.

Adding a Top-Level Menu

If you want to add a new page, such as Change Management, you can do so by adding a top-level menu. This creates a new tab on the menu bar at the top of PWA and also creates a new page formatted similarly to the other pages in PWA (such as the Resource Center page). The new tab will not be present until you create submenus for it. To add a new menu tab and page perform the following steps:

> **NOTE**
>
> Both top-level menus and submenus are not available until you log off PWA and then log back on.

1. Select Menus under Configuration Options in the side pane and click Add Custom Menu. The Add Custom Menu dialog box displays, as shown in Figure 19.24.

2. In the Add Custom Menu dialog box, select the Add a Top Level Menu radio button.

3. Add the title for the menu and ToolTip.

4. Click OK to save the menu. The menu name is added at the bottom of the menu list.

5. Select the top-level menu from the menu list and click Add Custom Menu.

6. In the Add Custom Menu dialog box, select the Add a Submenu radio button, as shown in Figure 19.25.

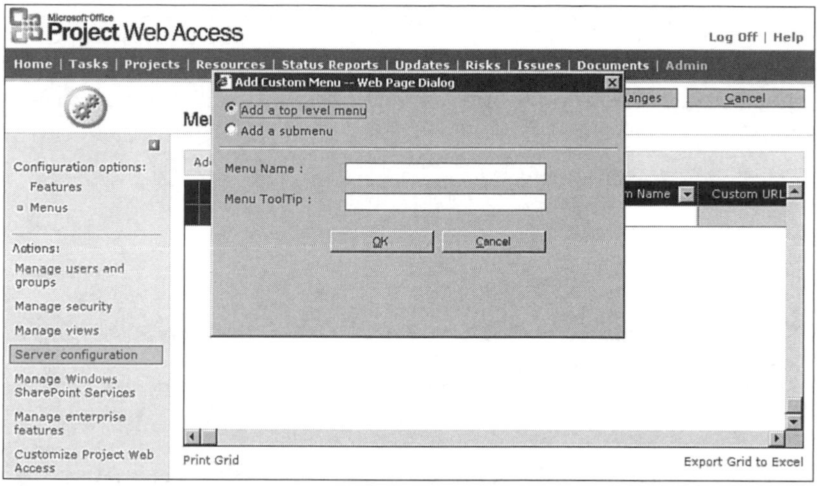

FIGURE 19.24   Adding a top-level custom menu.

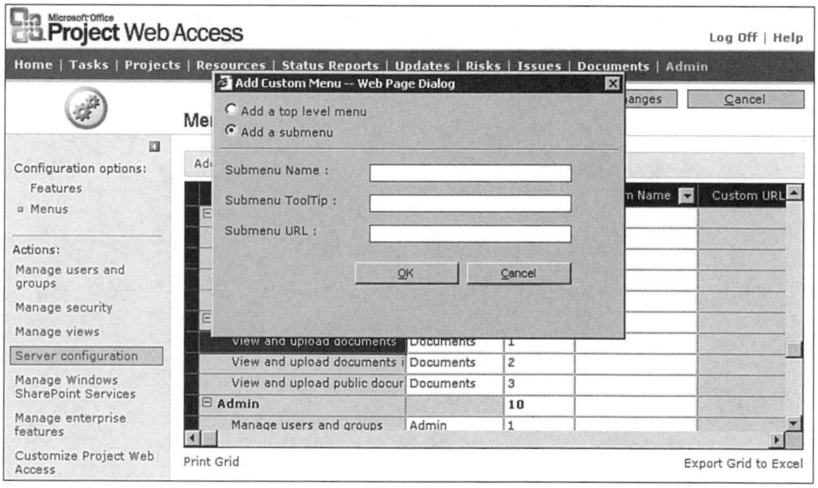

FIGURE 19.25   Adding a custom submenu to an existing top-level menu.

7. Add the title for the submenu, ToolTip, and URL.

8. Click OK to save the submenu.

If you need to modify top-level menus or submenus, perform the following steps:

1. To move a submenu to a different top-level menu, in the Menu column, select the name of the menu to which you want to move the submenu.

2. To change the order of menus in the top-level navigation or to change the order of submenu items within a top-level menu, type new numbers in the Order column.

3. To change the label of a top-level menu or submenu, type the name in the Custom Name column.

4. To create or change a ToolTip for any item, type ToolTip text in the Custom ToolTip column.

5. Click Apply Changes to update the entries on the Menus page.

6. Click Save Changes.

NOTE

You must log off PWA and then log back on to apply the menu changes.

Using the Manage Windows SharePoint Services (WSS) Function

The Manage Windows SharePoint Services function allows you to specify the server running Windows SharePoint Services, change the settings used for provisioning SharePoint team websites, manage SharePoint sites, synchronize users, and identify a portal server.

Connecting to Windows SharePoint Server

Use this function to connect Project Server to the server running WSS. To connect to a Windows SharePoint Server, follow these steps:

1. Select Manage Windows SharePoint Services under the Admin tab.

2. In the side pane under Options, select Connect to SharePoint Server. The Connect to SharePoint Server page displays, as shown in Figure 19.26.

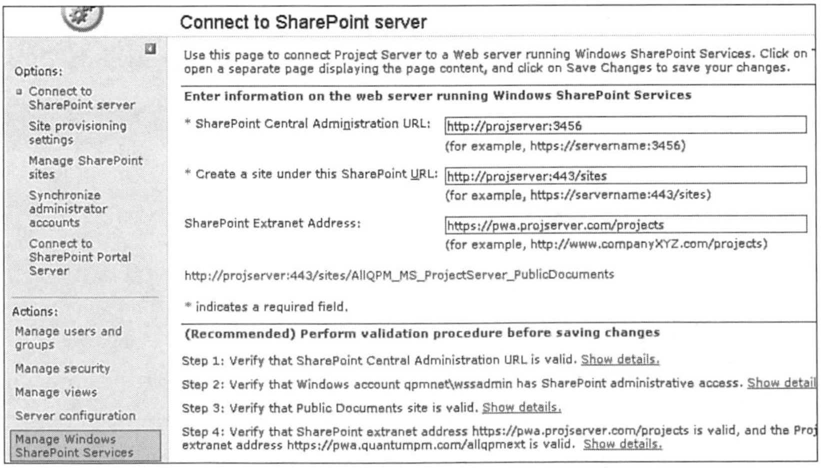

FIGURE 19.26   The Connect to SharePoint Server page.

3. Under Enter Information on the Web Server Running Windows SharePoint Services, in the SharePoint Central Administration URL box, type the Uniform Resource Locator (URL) for the SharePoint Central Administration page. You may want to click on the Test URL hyperlink to make sure that you typed a valid URL.

4. In the Create a Site Under This SharePoint URL box, type the SharePoint Managed Path URL for the server running Windows SharePoint Services that will host the site collections for projects.

> **NOTE**
>
> The SharePoint Managed Path is the URL for the server running Windows SharePoint Services with /sites appended to it. The extranet address is also a SharePoint Managed Path URL.

5. Type the extranet address for the server running Windows SharePoint Services in the SharePoint Extranet Address box, if desired.

6. You may review the validation procedures before saving the changes. Click Save Changes.

Setting Site Provisioning

Use this feature to set how Project Server should provision websites associated with projects. This sets up the website URL for the project workspace and associated risks, issues, and documents. To modify Windows SharePoint Services team website provisioning settings, follow these steps:

1. Select Manage Windows SharePoint Services under the Admin tab.

2. In the side pane under Options, select Site Provisioning Settings. The Windows SharePoint Services Team Web Site Provisioning Settings page displays, as shown in Figure 19.27.

3. Enter the following Root Web Site Settings:

> **NOTE**
>
> The site owner and email are defined during setup.

- Set the site template language from the drop-down list.
- Set the site template for Project Server Team sites from the drop-down list.
- Enter the secondary site owner and email if desired.

4. Set the provisioning method by selecting either the Automatically Create a Team Web Site for the Project When a Project Is Published to Project Server or the Manually Create a Team Web Site for Each Project in Project Server radio button.

19

FIGURE 19.27   The Windows SharePoint Services Team Web Site Provisioning Settings page.

> **NOTE**
>
> The SharePoint sites have their own user list used to set permissions on the site. Project Server can automatically add users to the sites based on the user permissions and role in the project schedule.

5. Set Grant User Access to the Project Team Web Sites to automatically add users to the public documents site and team sites based on permissions in Project Server.

6. Click Save Changes.

Managing SharePoint Sites

The Manage Windows SharePoint Services Sites option can be used to verify that a WSS site has been provisioned for a project, provision a new site for a project, delete a site, and synchronize user access to a team site. You can also navigate to the site administration page on the web server running Windows SharePoint Services. To manage SharePoint Services sites, do the following:

1. Under the Admin tab, select Manage Windows SharePoint Services.

2. Under Options in the side pane, select Manage SharePoint Sites. The Manage Windows SharePoint Services Sites page displays, as shown in Figure 19.28.

> **NOTE**
>
> The site grid contains a list of all published projects. Other versions of the project do not create WSS sites.

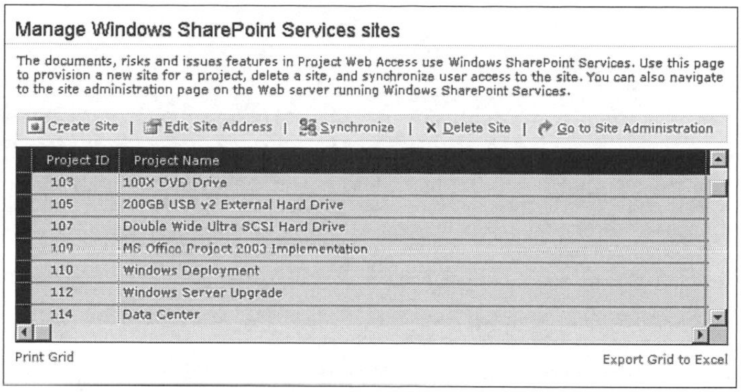

Manage Windows SharePoint Services sites

The documents, risks and issues features in Project Web Access use Windows SharePoint Services. Use this page to provision a new site for a project, delete a site, and synchronize user access to the site. You can also navigate to the site administration page on the Web server running Windows SharePoint Services.

| Create Site | Edit Site Address | Synchronize | X Delete Site | Go to Site Administration |

Project ID	Project Name
103	100X DVD Drive
105	200GB USB v2 External Hard Drive
107	Double Wide Ultra SCSI Hard Drive
109	MS Office Project 2003 Implementation
110	Windows Deployment
112	Windows Server Upgrade
114	Data Center

Print Grid   Export Grid to Excel

FIGURE 19.28   The Manage Windows SharePoint Services Sites page.

Creating a Project Site

Use the Create Site function if manual provisioning is selected to create sites as required. Perform the following steps, to create a project site:

> **NOTE**
>
> If automatic provisioning is selected, all projects will have sites established unless for some reason the system could not create a site (for example, the network goes down while the project manager is creating a project). If the site is not provisioned, select the Create Site option to create the site for the project.

1. Highlight the project from the list of projects displayed in the grid.

2. Select Create Site from the menu. This creates a WSS site for the project and adds users to the site based on permission in Project Server.

Editing a Site Address

If you need to move a site to another website, use this feature. To edit a site address, do the following:

1. Highlight the project from the list of projects displayed in the grid.

2. Select Edit Site Address from the menu.

3. Enter the new URL in the Edit Site Address dialog box.

4. Click OK.

> **NOTE**
>
> To change a site address, the new site must be created with the Project Workspace template prior to editing the address.

19

▶ **SEE** "WSS Project Workspace Customization," **PAGE 732**.

Synchronizing Site Users

Project WSS site users are automatically updated when the project is published if the setting is selected in the provisioning options. An administrator may need to use this function to synchronize sites if the Project Server user permissions change and would affect the WSS security groups.

▶ **SEE** "Risks, Issues, and Documents Using Windows SharePoint Services," **PAGE 441**.

Follow these steps to synchronize users:

1. Highlight the project from the list of projects displayed in the grid.

2. Select Synchronize from the menu.

> **NOTE**
>
> When you use the Synchronize option, users will be added to the appropriate site group based on the permissions and role in the project schedule. Any custom changes to a user's site permissions will be lost. Modified site group permissions will not be lost during synchronization.

3. Click OK.

Deleting a WSS Site

At times, you may need to delete a WSS site. For example, you may want to delete the WSS site attached to that project if you delete the project from the Project Server database. Perform the following steps to delete a project site:

> **NOTE**
>
> Deleting a site permanently deletes all content contained in the site.

1. Highlight the project from the list of projects displayed in the grid.

2. Select Delete Site from the menu.

3. Click Yes in the verification dialog box to delete the site.

Using the Manage Enterprise Features Function

The Manage Enterprise Features function allows you to run the build process for the Online Analytical Processing (OLAP) cube, update resource availability information, check in projects and resources, and add or delete project versions. In some cases, you may want to allow more than just administrators to run some of these functions, other than updating the OLAP cube. For example, you might want to allow resource managers to be able to check in resources who have been checked out of the Enterprise Resource Pool. However, you will want to guard the permissions for running of the OLAP cube and updating of the resource tables: These functions can significantly slow down the Project Server if they are run during the day, especially as your Project Server database gets larger. The following sections describe each of the functions available.

The Update Resource Tables and OLAP Cube

Under the Update Resource Tables and OLAP Cube feature, there are two particular functions you can perform:

- Updating the OLAP cube, which brings in the latest resource and project information from the Project Server database to Portfolio Analyzer views you have created. The Portfolio Analyzer views show static data based on this update process.

- Updating resource availability, which updates the availability information in View Availability in the Resource Center of PWA and other reporting locations in Project Server.

The two functions may be run separately. For example, you may want to show availability information for resources frequently, but the static view from the OLAP cube may need to be run only once a week.

> **TIP**
>
> Set up and follow written standards to indicate when you will update the Portfolio Analyzer views and the resource availability for your organization.

Figures 19.29 and 19.30 show you the sections of the Update Resource Tables and OLAP Cube screen where you update the OLAP cube and resource availability.

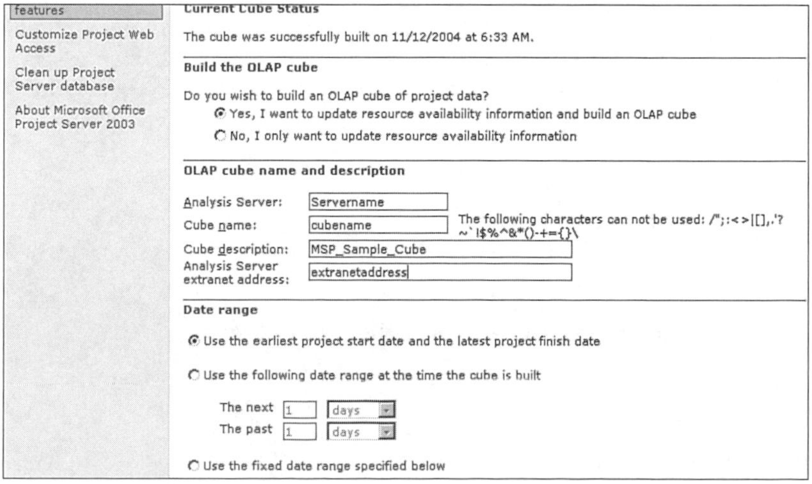

FIGURE 19.29   Updating the OLAP cube.

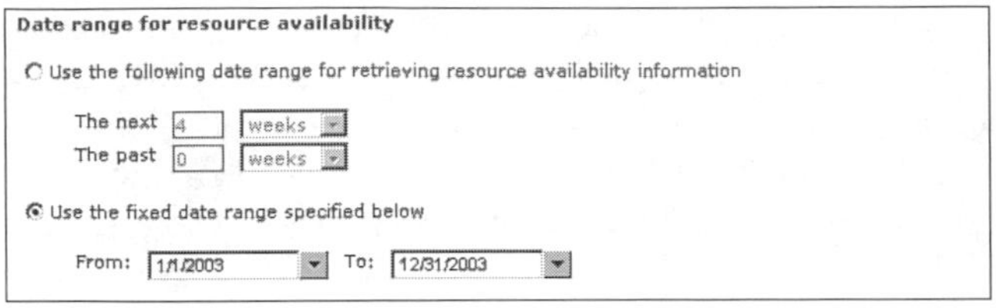

FIGURE 19.30   Section to update resource availability.

First, it's important to understand how the OLAP cube works. The OLAP cube is created by an additional service called Analysis Services, which is part of SQL Server 2000. Data displays in the Portfolio Analyzer views, only after tables in Analysis Services are updated from the Project Server database. These tables are updated only from project information being published into the Project Server database and the OLAP cube function being run (by clicking Update Now or by scheduled updates being set on this Update Resource Tables and OLAP Cube screen). It's also important to understand that the data being published to the Analysis Services tables may be limited by your entering a date range for the data. If you have a lot of data, it is probably a good idea to limit the date range for the data that can be shown in Portfolio Analyzer.

> **NOTE**
>
> Some organizations do not understand the importance of the Publish function in Project Server. Project managers must use the Collaborate, Publish function in Project Professional to include project information in Portfolio Analyzer views. Saving a project is not enough.

> **NOTE**
>
> You must set up the Analysis Services correctly and set permissions for users and groups on the Analysis Services server for everyone needing access to Portfolio Analyzer. Many organizations forget this part of the process after they have run the OLAP cube. If users have not been given permission on Analysis Services or if it has not been installed correctly, users will see a message saying that they do not have permission for the Portfolio Analyzer view after they select it on the Resource Center or Project Center pages.

Building the OLAP Cube

You must build the OLAP cube to update the data for a Portfolio Analyzer view. To build an OLAP cube, follow these steps:

1. Select Manage Enterprise Features under the Admin tab.

2. Select Update Resource Tables and OLAP Cube under Enterprise Options in the upper-left side pane.

3. Click on the radio button for Yes, I Want to Update Resource Availability Information and Build an OLAP Cube under the Build the OLAP Cube section.

4. Complete the information for the Analysis Server and the cube you are building under OLAP Cube Name and Description as follows:

- **Analysis Server**—Enter the name of the server running Analysis Services.

- **Cube Name**—Enter a name to describe the cube. This can be any name you want to help you identify the cube. You can have more than one cube, so you will want to make this distinctive.

> **NOTE**
>
> When you are updating a cube to get more current information, make sure that the correct cube name is in this field. You may have more than one cube, and you could accidentally update the data for the wrong cube.

- **Cube Description**—Enter a more detailed description of the purpose of the cube.

- **Analysis Server Extranet Address**—Enter the Analysis Services server's extranet address. This is optional; use this only if Portfolio Analyzer may be accessed from an extranet.

5. Enter the date range for the projects that will be in the cube in the Date Range field. You have three options for entering the date range:

- **Use the Earliest Project Start Date and Latest Project Finish Date**—Builds a cube for all projects within Project Server. This may be useful when you first start using Project Server, but if you start having large and numerous projects over time, you might want to consider one of the other options to limit the processing time for building the cube.

- **Use the Following Date Range at the Time the Cube Is Built**—Enter the number of days (or weeks or months) before and after today's date to indicate the date range for the projects in the cube. Selecting this option and setting a date range that provides your organization the best forward and backward project visibility is the recommended approach.

- **Use the Fixed Date Range Specified Below**—Enter the exact date range in the From and To fields to indicate the dates of the project data you want to be reflected in the cube.

6. Enter the date range for reflecting resource availability in the Date Range for Resource Availability field:

> **NOTE**
>
> If you enter a date range for building the cube and you enter a date range for resource availability that is smaller than the cube's date range, the cube's date range will be used for resource availability.

19

- **Use the Following Date Range for Retrieving Resource Availability Information**—Enter the number of days (or weeks or months) before and after today's date to indicate the date range for the resource availability to be reflected in the cube.

- **Use the Fixed Date Range Specified Below**—Enter the exact date range in the From and To fields to indicate the availability data to be reflected in the cube.

7. Set how often you want the OLAP cube to be updated. You can set a date/time when you want to have the cube updated automatically, or you can update the cube manually. You have two options:

   - Enter the number of days, weeks, or months in the Update Every fields, and enter the date and time the first build should occur in the Start Update On field.

   - Click the radio button for Update Only When Specified, and click Update Now if you want to manually update the cube. You might use this when you first start using Project Server, but eventually you will want to set a scheduled date and time.

8. Click Save Changes.

You can also just update resource availability without building the OLAP cube for all the other information in the Project Server databases, and thus it will take less time to run. To do so, you go through the same process described previously, but under the Build the OLAP Cube section, select the radio button for No, I Only Want to Update Resource Availability and make sure that you set the date range as described previously.

> **TIP**
>
> Consider how often you need the data for resource availability and Portfolio Analyzer views to be updated. You might want to run the cube once a week during hours the system is not used much. Make sure that you document when and why you update the cube when you do.

Check In Enterprise Projects

This function allows an administrator to force a check-in of a project to the Project Server database. The project reverts to the last version saved to the database, and any changes since that save will be lost. This may be required if the client or server goes down, such as during a network outage, when the project is checked out.

> **TIP**
>
> Make sure that you educate the project managers so that they can check in their own projects in the Project Center using the Check in My Projects feature.

▶ **SEE** "Using Project and Resource Centers," **PAGE 345**.

To check in a project, follow these steps:

1. Select Manage Enterprise features under the Admin tab.

2. In the side pane under Enterprise Options, select Check in Enterprise Projects. The Check in Enterprise Projects page displays, which consists of a grid listing projects currently checked out.

3. Select the project (or projects) that you want to check in, and then click Check-In.

Check In Enterprise Resources

This function allows an administrator to force a check-in of a resource to the Project Server database. The resource data reverts to the last version saved to the database, and any changes to a checked-out resource will be lost. This may be required if the client or server goes down when the resource is checked out.

To check in a resource, follow these steps:

1. Select Manage Enterprise Features under the Admin tab.

2. In the side pane under Enterprise Options, select Check in Enterprise Resources. The Check in Enterprise Resources page displays, which consists of a grid listing resources currently checked out.

3. Select the resource (or resources) that you want to check in, and then click Check-In.

Using Versions

A *version* is a complete copy of a project that is saved to the Project Server database. Versions can be created for a project only if a published version is in the Project Server database. Versions are best used to create snapshots of project data over time and to evaluate schedule options for a particular project.

Follow these steps to add a custom version:

1. Under the Admin tab, select Manage Enterprise Features.

2. In the side pane under Enterprise Options, select Versions. The Versions page appears, which consists of a grid listing the available versions, as shown in Figure 19.31.

3. Select Add Version from the top menu. This displays the Add Version page to name the version, set the archive option, and set the Gantt Bar name to indicate the bar format you want, as shown in Figure 19.32.

4. Enter a name for the version.

5. Select Yes or No in the Version Archived drop-down list.

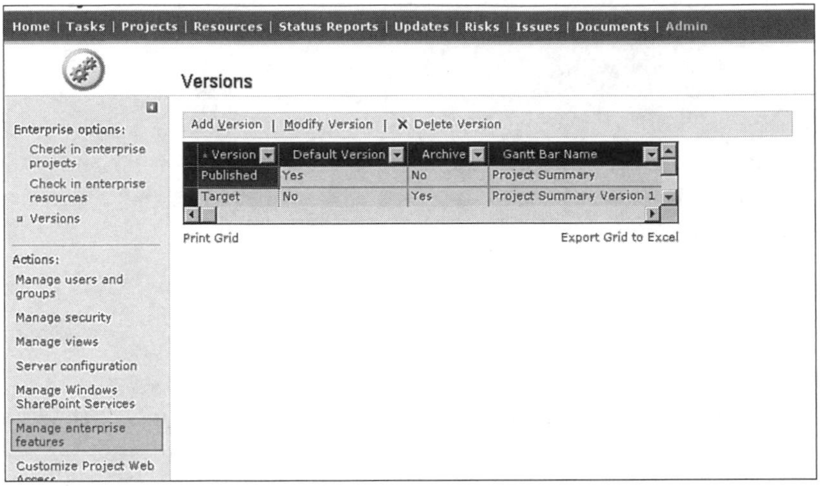

FIGURE 19.31   The Versions page.

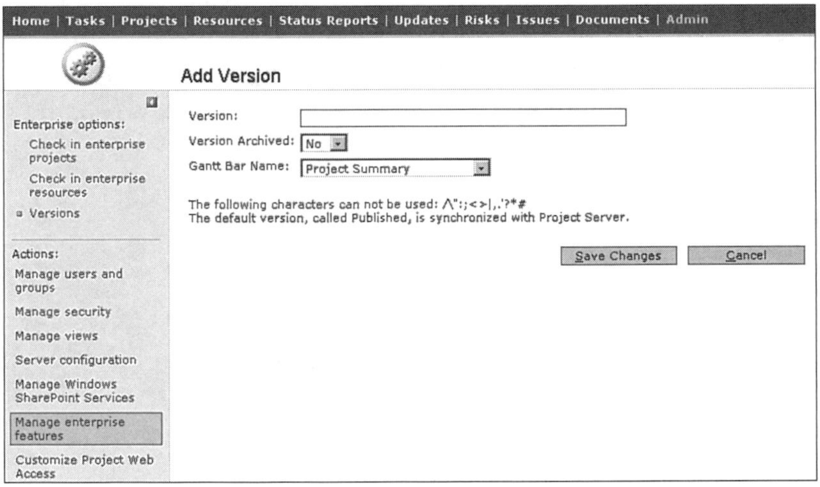

FIGURE 19.32   The Add Version page.

> **NOTE**
>
> If you set the version as an archived version, a project saved as that version shows the resource assignments as they existed at the point the project was saved to the version. The next time this version of the project is opened, the project will not show the current assignments of the resources. If you save the project as a nonarchived version, the summary resource assignments will be updated to reflect current resource allocations.

6. Select a Gantt Bar Name from the list. The Gantt Bar Name displays a particular Gantt Bar format when the project version is displayed in the Project Center.

> **NOTE**
>
> Predefined Gantt Bar formats are available for five versions. The published version uses the Project Summary format. Gantt Bar formats are described further in "Using the Customize Project Web Access Function" later in this chapter.

7. Click Save Changes.

Follow these steps to modify a version:

1. Under the Admin tab, select Manage Enterprise Features.

2. In the side pane under Enterprise Options, select Versions. The versions page displays, which consists of a grid listing the available versions.

3. Highlight the version to modify and select Modify Version from the top menu. This displays the Modify Version page to change the name of the version, set the archive option, and select the name for the Gantt Bar format.

> **NOTE**
>
> You cannot change the name of the version if a published project is also saved to the version.

4. Enter a new name for the version.

5. Select Yes or No in the Version Archived drop-down list.

6. Select a Gantt Bar Name from the list.

7. Click Save Changes.

To delete a version, do the following:

1. Under the Admin tab, select Manage Enterprise Features.

2. In the side pane under Enterprise Options, select Versions. The Versions page displays, which consists of a grid listing the available versions.

3. Highlight the version to delete and select Delete Version from the top menu.

> **NOTE**
>
> You cannot delete a version if a published project is also saved to the version. Use Cleanup Project Server database to delete the projects saved to the version prior to taking this action.

4. Click OK to remove the version from the database.

Using the Customize Project Web Access Function

The Customize Project Web Access function allows you to change the look and capabilities of several screens within PWA. The first function, Tracking Settings, is one of the most important functions you will set when you configure PWA. You will want to use the last function, Notifications and Reminders, to set your email server. You may leave the other functions with their defaults with no issues.

The Tracking Settings Function

The Tracking Settings functions allows you to set how you want people to track time on the Tasks page. You also have a choice between setting up Managed and Non-Managed Time Periods as well.

▶ **SEE** "Time Tracking in Project Web Access," **PAGE 317**.

▶ **SEE** "Time Period Settings," **PAGE 253**.

Gantt Chart Formats

The Gantt Chart Formats function allows you to change the color, style, and other characteristics of the Gantt charts you see in PWA, as shown in Figure 19.33. Use this if your organization is used to seeing the chart information differently from the default.

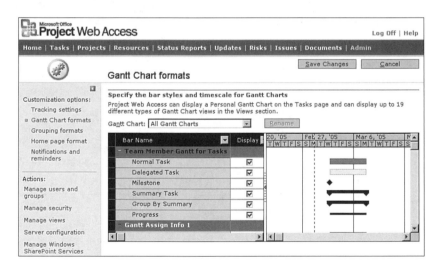

FIGURE 19.33 The Gantt Chart Formats page.

To rename the Gantt chart, follow these steps:

1. Under the Admin tab, select Customize Project Web Access.

2. In the Customization Options section in the upper-left pane, select Gantt Chart Formats. The Gantt Chart Formats page displays, as shown previously in Figure 19.33.

3. Click on the arrow next to the Gantt Chart field. A drop-down box appears. Select the Gantt chart you want to rename. Only the Gantt chart selections for that particular Gantt chart appear.

4. Click Rename. The field name changes to New Name for Gantt Chart, and you can type the new name in the field, as shown in Figure 19.34. Click on the green check mark now showing next to the field to accept the change.

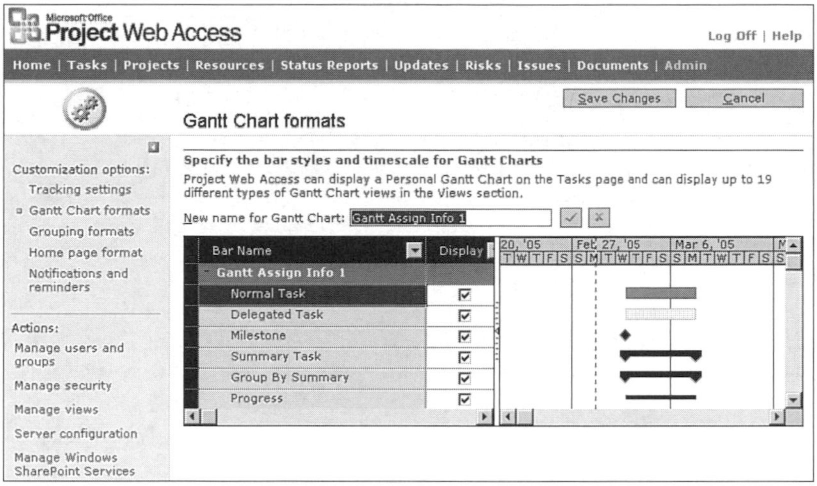

FIGURE 19.34   Renaming the Gantt chart.

To change the bar styles, perform the following steps:

1. Select Customize Project Web Access.

2. In the Customization Options section in the upper-left side pane, select Gantt Chart Formats. The Gantt Chart Formats page displays, as shown previously in Figure 19.33.

3. Select the Gantt chart bar or symbol you want to change. Choose from the selections in the columns that display to make changes for each Gantt chart bar or symbol. Note that to see all these format capabilities, you will need to scroll on the right side of the grid.

4. Click Save Changes to keep the changes.

Grouping Formats

The Grouping Formats function allows you to change the color and pattern of the bars that separate groups in various views in PWA. For example, in Figure 19.35, you see the groupings in the Project Center for the first group of Strategic Alignment, second group of Project ROI, and third group of Project Exposure.

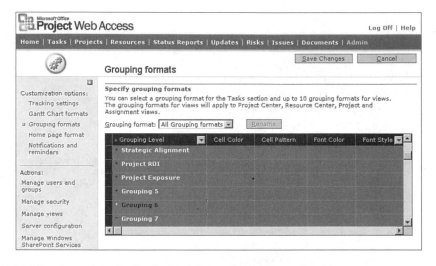

FIGURE 19.35   Groupings in the Project Center in the Grouping formats page.

You can change the color, pattern, and other characteristics of the grouping row via the Grouping Formats. Also, you can create a custom grouping format for a view using this feature.

To rename a grouping, follow these steps:

1. Under the Admin tab, select Customize Project Web Access.

2. In the Customization Options section in the upper-left side pane, select Grouping Formats. The Grouping Formats page displays, as shown in Figure 19.36.

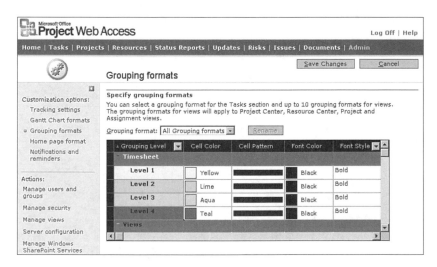

FIGURE 19.36   The Grouping Formats page.

3. Click on the arrow next to the Grouping Format field. A drop-down box appears from which you can select the Grouping format you want to rename.

4. Click Rename. The field name changes to New Name for Grouping Format, and you can type the new name in the field. Click on the green check mark that is now showing next to the field to accept the change.

Changing Grouping Colors and Patterns

To change the grouping colors and patterns, perform the following steps:

1. Select Customize Project Web Access.

2. In the Customization Options section in the upper-left side pane, select Grouping Formats.

3. The Grouping Formats page displays as shown previously in Figure 19.36. Select the grouping level/sublevel you want to change by selecting the Grouping Level row. Choose from the following kinds of changes you can make for each grouping level:

   • Click on the color in the Cell Color column for the grouping level to see a drop-down list, and select the group level cell color you prefer. In some cases, the color you have chosen may not allow you to select a color other than black.

   • Click on the pattern in the Cell Pattern column for the grouping level to see a drop-down list, and select the cell pattern you prefer.

   • Click on the color in the Font Color column for the grouping level to see a drop-down list, and select the font color you prefer.

   • Click on the font style in the Font Style column for the grouping level to see a drop-down list, and select the font style you prefer.

4. Click Save Changes to keep the changes.

The grouping levels are handy for special situations for setting views for easier readability. For example, you might change the Grouping 1 format name to RBS Levels. Then, when you set up a special Resource Breakdown Structure (RBS) view for the Resource Center using the Manage Views selection under the Admin tab, you can set that special grouping for RBS views. On the special view you create, you would select the special grouping you selected to display on the view, as shown in Figure 19.37.

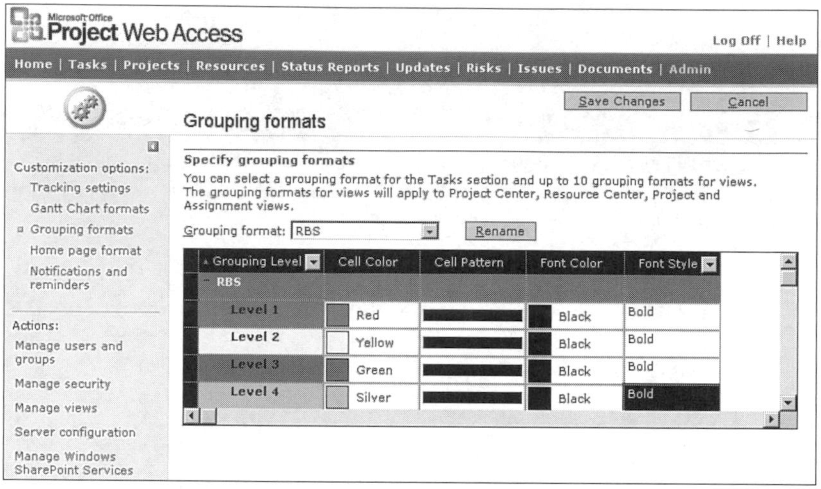

FIGURE 19.37   Creating a special grouping for a view.

The Home Page Format Function

The Home Page Format function allows you to add links and content to the PWA home page. Many organizations use this function to add a link to their PMO home page, special templates, or other areas they want PWA users to access.

Adding a Link to the PWA Home Page

To add a link to the PWA home page, follow these steps:

1. Under the Admin tab, select Customize Project Web Access.

2. In the Customization Options section in the upper-left side pane, select Home Page Format. The Home Page Format page displays, as shown in Figure 19.38.

3. Enter a descriptive name in the Link Name field.

4. Enter a URL for the link in the URL field.

5. If you want to add another link, click Insert Row.

6. If you want to delete a link, click Delete Row.

7. Click Save Changes at the bottom of the page when you are finished. The link appears at the bottom of the home page under the section called Links.

To add content to the PWA home page, do the following:

1. Under the Admin tab, select Customize Project Web Access.

2. In the Customization Options section in the upper-left side pane, select Home Page Format. The Home Page Format page displays, as shown previously in Figure 19.38.

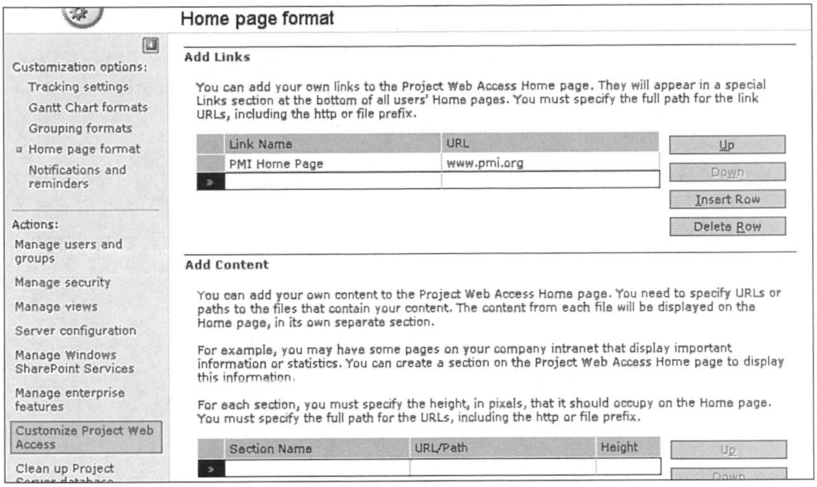

FIGURE 19.38   The Home Page Format page.

3. Enter a descriptive name in the Section Name field. For instance, if this included a dashboard of operations spending, you might name this Operations Spending by Department.

4. Enter a URL for the link of the content in the URL/Path field.

5. If you want to add another link for more content, click Insert Row.

6. If you want to delete a link, click Delete Row.

7. Click Save Changes at the bottom of the page when you are finished.

The content appears at the bottom of the home page under the section name you gave the content.

> **NOTE**
>
> If you have many different sections on the home page (including Tasks, Risks, and Issues), the home page users will not see the additional links or content when they first see the screen. Users will need to scroll down, so consider design and usability if you decide to use these features.

Notification and Reminders

The Notification and Reminders function allows you to set the email servers that will manage the email notifications sent out by Project Server. Regular email notifications may be sent out to team members once a day to remind them of tasks due or in progress. Also, emails are sent out according to reminders set by task members and project managers.

▶ **SEE** "Managing Alerts," **PAGE 305**.

Some organizations have chosen to not use emails by leaving the SMTP Mail Server field blank. If you do leave the email set up, make sure that your organization provides training so that team members understand how to manage email reminders.

Follow these steps to set up the email:

1. Under the Admin tab, select Customize Project Web Access.

2. In the Customization Options section in the upper-left side pane, select Notifications and Reminders. The Notifications and Reminders page displays, as shown in Figure 19.39.

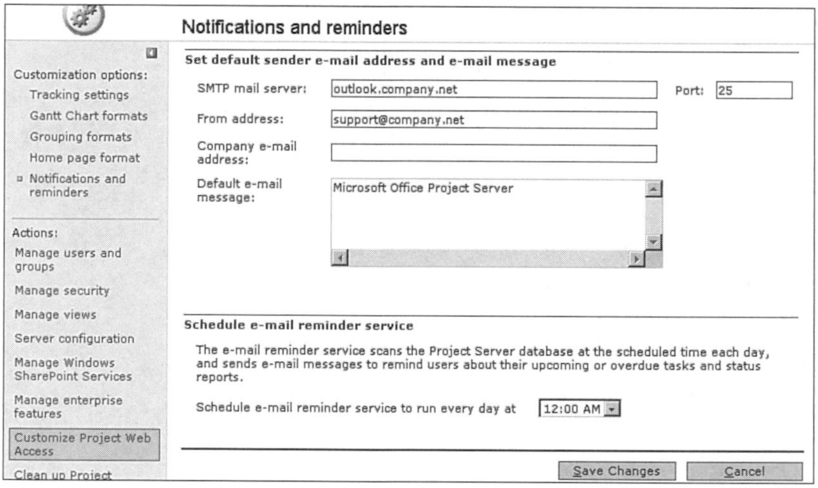

FIGURE 19.39   The Notifications and Reminders page.

3. Under the Set Default Sender Email Address and Email Message section, enter the SMTP mail server in the SMTP Mail Server Field. Also, verify the port number in the Port field.

4. Enter the return messages email server address in the From Address field.

5. Enter the company email host and domain information for your company email (such as "company.com") in the Company Email Address field. If you do not specify a full email address when adding a user to Project Server, this feature adds the host and domain information to the user name or ID to complete the user's email address.

6. Enter a message in the Default Email Message field. Enter a message explaining that the notifications sent out are from the Project Server and cannot be replied to. Some organizations enter a message similar to the following: "Do not reply to this message. The following information provides status information for you from Microsoft Office Project Server. Contact your project manager if you have any questions."

7. Under the Schedule Email Reminder Service section, enter the time when the scheduled email reminders will be sent out to team members. Most organizations leave the default at 12:00 a.m. To change the time, click on a different value in the drop-down list.

8. Click Save Changes when you are finished.

Using the Clean Up the Project Server Database Function

Occasionally, it may be necessary to create more space in the Microsoft Office Project Server 2003 database or to remove redundant or old information from users' Project Web Access views. Task assignments, task updates, projects, to-do lists, resources, and status reports can be removed on time-based or specific resource-based criteria. To perform database cleanup, use the Clean Up Project Server Database administration function.

Deleting Task Assignment Data

Perform the following steps to delete task assignment data:

NOTE

Assignment data is permanently deleted from the MSP_Web_Tables. This operation does not delete the tasks from the MS Project schedule in Project Professional.

---

1. Under the Admin tab, select Clean Up Project Server Database. The Clean Up Project Server Database page displays, as shown in Figure 19.40.

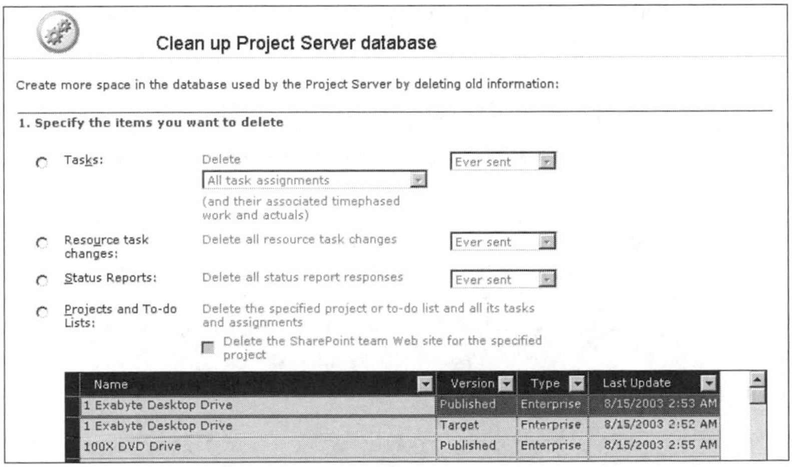

FIGURE 19.40   The Clean Up Project Server Database page.

2. Select the Tasks radio button under the Specify Items You Want to Delete section.

3. Select All Task Assignments or Only Completed Task Assignments from the Delete drop-down list.

4. Set the time frame criteria for task assignments to delete by choosing Ever Sent, Older Than, or Sent Between from the list.

> **NOTE**
>
> If Older Than or Sent Between is selected, additional date criteria can be entered.

5. Select the option to delete the task assignments for all users or a specific user under the heading If Necessary, Specify the Users Whose Items Should Be Deleted.

6. Click Delete to permanently delete the assignments from the MSP_Web_tables.

To delete resource task changes, follow these steps:

> **NOTE**
>
> Resource task changes are entries in the Updates page. Project Server retains a complete history of all changes submitted.

1. Under the Admin tab, select Clean Up Project Server Database. The Clean Up Project Server Database page displays, as shown previously in Figure 19.40.

2. Select the Resource Task Changes radio button under the Specify Items You Want to Delete section.

3. Set the time frame criteria for resource task changes to delete by choosing Ever Sent, Older Than, or Sent Between from the list.

> **NOTE**
>
> If Older Than or Sent Between is selected, additional date criteria can be entered.

4. Select to delete the resource task changes for all users or a specific user under the heading If Necessary, Specify the Users Whose Items Should Be Deleted.

5. Click Delete to permanently delete the resource task changes.

To delete status reports, do the following:

1. Under the Admin tab, select Clean Up Project Server Database. The Clean Up Project Server Database page displays, as shown previously in Figure 19.40.

2. Select the Status Reports radio button under the Specify Items You Want to Delete section.

3. Set the time frame criteria for status reports to delete by choosing Ever Sent, Older Than, or Sent Between from the list.

> **NOTE**
>
> If Older Than or Sent Between is selected, additional date criteria can be entered.

4. Select to delete the status reports for all users or a specific user under the heading If Necessary, Specify the Users Whose Items Should Be Deleted.

5. Click Delete to permanently delete the status reports from the database.

Projects and to-do lists may be deleted if they are no longer valid or need to be saved (prior to deleting) and archived from the Project Server database. Perform the following steps to delete projects and to-do lists:

> **NOTE**
>
> Projects or to-do lists will be permanently deleted from the database along with the associated assignments in PWA for all team members.

1. Under the Admin tab, select Clean Up Project Server Database. The Clean Up Project Server Database page displays, as shown previously in Figure 19.40.

2. Select the Projects and To-Do lists radio button under the Specify Items You Want to Delete section.

3. Select the project or to-do list from the grid.

> **NOTE**
>
> To permanently delete the SharePoint team website for the specified project, check the box.

4. Click Delete to permanently delete the project or to-do list.

Resources may be deleted if they should no longer be available in the Enterprise Resource Pool for assignment. Resources are not deleted from the database. They are set to be inactive to prevent access, and no future assignments can be made. Any associated historical information, such as timesheet entries (actuals), status reports, and so on, remains in the database, and the resources are removed from the Enterprise Resource Pool. To delete a resource, follow these steps:

1. Under the Admin tab, select Clean Up Project Server Database. The Clean Up Project Server Database page displays, as shown previously in Figure 19.40.

2. Select the Resource radio button below the project grid under the Specify Items You Want to Delete section.

3. Select the resource from the drop-down list.

19

> **NOTE**
>
> A deletion comment can be entered in the text box provided. The default comment is "Deleted M/D/YYYY."

4. Type a comment in the Deletion Comment text box.

5. Click Delete.

The About Microsoft Office Project Server 2003 Page

The About Microsoft Office Project Server 2003 page reports the number of Project Server users and Product ID. The number of users is calculated by counting the number of active Project Server user accounts that have permission to log on. This would not include inactive or generic resources.

To access this page, select About Microsoft Office Project Server 2003. The page is display-only and cannot be changed.

Best Practices

Administration of Project Server 2003 is a critical function and requires not only application knowledge but also project management and organizational process knowledge. The following best practices will minimize problems and simplify maintenance of the system:

- Restrict Project Server administration functions to trained users who understand the consequences of their changes.

- Set all the Account Creation features in Server Configuration to Deny.

- Remove unused features from the PWA interface through server configuration/group permissions. For example, if you are not using the Delegate Task feature on the Tasks page, Deny that permission in the Server Configuration permissions area.

- Create resource administration processes to include step-by-step procedures for adding, modifying, and deleting a resource.

- Set the availability from date to date of hire when adding resources to the Enterprise Resource Pool.

- Remove views that your organization will not want to use from all categories.

- Create basic views with custom fields and allow users to modify and save links instead of creating multiple views with the same information. Users can Save Links in the Project Center and Resource Center of PWA.

- Document the baseline configuration and implement strict configuration control processes for the application to ensure changes are well managed and communicated to the users.

- Create a data retention policy and perform database cleanup using these rules.

- Keep it simple and always keep maintainability in mind.

PART VI

Using Microsoft Office Project Professional 2003 Enterprise Features

IN THIS PART

CHAPTER 20   Building Custom Enterprise Configuration   537

CHAPTER 21   Building Project Team and Resource Substitution   563

CHAPTER 22   Project Team Collaboration   589

Building Custom Enterprise Configuration

IN THIS CHAPTER

- Introduction to Microsoft Office Project Professional

- Enterprise Options

- Customizing the Enterprise Global Template

- Best Practices

Enterprise thinking and enterprise-level project management are management of projects, resources, and their interrelationships, at the team, organization, or enterprise level.

Enterprise configuration allows you to manage not just the separate projects on the desktop, which can create duplication and conflict of information, but also complete project enterprise integration and visibility.

Microsoft Project 2003 provides the base repository, collaborative user interface, and great reporting capabilities to support enterprise-level configuration and project management.

Introduction to Microsoft Office Project Professional

The enterprise project concept is common in project management. Microsoft Project 2003 provides solutions for managing and reporting on resources and projects for an entire enterprise. Microsoft Project 2003 has Project Professional and Project Web Access (PWA) as its main user interface components. Microsoft Office Project Professional 2003 provides the capability to create and maintain project schedules both in a standalone mode and in collaboration with your project team through the integration with Microsoft Project Server 2003. PWA is used by team members for collaboration, status and time reporting, modeling, analysis, and so on. Project managers access PWA to accept updates from resources, request or review status reports, and use other collaborative functions of Microsoft Project. Project Professional is used for all main functions of project management and contributes to the enterprise model of Project Server. Microsoft Project 2003 contains the following components that make it an enterprise solution management system:

- Enterprise-level resource management provides a single repository for all resources.

- Enterprise-level portfolio management enables project and resource analysis and modeling across multiple projects.

- Intricate security model provides control over access, viewing, updating, and publishing of enterprise project information.

- Advanced reporting capabilities allow better inner-team communication and status reporting.

- Collaboration and global template capabilities help standardize and streamline communication and enterprise processes for more accurate and consistent data.

The enterprise concept of Project Professional includes the Enterprise Global, Enterprise Resource Pool, Enterprise Global template, Enterprise Outline Codes, Enterprise Custom Fields, and custom objects.

In a standalone mode, Project provides powerful planning and scheduling functionality to define work, organize it, make resource assignments, track progress against baseline estimates, and perform numerous analysis tasks. With the integration to Project Server 2003, all these features are expanded to provide a truly enterprise project management system. Additional functions to collaborate with your project team, establish enterprise standards, and create an Enterprise Resource Pool are also included. Access to project schedules, the save baseline function, and other enterprise controls ensures data integrity and consistency in the system.

Enterprise Options

The Enterprise Options feature is available in Project Professional by selecting Tools, Enterprise Options. Enterprise Options provides access to the enterprise configuration functionality of Project Professional. Enterprise Options is your portal for configuring the enterprise-level options for your Microsoft Project configuration.

Microsoft Office Project Server Accounts

You can now work on project files in three modes: local desktop, connected to a project server instance, and offline with a Project Server schedule.

When Project Professional is installed, a single account is created called My Computer, as shown in Figure 20.1. This account is used to work in the local desktop mode. When using this account, the local Global template is used as the template in all new project files created. The Global template is usually located in the \Program Files\Microsoft Office\Office11\1033 directory.

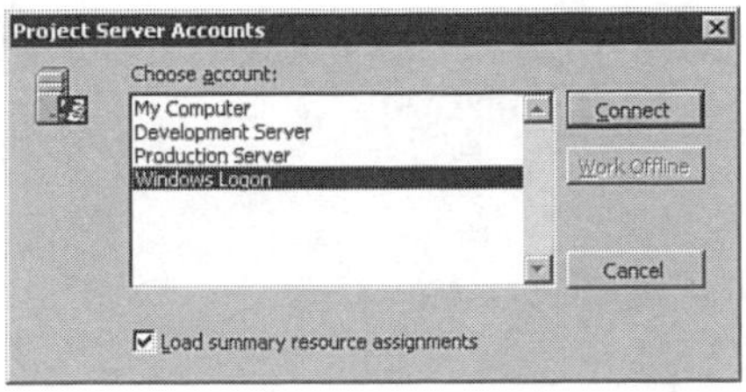

FIGURE 20.1   The Project Server Accounts dialog box allows you to select an account to connect to.

To configure Project Professional to work with a specific Project Server 2003 instance, you must create an account to use the collaborative features of an enterprise installation. To set up an account, follow these steps:

1. From the Start menu select All Programs, Microsoft Office, Microsoft Office Tools, Microsoft Office Project Server Accounts. Or within Project Professional, select Tools, Enterprise Options, Microsoft Office Project Server Accounts from the menu. This displays the available accounts table.

2. Click the Add button, and the Account Properties dialog box appears, as shown in Figure 20.2.

3. Enter a name for the account. This should be a descriptive name to identify the specific Project Server that the account references. For example, use **Production Project Server** or **Development Project Server**.

4. Enter the proper URL to the project server. Click the Test Connection button to confirm that the URL points to a valid Project Server instance. This validates only the URL; it does not validate the account permissions for the specific user.

5. Specify the account as a Windows Account or a Project Server Account. If using a Project Server account, you must also enter the username.

6. Specify the Project Server account that is used when you start Microsoft Office Project 2003 by checking Set As Default Account in the account properties.

7. To save the account information, click OK.

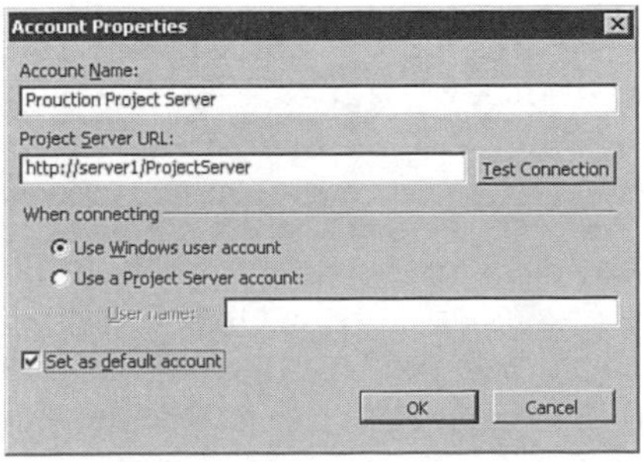

FIGURE 20.2   The Account Properties dialog box allows you to create new Project Server accounts.

NOTE

On creating a Project Server account, the following registry is added:

```
[HKEY_CURRENT_USER\Software\Microsoft\Office\MS Project\Profiles\Project Server]
"Name"="Project Server"
"Path"="http://server1/projectserver"
"AccountType"="0"
"UserName"=""
"Default"="No"
"GUID"="{F5FCAE4C-8FE6-46D2-BA27-A9187ABC2B50}" (This is an example. The GUID will
be unique for each project server account.)
"EntGlobalLastMod"=""
"ServerAllowsMasterProjects"="No"
"ServerAllowsLocalBaseCals"="No"
"ServerProtectsActuals"="No"
"DisableMacros"="No"
"DisableProjInfoGrid"="No"
"DisableSaveAsGrid"="No"
"CachedGlobalCPID"="0"
"LastDBBootCPID"="0"
```

The folder for offline project files is also created using the GUID in the preceding example for
the folder name at C:\Documents and Settings\<User>\Application Data\Microsoft\MS Project.

The new account then appears on the Project Server Accounts dialog box. To set the
starting options for Project, select Automatically Detect Connection State or Manually
Control Connection State. The Automatically Detect Connection State option automatically connects to the default account when you start Project. If the server is available, it
connects to the enterprise Project Server. If the server is unavailable, it starts in the offline
mode for that account.

Manually Control Connection State presents the Project Server Accounts dialog box from
which you can select the name of the account you want to use. This should be used if
you use multiple Project Server accounts, you require the option to load resource
summary data, or you require to work offline in local desktop mode. The specified default
account is highlighted in the manual connection mode as shown in Figure 20.3.

Use the Project Server Accounts dialog box to modify account properties as necessary—for
example, if the project server was moved and a different URL is used, or if you are using
various Project Server accounts to test permissions on group security.

After the accounts are created, you must connect to the specific project server before you
can work offline with that account. On initial connection, the registry is modified to
include additional information of the profile and copy the Enterprise Global template to
C:\Documents and Settings\User\Application Data\Microsoft\MS Project\11\1033 under
the GUID matching the offline folder name.

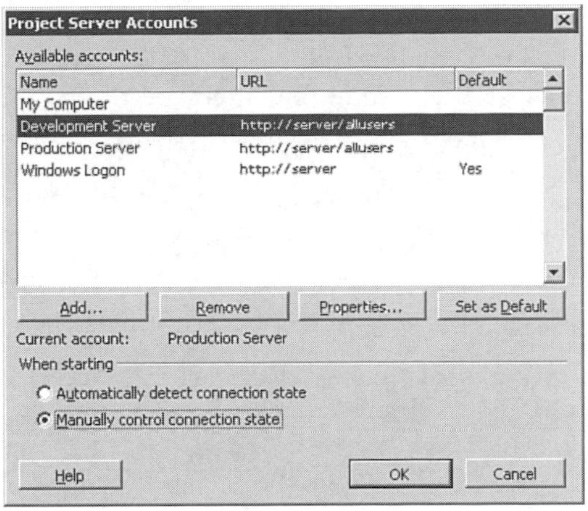

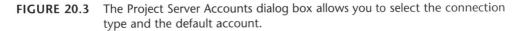

FIGURE 20.3 The Project Server Accounts dialog box allows you to select the connection type and the default account.

Connection to Project Server Accounts

On starting Project Professional, depending on the Control Connection State setting, Project connects to the default account or presents the Project Server Accounts dialog box from which you can select the name of the account you want to use. In the manually controlled connection state, you also have the option to load or not load resource summary data.

Tools Plus Options

Setting the options that control the behavior of Project Professional 2003 in a Project Server 2003 environment requires an understanding of the interaction of the global templates and the specific options. When Project Professional is set up to connect to a Project Server 2003 instance, there are three global template files: Local Global, Non-cached Enterprise Global template, and the Cached Enterprise Global template. Project loads dependent on the connection. Some possible connection scenarios follow:

- **Example 1**—Connected to My Computer account in the offline mode uses the local global file located in the folder C:\Documents and Settings\User\Application Data\Microsoft\MS Project\11\1033.

- **Example 2**—Connected to a Project Server account in the connected state merges the Enterprise Global template stored in the Project Server database with the Local Global template.

- **Example 3**—Connected to a Project Server account in the offline state merges the Local Global template with the Enterprise Global template for that instance stored in the folder C:\Documents and Settings\User\Application Data\Microsoft\MS Project\11\1033 with the filename of the GUID. The cached Enterprise Global template is updated with a newer version when connected to the server and the time stamp differs between the templates. Only the most current Enterprise Global Template is retained on the local machine.

20

The Enterprise Global template does not control the environment options except for setting the currency symbol provided by the Project Server configuration feature by selecting Enforce Single Currency As Specified in the Enterprise Global Template option is elected. The following sections provide details of the environment options and precedence.

The View Tab

The View tab allows you to establish settings regarding the way things appear in Project Professional. Table 20.1 outlines the features available in Options when the View tab is selected, as well as what template those features apply to.

TABLE 20.1   Enterprise Environment Options—View Tab

Environment Options	Project File	Local Global	Enterprise Global	Software Policy #
Default View		X		X
Date Format		X		X
Show				
Status Bar		X		X
Scrollbars		X		X
OLE Links		X		X
Indicators				
Windows in Taskbar		X		X
Entry Bar		X		X
Project ScreenTips		X		X
Cross-project Linking Options for "Project 1"				
Show External Successors		X		
Show External Predecessors		X		
Show Links Between Projects Dialog on Open		X		
Automatically Accept New External Data		X		
Currency Options for "Project 1"				
Symbol			X	
Placement	X			
Decimal Digits	X			
Outline Options for "Project 1"				
Indent Name	X			
Show Outline Number	X			
Show Outline Symbol	X			
Show Summary Tasks	X			
Show Project Summary Task	X			

The General Tab

The General tab in the Options window allows you to control what features of Project Professional appear. For example, you can select the option Open Last File on Startup, which means that the last .mpp file you viewed before closing Project Professional will open automatically the next time you connect to Project Server. Table 20.2 outlines the features available to you when selecting the General tab on the Options window and the template the features apply to.

TABLE 20.2 Enterprise Environment Options—General Tab

Environment Options	Project File	Local Global	Enterprise Global	Software Policy #
General Options for Microsoft Office Project				
Display Help on Startup		X		X
Show Startup Task Pane		X		X
Open Last File on Startup		X		X
Prompt for Project Info for New Projects		X		X
Set AutoFilter on for New Projects		X		X
Recently Used File List		X		X
Planning Wizard				
Advice from Planning Wizard		X		X
Advice About Using Microsoft Office Project		X		X
Advice About Scheduling		X		X
Advice About Errors		X		X
General Options for "Project 1"				
Automatically Add New Resources and Tasks	X	*		*
Default Standard Rate	X	*		*
Default Overtime Rate	X	*		*

X—Software Policy using Project 2003 administrative template

*—Default setting

20

The Edit Tab

The Edit tab in the Options window allows you to control the editing features of Project Professional. For example, you can select the option Edit Directly in Cell, which allows you to edit directly in the cell of the grid (and not have to do it in the top bar). Table 20.3 outlines the features available to you when selecting the Edit tab on the Options window and the template the features apply to.

TABLE 20.3 Enterprise Environment Options—Edit Tab

Environment Options	Project File	Local Global	Enterprise Global	Software Policy #
Edit Options for Microsoft Office Project				
Allow Cell Drag and Drop		X		X
Move Selection After Enter		X		X
Ask to Update Automatic Links		X		X
Edit Directly in Cell X		X		
View Options for Time Units in "Project 1"				
Minutes	X	*		*
Hours	X	*		*
Days	X	*		*
Weeks	X	*		*
Months	X	*		*
Years	X	*		*
Add Space Before Label	X	*		*
Hyperlink appearance in "Project 1"				
Hyperlink Color	X	*		*
Followed Hyperlink Color	X	*		*
Underline Hyperlinks	X	*		*

X—Software Policy using Project 2003 administrative template
*—Default setting

The Calendar Tab

The Calendar tab in the Options window allows you to control what calendar features of Project Professional are used for your project files. For example, under the Calendar tab you can set options such as what day the week starts on, the default start time, and so on. Table 20.4 outlines the features available to you when selecting the Calendar tab on the Options window and the template the features apply to.

TABLE 20.4   Enterprise Environment Options—Calendar Tab

Environment Options	Project File	Local Global	Enterprise Global	Software Policy #
Calendar Options for "Project 1"				
Week Starts On	X	*		*
Fiscal Year Starts In	X	*		*
Use Starting Year for FY Numbering	X	*		*
Default Start Time	X	*		*
Default End Time	X	*		*
Hours Per Day	X	*		*
Hours Per Week	X	*		*
Days Per Month	X	*		*

X—Software Policy using Project 2003 administrative template
*—Default setting

The Schedule Tab

The Schedule tab in the Options window allows you to customize what features of Project Professional are used for scheduling in your project files. For example, you can select the default scheduling unit for resource assignments and whether you want to see a percentage or a decimal number. Table 20.5 outlines the features available to you when selecting the Schedule tab on the Options window and the template the features apply to.

TABLE 20.5   Enterprise Environment Options—Schedule Tab

Environment Options	Project File	Local Global	Enterprise Global	Software Policy #
Schedule Options for Microsoft Office Project				
Show Scheduling Messages		X		X
Show Assignment Units As a Percentage or Decimal		X		X
Scheduling Options for "Project 1"				
New Tasks	X	*		*
Duration Is Entered In	X	*		*
Work Is Entered In	X	*		*
Default Task Type	X	*		*
New Tasks Are Effort Driven	X	*		*

20

TABLE 20.5   Continued

Environment Options	Project File	Local Global	Enterprise Global	Software Policy #
Autolink Inserted or Moved Tasks	X	*		*
Split In-Progress Tasks	X	*		*
Tasks Will Always Honor Their Constraint Dates	X	*		*
Show That Tasks Have Estimated Durations	X	*		*
New Tasks Have Estimated Durations	X	*		*

X—Software Policy using Project 2003 administrative template
*—Default setting

The Calculation Tab

The Calculation tab in the Options window allows you to customize what features of Project Professional are used when performing calculations in your project files. For example, you can select a manual calculation mode that prevents Project Professional from running automatic recalculations while you are working with your project file. This can be particularly useful if you are using the built-in function for leveling resources and don't want to see recalculation after each minor change you make. Table 20.6 outlines the features available to you when selecting the Calculation tab on the Options window and the template the features apply to.

TABLE 20.6   Enterprise Environment Options—Calculation Tab

Environment Options	Project File	Local Global	Enterprise Global	Software Policy #
Calculation Options for Microsoft Office Project				
Calculation Mode		X		X
Calculate		X		X
Calculation Options for "Project 1"				
Updating Task Status Updates Resource Status	X	*		*
Move End of Completed Parts After Status Date Back to Status Date	X	*		*

TABLE 20.6 Continued

Environment Options	Project File	Local Global	Enterprise Global	Software Policy #
And Move Start of Remaining Parts Back to Status Date	X	*		*
Move Start of Remaining Parts Before Status Date Forward to Status Date	X	*		*
And Move End of Completed Parts Forward to Status Date*	X	*		
Edits to Total Task % Complete Will Be Spread to the Status Date	X	*		*
Inserted Projects Are Calculated Like Summary Tasks	X	*		*
Actual Costs Are Always Calculated by Microsoft Office Project	X	*		*
Edits to Total Actual Cost Will Be Spread to the Status Date	X	*		*
Default Fixed Costs Accrual	X	*		*
Calculate Multiple Critical Paths	X	*		*
Tasks Are Critical if Slack Is Less Than or Equal To	X	*		*

X—Software Policy using Project 2003 administrative template
*—Default setting

The Spelling Tab

The Spelling tab in the Options window allows you to customize the Autocorrection and Ignore options for spelling within the project files. Table 20.7 outlines the features and selections available to you when choosing the Spelling tab on the Options window and the template the features apply to.

20

TABLE 20.7   Enterprise Environment Options—Spelling Tab

Environment Options	Project File	Local Global	Enterprise Global	Software Policy #
Ignore Words in UPPERCASE		X		X
Ignore Words with Numbers		X		X
Always Suggest		X		X
Suggest from User Dictionary		X		X

The Collaborate Tab

The Collaborate tab in the Options window allows you to customize features used for collaborating using Project Professional. For example, you can select what assignments, if any, Project Professional should publish when you save a project file. Table 20.8 outlines the features available to you when selecting the Collaborate tab on the Options window and the template the features apply to.

TABLE 20.8   Enterprise Environment Options—Collaborate Tab

Environment Options	Project File	Local Global	Enterprise Global	Software Policy #
Collaboration Options for "Project 1"				
Collaborate Using	X	*		*
Project Server URL	X	*		*
Identification for Project Server				
Windows User Account	X	*		*
Microsoft Office Project User Name	X	*		*
Email Address	X	*		*
Allow Resources to Delegate Tasks Using Project Server	X	*		*
"Publish New and Changed Assignments" Updates Resources' Assignment When				
Start, Finish, % Complete or Outline Changes	X	*		*
Any Task Information Changes	X	*		*
On Every Save, Publish the Following Information to Project Server				
New and Changed Assignments	X	*		*
Project Summary	X	*		*
Including Full Project Plan	X	*		*
X—Software Policy using Project 2003 administrative template				
*—Default setting				

The Save Tab

The Save tab in the Options window allows you to customize the save options available to you in Project Professional. For example, you can select the Auto Save interval so that Project Professional saves your projects every X minutes. Table 20.9 outlines the features available to you when selecting the Save tab on the Options window and the template the features apply to.

TABLE 20.9   Enterprise Environment Options—Save Tab

Enterprise Options	Project File	Local Global	Enterprise Global	Software Policy #
Save Microsoft Office Project		X		X
File Locations		X		X
Auto Save				
Save Every		X		X
Save Active Project Only		X		X
Save All Open Project Files		X		X
Prompt Before Saving		X		X
Database Save Options for "Project 1"				
Expand Timephased Data in the Database		X		X

The Interface Tab

The Interface tab in the Options window allows you to customize the interface options available to you in Project Professional. For example, you can select which of the indicators you want to appear in your project file. Table 20.10 outlines the features available to you when selecting the Interface tab on the Options window and the template the features apply to.

TABLE 20.10   Enterprise Environment Options—Interface Tab

Enterprise Options	Project File	Local Global	Enterprise Global	Software Policy #
Show Indicators and Option Buttons For				
Resource Assignments		X		X
Edits to Start and Finish Dates		X		X
Edits to Work, Units, or Duration		X		X
Deletions in the Name Column		X		X

20

TABLE 20.10 Continued

Enterprise Options	Project File	Local Global	Enterprise Global	Software Policy #
Project Guide Settings				
Display Project Guide		X		X
Project Guide Functionality and Layout Page	X	*		*
Project Guide Content				
Use Microsoft Office Project's Default Content	X	*		*

The Security Tab

The Security tab in the Options window allows you to customize your security setup for Project Professional. For example, you can set the privacy options to remove information such as Author, Company, Last Saved By, and so on, from a newly created project file. Table 20.11 outlines the features available to you when selecting the Security tab on the Options window and the template the features apply to.

TABLE 20.11 Enterprise Environment Options—Security Tab

Enterprise Options	Project File	Local Global	Enterprise Global	Software Policy #
Privacy Options for "Project 1"				
Remove Information from File Properties on Save	X			
Macro Security		X		X

Using the Organizer

The Organizer is a utility provided in Project to copy, rename, or delete objects in project schedules and templates. This allows the user to share objects from one file or template to another file or template. Table 20.12 demonstrates the objects contained in a project file/template.

TABLE 20.12 Project Objects

Objects	Description
Views	Used to display project data for reporting, modifying, and organizing information. There are six types of views in Project: Calendars, Charts, Diagrams, Forms, Sheets, and Usage (time-phased data).
Reports	Used to query specific project information and output to the screen or printer.

TABLE 20.12   Continued

Objects	Description
Modules	Macros using VBA and can be of the type, module, userform, or class module.
Forms	Forms are used to present detailed task or resource data.
Tables	Used to define the data columns from task or resource fields.
Filters	Used to limit or highlight data presented to defined conditions.
Calendars	Used to identify working times for projects, resources, and tasks.
Toolbars	Used to rearrange and modify existing toolbar buttons, menus, and menu commands or to create new ones.
Maps	Used to define the field mapping for import and export to other file types.
Fields	Custom fields defined in the project.
Groups	Used to group resource or task data to create rolled-up totals for the condition specified.

TIP

When creating or modifying an object, maps, toolbars, and macros are saved to the Local Global template. All other objects are saved in the active project file.

To access the Organizer, select Tools, Organizer. The Organizer dialog box appears, as shown in Figure 20.4.

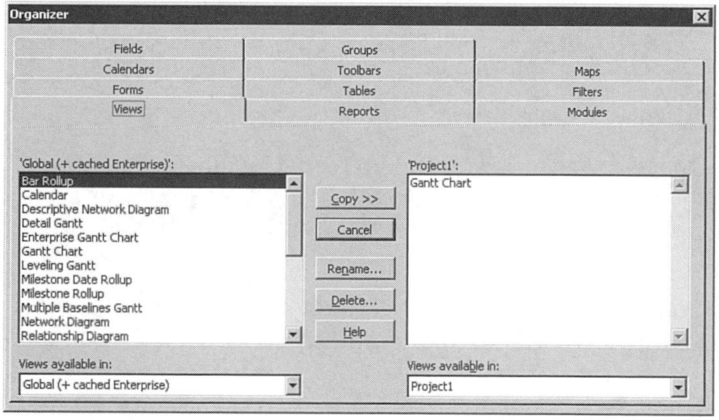

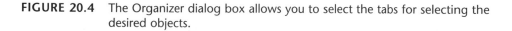

FIGURE 20.4   The Organizer dialog box allows you to select the tabs for selecting the desired objects.

The Organizer dialog box has a tab for each type of object and a radio button to select task or resource objects on appropriate objects. Two windows list the object names based on the file selected in the drop-down list at the bottom of each window. The global template being used and any open project files will be listed. From this interface you can copy, rename, or delete objects.

20

> **TIP**
>
> An object used within a project file becomes a unique object in that file. Any changes to objects or any new objects are stored in the project file object and not the global object. The exceptions are maps, modules, and toolbars.

To copy an object from one file to another, perform the following steps:

1. Open the source file for the object and the target file where you want to copy the object.

2. Select the files from the pick-list at the bottom of each object list. Select the source file for one and the target file for the other.

3. Select the tab that contains the object to copy. Select the radio button for Task or Resource, if applicable.

4. Select (highlight) the object name(s) from the list for the source.

5. Click the Copy button.

To delete or rename an object, perform the following steps:

1. Open the source file for the object you want to delete or rename.

2. Select the file from the pick-list at the bottom of an object list.

3. Select the tab that contains the object to delete or rename. Select the radio button for Task or Resource, if applicable.

4. Select (highlight) the object name(s) from the list.

5. Click the Delete or Rename button. Enter a new name for the object if renaming.

Tools Plus Enterprise Options

Project Professional provides access to enterprise functions to manage Project Server accounts, the Enterprise Global template, and the Enterprise Resource Pool, and to import projects or resources to the enterprise environment. These functions can be located using the Tools, Enterprise Options menu.

Microsoft Project Server Accounts

You access Project Server accounts by selecting Tools, Enterprise Options, Microsoft Project Server Accounts. The Project Servers Accounts dialog box opens, allowing modification of your accounts.

▶ **SEE** "Microsoft Office Project Server Accounts," **PAGE 538**.

Open Enterprise Global Template

The Enterprise Global template is similar to your Local Global template but allows you to create enterprise standards for project schedules. When a user connects to Project Server, the Enterprise Global template is merged with the Local Global template to create the Global (+ noncached Enterprise) template.

To modify the Enterprise Global template select Tools, Enterprise Options, Open Enterprise Global.

> **NOTE**
>
> You must connect with an account that has permission to Save Enterprise Global to modify it.

The Enterprise Global template opens as a Checked-out Enterprise Global and displays as a blank project schedule. When the template is opened, you can create or add custom views, tables, reports, filters, groups, forms, modules, calendars, toolbars, maps, and fields that are then available to all users connected to the Project Server.

> **NOTE**
>
> The Enterprise Global template resides in the Project Server. Each version of the Global template is retained in Project Server to enable version archiving. The most recent template is the active Enterprise Global.

Project must be closed and reopened to access the modifications in the Enterprise Global template.

> **NOTE**
>
> To transfer an item from a project file to the Enterprise Global template, open both files and use the Organizer to copy the item to the template.

Open Enterprise Resource Pool

To modify the Enterprise Resource Pool select Tools, Enterprise Options, Open Enterprise Resource Pool. This presents the Open Resources dialog box as shown in Figure 20.5.

To filter the resources, select an Enterprise Outline Code and select the value. Only defined outline codes can be used. Click the Apply Filter button to filter the list based on the selections.

To include inactive resources, check the Include Inactive Resources box and click Apply Filter.

To select individual resources, select the box next to the resource name. Use Select/Deselect All to include all resources in the list.

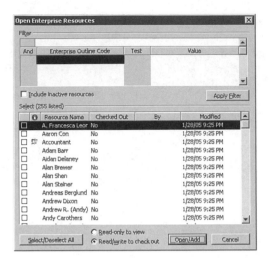

FIGURE 20.5   The Open Enterprise Resources dialog box displays the resources the user has permission to see in the Enterprise Resource Pool.

The Open/Add button opens the Enterprise Resource Pool and presents the selected resources in the Resource Sheet view. Resource attributes can then be modified, or new resources can be added.

Import Project to Enterprise
The Import Project to Enterprise option saves an existing local project file to the Project Server. When executed, the Import Project Wizard is initialized. Resources in the project file are automatically mapped to enterprise resources, provided that the names match. If resources are not matched, they are identified as local resources in the project file. Tasks are then listed, and local task custom fields can be mapped to enterprise task custom fields.

The Import Resources to Enterprise Option
The Import Resources to Enterprise option adds resources from a project file to the Enterprise Resource Pool. The Import Resource Wizard allows mapping of local custom fields to enterprise fields and setting of resource attributes as desired.

The Backup Enterprise Global Template
The Enterprise Global template can be saved as a Microsoft Project template file. To back up the Enterprise Global template, select Tools, Enterprise Options, Backup Enterprise Global. The Save As dialog box opens where you can select the folder and enter a name for the backup.

The Restore Enterprise Global Template
The Enterprise Global template can be restored from an Enterprise Global backup file. To restore an Enterprise Global template, select Tools, Enterprise Options, Restore Enterprise Global. The Restore Enterprise Global dialog box appears as shown in Figure 20.6.

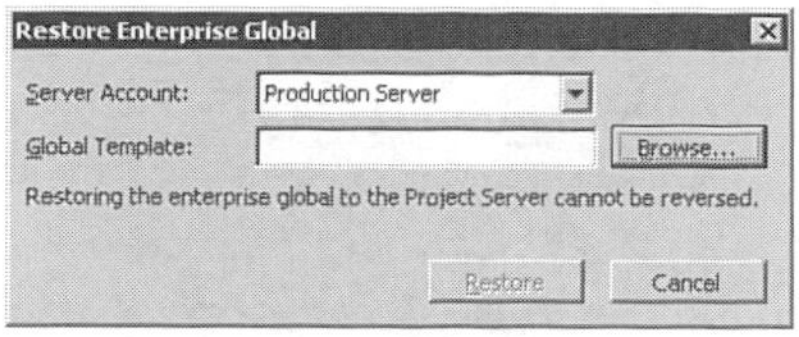

FIGURE 20.6   The Restore Enterprise Global dialog box.

Select the server account where you want to restore the template to. All Project Server accounts identified will be listed in the pull-down list. Select the backup file location and name using the Browse button. Select Restore to load the backup file to the Project Server. The restored global cannot be removed; however, you may restore again.

> **NOTE**
>
> The Work Breakdown Structure (WBS) is a local project file field. Enterprise Global cannot be restored if it contains local fields. Use the Organizer to delete those fields and repeat the restore process.

Customizing the Enterprise Global Template

The Enterprise Global template is a critical part of an enterprise configuration. Enterprise standards, custom objects (Views, Reports, Modules, Forms, Tables, Filters, Calendars, Toolbars, Maps, Fields, and Groups), and the currency symbol are established in the template. These enterprise standards are applied to all projects and can be modified only by an authorized user with Save Enterprise Global permission.

Setting the Currency Symbol

To define the currency symbol in the Enterprise Global template, perform the following steps:

1. Open the Enterprise Global template by selecting Tools, Enterprise Options, Open Enterprise Global.

2. Select Tools, Options and select the View tab.

3. Under the Currency options, enter the currency symbol.

4. Save the Enterprise Global template.

> **NOTE**
>
> The currency symbol is the only environment option that can be set in the Enterprise Global template. All enterprise projects will inherit this setting if enterprise features are enabled and the Enforce Single Currency As Specified in the Enterprise Global Template option is selected on the server configuration in PWA.

20

Customizing Enterprise Fields

Enterprise-level custom fields are similar to Project custom fields but are standard across all projects and have some unique attributes. Enterprise custom fields include task, resource, and project-level custom fields and outline codes. The following sections provide detailed instructions on how to create enterprise custom fields.

To customize enterprise fields you must first open the Enterprise Global template. Within the checked-out Enterprise Global template, select Tools, Customize, Enterprise Fields. The Customize Enterprise Fields dialog box appears presented as shown in Figure 20.7.

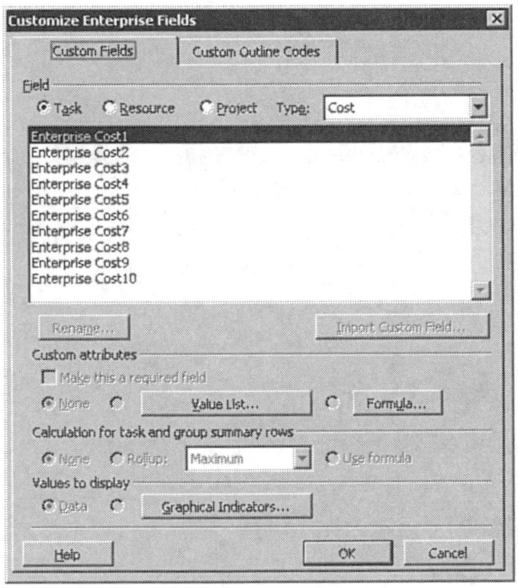

FIGURE 20.7   The Customize Enterprise Fields dialog box in Project Professional.

Customizing Enterprise Outline Codes

Outline codes are hierarchical codes that use a code mask to define each level in the structure. There are 30 definable outline codes for each type, project, resource, and task. Enterprise Resource Outline Code 30 is predefined as Resource Breakdown Structure (RBS) and is used in the Project Server security model. Enterprise Resource Outline Codes 20 to 29 are multivalue codes that allow selection of one or more values from the lookup table. Project and Resource Enterprise Outline Codes are included dimensions in the OLAP Portfolio Analyzer cube built for the Project Server. To customize an outline code, perform the following steps:

1. Select the Custom Outline Codes tab.

2. Select the type of code (Project, Resource, or Task) by selecting the radio button.

3. Highlight the outline code from the list to customize.

4. Click the Rename button, replace the code name with a suitable alias, and click OK.

5. Select Define Code Mask, and the Outline Code Definition dialog box appears, as shown in Figure 20.8.

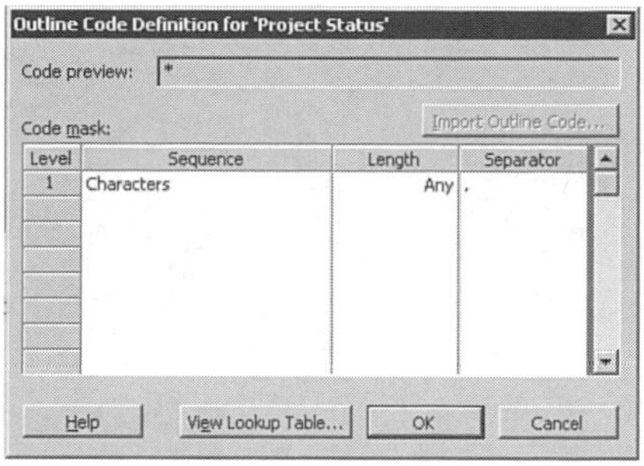

FIGURE 20.8   The Outline Code Definition dialog box.

6. Enter the sequence, length, and separator for each outline level by highlighting the cell and entering a value.

> **NOTE**
>
> The separator can be selected from the predefined list, or you can use any special character by typing in the value.

7. Edit the lookup table and enter values for the outline code. Use the arrows to indent or outdent values in the table. Add a definition for the code by selecting the cell and entering a value. Code tables may be shared with another outline code by selecting the Share Another Code's Lookup Table check box and clicking Choose Outline Code. Project, resource, and task codes can be shared across types.

> **NOTE**
>
> The following items should be considered when creating outline codes:
>
> - Define level one as the code name and indent all other entries to create a summary level rollup when grouping.
> - The code table is sorted alphabetically when saved. Use number prefixes if presentation order is desired.
> - Do not use special characters in the outline code value. This may cause errors in the OLAP cube when built.
> - Definitions are appended to the code value in the field selection presentation.
> - Field values are the concatenated string of all levels for the selected code.
> - PWA view's grouping titles use the definition if defined.

8. Set the rules for the code.

9. Select Make This a Required Code to enforce a selected value for all projects saved to the Project Server.

10. Select Only Allow Selection of Codes with No Subordinate Values to force users to select only the lowest level codes in the lookup table.

20

11. On Resource Outline Codes, select Use This Code for Matching Generic Resources to include the outline code in the match function in the Build Team function and Resource Substitution Wizard.

Customizing Enterprise Custom Fields

Enterprise custom fields can be defined for storing task, resource, or project information. Each category contains the same type and number of custom fields. Table 20.13 describes the enterprise custom fields available.

TABLE 20.13   Enterprise Custom Fields

Field Name	Field Data Description
Cost	Cost formatted number. Negative values are formatted as ($5.00).
Date	Valid date value.
Duration	Valid duration value.
Flag	Yes/No value.
Number	Any positive or negative number.
Text	Alphanumeric, up to 256 characters.

To customize an enterprise field, perform the following steps:

1. Select the Custom Fields tab.

2. Select the field of code (Project, Resource, or Task) by selecting the radio button.

3. Select the type of code from the list to customize (Cost, Date, Duration, Flag, Number, or Text).

4. Highlight the field name from the list to customize.

5. Click the Rename button, replace the code name with an appropriate alias, and click OK.

6. Select Make This a Required Code to enforce a value for all projects saved to the Project Server.

7. Under Custom Attributes, select the following:

   - **None**—Allows users to enter free-form values

   - **Value List**—Specifies allowed values for list

   - **Formula**—Calculates the value based on other project fields

> **NOTE**
>
> The following items should be considered when creating enterprise custom fields:
>
> - Value lists for enterprise custom fields cannot be appended by users.
> - Enterprise custom field formulas cannot reference local project custom fields.
> - Task-level custom fields are not available in Project Center views.

8. Set calculation for task and group summary rows by selecting None, Roll-up, or Formula. The default value is None.

> **NOTE**
>
> The following items should be considered when creating formulas:
>
> - With calculation set to None, summary task values can be set manually.
> - The calculation for task and group summary rows for text fields is available only using the formula if defined.
> - The field type determines the rollup calculations available.

9. To create a value list, select the radio button for Value List and select the Value List button to enter desired values. The Value List dialog box opens as shown in Figure 20.9.

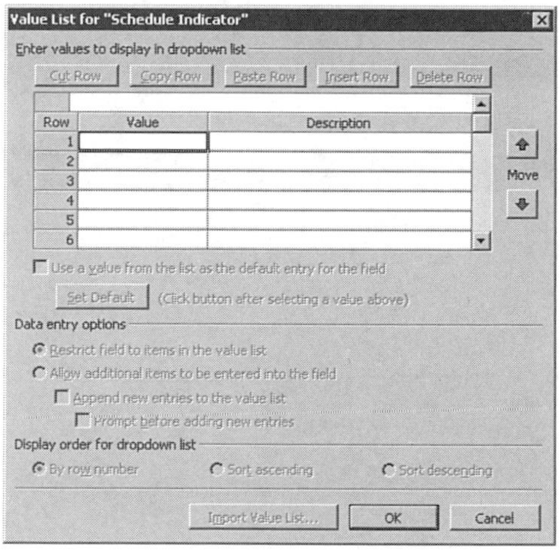

FIGURE 20.9   The Value List dialog box.

10. Enter values by selecting the cell and entering the data value. Enter description text as desired.

11. To set a default value, select the row that contains the default value, select the Use a Value from the List As the Default Entry for the Field check box, and click the Set Default button. The row text becomes red to denote the default value.

12. Value lists can be displayed by row number or by ascending or descending order of the values by selecting the associated radio button.

13. Field values can be displayed as data (the value) or graphical indicators based on user-defined conditions.

14. To define graphical indicators, click the Graphical Indicators button. The Graphical Indicators dialog box appears, as shown in Figure 20.10.

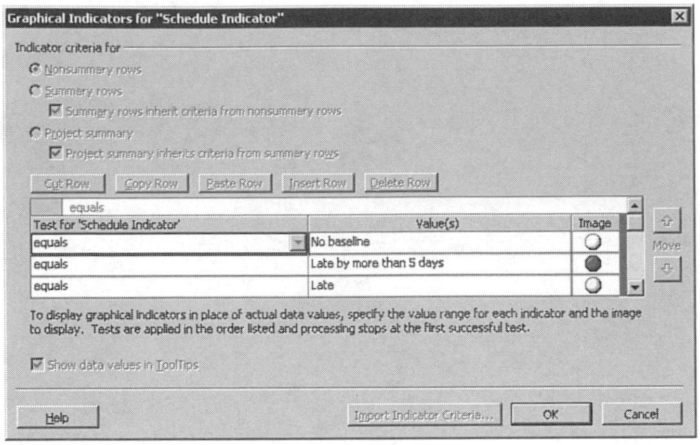

FIGURE 20.10   The Graphical Indicators dialog box.

15. Enter a test by selecting one of the conditional statements from the drop-down list.

16. Enter a value to measure against. You can enter text or select a project field.

> **NOTE**
>
> The Value field can contain a wildcard (? or *).

17. To create a calculated custom field, select the Formula radio button.

18. To open the formula dialog box, click the Formula button.

19. Enter the formula for the field and click OK.

20. Set the calculation method for task and group summary rows by selecting None, Roll-up, or Formula.

Adding Custom Objects

The Enterprise Global template is distributed to all Project Professional users, and any objects within the template are available. These objects can be permanently changed only by the administrator with Wave Global permissions. In a user session, objects can be modified but will not be saved on exit. There are two ways to add objects to the Enterprise Global template: Use the Organizer to copy objects from existing projects or build the objects directly in the Enterprise Global template. On installation, the Enterprise Global template contains the following two objects:

- Enterprise Gantt (View)

- Enterprise Entry (Task Table)

The Enterprise Resource Pool is not stored as a project and does not contain objects. Build a resource table and associated view to contain the custom resource fields to simplify adding or modifying enterprise resources.

Best Practices

- Set Project to manually control connection state. This allows selecting to connect to the desired account and gives the user an option to not load resource summary data.

- Use Software Policy to establish Project 2003 default options.

- Create and use enterprise project templates for all future projects. Set options in the templates.

- Create enterprise templates prior to setting custom fields as required.

- Validate custom field formulas in a project prior to adding to the Enterprise Global template.

- Create custom objects in the Enterprise Global template to standardize process and views.

- Allow the Enterprise Global template to be saved by the primary and backup administrator only.

CHAPTER 21

Building Project Team and Resource Substitution

IN THIS CHAPTER

- Building Project Teams
- Performing Resource Substitution
- Best Practices

The Enterprise Resource Pool is a central pool of your resources stored in the Project Server database. The Enterprise Resource Pool enables you to plan and balance the capacity of your resources across multiple projects, identify conflicts between task assignments in different projects, and view resource allocation information across multiple projects. You can use the Build Team feature in Project Professional to add resources in the Enterprise Resource Pool to projects.

Before building a project team and optimizing your resource assignments you need to have your Enterprise Resource Pool defined and created. The Enterprise Resource Pool contains all your enterprise resources with all their attributes that can be used to make selection of appropriate resources for your project teams more efficient.

When all your enterprise resources have been identified, approved, and procured, you can build your project team by entering the resource information into the project plan.

▶ SEE "Enterprise Resource Pool," **PAGE 191**.

Building Project Teams

Staffing projects involves assigning resources to tasks from a pool of available resources. Because resources are required to have the specific skills necessary for the tasks to which they are assigned, it is important to identify required skills for all resources in your Enterprise Resource Pool.

Skills are Enterprise Resource Outline Codes with the Use to Match Generic Resources property enabled. Microsoft Office Project Server 2003–based EPM solution allows a maximum of 29 skill codes per resource. Ten of the 29 skill codes are defined as multi-value outline codes (Enterprise Resource Outline Code 20 to 29). Each multivalue Enterprise Resource Outline Code sets a limit for number of skills being selected within the single Enterprise Resource Outline Code. Each resource can be assigned a maximum of 255 skill values within each multivalue Enterprise Resource Outline Code.

You can assign resources to projects by using the Build Team feature in Project Web Access (PWA) or the Build Team from Enterprise feature in Microsoft Office Project 2003 Professional client. This chapter focuses only on project team-building features provided by the Microsoft Office Project Professional 2003 client.

You can build teams for projects based on many different parameters, including resource skills, location, availability, and/or current workload.

Your final project team can be a collection of many different resources. Your project team resources can be either proposed or fully committed individual resources—individuals who meet the skill and availability requirements for staffing the project and subsequent task assignments—or generic resources—resources that represent general categories and skills required for the task.

▶ **SEE** "Enterprise Global Codes," **PAGE 163**.

Table 21.1 shows Project Server 2003 global and category permissions required to build a project team.

TABLE 21.1   Permissions Required to Build Project Team

Permission Type	Permission	Description
Category	Assign Resources	Determines the list of resources the user is allowed to add to a project team.
Category	Build Team on Project	Determines the list of projects to which the user is allowed to add resources. This permission also requires that users have permission (at the category level) to access the specific projects and resources that need to be accessed to build the project team or assign resources.
Category	See Enterprise Resource Data	Allows a user to view resources and resource data stored in the Enterprise Resource Pool, including the Build Team, Resource Center, and Portfolio Modeler features.
Global	Assign Resource to Project Team	Allows a user to use Build Team in Project Professional and assign resources to projects.
Global	Build Team on New Project	Allows a user to use Build Team to add resources to a project that has not been saved to the Project Server database.

> **NOTE**
>
> For detailed information about all permissions, see Appendix C, "Project Server Permissions," in the *Microsoft Office Project Server 2003 Administrator's Guide* available from http://go.microsoft.com/fwlink/?LinkID=20236.

Identifying the Right Resources for Your Project

When you add resources to project teams, you can prefilter resources by availability and time period to ensure that the resources you assign are available for the assigned tasks.

Before you can assign enterprise resources to your project tasks, you must use the Build Team feature available in the Project Professional client to select the resources from the Enterprise Resource Pool. You can also use the Build Team feature to replace resources currently assigned to your tasks in your project plans. Figure 21.1 shows the Build Team dialog box.

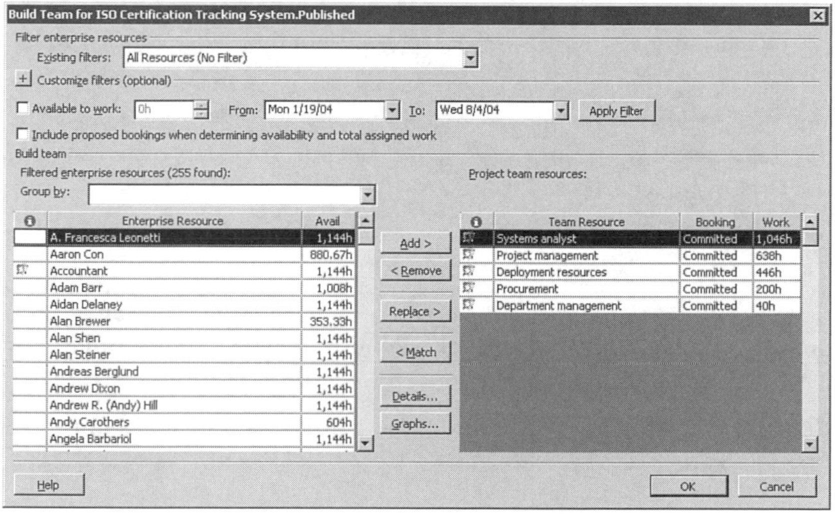

FIGURE 21.1 In the Build Team dialog the enterprise resources are displayed on the left side, and the project team resources are listed on the right.

> **TIP**
>
> For performance reasons, if you have permission to view more than 1,000 resources from your Enterprise Resource Pool, a prefilter dialog automatically displays. If this happens, you need to either select an existing filter or create a customized filter in the dialog to limit the number of resources displayed. These filters are based on enterprise custom outline code fields defined and created based on your business requirements.
>
> If the number of resources matching the criteria is still more than 1,000, the prefilter dialog displays a second time. Either add additional criteria to further limit the number of resources or just click OK, and all the resources will display.
>
> If there are no resources displayed matching the selection criteria you entered, an alert appears, which states that no resources meet your criteria.

Selecting and Grouping Resources Based on Skills

Before you can add any resource—generic or individual—to your project team, you need to choose the appropriate resources to add from possibly a large Enterprise Resource Pool containing thousands of resources. If you want to select your project resources based on skills, you may want to first organize or group your enterprise resources listed on the left side of the dialog box by their skills or any other available resource attribute you may have defined, such as Location. This simple step makes selection of resources with the right skills for your project a lot easier. After your enterprise resources are grouped based on their skills, you can then select resources with desired skills and add them to your project team or perhaps replace the generic resources in your project team with individuals with the right skills.

You can also use the Group By list to select a different grouping format not based on resource skills in which you want to have your enterprise resources organized. For example, you can use RBS enterprise outline code to group and display your resources based on how your organization's Resource Breakdown Structure (RBS) is defined.

Three types of indicators and four possible types of resources can be displayed in the Build Team dialog box:

- A single-head icon in the Indicator column designates a local resource to the project that does not exist in the Enterprise Resource Pool. Local resources can appear only in the list on the right.

- A double-head icon in the Indicator column indicates a generic resource in the Enterprise Resource Pool.

- Both a single- and a double-head icon in the Indicator column indicates a generic resource defined locally in the project and not a generic resource from the Enterprise Resource Pool.

- No icon in the Indicator column denotes an enterprise resource defined in the Enterprise Resource Pool.

> **NOTE**
>
> Any enterprise resources already part of the project team—listed on the right—are grayed out in the resource list in the left pane.

Figure 21.2 shows an example of enterprise resources organized and grouped by their skills.

To use the Build Team from Enterprise feature and select resources for your project team follow these steps:

1. Open Project Professional and connect to your Project Server.

2. From the menu, select Tools, Build Team from Enterprise to open the Build Team for *Project Name* dialog.

3. To organize and group your enterprise resources by their skills, in the Group By list box, select one of the skill enterprise outline codes.

4. Choose appropriate resources with required skills and use the Add button to add them to your project team.

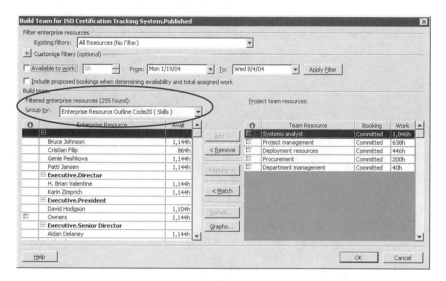

FIGURE 21.2   Use the Build Team for *Project Name* dialog with grouped enterprise resources displayed on the left side to simplify the project team selection based on skills.

Selecting Resources Based on Availability, Current Workload, and Other Criteria
After your enterprise resources are grouped based on their skills, you can apply additional criteria to filter the list of resources displayed further. The criteria can include number of work hours a resource should be available within a specific time frame. You can also use many predefined filters available from the Existing Filters list box or define your own custom filters using the Customize Filters (Optional) feature.

Selecting Resources Using Existing Predefined Filters   To select resources using existing predefined filters, open the Build Team dialog box and, under Filtered Enterprise Resources, select a filter from the Existing Filters drop-down list. Figure 21.3 shows an example of the existing filters to choose from.

NOTE

For more information about the use of existing predefined filters and how to create your custom filters, click the Help button to open the Build Team dialog box topic in the Project Professional Help window. The help information covers "how to" instructions as well as provides a detailed description of all available existing filters.

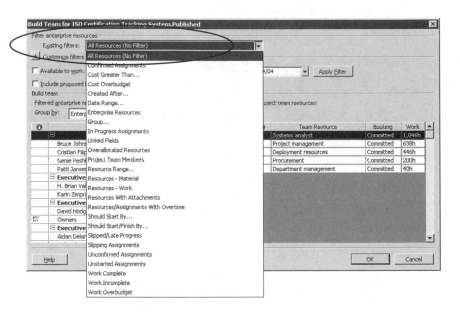

FIGURE 21.3   Use the Build Team for *Project Name* dialog and select from the list of predefined filters to limit the size of your enterprise resource list.

Selecting Specific Resources Based on Custom Filters   To select specific resources using
custom filters, perform these steps:

1. Remove the generic filter, if it is active.

2. Open the Existing Filters list.

3. Expand the Customize Filters button.

4. Build. the filter by defining and selecting the field you want to test. Select the test
   you want to apply to the field and, finally, type the value for which you want to
   test.

> **NOTE**
>
> You must type the value(s) for the custom filter. There is no list to choose from. Also, when you
> are entering the value for an Enterprise Custom Outline Code, you must include the correct
> separator value. For example, if you are using RBS code for the field name and your organization
> is using a period (.) as the separator between the organization and the location, you need to
> enter **<company>.<location>** for the custom filter to work properly.

5. Click the Apply Filter button to apply the custom filter.

6. You can then select any resource from the prefiltered enterprise resources and add
   them to your project team.

Figure 21.4 shows an example of a custom filter being defined.

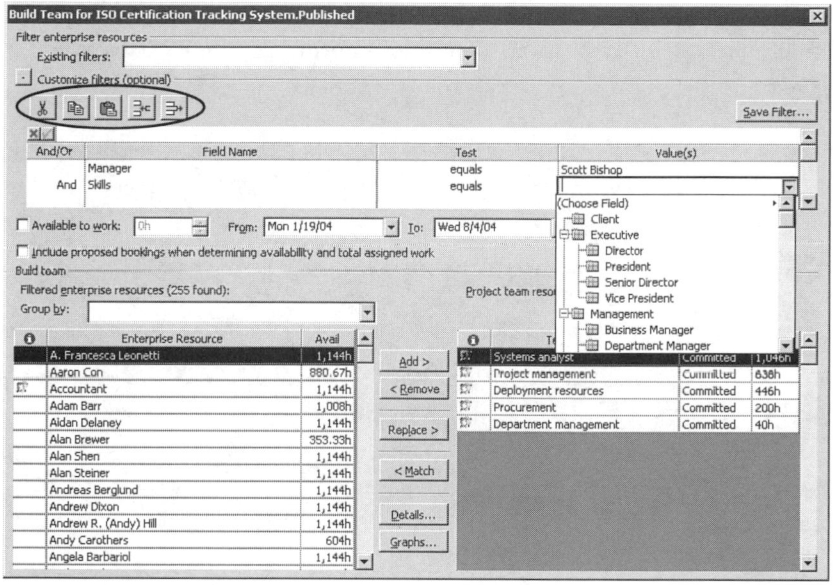

FIGURE 21.4 Use the Build Team for *Project Name* dialog to define your custom filters to limit the size of your enterprise resource list.

NOTE

To remove the filters, open the list at the top of the dialog and select All Resources (No Filter) .

Selecting Resources Based on Number of Work Hours Available   You can also select resources based on their current workload and availability. This filter is always available, no matter whether other filters are applied to the list of your enterprise resources. The filter searches through the nonmaterial resources returned from the Enterprise Resource Pool and selects resources with remaining availability equal to or greater than the number entered for the "work required" value between the dates specified.

Select the Available to Work check box to specify whether a resource should be filtered for work availability during a specific period of time. To use this option, specify the amount of time the resource will be required to work—for example, 300 hours (300h)—and then use the From and To calendar options to specify the period of time during which they will be needed. When you are finished, click the Apply Filter button. Figure 21.5 demonstrates how the Available to Work feature works.

Determining Future Resource Availability Based on Current Workload   To determine the future resource availability based on the resource's current load, follow these steps:

1. In Project Professional, from the menu, select Tools, Build Team from Enterprise.

2. Select the enterprise resources that you want to determine the availability for and then click Graphs.

3. Choose the Remaining Availability, Work, or Assignment Work graphs to get an idea of which enterprise resources are available for other assignments based on their current workload.

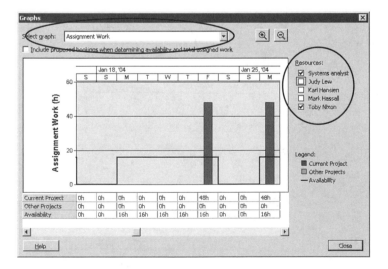

FIGURE 21.5   The Build Team for *Project Name* dialog shows the prefiltered enterprise resource list based on a defined minimum work availability (300h) between two specific dates.

Figure 21.6 shows the Graphs dialog with availability information for selected enterprise resources.

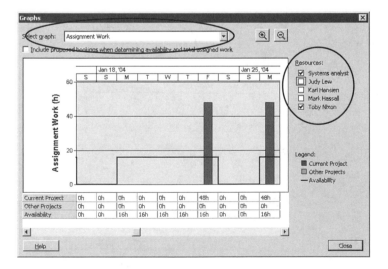

FIGURE 21.6   The Graphs dialog shows future availability and current assignment work information for the selected enterprise resources.

21

> **NOTE**
>
> You can select multiple resources from the list and then click Graphs to display availability for all the selected resources. You can also later interactively deselect and select the resources in the Graphs dialog box to focus on current work and availability of a single resource.

Including Proposed Bookings for Resources When Determining Availability   To include the proposed bookings for resources when determining their availability, select the Include Proposed Bookings When Determining Availability and Total Assigned Work check box to indicate whether the proposed assignments should be considered when filtering for availability and work. Figure 21.7 shows the Build Team for *Project Name* dialog where you can make a choice regarding proposed bookings.

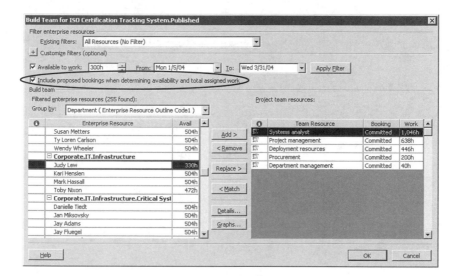

FIGURE 21.7   Check this box to include proposed assignments in the total of the current work assignment.

Adding Generic Resources to Your Project Team

Adding generic resources to your project team is a common task for project managers. Before adding individual resources to a project team you may know already the skills required for your project team.

It makes sense to first add the generic resources to your project team, making sure that you identified all required skills for your project, and then, later on, when you have more information about individual resource availability, replace these generic resources with individuals using tools such as the Build Team from Enterprise or Resource Substitution Wizard.

One tool you can use to assign generic resources based on the skill set defined in your project is the Build Team from Enterprise feature. Figure 21.8 shows the Build Team from

Enterprise dialog box displaying a filtered list of generic resources ready to be added to your project team.

To add generic resources to your project team, perform these steps:

1. In Project Professional, from the menu, select Tools, Build Team from Enterprise.

2. Under Group By, select a predefined Generic filter.

3. Collapse the No Entry list to display all generic resources.

4. From the list of generic resources on the left side, select a resource.

5. Click the Add button to add the generic resource to your project team.

6. Continue this process until you have added all generic resources required to your project team.

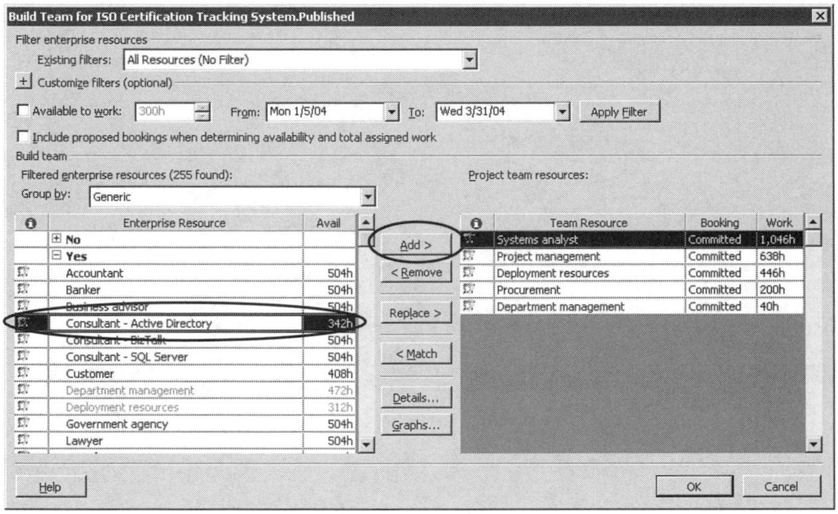

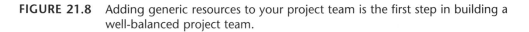

FIGURE 21.8   Adding generic resources to your project team is the first step in building a well-balanced project team.

Adding Individual Resources to Your Project Team

Sometimes it is desirable to have a project team defined as a mix of generic and individual resources. As the resource availability and workload information becomes clearer, more generic resources are replaced with individual ones.

In some cases, perhaps when the Enterprise Resource Pool is not that big and every project manager knows every person's name, you can start building your project team using individual resources from the beginning.

If you already identified the correct individual resources in your Enterprise Resource Pool to add to your project team, use the Build Team from Enterprise feature to add individual resources to your project team.

Figure 21.9 shows the Build Team from Enterprise dialog box displaying a filtered list of individual resources ready to be added to your project team.

1. In Project Professional, from the menu, select Tools, Build Team from Enterprise.

2. Under Group By, select a predefined Generic filter.

3. Collapse the Yes entry list to display all individual resources.

4. From the list of individual resources on the left side, select a resource.

5. Click the Add button to add individual resources to your project team.

6. Continue this process until you have added all individual resources required to your project team.

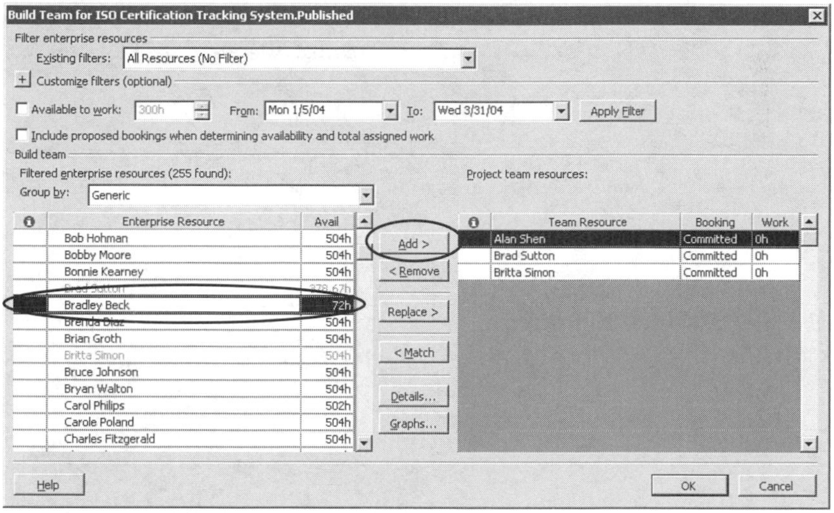

FIGURE 21.9   Adding individual resources to your project team is sometimes performed at the beginning of building your project team.

Matching Skills of Generic Resources with Individual Resources

After some more negotiation and a few meetings you now know the correct individual resources in your Enterprise Resource Pool to add to your project team. You can use the Build Team from Enterprise feature to replace generic resources already identified in your project team with individual resources based on the skill match.

This action is often performed when your project plan started as a template and the designers of the project template defined the skills required to perform each detailed task. Figure 21.10 shows the Build Team from Enterprise dialog box displaying a list of individual resources ready to be matched with generic resources from your project team.

To replace generic resources with individual resources, follow these steps:

1. In Project Professional, from the menu, select Tools, Build Team from Enterprise.

2. Select the generic resource you want to replace from the list under Project Team Resources.

3. Click Match to have Build Team from Enterprise find all the resources in the Enterprise Resource Pool that have the same required skill. All individual resources from the Enterprise Resource Pool that match the skills defined by the generic resource are displayed in the left pane under Filtered Enterprise Resource.

4. Select the individual resource you want to substitute for the generic resource and then click the Replace button to add this individual resource to the project team and replace the generic resource in the project team.

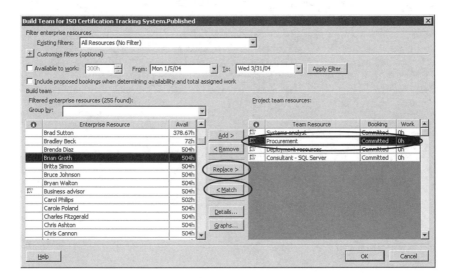

FIGURE 21.10   Replace generic resources with individual resources based on matching skills and build your project team with individual resources.

How the Resource Matching Feature Works

Resource matching can be a useful and powerful technique to select resources with the right skills, but the resource matching functionality has a limitation. If multiple Enterprise Global Resource Outline Codes are set to Use for Matching Generics, every one of those codes is included in the "match" function's filter query. Therefore, the default query can be pretty large for the match. The user can then reset the AND/OR condition and rerun the filter for submatching purposes. Your managers often need to make decisions about resource assignments based on multiple criteria.

Custom filters may be used to modify the default filter conditions that enable you to define unique resource requirements when building your project team from resources in your Enterprise Resource Pool. Unlike the functionality provided by resource matching, a custom filter can be based on multiple criteria that use AND or OR logical operators.

Resource matching also uses different test criteria depending on the skill code used to find a match:

- Single-value skill code match uses the test "equals" within the query filter when building project team in PWA or the Project Professional client.

- Multivalue skill code match uses the test "contains" within the query filter when building project team in PWA and Project Professional. This test returns all matches that have a partial match within the multivalue codes.

    ▶ **SEE** "Portfolio Management Using Portfolio Analyzer and Portfolio Modeler," **PAGE 393**.

Replacing Existing Project Resources

You can also replace existing individual resources with new individual resources or, if necessary, existing generic resources with new generic resources.

To replace individual resources with different individual resources, perform the following steps:

1. In Project Professional, select Tools, Build Team from Enterprise from the menu.

2. Select the individual resource you want to replace from the list under Project Team Resources.

3. Select the new individual resource you want to substitute for the individual resource already in your project team and then click the Replace button to replace the existing individual resource in the project team with the new one.

Removing Team Members from a Project

To remove existing resources from your project team, use the Build Team from Enterprise feature. To remove team members from the project team, perform these steps:

1. In Project Professional, from the menu, select Tools, Build Team from Enterprise.

2. In the Project Team Resources list, select the resource that you want to remove and click the Remove button.

NOTE

If the resource on your project team is the right resource, but the resource's data is incorrect, consider modifying the resource's information in the Enterprise Resource Pool first instead of removing the project team member from the project team.

You can also use the Assign Resources feature, which preserves actual work associated with existing, already assigned resources but moves any remaining work to the new resource.

Using the Build Team Feature in a Wide Area Network Environment

If your Project Professional client is connected to Project Server over a Wide Area Network (WAN), filtering for resource availability using the Build Team feature can become very slow, especially if your connection experiences a high degree of latency. You can improve the performance of your Project Professional client over a WAN by disabling the capability to filter for resource availability in the Build Team dialog box.

Figure 21.11 shows the Project Server Accounts dialog box with the Connecting Across a WAN check box selected.

To disable filtering for resource availability when using the Build Team feature, follow these steps:

1. Open the Project Professional client.

2. In the Project Server Accounts dialog box, select the Connecting Across a WAN check box.

3. Click OK.

4. Close and then restart the Project Professional client. You will not be able to filter for resource availability using the Build Team feature.

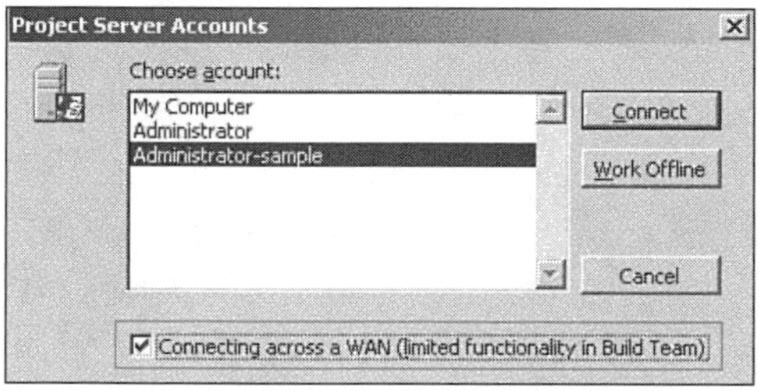

FIGURE 21.11   Disable filtering for resource availability by selecting the Connecting Across a WAN check box.

Performing Resource Substitution

The Resource Substitution Wizard is a tool that you can use to assign specific resources to project tasks. The Resource Substitution Wizard is available by selecting Tools, Substitute Resources from the Project Professional menu. The Resource Substitution Wizard can work with resources allocated across more than one project.

You can use the Resource Substitution Wizard in Project Professional to reassign or replace named and generic resources in one or more projects. The resource substitution performed is based on a comparison of the skill demands defined in the project and the skills of the resources defined in the Enterprise Resource Pool.

The Resource Substitution Wizard also can be used to develop and test different scenarios for resource allocation across multiple projects. This assists you in determining the best resource allocation scenario for your project portfolio. You can subsequently save the best scenario results in a project version created for these purposes.

▶ **SEE** "Using Portfolio Modeler to Analyze Projects," **PAGE 424**.

Skill-Based Scheduling Overview

This section defines what skill-based scheduling is and when it is appropriate to use it.

You can associate skill sets and skill levels with your enterprise resources. To do that, you first use Enterprise Resource Outline Codes based on your business requirements for resource management. These Enterprise Resource Outline Codes reflect the skills and skill levels identified for your enterprise resources. After you associate the skills and skill levels with your resources, you can use resource substitution as well as filtering and grouping to identify resources with the required skill set and skill levels for your projects.

Not all organizations require the ability to perform skill-based scheduling. Smaller organizations with a small, reasonably static, and well-defined resource pool perform resource scheduling based on skills informally; perhaps even without defining any resource skill sets at all. This may be a situation of a small to medium size organization with up to 500 resources defined in the Enterprise Resource Pool. Project managers have been working with the same enterprise resources for some time and know whom to ask for when it comes to their project teams.

The next scenario is when you may really need the ability to do skill-based scheduling in your organization. Perhaps in this case you are a multinational corporation with many office locations across the world. You use the concept of virtual teams for many of your projects, and a lot of project work is done remotely. Your Enterprise Resource Pool has 20,000 resources defined. In this case, you definitely need a tool that helps you with the resource selection process and making sure that the selected resources are the best match possible.

Preparing to Use the Resource Substitution Wizard

Before you start using the Resource Substitution Wizard feature, it is important to consider the following:

- The Resource Substitution Wizard is probably the most effective when you replace generic resources with individual resources early in a project life cycle. It is recommended that you use the Resource Substitution Wizard feature with projects based on enterprise project templates that have project teams defined using generic resources.

- The Resource Substitution Wizard is not an effective tool for substituting resources in projects that are in progress and for which actual task assignment progress has been already reported and saved.

- It is imperative that you review and analyze the results of the Resource Substitution Wizard before you commit to them by saving or publishing the project changes to your Project Server.

Several tasks need to be completed before you run the Resource Substitution Wizard:

- All resources that will be used by the wizard must exist in the Enterprise Resource Pool.

- At least one Enterprise Resource Outline Code must have been defined as a skill code to be used with the Resource Substitution Wizard by selecting the Use This Code for Matching Generic Resources box.

- Resources in the Enterprise Resource Pool have valid entries set for at least one Enterprise Resource Outline Code designated as a skill code.

- Project tasks have resources assigned, either generic or individual, that have valid entries set for at least one Enterprise Resource Outline Code designated as a skill code.

NOTE

Only a limited number of advanced Project Server, Project Professional, and PWA users typically work with the Resource Substitution Wizard and the Portfolio Modeler features. These are sophisticated features used only in specific scenarios and require a high organizational project management maturity level.

Although both features perform skill-based scheduling, their purposes are different, and results are not identical.

Table 21.2 lists the Project Server 2003 permissions required for Project Professional and PWA users to work with skill-based scheduling features.

TABLE 21.2   Permissions Required to Work with Skill-Based Scheduling Features

Permission Type	Permission	Description
Category	See Enterprise Resource Data	Allows a user to view resources and resource data stored in the Enterprise Resource Pool, including the Build Team, Resource Center, and Portfolio Modeler features
Category	Open Project	Allows a user to open a project from the Project Server database in Project Professional 2003 and/or use the Portfolio Modeler feature from PWA or Project Professional 2003
Global	View Models	Allows a user to use Portfolio Modeler from PWA or Project Professional 2003

NOTE

For detailed information about all permissions, see Appendix C, "Project Server Permissions," in the *Microsoft Office Project Server 2003 Administrator's Guide* available from http://go.microsoft.com/fwlink/?LinkID=20236.

Limitations of the Resource Substitution Wizard

The Resource Substitution Wizard enables substitution of generic resources for individual resources prior to a project start. It is typically used as part of the organizational strategic resource capacity planning.

You should not run the Resource Substitution Wizard against projects that already have started and have many project tasks already in progress. The scheduling engine used by the Resource Substitution Wizard does not account for the progress on individual assignments when performing calculations. This issue does not affect project start dates or the resource freeze horizon and only affects task assignments.

> **NOTE**
>
> For a detailed description of this limitation, review Microsoft Knowledge Base article number 828826. Microsoft Knowledge Base articles on Microsoft Office Project Server 2003 is available from http://support.microsoft.com/search/?adv=1&spid=2526.

It is important to understand that this limitation does not affect the resource substitution process of the Project Professional scheduling engine. When the scheduling engine in the Project Professional client evaluates a project that has significant task progress recorded, all forward dates might be considered invalid by the scheduling engine used by the Resource Substitution Wizard. As a result, the scheduled dates reported by the Resource Substitution Wizard for in-progress tasks might be inaccurate.

If you absolutely have to use the Resource Substitution Wizard on projects in progress, use it very carefully for resource substitution on any task in progress unless its completion percentage is either 0 or 100. This will effectively avoid the progress issue described previously.

> **CAUTION**
>
> The Resource Substitution Wizard process allows you to select projects that are in progress. You can run the tool against in-progress projects for testing and what-if scenario purposes, but it is recommended that you do not save the project when you are finished.
>
> When you use the Resource Substitution Wizard, consider also running it against a separate version of all in-progress projects to avoid saving your changes to the published projects.

If you think that this is not a realistic scenario for any in-progress project, you are probably correct. It is recommended that the Resource Substitution Wizard be used only with projects that either have not started or are complete.

> **NOTE**
>
> For more details on the Resource Substitution Wizard, review the *Microsoft Office Project Server 2003 Project Manager's Guide*, Chapter 12, available from http://www.microsoft.com/technet/prodtechnol/office/proj2003/reskit/default.mspx.

Using the Resource Substitution Wizard

The Resource Substitution Wizard is available under the Tools menu in the Project Professional client. Select Substitute Resources after you connect to your Project Server and then select the Substitute Resources submenu.

The Resource Substitution Wizard helps you to complete the following tasks:

- Replace one or more generic resources with one or more actual resources that have the same resource skills attributes associated with the generic resource.

- Substitute a specific resource (generic or individual) for another resource if the specific resource assigned to a task is overallocated.

You can guide and control the resource substitutions that the Resource Substitution Wizard makes as well as the time frame for the resource substitutions on project task assignments.

The Welcome Screen

The Welcome screen, shown in Figure 21.12, is an initial page that describes the steps in preparing the Resource Substitution Wizard. Review it and then click the Next button.

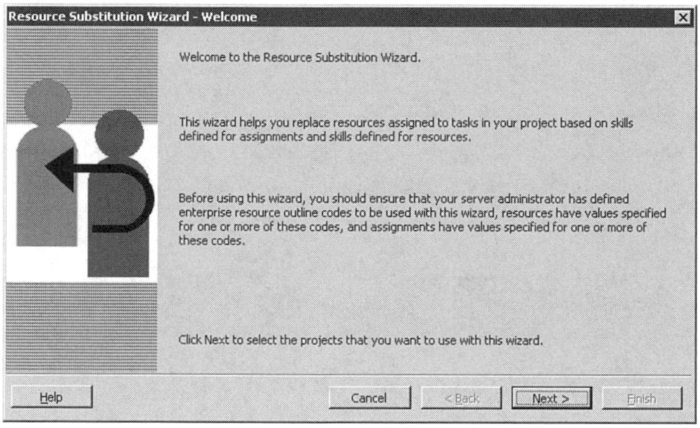

FIGURE 21.12   The Resource Substitution Wizard Welcome screen.

Step 1—Choose Projects

The list of projects to choose from contains all currently open projects.

In this dialog box, select only the projects that you want to consider in your scenario, clear all other projects, and then click Next (see Figure 21.13).

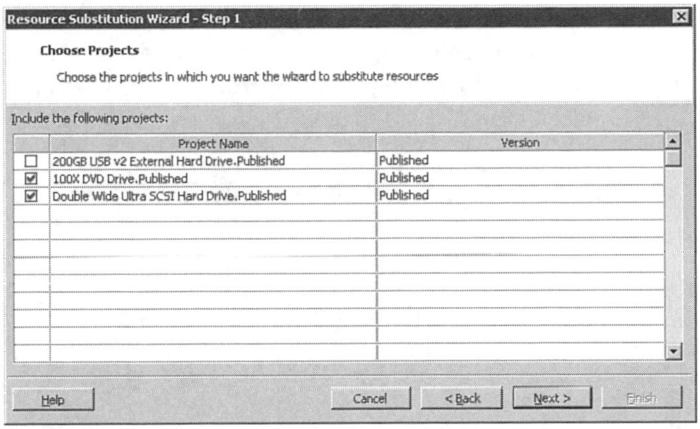

FIGURE 21.13   The Resource Substitution Wizard Choose Projects screen.

Step 2—Choose Resources

The Choose Resources screen, shown in Figure 21.14, defines the resources that will be considered when the resource substitution process takes place. Three options can be made, but you can choose only one for any run of the Resource Substitution Wizard:

- **In the Selected Projects**—This option is useful when you want to evaluate several projects and resource assignments between projects to achieve a better balanced resource load. The Resource Substitution Wizard selects only resources from project teams already associated with the selected projects.

- **At or Below the Following Level in the Resource Breakdown Structure**—This option is useful when you want to allow the Resource Substitution Wizard to work with a wider range of resources than just those on the project teams of the projects being analyzed. This range is specified in the drop-down menu.

  This option requires properly defined Resource Breakdown Structure (RBS). If your organization does not have RBS defined, you cannot use this option.

- **Specified Below**—This option allows you to select specific resources to be considered for substitution. Use this option when you want to evaluate specific resource overallocation conditions or to determine the effects of adding more specific resources to your project team.

  Selecting the Add button initiates the Build Team dialog, and new or additional resources can be added to the list of available resources for the Resource Substitution Wizard.

If you select the Allow Resources with the Proposed Booking Type to Be Assigned to Tasks option, resources with proposed bookings/assignments will be considered for resource substitution. If you choose to include proposed bookings in your scenario, some resources may become overallocated later if the proposed bookings become committed bookings.

The Resource Freeze Horizon option is a date selected from a calendar control that provides the date before which no resource assignments will be reviewed or changed—that is, the date before which all assignments will be frozen. This date applies regardless of which resource selection parameters are made.

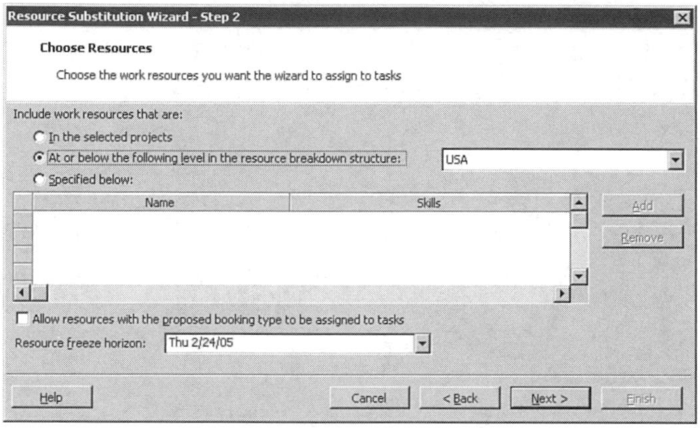

FIGURE 21.14   The Resource Substitution Wizard Choose Resources screen.

Step 3—Choose Related Projects

Next, you select the projects to be included in the scope of the substitution scenario when it is run, as shown in Figure 21.15. The Resource Substitution Wizard identifies projects associated with the open project through cross-project links or shared resources.

When determining the related projects, the wizard looks for projects with the following relationships to those projects selected in the Step 1—Choose Projects screen:

- Shares a common resource
- Cross-project links

After the directly related projects have been identified, the Resource Substitution Wizard then continues with identifying the indirect links between projects. Indirectly linked projects give you another set of projects to consider for your scenario.

For example, Project A uses Boris and Charles as resources for some tasks. The Resource Substitution Wizard may find Project B that uses Boris and Christian as resources for some tasks, so a direct link is established between Projects A and B because they share a common resource (Boris). The Resource Substitution Wizard then finds Project C that uses Christian and Stuart for some task assignments. This relationship constitutes an indirect link between Projects A and C. It is due to the fact that if the Resource Substitution Wizard reschedules some task assignments in Projects A and B then there can be a possible impact created on Project C—Project C shares resource Christian with Project B, and Christian's assignments in Project C can be impacted by changes in Projects A and B.

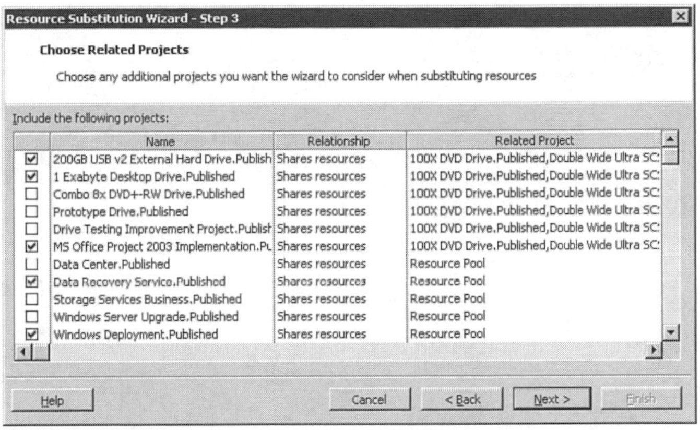

FIGURE 21.15   The Resource Substitution Wizard Choose Related Projects screen.

Step 4—Choose Scheduling Options
You can specify scheduling options for the selected projects included in your scenario. Use this screen to specify the relative priority of each project and to specify the source for resources considered for substitution.

The options for resource source are

- Use resources in project.

- Use resources in pool.

Your selection determines the scope of the resource pool that the Resource Substitution Wizard uses when calculating the best resource fit. For each selected project, the Resource Substitution Wizard uses the resources defined in the project team, or it uses the combined resource pool from all the project teams.

At this point the Priority for all projects in your scenario is set as well. This is a field with a value range of 1 to 999. It is set at the project level and defaults to a value of 500. Higher priority projects have a higher value assigned. When resources are allocated by the Resource Substitution Wizard, the higher priority projects get their resources assigned first, and if there is any resource assignment conflict, the higher priority project always wins.

The Level Resources with the Proposed Booking Type setting indicates whether the proposed resources should be leveled along with the committed resources. By default, this check box is not selected. Figure 21.16 demonstrates how to choose scheduling options in Step 4 of the Resource Substitution Wizard.

Step 5—Substitute Resources
The Substitute Resources screen, shown in Figure 21.17, shows the current Resource Substitution Wizard scenario settings selected in all previous screens. It shows the projects selected, the resource pool selected, and the resource freeze horizon date chosen.

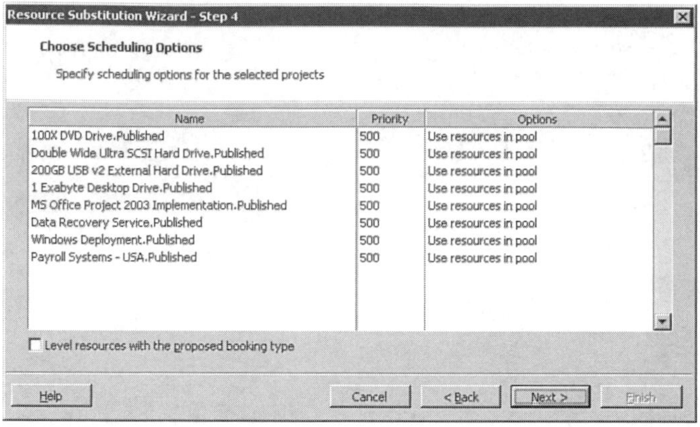

FIGURE 21.16   The Resource Substitution Wizard Choose Scheduling Options screen.

If you are happy with all the settings displayed, click on the Run button to start the substitution process. Progress status feedback is shown while the Resource Substitution Wizard is running and can be canceled while it is executing. When the substitution process finishes, the Next button that was grayed out previously should become available and can be selected to continue to the next step.

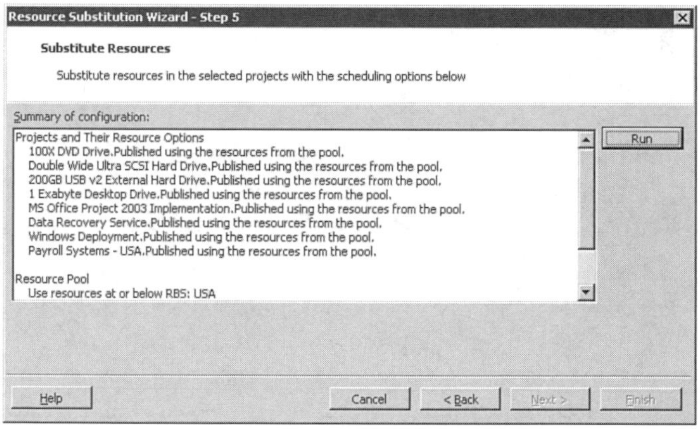

FIGURE 21.17   The Resource Substitution Wizard Substitute Resources screen.

Step 6—Review Results

When the resource substitution process finishes, it displays the results of the substitution. Figure 21.18 demonstrates the results of the resource substitution. The dialog shows each task for each project included in your scenario that was processed, and for each task it shows the following information:

- **Task**—The name of the task as displayed in the Project Professional plan.

- **Skill Profile**—Determined by the first generic resource assigned to the task. If needed, this can be changed in the Task Usage view.

- **Assigned Resource**—The substituted resource assigned to the task by the Resource Substitution Wizard based on the best option to complete the project tasks on time, given the selected resource pool.

- **Requested Resource**—The original resource assigned to the task in the plan currently stored in Project Server database.

- **Request/Demand**—An indication of how that specific assignment was set in the project plan—demanded (D) or requested (R).

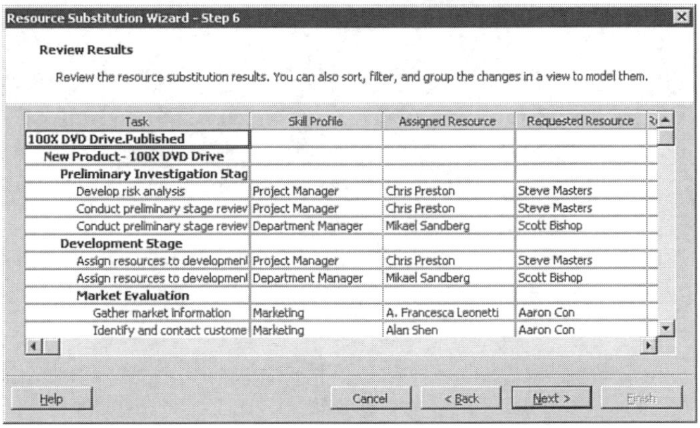

FIGURE 21.18   The Resource Substitution Wizard Review Results screen.

Step 7—Choose Update Options

The next step of the Resource Substitution Wizard determines what happens with changes suggested by the Resource Substitution Wizard.

Choose the options that you want to use to save your resource substitution results. You can either update the projects selected for your scenario directly or save the scenario configuration information to a text file for future review. If you choose to save the scenario configuration information to a file, the file information will look similar to the Review Results screen of the Resource Substitution Wizard.

If the Cancel button is selected, the wizard is stopped, and no further action is taken. Figure 21.19 demonstrates the Choose Update Options screen of the Resource Substitution Wizard.

> **CAUTION**
>
> When the Update Projects with Result of the Wizard check box is selected, the suggested changes to each of the task assignments will be made in all relevant project plans. This does not alter any project plan permanently yet. After that, the project manager must select to save the project plan changes before the changes are written and saved to the Project Server database.

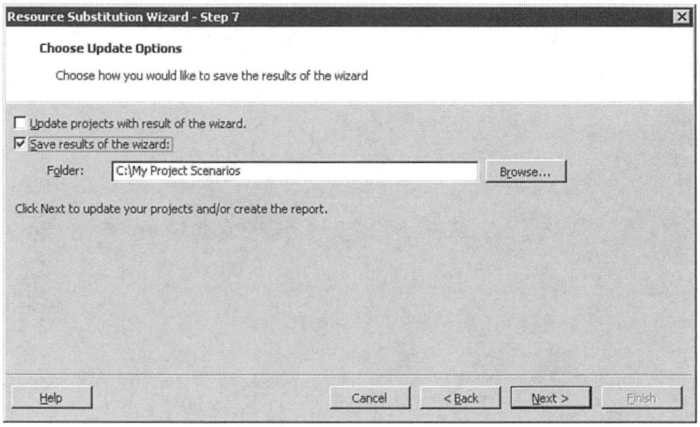

FIGURE 21.19   The Resource Substitution Wizard Choose Update Options screen.

Step 8—Finish

The final screen of the Resource Substitution Wizard displays progress on the update process and provides reminders. This screen enables you to stop updates to projects and return to the Resource Substitution Wizard. When all changes have been made, the wizard screen should be closed using the Finish button. It is still possible at this point to review and rerun the wizard by selecting the Back button to return to the previous screen.

> **CAUTION**
>
> The suggested changes to your project plans in your scenario have not been saved back to the Project Server database yet. This last step must be performed by project managers saving each open project plan.

After you finish running the Resource Substitution Wizard, you might want to level your projects to review how the resource assignment changes that the Resource Substitution Wizard suggested affect the project's finish dates and resource utilization (see Figure 21.20).

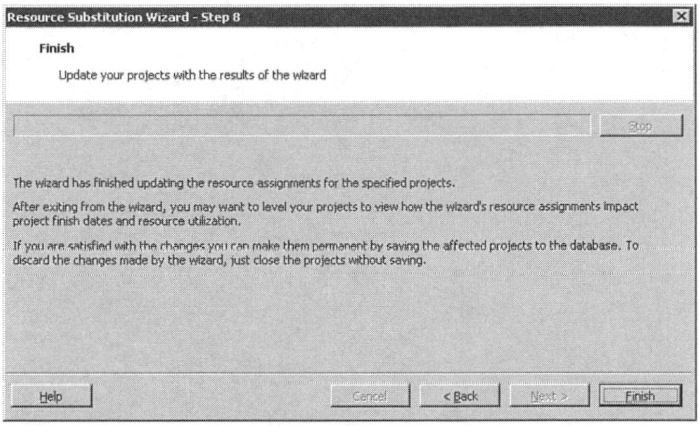

FIGURE 21.20   The Resource Substitution Wizard Finish screen.

Best Practices

- Before building a project team and optimizing your resource assignments, you need to define and create your Enterprise Resource Pool.

- You can build teams for projects based on many different parameters, including resource skills, location, availability, and/or current workload.

- Improve the performance of the Project Professional client over a WAN by disabling the capability to filter for resource availability in the Build Team dialog box.

- Run the Resource Substitution Wizard only against a scenario with projects that have not started yet. If possible, do not include projects with tasks in progress for which actual work has been reported in your Resource Substitution scenario.

- If you run the Resource Substitution Wizard scenario with in-progress projects, do not save the project results.

CHAPTER 22

Project Team Collaboration

IN THIS CHAPTER

- Overview of Collaboration Features

- Team Collaboration in Small Organizations

- Team Collaboration in Large Organizations

- Effective Use of Project Team Collaboration Tools

- Team Collaboration on Management of Risks

- Collaboration Features for Issues Management

- Collaboration Features for Documents Management

- Updating Project Progress

- Best Practices

Scope, schedule, quality, and cost management are only some of the areas that project managers are in charge of when managing projects. They also have to produce and gather numerous documents, reports, memos, messages, and other project-related artifacts for and from team members, customers, sponsors, and stakeholders.

Overview of Collaboration Features

The project manager is responsible for three key pieces of information for each project:

- **Issues**—Problems or events arising and developing during the project lifecycle.

- **Risks**—Future events or conditions that can have negative effects on the outcome of a project.

- **Document artifacts**—Project charter, proposals, minutes of meetings, progress reports, and other items related to the project.

Every day, organizations around the world generate an incredible amount of documents. A significant portion of these documents is related to project development. For any organization, collecting, organizing, maintaining, archiving, analyzing, and indexing these documents properly is a time-consuming and complex effort.

Windows SharePoint Services (WSS), which integrates with Microsoft Office Project Server 2003 and provides a platform for risks, issues, and document-related features helps project managers handle all necessary document artifacts, business processes, and project teams. All team members on any project team derive the most value from the information sharing.

WSS provides risks and issues tracking features, as well as a document library for each project published to Project Server. Public libraries that are not project-specific can be created as well. Websites that are automatically created for projects can be particularly attractive to server administrators when you consider the manual alternatives.

Using file shares that provide a hierarchical directory structure as a means of organizing project artifacts has some limitations. There is only one path to any given artifact item, and on top of that, users must know the name of the server the item is stored on, as well as the name of the share and directory structure of folders on the server. When you add other data sources such as other corporate websites, email servers, and databases to the mix of information available, artifact search and retrieval becomes challenging, if not impossible. With files stored all over the network, archiving and preserving the valuable knowledge of the company is difficult.

After project-related information grows to a substantial size, the overhead of managing a standalone project website on top of other project work can become increasingly difficult. One key reason why standalone project websites may fail is the inability to effectively provide the information and facilitate team collaboration for even small organizations because of the effort required.

Coordinating the efforts of a project team takes foresight and planning—that is what project managers master. The ideal time to agree on and enable project team communications is right after your project team is chosen. You can select from the online team collaboration solution supported by Project Server 2003 or use other means to communicate.

By publishing project information to Project Server and using the Microsoft Office Project Web Access (PWA) client, you can distribute project information and collaborate online with your project team members, customers, and stakeholders.

Team Collaboration in Small Organizations

Small workgroups sometimes can get by using less formal team collaboration based on a combination of email, file servers with shares, and data on their own hard drives. Because all your project team members are probably already familiar with these tools, their use becomes the *modus operandi* for small project team information sharing.

What may be lacking in this collaboration system is an audit trail of all project team actions and efforts.

Furthermore, as size and complexity of a project grows, so does the potential number of issues, risks, and related documents—small organizations can have fairly sophisticated team collaboration requirements as well.

It is imperative for project managers to be able to track all information relevant to any project risks and issues identified, who is responsible for the issue or risk resolution, and how and when the issues or risks are resolved. Without a centralized project space to collect and store this information, it can get overlooked or lost, and project performance can be negatively impacted.

Team Collaboration in Large Organizations

In a large organization, information sharing and team collaboration requirements typically become more complex. Comprehensive indexing, intuitive search capabilities, and the ability to manage and analyze large volumes of project-related information across many data stores are the key requirements. Businesses also need advanced document management, including well-defined publishing processes and versioning to ensure that the data and information they are collaborating on are complete and up-to-date. Using WSS-based features, organizations can aggregate content from multiple data sources for projects and programs into a portal website, creating personalized digital dashboards, regardless of where the data resides.

Large projects require a lot of attention and require your project teams to focus on different areas. You need to collaborate not only with your project team members but also with your clients and other stakeholders. You need to be able to answer the following questions:

- How are you going to communicate with your project team, clients, and stakeholders?

- How do you create a single project calendar and share it with all your stakeholders?

- Can you publish project documents for review?

- How are you going to handle project issues and risks tracking?

The answers may be found in setting up a WSS website for each project accessible to all on your project team and your stakeholders. You can use this project website to post meeting agendas and minutes, post related project documents, track project issues and risks, hold online discussions, and more.

Other technologies are available from Microsoft that can help you with effective team collaboration. For example, if you are using the concept of virtual teams where your project team members are not in the same location, you can use Microsoft Office Live Meeting for online meetings.

The relevant project information that the project manager should maintain typically comes from many different sources, such as individual project team members, clients, stakeholders, external consultants, accounting, HR systems, and other data sources. One of the technical challenges for Enterprise Project Management (EPM) system designers and project managers today is creating a project-centric environment that promotes project team collaboration. In this project-centric collaboration space, all relevant project management data is collected and organized with appropriate tools for filtering and sorting available as well as appropriate role–based security.

Based on the findings from Forester Research Report, most large companies go through four collaboration phases:

- Traditional collaboration
- Experimentation
- Increase in tools
- Enterprise strategy and standardization

Although the desired state of team collaboration for any large organization is enterprise strategy and standardization, the majority of large companies are stuck in the first two phases. The question is how do you get to the next phase?

NOTE

The free Forester Research Reports referred to in this chapter are available from the following Microsoft website: http://www.microsoft.com/business/productivity/collaboration/Reports/default.mspx.

Based on another Forester Research Report available from the previously referenced Microsoft website, the most significant and most common challenges of rolling out team collaboration software relate to people and human behavior rather than technology. Organizations commonly face the following roadblocks to successful team collaboration rollouts:

- People resist sharing their knowledge.

- Users are most comfortable using email as their primary electronic collaboration tool.

- People do not have incentive to change their behavior.

- Teams that want to or are selected to use the software do not have strong team leaders.

- Senior management is not actively involved in or does not support the team collaboration initiative.

TEAM COLLABORATION

Based on the article by Dan Webb from Team Analytics, "ineffective team collaboration is probably one of the primary contributors to costly rework and delivery failure in IT projects. Team collaboration is about sharing knowledge and reaching consensus within the team. Consensus results from effectively detecting and resolving conflicts in data, perceptions, interpretations, and actions."

The article titled "Leveraging the Power of Project Team Collaboration" is available from the following Microsoft website: http://office.microsoft.com/en-ca/assistance/HA010788211033.aspx.

Dan Webb also suggests in the previously referenced article that "A key human-factors challenge for project managers is to make sure that all crucial information related to the project has been validated by at least two team members who agree about the validation, and that the information has been effectively integrated by the stakeholders whose successful performance depends upon it. Team members need access to crucial information, and they need support for communicating clearly and reaching agreement easily. Clear communication and ease of agreement can never be assumed without some appropriate test for that condition."

Effective Use of Project Team Collaboration Tools

This section focuses on how project team collaboration is facilitated for users of a Microsoft EPM solution. The PWA client with all its modules can be definitely considered a collaborative tool. As a matter of fact, the PWA client is all about project team collaboration. It lets you send and receive updates to and from team members via a web page to help you understand project status and issues. It has several features that you and your project team can use to communicate about your project. Many of these forms of communication, including when and to whom they are used, should have been addressed in the Communications Management Plan. The Communications Management Plan makes sure that you have a consistent method of using them during the project executing and controlling phases.

You may want to create a project-centric home page, where your project team members and customers can see announcements, client status reports, and any other item you want to help communicate project activities and status.

> **NOTE**
>
> You and your team may want to use the To-Do Lists feature to track and/or assign tasks at a lower granularity than a project schedule. Team members can submit status reports that supplement task updates in the Tasks page.

▶ **SEE** "Project Web Access Collaboration," **PAGE 293**.

Team members can create and track risk items for a project, specify tasks impacted by the risks, and be assigned risk response actions. As issues arise during the execution of the project, they can be logged and tracked until they are resolved. Documents associated with projects can be stored in the document library and can be collaboratively reviewed and updated by the project team.

> **NOTE**
>
> The following Microsoft website lists Microsoft technologies available for Team Collaboration Solutions: http://www.microsoft.com/business/productivity/decision/teams/tech.mspx.

Next, you review the team collaboration features available to your project managers that are also exposed through the Project Professional client interface. The three main collaboration modules you will review are risks, issues, and documents as shown in Figure 22.1.

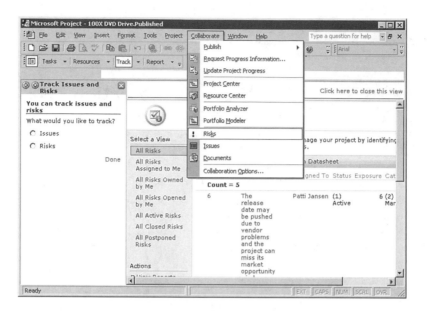

FIGURE 22.1   List of modules available in the Project Professional client under the Collaborate menu. Risks, issues, and documents can be accessed from the Project Professional client as well as PWA.

Team Collaboration on Management of Risks

Risks are potential future events or conditions that can have negative effects on the outcome of a project. *Risk management* is the processes and procedures that enable managers to identify risks, assess them, and arrive at plans for handling them.

Some form of risk management is appropriate for nearly all projects. The extent to which it is used varies from project to project depending on the importance of the project, size and complexity of the project, and level of uncertainty associated with it.

Risk Overview

Risk management should be proactive. If implemented correctly, it helps to anticipate where a process or task may fail. If a project manager suggests that a task will take two weeks, but the resource assigned to it says it may take up to four weeks, the proactive project manager may want to create a risk item with a link to the task. After that, everyone who needs to can see the discrepancy. The reactive project manager may decide and hope that a problem does not occur before doing anything. When the problem occurs, in this example the task already took four weeks to finish, it may be too late to do anything—the impact on other project tasks has already occurred.

A project risk management plan must be developed by the project team, and its level of detail should be appropriate to the size and importance of the project. For example, building a backyard patio doesn't require sophisticated risk analysis. On the other hand, building a high-rise condominium building complex for 15,000 people requires a sophisticated risk management plan—the failure of one of the major subcontractors can lead to significant and costly delays, not to mention many unhappy customers.

Risk is the possibility of an event that, if it occurred, would have a negative effect on a project. After a project begins, new events that were difficult to anticipate might create new risks. For example, unseasonably cold weather might seriously impact the end date of a construction project in southern California.

This section of the chapter further discusses what you can do to prepare for risks.

The steps involved in preparation of a risk management plan in the context of the EPM solution include the following:

- **Identify high-risk tasks**—Identify tasks likely to take longer than expected, end beyond their finish dates, delay the start or finish of related tasks, or delay the project finish date.

- **Identify resource risks**—Resource risks include resources working near, at, or over their maximum availability. These resources can delay the project if they become unavailable. Identify also resources with specialized skills that the project absolutely depends on.

- **Identify project budget risks**—To see overbudget tasks that are likely to cause the entire project to go over budget, identify your project budget risks.

- **Specify risk probability**—Using the Project Server Risks module, you can specify the probability of a risk event that could impact negatively your project budget or cause a significant project delay.

- **Involve your resources in identifying additional risks**—You may need additional resources that can help you identify additional risks. The resources that can best help you identify these additional risks are key people involved in planning and running the project and working on the tasks. In your project plan, look first at the critical path tasks and then at noncritical tasks.

Using the Project Professional client, look specifically for

- **Tasks that your project team has little or no expertise in**—The duration and cost estimates for these tasks may not be accurate.

- **Task estimates that look too optimistic**—Ask your estimators how confident they are in their estimates, especially for critical tasks.

- **Tasks for which you have few resources available or that require resources with special skills**—Especially look at parts of the schedule where these resources are fully allocated, overallocated, or might become unavailable.

- **Tasks with several predecessors**—The more predecessors a task depends on, the greater the chance that one of its predecessors finishes late and delays the successor task. You might not be able to identify all your project risks if you analyze only the project schedule alone. Meet with your key project resources and ask them to help you with identification of additional risks.

Risk Tracking Using Project Server

Using the risk tracking feature in the Project Professional or PWA client, project managers can record, update, review, and escalate project risks for their projects. Team members can keep track of risks assigned to them for resolution.

> **NOTE**
>
> The Risk module in Project Professional does not provide cross-project risk tracking and reporting or sophisticated risk analysis tools based on Monte Carlo analysis.

The Risk module interface exposed in the Project Professional client is the same interface available in the PWA client. You might prefer to use Project Professional for risks, however. Perhaps as a project manager you do most of your project plan work in the Project Professional client, and there is no reason for having to open another client interface if you can do your work in the Project Professional client.

When risk items are created, project managers can specify for each risk item the following default attributes:

- **Title**—A text field that can be used to provide a description of a risk

- **Assigned To**—The person responsible for handling or managing the risk

- **Status**—Whether the risk is active, closed, or inactive

- **Category**—The risk type

- **Due Date**—Risk resolution due date

- **Owner**—Person owning the resolution of the risk

- **Probability**—The degree of probability that the risk will occur, ranging from 0% to 100%

- **Impact**—How significant the risk would be relative to affecting the outcome of a project

- **Cost**—The cost of the risk to the project, in monetary terms, should the risk actually affect the outcome of a project

- **Description**—A text field that can be used to provide descriptions of a risk

- **Mitigation Plan**—The plan to mitigate or minimize the impact of the risk, should it occur

- **Contingency Plan**—The fallback plans, should the risk occur

- **Trigger Description**—A text field that can be used to provide descriptions of a risk trigger

- **Trigger**—The events that cause a risk to actually affect the outcome of a project, including dates, exposure, or incomplete tasks

In addition to the default risk attributes in the preceding list, you can link the risk to other risks, issues, documents, and project tasks.

Collaboration Features for Risk Management in Project Professional

The Risks page helps you document and track the risk events that could negatively affect your project. You must have WSS installed to use the Risks feature.

> **NOTE**
>
> To access the Risks module, select Risks from the Collaboration menu bar.

The first page that displays for risks is a list of all projects you are assigned to or own. Depending on your security permissions, you may view a list of all projects or a subset of projects. Select the hyperlink for the project you want to see risk items for.

▶ **SEE** "Creating Risks," **PAGE 455**.

Collaboration Features for Issues Management

One of the most important tasks of any project manager is the management of unforeseen problems and issues that arise during the project life cycle. Issue management and tracking is another integral part of the project management discipline.

Overview of Issues Management

It is also important to understand that issue tracking is not the same as identifying and tracking risks. Risks deal with events in terms of their future effect on a project. Issues are about current problems that are occurring and need to be dealt with immediately.

In the Project Professional client, the Issues module can be used to capture items not identified as task assignments in projects. Project team members can participate in issue discussion together with project managers, resource managers, and team leads. This enables project managers or others responsible for issue resolution to determine the best strategy to deal with any issues before they become major problems.

Issue Tracking Using Project Server

Your project teams can create and track issues that arise throughout the project life cycle by using the Issues module.

Issues can be associated with projects, tasks, documents, and other issues. Summary of newly assigned issues appear on team members' home pages. You can also configure email notifications to alert you when issues have been opened, assigned to you, or updated. Depending on the actions taken to resolve issues, they can be flagged as active, closed, or postponed.

> **TIP**
>
> Before you can create and track issues, a web server running WSS must be set up and config-
> ured properly for Project Server 2003 and a site must be created, manually or automatically, for
> your project on this server.
>
> Depending on the permissions settings associated with your role in the organization, you may
> be able to view, open, edit, or close issues or customize a project's issue form. For example, as a
> project manager, you typically can add additional fields or attributes to all project issues or
> define new issue views.

Viewing and Creating Issues in Project Professional

In the Project Professional client, select Collaborate, Issues from the menu.

When issue items are created, project managers can specify for each issue item the following default attributes:

- **Title**—A text field that can be used to provide a description of an issue

- **Assigned To**—The person responsible for handling or managing the issue

- **Status**—Whether the issue is active, closed, or inactive

- **Category**—Specifies the issue type

- **Owner**—The person owning the resolution of the issue

- **Priority**—The priority of the issue

- **Due Date**—Issue resolution due date

- **Discussion**—A text field that can be used to provide a relevant discussion about the
  issue

- **Resolution**—Describes final resolution of the issue

As previously discussed, you can associate issues with documents, projects, tasks, and
risks, as well as with other issues. This can be an efficient way of integrating all the issues,
documents, reports, graphics, risks, and so forth for easy navigation and browsing.

▶ **SEE** "Issues," **PAGE 462**.

Collaboration Features for Documents Management

In today's world, little could happen with projects without some form of document
collaboration provided for your project team. Project Server 2003 provides a robust document collaboration workspace, which comes with some document management features
such as documents versioning, check-in and check-out functions, and read-write access
control.

Documents Management—A Stringent Necessity for Any Project Team

Collaboration within a project team using documents can be at times challenging, and most organizations have recognized these challenges by introducing a document management system that facilitates documents collaboration in a coordinated manner.

Without a proper document management system in place, a number of things can go wrong. If you collaborate with your project team members on documents, you probably can come up with your own examples of what can go wrong in the process of document collaboration. This may include

- Multiple versions of a document floating around, creating redundancy, confusion, and extra work.

- Confusion about document ownership and version. For example, one team member might waste time researching and writing about a particular issue that another team member already covered in a different version of the same document.

- Overlooked comments and notes when a document is passed around and change tracking is not turned on.

- Wasted time compiling comments and notes from multiple copies of a single document.

To minimize the negative effects of an inadequate documents management system, you may consider some options presented in the following discussion.

Options for Document Collaboration

To solve your problems with document collaboration and bring better consistency and clarity to your projects, consider several basic collaboration and document management methods discussed in the following sections.

Managing Paper Documents

In spite of high hopes about a "paperless office," many people still rely on paper documents most of the time. In fact, people seem to use more paper than ever before.

Using paper documents is supposed to be straightforward. You give the document to a project team member who edits it or attaches comments and passes it on. No complex software package is required, and if you stick to one copy of the document and one file folder per project, it should be reasonably easy to keep everyone's contributions together.

On the other hand, paper documents can be easily lost or misplaced. They also are not that great if only part of the project team works in the same office and if all team members cannot see all comments and notes as the comments are added.

Managing Email Messages and File Attachments

When you need quick feedback, an email message is the way to go. New messages in your Inbox are difficult to ignore, and the information comes to you rather than you searching for it. Email gets most people's attention, and they can choose to send a reply just to you or to everybody on the project team.

If you want to collaborate on a larger, more formal document with your project team, you can send a document as an attachment. Use the tracking and reviewing features to see who made what changes.

Working with the Meeting Workspace Feature in Microsoft Office Outlook 2003

The Meeting Workspace consists of one or more pages that contain meeting details and lists of related information required when planning, conducting, or following up on a meeting. The Meeting Workspace is a website for centralizing all the information and materials for meetings. Before the meeting, you can use a workspace to publish the meeting agenda, documents you plan to discuss, and meeting attendee list. It is also a natural place to store everything related to your project. You can post meeting agendas and minutes, capture and record important decisions, track task progress, and many other things. You are always guaranteed to have the latest document version, and you don't need to send large file attachments to all team members via email.

To use a Meeting Workspace, send a meeting request to invite your team to the meeting. In the meeting request, include a hyperlink that points to the workspace where invitees can go to learn details about the meeting and review the related materials.

> **NOTE**
>
> A Meeting Workspace is a special type of WSS subsite under a parent SharePoint site, as shown in Figure 22.2.

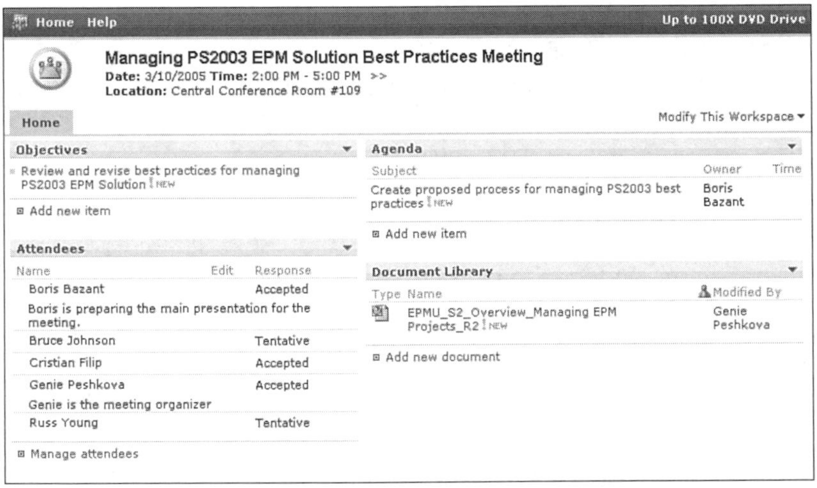

FIGURE 22.2   An example of a Meeting Workspace created by sending a meeting request in Microsoft Office Outlook 2003.

Working with the Document Workspace Feature in Microsoft Office 2003

A Document Workspace site is a WSS site centered on one or more documents. Project team members can collaborate on the document, either by working directly on the Document Workspace copy or by working on their own copy, which they can update periodically with changes that have been saved to the document copy stored on the Document Workspace site.

Because a Document Workspace is a WSS site, project team members can use all available WSS features—for example, using the Tasks list to assign each other to-do items, using the Links list to create hyperlinks to original resources, and storing related or supporting documents in the document library.

You can create a Document Workspace when you send a shared document attachment via email. The sender of the shared attachment becomes the administrator of the Document Workspace, and all the email recipients become members of the Document Workspace, where they are granted permission to contribute to the site.

Another way to create a Document Workspace is to use the Shared Workspace task pane (select the Tools menu first) in Microsoft Office programs. You can also use commands on a WSS site to create a Document Workspace.

When you create a Document Workspace from a shared attachment, the site inherits the name from the document on which it is based. When you create a Document Workspace from the Shared Workspace task pane or by using commands on a WSS site, you specify a name for the site.

NOTE

Using the Shared Workspace task pane, you can create Document Workspaces in Microsoft Office Word 2003, Microsoft Office Excel 2003, Microsoft Office PowerPoint 2003, and Microsoft Office Visio 2003 only.

When you create a Document Workspace, your Office document is stored in a document library in the new Document Workspace, where your project team members can access it by opening it in their web browser or in a Microsoft Office program. Figure 22.3 shows an example of a Document Workspace created for a Microsoft Office Word 2003 document.

How to Improve the Document Collaboration Process

This section discusses how you can improve the quality and consistency of your project team document collaboration. High-performing project teams know that without efficient document collaboration it is virtually impossible to run a successful project. Following are recommendations based on years of experience, lessons learned, and feedback from project teams:

- **Periodically evaluate your document and team collaboration processes**—You might want to ask your project team members what types of problems they experienced with document collaboration. Analyzing a problem that may seem random, such as someone revising a wrong document version, can help you find collaboration process steps that need to be fixed to make sure that they do not happen again. Your project team will not work better because you ask your team members to try harder—many other people are probably asking them to do the same all the time. Your teamwork can improve if and when better processes are in place.

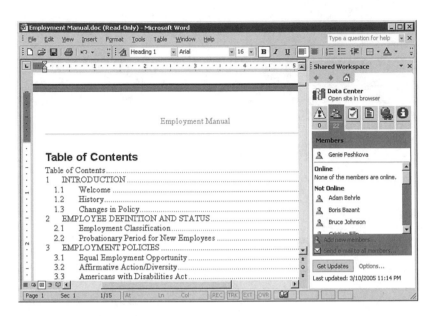

FIGURE 22.3   An example of a Document Workspace created for Employment Manual document.

- **Assign a project leader**—Every project and project-related document needs an owner. Otherwise, the document might not serve its purpose well. For example, a project team member posts a financial spreadsheet on a project intranet site. Team members are then instructed to periodically update the spreadsheet data. A few weeks later, only a few people are updating the spreadsheet data, and a few weeks after that nobody on the project team is sure why they are supposed to update this spreadsheet. Because the document has no owner assigned, team members don't even know whom to ask for guidance and decide to ignore it. Make sure that you establish clear ownership of each project and related documents!

- **Set the expectations for your team members**—A project leader needs to get a commitment from the project team members. If you send task assignments that include document updates with expected finish dates to your team members, do not assume that the tasks will get done on time unless your team members confirm it. Team members might be facing other difficult deadlines on other projects that make your document updates lower on their priority list. When you confirm expectations and task assignment finish dates, you are much more likely to stay in control of your project.

- **Establish consistent conflict resolution mechanism**—Many books have been written about reaching a consensus and negotiations, but knowing a few basic rules can help.

Senior management must first set the consistent standard for conflict resolution. Sometimes one project team member can be the tie-breaker. In other cases, the whole project team can vote. It is advisable that subject matter experts such as the lead designer or legal counsel need to have the last word in their areas of expertise.

- **Keep records of your project progress**—If you use email as your document collaboration vehicle, you can send messages, with optional attached documents, back and forth until all related issues are resolved. You can save the email thread and use it as an audit trail of the decisions made along the way. Comments and changes added within the document are also important for good record keeping. Save document copies with all comments and changes as a record, and then accept or reject all tracked changes and comments before the documents are ready for publishing.

- **Encourage communication and participation**—Heavy-handed methods may help you reach a consensus quickly, but they defeat the purpose of a team collaboration. Team collaboration is about taking full advantage of all unique skill sets and backgrounds of your project team members. Make sure that your conflict resolution methods encourage communication and participation, not artificial consensus that will not last long.

- **Acknowledge other opinions and explain reasoning**—Usually the owner of the document or project is the person designated to compile the results after all comments are processed. The owner might need to respond to each concern and comment, or she might be able to make the decision without further team input. Even if the owner has the authority to make the final decisions, it's important to understand everyone's concerns and document how decisions were arrived at.

  The Meeting and Document Workspace features provide a space for keeping a collection of project documents, additional information such as detailed technical research, prior versions of documents, team member names and their contact information, and notices about upcoming meetings.

- **Keep your document collaboration processes lean and flexible**—Not all problems can be resolved effectively and quickly through document collaboration. Many times, you need to pick up the phone, walk down the hall to talk to somebody on your project team, or schedule and attend a team meeting—that is, after all, what project managers do most of the time.

- **Focus on document version control**—Poor document version control can lead to a lot of waste and frustration. It is a good idea to set some ground rules before starting to collaborate on any complex document.

  If you are collaborating on a document through email, establish rules for how to use the To and Cc lines and make sure that all your team members understand when to use Reply or Reply to All.

  If you are collaborating on a Microsoft Office document, protect the document from unauthorized changes including the Track Changes feature being turned off. You can also require anyone who changes a document to add her name, the date of change, and a version number to a header or footer of the document.

22

Need for effective version control helps to make an argument for online document collaboration. When you store a document in a Meeting or Document Workspace or project document library, everyone on the project team can always see the latest document version. Any team member can check out documents, make changes, and check them back in. You can see who has the document checked out and who has made changes. You can also see the document history and older document versions at any time.

Using Document Libraries

You can configure a space for project documents by creating a WSS site for each project in your project portfolio. These project sites may be created automatically or manually when a project is published to Project Server 2003.

The project manager or anybody else with appropriate permissions can then set up a document library. A *document library* is a document folder with a collection of documents. The default template for the documents in each library can be configured, if required. By default, administrators as well as project managers can define the document properties required and who has access to the project documents. Each document's creator defines information about the document, which appears in the contents list for the library.

Two different types of document libraries are available in Project Server 2003:

- **Project document library**—Stores documents related to a specific project. Each project can have multiple document libraries configured. Authorized users can create additional document libraries for the project. Project managers, who by default have design list permission on WSS, can make changes to specific document libraries.

- **Public document library**—Stores documents accessible to all users in the organization. The server administrator configures the access to documents in this library. Although any user can contribute documents to this library, only an authorized user can create and customize public document libraries.

> **NOTE**
>
> Before you can work with documents, a web server running WSS must be installed and configured properly for Project Server 2003, and a project-specific site must be created for each project in your portfolio.

Viewing Documents in Project Professional

If you want to view documents in the Project Professional client, select Collaborate, Documents from the menu.

Document libraries features include the following:

- **Alert notification**—The PWA client uses alerts to notify you through email about additions, deletions, and changes to document libraries. You can receive alert results immediately, or request alerts daily or weekly.

- **Document versioning and document check-in and check-out**—With document versioning, a backup copy of a file is created whenever the file is saved to a document library. Users can also check out a document to lock it while editing, preventing other users from overwriting or editing it inadvertently.

Three groups of document libraries are accessible to you and your project team members via the Project Professional client:

- **My Projects**—This library group shows documents related to your specific projects. Each project can have multiple libraries associated with it. Authorized users can create additional document libraries for the project. Project managers, who by default have design list permission in WSS, can define properties for each document library or create new document libraries. Team members can create, upload, and edit documents in existing document libraries. To configure these permissions for creating, uploading, and editing documents for other users, go to the WSS server administration module.

- **Public**—This library group stores documents accessible by all users in your organization. The administrator defines who has access to documents in this library group. By default, every user has permissions to create and customize public document libraries.

- **Other Projects**—This library group stores documents related to additional projects that an administrator gives you permission to view.

    ▶ **SEE** "Documents," **PAGE 468**.

Updating Project Progress

Whether your project team members are in the same office building or in a different country, collaborating on shared projects and updating them can be a challenge. Managing all changes made to all shared documents by each project team member can quickly become a logistical nightmare. The consequences of mismanaging document changes and project progress information can be serious. They may include duplicated task effort, unauthorized project changes, and inconsistent task work.

With this in mind, it is important to design and maintain an adequate progress tracking system for your project portfolio.

Tracking Project Changes

Some project teams track changes and updates by email or in periodic status meetings. Project managers collect the update and change information first and then update and republish their project plans for the rest of the project team. This method may work for smaller less formal project teams, but it can be difficult to scale up for large, more formal ones.

Other project teams may decide to use team collaboration features available in Project Server 2003 software. This tracking system can work well if everyone on the project team uses those features consistently.

Collaborating on projects with team members has come a long way from the days when project team members passed around floppy disks or paper folders. Today, many collaborative technologies are available to choose from, enabling you to keep your project-related documents on an intranet or extranet, and you can collaborate and communicate project updates and changes across the world.

However, when it comes to project progress tracking, one thing remains the same. To collaborate and track your project progress effectively, you should stay informed of changes, additions, and deletions to project task and resource assignments, documents, and other related project artifacts.

Updating Project Progress Workflow

This section focuses on the role of the project manager in the project update process. If your role in your organization is a project manager, you can use the Updates page in the PWA client to review, accept, or reject task updates or requests sent by your team members.

The Updates page contains a listing of all task updates sent by your team members working on projects controlled by you, whether they are newly created tasks, delegated tasks, or updates for a task's actual progress.

You as a project manager then have the option to accept or reject the updates from your resources before committing the changes to the appropriate project plan, as part of the overall plan update cycle.

> **NOTE**
>
> This process ensures that the project manager remains the gatekeeper of the project plan. All updates have to pass through and be accepted by the project manager before the updates are saved to the plan. This maintains the integrity of the project plan and gives the project manager needed control over his resource assignments.

The Updates page is available to project managers and those who have the permission to view the Updates page. The ability to manage task changes is set by the system administrator.

The activities that can be carried out from the Updates page include

- Viewing task changes and updates from resources
- Accepting or rejecting these changes and updates and saving them into the appropriate Project Professional plan

- Setting up rules that allow automatic updating of task changes according to set criteria

- Viewing of a task update archive, listing historical changes to tasks made by the project manager

    ▶ **SEE** "Using the Updates Page," **PAGE 336**.

For the project manager to track the project progress and report that progress to senior management, she must save the task changes and updates submitted by project team resources back into the Project Professional plan.

After all changes and updates are saved in the project plan, the project manager then makes necessary adjustments to the project plan to meet the project requirements and republishes the plan, including all changes to resources assignments, back to the Project Server.

Figure 22.4 describes the flow of these activities in relation to the entire plan update cycle process. The part of the cycle carried out by the project manager using the Updates page and the Project Professional client are highlighted in white. The grayed out areas are other parts of the process performed by the project team members.

After the project manager processes all task updates and changes—rejecting or accepting them—in the Updates page, the updated information is transferred to the project plan by clicking the Update button.

For the tasks accepted by the project manager, the relevant project plans will be opened and the changes automatically applied to the appropriate plan.

Not until the plan is saved are the task changes and updates permanently saved in the project plan.

Updating and Saving Task Changes into Project Schedules

As a project manager, you must save the task updates and changes submitted by your resources back into your project schedule.

The Project Professional client must be installed on the machine used for updates processing. If the Project Professional client is not running, it will automatically be launched and a connection to the Project Server will be established to update relevant enterprise project plans. If any updates cannot be completed, an alert is displayed.

When you accept a change, the relevant project schedules open and the changes are applied automatically to all relevant open plans. The plans remain open with icons in the information column indicating the tasks where these changes have had an impact. Until you save the plans, the changes and updates do not become permanent.

After all the updates and changes are saved to the plans, you should republish the plans to Project Server and save the updated project schedules.

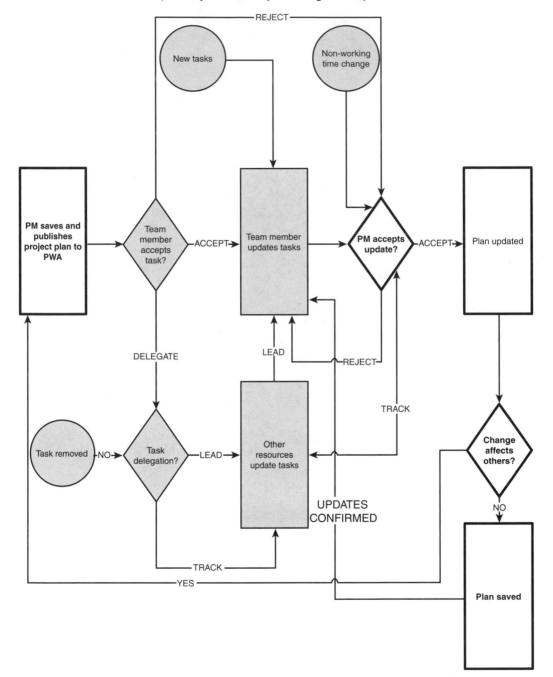

Update Cycle From Project Managers Perspective

FIGURE 22.4   The schematic workflow of task update information and the role a project
manager plays in this process.

Setting the Status Date

After you save the latest actual information to your project plan, it is important to reset the project status date. Anybody who needs information about the project progress then knows when your plan was updated the last time. To do so, select Project, Project Information from the menu.

Enter the date in the Status Date field. This date is usually set to the last day with actual work reported for your last reporting period, as shown in Figure 22.5. Any task updates and changes you have entered through the end of that day will be reflected in any reports or schedule updates.

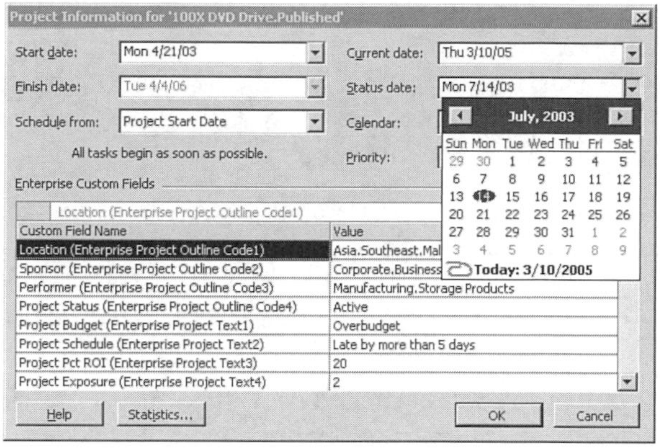

FIGURE 22.5   The dialog box where you reset your status date for the next reporting period.

Publishing the Project

For the project information to be made available in PWA, you first must save and publish project information to Project Server. By doing so, project managers make project information available to team members, stakeholders, and anyone who has been granted the appropriate permission to view project information.

There are two ways of publishing project information on the server: manually and automatically.

To publish project information manually, follow the process described by the following steps:

1. The project manager develops the project schedule in Project Professional; this includes assigning resources to tasks.

2. The project manager saves the project to the server and publishes all information. After all project information is published, team members receive their task assignment, and these are visible on each team member's Tasks page. Also, now all project information is visible in PWA to all users with appropriate permission.

3. Every time a project needs to be updated, the project manager operates the changes needed and then publishes all information again.

Project Professional offers users four choices when it comes to publishing information on the server:

- **Publish All Information**—Publishes all information that exists in the project schedule, including task assignments, updates of project information, and updated status. This option updates information about the project and assignments in Project Center, Project views, and Tasks assignments.

- **Publish Project Plan**—Used to publish the most current project information so that team members and other stakeholders can have access to it. This option refreshes the information in Project Center and Project views.

- **New and Changed Assignments**—Informs team members of the latest project updates by publishing new and changed assignments. This option refreshes the information on the Tasks page and Assignments views. You may choose this option to refresh the information on team members' Tasks pages on a regular basis (for example, every week on Monday morning).

- **Republish Assignments to Refresh Data on Team Members' Tasks Page or Force and Update Assignment Information**—Use this option after a team member hides a task and then needs to see it back on her Tasks page. The second way of publishing project information on the server is to choose the Automatic option.

To publish project information to Project Server automatically, from the Project Professional menu, select Tools, Options to open the Options dialog box; then select the Collaborate tab. Under On Every Save, Publish the Following Information to Project Server, select from the following:

- To automatically publish new and updated assignments, select the New and Changed Assignments check box.

- To automatically publish project summary information, select the Project Summary check box. This operation has the same effect as selecting Project Plan from the Collaborate menu in Project Professional.

- To include the full project plan with the project summary information, select the Including Full Project Plan check box. This is the same as selecting All Information on the Collaborate menu in Project Professional.

It is important to mention here that the Publish feature also has the effect of flagging resources as Committed. If assignments are not published on the server for a particular project, the result is that resources assigned in that project are flagged as Proposed. In this case, the "proposed" resources do not receive any task assignments on their Tasks page. This could be an effective method to perform a quick "what-if" analysis regarding task assignments and their effect on the overall resource allocation.

Updating the Project

After setting the status date, the next important step is to reschedule any work that was scheduled to be completed but for whatever reason did not get completed. It is imperative to understand and analyze carefully the impact of the last update on your project plan. As a result of the last update, you may need to make some changes to your plan before moving on.

When you consider your options for schedule corrections due to changes caused by accepted and saved actual updates, the following list provides some suggestions to choose from (in order of preference), with the caveat that you may not have some of these options available in your situation:

- Review the project critical path first. Also, after making any adjustments to your critical tasks, review the critical path again to see whether it has changed.

- Check the updated tasks and review Remaining Work to perform a sanity test. Make sure that the resource has accurately updated the assigned tasks and reduced remaining work still required as appropriate.

- Ask your resources whether they have ideas to get the work done quicker (perhaps using some efficencies not thought of yet). You can then reduce the Remaining Work estimate on the task to account for those newly identified efficiencies.

- Ask resources to work overtime. You can consider one of two options to change the schedule: Increase the number of units of the resource assigned to the tasks to account for overtime, or reduce the Remaining Work and add the time to Overtime Work.

- Break a critical task into smaller tasks that can be worked on simultaneously by different resources.

- Add more resources to get the task or tasks done faster. In some cases, you may not have this option. You can assign another resource to the task (the task needs to be an effort-driven task to show that the additional resource will help reduce the duration of the task).

- Revise task dependencies to allow more parallel scheduling (Fast Tracking).

- If actual updates caused overallocation of some of your resources, try to find another time, when the overallocated resources can do the work without being overallocated. You may also need to adjust the task dependencies, not because real dependencies exist, but to make sure that the resources can work on the tasks at a different time. This technique often increases the project time frame and therefore is often not the most efficient option.

Select Tools, Tracking, Update Project from the menu. Then click on Reschedule Uncompleted Work to Start After and enter a date. This action may change the finish date for some tasks, as shown in Figure 22.6.

With the changes saved into the project plan, you can then analyze and adjust the project schedule as required and publish the plan, including any changes to resources assignments, back to the Project Server—that is the last step in the update cycle.

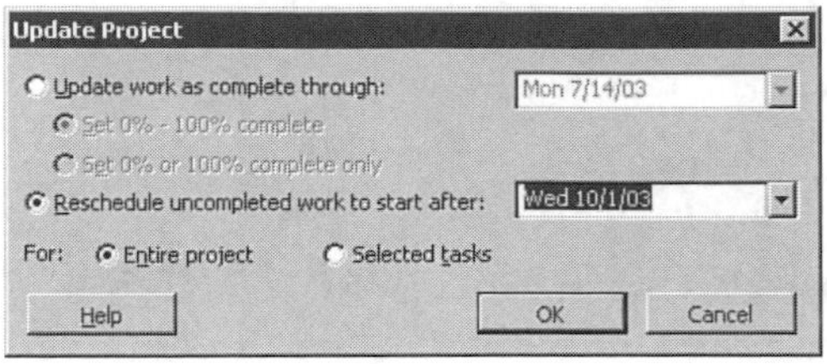

FIGURE 22.6   Reschedule uncompleted work and make sure that it gets done in the future.

Best Practices

- Always prepare a contingency plan for your project.

- Involve your resources in identifying all possible risks.

- Associate issues with documents, projects, tasks, and risks, as well as with other issues. This is an efficient way of integrating all the issues, documents, reports, graphics, risks, and so forth for easy navigation and browsing.

- Periodically evaluate your document and team collaboration processes.

- Keep your document collaboration processes lean and flexible.

- Focus on document version control.

- Design and maintain an adequate progress tracking system suitable for your organization and project portfolio.

- Understand and analyze carefully the impacts of all changes and updates on your project portfolio plans.

PART VII

Enterprise Project
Management Integration
with Microsoft Office
Applications

IN THIS PART

CHAPTER 23   Project Web Access and Project
Professional Integration with Office   **615**

CHAPTER 24   Project Workspace Integration with Office   **635**

Project Web Access and Project Professional Integration with Office

IN THIS CHAPTER

- Project Web Access and Project Professional with Individual Office Applications

- Best Practices

Microsoft's Enterprise Project Management (EPM) solution was designed to work and seamlessly integrate with applications in the Microsoft Office System, including Microsoft Office Excel 2003, Microsoft Office PowerPoint 2003, and Microsoft Office Visio 2003. This enables you to effectively communicate, collaborate, and share project information with a wider audience, using the Microsoft Office System's comprehensive, integrated system of programs that work together to analyze, publish, and share business data.

Prior to discussing EPM/Office integration, it is important to briefly mention Office Editions, which have different levels of integration with EPM. For example, to use Office Web Components in full interactive mode to create Portfolio Analyzer views, a valid end-user license for a Microsoft Office 2003 Edition, Microsoft Office Project Professional 2003, or any Microsoft Office System program is needed. Additionally, Windows SharePoint Services (WSS) versioning and check-in/check-out are fully integrated only with Office 2003. Because it has the greatest degree of integration, the information contained in this chapter and Chapter 24, "Project Workspace Integration with Office," is based on Microsoft Office 2003.

> **NOTE**
>
> Any reference to Office in this chapter implies the Microsoft Office Professional Edition 2003: Access, Excel, Outlook, PowerPoint, Publisher, and Word.

Project Web Access and Project Professional with Individual Office Applications

Integration with individual Office applications and the EPM solution is a big topic. Outlook and Excel each have numerous points of integration, and Visio has some integration features that can be useful for communicating project information graphically within the EPM solution. The discussion in this section highlights some of the most useful integration features between the EPM solution and the Office application suite.

Project Web Access Integration with Outlook

Outlook integration with the EPM solution encompasses far more than emailing project plans to team members and getting email notifications from Microsoft Office Project Server about updated tasks. Outlook integration is centered on team members, allowing them an alternative to working with Microsoft Office Project Web Access (PWA).

About the Project Web Access Add-in for Outlook Integration Wizard

Team members can use PWA to view and work with their task assignments that have been published to Project Server 2003; however, they may prefer to work with their project tasks in Outlook instead. Because people already keep track of their appointments and tasks in Outlook, they might feel it's an added burden to work with the PWA interface. Working in Outlook may also assist team members to focus on getting their work done. The EPM solution provides the Project Web Access Add-in for Outlook Integration Wizard to easily import project tasks to Microsoft Outlook 2000 or later and assist team members in keeping project managers updated.

The Project Web Access Add-in for Outlook Integration Wizard is a Component Object Model (COM) add-in downloadable from the Tasks page in PWA 2003. In addition to downloading and executing the Project Web Access Add-in for Outlook Integration Wizard, you must have two other requirements to access and work with Project Server data in Outlook: A valid PWA account and Microsoft Outlook 2000 or later installed on your local computer.

After utilizing the wizard to install the Project Web Access add-in for Outlook, you can import your assigned tasks from the Project Web Access timesheet to the Outlook calendar. In the Outlook calendar, tasks can be viewed alongside existing appointments, and you can report progress on those tasks to Project Server directly from Outlook.

Project Web Access Add-in for Outlook Setup

To connect PWA and Outlook you must be a local administrator on the workstation, or your Windows policies must allow you to perform the installation. To activate the COM add-in on the workstation with Outlook, follow these steps:

> **TIP**
>
> It is a good idea to close Outlook and even perform a restart of the workstation before you proceed with the wizard because Outlook may have a background process running that may prevent the installation from completing unless you do a restart after the wizard.

1. Log on to PWA and click Tasks on the menu bar.

2. Click the View and Report Your Tasks from your Outlook Calendar link on the Work with Outlook screen (this link may also appear on the PWA home page as Work with Outlook to Share Calendar and Task Information). Click the Download Now button to begin the download of the Outlook add-in. When you click on this link, you may be prompted to accept ActiveX controls (depending on your security settings). Click Yes to allow the ActiveX component to proceed.

3. In the File Download dialog box, select Open to begin installing the add-in.

4. The Microsoft Project Web Access Add-in for Outlook Setup Wizard begins. Follow the instructions in the wizard to finish the setup.

23

If the installation completes successfully, you see the Microsoft Office Project Help dialog box when you open Outlook (see Figure 23.1). Microsoft Office Project Help is a handy reference for the Project Web Access add-in for Outlook and contains topics such as setting a date range for imported assignments and updating PWA assignments automatically and manually.

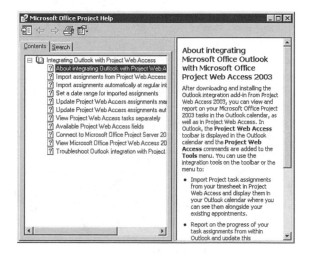

FIGURE 23.1   When opening Outlook for the first time after the Project Web Access add-in for Outlook is installed, Microsoft Office Project Help displays.

TIP

Integration help for Outlook and PWA can be opened at any time from within Outlook by selecting Tools, Project Web Access, Help from the menu. The title of the help window, Microsoft Office Project Help, can be somewhat misleading.

Connecting Outlook to Project Server

To share data with Project Server, Outlook must have a valid connection to your Project Server installation. To create a connection between Outlook and Project Server, open Outlook and follow these steps:

1. Select Tools, Options from the menu.

2. In the Options dialog box select the Project Web Access tab.

3. On the Project Web Access tab, under the Project Web Access Login heading, select the Enter Login Information button.

4. Enter the URL for your Project Server installation, such as http://*yoursevername*/ *projectserver*. You can test your connection by clicking the Test Connection button.

5. The default connection type is Windows Authentication. Keep that option if you use your Windows account to log in to Project Server. Otherwise, select Project Server Authentication and enter your PWA username.

6. Click OK to return to the Project Web Access tab in the Options dialog box. Other options here allow you to schedule Outlook to automatically import your assignments to the Outlook calendar and to automatically submit saved updates to PWA.

7. Click OK again to complete the Project Web Access add-in for Outlook connection setup.

The Project Web Access add-in for Outlook setup is now complete.

Project Task Import and Review in Outlook

After project task assignments are imported, they can be viewed and updated from within Outlook. The Project Web Access Add-in for Outlook Integration Wizard adds several new menu items under the Project Web Access submenu of the Tools menu. This section discusses two of them:

- **Import New Assignments**—Imports project tasks assigned to you into your Outlook calendar. A dialog box displaying a list of your tasks appears showing new assignments from PWA. Click OK to complete the task import.

- **Update Project Web Access**—Sends your updated tasks to Project Server and the appropriate project managers for their acceptance to the project schedule.

Appointment reminders appear if any of the new assignments are due in the current calendar period. As with any Outlook reminder, you can review and dismiss them individually or select Dismiss All to eliminate all reminders.

To review only your project tasks in the Outlook calendar, follow these steps:

1. Select any Calendar view.

2. From the menu, select View, Arrange, By-Current View, and Active Project-Related Appointments.

3. In the calendar, double-click an appointment to see details about the assignment.

Reviewing and Submitting Actual Work with the Project Web Access Add-in for Outlook

Your assignments can be updated within Outlook using the Project Server menu controls. Simply select the Calendar view and set the time frame to review the assignments within the date range you want to see. To see the assignment details, double-click it to view the assignment in the Project Web Access Appointment dialog, which has three tabs. Click the Project Web Access tab and maximize the frame to see your task timesheet as shown in Figure 23.2.

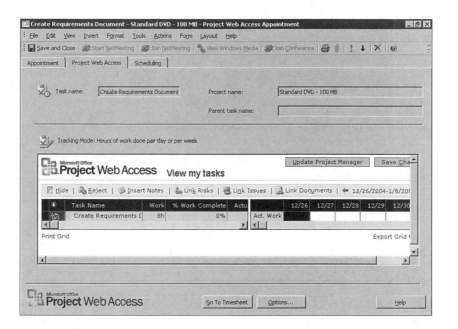

FIGURE 23.2   Project Web Access tab of the Project Web Access appointment dialog.

Input your Actual Work and, if necessary, update the Remaining Work for the task and click the Update Project Manager button to submit the work effort directly from this dialog box. Alternatively, you can use the Save Changes button and process all your task updates to Project Server at once. To update all your tasks simultaneously, select Update Project Web Access on the toolbar, or from the menu select Tools, Project Web Access.

Importing a Task List from Outlook

Many people use Outlook to track lists of tasks. The EPM solution makes it easy to import these tasks directly from Outlook to begin a project schedule.

Start your task list in Outlook. Double-click any task to access the Properties dialog box and additional information you can input about the task—for example, you can add notes (on the Task tab) and Total Work (on the Details tab).

Here's the procedure to import an Outlook task list into a project:

1. Input the task information into the Tasks list in Outlook. You can input a start date, due date, and notes in the Properties dialog box, if applicable.

2. In Project Professional, open a blank project or the project into which you want to import the Outlook task list.

3. From the menu, click Tools, Import Outlook Tasks. The Import Outlook Tasks dialog box appears. Select the tasks to be imported.

4. Click the check box for each task you want to import or click Select All to select every task in the list.

5. Click OK to import the Outlook tasks into Project Professional.

   • Project ignores the start date for your imported tasks. It sets the start date of the tasks to the start date of the project.

   • Outlook tasks are imported into your project file in alphabetical order and can be dragged into the proper sequence after they appear in your project file.

More Ways to Work with Outlook

In addition to the Project Web Access add-in for Outlook, there are a couple of other integration points between Outlook and EPM. On the bottom of the Work with Outlook screen, which you get to by clicking the View and Report on Your Tasks from Your Outlook Calendar link on the PWA home page, there are two links under the heading More Ways to Work with Outlook. Those links are Display Project Web Access in Outlook and Display a Digital Dashboard in Outlook.

Display Project Web Access in Outlook   Clicking on the Display Project Web Access in Outlook link, you may be prompted to accept ActiveX controls (depending on your security settings); click Yes to allow the ActiveX component to proceed. Next, the Display Project Web Access Page in Outlook—Web Page dialog box appears offering you the three options for displaying PWA in Outlook (see Figure 23.3).

The first option, As a New Outlook Shortcut, creates a new *shortcut*—an icon and associated name—in the Shortcuts pane in the Navigation pane on the left side of the main Outlook window that offers quick access to folders.

NOTE

Note that new shortcuts are added to the first shortcut group. If you want the shortcut to appear in another group, click the shortcut and then drag it to the shortcut group you want.

The second option, As the Home Page to an Existing Outlook Folder, has an associated drop-down list that displays your existing Outlook folders and lets you choose with which folder PWA should associate itself. Clicking the Show Home Page for the Folder By Default check box causes PWA to display when you click the folder from the Navigation pane.

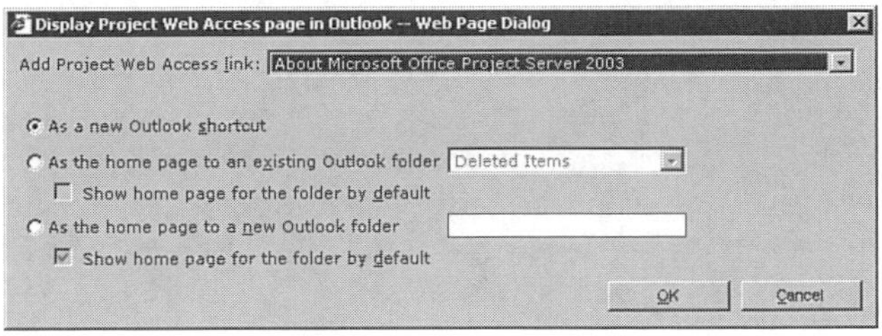

FIGURE 23.3   The Display Project Web Access page in the Outlook—Web Page dialog gives you the options to automatically create easy methods to access PWA in Outlook.

Using the last option, As the Home Page to a New Outlook Folder, you can tell Outlook to create a new folder in the Navigation pane, and, by clicking the Show Home Page for the Folder By Default check box, you can choose to have PWA opened in Outlook when you click the folder.

> **TIP**
>
> If you select either of the last two options from the Display Project Web Access Page in Outlook—Web Page dialog and find that instead of setting up a link to the PWA home page, it sets up a link to a page displaying the Product ID for Project Server and the Number of Project Server Users, you can manually edit the link. Right-click the folder from the Navigation pane in Outlook. In the Properties dialog box, click the Home Page tab and correct the URL in the Address box.

Display a Digital Dashboard in Outlook   The second link on the bottom of the View and Report on Your Tasks from Your Outlook Calendar page allows you the same three options as discussed in the preceding section, but instead of displaying the PWA home page, you can input the URL to your previously created digital dashboard and have it displayed when you click the folder or shortcut in Outlook (see Figure 23.4).

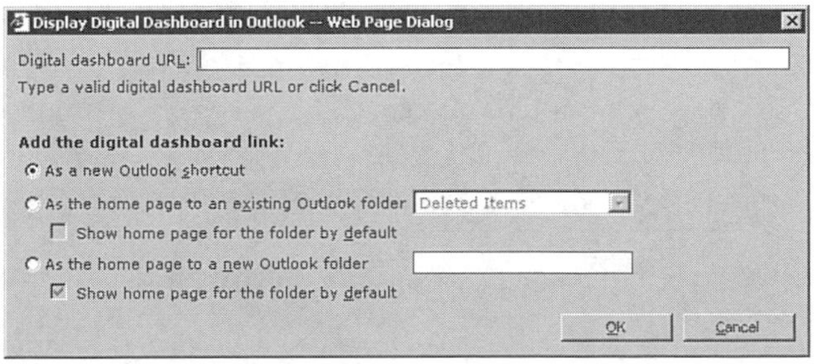

FIGURE 23.4   The Display Digital Dashboard in Outlook—Web Page dialog showing the three options for how to access your previously created digital dashboard.

Project Server Integration with MAPI Email

In addition to the Outlook integration items reviewed earlier in this chapter, there are many integration points between Project Server and any MAPI-compliant email system, such as Outlook. Although worth mentioning, these integration points are not specific to Outlook and Project, and, therefore, are beyond the scope of this chapter. Project Help is an excellent resource to further explore the MAPI email and Project Server integration features listed here:

- Emailing your project plan

- Routing your project plan

- Email notifications to team members sent from Project Server on new tasks/task updates

- Email to project manager when tasks have been updated

PWA Integration with Excel

Beyond Outlook, Excel has perhaps the greatest number of integration options with the EPM solution. This section details the features specific to Project Web Access. Project Professional integration with Excel is a large topic and has been covered well in other reference books—for example, *Special Edition Using Microsoft Office Project 2003*, copyright 2004, Que Books.

Export PWA Grid to Excel

Appearing at the bottom-right side of every PWA ActiveX data grid is the Export Grid to Excel link, as shown in Figure 23.5. When you click this link, you may be prompted to accept ActiveX controls (depending on your security settings); click Yes to allow the ActiveX component to proceed.

Excel opens on your local desktop, and the grid data displayed in the PWA interface is displayed in Excel (see Figure 23.6).

> **NOTE**
>
> The Excel export function adds a username and time stamp to the exported data. This can be a handy feature if, for example, you're taking a snapshot of data from a project for historical purposes.

Exporting to Excel is a simple, one-step procedure; however, keep in mind a couple of details to make the export more efficient. First, make sure to set up the data in the PWA grid that you really want to see in Excel. PWA grids won't allow you to add or take away columns from the display, so you'll have to do that in Excel (or use the Print Grid functionality explained in the next section), but you can sort your data, group your data, and filter it. After the data is exported to Excel, you can work with it like you would any other data that appears in an Excel worksheet because this is static data and there is no dynamic data connection.

▶ **SEE** "Exporting a Portfolio Analyzer Table to Excel," **PAGE 624**.

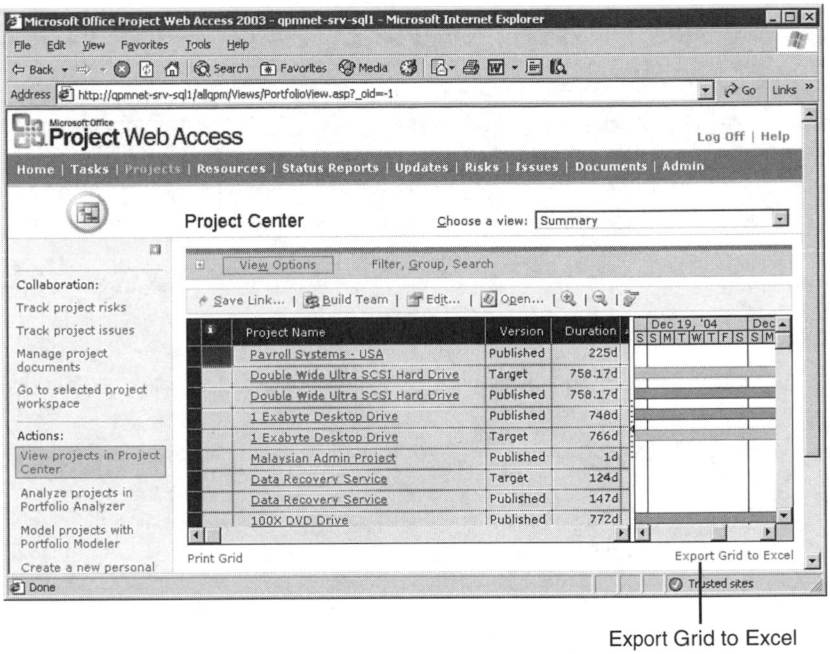

Export Grid to Excel

FIGURE 23.5 The Export Grid to Excel link appears at the bottom-right corner of every PWA grid and gives you quick access to this Excel/PWA integration feature.

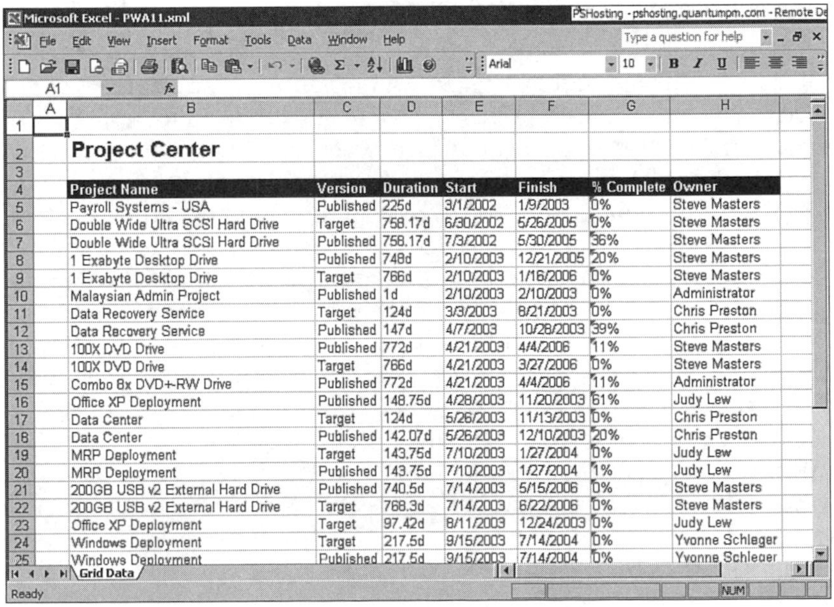

FIGURE 23.6 The result of clicking the Export Grid to Excel link. The formatting of the spreadsheet is automatically set when you click the link.

> **NOTE**
>
> Before Service Pack 1 for Project Server 2003 there was an issue with the Export Grid to Excel feature. When the link was clicked, an error message would display in PWA, and Excel would continue to run in the background. In other words, when you tried to export a project plan that contained more than eight outline levels using the Export Grid to Excel feature in PWA, a hidden instance of Excel remained running, and you received the following error message:
>
> "An error occurred while exporting the grid data to Excel. Because of this error, you can only copy XML data to the Clipboard. Do you want to continue?"
>
> This feature depends on an ActiveX control (pjprint.dll) that may not be available because of your IE security settings. This DLL is marked as "Safe for Initialization" but as "Unsafe for Scripting."
>
> Confirm that the IE security settings for the zone in which your Project Server website is listed are set as follows:
>
> The value for Initialize and Script ActiveX Controls Not Marked as Safe must be set to either Enable or Prompt.
>
> (To check your settings in Internet Explorer, select Tools, Internet Options, and then select the Security tab. Select the Zone in which Project Server is listed; then click the Custom Level button.)

Using the Print Grid Function to Export to Excel

Just glancing at the Print Grid link that appears at the bottom of every PWA grid control, you might expect that it's a simple print function. It is indeed simple, but it comes with a lot more functionality than is implied in its name. For example, using this web-based interface, you can arrange and format columns before you export the data to Excel.

Clicking the Print Grid link causes a new browser instance to open in front of your PWA browser screen. The lower portion of this new browser window holds a simple HTML, printer-friendly table with the same grid data you were looking at when you clicked the link. The upper portion of the screen gives you options to Arrange Columns and Format Columns. The toolbar below these options holds a Print Grid link, an Export to Excel link, and a Reformat Grid link. Using Arrange Columns, you can change the order of your columns in the display and exclude columns. If you click the Format Columns button, you get options to prevent column wrapping, use the default column width, or set a specific column width in em units, pixels, points, or a percentage. You also can choose the column alignment: Default, Left, Center, or Right. After you set your options for each column and decide which ones you really want to export, click the Reformat Grid link to see your changes in the web interface. Finally, click the Export to Excel link and click Yes on the ActiveX warning, and your data will appear in Excel, or click the Print Grid link to send the report directly to your printer.

Exporting a Portfolio Analyzer Table to Excel

Excel PivotTables summarize data in cross-tabular calculations and offer impressive flexibility for quickly changing the layout of the data. Several good references on dealing with PivotTables in Excel are available—for example, *Special Edition Using Microsoft Office Project*

2003, copyright 2004, Que Books, which contains an excellent discussion of PivotTable functionality. Additionally, Excel 2003 contains Help articles on how to use PivotTables effectively. Look for the article "Ways to Customize PivotTable Reports" in Excel Help topics. This section discusses how to create a simple PivotTable while avoiding repetition of the information that's already available.

Creating a PivotTable in Excel from a PWA Portfolio Analyzer view involves exporting the data and then altering the PivotTable in Excel to present the data exactly as you want it to appear. The export process creates a simple PivotTable that you can edit to fine-tune the display of data.

The basic, no frills, export to Excel is a simple process. Of course, there are options, which this chapter reviews, that make it flexible so that it can fulfill the needs of most any user in your organization. To export the current Portfolio Analyzer table to Excel, follow these steps:

1. In the toolbar, click the Export to Microsoft Office Excel icon (see Figure 23.7).

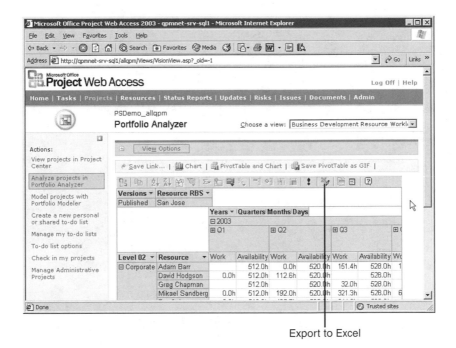

Export to Excel

FIGURE 23.7   The Export to Excel button on the PivotTable toolbar.

2. When Excel opens, click the button to Enable automatic refresh. If you click the button to Disable automatic refresh, the PivotTable framework will attempt to display in Excel, but you won't see any data.

3. The PivotTable displays in Excel, as shown in Figure 23.8.

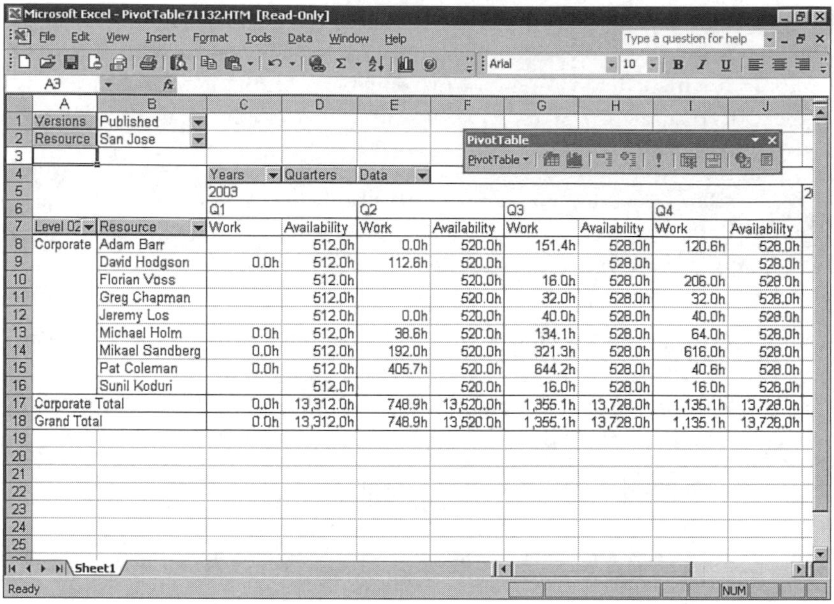

Versions	Published								
Resource	San Jose								
		Years	Quarters	Data					
		2003							
		Q1		Q2		Q3		Q4	
Level 02	Resource	Work	Availability	Work	Availability	Work	Availability	Work	Availability
Corporate	Adam Barr		512.0h	0.0h	520.0h	151.4h	528.0h	120.6h	528.0h
	David Hodgson	0.0h	512.0h	112.6h	520.0h		528.0h		528.0h
	Florian Voss		512.0h		520.0h	16.0h	528.0h	206.0h	528.0h
	Greg Chapman		512.0h		520.0h	32.0h	528.0h	32.0h	528.0h
	Jeremy Los		512.0h	0.0h	520.0h	40.0h	528.0h	40.0h	528.0h
	Michael Holm	0.0h	512.0h	38.6h	520.0h	134.1h	528.0h	64.0h	528.0h
	Mikael Sandberg	0.0h	512.0h	192.0h	520.0h	321.3h	528.0h	616.0h	528.0h
	Pat Coleman	0.0h	512.0h	405.7h	520.0h	644.2h	528.0h	40.6h	528.0h
	Sunil Koduri		512.0h		520.0h	16.0h	528.0h	16.0h	528.0h
Corporate Total		0.0h	13,312.0h	748.9h	13,520.0h	1,355.1h	13,728.0h	1,135.1h	13,728.0h
Grand Total		0.0h	13,312.0h	748.9h	13,520.0h	1,355.1h	13,728.0h	1,135.1h	13,728.0h

FIGURE 23.8 Finished PivotTable export to Excel with the floating PivotTable menu.

TIP

To access the Export to Excel button, the toolbar must be displayed on the PivotTable you're viewing. If you don't see it, right-click a blank area of the table and select Toolbar from the context menu.

Importing External Data into Excel

Two other options within Excel integrate with EPM. They both exist on the Data menu in Excel:

- PivotTable and PivotChart Report
- Import External Data

You can use these functions to create a connection to an external data source and import data into Excel. To integrate these functions with the Project Server database, you need to have intimate knowledge of the Project Server database architecture to produce a meaningful data set. Because of the complexity of this task, a discussion of these functions is beyond the scope of this book.

Displaying Timescaled Data in Excel

Using the Analyze Timescaled Data Wizard in Project Professional, you can export and display timephased or timescaled information in an Excel 2003 graph or chart. Timescaled data is task, resource, or assignment information distributed over time.

> **NOTE**
>
> The Analyze Timescaled Data Wizard does not export resource assignment information.

To begin using the Analyze Timescaled Data Wizard, follow these steps:

1. Make sure that you have a Gantt Chart view selected in Microsoft Office Project, and if you want to analyze data from only certain tasks, select those tasks before starting the wizard. Click the Analyze Timescaled Data in Excel button on the Analysis toolbar.

2. In the Analyze Timescaled Data Wizard Step 1 of 1 screen, select the option to export data for the whole project or selected tasks.

3. In the subsequent steps of the wizard select the fields, date range, and units you want to export, and select whether you want Excel to graph the data.

4. Finally, click the Export Data button on the last wizard screen.

> **TIP**
>
> The Analyze Timescaled Data in Excel button appears on the Analysis toolbar. If you don't see it, from the menu, select View, Toolbars, and then click Analysis.

Project Professional Integration with Visio

Using Microsoft Project's export to Visio functions, you can create graphics that can be imported into a Visio diagram for enhancement, annotation, and inclusion in another document. Another use for these graphics could be communicating project information in a visual format to team members by displaying the graphics in the project's workspace.

> **NOTE**
>
> Technically, the features reviewed in this section do not require Project Server and can be done with any Microsoft Office Project offering (2000 or later). These features are worth mentioning here because they assist with communication and collaboration, which are two of the main motives for implementing EPM. Also, these functions are not examined in other resources.

Visio WBS Chart Wizard

In previous versions of Project Server, the WBS tool was a third-party add-on. With Microsoft Project 2003, you can display project information in a Visio chart with a few simple clicks.

> **TIP**
>
> The Visio WBS Chart Wizard button appears on the Analysis toolbar. If you don't see it, from the menu, select View, Toolbars, and then click Analysis.

To begin the Visio WBS Chart Wizard, follow these steps:

1. To create a chart for all tasks or tasks based on an outline level, click Launch Wizard.

2. In the next wizard step, select an option for how much of the project you want to display in the WBS—the entire project or selected tasks.

3. Click Finish to create the Visio WBS Chart.

> **TIP**
>
> If you want to include only selected tasks in the Visio WBS chart, first change the value in the Include in WBS Chart field to Yes for those tasks.

Importing Project Schedule Data to a Visio Timeline

Presentations for customers and upper-management should be designed to be clear, yet thorough. You want to offer a schedule that is readable and presents only the milestones and necessary high-level information. Your Microsoft Project schedule can be presented in a simple format by exporting the timeline data to Visio.

Using the Import Project Data Wizard, you can quickly and easily import your project information into Visio 2003 (see Figure 23.9). Subsequently, you can cut and paste your timeline from Visio into PowerPoint or display it as a graphic on your project workspace. Follow these steps to import your project schedule to a Visio timeline:

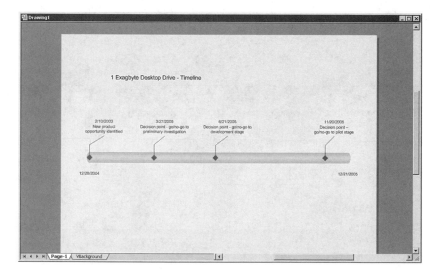

FIGURE 23.9   Microsoft Project information presented as a Visio timeline.

1. Before beginning the wizard in Visio, save your Project Server–based project schedule as a file on your local computer and remember the location. (The wizard will not allow you to import a project schedule that is currently open in Microsoft Project.)

2. In Microsoft Visio, from the menu, select File, New, Project Schedule, and then select Timeline (choose Timeline [Metric] or Timeline [US Units] if those options appear).

3. On the Timeline menu, click Import Timeline Data.

4. On the first Import Timeline Wizard screen, enter or browse for the Project (MPP) file you saved to your local computer for use in creating the Microsoft Office Visio timeline and then click Next.

5. On the next Import Timeline Wizard screen, select the task types you want to import. See the description at the bottom of the screen for details about each task type.

6. On the third Import Timeline Wizard screen, select the shape types you want to use for the timeline, as well as for the milestones and intervals that appear on your timeline. You can also click the Advanced button to set the timescale and display options for your Visio timeline. Choose your options; then click Next.

7. Click Finish to create a Visio timeline with the properties you specified in the Import Timeline Wizard.

8. To change the shape types for any or all of the timeline types, milestones, and interval shapes, right-click the shape on the drawing page and then click Set Timeline Type, Set Milestone Type, or Set Interval Type.

NOTE

If you have shapes on the current drawing page, Visio places the timeline on a new page in your current drawing.

Exporting a Visio Timeline to a Project Schedule

You can also export your timeline data created in Visio to Microsoft Project. This is handy if you want to create your timeline in a graphical interface and let Project Professional pull it into a schedule for you. Creating a timeline in Visio and then exporting it to Microsoft Project is a two-part process.

First, follow these steps to create your timeline in Visio:

1. From the menu, select File, New, Project Schedule, and then Timeline.

2. From the Timeline Shapes panel, click and drag a timeline shape onto the drawing page. The Configure Timeline dialog box opens prompting you to specify the time period, scale, and time format. You can also turn off the option to have Visio automatically adjust the dates when you move markers, interval shapes, or milestones on the timeline. This box is checked by default. Click OK to close the Configure Timeline dialog box.

3. Drag and drop milestone and interval shapes onto your timeline to show important tasks, events, and processes. When you do so, the Configure Milestone dialog box automatically opens prompting you to enter a description, date, and time format. After you have selected your options, click OK.

4. Using intervals, you can outline the phases or summary tasks for your project. From the Timeline Shapes panel, drag an interval shape onto your timeline. The Configure Timeline dialog box opens prompting you to specify the interval start date, start time, finish date, finish time, description, and a format. Click OK.

5. By adding an Elapsed Time or Today marker shape to your timeline you can show the elapsed time or the current date.

6. If milestone descriptions overlap or interval text is not visible, move them by dragging their control handles (yellow diamond).

NOTE

Visio allows you to export only one timeline at a time. If your drawing contains more than one timeline on the page, select the one to export. This rule does not apply to expanded timelines. If the timeline you are exporting includes an expanded (child) timeline that contains more data (such as milestones) than appears on the parent timeline, a dialog box asks whether you want to export all markers on the timeline's expanded child timeline.

To export your completed Visio timeline to Microsoft Project follow these steps:

1. If your timeline is not already open in Visio, open the file in Visio that holds the timeline you want to export and then select the timeline by clicking the border.

2. On the Timeline menu click Export Timeline Data.

3. The Export Timeline Data dialog box displays. In the Save In drop-down box, navigate to the folder to which you want to export the file.

4. In the File Name box, input the filename you want to use for your Project file. The Save As type should default to Microsoft Project file (*.mpp). If not, select it, and then click OK. Visio displays a notification when the export is completed confirming that your Project file has been created.

CAUTION

When exporting a timeline to Project, the tasks will be created with a Start No Earlier Than constraint. If this is not what you prefer, simply select all the imported tasks when you are viewing the project in Project Professional and reset the constraint type in the Task Information dialog box to As Soon As Possible.

Importing a Gantt Chart from a Project Schedule

A new feature of Microsoft Office Project 2003 is the Copy Picture to Office Wizard, which resides on the Analysis toolbar. This function is self-explanatory—it assists you in copying a picture of the active view of your project to a new document in most of your favorite Office programs. Your choices for the target application are PowerPoint, Word, or Visio (version 2000 or later). The wizard steps you through the entire exporting procedure.

Your project schedule can also be presented in a formatted Gantt chart by using Visio. You might prefer using a Visio-generated graphic rather than one generated from Project to send to stakeholders who might not have Project Professional on their computers. With a Gantt chart import, you'll get more detail than you would with an exported time-line, which might be useful for team meetings. Here's how to create your schedule in Visio and then export it to Project:

1. Before you begin, save your Project Server–based project schedule as a file on your local computer and remember its location.

2. From the Visio menu, select File, New, Project Schedule, Gantt Chart. A dialog box opens for Gantt Chart Options. In this process, you will want to import your data from a previously created Project file, so click Cancel.

3. On the Gantt Chart menu, click Import.

4. The first Import Project Data Wizard page asks where your data is stored; click Information That's Already Stored in a File and click Next.

5. The next Import Project Data Wizard page opens. Select Microsoft Office Project file and click Next.

6. On the next Import Project Data Wizard screen, enter the name of or browse for the Project (MPP) file you saved to your local computer before beginning the import process and then click Next.

7. The next Import Project Data Wizard screen asks you to specify your timescale and duration options. You can also click the Advanced button to set the display options for shapes in your Visio Gantt chart. After selecting your options, click Next.

8. On the next Import Project Data Wizard screen, select the shape types you want to use for the Gantt chart and click Next.

9. Click Finish to complete the wizard and create the Gantt chart from the data file that you specify.

TIP

Gantt charts you import to a currently open drawing may have different colors than your original drawing. To change the color scheme for your new drawing, right-click a blank area on the drawing page and then click Color Schemes.

Exporting a Visio Gantt Chart to Project a Schedule

You can also export a Visio-created Gantt chart to Microsoft Project. This is handy if you want to create your Gantt chart in a graphical interface and let Project Professional pull it into a schedule for you. Follow these steps to create a Gantt chart in Visio and export it to Microsoft Project.

First, create your Gantt Chart in Visio:

1. From the menu, select File, New, Project Schedule, Gantt Chart.

2. The Gantt Chart Options dialog displays. This dialog has a Date tab and a Format tab. On the Date tab, enter the number of tasks you want to start with, the time units you want your chart displayed in, and the timescale range for the project.

3. On the Format tab, select the options you want for the appearance of summary bars, task bars, and milestones. These can be changed later by clicking Gantt Chart on the Visio menu bar, clicking Options, and then selecting the Format tab.

4. The Gantt chart displays. Change the default task names to meaningful names for your project and set task durations, start dates, and finish dates.

> **NOTE**
>
> Similar to Project Professional, you cannot change the date for a summary task, which is a rollup of the tasks dates below it. Also similar to Project Professional, you can change the start date by clicking and dragging it to a different location. This works with the duration, too: Click the right end of the task bar and drag it to a new location.

5. You can add more blank task rows to the Gantt chart by clicking and dragging the center selection handle on the bottom of the Gantt chart frame. As you're dragging, an empty space is created. When you release the mouse button, this area fills with task rows.

> **TIP**
>
> By clicking and dragging the task rows, you can reorder the tasks in a Gantt chart.

6. You can add milestones to the Gantt chart in two ways. You can change an existing task's duration to 0, or you can drag a Milestone shape onto the Gantt chart.

7. Finally, create the dependencies between tasks. Click the taskbar or milestone that you want to set as the predecessor task; then press Shift and click the successor task or milestone. Right-click one of the shapes and in the context menu click Link Tasks.

TIP

Task dependencies can also be set in four other ways:

- Select two or more tasks and click Link Tasks on the Gantt Chart menu.
- Select two or more tasks and click the Link Tasks button on the Gantt Chart toolbar.
- Click and drag the control handle (click the task bar and look for the yellow diamond shape) on the right end of one task bar and glue it to a connection point (small x—a red box appears around the connection point when the connection is complete) on the left end of the successor task bar.
- From the Gantt Chart Shapes pane, drag a Link Lines shape to the chart and connect its endpoints to the connection points (small x) on the two task bars you want to link.

To export your completed Gantt chart from Visio to Project, follow these steps:

1. If your Gantt chart is not already open in Visio, open the file that holds the chart you want to export and then select the chart by clicking the border.

NOTE

You can export only one Gantt chart at a time. If you have more than one Gantt chart on the drawing page, select only the chart you want to export.

2. On the Gantt Chart menu, click Export.

3. On the Export Project Data Wizard screen, choose Microsoft Office Project file (.mpp) and click Next.

4. On the second Export Project Data Wizard screen, browse to the folder location where you want to save your project data and type a filename in the File Name box. Click Save; then click Next.

5. Click Finish to export your project data.

NOTE

To export data to Microsoft Office Project, you must have Microsoft Office Project 2000 or later installed on your computer.

Best Practices

- Use the Print Grid link to format your PWA information and display only the information you need before you export to Excel.
- Use the Analyze TimePhased Data in Excel Wizard to export your data to Excel and review in chart form for important information you may be missing in Project Professional.

- Use the Visio WBS Chart Wizard in Project Professional to create a WBS for your project.

- If you are a visually oriented person, use Visio to create your project schedule and/or timeline and export it to Project Professional. This information can be communicated easily with your project team by posting the image on the project's workspace.

CHAPTER 24

Project Workspace Integration with Office

IN THIS CHAPTER

- The Project Workspace and Shared Office Integration
- Integration with Individual Office Applications
- Best Practices

Windows SharePoint Services (WSS) is tightly integrated with Microsoft Office, more than can be covered in one chapter of a book. Moreover, this entire book is dedicated to the EPM solution, in which WSS plays a core role. Therefore, this chapter's focus is limited to WSS as it is implemented in the EPM solution (the project workspace) and the important integration points with Microsoft Office. For more information about WSS in general, Microsoft offers two important references that pertain to Office integration: "The Integration Guide for Microsoft Office 2003 and Windows SharePoint Services" and "Good Better Best…," the latter being a guide to the specific features of WSS that work with each version of Office. Both these documents are found on the Microsoft website. This chapter first reviews project workspace integration points shared across Office products and then discusses the integration that applies to individual Office products.

> **NOTE**
>
> Any reference to Office in this chapter implies the Microsoft Office Professional Edition 2003: Access, Excel, Outlook, PowerPoint, Publisher, and Word.

The Project Workspace and Shared Office Integration

This chapter first covers integration between the project workspace and Office in general—points of integration with two or more Office programs—and then delves into integration specific to individual Office programs. The chapter also reviews document workspaces, document libraries, and web discussions.

Saving a Document to a Workspace

An essential element of the project workspace is the capability to host documents pertinent to the project in a document library. Document libraries then become a good tool for storing project collateral or artifacts. But if you want team members to collaborate on a document, the project workspace offers the capability to create an entire site around a document—a document workspace. This allows team members to easily collaborate on the document.

WSS is all about enhancing collaboration, and there's no better example of that than document workspaces. A *document workspace* is a WSS site created around one or more documents. The enhanced capabilities of a document workspace include those that every WSS document library has—document check-in/check-out and versioning—but there are also other WSS features, such as task lists, links to other content/references, and presence information for real-time collaboration. Figure 24.1 shows the home page of a document workspace. Like any other WSS site, you can customize a document workspace site using a web browser.

NOTE

Access and Publisher do not support integration with the document workspace feature.

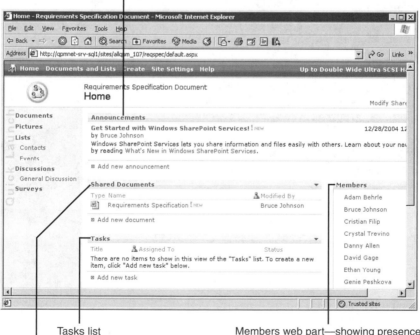

FIGURE 24.1   A document workspace looks and functions like other WSS sites but contains other elements designed to facilitate collaboration around a document or group of documents.

Document workspaces can be created in a couple of ways. The most common way is emailing a shared attachment. When you create an attachment to an email, the Attachment Options pane is displayed allowing you to choose whether to send a shared attachment or a regular attachment (see Figure 24.2). If you choose shared attachment, you get to choose where to create the document workspace. To make the location selection, follow these steps:

1. Click the drop-down list under the heading Create Document Workspace At.

2. Choose an existing WSS site from the list or choose the (Type New URL) option.

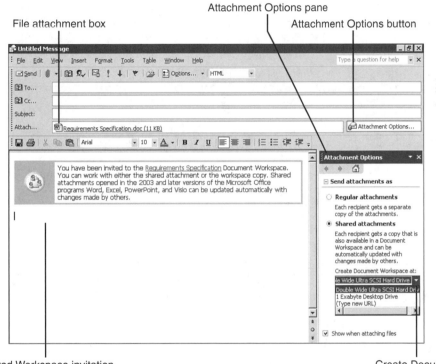

FIGURE 24.2   Email with shared attachment option.

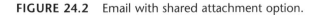

If you don't see the Attachment Options pane and you have the EPM solution implemented, look for the Attachment Options button at the right end of the attachments box.

When you send your email with the shared attachment, four things happen:

1. Your document workspace is created with the name of the document used as the name of the site.

2. Your email recipients are automatically added as members of the site with permission to contribute to the site.

3. You are added as the administrator of the site.

4. You get an email confirmation of the site's creation.

Members of the document workspace can work together on the document. When members are online, they can work on a local copy of the document. Periodically, the Office document they are working in checks for updates. Any changes saved to the copy of the document workspace can be merged with their local copy, or, if the changes conflict, members can choose which copy to keep. Finally, they can save their changes to the document in the document workspace, where everyone can integrate them into their copy of the document.

NOTE

You can also create the document workspace from the Shared Workspace task pane in Microsoft Office Word 2003, Microsoft Office Excel 2003, Microsoft Office PowerPoint 2003, and Microsoft Office Visio 2003. When you create the workspace using this method, you can specify the name for the site. Members can access the document by navigating to the document library of the document workspace site in a browser.

Document workspaces are an easy way to facilitate collaboration among project team members. The ease with which they can be created and the capability to create them within almost any Office application could quickly make them a favorite tool of the project team.

CAUTION

One concern your organization should address before allowing everyone to create document workspaces is management. The proliferation of document workspaces could be a real problem for the organization if some controls or standards are not followed. Here are some considerations:

- Who should have permission to create document workspaces
- Quotas on WSS sites (set on the WSS Central Administration page)
- How long WSS sites are maintained before they are archived
- Navigational issues with WSS sites that get "buried" at the bottom of the hierarchy
- Storage impacts—the size on the disk that each document workspace site consumes

When you create a document workspace site, it is created as a subsite of the existing WSS site that you choose. After a subsite is created and team members are finished collaborating on the document, the subsite is easily forgotten, and hunting down document workspace sites buried under project workspaces involves manually opening each project workspace site, selecting the Documents & Lists navigation link on the upper menu bar, clicking Documents Workspaces under See Also on the Actions pane, and reviewing the entries in the Sites and Workspaces page. Not easy to do, if you have hundreds of project workspaces.

Fortunately, the command-line utility, stsadmin, with its enumsubsites command solves the problem of finding subsites, but it doesn't allow you to see the data that's there to assist in making a disposition decision. At this point, you may want to review the third-party web parts available to help find these needles in the haystack. Check out the Microsoft Office FrontPage 2003 Customization Kit for SharePoint Products and Technologies website for available web parts.

Before leaving the discussion about document workspaces, it is worth mentioning the other features contained on the Shared Workspace task pane of the Office products that share this feature. Because a document from a document workspace is really a document from a document library contained in a WSS site, the Shared Workspace task pane contains all the functionality of a document in a document library in WSS. Several practical features on the pane work hand-in-hand with the WSS document workspace. Figure 24.3 shows that, in addition to having a link to open the site in your browser, several site management links on the Shared Workspace task pane give you options to delete the workspace site, delete the document, change the site title, change other site settings, and disconnect the open document from the workspace. This last option disassociates the document from its document workspace and releases the document's connection with the workspace. The application will no longer automatically check the workspace for updates, and your local copy will be detached from the document workspace. To complete the disconnection, you must close the document and save it.

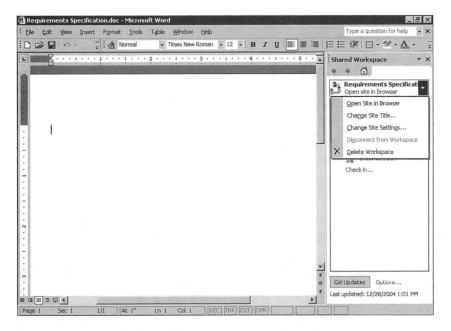

FIGURE 24.3   Site management options on the Shared Workspace task pane.

The Shared Workspace task pane also has six tabs that integrate with the project work-space, as shown in Figure 24.4. The Status tab gives you the current status on document updates. The Members tab tells you who's online—the drop-down list on each name gives you other collaboration options, for example, scheduling a meeting, member administra-tion options, and, where appropriate, the ability to Edit Site Group Membership.

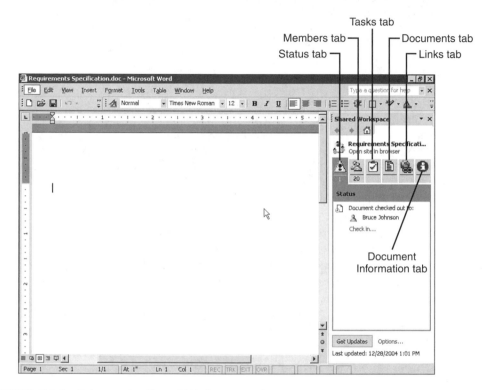

FIGURE 24.4   Tabs on the Shared Workspace task pane.

The Tasks tab allows you to assign tasks to workspace members. Other documents in the workspace's document library can be seen and opened from the Documents tab. The Links tab allows you to create links to relevant content and, finally, the Document Information tab displays information about the current document.

Saving a Document, Versioning, and Check-In/Check-Out

Project workspace document libraries provide a great deal of integration with Office prod-ucts in the form of a rich document management environment for project-based docu-ments, including versioning and check-in/check-out features. Provided that you have the proper permissions, you can save a document to a project workspace from your Office application, add versioning comments, and set document properties (metadata such as status and other custom properties). The one challenge to all this integration is easy access to your project workspaces. Setting up your project workspaces as items in My Network Places so that you can access them in the Save dialog box from your Office application is one way to make it easy. If you don't have the project workspace already set up in My Network Places, you can set it up from the Save As dialog box in your Office application (see Figure 24.5). Here's how:

1. In the Save As dialog box, click the My Network Places icon on the My Places bar.

2. On the toolbar, click the Create New Folder icon.

3. Follow the steps to create a New Network Place in the wizard.

> **TIP**
>
> When you get to the What Is the Address of This Network Place Wizard screen, you have to type in the URL of the project workspace. If you don't remember the number that the project work-space was created with, you'll have to navigate to it in a browser and copy it to the Clipboard so that you can paste it back into the wizard screen. The alternative to this document save process is to start your document directly from the document library by clicking the New Document link on the library's toolbar. Using this method, your document will be created with the default document template the administrator of the project workspace site has chosen—probably a Word template.

My Places bar   Create New Folder icon

My Network Places

FIGURE 24.5   The Save As dialog box set up with project workspace places.

When you choose a Network Place to save your document to, make sure that the location you're saving to is a document library. If you're not in a document library but instead one level up in the hierarchy and you have the permissions to do so, you can save to that folder. Doing so means that your document will not appear in the default document library view when you go to the project workspace. If this happens, the easiest solution is to click the Explorer View link on the Action bar in the document library; click the project's name in the Other Places drop-down list in the Explorer view. Your newly saved document should appear here along with other folders from the workspace such as Shared Documents, Lists, and so on. From here, because you're in Explorer view, simply drag your document to the document library where you want it to be located.

Web Discussions

Using web discussions, you can comment on a document without having to open the document and share comments with your team members. Additionally, team members can use web discussions to comment on a document without having the facility to edit the document. This feature has limited usefulness, so it is not covered in this chapter. If you are interested in web discussions, there's good documentation in *Special Edition Using Microsoft Office 2003*, copyright 2004, Que Books.

Integration with Individual Office Applications

In addition to the integration points between project workspaces that most Office products share, discussed in the previous section, Outlook and Excel have some integration with project workspaces that is unique. Project workspaces use a lot of email functionality, and you can control some of that email and interact with project workspaces through Outlook, which is a part of the EPM solution. Excel has many integration points because it's a good choice for dealing with lists of information—the building blocks of a project workspace site. The next section highlights some of the unique integration points that Outlook and Excel share with project workspaces.

Project Workspace Integration with Outlook

Because Outlook is considered to be part of the EPM solution, it's natural to expect a lot of integration with project workspaces. Some of the integration features are useful but perhaps not easily discovered, such as the topic of the next section: creating and managing SharePoint alerts in Outlook.

Creating and Managing SharePoint Alerts in Outlook

Because you can create alerts and manage them in project workspaces, you might not think about having the ability to do the same in Outlook. However, this feature does exist, and after people discover it, they find it easier to work with their alerts consolidated in one place instead of going to individual project workspaces. To access this feature in Outlook, follow these steps:

1. Choose Tools, Rules & Alerts from the menu.

2. On the Rules & Alerts dialog box, click the Manage Alerts tab.

From this interface, you can create new alerts, view and modify properties, delete alerts, and create an Outlook rule to automatically deal with the notification you get from an alert.

Creating a Meeting Workspace from Outlook

A *meeting workspace* is an entire WSS site devoted to providing a structure for all your meeting needs. Meeting workspaces provide lists and document libraries so that you can post meeting agendas, post meeting minutes, record objectives, record decisions, track tasks, save documents, and host discussions. Some project managers find it convenient to use meeting workspaces for their formal project meetings, such as a Project Kickoff meeting. To create a meeting workspace from Outlook, follow these steps:

1. From the Outlook menu, choose File, New, Meeting Request.

2. Click the meeting workspace button (see Figure 24.6).

3. Check the default settings. To change the location or template, click the Change Settings link.

4. When you are satisfied with your selections and you've completed the other information for the meeting request, click the Create button on the meeting workspace pane.

Default Create a Workspace settings

Meeting Workspace pane

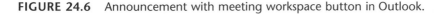

Meeting Workspace button

Change Settings link

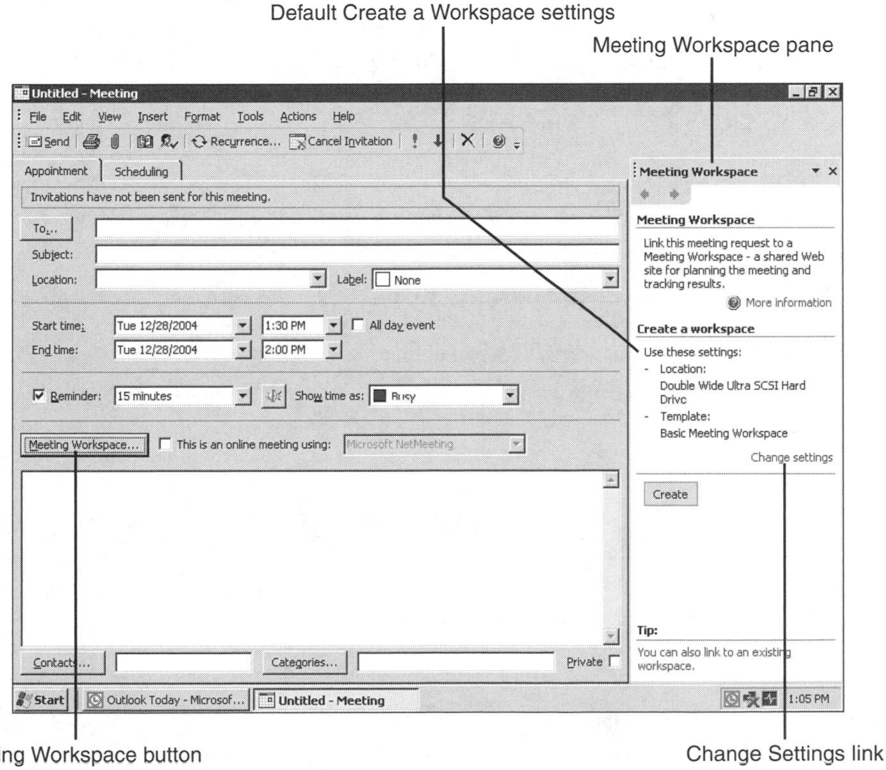

FIGURE 24.6   Announcement with meeting workspace button in Outlook.

CAUTION

The same caution applies here as it does for document workspaces: When you create a meeting workspace site, it is created as a subsite of the existing WSS site that you choose. After a subsite is created and the meeting is over, the meeting workspace is easily forgotten, and hunting down meeting workspace sites buried under project workspaces involves manually opening each project workspace site, selecting the Documents & Lists navigation link on the upper menu bar, clicking meeting workspaces under See Also on the Actions pane, and reviewing the entries in the Sites and Workspaces page. Not easy to do, if you have hundreds of project workspaces.

Fortunately, the same solution exists as for the similar problem with document workspaces. The command-line utility, `stsadmin`, with its `enumsubsites` command, solves the problem of finding subsites, but it doesn't allow you to see the data that's there to assist in making a disposition decision. At this point, you may want to review the third-party web parts available to help find these needles in the haystack. Check out the Microsoft Office FrontPage 2003 Customization Kit for SharePoint Products and Technologies website for available web parts.

Viewing Shared Events and Contact Lists from Within Outlook

If events and contact lists are important enough to your project that you enter them into the project workspace, perhaps you want to consider seeing them in Outlook, too, as shown in Figure 24.7. After an event list is "imported" into Outlook, you can display it side-by-side other calendars. Contacts and events are updated automatically when new items are added to the project workspace site.

Viewing Project Workspace Events

To add an event list to Outlook, you first need to open the project workspace in your web browser. Perform the following steps:

1. Open the project workspace's Events list that you want to access within Outlook.

2. On the menu bar, click Link to Calendar.

3. In the dialog box that opens, click Yes to add the project workspace's Events list to Outlook.

NOTE

If you don't see the Link to Calendar link in Step 2, you may be viewing the web part for the Events list on the project workspace home page. If that's the case, click the Events link in the header bar for the web part to navigate to the Events list.

Viewing an Events List in Outlook

In your Calendar view, under Other Calendars on the Navigation pane, select the check box for the project workspace entry you want to view. To view the Calendar side-by-side with another calendar, simply click the check boxes to display the calendars you want to see. Finally, clear the check boxes for calendars you do not want to be displayed.

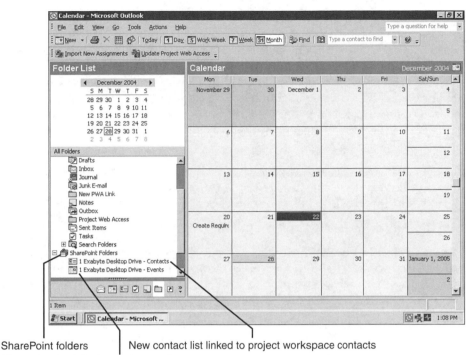

SharePoint folders   New contact list linked to project workspace contacts
New calendar linked to project workspace events

FIGURE 24.7   SharePoint folders displayed in Outlook with a shared contact list and a shared calendar from a project workspace.

NOTE

If you try to edit an event in an Events list that belongs to a project workspace event list or a contact from the project workspace Contact list, you get a message letting you know that in Outlook the item is read-only and asking whether you want to save a copy of the item in the default folder for the item. If you answer yes, your changed item is copied (with your changes) to either the Outlook Contacts folder or the Outlook Calendar, depending on which type of item you are working with. To edit the original event or contact, you have to go to the project workspace site.

Project Workspace Integration with Excel

When it comes to working with lists in project workspaces, Excel is unmatched in the number of features available. Not only can you manage the data from a list in Excel, you also can synchronize the data with your local copy of the online list, publish a list to your project workspace, and, finally, from the project workspace, import a local spreadsheet as a new list.

Publishing an Excel List to a Project Workspace

One way to create a new list in a project workspace is to create the list first in the familiar Excel spreadsheet format and then publish it to the project workspace. If you're creating a list with many columns, you may prefer this method to creating the list in the web browser, which involves creating each column step-by-step and selecting the options individually for each column. You could also perfect your list in an iterative fashion using this feature, publishing and deleting your list until you get it right. To publish your active list from the data on the current Excel worksheet page to a project workspace, follow these steps:

1. If you haven't already created your data as a list, select the data. On the Data menu, point to List and then click Create List. If the data range includes headers, click in the My List Has Headers check box and click OK.

2. On the Data menu, select List, Publish List.

3. In the Publish List to SharePoint Site—Step 1 of 2 Wizard screen, type the URL of the project workspace site and, if you want to update any changes to the project workspace when you synchronize, select the Link to the New SharePoint List check box. Also type a name and description and click Next.

4. The next wizard step allows you to review the column data types that will be created on the SharePoint site. After you are satisfied, click Finish, and your list will be published to the project workspace.

> **NOTE**
>
> If you used the linked list option, your list is created with an ID column, which displays in Excel. While the list remains linked, this column will be read-only.

Importing a Spreadsheet As a New List

Just as you can export data from a local list contained in a spreadsheet, you can create a new list in a project workspace by importing an Excel spreadsheet. Follow these steps to import a spreadsheet as a new list:

1. Open your project workspace in Internet Explorer and click Create on the menu bar of the project workspace where you want to create the new list.

2. Under the Custom Lists header, click Import Spreadsheet.

3. Enter a name and description on the New List definition screen.

4. In the Import from Spreadsheet section, type the location of the file or click the Browse button.

5. Click Import. Excel opens your spreadsheet so that you can specify the range of data to be imported.

6. In the spreadsheet, select the range of cells you want to import. Click Import when you are finished specifying the range.

Using the Import Spreadsheet As a New List feature is an alternative to publishing your list to the project workspace from Excel. Publishing the list from Excel is probably the most efficient choice if you have been working with the list and still have it open in Excel. The Publish from Excel option also gives you choices about how to import your data, such as specifying the data types for your columns.

Synchronizing a List Between Excel and the Project Workspace

You may decide that you want to work with a list offline. To synchronize the data in a list that you have permission to access offline after you have taken a list offline and edited it, follow these steps:

1. On the worksheet, click the published list.

2. On the List toolbar, click List and then click View List on Server.

3. You then have two options for how to work with the list from the List toolbar. You can click Discard Changes and Refresh, which removes any changes you have made locally, or you can click Synchronize List to publish your local changes and import any changes that have been made to the list on the project workspace.

> **CAUTION**
>
> It's important to remember that synchronization is not automatic, as you might expect if you've worked with importing contact or events lists into Outlook from a project workspace. In fact, Excel won't prompt you to synchronize when the list is saved or closed locally. You get a notification only if you open the file that contains unsynchronized changes.

Best Practices

- Collaborate on project documents using a document workspace instead of emailing attachments.

- Archive and delete document workspaces and meeting workspaces when they are no longer needed.

- Create document workspace items in My Network Places for easy access when saving documents to the project workspace.

- Use the Publish from Excel option to iteratively refine new project workspace lists.

- If you prefer to work disconnected from the project workspace, for example, to create a list of project risks, use the list synchronizing feature of Excel to synchronize your locally saved copy with the project workspace copy.

PART VIII

Server Maintenance and Configuration Management

IN THIS PART

CHAPTER 25   Server Maintenance and Configuration
Management   651

CHAPTER 26   Capacity Planning   683

Server Maintenance and Configuration Management

IN THIS CHAPTER

- Server Components Overview
- Monitoring Project Server and Windows SharePoint Services
- Maintaining Project Server 2003 SQL Server Databases
- Disaster Recovery
- Testing and Troubleshooting
- Managing Terminal Services
- Patching
- Best Practices

This chapter is intended to be a guide for system administrators and is broken down into sections designed to provide basic details and recommendations for configuring, maintaining, and troubleshooting a Microsoft Office Project Server 2003 system post-installation. Additionally, there is an emphasis on developing and practicing a proactive approach to maintenance and monitoring. This chapter is not meant to be an all-inclusive manual. Rather, it is geared to provide useful information to any organization, independent of size, skills, and resources.

Server Components Overview

This section contains an overview of the different components that comprise a full installation of Project Server 2003. In addition, it outlines the recommended software versions that will help facilitate the overall reliability, security, and manageability of the system. These include the following:

- Active Directory and Windows Server 2003
- Internet Information Services 6.0
- SQL Server 2000
- Analysis Services
- Windows SharePoint Services (WSS)
- Session Manager
- Views Processing

Understanding how these components fit together provides a foundation for maintaining and troubleshooting the Project Server implementation.

Active Directory and Windows Server 2003

Microsoft Windows 2003 Server, Standard or Enterprise, is the operating system most highly recommended for Project Server 2003 implementations. All Windows 2003 Server versions, except the Web Edition, include the latest version of Active Directory (AD). AD is a directory service that provides the capability to integrate and manage users, groups, and computers from a central location and provides a system to assign permissions to resources across the enterprise. AD was originally introduced in Windows 2000 and has since been updated and refined to offer network administrators scalability, accessibility, and functionality to manage the service requirements of enterprise computing environments.

The main benefits to Project Server 2003 offered in the latest flavor of AD include easier management of users, groups, and organizational units, as well as providing increased security. Additionally, you can now rename a domain and still maintain the global unique identifier (GUID) and security identifier (SID) of the domain. Although this was possible in Windows 2000, there were considerable restraints. Changing the name of a domain can be an exceptionally useful feature that greatly simplifies scenarios such as renaming a newly acquired organizational domain to match an existing AD infrastructure. In the Project Server world, this may be useful in support of corporate reorganizations, mergers, or the combining of two separate departments, and so on. The new Group Policy Management Console (GPMC) snap-in is indispensable to maintaining a large number of users.

Internet Information Services (IIS) 6.0

Internet Information Services (IIS) is Microsoft's popular Web Server software and is a requirement for the Project Web Access (PWA) feature of Project Server. The latest implementation of IIS in the Microsoft family is highly recommended for Project Server 2003. Besides the security and reliability improvements, IIS 6.0 adds ASP.NET integration, which is extremely useful when designing customizations to Project Server code.

Structured Query Language (SQL) Server 2000

SQL Server 2000 is Microsoft's relational database engine that is the backbone of Project Server 2003 and Windows SharePoint Services. Project Server 2003 requires either the Enterprise or Standard version of the software. The Standard version has all the features of the Enterprise version with the exception that the Enterprise version allows for a scalable solution, such as clustering. The Enterprise version is required if you have potential external (outside your firewall) PWA users and want to provide PWA Portfolio Analyzer views through a single exposed port. See the following section "Analysis Services (AS)" for more information on Portfolio Analyzer.

Analysis Services (AS)

Analysis Services (AS), often referred to as *Online Transaction Processing (OLAP) Services*, comes with SQL Server 2000 and is advertised as a multidimensional database server. Project Server 2003 uses AS to analyze all the different dimensions of data in the Project Server database and display that data in an informative and often three-dimensional graphical view. Components such as the Portfolio Analyzer use the OLAP cube built by AS. As with SQL Server 2000, Analysis Services comes in Standard and Enterprise versions. Project Server 2003 requires the Enterprise version of Analysis Services if you intend to display Portfolio Analyzer views via PWA over an extranet on port 80 without the use of a Virtual Private Network (VPN). Without the Enterprise version, you have to expose port 2725 to allow the browser Portfolio Analyzer ActiveX control to access Analysis Services.

Session Manager

The Session Manager is a unique component for Project Server 2003 that monitors and maintains a user's session information, such as the current PWA panes being viewed and recently viewed PWA pages. It utilizes Remote Procedure Calls (RPC) to communicate with IIS. IIS has similar functionality built in (workable in single IIS server implementations); however, the Session Manager provides this flexibility in a load-balanced or web farm solution. You can offload this service to increase availability, reliability, and performance regardless of the state of the server running Project Server 2003.

Views Processor (VP)

The process of publishing a project to the Project Server is database and processor intensive. The Views Processor was created to improve the performance and scalability of the views generation process. This process contains three subcomponents: Views Notification Service, View Processor, and View Manager. The Views Notification Service monitors the ViewDrop folder for an XML metadata file indicating that views processing should be performed for a specific project within the database. It opens and checks the XML file and, if validated, passes it on to the View Processor. The View Processor performs a check that removes duplicate publish requests for projects by project and/or user. Finally, the View Manager writes the views to the Project Server database by transforming the data it pulls from the project file to be published into view information in the enterprise project database.

Windows SharePoint Services (WSS)

Windows SharePoint Services (WSS) is an optional web-based application used to add document management, issue tracking, and risk management to Project Server 2003. Microsoft provides this application free with Project Server. WSS for Project Server 2003 requires Windows Server 2003. It is provided with Project Server to provide project-centric collaboration sites.

Monitoring Project Server and Windows SharePoint Services

Reliability, performance, and security are vital to any organization. A proactive approach to managing your infrastructure requires real-time monitoring. This section outlines several recommendations for monitoring Project Server, WSS, and their components and is intended to complement your existing monitoring processes. As any system administrator knows, the first step in resolving any problem is becoming aware that a problem exists. Waiting for your user base to report an issue is a reactive approach and can result in unnecessary and redundant calls to your help desk.

Windows 2003 Server Log File Monitoring

These days log management is an essential skill for any IT administrator or network security professional, and a Project Server administrator is no exception. It includes the monitoring, collection, consolidation, and analysis of log files and is a necessary and vital component to maintaining a healthy and secure system. With the vast amounts of log data being passed to a system, these activities can be a burden. Understanding where Project Server 2003 logs its information, warnings, and errors can help to reduce the effort and provide a valuable proactive troubleshooting tool.

Real-Time Monitoring

Real-time monitoring provides a proactive approach to diagnosing potential problems with Project Server 2003 and should be considered a cornerstone in any organization's network security plan. The presence of a strong event monitoring strategy provides a substantial advantage in identifying problems and potential threats early on instead of investigating them after the fact. Consider real-time monitoring to be a sort of "early warning" system.

The Microsoft Windows 2003 Server family provides an extensive mechanism for event log monitoring. If you've administered Windows Servers before, you are no doubt familiar with the Event Log Viewer built in to the operating system. To find this valuable tool, select Start, Run; type in **eventvwr**; and click OK. The Event Viewer window is launched, as shown in Figure 25.1.

Project Server 2003 events are stored in the application log and have a source of Microsoft Project Server Tracing Eventlog Provider. If your Project Server hosts many other applications, you may want to create a custom filter and key off of this source.

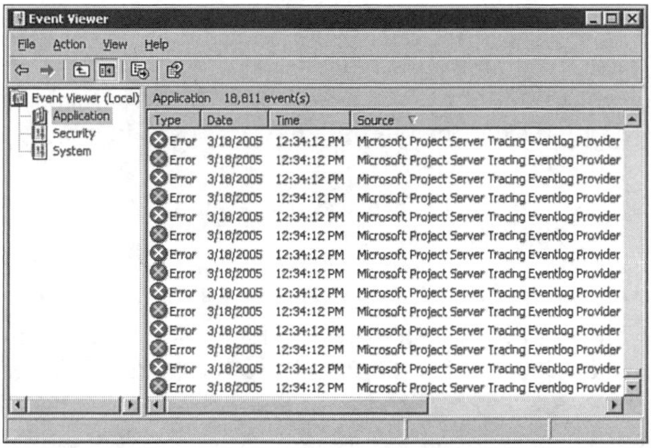

FIGURE 25.1   Event Viewer filtered by Microsoft Project errors only.

The application log is useful for tracking issues related to the access and publishing of projects and views in Project Server. If you start to notice high numbers of Error events, it is time to investigate further. Project Server error events almost always contain the following elements:

- **Date and time**

- **Source**—Usually Microsoft Project Server

- **Event ID**

- **User**—Most commonly reports NT AUTHORITY\LOCAL SERVICE

- **Computer**—Typically the Project Server itself

- **Description**—Contains the service or offending component name and descriptive error code

> **NOTE**
>
> Not all Project Server–related errors contain Microsoft Project Server as the source. Pay close attention to errors related to any of the related components listed at the beginning of this chapter.

The other important log to monitor for Project Server is the security log. This log contains the successful, and more importantly, the failed attempts to authenticate on the Project Server. Monitor this log carefully for potential illegal attempts to access your system.

> **TIP**
>
> Several third-party tools can monitor the event logs in Windows and alert you to potential problems real-time. Do a search online using the keywords "Event Log Management software" for suggestions and potential software solutions.

Internet Information Services (IIS) Log File Monitoring

Depending on your organization, you may have a web administrator who is already familiar with the IIS logging portion of this chapter. This section outlines some recommendations for monitoring and logging entries in IIS 6.0, as well as highlighting basic, normal Project Server type entries.

The Importance of IIS Logging

Keeping good IIS logging information is important primarily because it will assist you in tracking down potential problems as well as provide a detailed record of transactions for security and monitoring purposes. IIS logs can contain a lot of useful information for recognizing unauthorized entries into the Project Server including IP addresses, information accessed, logon information, and so on. In addition to the security benefits, these logs contain error entries and time stamps that assist in identifying performance problems and other potential project server issues.

Log File Formats and Locations

IIS provides the following formats for logging:

- **National Center for Supercomputer Applications (NCSA) common log file format**—Log entries are typically smaller in size, which reduces the amount of disk space required.

- **Microsoft Internet Information Services (IIS) log file format**—More detailed than NCSA format, and log files can become large. Performance on a busy server can be negatively impacted by lengthy entries.

- **World Wide Web Consortium (W3C) extended log file format**—Same traits as the IIS format; however, it allows for customization of the fields being tracked. This is the default format for most IIS servers and the most recommended format.

- **ODBC logging**—Allows writing to an ODBC-compatible database. Log files are compact, and data can be read much more quickly than a standard text-based log file. However, ODBC logging is processor intensive and requires tracking software capable of reading from the database.

- **Centralized binary logging**—Used to combine logging information from multiple websites to a single log file. This format records the log with an .ibl extension. You need an application capable of reading this format. Tools available in the IIS 6.0 Resource Development Kit can read this format.

> **TIP**
>
> Microsoft provides a tool called CONVLOG.EXE that can convert log files from one format to another. It is located in the \%WinDir%\System32 directory.

Each website under IIS is assigned a logging folder based on the type of service. This folder name can be found by following these steps:

1. Launch the IIS Manager from Administrative Tools, Internet Information Services (IIS) Manager.

2. Expand the folder called Web Sites; then highlight a website instance such as Default WebSite and right-click on it.

3. Choose Properties.

4. Click the Web Site tab, and then click the Properties button.

You should see the Log file name listed toward the bottom of the window. The actual logs are stored in \%WinDir%\System32\Logfiles\[folder name].

Recommended Logging Options

For the most part, the default logging options are sufficient. You should add one extra field labeled "Time Taken (time-taken)," because this field can shed some light on slow response times through PWA. Follow the same steps you used previously to find the log folder name to modify the logging properties. Table 25.1 lists recommended settings.

TABLE 25.1 Logging Options

Field Type	Actual Field Name	Description
Client IP Address	c-ip	IP address of the client that accessed the server
Date	Date	Date on which the activity occurred
Method Used	cs-method	HTTP request method
Protocol Status	sc-status	HTTP status code, such as 404
Protocol Substatus	sc-status	HTTP substatus code, such as 2
Server IP	s-ip	IP address of the IIS server
Server Port	s-port	Port number to which client is connected
Time	Time	Time the activity occurred
Time Taken	time-taken	Time taken (in milliseconds) for the transaction to be completed
URI Query	cs-uri-query	Query parameters passed in request (if any)
URI Stem	cs-uri-stem	Requested resource
User Agent	cs(User-Agent)	Browser type and version used on the client
User Name	c-username	Name of an authenticated user (if available)
Win32 Status	sc-win32-status	Error status code from Windows

When troubleshooting, you may find other fields helpful, but be aware that writing longer log files decreases the overall response time of the server.

Typical Project Server Entries

The most common Project Server entries almost always look like the following:

```
{Date}{Time}{Method}{Project Server URL}{Port}{DOMAIN\username}
➥{referring IP address}{Browser and OS info}{Status or Error codes}
```

25

For example:

```
2005-01-01 00:37:14 192.168.5.150 POST /ProjectServer/logon/PDSRequest.asp - 80
➥domain.local\joeuser 192.168.1.1 Mozilla/4.0+(compatible;+MSIE+6.0;+Windows+NT+
➥5.2;+.NET+CLR+1.1.4322) 200 0 0
```

In the preceding example, IIS returned a status code of 200, which translates to "OK. The client request has succeeded." For a list of other IIS status codes, try referencing Microsoft Knowledge Base article 318380. As with most content on the web, a search may be necessary if the preceding article is unavailable.

Monitoring SQL Server 2000

This section outlines recommendations for monitoring usage, performance, database connections, and log files associated with SQL Server 2000 as it relates to Project Server 2003.

Establishing a Baseline

An important element to monitoring SQL Server is creating a baseline. Over time, performance will degrade, and without a solid baseline it is difficult to troubleshoot problems. Keep in mind four key areas when monitoring performance and creating baselines:

- **System resources**—Physical capacity hardware

- **Workload**—Volume of activity

- **Throughput**—Amount of queries in a given time period

- **Contention**—Resources competing for the same data

Project Server relies heavily on SQL Server performance, and most bottlenecks can be traced to one of the four key areas just mentioned. It is recommended that you use the built-in Windows performance monitoring (PERFMON.EXE) tool and the SmokeTest utility, freely available from Microsoft, to create your baseline. The SmokeTest utility tests the basic functionality of a Project Server 2003 installation, but it also has the capability to put a valid load on the system. The following list represents Microsoft's recommended counters for monitoring SQL using PERFMON.EXE:

- **Memory**—Pages/sec

- **Network Interface**—Bytes total/sec

- **Processor**—Disk Transfers/sec

- **SQLServer:Access Methods**—Full Scans/sec

- **SQLServer:Buffer Manager**—Buffer Cache Hit Ratio

- **SQLServer:Databases**—Log Growths

- **SQLServer:Databases Application Database**—Percent Log Used

- **SQLServer:Databases Application Database**—Transactions/sec

- **SQLServer:General Statistics**—User Connections

- **SQLServer:Latches**—Average Latch Wait Time

- **SQLServer:Locks**—Average Wait Time

- **SQLServer:Locks**—Locks Waits/sec

- **SQLServer:Locks**—Number of Deadlocks/sec

- **SQLServer:Memory Manager**—Memory Grants Pending

- **SQLServer:User Settable**—Query

> **NOTE**
>
> A more detailed explanation on what each counter monitors and how to create a baseline chart can be found in the book *Microsoft SQL Server 2000 Operations Guide* published by the Microsoft Corporation, 2002.

Tracing Events Using SQL Profiler

SQL Server 2000 includes a powerful tracing tool called SQL Profiler. The SQL Profiler can monitor the server and databases providing an effective method of tracking activities and events associated with a SQL instance. This can be especially useful when trying to troubleshoot performance issues with Project Server. For example, you can monitor the activities of connected users allowing the ability to track concurrent usage and memory overhead.

Monitoring Connections to Project Server 2003   Using SQL Profiler, you can monitor connections to the Project Server 2003 database. To do this, launch the SQL Profiler from the Tools menu in Enterprise Manager and perform the following steps:

1. Choose File, New, Trace.

2. Type in your SQL server name and click OK.

3. Give your trace a name and click the Events tab.

4. Under the Selected Event Classes column, remove everything but the one labeled Sessions – ExistingConnection.

5. Click the Run button.

You see a results window like the one shown in Figure 25.2. Users with open Project Professional sessions will show up with an `EventClass` of `ExistingConnection` with the login name of the Project role defined during the installation. Two application-level user logins are created by default during installation: `MSProjectServerUser` and `MSProjectUser`. `MSProjectServerUser` is used by Project Server's web application to log on to the database (these connections are defined as a pool, so you may see several over time). Project Professional (the desktop client) uses the other application-level login (`MSProjectUser`). You can count the unique `processIDs` associated with `MSProjectUser` login entries to get an idea of concurrent connections to the Project Server database.

NOTE

The default usernames, `MSProjectServerUser` and `MSProjectUser`, can be modified during installation so that they may be different in your implementation. Check the security logins using Enterprise Manager to verify.

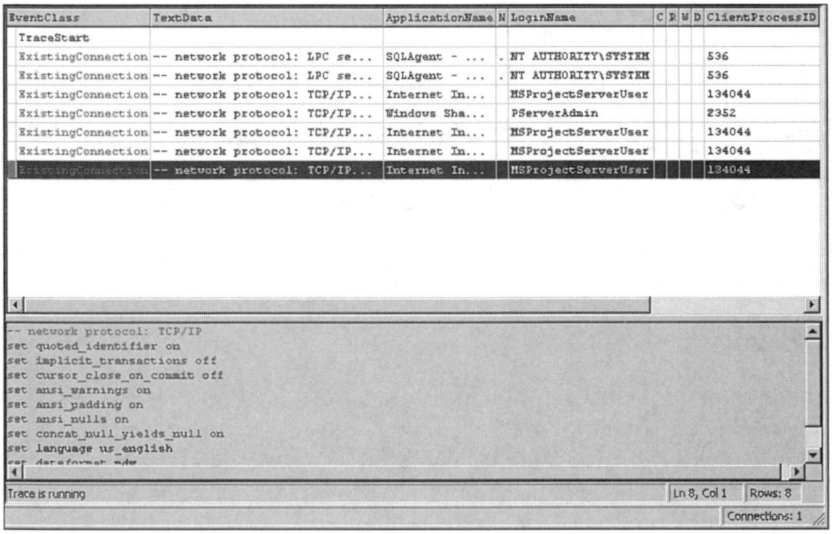

FIGURE 25.2 The results of this trace show one active connection (from Project Server) to the Project Server DB.

NOTE

Each active session of Project Professional shows up with multiple rows in Figure 25.2. Look at the `ClientProcessID` column to determine unique connections. Additionally, this type of trace only tells you the current connections when the trace was executed. It will not pick up any new connections that occur after the trace was started.

Analysis Services Monitoring

This section outlines recommendations for monitoring Analysis Services as it relates to Project Server 2003.

Enterprise and Standard Edition Differences

Just like SQL Server 2000, Analysis Services (AS) comes in a Standard and an Enterprise edition. Project Server uses both versions the same with the exception of implementations that include an extranet (outside your firewall) component. AS Standard transmits OLAP cube requests over port 2725, which is typically closed on the firewall. This issue results in an error, like the one shown in Figure 25.3, for computers accessing Portfolio Analyzer views from outside the firewall. For more information on extranet implementations, see the *Project Server 2003 Installation Guide* and the *Project Server 2003 Configuration Planning Guide* published by Microsoft.

> **Unable to access the Microsoft Office Project Portfolio Analyzer OLAP cube.**
>
> The cube may not exist, or you may not have permissions to access the cube.

FIGURE 25.3   This OLAP error can appear if permissions are applied incorrectly to the OLAP cube or if the wrong edition of AS is used.

The Enterprise edition allows for these transactions to use port 80 or port 443.

Monitoring Log Entries

From the monitoring standpoint, Analysis Services can be monitored from the event logs in Windows 2003 Server. Entries show up under the application logs in the Windows Event Viewer (EVENTVWR.EXE). Typical implementations of Project Server schedule a nightly build of the OLAP cube. By monitoring the event logs, you can actively alert and troubleshoot potential failed builds. The following is a log entry example of a failed cube build:

```
Event Type:Error
Event Source:    Microsoft Project Server Tracing Eventlog Provider
Event Category:    None
Event ID:    2
Date:        1/31/2005
Time:        4:52:19 PM
User:        NT AUTHORITY\LOCAL SERVICE
Computer:    PROJECTSERVER1
Description:
Component: MSP Resource Availability Refresh and OLAP Cube Creation Component
➥(ProjOLAP)
File: PROJOLAPProcess
Line: 1
Description: <Description><![CDATA[DSO.Server.Connect failed with error
➥message 'Cannot open connection to Analysis server 'PROJECTSERVER2'.
Unable to connect to the Analysis server. The server name 'PROJECTSERVER2' was
➥ not found. Please verify that the name you entered is correct, and then try
➥again' Error Number : '-2147221424]]></Description>
```

▶ **SEE** "Troubleshooting Analysis Services Errors," **PAGE 671**.

25

Maintaining Project Server 2003 SQL Server Databases

Depending on your organization, you may have a database administrator (DBA) who is already comfortable with maintaining SQL databases. This section outlines recommendations for maintaining the Project Server 2003 databases in SQL Server 2000 and is meant to be more of an overview and a checklist than a detailed how-to. Typical DBA tasks still apply.

Database Lists and Functions

A typical Project Server 2003 implementation includes three main databases. Table 25.2 lists these databases and their functions.

TABLE 25.2 Project Server Databases

Database	Description
Project Server DB	Contains the views, resource, outline codes, and project tables, as well as tables linking projects and tasks to WSS content.
WSS Config DB	Contains the connection and settings information for WSS.
WSS Content DB	Contains the issues, risks, and documents associated with the Project Server DB. Several content databases can be on a server.

In addition to these databases, it is important to include your msdb and master databases in any backup strategy you implement. Without these two databases, it can be more difficult to recover from a complete system failure.

Database Settings

The majority of the defaults in SQL Server 2000 are sufficient for Project Server 2003. One important property to determine early is the recovery model. SQL Server 2000 provides three recovery models, shown in Figure 25.4, located in database properties under the Options tab: Simple, Bulk-Logged, and Full. Only the Simple and Full recovery modes are recommended for Project Server 2003.

Simple Recovery Considerations

The Simple Recovery model is recommended for small implementations where database size and backup capabilities are a concern. Using the Simple Recovery model results in simpler backup and restore procedures. The main disadvantage is that you cannot restore to a specific moment in time but only to the time of the last backup. Organizations that choose this model typically back up nightly and can tolerate some data loss. In this model, when a restore is necessary, data entered since the last backup is lost.

Full Recovery Considerations

The Full Recovery method is recommended for larger organizations that can facilitate real-time backups throughout the day. The main advantage to this model is the capability to restore to a specific moment in time, which provides the capability to recover right up to the point of failure. The biggest disadvantages are the large transaction logs generated and the extra resources required to store, maintain, and confirm valid backups throughout the day. This method requires more thoughtful backup and recovery planning, or you will not have what you need, when you need it.

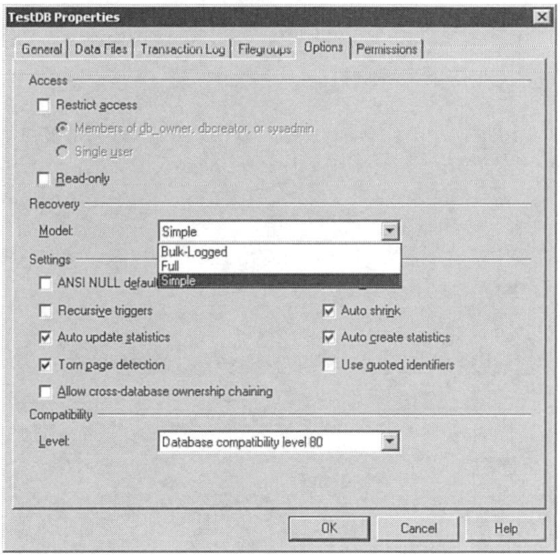

FIGURE 25.4   The Options tab under database properties allows you to set the database recovery mode.

Database Maintenance Plans

MAINTENANCE PLAN WIZARD

Jobs created either with the Maintenance Plan Wizard or manually will not run automatically unless the SQL Server Agent (SQLSERVERAGENT) Service is running. By default, it is set to the manual state. It is suggested that you set this service to start automatically in the Services snap-in provided in Windows Server 2003; otherwise, you need to manually start these services each time you restart SQL server.

SQL Server 2000 provides a wizard for creating maintenance plans. You should create at least two maintenance plans in Enterprise Manager to help maintain the Project Server 2003 databases. The first one should include at least the master and msdb databases and should contain an integrity check and backup schedule at the very least. The second should include the three main databases needed by Project Server, listed in Table 25.2, and contain an optimization schedule, integrity check, and backup schedule at a minimum. The following is a list of suggested settings for the Project Server maintenance plan:

- Optimization

- Integrity Check

- Complete Backup

- Transaction Log Backup

- Ensuring that the Maintenance Plan Worked

Optimization

There usually is no need to frequently Reorganize Data and Index Pages or Update the Statistics Used by the Query Optimizer for the Project Server databases unless you start noticing a decrease in performance. Figure 25.5 illustrates the options available under the Optimization tab.

▶ **SEE** "Establishing a Baseline," **PAGE 658**.

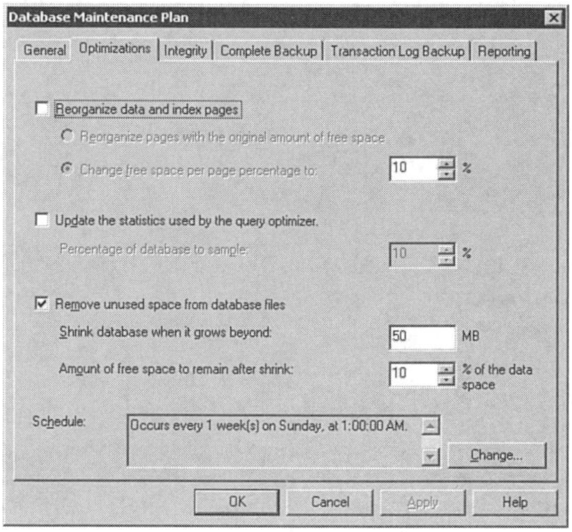

FIGURE 25.5   Under the Optimizations tab, an important option is Remove Unused Space from Database Files.

You should Remove Unused Space from the Database Files on a regular basis. Although these databases are dynamic in design and will grow periodically to accommodate requests, they will not shrink unless you tell them to. Shrinking the database files allows you to free up resources for other databases to use.

The optimization portion of this maintenance plan does not need to run often. Depending on the size of your organization and the physical hardware of the server, running this job once a week or even once a month is sufficient. Optimizations can be resource intensive, so it is recommended that you run them sparingly and at low load times on the server.

Integrity Check

Figure 25.6 shows suggested settings on the Integrity tab. Integrity checks should be run fairly frequently; typically once a week is sufficient. Checking the box to allow SQL to Attempt to Repair Any Minor Problems is recommended. "Minor problems" are not data errors, and this option will allow SQL to maintain the pages where the data is stored preventing fragmentation or other problems.

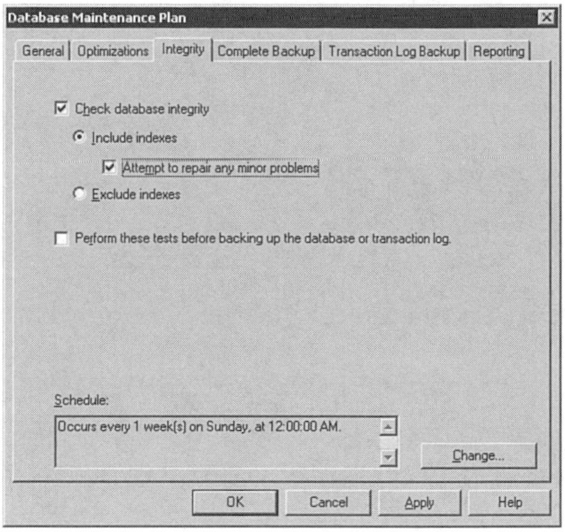

FIGURE 25.6   It is important to check the SQL logs after running an integrity check to identify potential database corruption.

The Complete Backup Tab

The Complete Backup tab, shown in Figure 25.7, allows you to schedule and verify database backups. It is recommended that you schedule a complete backup at least once a day during off-peak hours. Running a backup during peak hours can impact performance significantly. If you choose to run your Project Server databases in simple mode, this is the single most important backup you will make. Back up to tape or disk, but be aware that if you back up to disk you need to offload the backups to a different server or risk losing your backups as well as your live databases to a hardware or software failure.

▶ **SEE** "Disaster Recovery," **PAGE 667**.

NOTE

Backup files can be similar in size to the actual database size. If you have physical hard disk limitations, be careful about keeping archived backups. Each time a complete backup is run, the job creates a new backup file appended with the date and time. This could cause insufficient disk space problems resulting in failed backups and production SQL errors. Storing backups off the production server is highly recommended.

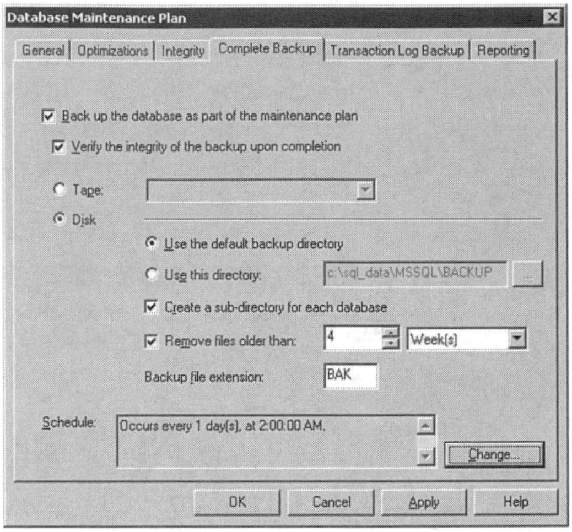

FIGURE 25.7   Set your backup schedule to match your backup recovery mode with this tab.

Transaction Log Backup

Figure 25.8 shows suggested settings on the Transaction Log Backup tab. This backup is necessary only if you choose the Full database recovery option. In Full mode, backups become very large, dramatically increasing the physical hard disk requirements of the server.

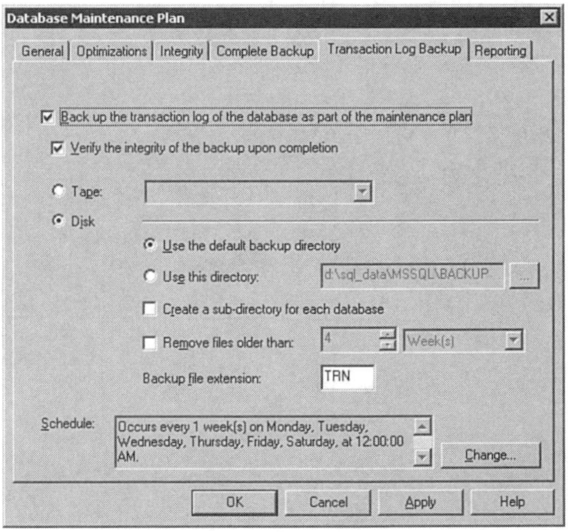

FIGURE 25.8   The Transaction Log Backup tab is unnecessary if the database is set up to use the simple recovery mode.

Ensuring That the Maintenance Plan Worked

You can use the Maintenance Plan Wizard to create reports and record job status to a text file in the SQL Logs directory. Additionally, you can have the report emailed to an operator or sent to a remote server. Figure 25.9 illustrates some of the settings available.

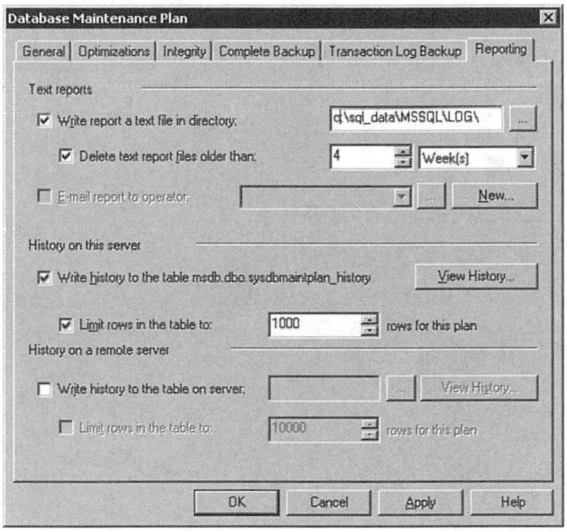

FIGURE 25.9   The reports generated by this part of the maintenance plan should be reviewed regularly.

> **NOTE**
>
> Maintenance plans are only a part of a total backup solution for the Project Server databases. They are meant as an aid for automating day-to-day maintenance activities, allowing the DBA to focus efforts on other business needs. Maintenance plans alone do not constitute a backup solution.

Disaster Recovery

The topic of disaster recovery could easily warrant an entire chapter on its own. Microsoft has published an excellent technical document specific to Project Server 2003 titled "Project Server 2003 Disaster Recovery Guide," and it is freely available from the Microsoft website.

> **NOTE**
>
> One vital element to a solid disaster recovery plan is testing your backups regularly. After all, backups are only as good as the restore. Just like any data, backups can go bad making restores impossible. Just because a backup appears to be successful doesn't mean a restore will be as well. Problems with indexes or tables in a database can result in restores failing, so *test your backups regularly*!

Testing and Troubleshooting

Over time, without proper proactive maintenance, any system will begin to degrade, and the performance of applications will suffer and may eventually break. This section is intended to be used by the system administrator who needs to know the basics of troubleshooting a Project Server 2003 installation. This section differs from the validation chapter of this book in that it outlines the typical tools and steps used to troubleshoot Project Server 2003 from a support standpoint. An assumption will be made that the Project Server implementation is validated and appears to be working prior to an issue arising.

The Application and Client Layers

Server issues are considered part of the *application layer* which, for the end user, consists mainly of PWA and WSS. For the system administrator, it also consists of SQL, Analysis Services (AS), Session Manager, Views Processing, and Internet Information Services (IIS) .

The *client layer* consists of the desktop components, such as Internet Explorer and Project Professional.

The first step to troubleshooting Project Server 2003 is to determine whether the issue is an application or client layer (that is, server or desktop) issue by discovering what component(s) the user is using when the error occurs. If the error occurs in the application layer, most of the following conditions should be true:

- The error occurs in PWA, WSS, or Project Professional (while publishing or saving a project).

- The error can be consistently re-created from multiple desktop locations.

- The error is not user specific. Other users can log on to the same client machine and receive the same errors.

If the error occurs in the client layer, these conditions should be true:

- Internet Explorer or Project Professional crash while working in the application.

- Errors appear to be user and/or desktop specific.

Troubleshooting the Application Layer

Several tools developed and distributed by Microsoft are designed to troubleshoot and reconfigure a Project Server 2003 implementation. As a system administrator, you will most likely use six key tools, listed and briefly described in Table 25.3.

> **NOTE**
>
> For more detailed information and instructions on use, consult the *Project Server 2003 Administrator's Guide* published by and downloadable from the Microsoft website.

TABLE 25.3   Troubleshooting and Configuration Tools for Project Server 2003

Utility	Description
SetTracing.exe	This utility is separate from the Tracing Service installed by Project Server. It allows Project Server alerts to be written to the Windows Event Viewer and/or a log file. Use this utility to create a log file to send to technical support for trouble resolution.
EditSite.exe	Allows you to test connectivity to all the key components of Project Server 2003. Additionally, it provides the ability to create new Project Server instances on the same server. This can be useful for testing and training environments.
Sec_audit.asp	PWA page designed to help administrators troubleshoot and view effective permissions on the Project Server. Also known as the View Effective Permissions tool.
psHealthMon.exe	Designed to help troubleshoot Project Server components that are responding slowly or not at all. It also has a notification component to alert you of potential problems.
PSCOMPlus.exe	Useful if the passwords or names of the AD accounts used for Project Server are ever changed. It allows you to reset the accounts used for connections to WSS and Analysis Services.
Proxycfg.exe	Command-line tool used to configure proxy settings for Project Server. Use this tool if a proxy configuration change is affecting Project Server.
SmokeTest.exe	This utility runs a sequence of tests to verify the basic functionality of Project Server and can also be used to put a controlled load on the system. Use this tool for both performance and functionality testing.

Using EditSite for Troubleshooting   EditSite should be the first utility run when a problem occurs on the application layer of Project Server 2003. After installing it, run editsite.exe. A window similar to Figure 25.10 opens and allows you to test connections to the main components of Project Server. This window also reveals all of the Project Server instances currently configured and their related connection information.

CAUTION

Be careful about changing any settings with EditSite unless the test results indicate a connection issue. Changing any settings to incorrect values will break Project Server.

Consult the Microsoft Knowledge Base online for appropriate steps to resolve any Failed test results. Typically, the main culprits for connection issues are the SQL accounts MSProjectServerUser and MSProjectUser.

Click the Test button to start a test. Figure 25.11 shows a results window.

Using the Project Server Health Monitor to Troubleshoot   The Project Server Health Monitor tool, shown in Figure 25.12, should be used to monitor thresholds for Project Server and can be left running on the Project Server or another server if the Views Notification service is located on another server. It is useful in tracking down latency or performance issues. Table 25.4 provides a description of what each tab is used for.

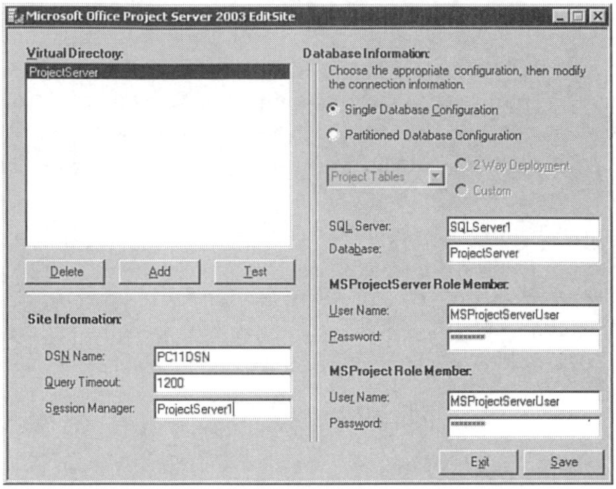

Figure 25.10   EditSite main screen.

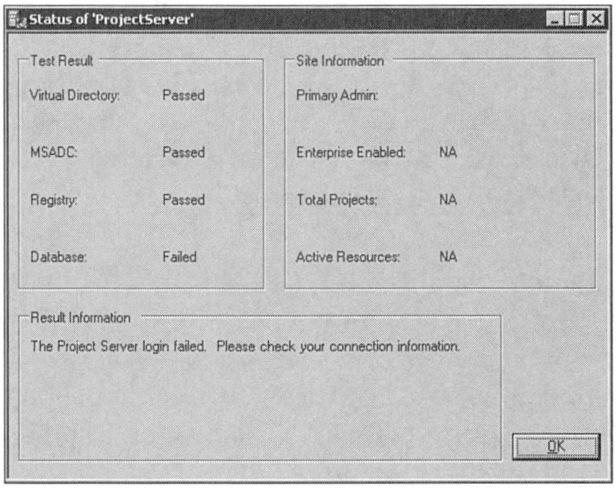

FIGURE 25.11   Notice the Failed entry to the SQL database in the results window from EditSite.

TABLE 25.4   Tabs in the Project Server Health Monitor

Tab	Description
Monitor	Monitors the current status of the server in real-time. Useful for determining possible root causes for latency issues.
ViewDrop	Sets the path information for the ViewDrop folders. This tab accepts both absolute and UNC paths.
PDS Info	Sets the PWA URLs to monitor. Each instance of the Health Monitor can monitor up to four sites at one time.
Admin	Sets the preferences for running the utility. This is also the tab to set the thresholds used to determine whether a notification is sent.

TABLE 25.4 Continued

Tab	Description
Notify	Sets who and when to notify when a threshold is exceeded.
Errors	Logs errors specific to the Health Monitor. This is useful when setting up the ViewDrop, PDS Info, Admin, and Notify tabs.

> **NOTE**
>
> In Table 25.4, under the Errors tab, when thresholds are exceeded, they will not show up in the Errors tab. They will be written to a log file or emailed depending on the settings in the Notify tab.

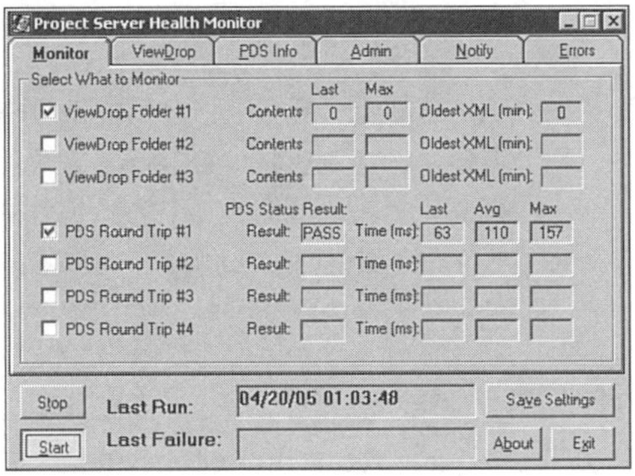

FIGURE 25.12 The Project Server Health Monitoring utility can provide a real-time troubleshooting view of performance.

Troubleshooting Analysis Services Errors Troubleshooting Analysis Services basically comes down to two things:

- Successfully building an OLAP cube

- Successfully connecting to the OLAP cube

If the cube fails to build, you should find errors in both the Windows Event Viewer and the Update Resource Tables and OLAP Cube page in PWA under the Admin, Manage Enterprise Features link. There are typically four main causes for a failed cube build. The first is forgetting to migrate the AS repository to SQL as outlined in the Post Installation tasks from the *Microsoft Office Project Server 2003 Installation Guide*. The second is incorrect credentials supplied in the Project Server database for accessing the cube. Use the PSCOMPlus utility to resolve this issue. Third, special characters may have been used in the Enterprise Resource Pool or Enterprise Outline Codes. Finally, incorrect or corrupted DSN information causes the OLAP build to fail. The DSN information tells Project Server how to talk to the SQL server. If you feel this is a possible cause, use the following steps to resolve it:

1. Launch EditSite.

2. Highlight your Project Server instance.

3. Change the DSN Name from PC11DSN to PC11DSN1 and click Save.

4. Change the DSN Name from PC11DSN1 back to PC11DSN and click Save.

5. Exit EditSite.

If your users encounter errors such as the one shown in Figure 25.12, there are typically three reasons:

- The user does not have permission to see the cube. This can be fixed by granting access to the group or user on the cube by using Analysis Manager, Manage Roles. Add a new role, give it a name, add the user or group, and select the MSP_PORTFOLIO_ANALYZER under the cube tab.

- The user is trying to access the cube from an external address, and you are running the Standard version of AS instead of the Enterprise version. The Enterprise version allows for connections using port 443 instead of the default port of 2725.

- The user's username and password on the desktop do not match her credentials on the server running AS. To resolve this, synchronize the credentials.

Figure 25.3 shows the typical OLAP error in PWA.

Troubleshooting the Session Manager   Symptoms of problems with the Session Manager usually are related to user logon issues. Because the Session Manager keeps track of where a user is in PWA and the credentials used to access Project Server, if it becomes unavailable, the user sees an error such as the one shown in Figure 25.13.

FIGURE 25.13   Error generated when Session Manager becomes unavailable.

Usually, restarting the Project Server Session Manager Service resolves most issues.

> **NOTE**
>
> If the Session Manager become unavailable in some load balanced scenarios, it may be necessary to manually re-point the IIS server(s) to a new Session Manager by modifying the following registry entry:
>
> ```
> HKLM\SOFTWARE\Microsoft\Office\11.0\MS Project\WebClient Server\
> ➥ProjectServer\Services\SessionMgr\{2A080D24-F2BA-4FF2-B0F2-FF1933F2A08D}
> ```

Troubleshooting Views Processing   The two main components to Views Processing that you may encounter problems with include the Views Notification service and the ViewDrop folder.

The Views Notification service is used to monitor the ViewDrop folder and take action when a new XML file is put there. Symptoms outlining problems with the Views Notification service usually result in a backlog of XML files in the ViewDrop folder. You can use the Project Server Health Monitor to confirm this problem, as well as take a look at the number of files in the ViewDrop folder. Problems with this service can usually be resolved by restarting it using the Services snap-in to MMC.

Problems with the ViewDrop folder are almost always related to the NTFS and/or the sharing permissions on the folder. Symptoms include being unable to publish changes or updates to a project, spooler errors, and the ViewDrop folder will be empty or unchanged for an extended time. Double-check the permissions to this folder if you encounter these symptoms. If the Views Notification service is not in a clustered or NLB setup and it is running on the same server as the Project Server, there should not be any sharing permissions, just NTFS.

Troubleshooting the Client Layer

The client layer can be difficult to troubleshoot because most desktop environments are not as well managed as server environments. Internet Explorer, for example, may have been loaded with third-party add-ins, and these add-ins may cause conflicts with the ActiveX controls for PWA.

Troubleshooting Internet Explorer   Some basic setup items are often missed on an individual desktop that will affect the way PWA and WSS work. The most common mistake is failing to set the security levels in Internet Explorer, shown in Figure 25.14. Make sure that the browser has the Project Server name listed as a trusted site and that Trusted Sites are using "low" security settings.

Click the Sites button to add or remove entries to the Trusted Sites. This brings up a window similar to the one shown in Figure 25.15.

ActiveX Controls for Internet Explorer   Project Server 2003 installs two ActiveX controls for Internet Explorer when you first connect to PWA: `Pj11enuC` Class and `PjAdoInfo3` Class. These controls can also be pushed to user desktops. If you encounter issues with the desktop browser, often the root cause is a corrupted ActiveX control. To reinstall these controls, perform the following steps:

1. Close all instances of Internet Explorer.

2. Find the Windows folder %Systemroot%\Downloaded Program Files.

3. Delete `Pj11enuC` and `PjAdoInfo3`.

4. Launch PWA again and re-download the controls.

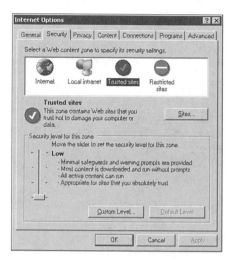

FIGURE 25.14   On the Internet Security tab, the Trusted Sites section should be set to use low security.

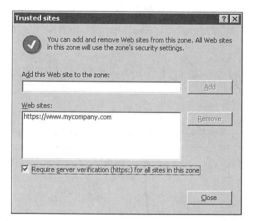

FIGURE 25.15   This list should contain your project server prepended with either an http:// or https:// .

Troubleshooting Project Professional 2003   Most users experience very little trouble with Project Professional, and the majority of problems can be traced to an incorrect patch level. Updating Project Professional by using Office Update (http://office.microsoft.com) is highly recommended. Service Pack 1 (SP1) for Project Professional needs to be installed on the desktop to properly connect to a Project Server 2003 patched with SP1.

Your users may also report occasional spooler errors when working with or publishing projects using Project Professional. The majority of the time these errors are caused by issues with the specific project, not the application or the server.

> **NOTE**
>
> For a comprehensive list of spooler errors, refer to the *Project Server 2003 Administrators Guide*, Appendix E, published by Microsoft.

Troubleshooting Portfolio Analyzer View Creation   If your project administrators complain that they are unable to create or modify a Portfolio Analyzer view, the most common reason is that the desktop does not meet the minimum requirements. Besides the minimum requirements to use PWA, the desktop also needs a fully licensed version of Microsoft Office XP or better. Without a Microsoft Office license, the Office Web Components (OWC) will be read-only.

Managing Terminal Services

Using Terminal Services for Windows 2003 Server is the recommended method for deploying Project Professional and Microsoft Office 2003. This section outlines the benefits, considerations, and other useful information regarding deploying Terminal Services for Project Server 2003.

Terminal Services Versus a Virtual Private Network (VPN)

VPNs are becoming an everyday necessity for most organizations with remote users to secure data and protect company resources. Unfortunately for remote users, VPNs tend to be slow, and these latency issues are magnified to the point of failure for managers using Project Professional to connect to Project Server. This is because the connection from the desktop application to the server contains a lot of query and response. If at any point a response is delayed (times out), the entire process fails. For this reason, latency kills the productivity of your project managers. This is where Terminal Services comes in. Terminal Services eliminates the latency problem for remote users and improves overall performance. Best of all, your data is still secure and in fact may be even more so because the actual sensitive data traffic all remains within the confines of your local area network (LAN). Many great resources can provide more detail on the security model and options of Terminal Services, including Microsoft's site online.

Benefits of Using Terminal Services for Project Server 2003

The biggest benefits of using Terminal Services will be seen when using applications such as Microsoft Project Professional; however, there are several other important advantages to consider. The following lists some of the benefits of using Terminal Services for both remote and local users:

- **Faster than VPN for remote users**—No latency issues for remote users because all the processing occurs on the server side.

- **Low bandwidth requirements**—Even users on slower dial-up connections can enjoy fast access to Office applications and connectivity to the Project Server. This is because Terminal Services really sends only screen views instead of the actual data.

- **Centralized support**—With Terminal Services, you are managing only one system rather than individual desktops, providing for better availability, service, and monitoring. Additionally, you can easily share a desktop with a remote user and troubleshoot real-time. You also ensure that your users are running all the latest security updates, patches, and enhancements eliminating the need to visit each desktop.

- **Availability and scalability**—With Terminal Services, your users can reach their data from anywhere, anytime using the Remote Desktop built into Windows XP or freely downloadable from Microsoft, even through an ActiveX browser plug-in. If your users are having a problem with their desktop, they can use another workstation, and it will look and feel exactly the same to them. Additionally, the system requirements on the user side are minimal. A computer with a Pentium 133 megahertz processor performs well because you'll be leveraging server architecture, which allows for faster performance and scalability. As your user load increases, simply add another Terminal Services to your network load-balanced (NLB) cluster.

- **Increased security**—Because the desktops are only receiving screenshots, your data remains on your LAN. Group Policy management allows you to protect key components of the server as well as provide some customization to the users, such as automatically setting their home page in Internet Explorer (IE) and collaboration settings in Project Professional.

- **Monitoring**—By having your users access through Terminal Services, you can easily monitor who is logged on to the system, what processes are running, and so on. This can be useful information for troubleshooting performance and other issues.

Considerations for Implementing Terminal Services

Before implementing a Terminal Services solution, careful architecture and planning should take place. Performance, availability, and training are just a few of the areas to take into account. The following is a short list of other important considerations:

- **Hardware requirements**—For smaller organizations, the hardware requirements may be cost prohibitive.

- **Single point of failure**—If the terminal server fails, all your users will be without access. This can be minimized by creating a failover by using Network Load Balanced (NLB) clusters using two or more servers. Before deploying Terminal Services, be sure to have a strong disaster recovery plan in place. A network failover should also be considered.

- **Single configuration**—You can have only one configuration of the applications on a Terminal Services. If your users require custom features to be installed, an additional terminal server will be required.

Installation Order and Application Server Mode

The installation order is important for deploying Project Professional and/or Microsoft Office on a Terminal Server. The server must have Terminal Services installed and enabled prior to installing any other applications. Project Professional automatically detects the implementation of Terminal Services on Windows 2003 and installs properly.

CAUTION

In Windows server versions prior to Windows 2003, you could choose the Remote Administration or the Application Server mode for Terminal Services. In Windows 2003, the Remote Administration mode is built-in. The terminal server must have Terminal Services Application mode installed for Project Professional to install correctly for use by remote users.

Group Policy and the Group Policy Management Console (GPMC)

The Windows Server 2003 implementation of Active Directory (AD) provides a key upgrade to managing Group Policy Objects (GPO) in the enterprise. GPOs can perform many management tasks including adding registry entries, enforcing security policies, and even performing software maintenance. The GPMC is a Microsoft Management Console (MMC) snap-in that can be used to create and enable GPOs. You need to download and install it from Microsoft because it is not included on the Windows Server disks or install.

TIP

Organization Units (OU) are useful when applying GPOs. OUs provide a tree structure, allowing you to apply GPOs similar to the way security groups are implemented. This may come in handy if you want to apply a restrictive policy to your Terminal Server users but don't want to lock out the administrator's functions. OUs can be created and managed using either the GPMC or the AD Users and Computers MMC snap-in.

CHECKING FOR ENFORCED GROUP POLICIES

After making any changes to an existing GPO, check to make sure that the updates are actually being enforced on the server or user. To do this, use the Group Policy Results Wizard built in to the GPMC. You can find this wizard by right-clicking the Group Policy Results folder. Although Windows Servers check and grab new or updated GPOs on a schedule, you may want to "push" the changes right away. You can do this by using the Group Policy Update (gpupdate.exe) command from a command prompt. Type **gpupdate** **/?** for a list of switches. The /force switch, in particular, is important.

25

You can use an .adm file to add a template to the GPO editor. These are text-based files that contain registry and security settings. By default, the GPO editor tries to read .adm files from the Sysvol on the domain controller, but you can add a template from any directory. If the .adm file is new or the time stamp is newer than one currently in the Sysvol, the GPO Editor automatically copies it to the Sysvol.

The following is an example of an .adm file that can be used to set the registry entries needed to connect Project Professional to the Project Server:

```
CLASS USER
CATEGORY "Project Professional Settings"
    POLICY "Microsoft Project 2003"
        KEYNAME "Software\Microsoft\Office\MS Project\Profiles\Windows Logon"
        EXPLAIN    "Set these settings for the hosting environment."
            PART "Project Server URL" EDITTEXT
                VALUENAME "Path"
                DEFAULT "http://servername/projectserver"
            END PART
            PART "Windows Logon Name" EDITTEXT
                VALUENAME "Name"
                DEFAULT "Windows Logon"
            END PART
            PART "Window Logon Account" CHECKBOX
                VALUENAME "AccountType"
                VALUEON "0"            ;REVERSED ORDER: 0,1
                VALUEOFF "1"
                DEFCHECKED
            END PART
            PART "Default" CHECKBOX
                VALUENAME "Default"
                VALUEON "Yes"
                VALUEOFF "No"
                DEFCHECKED
            END PART
            PART "AutoConnect" CHECKBOX
                KEYNAME "Software\Microsoft\Office\MS Project\Settings"
                VALUENAME "AutoConnect"
                VALUEON "Yes"
                VALUEOFF "No"
                DEFCHECKED
            END PART
    END POLICY
END CATEGORY
```

Copy and paste this code into a text file and rename it with a descriptive name and an .adm extension. After the GPMC is installed, follow these steps to add the template to the GPO Editor:

1. From Administrative Tools open the GPMC.

2. Right-click on the appropriate folder level that you want to create a GPO for and choose Create and Link a GPO Here.

3. Give the new GPO a name and click OK.

4. Right-click on the new GPO and select Edit. This launches the GPO Editor.

5. Under User Configuration find the Administrative Templates section, right-click, and select Add/Remove Templates.

6. Click the Add button.

7. Navigate to the location of your .adm file, highlight it, and click Open.

Now that you've added the template, you need to perform a few more steps to see it in the editor to modify:

1. From the GPO Editor, highlight the Administrative Templates section under User Configuration and then click the View menu toward the top of the window.

2. Select Filtering.

3. Remove the selection on the Only Show Policy Settings That Can Be Fully Managed option.

4. Click OK.

You should now see the template you created and can modify it at will. Make sure that when you are finished making changes that you enforce the policy in the GPMC by right-clicking it and choosing Enforced as shown in Figure 25.16.

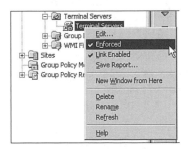

FIGURE 25.16   GPMC menu highlighting a GPO.

Patching

Patching should be considered an ongoing and vital maintenance activity. Keeping the operating system (OS) and other applications up-to-date is essential to maintaining a healthy and secure system. This section describes the main points for maintaining a patched Project Server system.

Windows Server 2003 Patch Management

The Windows Update Services (WUS) or Software Update Services (SUS) have become a staple for most Windows users since the days of NT 4 and Windows 98. Over the years it has evolved into an automated process built in to the operating system, but, as any Windows server administrator will tell you, it still is only a partial solution to keeping your OS patched. Security updates and application enhancements have become a weekly ritual for most server administrators. Unfortunately, despite the best efforts of programmers to release well-tested patches, automating updates to a production Project Server 2003 system using Windows Update is not recommended. Applying an untested patch to a production system could result in the entire system failing, resulting in downtime and all of its inherent issues.

A solid patch management strategy involves the following elements:

- Performing verification of a solid disaster recovery plan.

- Performing a risk assessment of whether to apply an untested patch to a production system. Ask whether this justifies the purchase of a test environment. Do the security concerns outweigh the potential downtime?

- Performing active scanning for newly discovered security vulnerabilities and patches.

- Defining maintenance windows so that users are aware downtime may occur.

- Managing personnel and software to deploy an "emergency" patch within 24 hours and a "critical" patch within 14 days.

- Performing a patch verification process.

Several software tools are available on the market today that provide security and patch management services, including Microsoft's Systems Management Server (SMS) and Software Update Services (SUS). Keep in mind that these tools do not replace the need to have a well-defined patch management plan.

> **TIP**
>
> Whenever possible, load new patches and application enhancements into a test environment identical to the production system and prior to applying them to production. In smaller organizations this may be cost prohibitive, in which case a solid disaster recovery plan is vital (see the "Disaster Recovery" section earlier in this chapter).

Applying Hotfixes and Service Packs to Project Server 2003

Hotfixes are generally a collection of files that correct a specific problem in the application. Microsoft defines a *service pack* as "a tested, cumulative set of all hotfixes, security updates, critical updates and updates. Service packs may also contain additional features for problems that are found internally since the release of the product and a limited number of customer-requested design changes or features." As of the writing of this chapter, Microsoft officially released Service Pack 1 (SP1) for Project Server 2003. This patch is highly recommended and provides several key fixes and enhancements.

One of the most important enhancements in SP1 is to the Views Notification service. Post SP1 includes the capability to run the Views Notification service on multiple servers, which allows for increased performance. The service is designed so that it does not have to be run on a dedicated server. The service is set to low priority by default to prevent it from taking up 100% of the processor. If this service is run on a dedicated server, be sure to increase the priority for better performance.

Hotfixes should be applied only if you are experiencing the specific problem it addresses, with the exception of security hotfixes. This is recommended because hotfixes are generally not as thoroughly tested prior to the cumulative release in a service pack.

CAUTION

SP1 updates only the default IIS Virtual Root folder. If you are running a custom installation of Project Server 2003 that includes a nondefault IIS Virtual Root, you will need to manually copy the post SP1 files into the other virtual root folder. Take care to back up any custom pages prior to overwriting them. For a list of updated files in SP1, refer to the documentation on the Microsoft website titled "Description of Project Server 2003 Service Pack 1."

25

Microsoft Baseline Security Analyzer Tool

IIS and SQL servers are prime targets for security attacks and therefore should be monitored on an ongoing and real-time basis. Security hotfixes and service packs should be applied regularly. In addition to the SMS tool mentioned earlier, the Microsoft Baseline Security Analyzer (MBSA), shown in Figure 25.17, can be useful to scan for updates to SQL Server, IIS, and Windows Server 2003. MBSA is a free download from Microsoft.

▶ **SEE** "Internet Information Services (IIS) Log File Monitoring," **PAGE 656**.

▶ **SEE** "Monitoring SQL Server 2000," **PAGE 658**.

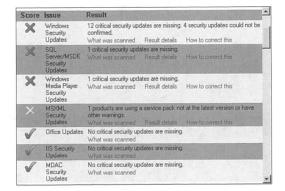

FIGURE 25.17   Sample output from the MBSA tool.

Best Practices

- Systems will degrade over time; therefore, monitor your Project Server to identify potential problems in performance and functionality. Taking this proactive approach to maintaining the system ensures reliability, efficiency, and up-time for your users.

- Numerous tools are built into the operating system, such as the Event Viewer (EventVwr.exe), and applications are available to assist in monitoring and troubleshooting. In addition, Microsoft provides several free utilities for testing, troubleshooting, and monitoring Project Server 2003. These utilities are freely downloadable from Microsoft.

- Create backups of the Project Server databases at least once every 24 hours. Larger organizations should consider more frequent backups. All organizations should consider the recovery mode options built into SQL Server 2000 and design a backup strategy accordingly. Verify and test backups regularly. Often, database backup corruption is not detectable until a restore is necessary.

- Document and maintain a solid disaster recovery plan. Make sure that you include testing in the plan. Good planning only goes so far. Servers do fail and databases do corrupt, but a solid disaster recovery plan alleviates the risks of data loss.

- Baseline your installations. This helps greatly in troubleshooting performance issues and can even help to distinguish between hardware and software problems.

- Leverage the advantages of Terminal Services. Speed, reliability, and manageability, as well as increased security, are tremendous benefits to any organization.

- Keep your servers and applications up-to-date. Install emergency patches within 24 hours and critical updates within 14 days. Install hotfixes only when necessary and service packs as they are released. Whenever possible, test all updates prior to implementing in a production environment.

CHAPTER 26

Capacity Planning

IN THIS CHAPTER

- System Hardware/Architecture Instance Design
- Planning for Growth
- Monitoring for Growth
- Ongoing System Concerns
- Federation
- Best Practices

Capacity planning is the act or process of planning for current and future application or system needs. Assumed in the concept of capacity planning is that minimal performance requirements (user perceived and/or system) must be protected. The goal of capacity planning is to achieve these performance requirements throughout the designated planning time frame (often the life span) of the application. Capacity planning can be approached in many ways; the following are representative options:

- **Option 1**—Examining the expected capacity requirements at the end of the target time frame and designing/procuring the architecture and hardware needed to meet those requirements.

- **Option 2**—Examining capacity requirements at the designated stages in the target timeframe, meeting the initial need through architecture and hardware, and laying out planned upgrades to meet the needs of the subsequent phases.

- **Option 3**—Understanding system scalability options, meeting the initial need through architecture and hardware, and enacting a performance monitoring program with alternatives for upgrading as specific bottleneck thresholds are reached.

For many companies, Option 1 is the de facto standard because many applications are not equipped to support the full monitoring (and its associated costs) of Option 3. Option 1 is also easier for initial budgeting and planning than either Options 2 or 3. In fact, the existing best practice guidance around Microsoft Enterprise Project Management (EPM) is to look out to the system needs two plus years from initial implementation and then meet those needs via Option 1. This is a reasonable approach from many angles. For example, the two years time frame is a good demarcation because it is reasonable to expect advances and upgrades in hardware performance and/or in application performance in new version releases within this time frame. These advances would make planning beyond a two-year time frame ineffective.

For many smaller companies, an initial investment in hardware or architecture to support needs that may not be realized over the next two plus years is simply not cost-effective. For these companies, Options 2 or 3 are much more rewarding.

TIP

Planning capacity requirements around deployment phases (and scoping hardware to match need) while monitoring the system performance for proactive action is usually the most cost-effective approach to an EPM solution deployment.

Unfortunately, in the world of enterprise systems, capacity planning is even more complex than you might initially consider because other factors play a significant role in performance over time. The performance of many (even most) large distributed applications is affected by the environment they are deployed in and changes to that environment. Many of these changes go unpredicted even in proactive IT environments. Knowledge of organization data and bandwidth patterns and of individual application architecture and usage all come together in capacity planning.

UNPLANNED NETWORK IMPACTS: THE CASE OF POINTCAST

In May 1996, PointCast Network was launched as the first personally tailorable, ad-supported news source delivered to your screensaver. It was a huge hit. Using a continuous polling and pulling application, news and advertisements were delivered directly to individual desktops. By September 1996, PointCast had 1.4 million users and was adding 250,000 new users a month. PointCast was a web phenomenon and a growing IT nightmare. Corporate gateways were hit in a double whammy. The popularity of the software itself meant that it was being downloaded repeatedly (once by each internal user interested in it, and many were interested in it). After the software was installed, each user controlled how frequently his information was updated (and most chose minutes). The corporate connection to the Internet jammed with traffic, and critical systems such as email were impacted. Network managers were initially taken unaware by the bandwidth demand, and corporate networks suffered, but eventually steps were taken to limit or block internal use of the software.

The PointCast scenario is an example of how one application impacted millions. Despite careful planning, unrelated applications can have a major impact on performance.

In addition, an implemented EPM solution has a special sensitivity to its own data and data complexity. The EPM solution is a mix of data repository, query, and analysis made more performance sensitive by the business knowledge layer being distributed on client machines. That means that the data complexity is not dealt with in a single server location but on each client station. The performance of each client station is a complex mix of the resources available on the local machine, network bandwidth, traffic volumes, and the complexity of the data served to it (which then requires more or less local machine resources to display and manipulate).

> **NOTE**
>
> In the world of EPM, data complexity can impact performance as much or more than user numbers and server/network bottlenecks. Data complexity can change over time due to user maturity and system goal changes. For example, the original vision may have been simply of supporting internal project management, but it is broadened over time by adding external vendor management and more refined resource forecasting.

In reality, at least some of Option 3 is a necessity for successful planning and implementation.

Instead of promoting any individual capacity planning option (1 through 3 mentioned previously), this chapter takes a different approach. This chapter provides some guidance on the components of capacity planning used in all three of the options, allowing you to mix and match to build a capacity plan that may be any combination of the three and is more appropriate to your organization.

> **NOTE**
>
> A large volume of material is already developed by Microsoft in support of capacity and installation planning. This chapter does not reiterate that information here but rather provides pointers to it as it is relevant in the following discussion.

System Hardware/Architecture Instance Design

This section deals with planning for a system at targeted user loads and scenarios for a specific point in time. The concepts in this section are appropriate for planning any initial installation the system needs at the two-year mark or any stage of a system life cycle. As such, this section refers to this as *instance planning*.

> **TIP**
>
> So many factors play into an enterprise system's performance (as noted in the introduction to this chapter) that estimation is exactly that, estimation. It is the best guess for hardware/architecture needs to support an estimated user volume, usage scenario set, network/hardware environment, and data complexity.

To plan for the needs of a system at any specific instance in time, you need to estimate system needs in the following areas:

- User numbers and types
- User location
- Peak/heavy usage scenarios
- Network environment
- Server environment
- Data complexity
- Client environment
- Data storage requirements
- Miscellaneous advanced areas

Each of these areas is important in and of itself. However, each area also touches, or is related to, many of the other areas as well. The interplay between the areas is one more complexity factor of capacity planning. Knowledge of these areas helps to design the instance hardware/architecture and application topology. Since the release of the first version of the Microsoft EPM solution (Microsoft Project Server 2002), Microsoft has maintained a set of six example environment scenarios and the suggested architecture and topology for each. Many of the scenarios are further refined. Common practice has been to go through the requirement need planning in each of the areas listed previously, choose the closest one of the six Microsoft published scenarios for a starting point in terms of suggested hardware architecture and application topology, and then modify as needed. This process is supported by the *Project Server 2003 Configuration Planning Guide*. This document is updated frequently and is an excellent resource.

The next few sections go into more detail in each of the areas specified previously.

> **TIP**
>
> Microsoft's detailed guidance for capacity planning is in the *Project Server 2003 Configuration Planning Guide* available at http://www.microsoft.com. Search by name—"Project Server 2003 Configuration Planning Guide"—because it is updated frequently.

User Numbers and Types

Types of users are defined by a combination of the interface they use to access project information and the scenarios they perform. The interfaces are either Microsoft Project Professional (ProjPro: the desktop thick client) or Project Web Access (PWA: the web interface). There are many typical user scenarios: project maintenance and updating, timesheet entry for project statusing, report viewing for analysis, and many others.

The number of each type of user comes into play in two ways:

- Data complexity
- Server load via peak usage scenarios

Data complexity is impacted by the number of team member resources in the database. These generally make up the majority of the PWA users. It is a generality, but the more resources there are (thousands versus hundreds versus tens), the more complex the security structure, resource selection, and assignments.

Server load is impacted because of the user number/type relationship to peak usage scenarios, as described in the "Peak/Heavy Usage Scenarios" section later in this chapter. User numbers are meaningful mostly in regard to server usage concurrency and its impacts on performance.

User Location and Connectivity

User location is important because of network impacts between the user and the servers. Network latency is the primary concern here, although bandwidth or traffic can come into play as well. Again, these are generalities, but if users are not collocated in the same building as the servers, frequently bandwidth and latency issues must be addressed. These mostly impact thick client (Project Professional) users (typically project managers); however, in some instances these can impact Project Web Access (PWA) users as well.

▶ **SEE** the "Network Environment" section, **PAGE 688**.

Peak/Heavy Usage Scenarios

Peak usage scenarios are periods of time during which many users are doing things that put significant loads on either servers or network infrastructures. Typical examples for the Project Server environment are

- Friday afternoon timesheet updates

- Monday morning project manager time approval and project progression

> **NOTE**
>
> *Project progression* is the process of updating the status of a project plan for the current reporting period. This process is critical to tracking an ongoing project.

The first scenario is primarily PWA related. An attempt should be made to realistically describe this scenario. For example, if there are 200 people in your company and the company rule is that everyone reports their time by 5:00 p.m. on Friday, define the peak usage scenario as 200 people entering time in 2 hours instead of 200 people entering time in 10 minutes—unless of course you can show that, in fact, 200 people *do* enter time between 4:50 p.m. and 5:00 p.m. In some extreme cases it may be less costly in equipment to consider requesting that the 100 people in Department A enter time by 4:00 p.m., and the 100 people in Department B enter time by 5:00 p.m.

The second scenario is primarily a project manager–focused scenario. In environments where PWA Timesheet functionality is used, the Monday following the time entry is typically when project managers review the time entered and apply it to the project plans to update current task status. This activity is typically called any one of several things: *updating the project*, *project progressing*, or *project progression*.

> **NOTE**
>
> In companies where PWA timesheets are not used, project progression is still performed but often less frequently.

Typically this scenario involves a much smaller set of users but places a more data-intensive load on the server.

Network Environment

The network environment (that is, the network connectivity) is primarily important in regard to latency and bandwidth availability.

Latency is the time it takes a packet of data to travel from a source computer to a destination computer. It is most relevant in regard to EPM between the client desktop and the SQL Server machine. This connection between the desktop thick client (which contains all the business logic) and the database server is very "chatty." In other words, many individual requests are made by the desktop client of the database server. Each request gets another set of information needed to build the project in the client machine memory. Network latency is added to each request and each response, compounding across the total of all request/response pairs.

> **NOTE**
>
> Microsoft is addressing the chatty nature of the connection between the desktop client (Project Professional) and the SQL database server in future releases of Project Server.

The network latency is most easily measured by opening a Windows Command Shell window on the desktop machine and typing **ping sqlservermachine**, where *sqlservermachine* is the SQL Server on which the Project Server database is installed. The ping returns the round-trip time for a series of test packets sent. The latency is the one-way delay or half of the reported round-trip time. Microsoft suggests that any latency greater than 30ms may (depending on data complexity) cause a perceptible delay in opening or saving projects. If network delays are determined to be impacting performance, the solution is to use an application such as Terminal Services, as shown in Figure 26.1, which allows the user to be "remotely" connected using the thick client (Project Professional), which is actually running on a desktop server located near the database server.

In a simplified way, you can think of the remote desktop as a camera view of a desktop on another personal computer somewhere distant from you. The camera view gets updated frequently, so it feels like it is living on your local machine even though what is actually happening is that you are seeing updates via screenshots passed to you from the remote machine. Passing only the screenshots from the remote machine reduces the amount of information that must travel back and forth to the client machine because all the heavy traffic is between the remote desktop and the SQL Server and does not include the client machine.

> **NOTE**
>
> The Terminal Services screenshot analogy is an oversimplification. Terminal Services algorithms have grown complex and leverage many "tricks" to reduce even further the amount of information that actually has to be sent between machines. In fact, full screenshots are rarely sent, a local cache is used, and only the changed portion of the remote screen is updated locally.

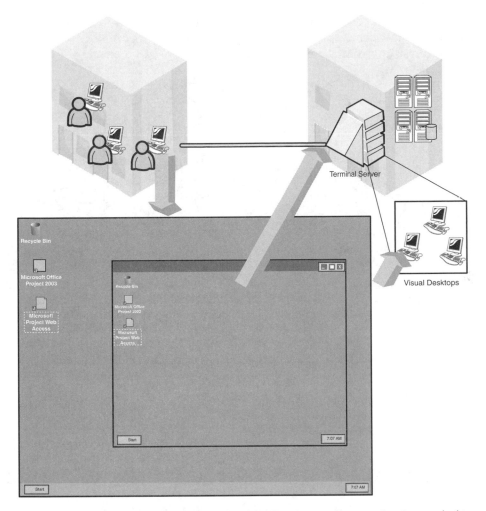

FIGURE 26.1   A user on a machine in the first building is actually remoting into a desktop (consider it a virtual desktop machine) in the server building.

Available bandwidth can also cause performance issues, as shown in Figure 26.2. An example of bandwidth availability impacting performance is as follows: Multiple users are in building A, and their servers are in building B. The two buildings are connected with a limited bandwidth connection. Users may see performance impacts whenever the available bandwidth is low, which may be an intermittent condition. For example, Project Server may appear very slow at 8:15, which happens to be when a deluge of people in building A arrive and log in to their email servers, using all available bandwidth between the buildings to sync their email.

Server Environment

Server environment is an area that may be impacted by topology (how many servers you have the application spread over) and what other applications share a server machine (for example, when loaded on the same machine, Microsoft's Internet Information Server and SQL Database Server continually fight over memory, dropping performance, unless SQL is configured to use only a fixed amount of memory).

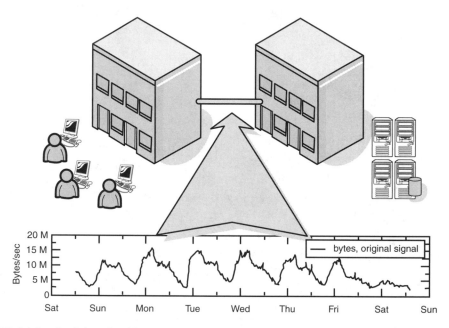

FIGURE 26.2   Peak bandwidth usage can impact user-perceived performance. The bandwidth usage shown is an example of bandwidth availability patterns even before Project Server is installed.

CAUTION

Be wary of servers being used for any other non–Project Server applications. You will likely have no control (and little to no visibility) over the resource loads placed on the server by these "foreign" applications. Foreign applications also severely hinder your ability to determine what is actually causing performance degradation when you are performing proactive performance monitoring.

Data Complexity

Data complexity can vary greatly and typically increases over time as companies develop more refined project management practices and commission more complex projects. A project file may be as simple as a handful of tasks, without any resources assigned, and with no predecessor or successor links. On the other end of the spectrum, a project file may be as complex as tens of thousands of tasks, with multiple people assigned to each, and a high degree of interdependencies such that delaying one task causes a change to many others.

As expected, there will be impacts to the amount of data delivered to and processed by the client machines. This in combination with user concurrency (during peak usage scenarios) impacts server loads.

Client-Side Environment

The available resources and power of the local desktop client machine are very much a factor for thick client (Project Professional) users. Project Professional contains all the business logic for schedule management, resource loading, and other project management operations. When a project is opened on the client machine, data is retrieved from the Project Server repository to the client machine in a series of transactions. Business rules are then applied and the data expanded in memory.

> **NOTE**
>
> *Complex data* is a term used throughout this chapter. Data can be complex in many ways:
>
> - Highly interconnected tasks (via dependency relationships)
> - High number of resources assigned to each task (resulting in a high volume of assignments)
> - High number of tasks
> - High number of task constraints
>
> Complex data requires more local resources, memory space, and processor time for the data to be *unrolled* into more accessible structures in local machine memory.

26

Data Storage Requirements

Data storage requirements are the physical disk space requirements for retaining the amount of data that will be kept over any period of time. Every resource defined and every project saved in the database uses physical space within the database(s) deployed with the EPM solution. The number of databases deployed depends on the architecture and features of the EPM solution deployed. Data storage estimates must take into account multiple areas:

- Data complexity
- The number of ongoing projects
- The number of resources
- The length of time data is to be retained

A five-task project plan with no resources takes up considerably less physical space than a 10,000 task plan with three resources assigned to each task (thereby creating 3 * 10,000 = 30,000 assignment objects).

The simplest way to develop a plan to estimate your physical space needs is to perform the following steps:

1. Stand up a single-machine installation.

2. Populate a test database with some resources and project plans that reflect the expected complexity of the instance environment. Use real project plans if possible.

3. Perform all the normal processes of publishing all projects and building OLAP cubes.

4. Increase the number of projects and resources while noting the physical database growth.

This mechanism mimics growth and allows an organization to better see the impact of data growth, especially the relationship between the number of concurrent assignments and the PWA administration settings for the date range to include for OLAP generation and the date range for resource availability calculation. These last two settings are both found in the PWA Administration web pages under the Manage Enterprise Features subpane. These two settings frequently bear the responsibility for causing the most database size variation. Each of these ranges may be designated as a sliding window of time. All tasks within this time range will be expanded in the database for reporting purposes. The expansion consists of creating a set of data records for each unique task/resource/day combination. This expansion is performed for the purposes of general OLAP analysis and resource availability reporting.

TIP

In the final estimations, don't forget project retention factors—that is, the period of time after project closure for which an organization desires to retain that project information online. Organizations frequently retain projects in the database for several years. Although these projects are likely closed and no longer regularly viewed, they still take up space in the database.

One aspect that is difficult to plan for is Windows SharePoint Services (WSS). Project Server can be set up to create a WSS subweb for each project created in Project Server. The WSS site is created from a template WSS subweb that can be modified. The WSS subweb site is a project team collaboration point for project life cycle documentation, project issues and risks, and anything else that a team finds helpful during a project. The simplest way to estimate the space needed for each of these sites is to look back at the artifacts historically created by projects, size them, and add an additional tolerance factor. The wildcard aspect of WSS sites is due to the fact that WSS sites can be created by a WSS administrator and be totally unrelated to projects. Many organizations find that these subwebs are useful collaboration points and create more for other uses. Because these subwebs are unplanned, coping with WSS database size and maintenance issues can come a lot earlier than originally planned.

CAUTION

SharePoint Portal Server (SPS) is commonly added at some point to provide simpler user-focused access and better search and indexing. With SPS, it is even easier for the number of sites to balloon. SPS implementation should be considered an enterprise implementation on its own and should be *very* carefully planned, or you may well find yourself with a "tiger by the tail."

Miscellaneous Advanced Areas

The EPM solution involves many server products and desktop applications. These in turn can be hosted on multiple machines in multiple hardware configurations. Microsoft continues to add to and refine its existing publicly posted documentation. These should be the first recourse when planning very large implementations. The following list is a set of advanced topics that are more relevant in very large implementations. Many can easily be small books in themselves. Most organizations planning very large implementations will have some experience in these areas, so they are listed here to make sure that they are not overlooked.

> **NOTE**
>
> Project Server and the EPM solution are now (and have been since the release of Project Server 2003) the most documented Microsoft solution in Microsoft's history.

- Using multiple network interface cards for isolating traffic between specific servers.

- Using Multiple SQL servers for partitioning the Project Server 2003 database (described in Microsoft documentation but rarely needed).

- Hyper-Threaded CPU concerns for single-threaded applications. (Some single-threaded applications actually lose performance on Hyper-Threaded CPUs.)

- Database replication and replication type compatibility issues.

- Saving disk and memory by using terminal server profile caching in large terminal server farms.

- SQL database tuning and disk architecture.

- SQL database machine overhead differences when comparing use of multiple SQL instances versus multiple SQL databases. (Record-locking and temp db chokepoints can make running databases under multiple instances of Microsoft SQL faster than running the same databases under a single instance of SQL.)

- Online/offline project and project data archiving strategies for performance and fast archive recovery.

Planning for Growth

The Microsoft EPM solution or Project Server system has been designed to be scaled out in many different ways to fit many different needs. This, as it turns out, is necessary because growth in usage of these systems sometimes occurs in unexpected ways. A carefully planned department-by-department rollout can be overtaken by enthusiasm or business need. As in many systems, frequently the pilot becomes the production system overnight, literally. Although some of this might be foreseeable, most of it isn't. The best defense is preparation. Carefully read the Microsoft documents that discuss the scalability scenarios of the system, understand the topology of the components, and know where your first

26

expansion points are. Do not relax into a comfort zone after the pilot or the first deployment. Make sure that system monitoring is established (as defined in the following section "Monitoring for Growth") as early as possible.

Monitoring for Growth

No matter how well you estimate your future needs, they are still estimates, subject to the reality that is the business environment. Microsoft's EPM solution is extremely scalable. There are always ways to address performance issues. Putting in place proactive monitoring allows an organization to respond when a performance degradation trend is identified, before the user community is severely impacted.

A solid monitoring program consists of two components:

- Tracking the changes made to the system

- Tracking the performance of the system

Each of these components is critical. Without tracking changes to the system, performance degradation can be assumed to be user or data complexity based when in fact it is not. Incorrect actions may be taken to remedy the degradation and time and money inefficiently spent.

In support of the change control aspect, the following system changes should be logged when any change is made:

- Any system updates via Service Packs (OS or application)

- Changes in Project Server availability and OLAP window data range sizes

- Additions/modifications to the Project Server Category/Group model

- Additions of new Enterprise Custom Fields (Task, Project, or Resource) or to the formulas used by them

- Additions/modifications of any customizations (triggers/stored procedures/ASP pages)

- Additions or changes to other applications sharing the Project Server–related servers

- Network changes between clients/servers and/or servers/servers

- Client changes (upgraded hardware/OS/application suites)

Tracking the performance of the system is currently a manual chore. At least check the following monthly (the preference would be weekly):

- The number of active projects in the database

- The total number of projects in the database

- The number of resources in the database

- The average number of assignments in the database

- The network latency (done via a command shell `ping`) between remote clients and the SQL Server

- The time it takes Project Professional to open the chosen test project during a low-usage time

- The time it takes Project Professional to open the chosen test project during a peak usage time (as defined by the peak usage scenarios for your organization—possibly a Friday afternoon time entry or a Monday morning project progression by project managers)

- The time it takes to display the PWA Detail Project view for the chosen test project

- The time it takes for the OLAP cube to build

Routinely logging or tracking the preceding items is drudgery, but the return can be enormous. Having and tracking the preceding information allows an organization to see trends in performance and understand and identify bottlenecks earlier. This information can then be used to make adjustments in architecture or to spot business or usage practices that are not as expected and either address the practices directly or adjust the capacity planning to account for them.

> **TIP**
>
> Routinely collecting performance information can be done by soliciting the user community to log performance by performing operations on a designated test project or test view during peak usage times. It is also worthwhile to look at the SmokeTest utility (a free download from Microsoft) to automate this activity. The SmokeTest utility can be found at
>
> http://www.microsoft.com/downloads/details.aspx?FamilyID=68fd51ba-2037-4c75-a529-1da948c24c0c&DisplayLang=en

Ongoing System Concerns

After a system goes into production, many operational situations arise. Good capacity planning tries to allow for these types of situations. The most common are discussed briefly here.

New Software Releases

As noted in the section "Monitoring for Growth" earlier in this chapter, network, machine, and application administrators should log any changes made to a production Project Server environment or system. This should be done in the context of an ongoing system monitoring or change policy.

Information Life Cycle—Archive and Retention Policies

Over time, the database sizes will expand; however, the information within the databases has a life cycle. Projects end; resources leave—these factors mean that pruning of information within the databases is appropriate. Data archival (pruning) policies must be promoted by IT but defined by the business. In addition, the impact of removal of a project or a resource from the repository must be well understood. Removing a project will change the resource loading for the period that that project spanned. Removing a resource should be done only after any projects that resource worked on have been removed from the system. These are important considerations that generally lead to a project retention policy on the order of one or two years. The retention of this information in the system must be accounted for in the physical storage space estimations for the time frames.

Business Need Changes

The EPM system is initially configured to meet the originally defined business needs. It is recommended to have the "whys" of the initial configuration design decisions (and any changes over time) documented. If business needs change or the sponsors and maintainers of the system move on, re-examination or modification of the system can still occur efficiently.

Defined business needs change more frequently than most allow for. Simple requests or formula changes from Finance, for example, can cause project schedule restructuring to better support reporting (which can cause performance impacts depending on how and where formulas are used; for example, formulas not carefully defined in Enterprise Task level custom fields can sometimes cause performance penalties). Large project creation may inspire creation of new roles (for example, resource managers may appear where before there was no such role). It is frequently not the original sponsors and system implementers who have to define the system changes to support the new business need. Having the history of the changes made to the system and why they were made helps prevent configuration changes that appear to address the current need but that may have been previously analyzed and ruled out due to subtle process impacts.

System Customization—Special Needs

Throughout the life of an EPM implementation there are business need changes, system augmentations, and new integration points with other systems. Any of these can lead to customization activity. As soon as customization is broached, a need for a test system arises so that the production system is not impacted until modifications are validated and quality assured. Capacity planning must address the possibility of a test system for completeness, even if no test system is initially deemed necessary.

Federation

A *federated EPM environment* is one in which multiple, individual instances of Project Server repositories exist (perhaps one for each department) and all these repositories integrate at some point or points for various purposes. The most common purpose is consolidated reporting across all repositories for rollup to all-inclusive corporate level reports. This is the simplest form of a federated environment because information for the corporate level reports is read-only, meaning that the department information is collected and aggregated but not changed by corporate. The information flow is unidirectional.

> **TIP**
>
> Microsoft has an excellent introduction to federation for reporting that includes code, available at http://msdn.microsoft.com/library. Search for "Solution Starter: Microsoft Office Project Server Enterprise Reporting."

All other forms of federation are much more complex because they typically require a bidirectional exchange of information between the environments. These bidirectional environments are almost always customized with programming integration points. An example of a business need that would demand a complex bidirectional flow of data is easy to find. The following set of assumptions defines a more complex federation environment:

- Each department has implemented its own EPM environment (one repository per department).

- Department resources typically work multiple projects.

- Resources staff projects run by other departments as well as their own department.

- Resources enter time in a single timesheet.

This federation environment can become amazingly complex as projects that the Department A worker is assigned to in Department B must exist not only in Department B's repository but also in Department A's so that the worker may enter her time in the Department A repository timesheet. Entries must then be propagated to Department B's project. Corporate rollup reporting must also be made to roll up only the Department B project because the Department A project would be a partial duplicate, and this is just the top level.

There are actually multiple ways to meet the four business statements presented previously, but all of them require customization of the tool. Since the first versions of Microsoft Project, Microsoft has provided ways for users to modify or customize the product. In fact, at the demand of the user community, Project was the first Microsoft desktop application to include a macro programming capability. This capability was then added to, enhanced, and evolved in each of the other desktop applications and ended up as Visual Basic for Applications (VBA), which was then, finally, retrofitted back to Project to replace the original macro language that had been the initiator of the concept. The point being is that the project management community was the first to recognize the benefit of having a base platform while understanding that the common base would not fit every need out of the box. This concept continues today as the Microsoft EPM solution is in fact a base set of tools that can be easily modified or tailored for individual company needs.

26

If your organization requires a federated approach and most especially if it determines that bidirectional flow of information in a federated environment is needed, it is highly recommended that you find a good Microsoft Project Partner to work with you. This will be an enormous time and frustration reducer even in the case of federation for reporting only. Whereas the Project Server database is open, with a published schema, the information saved within the database is still raw information (because the business rules live in the thick client Project Professional), and some of the information is not intuitively producible, as shown in Figure 26.3.

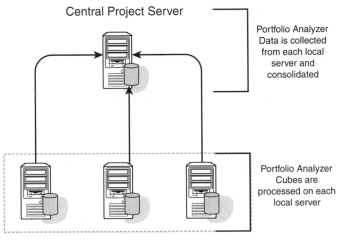

FIGURE 26.3 Here, multiple Project Server repositories are in use with a central Project Server collecting the information from each of the local repositories for centralized reporting purposes.

Best Practices

- Establish data archival and retention requirements so that they can be used in understanding data storage needs.

- If possible, load a test database with typical project sizes and complexities to better understand how your database will grow as projects are added to it. Don't forget to publish the projects, set the availability and OLAP calculation window time frames, and build the cube.

- Expect system performance to change over time; enact regular system monitoring and logging to address performance needs proactively.

- Monitor WSS database growth carefully because user acceptance of WSS can sometimes vastly surpass any expectations.

PART IX

Industry Configuration Examples

IN THIS PART

CHAPTER 27 Industry Examples for Microsoft Office
Project 2003 Configuration   **701**

Industry Examples for Microsoft Office Project 2003 Configuration

IN THIS CHAPTER

• Customizing Project Web Access and Views Configuration

• Customizing Enterprise Global Custom Outline Codes

• Generic Enterprise Outline Codes for Projects

• Custom Outline Code for Resources

• Examples of Generic Enterprise Custom Fields

• Research and Development Examples

• Government Agency Examples

• Air Industry Examples

• Healthcare Sector Examples

• Oil and Gas Industry Examples

• Construction Industry Examples

• Pharmaceuticals/ Biopharmaceuticals Industry Examples

• Information Technology Examples

• Best Practices

This chapter presents some examples of configuration for different industries. These examples are generic and may not be suitable for a specific organization, even if the organization in question operates in the industry described.

Moreover, these examples are meant to provide guidance for the deploying organization and not be construed as industry standards.

Customizing Project Web Access and Views Configuration

It is important to understand that Project 2003 was designed with flexibility in mind, and it can be configured to adapt and respond to a wide range of requirements. The Project 2003 repository makes it possible to view project and resource data in many different ways to satisfy users' specific interests and responsibilities.

All Project Web Access (PWA) views, including Portfolio Analyzer Views, are customizable by the deploying organization, and they are specific to each of them.

> **NOTE**
>
> Because of the large number of individual variations of project management methodologies, specific views, administrative settings, and entry tables cannot be recommended for a specific sector. These settings are particular to each deploying organization.

Most administrative settings are, just as the views, specific to each organization, and they cannot be tied to a specific sector or industry.

Notwithstanding that settings are specific to each organization, when customizing PWA a few recommendations are valid for most organizations, and these are presented in the following sections.

Managed Time Periods Versus Nonmanaged Time Periods

This setting applies to organizations that need to "lock down" accounting periods for cost synchronization with an account system and/or need to analyze accurately the Earned Value performance. If the organization does not require strict accounting interfaces for the EPM system, the Managed Time Periods option is not necessary.

Tracking Settings

Time reporting and tracking are paramount for capturing the actual effort input for each project and provide a more objective estimation of the project progress.

Project 2003 can be configured to track work performed by resources in three ways:

- **Percent of work complete**—Resources report the percent of work complete, between 0 and 100%. This is the preferred method for organizations deploying an EPM solution in an R&D environment.

- **Actual work done and work remaining**—Resources report the actual work done and the work remaining to be done on each task. This method is recommended for organizations in healthcare, oil and gas, and product development.

- **Hours of work done per day or per week**—Resources report the hours worked on each task during each time period. This method is recommended for any organization that needs to track with accuracy the work effort of each project participant. This method is not recommended for R&D organizations.

Locking Down Defaults

It is recommended to use Force Project Managers to Use the Progress Reporting Method Specified Above for All Projects because this provides consistency and coherence in use of Project 2003 throughout the enterprise.

Use Allow Project Managers to Change the Default Method for Reporting Progress If a Different Method Is Appropriate for a Specific Project only if the deploying organization has a high level of maturity of project management and there is a solid project management knowledge base within the company.

Project Web Access and Portfolio Analyzer Views

Time reporting and tracking, actual work, and resource availability are just a few example areas where PWA views can easily be customized. This enables the organization to report on various attributes for projects and resources in a consistent manner.

Lack of this information may drive late identification of projects' needs and requirements and force decisions that are not always fact-based.

The following views are the most common ones that we recommend:

- **Temporal requirements for management reports**—Resources Versus Time, Work Versus Time, Skill Sets Versus Time, and so on

- **Functional requirements**—Resources Versus Projects, Resources Versus Tasks, Department Loading, Actual Work Versus Work, Actual Work Versus Baseline Work, and so on

- **Portfolio requirements**—Project Dimensions, Project Priority List, Project Synchronization, Project Metrics, and so on

Customizing Enterprise Global Custom Outline Codes

When designing the custom outline codes and fields, a number of questions must be answered to produce a meaningful structure that in turn results in useful reports.

Some of these questions are

- What is the appropriate level of detail needed?

- How many sublevels will be used, and what is the level of detail required?

- How often are the project and resource outline codes values expected to change over time?

- Are there outline codes that can be shared by projects and resources?

When developing these custom codes and fields it is important to remember a few basic rules:

- The enterprise system is meant to standardize collection, management, and reporting of data, and, therefore, anyone who has a stake in the system must participate in the development of these codes and fields. Customizing the views in PWA involves the delicate act of balancing the needs of the individual user with the requirements at a corporate level.

- Clearly define the grouping element. It should not include more than one type of project or resource for any code or field defined. For example, do not mix Project Life cycle values with Project Status values.

- Have clear, objective criteria for assigning an outline code value to a project or a resource. The object of the exercise here is to eliminate ambiguity in reporting, not to create it.

In designing custom outline codes and fields it is recommended that whenever possible you use shared outline codes for projects and resources that can be assigned the same value.

27

For example, Resource Location and Project Location may share the same value. For example, consider a healthcare management organization that operates in two states: Colorado and Washington. This fictitious organization would have offices in Denver, Vail, Colorado Springs, Seattle, Tacoma, and Redmond.

In this case the deploying organization may choose to organize its projects by location.

As such, the Project Location custom outline code may have the following structure:

- Colorado
  - Colorado Springs
  - Denver
  - Vail
- Washington
  - Redmond
  - Seattle
  - Tacoma

Following the same structure, the deploying organization may choose to create another outline code, named Resource Location. In this case, the values would be identical for both the project and resource location.

Therefore, the deploying organization needs to maintain only a single list of values for project location because the Resource Location value list would be shared with the project location.

The advantage of sharing the value list for two or more outline codes is that it ensures consistency and avoids duplication and redundant work.

Also, for deploying organizations that do business worldwide, it is recommended to group different locations by state, province, or county, and then by country and/or continent. This grouping facilitates the search for a specific location when assigning a value to projects or resources, or when reporting project or resource distribution by location.

In this case, the four recommended levels for project and/or resource location are as follows:

- Level 1: Continent
- Level 2: Country
- Level 3: State/Province/County/Prefectures
- Level 4: City

It is worth mentioning here that a project can be assigned a location based on five differ-ent principles:

- Location of the performing organization where the project is budgeted
- Location of the sponsoring organization
- Location of the paying client
- Location of the project manager
- Location of the project management team

Regardless of which method is employed, it is essential to apply the same principle to all projects to generate proper reports.

Generic Enterprise Outline Codes for Projects

Most deploying organizations identify and develop custom outline codes that meet their reporting needs. Although each organization has specific requirements, a significant number of custom outline codes are used by companies regardless of their field of activity. Among those codes are Project Location, Project Status, and Project Type.

It is important to remember that these outline codes are provided here as guides and not as "must haves." It is up to the EPM deploying team to decide which codes should be used.

As discussed in Chapter 3, "Knowing Product Limits and Overcoming Them," each orga-nization must carefully consider which codes are relevant and what the reporting require-ments of various stakeholders are. It has been our experience that most organizations that want to deploy an EPM solution will most likely have a need for certain outline codes that are common across industries.

Project Location

Project location was discussed previously, and it is always a good idea to have projects grouped by their geographical distribution. Grouping projects by location helps not only the executives and portfolio managers but also product development, sales, and market-ing managers. For example, grouping projects by location can help identify the workload for various locations, help analyze the proximity of vendors and suppliers, and help an organization balance the financial burden represented by each project.

Project Status

An enterprise project outline code, which we recommend using, regardless of industry, is the Project Status. Project Status represents an important classification for a project port-folio because it provides important information with regard to project pipeline loading.

27

For example, a project pipeline that has many projects in the execution phase but few that are closed or canceled is a sign of an unbalanced pipeline and that these projects may be lingering in the execution phase when they should actually be closed or canceled.

Examination of the project pipeline loading is also the first indicator of the resource needs, and it is an important tool for future balancing and synchronizing the projects and resource requirements with organizational availability of all resources (human, financial, material).

The following is an example of a Project Status outline code:

- Initiated
- Approved
- In Execution
- On Hold
- Canceled
- Closed

Grouping Projects By Project Type

Often organizations initiate projects to address an issue or a change that has been legislated by government or mandated by a professional organization or a certification agency. Most of the time, these projects face tight deadlines that cannot be modified. Alternatively, organizations initiate projects as a response to a business need discretionary to the organization. In such cases, it is useful for portfolio managers to group the projects into the following three major categories:

- Government Legislated
- Nongovernment Mandatory
- Discretionary

CAPTURING DIFFERENT TYPES OF WORK

Project Server 2003 offers the possibility to capture time spent by resources on almost any work initiative in an organization. Portfolio managers and resource managers find it particularly useful when they can get visibility and understand the level of effort that resources are allocating to each activity by type.

For example, an organization wants to know how much effort is allocated to project work versus nonproject work. In this case, the deploying organization may group work initiatives into two major categories: project and nonproject work. Otherwise, the organization may choose to further detail the nonproject work into four other categories: administrative, maintenance, support (help desk), and service requests (or work orders).

The custom outline code could be named in this case Type of Work. The code could have the following structure:

- Administrative
- Project
- Maintenance
- Support
- Work Orders

Grouping Projects By Sponsoring Division

Project Sponsoring Division is a particularly useful outline code for organizations in which projects are executed by a different division than the sponsoring division. This gives portfolio managers the necessary tools to group projects by various sponsoring divisions within the organization. When organizations decide to employ the Project Sponsoring Division outline code, it is advisable to employ a second code as well: Project Performing Division.

Project Performing Division

Project Performing Division is an outline code that allows functional and portfolio managers to identify project workload by performing organization. In many cases, the sponsoring and the performing organization value would be identical. In this case, we suggest using the sharing feature of the two outline codes.

Project Priority

Almost all deploying organizations have a need to group projects by their respective business priority within the company. Most common values for this outline code are represented in the following list, in three different approaches:

- Project Priority (most typical)
  - High
  - Medium-High
  - Medium-Low
  - Low
- Project Priority (typical for organizations with a relative small number of projects, under 50):
  - Values 1 through 3
- Project Priority (typical for large organizations, with a large number of projects):
  - Values 1 through 10, 100, or 1,000

Custom Outline Code for Resources

Resources can also be grouped into meaningful categories. The most common categories include resources by the following:

- Resource breakdown structure (RBS)
- Location
- Skill set
- Certification
- Employment type

Resources by RBS

Resources by RBS is a code that not only helps the deploying organization to maintain a clear view of the distribution of resources throughout the enterprise but also interacts with the security model of Project 2003.

Maintenance of the RBS code can be costly, especially for large organizations that often reorganize their organizational structure.

When developing the resource breakdown structure, the deploying organization must consider the fact that Project 2003 RBS does not support mapping of dual-reporting or dotted-line reporting structures that often exist in an organization. In this case, an individual resource should be placed under the functional grouping that is financially responsible for his or her pay.

It is recommended that the RBS in Project 2003 be kept up to date to ensure proper reporting of resource availability.

Resources by Location

The Resources by Location grouping is useful for large organizations that operate in various geographic locations. Classifying the resource pool by geographic location helps the deploying organization understand the distribution of its resources and make informed decisions when it comes to balancing the work force.

Resources by Skill Set

One major challenge in today's project world is matching the skill set requirements of the projects with those available in an organization.

Project 2003 helps all stakeholders involved in the management of resources to determine what skill sets will be needed, in what projects, for how long, and when.

When forecasting the resource requirements is done properly, it allows project managers to achieve the goals of the projects they lead on time and within the allocated budget. It also allows the resource managers to consider all options when allocating resources to projects or to consider trade-offs when there is a shortage of a certain skill set.

When developing the skill set outline code, it may be useful to take into account the use of multivalue outline codes. The advantage of these codes is that they allow allocation of multiple skill sets to a particular resource. Multivalue outline codes also support multiple levels because skill sets can be grouped in meaningful structures.

> **CAUTION**
>
> When developing the skill set list, make sure that you list only skills relevant for the organization and at a level of detail that does not render the results of searching and filtering useless.

Resources by Certification

In many organizations, certain job functions can be performed only by certified workers. Depending on the size and scope of the resource pool, it may be a good idea for a deploying organization to develop such a resource outline code to facilitate identification of a certain type of resource.

> **NOTE**
>
> This chapter does not list any example values because they are specific to each profession, industry, and organization.

Resources by Type

A common way of grouping the resources is by type of employment. Today, more organizations consider various types of employment for their resources. The following is an example of type of employment values that could be used in an enterprise environment:

- Full-time employment
- Part-time employment
- Contractor
- Consultant
- Seasonal

Examples of Generic Enterprise Custom Fields

Most portfolio managers and executives seek answers to questions such as the following:

- Which projects are on schedule, and which ones are not? If there are projects not on schedule, how much behind (or ahead) are they in comparison to the baseline?

- Which projects are within the budget, and which ones are not? If there are projects not within the approved budget, how much over are they in comparison to the baseline?

To answer questions such as these, the deploying organization may use the traffic light indicators for schedule and budget performance.

Enterprise Custom Field: Schedule Indicator

The basis for the schedule formula is Planned Start/Finish against Baseline Start/Finish expressed as a percentage of Baseline Start/Finish.

The rules are

- If Planned Start/Finish is over the baseline by greater than 20%, the project is late and will not finish on schedule.

27

- If Planned Start/Finish is over the baseline by greater than 10%, the project is somewhat late and may not finish on schedule or could finish late by a manageable percentage).

- If Planned Start/Finish is over the baseline by 10% or less, the project schedule is within tolerance (green ball indicator).

Any and all projects that have not been baselined will be indicated as such No Baseline.

Given these rules, the following is the schedule formula:

```
IIf([Baseline Finish]>#1/1/2900#,"No Baseline",
IIf(((ProjDateDiff([Start],[Finish])-ProjDateDiff([Baseline Start],
[Baseline Finish]))/(ProjDateDiff([Baseline Start],
[Baseline Finish])))*100>20,"  +" & ((ProjDateDiff([Start],
[Finish])-ProjDateDiff([Baseline Start],
[Baseline Finish]))/(ProjDateDiff([Baseline Start],
[Baseline Finish])))*100 & "%",
IIf(((ProjDateDiff([Start],[Finish])-ProjDateDiff([Baseline Start],
[Baseline Finish]))/(ProjDateDiff([Baseline Start],
[Baseline Finish])))*100>10," +" & ((ProjDateDiff([Start],
[Finish])-ProjDateDiff([Baseline Start],
[Baseline Finish]))/(ProjDateDiff([Baseline Start],
[Baseline Finish])))*100 & "%",IIf(((ProjDateDiff([Start],
[Finish])-ProjDateDiff([Baseline Start],[Baseline Finish]))
/(ProjDateDiff([Baseline Start],[Baseline Finish])))*100>0,"+" &
((ProjDateDiff([Start],[Finish])-ProjDateDiff([Baseline Start],[
Baseline Finish]))/(ProjDateDiff([Baseline Start],[Baseline Finish])))*100 &
"%",IIf(((ProjDateDiff([Start],[Finish])-ProjDateDiff([Baseline Start],
[Baseline Finish]))/(ProjDateDiff([Baseline Start],
[Baseline Finish])))*100=0,"0%",((ProjDateDiff([Start],
[Finish])-ProjDateDiff([Baseline Start],[Baseline Finish]))/
(ProjDateDiff([Baseline Start],[Baseline Finish])))*100 & "%")))))
```

CAUTION

The preceding formula does not apply to tasks. It applies only to project duration, and it shows the percentage increase in duration. Also, note that if you slip the start date out, the formula will not show any problems as long as the duration of the project is the same.

Enterprise Custom Field: Budget Indicator

Budget performance is another important indicator for the health of the project. Different organizations have different requirements, and their tolerance to budget overruns varies. For example, consider the case of an organization that flags as "green" any project that is under budget, "yellow" any project that has a budget overrun up to 20%, and "red" any project that has a budget overrun of 20% or more. In this case, the short formula is

```
Switch(Len(CStr([Baseline Finish]))<3,"No baseline",
([Cost]+1)/([Baseline Cost]+1)>1.2,"Overbudget by 20% or more",
([Cost]+1)/([Baseline Cost]+1)>1,"Overbudget",True,"Under budget")
```

Other custom fields can be designed by each deploying organization to suit the organization's specific need. Some of the more common custom fields are

- Project's Billable Rate

- Project ROI

- Project Brief Description

Research and Development Examples

Research and Development (R&D) is one area where organizations deal predominantly with projects. Most of the work happening in an R&D environment is project work, and within the R&D organizations have various project methodology, life cycle, and management requirements that make them unique. But even with a wide range of needs and methodologies, there is commonality in diversity.

CAUTION

All examples in this chapter are for the guidance of deploying organizations. Organizations should assess the applicability of these examples, including the values described, and should not rely exclusively on the values presented here.

The most common resource outline codes for the R&D sector are Project Location, Project Status, Project Life cycle, Resource RBS, Resource Skill Set, and Resource Role. Note that the values for these codes are for orientation purposes and may not be suitable for every organization.

Project Location

Organizations that operate in an R&D environment often find that their portfolio of projects can be easily grouped by the location where they are undertaken. Understanding the geographical distribution of the projects, for example, can help organizations leverage local resources or balance their portfolio from a financial perspective by relocating projects from locations with high operating costs to locations with lower costs. Each organization maintains its own list of locations, and respective values form the structure of the Project Location outline code.

Project Status

Extremely important for an organization operating in the R&D sector is to have a clear understanding of its portfolio of projects from the perspective of their status. This helps the organization balance its pipeline of projects and make sure that resources (material, financial, and human) are properly allocated to projects. An example of grouping projects by the status is presented here:

- Initiated
- Approved
- In Execution
- On Hold
- Canceled
- Closed

Project Life Cycle

In many R&D organizations after the management of an organization has approved development of a new product, triggered by internal portfolio management or external market research, time to market becomes a critical success factor. A broad and flexible project management tool is needed to optimize the use of resources and the network of activities, including the interdependencies between them. The Project Life cycle outline code illustrates the transition of a project from one phase into another:

- Initiation
- Planning
- Detailed Planning and System Design
- Prototype Construction/Fabrication
- Prototype Testing
- Manufacturing Facilities Testing
- Limited Production
- Final Design Release
- Closing

Resource RBS

Resource RBS is used for mapping the organizational structure of the deploying organization. The Enterprise Outline Code 30 for resources is reserved by Microsoft Project to designate the RBS.

When designing the RBS make sure that it is accurate at all times. We also suggest developing a maintenance plan of this code, such as every time there is a change in the organizational structure of the company, that change is reflected immediately in the structure of this code. Any changes to this code should be coordinated with the executive management of the company and with the Human Resource department. Also, make sure that changes to the RBS are not made before organizational changes are communicated to the entire company.

Because each RBS structure is specific to the organization, we cannot recommend a specific structure. It is, however, highly recommended that you use this code.

Resource Skill Set

An important task for the project manager is the selection of appropriate resource skill sets and the planning of resources to avoid overload. This is of particular interest to R&D projects because in most of the cases it involves prototyping and testing activities that require specific skills. R&D projects are often characterized by overlapping phases and heavy use of cross-functional resources. As such, it becomes useful for project and resource managers to assess the pool of skill sets available in the organization, such as the following:

- Drafter
- CAD Designer
- ProE Designer
- Systems Engineer
- Mechanical Engineer
- Electrical Engineer
- Chemical Engineer
- Mechanic
- Technologist
- Foreman
- Welder
- Tester

Resource Role

Development of a project schedule often requires in the beginning the use of generic resources rather than specific resource names. To help project and resource managers identify the appropriate resource that will be assigned to project tasks, the organization may choose to group available resources by their role. The following is an example of roles common in almost all projects:

- Project manager
- Technical manager
- Account manager
- Product manager
- Subject matter expert
- Team lead
- Resource manager
- Portfolio manager
- Senior manager
- Team member
- Administrative support

27

Government Agency Examples

Project management in government agencies at the federal and local level is often governed by specific and strict policies and methodologies that dictate the configuration of Project 2003. Setting up the project and resource outline codes for projects and resources requires strict adherence to project management methodology and almost perfect synchronization with skill set and roles databases maintained usually by Human Resources departments.

The following sections provide examples of outline codes and fields that can be used for grouping projects and resources.

Project Type

Portfolio managers in any government agency need to always have a clear understanding of what type of projects exists in the organization. This can be easily achieved if projects are grouped by the authority that authorized them. For instance, undertaking a project in response to a piece of legislation can be construed as a "Government legislated" initiative. On the other hand, a project initiated in response to an organization's strategy to improve service can be deemed as "Discretionary," as presented in the following example:

- Government Legislated

- Nongovernment Mandatory

- Discretionary

Project Strategic Alignment

Project Strategic Alignment can be a useful outline code for organizations to make sure that all projects are aligned to major organizational business directives and initiatives. Usually these directives are outlined in the governance documents of the organization. An example of a Project Strategic Alignment outline code is as follows:

- Project Management Quality Improvement

- Improve Web Access for Public Records

- Integration of All eServices Offered on Agency's Website

Project Funding

An important outline code for project grouping is the source of funding. Most government agencies have a mix of public and private funding available for projects. Most projects fit in one of the following three categories:

- Public Funding

- Private Funding

- Public-Private Funding

Project Areas

Government agencies at the federal or local level need to group projects that they undertake by areas of application or activity. These areas sometimes coincide with a major department structure of that agency, and, in this case, it is strongly recommended that the project grouping area follow the structure already in place. If such a structure is not appropriate, consider the following possible grouping:

- Residential

    - Assessment and Taxes

    - Planning and Building

    - Licenses and Permits

- Business

  - Assessment and Taxes

  - Planning and Building

  - Licenses and Permits

Project Scope

Furthermore, projects can be grouped by their scope, which can be identified through sampling of existing projects. An example of a government agency's grouping of projects by scope is presented here:

- City Infrastructure

- City Buildings

- Private Buildings

- Codes and Standards

- Water Supply

- Law Enforcement

- Parking

- Parks and Recreation

- Electricity and Hydro

- Housing

Air Industry Examples

Understanding the project portfolio is a must for today's airline industry organizations. Strong competition, rising fuel prices, and investors' concerns are factors that organizations must take into consideration when managing their portfolio of projects. Challenges faced by these organizations require that projects must undergo tough management analysis and, hence, the necessity to view the portfolio of projects and the resource pool grouped by various characteristics.

Some of the most representative outline codes for projects and resources are presented in the following sections.

Project Portfolio Sector

Many organizations operating in the air industry sector tend to group their portfolio of projects by the sector of activity. An example of potential values for grouping projects by sector is as follows:

- Commercial Passenger Domestic

- Commercial Passenger International

- Charter

- Cargo

- Maintenance and Technical Support

- Planning and Cost Management

- Operations

- Reservations

- Security

- IT Support

- Administration

Project by Aircraft Manufacturer

Most airlines operate with a mix of aircrafts that allows them to operate on different routes in the most effective manner. When grouping the portfolio of projects by aircraft manufacturer, an airline can easily identify the required skill set for operations, maintenance, and commercial activities. As such, projects can be classified according to the manufacturer:

- Airbus
- ATR
- Beech
- Boeing
- Bombardier

- Cessna
- Embraer
- Fokker
- Gulfstream
- Lockheed

Project Portfolio by Global Alliances

Some organizations may need to group their portfolio of projects by global alliances as illustrated in the following example:

- Star Alliance
- One World
- Sky Team

- Qualiflyer Group
- Others

Projects by Aircraft Type

Commercial operations involve strict management of network routes with the aim of maximizing the load factor. Having the right mix of aircrafts allows airlines to deploy the appropriate aircraft on each route. As a result, the need to group the projects by aircraft type is essential in management of route networks. For example

- Short Range
- Medium Range
- Long Range

- Extended Long Range
- Commuter

Resource Skill Set

Just as airlines need to understand the project portfolio by aircraft type, most resource managers need to understand what skill sets are needed and what is the appropriate mix needed to achieve maximum efficiency of operations. An example of the resource skill set needed for an airline is as follows:

- Management and Executives
- Training and Development

- Computer Specialists
- Aerospace Engineers and Technicians

- Flight Attendants
- Customer Service
- Reservation and Ticket Agents
- Cargo and Freight Agents
- Pilots, Copilots, and Flight Engineers

- Commercial Pilots
- Airfield Operations
- Transportation Inspectors
- Baggage Handlers and Material Moving Workers

Healthcare Sector Examples

More and more healthcare facilities need to better manage their portfolio of projects. Most of the projects aim to decrease the overall operating costs while improving quality of care, or address issues related to technology, facility, and information management.

Having a clear view of project pipeline and resources distribution allows healthcare organizations to manage more effectively the budgets they own and to maximize the benefits.

Some of the most common project outline codes for the healthcare sector are presented in the following sections. These examples illustrate solutions that some organizations have implemented and are proven to be efficient.

Projects by Healthcare Area

Healthcare providers have a specific way of organizing their activities.

- Laboratory and Transfusion
- Pharmacy
- Surgery and Intensive Care

- Cardiology
- Patient Care
- Ambulance Services

Projects by Branch

Although every healthcare provider has a specific way of organizing its activities, projects can be grouped in a portfolio by the medicine branch, as follows:

- Public Health
- Primary Care
- Aging
- Dentistry
- Emergency/Trauma/Paramedics
- Surgery
- Intensive Care
- Cancer
- Cardiology

- Dermatology
- Diabetes
- Neurology
- Ophthalmology
- Pediatrics
- Radiology
- Rehab
- Laboratory

Projects and Resources by Sector

An outline code that can be shared by projects and resources is the Sector (or Area). The intent here is to allow portfolio managers to group both projects and resources by the same values in such a way that it identifies the amount (or percentage) of resources spent in a sector and correlates those numbers with the projects undertaken in each sector, or area:

- Acute Care
- Continuing Care Residential
- Continuing Care Community
- Mental Health
- Public Health
- Corporate Support

Resource Skill Set Classification

Generic resource classification presented in this section illustrates the way in which a healthcare organization may want to group the resource pool:

- Healthcare Specialists
- Technologists and Technicians
- Administration
- Support
- Therapists
- Aides
- Physicians
- Surgeons
- Management

Oil and Gas Industry Examples

The oil and gas industry is characterized by a large amount of capital expenditures for upstream exploration and production. The industry's growth in capital expenditures far outstrips spending in other industries, therefore creating a necessity for oil and gas companies to monitor closely their portfolio of active projects, as well as the resource pool.

Project Location

Project Location is one of the most common and useful project outline codes. Depending on the number of locations existent for projects, the deploying organization may choose to branch out one of the levels of the outline code. For example, under the level 1 "Continent," you may have more countries listed, and under each level 2 represented by a country, you may have more regions or cities/towns listed.

The outline code may have the following generic structure:

- Continent
  - Country
  - Region
  - City/Town/Drilling Location

Projects by Type of Capital Expenditures

As the existing reserves are used, finding and developing new supplies becomes increasingly expensive, and the project costs associated with these activities rise. Understanding how the projects are distributed according to the type of capital expenditures helps an organization balance its portfolio. An example of a project outline code that groups projects by type of capital expenditures is as follows:

- DCS
- PLC
- SCADA
- Safety System
- AC Drives
- Control Valves
- On/Off Valves
- Transmitters

- Flowmeters
- Analytical
- CPM
- EAM
- PAM/CM
- APC
- HMI & OCS
- Other

Projects and Resources by Area of Capital Expenditures

Another useful way of grouping projects and resources alike is the shared code Project and Resource by Area of Capital Expenditures. An example of the outline code is as follows:

- IT and Business
- Manufacturing

- Electrical
- Mechanical

In the same way that an organization groups its projects by location, it is important to understand the geographical distribution of the work force. Hence, a Resource Location outline code could share the values with the Project Outline code.

Project Area

Most oil and gas organizations may organize their portfolio of projects by area of activity. Such a code could have the following structure:

- Drilling
- Production
- Specialty Services
- Engineering

- Maritime
- Management and Administration
- Electrical
- Purchasing

Project Status

For any organization, not just oil and gas, it is a good idea to have the portfolio of projects classified by their status, as in the following example:

- Initiated
- Approved
- On Hold

- In Execution
- Canceled
- Closed

Project Phase

Grouping projects in a portfolio by the phase they are in constitutes a great tool for managers to ensure that resources, human and financial, are synchronized and aligned with project schedules and goals. The following code structure presents a branched-out outline code. Note that branching out is not a requirement but an exemplification of how an organization may choose to structure its portfolio of projects.

- Planning
- Detailed Engineering
    - General
    - Jacket
    - Piling
    - Topsides
- Structural Engineering and Drafting
- Mechanical/Process Engineering and Drafting
- Electrical Engineering and Drafting
- Instrument Engineering and Drafting
- Procurement

- Fabrication
    - General
    - Jacket
    - Piling
    - Topsides
- Transportation
    - General
    - Jacket
    - Piling
    - Topsides
- Installation, Hookup, and Commissioning

Resources Skill Set

The other important code is the Skill Set for resource. The following values exemplify the register of value for the Resource Skill Set code. It is worth mentioning here that the deploying organization may choose to use the multivalue outline codes. In this case, if skill set values are used to match generic resources, keep in mind that only one skill set value will be used in matching resources.

- Ballast Control Tech
- Barge Engineers
- Derrickman
- Directional Driller
- Driller
- Drilling Consultant
- Drilling Superintendent
- Dynamic Position Officer
- Entry Rig Roustabout
- Floorhand
- Instrument Tech
- Motorman
- Offshore Crane Operator

- OIM
- Radioman
- Rig Electrician
- Rig File Clerk
- Rig Manager
- Rig Mechanic
- Rig Mover
- Rig Welder
- Roustabout
- Safety Training Rep
- Storeman
- Subsea Engineer
- Toolpusher

Construction Industry Examples

During the execution of a construction project, the stakeholders involved, particularly the main contractor, project manager, and project management team, are typically required to achieve project goals in a number of specific areas. Some activities and goals are common to all projects, whereas others include requirements that are mandatory on specific projects.

Strict management of the schedules for construction projects is dictated in part by the tight budget and the narrow margin of profit. Although each construction is unique in its concept, design, and architectural solution, the activities involved in finalizing a construction can be detailed with a high level of accuracy, and the timing of required resources can be scheduled with a high level of confidence.

Some of the more often used project outline codes for organizations operating in the construction business are highlighted in the following sections.

Project Status

For large organizations that manage a significant number of construction projects at any given time, it is necessary to group various projects by the phase they are in, or by construction goal/component. For example

- Initiated
- Approved
- In Execution

- On Hold
- Canceled
- Closed

27

Project Phase

Portfolio managers will find it useful to group their projects by their respective phase. Most organizations these days use a stage-gate model for the development of their projects. Transitioning a project from one stage to another most often requires organizational approval and, to make a good, informed decision, the management of a company needs to have a clear view of how many projects there are in every stage of their life cycle. Following is an example of values that can be used for grouping projects by their respective phase:

- Initiation
- Planning
- System Design
- Construction
- Commissioning
- Closing/Cleanup

Projects by Types of Construction

Contractors and construction companies normally specialize in one or more of the following types of construction, which can constitute the basis for grouping your organization's portfolio of projects:

- General Building
- Highway
- Heavy Constructions
- Utilities
- Specialty

Projects by Construction Component

Another useful outline code is the Project Component, which may in turn provide valuable information regarding distribution of the work force and financial resources. An example of how portfolio managers may choose to group the portfolio of projects by construction component is as follows:

- Site Development
- Civil Structures
- Thermal Systems
- Flow Systems
- Storage Systems
- Electrical Systems
- Mechanical Systems
- Environmental Systems
- Instrumentation and Control
- Auxiliary Systems

Resources by Skill Set

Along with the other generic resource outline codes already presented in the beginning of this chapter, the deploying organization may find it useful to organize its generic resources by skill set category. This type of classification helps project managers estimate the skills demand for their projects and allows resource managers to develop an optimum skill set mix. A sample of skill sets used in the construction industry is presented here:

- Design-Build
- General Construction
- Heavy Duty Construction
- Transportation
- Construction Management
- Concrete
- Demolition/Wrecking
- Electrical
- HVAC
- Excavation/Foundation

- Glazing/Curtain Wall
- Waste
- Masonry
- Mechanical Work
- Painting
- Roofing
- Sheet Metal
- Steel Erection
- Utilities
- Wall Ceiling

Resources by Construction Management Position

An important resource outline code is identification of management positions because these positions are often critical to the success of the project. Having the right mix of management positions allows organizations to effectively manage multiple projects and minimize risks to the project. The following is a sample of values used for grouping management resources available by their position in the organization:

- Project Manager
- Project Engineer
- Estimator
- Superintendent
- Foreman

- Office Manager
- Expediter
- Safety Specialist
- Inspector

Resources by Core Construction Skills

It is critical for a construction company to identify who in the company has a certain skill because it is an important tool in the management of people and their careers. The following is a sample list of values that can be used in grouping resources by their core skills:

- Blueprint Reading
- Layout
- Tool Usage
- Construction Materials

- Concrete
- Plumbing
- Electrical

27

Pharmaceuticals/Biopharmaceuticals Industry Examples

Research and development in the pharmaceuticals and biopharmaceuticals sector plays a strong role in revolutionizing the way illnesses are prevented, diagnosed, treated, and cured. Contributors to these efforts are found throughout the sector's major segments, which include brand-name drug manufacturers, generic drug manufacturers, firms developing biopharmaceutical products, nonprescription drug manufacturers, and firms undertaking research on a contract basis. Universities, hospitals, and research centers also play a pivotal role in the research and development activities of this sector.

Most of the organizations within the industry choose to group their portfolio of projects based on the following criteria:

- Project Phase
- Project by Core Technologies
- Projects by Emerging Biopharmaceuticals
- Projects by Core Support Area
- Resource Distribution of Medical and Clinical Staff
- Resources by Skill Set

Project Phase

To ensure proper balance of the project pipeline and its synchronization with financial, material, and human resources, portfolio managers would need to see the portfolio of projects grouped by their respective phase. Due to high costs and long development cycles associated with the development of new drugs, it is imperative that portfolio managers understand exactly how many projects are in each phase at any given time. Following is a example of portfolio grouping of projects by their phase:

- Lead Identification
- Pre-Clinical
- One Trial
- Two Trial
- Final Trial
- Submission/Launch
- Commercial Program

Projects by Core Technologies

The biotechnology industry is characterized by certain core technologies around which the major projects are undertaken. Organizations may find it useful to group their portfolio of projects by their core technologies. Following is an example of portfolio grouping of projects by core technologies:

- Genomics
- Combinatorial Chemistry
- High Throughput Screening
- Bioinformatics

Projects by Emerging Biopharmaceuticals

Pharmaceutical companies usually employ leading-edge technologies in development of their products, and with that the amount of financial, material, and human resources needed for those projects is significantly high. To properly synchronize the project pipeline with resources available, portfolio managers may need to view certain projects grouped by underlying technology, as presented in the following example:

- Mimetics and peptidomimetics
- Glycotherapeutics
- Fully Human Monoclonal Antibodies

- Antigen Vaccines
- Vector Vaccines
- Gene Therapy

Projects by Core Support Area

A significant view that may be created for portfolio managers is to group projects by their core support area. It provides significant information about the number of projects active or not in various core areas and hence portfolio managers can ensure that their portfolio of projects is balanced and addresses all business needs. Following is an example of grouping projects by their core support area:

- Discovery
- TOX/ADME
- Medical
- Clinical Pharmacy

- CM & C
- Marketing & Sales
- Regulatory
- Legal

Resource Distribution of Medical and Clinical Staff

Resource managers and portfolio managers must identify the skill sets available to them for project work and the organizational distribution of those skills throughout the company. As such, most common skill sets and occupational areas are described as follows:

- Pharmacokinetic
- Pharmacodynamic
- Dose Ranging
- Dose Safety and Efficacy

- Drug Interaction
- Renal Effects
- Hepatic Effects
- Bioequivalency

Resources by Skill Set

Synchronizing the portfolio of a project with resources available in the organization is most of the time a fine act of balancing skill sets with tasks required for the projects. To assist project and resource managers in finding the appropriate resource for any given

27

task, the organization may find it useful to identify and group available resources by skill set. It is worth mentioning here that the deploying organization must decide what skill sets are relevant to the business to ensure that the list of available skills does not grow to unmanageable proportions. The list of skills must be meaningful and relevant to the business of the organization. It must be developed as an aid in identifying the proper resources and not necessarily as a repository of all available skills in the organization. The following is an example of how resources could be grouped by their skill set:

- Scientist
- Bioinformatics
- Biostatistics/Mathematical Modeling
- Pharamacogenomics
- Immunology
- Integrative Genomics & Viral Host Cell
- Project Manager
- Chemoinformatics

- DART Neurogenomics
- Peptide Synthesis
- Product Manager
- Product Support Engineer
- Quality Systems Engineer
- Principal Pharmaceutical Scientist
- Analytical Method Development
- Research Scientist

Information Technology Examples

In today's economy, more companies are demanding that their IT organizations make wise investments and demonstrate IT's value to the business not just by traditional IT measurements such as uptime and throughput but also by proof of this value in the form of business metrics. For projects, these business metrics can be easily collected and reported.

The following section lists the project and resource outline codes that can help IT managers manage their portfolio and balance the workload with the available resources.

Project Location

As previously discussed in this chapter, grouping the portfolio of projects by geographic distribution is a good start for any organization.

Project Status

Portfolio and senior managers in any organization need to know at any given time how many projects are currently active versus the ones that have been canceled or closed. It is important to understand this mix of projects to direct the necessary funds to active projects and make sure that the canceled or closed projects do not incur any more charges. IT organizations are no different from any others, and grouping projects by their status is always a helpful view for decision makers. Following is a sample of how projects can be grouped by their respective status:

- Initiated
- Approved
- In Execution

- On Hold
- Canceled
- Closed

Project Life Cycle

Understanding your project portfolio from the perspective of project life cycle is important for an IT organization to ensure proper utilization of financial, material, and human
resources. It also has a positive impact on ensuring a healthy project pipeline and identifying potential problems well in advance, such as all the necessary steps needed to correct
an unbalanced pipeline. Following is an example of how projects can be grouped in a
portfolio by life cycle:

- Project Planning, Feasibility Study
- Systems Analysis, Requirements
  Definition
- Systems Design

- Implementation
- Integration and Testing
- Acceptance, Installation, Deployment
- Maintenance

Project Portfolio by Area

In many IT organizations there is a need to group projects in a portfolio by area that they
are addressing. For example, understanding how many projects are undertaken in the
Help Desk area allows decision makers to ensure the appropriate level of staffing and
financing. Following is an example of possible values for grouping projects in a portfolio
by area:

- Hardware
- Software
- Business Practices

- Corporate Strategy Alignment
- Help Desk
- Procurement

Resources by Skill Set

It is equally important for IT organizations to properly identify resources available for
project and nonproject work. To achieve this goal, a deploying IT organization may
choose to use the skill set outline for resources.

> **NOTE**
>
> Given the wide variety of software applications and skill sets associated, it is recommended to
> use the multivalue fields outline codes.

27

Many IT organizations try to compile a list of the skill sets available to make sure that project work demand is properly met. This is particularly useful to resource or functional managers who need to anticipate staffing levels and coordinate the workload with multiple project managers. Project and resource managers can achieve a better coordination of projects and resources when there is a clear understanding of various skills required. The following is a list of IT skill sets that may be used as a starting point in the development of such a list:

- IT Manager
- Network Administrator
- Windows/Linux Administrator
- Database Administrator
- System Administrator
- C++ Developer
- Java Developer
- PHP Developer

- Web Design Specialist
- Graphic Design Specialist
- Help Desk
- Business Analyst
- IT Work Flow Configuration
- Quality Systems Engineer
- Software Tester

Best Practices

- When designing and developing the structure of the enterprise outline codes and fields, keep in mind that these are limited in number and that they must satisfy the entire project management community in an organization. Therefore, you should use the limited number of codes and fields available wisely.

- It is difficult to delete an outline code after it has been used for either projects or resources. Do not delete outline codes and fields that have projects and resources associated with them. First, remove the association of projects or resources with the values of the code that you want to delete, and only after that can you delete an outline code or a field.

- When developing the list of skill sets try to stay focused on only those skills needed for proper scheduling and resource management. Resist the temptation to list every single skill that a resource has. If you do that, you may end up with a long list of skills that is difficult to manage.

- When designing the enterprise views for the Portfolio Analyzer, keep in mind that this is a fully interactive tool and the end user can manipulate the data displayed. Unlike Project Access Views, the end user has access to all fields available. Therefore, design only those views required at the corporate level, leaving specific views to be created by the end users.

PART X

Customizing Microsoft Office Project Server 2003

IN THIS PART

CHAPTER 28   Enterprise Project Management
Customization   731

CHAPTER 29   Extending Enterprise Project Management
Through Customization Overview   793

CHAPTER **28**

Enterprise Project Management Customization

IN THIS CHAPTER

• Windows SharePoint Services Customizing the Project Workspace

• Customizing PWA

• Using VBA Macros

• Best Practices

Although Microsoft's Enterprise Project Management (EPM) solution is a robust, complete EPM system, the one-size-fits-all approach won't cover every organization's needs. An organization might need even greater reporting capability, another organization might want a custom project initiation tool, still another might be happy with the scheduling part of the EPM solution, but might have different needs around the collaboration tools. This chapter and Chapter 29, "Extending Enterprise Project Management Through Customization Overview," are here to help you understand the customization options available. Each section in the next two chapters covers a different customization alternative:

• **Customizing the WSS Project Workspace**—By default, project workspaces are created for every project initiated within Project Server, and they come with useful tools to track issues, risks, and share documents. The default installation may not exactly fit your needs, and you'll want to consider customizing the WSS Project Workspace.

• **Customizing PWA**—Presenting a specialized, high-level view of the information in the Project Server database is one example of what you can do with Customizing PWA.

• **VBA macros**—Some organizations require the same setup for every schedule at project initiation and might find that VBA macros give them the automation required to get the process going quickly and smoothly.

- **PDS**—Using the PDS, you can automate and control tasks that Project Server normally does behind the scenes.

- **SharePoint Portal Server**—Project workspaces are a great tool made to assist in team collaboration for an individual project. But if you want the ability to search across WSS sites and aggregate WSS sites, you'll want to integrate EPM with SharePoint Portal Server.

- **Extending the cube**—The out-of-the box Portfolio Analyzer provides a myriad of information, but it might not provide the precise data point you need. If not, you'll want to extend the OLAP cube.

Windows SharePoint Services offers a wide array of options for customizing the EPM solution; therefore, it is a good place to begin.

Windows SharePoint Services Customizing the Project Workspace

Windows SharePoint Services (WSS) is a great collaboration tool that you can download from the Microsoft website as a complement to your existing Project Server implementation. WSS can also be installed as an option when installing Microsoft Project Server 2003. WSS can serve as a perfect place for your team to get the latest updates on project progress, track requirements, and track risks, issues, documents, and other items you may choose to implement. WSS sites are created whenever a new project plan is published to Project Server and are project specific. WSS also allows you to create new sites that are not associated with a project in Project Server. You can use the large array of settings provided on the WSS site to customize each one to the specific needs and requirements of your project.

▶ **SEE** "Windows SharePoint Services," **PAGE 35.**

▶ **SEE** "Collaboration Using Windows SharePoint Services," **PAGE 442.**

This section discusses the different settings you can use to customize your specific project workspace, as well as the server-side template creation. This section is not meant to cover every nuance of WSS; a large amount of information already is available on this topic.

> **NOTE**
>
> For additional information on the use, administration, and customization of WSS, refer to *Microsoft Windows SharePoint Services 2.0 Administrator's Guide* and the Microsoft Windows SharePoint Services Software Development Kit. Both of these reference materials can be downloaded from the Microsoft website.

WSS Project Workspace Customization

WSS project workspaces are automatically created for every project published to Project Server and contain many useful features, such as lists, discussions, document libraries, and so on. Because each organization and projects within the organization have different needs and requirements, it is important to learn to customize the project workspace to meet those specific needs.

> **NOTE**
>
> You can also set the creation of project sites to manual, which requires your Project Server administrator to create the site using the Admin tab of PWA every time a new project is published. Manual WSS site creation may be a good practice for companies that do not want WSS sites created for every project in their portfolio.

You can access the project workspace through Project Web Access (PWA) by highlighting the project in the Project Center and clicking the Go to Selected Project Workspace button.

▶ **SEE** "Collaboration Using Windows SharePoint Services," **PAGE 442**.

> **NOTE**
>
> Some list items from the project workspace, such as risks, issues, and documents, are displayed directly in PWA as tabs in the top menu. When any of these items are selected for a specific project, the page displayed is the selected list page of the project workspace within the PWA frame. You can customize the items that appear in the top menu and add additional lists, discussions, surveys, and so on using the Admin functionality in PWA as well as custom implementation.

When you access a WSS project workspace, on the Home page you see the quick launch bar, the top navigation menu, and the main content frame, as shown in Figure 28.1. The quick launch bar is used for shortcuts to items such as lists that you create using the WSS Create function. The top navigation menu provides the different options you have in customizing the WSS workspace and also gives you access to all the existing lists and libraries. And finally, the main content frame is used to display different web parts that are either predefined (such as Announcements, Links, and so on) or that you can create yourself.

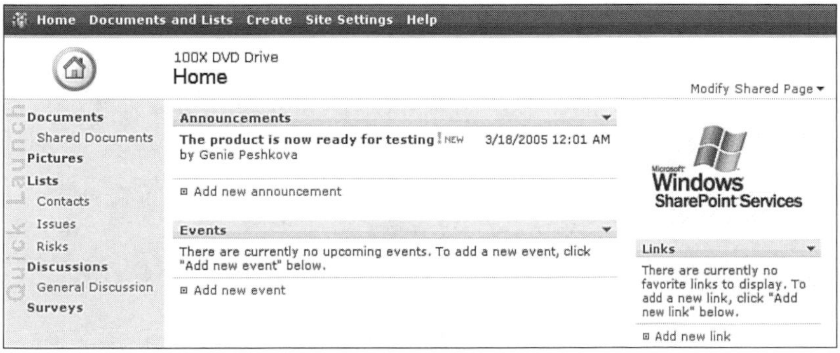

FIGURE 28.1   The Home page provides a quick reference to the purpose of the WSS site, displaying important messages, links, and events.

▶ **SEE** "Extending Enterprise Project Management Through Customization Overview," **PAGE 793**.

The Home Page

The Home page is the first page you see when accessing a project workspace WSS site. The WSS site Home page, as any other website Home page, can be used to provide users with information about the site, its purpose, tools, and information available to them. WSS also allows you to customize the look and feel of the content that appears on the Home page, which is discussed in the following sections.

The Standard Home Page   The standard (out of the box) Home page includes the following items in the quick launch bar:

NOTE

When creating document libraries, lists, discussions, or surveys, the Creation Wizard allows you to specify whether you want this particular item to appear on the Home page. When this option is selected, a shortcut link is created in the quick launch bar on the left.

- **Documents**—Lists links to all document libraries available in this WSS site. By default, each WSS workspace contains the Shared Documents library. The Shared Documents library can also be accessed using the Documents menu tab and selecting the specific project.

- **Pictures**—Lists links to all picture libraries available in this WSS site.

- **Lists**—Lists links to all lists available on this WSS site. The standard lists include Contacts, Issues, and Risks. Risks and Issues are also available as menu tabs in PWA.

- **Discussions**—Lists all discussion topics available for this WSS site. The default discussion that comes with the standard WSS template is the General Discussion.

- **Surveys**—Lists all surveys available on the current WSS site.

The main content frame includes

- **Announcements**—Provides a link to create new announcements that will be displayed on the Home page. The Announcements area is useful for drawing the user's attention to important details about the project.

- **Events**—Provides a link to create new events to be displayed on the Home page. The Events area can be used to highlight things such as upcoming demos, seminars, training sessions, client review, and so on.

The right side of the Home page contains the following:

- **The WSS site image**—By default shows the Windows SharePoint Services image, but it can be easily modified to display a logo of the project the site is related to, or any other relevant graphic.

- **Links**—Provides a link for creating new links. Links can be an effective way to provide reference information frequently used by your project team and to keep external information resources organized in one central location.

Customizing the Home Page   One of the benefits of WSS is that it is highly customizable to satisfy the needs of most project teams.

> **NOTE**
>
> You must be a WSS project site administrator to customize any of its site structure. By default, your Project Server administrator and the project manager of the specific project are the two people who have administrator rights for that specific WSS site. You may also modify the permissions for your project site to grant other team members a Web Designer permission, which allows them to modify the structure of the site and create new lists and document libraries.

To customize the main content frame of the WSS Home page, in the upper-right corner of the page click Modify Shared Page. This provides the following menu selections, as shown in Figure 28.2:

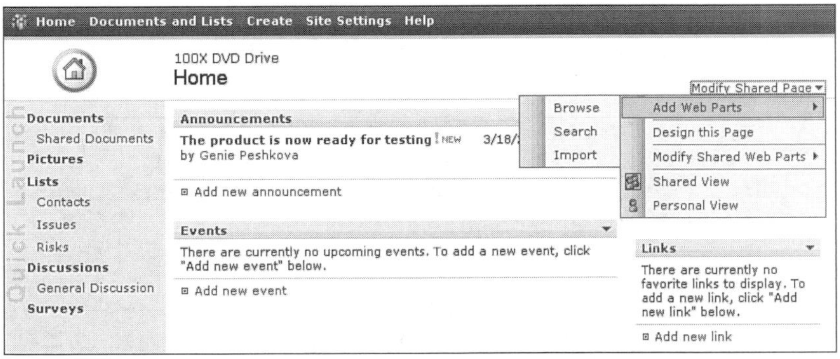

FIGURE 28.2   Modifying the shared page selection menu.

- **Add Web Parts**—Allows you to add more content web parts to be displayed on the Home page. As mentioned earlier in this section, Announcements and Events are the two web parts included in the default WSS site template. You may browse, search, or import web parts using this option.

  Selecting Browse displays the list of all web parts currently available, such as Announcements, Contacts, Members, and so on, as shown in Figure 28.3. Select the web part you want to add to the Home page, and also specify a web part zone as the location (left or right).

  The Search function under Add Web Parts allows you to search other sites for web parts to import. This works well if you know the name of the web part you want to locate.

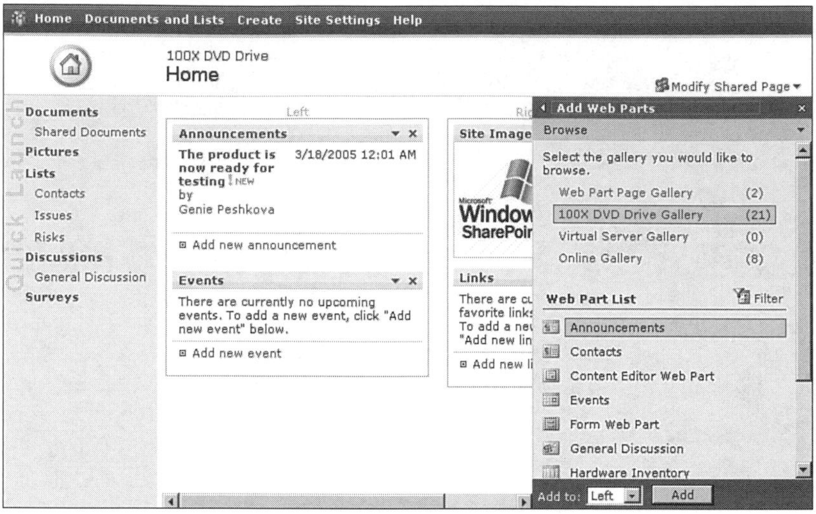

FIGURE 28.3   Web parts are an effective way to import additional tools to increase your project team productivity and collaboration.

You may also import a new web part that either you or someone else have custom created. An example of such a web part may be a calendar web part that integrates with your team Microsoft Outlook calendar. To import a new web part, click the Import link, Browse to the web part file on your local drive, and click the Upload button. After the web part is uploaded, be sure to click the Import button to add the web part to your WSS project site. When this action is completed, you may add it using the Browse function described previously.

- **Design This Page**—Allows you to modify the look, feel, and content displayed on the WSS site Home page for the specific site. Selecting this option creates a drop-down above each area of the main content frame, as shown in Figure 28.4. When you click the arrow in the upper-right corner of a web part you can do the following:

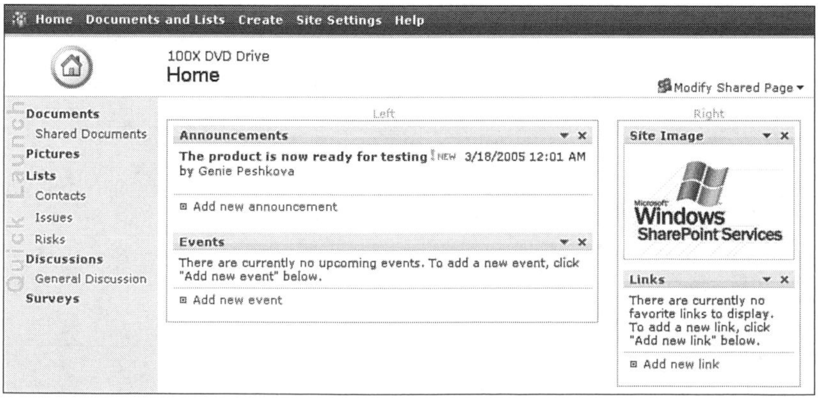

FIGURE 28.4   Left and Right web part zones designate the location for a specific web part.

- **Minimize**—Allows you to compress the selected web part. Minimization hides the content of the web part itself (for example, the list of all existing Announcements), but it still shows the header. The users then can click on the header hyperlink to view the items of the specific web part.

- **Close**—Allows you to "hide" the web part from the Home page, without actually deleting it. This option allows you to retain any settings you have set up for the web part. You may re-add the web part by using the Add Web Parts link under Modify Shared Page.

- **Delete**—Permanently deletes the web part, which erases all the settings you had set up. This operation does not delete the actual data of the web part. Be cautious when permanently deleting any items to ensure that no information loss occurs. You may re-add the web part by using the Add Web Parts link under Modify Shared Page.

- **Modify Shared Web Part**—Allows you to customize the appearance, layout, toolbar type, and other options. The Layout area allows you to specify the part of the screen and the order in which you want the web part to be displayed. The options available to you may vary depending on the web part you are working with. Take some time to get familiar with the different settings available to you in modifying a web part.

> **NOTE**
>
> The Modify Shared Web Part option may also appear as Modify My Web Part. Only one option may appear at a time. The option showing depends on whether you have a Shared View or Personal View currently selected. By default, WSS displays the Shared View when you arrive on the WSS Home page.

- **Connections**—Allows you to connect the web parts together, get filter/sort from another web part, or get data from one web part to another.

- **Help**—Links you to the WSS web part help page.

- **Modify Shared Web Parts**—Provides the list of all current web parts included on the Home page. Selecting a specific web part from the list displays the same options as provided by the Modify Shared Web Part function that you select for individual web parts.

> **NOTE**
>
> The Modify Shared Web Parts option may also appear as Modify My Web Parts, as mentioned earlier in the chapter. The Personal or Shared View dictates which of the options appears.

- **Shared View**—Displays the view that all users who visit the WSS site see. This is the public view, and by customizing the content, you can control the information sharing.

28

- **Personal View**—Allows you to set up a personal view that only you can see. This option can be particularly useful for personal links, reminders, or any other web parts, such as a personal calendar.

Documents and Lists

Documents and lists in a WSS site can be accessed in two ways: from the Home page left side item menu and from the top navigation menu by selecting Documents and Lists. The Documents and Lists page contains all the lists and libraries currently created for the site, as shown in Figure 28.5. It also provides important information such as item description, number of items in the specific category, and last modified information for historic purposes.

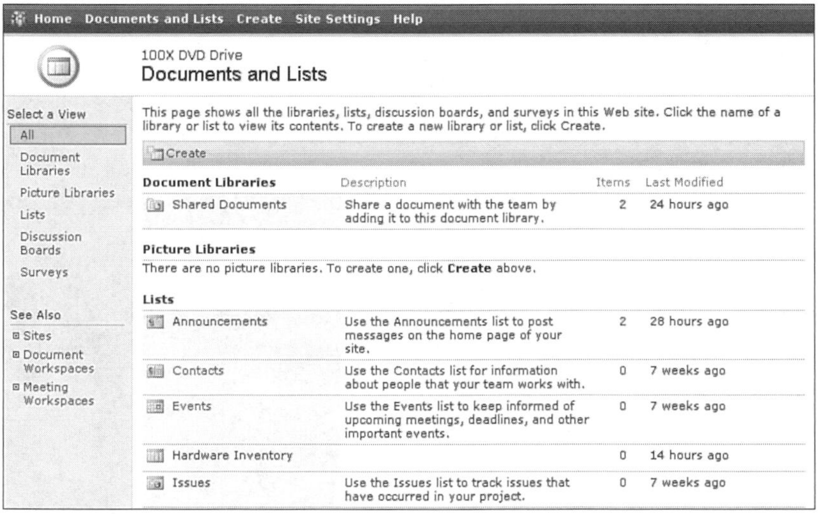

FIGURE 28.5   The Documents and Lists page is broken down into content areas to separate the different item types.

Clicking the hyperlink of each item takes you to the page for that specific item, where you can add new items, create alerts, and modify the columns and settings.

The Documents and Lists page also provides the See Also area, which contains links to

- **Sites**—Lists all subsites created under the current WSS site.

  ▶ SEE "Web Pages," **PAGE 747**.

- **Document Workspaces**—Lists all the document workspaces associated with this site. A Document Workspace is a subsite of the project WSS site that is used for collaborating on any work-related documents. This provides a central location for communicating regarding a specific document that is associated with your project.

- **Meeting Workspaces**—Lists all the meeting workspaces associated with this site. Meeting workspaces allow you to organize all the necessary components for the meeting, including a central location for the agenda, attendees and their responsibilities, documents to review, and so on.

  ▶ **SEE** "Project Team Collaboration," **PAGE 589**.

Documents and Lists Actions

Each item under Documents and Lists has the Actions menu. The Actions menu is located in the left side pane and can be seen on each item's page—for example, Announcements, Risks, Issues, and so on—as shown in Figure 28.6.

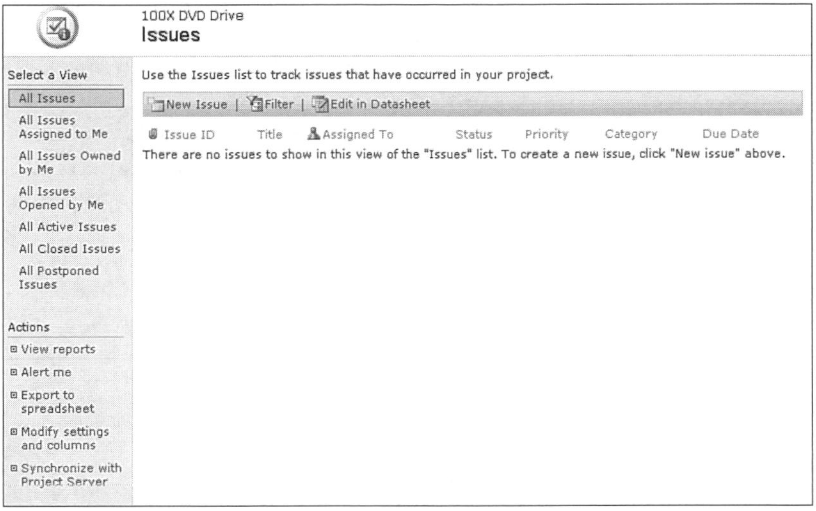

FIGURE 28.6   The Actions menu provides important options for customizing individual documents and lists.

For each list you can perform the following actions:

- **View Reports**—Takes you to the Reports page for the selected list. The Reports page contains the list of predefined reports and is available only for the standard lists included in WSS, such as Issues and Risks.

- **Alert Me**—Allows you to set up and customize the type of alerts you want to receive for this document library or a list.

- **Export to Spreadsheet**—Provides the option to export the current view to an Excel spreadsheet.

- **Modify Settings and Columns**—Allows you to customize the general settings for the item and perform customization actions on its columns.

- **Synchronize with Project Server**—Allows you to synchronize a list you modified outside the WSS site (using Excel or Access) with the WSS site. This option is also available only for predefined WSS lists, such as Risks, Issues, and Documents.

View Reports   The View Reports function allows you to create one of the several predefined reports for a standard WSS site list. These reports can be used for analyzing the selected list by categories, over a date range, and others.

> **NOTE**
>
> The View Reports option is described in detail in Chapter 18, "Risks, Issues, and Documents Using Windows SharePoint Services (WSS)," for each one of the standard WSS lists.

Alert Me   The Alert Me function is a new feature introduced in Project Server 2003, and it allows you to set up custom email notifications for each list or document library. This function is especially useful for monitoring changes made to the list or document library without having to check back to that page for updates. The Alert Me function can also be applied at the item level. For example, you can set up an alert for one specific risk item and not the entire list.

▶ **SEE** "Managing Alerts," **PAGE 305**.

Export to Spreadsheet   The Export to Spreadsheet function is a convenient feature because it allows you to capture a snapshot of the current view of the list or document library. It can be used for taking your work offline, performing analysis using Excel functionality, or for historic purposes.

> **NOTE**
>
> The Export to Spreadsheet function exports only the columns present in the current view. Many views do not contain all the columns of a specific list or library. One solution is to create a special Export to Excel view that includes all the columns present for that list or library and then to apply the Export to Spreadsheet function.

Modify Settings and Columns   Modify Settings and Columns is a powerful feature that allows you to easily customize any list or library you create within WSS. The Modify Settings and Columns feature can also be used on already existing lists, such as Risks, Issues, and Documents, which you can customize further to better fit your business processes.

▶ **SEE** "Risks, Issues, and Documents Using Windows SharePoint Services (WSS)," **PAGE 441**.

Modify Settings and Columns consists of three main areas, as shown in Figure 28.7:

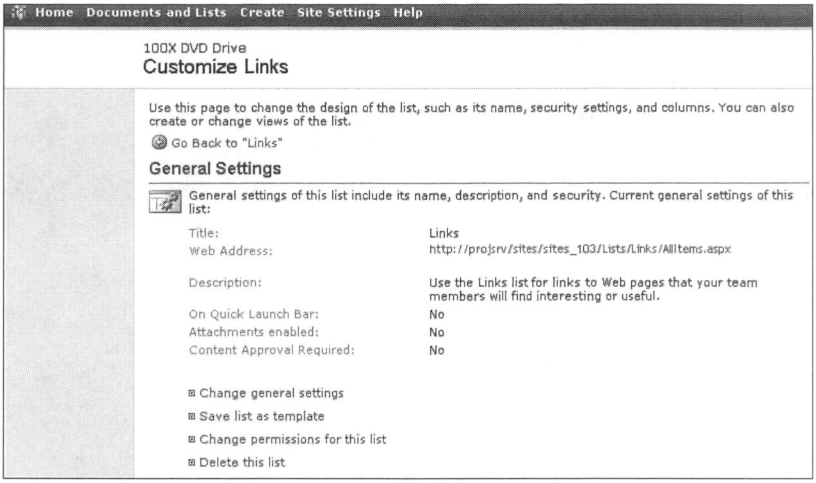

FIGURE 28.7   Use Modify Settings and Columns to customize any list or library on your WSS project workspace site.

- **General Settings**—Used for administration of general list settings, such as name, description, and permissions.

> **NOTE**
>
> The General Settings area of the custom-created lists provides you with the ability to save that list as a template. This functionality is not included for the predefined lists, such as Risks, Issues, and Documents.

> ▶ **SEE** "General Settings," **PAGE 448**.

- **Columns**—Used for creating, modifying, deleting, and reordering the columns that appear in the list or library.

- **Views**—Used for creating, modifying, and deleting the views available in the left side pane of each list or library.

> ▶ **SEE** "Modifying Settings," **PAGE 447**.

Synchronize with Project Server   The Synchronize with Project Server option is available only for the standard WSS lists, such as Risks, Issues, and Documents. This function is used to synchronize the changes you have made to the specific list offline, using Excel or Access. This function is especially useful for traveling—for example, taking the list to review and modify at meetings.

> **NOTE**
>
> The Synchronize with Project Server function is described in detail in Chapter 18 for each one of the standard WSS lists.

The Create Link

The Create link is located in the top navigation menu of the WSS site and is used for creating any new content that will appear on your site. The Create page provides the capability to create the following types of content, as shown in Figure 28.8:

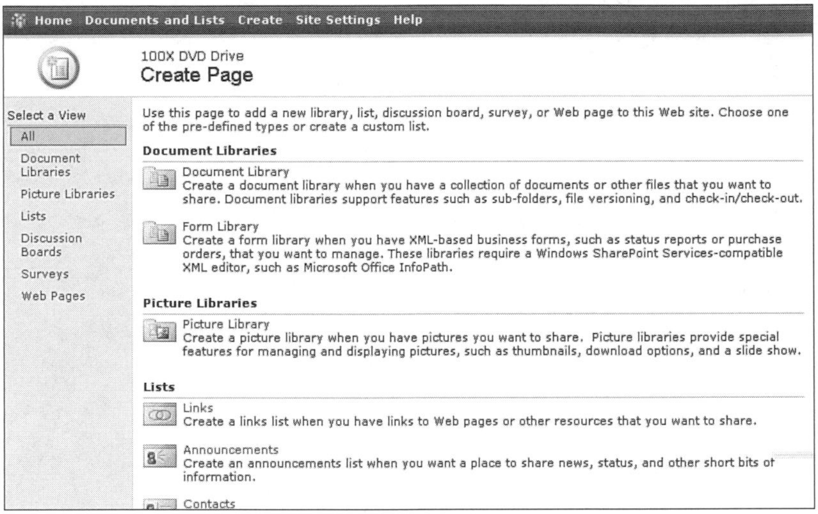

FIGURE 28.8   Use the Create function for adopting new tools to enhance your project team collaboration and communication.

- **Document Libraries**—Provides a template for creating new document libraries. You can customize each document library to include any information you need, and not just the document to upload. Document libraries also provide the ability to perform version control, check-out, and many other options.

- **Picture Libraries**—Provides a template for creating libraries used specifically for graphics.

- **Lists**—Allows you to create a specific type of list. The available choices are links, announcements, contacts, events, tasks, and issues. All these lists come from the standard template, but they can be modified to fit your specific needs.

- **Custom Lists**—Provides three options for custom list creation: Custom List, which consists of multiple custom-defined columns; a Custom List in a Datasheet View, which is similar to the custom list, except it appears in a form of a spreadsheet within the site frame; and Import Spreadsheet, which allows you to import a spreadsheet created using an application compatible with WSS.

- **Discussion Boards**—Provides a template for creating new discussion boards and customizing their settings.

- **Surveys**—Provides a template for creating a survey.

- **Web Pages**—Allows you to create additions to the current WSS project workspace. It provides three options: Basic Page, which adds another page to the project site; Web Part Page, which adds another page to the project site specifically intended for displaying web parts (similar to the Home page); and Sites and Workspaces, which allows you to create a document workspace, a meeting workspace, or a project site subsite.

WSS provides two main types of content templates: libraries and lists. The libraries include document libraries, form libraries, and picture libraries. The lists include links, announcements, contacts, events, custom lists, discussion boards, surveys, and custom lists. It is important to know which items belong to which category because all items in each category have fundamental similarities of how they are created and the options they provide.

Document Libraries   Document libraries are an ideal place to store all documentation related to your project. This provides your project team with one central, web-based location for accessing, modifying, and tracking documents. It is common in many organizations that the document collaboration locations are not well defined, which results in many team members keeping copies of the documents on their local hard drives. This practice hinders information sharing and, therefore, decreases team productivity and efficiency.

> **TIP**
>
> To improve collaboration on documents even further, consider adding additional columns to the document library you are creating. For example, a status field may be a useful way to find out the state of the documentation that can tell other users whether the document is a draft, ready for review, or the final version. You may also want to add a comments area that is used for additional communication of details about the document. Another possibility is adding a % Complete field that allows team members to track the progress of the document.

▶ **SEE** "Modify Settings and Columns," **PAGE 740**.

Figure 28.9 shows an example of a modified document library template.

> **CAUTION**
>
> Providing too many fields for users to fill out may turn people off to using a specific library, so take time to analyze your project needs and configure your document libraries accordingly.

▶ **SEE** "Documents," **PAGE 468**.

Picture Libraries   Picture libraries are similar in nature to document libraries and are used for storing images related to the project. This may be a good place to maintain all project-related logos, screen mockups for software projects, site pictures for construction projects, and so on.

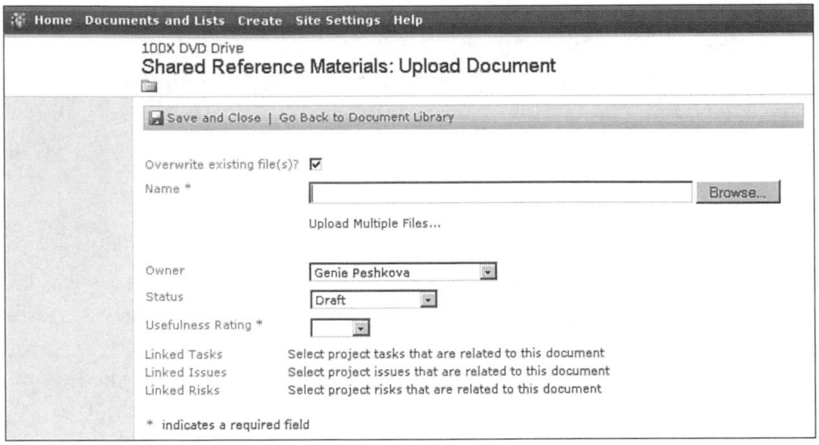

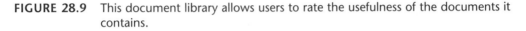

FIGURE 28.9   This document library allows users to rate the usefulness of the documents it contains.

Picture libraries also provide an image editor that allows you to modify images within the library itself.

Besides the actions that relate to all lists and libraries, picture libraries also provide an option to see a slideshow and to view all the folders. As with document libraries, you can customize the columns present in the picture library to fit the needs of your project.

▶ **SEE** "Modify Settings and Columns," **PAGE 740**.

Lists   Lists provide a number of predefined lists that you can use for creating new lists of that type. The available types are

- **Links**—Creates a new Links list that includes a title of the item and the date of last modification. You can use Modify Settings and Columns to modify the fields it contains.

- **Announcements**—Creates a new Announcements list that includes an item title and last modified columns. You can use Modify Settings and Columns to configure the columns displayed in this list according to your needs.

- **Contacts**—Creates a new Contacts list based on the existing WSS Contacts template. This template includes Last Name, First Name, Company, Business Phone, Home Phone, and an Email Address. The Contacts list also provides an option to link the list to Outlook and to Import Contacts. The Contacts list is a great way to keep the project team and client contact information available as a project resource. You can customize the columns displayed in the Contacts list using the Modify Settings and Columns feature.

- **Events**—Creates a new Events list that provides some predefined general events fields. The Events list includes the event title, begin and end date and time, description, location, recurrence, and indication for a meeting workspace. The Events list, as does the Contacts list, provides the capability of linking it to Microsoft Outlook.

You can customize the columns displayed in the Events list using the Modify Settings and Columns feature.

- **Tasks**—Creates a new Tasks list that provides predefined fields for a generic task type. The task fields include task title, priority, status, %complete, assigned to, description, start date, and due date. It also provides some predefined views: My Tasks (filters all tasks assigned to you), Due Date (sorts all tasks by the due date), Active Tasks (filters and displays tasks only with Active status), and By Assigned To (groups the tasks by the person they are assigned to). You can customize the columns and views for the Tasks list using the Modify Settings and Columns feature.

- **Issues**—Creates a new Issues list based on the WSS standard Issues template. You can use Modify Settings and Columns to customize the columns and views for the Issues list.

- **Risks**—Creates a new Risks list based on the WSS standard Risks template. You can use Modify Settings and Columns to customize the columns and views for the Issues list.

> ▶ SEE "Issues," **PAGE 462**.

Lists are a simple way to add more functionality to your WSS project site, but often the predefined templates, even after modifications, do not meet the needs of the project. For those situations, it is suggested that you use the custom lists.

Custom Lists   Custom lists allow you to use your creativity and apply your business processes to the WSS project sites to provide a more efficient working environment for the rest of your project team.

You can create three types of custom lists:

- **Custom List**—Allows you to create any type of custom list to meet the needs of your project, as shown in Figure 28.10. An example of a custom list might be an inventory list used for tracking equipment used for your project. Another example would be tracking defects (bugs) in a software development project.

- **Custom List in Datasheet View**—Same functionality as the custom list, only instead of it being in a list view, it is presented as a spreadsheet embedded in the site frame. This format may be useful for lists that get edited a lot because you do not have to go through the process of opening each item individually. The Datasheet view is also useful for viewing all items on one page.

- **Import Spreadsheet**—Allows you to create a new list by importing an existing spreadsheet created using an application compatible with WSS. Some of the compatible formats are Microsoft Excel spreadsheet or an XML schema document. When importing an Excel spreadsheet, it provides you with an option of Range Type (you can select a name range, a range of cells as you would in Excel, or a list range). The import of data is based on columns and rows to determine how the data is distributed.

> ▶ SEE "Project Workspace Integration with Excel," **PAGE 645**.

28

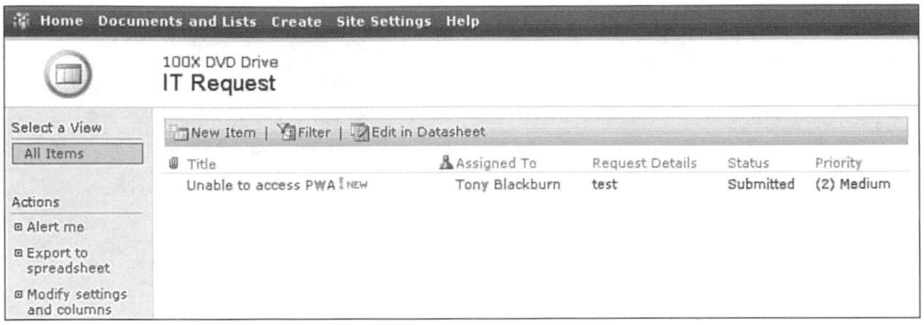

FIGURE 28.10   Custom list for tracking IT requests.

Discussion Boards   Discussion boards have become more popular since the bloom of the Internet, and they are even more effective in improving team communication today. It is possible that during the project life cycle, issues may come up that require the involvement of part of a team or even an entire team. Discussion boards are an efficient way to get input from the rest of the team and keep track of everyone's posts. It is also often difficult to get the entire team together for a meeting, and emailing can be cumbersome because the email chain may become long and unmanageable. That is where the discussion boards play their role. Their benefits are that they do not require all members of the discussion to be present, they allow for historical tracking of posts and decisions, they provide the capability to set up email alerts that notify you when a new post has been added, and many others.

Discussions in a WSS project site allow for two different views: flat and threaded. The threaded view displays a tree of responses. The flat view puts each reply to the main topic as its own "node" (thread). You can find many creative ways for using the discussion boards to fit the needs of your project, as shown in Figure 28.11.

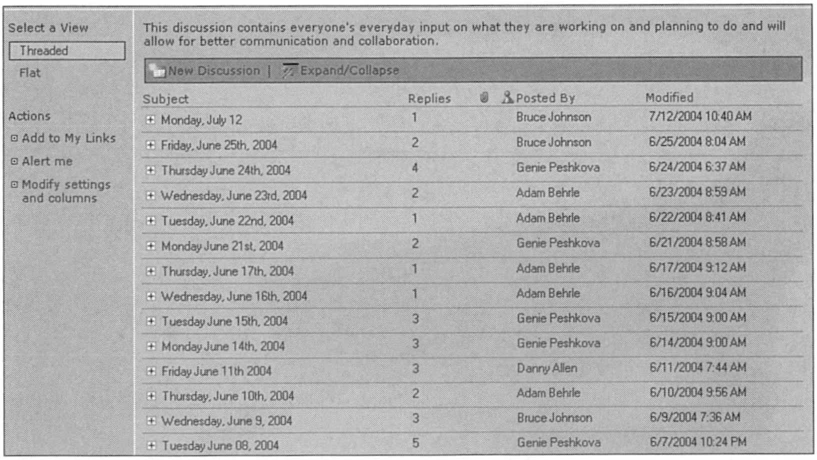

FIGURE 28.11   A discussion board is used for keeping track of the journal entries for a project team to raise awareness of everyone's daily activities.

Surveys   Surveys are another effective way to get team input on a particular subject. For example, surveys can be used to find out the general comfort level of the project progress or adaptation of new technology. The WSS Survey template provides a chain of question-oriented columns that allow for the same types of columns as any other lists in the WSS project site.

▶ **SEE** "Modifying Settings," **PAGE 447**.

The Survey template includes some other useful functionality such as a graphical summary of responses and the capability to view all responses at once. This can become a great analytical tool and a way to find out team members' opinions without putting anyone on a spot.

Web Pages   The Web Pages type of Create feature allows you to create three different types of pages:

- **Basic Web Page**—Allows you to create a new simple web page that contains some text formatting in addition to the existing pages in your WSS project workspace. When creating this page, the default save location is the Shared Documents library. A basic web page is automatically added to the Project Workspace's Shared Documents library, unless the location is changed in the drop down when it's created. The page creation screen provides you with a text editor to enter any information in whatever format you choose, as shown in Figure 28.12.

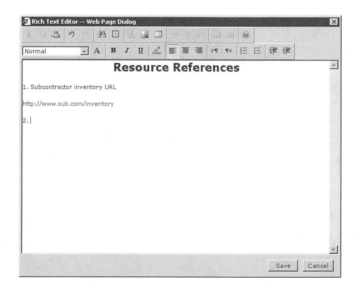

FIGURE 28.12   Creating a new reference page.

- **Web Part Page**—Allows you to create a new web page specifically designed to contain WSS web parts. The Creation Wizard for the web part page allows you to specify the page URL as an extension of your project workspace URL. The wizard also provides options for page layout—that is, whether the page needs to have a header and footer, a right or a left content area, and so on. After the web part page is created, you can use the Modify Shared Web Page link to import, search, or browse any web parts to include on your new page.

- **Sites and Workspaces**—Allows you to create a child site to your current project workspace. This child site is called a subsite.

When creating a subsite, you have the choice of inheriting the permissions from the parent site, which means that the user roles set in your project workspace will be shared with the child site.

The wizard for site and workspace creation also provides a list of templates to apply to the new site. The templates include the following:

- **Team Site**—Creates a WSS team site. The Team Site template contains document library, announcements, events, contacts, and quick links. Team sites are generally used for team organization and can be a great way to coordinate the team for a specific project. You can modify the site using the same functionality as you would a regular WSS project workspace site.

- **Blank Site**—Creates a blank WSS-enabled site. The blank site can be modified using any WSS-compatible web page building software to add lists, libraries, or any other items that you may need. This template is great for using as a clean slate for making your own design and layout.

- **Document Workspace**—Creates a WSS site used as a document workspace. The Document Workspace template includes a document library, tasks list, to-do items list, and links. You can customize the document workspace site the same way you would a regular WSS project workspace site.

- **Basic Meeting Workspace**—Creates a WSS site for organizing meetings. The Basic Meeting Workspace template includes a document library and objectives, attendees, and agenda lists. You can customize the basic meeting workspace site the same way you would a WSS project workspace site.

- **Blank Meeting Workspace**—Creates a blank WSS site for a meeting workspace. This template allows you to customize it to your personal needs and does not include any predefined templates.

- **Decision Meeting Workspace**—Creates a WSS site for a decision meeting workspace. This template includes a document library and objectives, attendees, agenda, tasks, and decisions lists. You can customize the decision meeting workspace site the same way you would a WSS project workspace site.

- **Social Meeting Workspace**—Creates a WSS site for organizing social occasions and events. The Social Meeting Workspace template includes a picture library and attendees, directions, image/logo, things to bring, and discussions lists. The social meeting workspace site is a great way to plan company social gatherings, such as Christmas parties and other social events.

- **Multipage Meeting Workspace**—Creates a WSS site for a meeting workspace. The Multipage Meeting Workspace template is the same as the Basic Meeting Workspace template, except that it includes two blank pages for you to customize. This template can be used for more intricate meeting planning.

- **Project Workspace**—Creates a WSS project workspace site. The Project Workspace template for the subsite includes all the functionality of the noncustomized parent site. You can customize the WSS project workspace subsite using the same features as you would for the parent WSS project workspace site. This template can be used to break up the parent site into smaller subsites for increased manageability and convenience.

Site Settings

Besides modifying the settings of individual lists and libraries, you can modify and manage the settings for the whole project workspace site. You can access the Site Settings feature by selecting Site Settings in the top navigation menu. The Site Settings page contains the following three main areas, as shown in Figure 28.13:

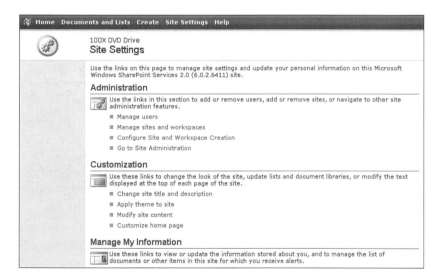

FIGURE 28.13   Modifying site configuration settings.

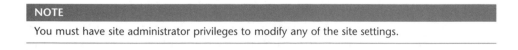

> **NOTE**
>
> You must have site administrator privileges to modify any of the site settings.

- **Administration**—This area is used for managing the site and allows you to manage users, subsites, and workspaces; configure site and workspace creation; and perform general site administration.

- **Customization**—This area is used for customizing the site settings, such as site name and description, site theme, site content, and the Home page customization.

- **Manage My Information**—This area is used for managing your personal information and the alerts for the overall site. You can also view other users' information here.

Administration   Administration is the first area under Site Settings and contains the following functionality:

- **Manage Users**—Provides the list of all current site users and lists their permission groups. WSS uses the Project Server security model. Here, you can add a new site user and grant him appropriate permissions.

  ▶ **SEE** "Permissions in WSS," **PAGE 444**.

  In Manage Users, you can also modify the permissions of any existing users, as well as a group of users (by selecting multiple users at once and clicking the Edit Site Groups of Selected Users link).

  You can also delete any current site user by selecting the user's name and clicking the Remove Selected Users link.

NOTE

Removing users removes them only from your project workspace site users list and does not permanently delete them from the database. If you removed a user by accident, you can add her using the Add Users button.

- **Manage Sites and Workspaces**—Provides a list of the current meeting and document workspaces, as well as any subsites. The list also includes the item description, date of last modification, and an option to remove the item permanently from the project workspace site.

  From the left side menu you can select to view All, Sites, Document Workspaces, or Meeting Workspaces. These options show the items of the selected type. Clicking the hyperlink of any specific item displays the edit page that walks you through the wizard for that specific item. You can modify options such as the type of template used. Clicking the Delete link next to the item name permanently deletes the item and all its content.

- **Configure Site and Workspace Creation**—Provides you with the ability to modify the general settings applied when a new subsite or workspace is created. This page lists all roles available for users of the WSS site; selecting the site group means that the users who belong to that group have a right to create a subsite (this includes the document and meeting workspaces associated with the WSS site).

- **Go to Site Administration**—Provides a list of functions that include customization for users and permissions, management and statistics, site collection galleries, and site collection administration for managing the top-level WSS site.

The Users and Permissions area allows you to do the following:

- **Manage Users**—Provides functionality to add, remove, edit, and add users to the existing site groups.

- **Manage Site Groups**—Allows you to create, modify permissions of, and delete site groups. This allows you to customize the type of access you give to your users.

- **Manage Anonymous Access**—Allows you to specify whether the authenticated Project Server users should automatically be granted access to the WSS site and allows you to select the group for permissions, such as Reader or Contributor.

- **Manage Cross-Site Groups**—Allows you to create a cross-site group that will give permission to the users belonging to that group access to your site and allows them to perform various actions based on the privileges you set.

- **Manage Access Requests**—Provides a setting to allow access requests. Access requests are used for sending an email notification to an email specified here, letting you know that a certain user does not have the rights he needs for your site so that you can choose whether to grant them. This is a great way of communicating about the access problems.

The Management and Statistics area allows you to do the following:

- **Save Site As Template**—Allows you to save the site as a template so that you can use it to define other sites with similar structure. This is a great way of defining a site template for a certain project type—for example, a software development project, which could potentially include a new list such as Defect Tracking. Site templates are beyond the scope of this chapter, but if you want to learn more about them, see the Microsoft website.

- **View Site Usage Data**—Provides a report of the usage data for the site.

> **NOTE**
>
> Usage processing must be enabled on your Project Server for you to be able to use the View Site Usage Data feature.

- **Manage Sites and Workspaces**—Allows you to create, modify, and delete subsites, meeting workspaces, and document workspaces for your WSS site.

- **Manage Web Discussions**—Allows you to select URLs to display for the web discussions associated with documents on your site. You may choose either All Web Discussions to view all URLs for the web discussions on your site or a specific folder of web discussions.

- **Manage User Alerts**—Allows you to remove users' alerts on your site. This is a great way to determine which users have different types of alerts set up and remove any of the unwanted ones.

28

- **Change Regional Settings**—Allows you to select the location (a region) to which the site applies, the time zone under which the site will operate, and the time format.

- **Delete This Site**—Allows you to permanently delete the WSS site and all its content. Be cautious when deleting sites to ensure that no information loss occurs.

The Site Collection Galleries area provides the Manage Web Part Gallery, Manage List Template Gallery, and Manage Site Template Gallery options. The Manage Web Part Gallery option allows you to review, edit, and upload new web parts for your WSS site. The web parts are used primarily on the Home page and provide various efficient ways to improve team collaboration. The Manage List Template Gallery option allows you to review, edit, upload, and delete new list templates for your WSS site. The list templates are used in creating custom lists and are an efficient way to create the same list on multiple WSS sites. The Manage Site Template Gallery option allows you to view, create, edit, and delete site templates available for WSS. WSS site templates are applied to each site at its creation and determine the type of content and the purpose the site is going to have.

MAKING YOUR TEMPLATE AVAILABLE FOR PROJECT WORKSPACE PROVISIONING

In WSS, you can modify the project workspace site and change the settings, content, and purpose of the site. After the site is customized to your needs, you can then save the site as a template and, by performing the steps described here, make it available as one of the template choices for creating a new site in the PWA Site Provisioning.

After you have customized the project workspace site, perform the following steps:

1. In the top navigation menu select Site Settings.
2. Under Administration select Go to Site Administration.
3. Under Management and Statistics, select Save Site As Template and provide a meaningful File name, Template title, and Template description.
4. Click OK and then click the Site Template Gallery link. This displays the Site Template Gallery page, listing all the site templates, including the one you just saved.
5. Download the template file you just created to your local drive and then copy it to your WSS server.
6. To upload the site template to WSS on your server, run the STSADM.EXE, which is located in C:\Program Files\Common Files\Microsoft Shared\web server extensions\60\BIN. Execute the file by the following command line.:

   ```
   stsadm.exe -o addtemplate -filename
   <nameOfYourTemplateFile> -title
   <TemplateTitle>
   ```

7. Perform an Internet Information Services (IIS) reset.

After the IIS reset is complete, your template will be available for selection as the template to be used for the project workspaces site of projects published in Project Professional. To select your new template, perform the following steps:

1. In PWA select Admin, Manage Windows SharePoint Services.

2. From the quick launch bar, under Options, select Site provisioning settings.

3. Select the Site template drop-down and select your template name.

This is a convenient way to create and add a new site template for the WSS sites without having to modify XML files on the server.

NOTE

The Manage List Template and Manage Site Template galleries are available only to the domain administrators.

The Site Collection Administration area allows you to do the following:

- **View Site Hierarchy**—Allows you to view the site hierarchy for all subsites created under the current WSS site, their URLs, and titles.

- **View Site Collection Usage Summary**—Provides information on storage, users, and activity information for your site. The storage shows the current storage used in MB, the percent of storage used by web discussions, and the maximum storage limit for your site. The Users area shows the total number of users currently allowed to access your site and any restrictions for the total number of users allowed. The activity is used for capturing the total number of hits to your site and the recent bandwidth use.

- **View Storage Space Allocation**—Shows the amount of storage used by each item in the document libraries, documents, and lists.

- **View Site Collection User Information**—Provides a list of users in the current site collection, their names, their usernames, and whether they are a site collection administrator. This feature also allows you to view the cross-site groups for this site collection.

- **Configure Connection to Portal Site**—Allows you to set up a connection to a portal site for accessing your WSS site by specifying the port web address and name.

Customization   The Customization area of the Site Settings is used for modifying the overall site look, feel, and functionality. The Customization area provides the following options:

- **Change Site Title and Description**—Allows you to modify the title and the description that appear for the site. The default title is the project name to which this WSS project workspace belongs to.

- **Apply Theme to Site**—Allows you to select a predefined color and look-and-feel theme. It allows you to preview each theme prior to applying it to your site. By default, the WSS project workspace site uses no theme. Some examples of the available themes are Arctic, Canyon, and Compass.

28

- **Modify Site Content**—Provides a list of all content (all libraries and lists) available on your site and allows you to customize each item (the same screen as the Modifying Settings and Columns). This feature also allows you to create new content, which takes you to the site Create page.

- **Customize Home Page**—Takes you to the WSS project workspace site in modify mode. Here, you can modify and delete the displayed web parts.

    ▶ **SEE** "The Home Page," **PAGE 734**.

Manage My Information   The Manage My Information area provides you with the functionality to modify the personal information displayed for your profile on the WSS site, the custom alerts that you have set up, and other users' information on this site.

The Manage My Information area provides the following options:

- **Update My Information**—Allows you to edit your personal information displayed on the WSS site, such as your name and email address. It also provides a link to the User Information list that contains all users who have rights for the WSS site and their display name, username, and email address.

- **My Alerts on This Site**—Allows you to add a new alert associated with a specific library or list on the WSS site. It also allows you to edit and delete any of the current alerts.

    ▶ **SEE** "Managing Alerts," **PAGE 305**.

- **View Information About Site Users**—Displays the User Information page that lists all site users and their display names, usernames, and email addresses. You can click each user's display name hyperlink to edit the user's information. It also provides a link to the Add Users page, which you can use to create new site users.

Saving Custom List As a Template

WSS provides you with the ability to save any custom list that you created as a template to import to another WSS site. This feature is especially useful if you reuse the same list template for certain types of projects and allows you to not have to re-create the list from scratch every time.

To save a custom list as a template, follow these steps:

1. On the WSS project site select Documents and Lists.

2. Click the name of the custom list to save as a template.

3. Under the Actions menu select Modify Settings and Columns.

4. On the Modify Settings and Columns page select General Settings. Select Save Link As a Template, which displays the Save As Template page, shown in Figure 28.14.

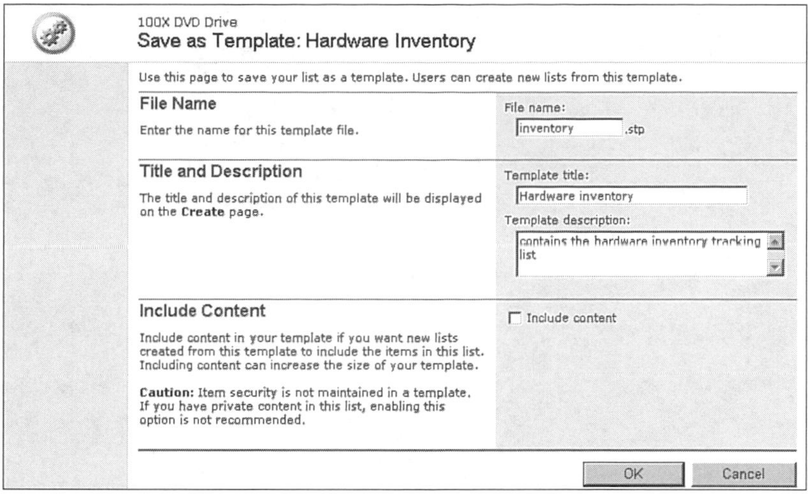

FIGURE 28.14   Provide a meaningful name and title for your list template.

5. Enter the name, title, and description for your list template.

6. Indicate whether to include the content of the current list by selecting the Include Content box.

7. Click OK, which displays a confirmation page for a successful template creation with a link to the List Template Gallery. Click on the link.

TIP

The List Template Gallery is a list template library automatically created for each WSS site. It generally does not appear in the Quick Launch bar, but you can access it by adding /_catalogs/lt/Forms/AllItems.aspx to your WSS site URL.

---

8. The List Template Gallery page displays all list templates that exist for this site.

9. On the List Template Gallery page, click the hyperlink name of your custom list template and click Save.

10. Save the template to your local drive to import it to another WSS site.

To create a new custom list based on your custom list template, follow these steps:

1. Access the List Template Library page for the WSS site where you want to create this custom list.

2. In the top navigation menu select Upload Template. Use the Browse button to navigate to the template file you saved on your local drive.

3. Click the Save and Close button.

4. The name of this new template (Hardware Inventory used as an example in this case) will appear under Create, Lists, as shown in Figure 28.15.

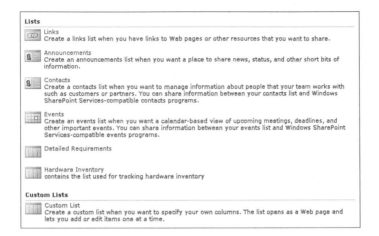

FIGURE 28.15   The Lists area of the Create page includes all predefined and custom templates that exist for the WSS site.

Creating Nonproject-Related WSS Sites

Creating WSS sites associated with a project is an excellent feature, which contributes to team collaboration and the management of project details. At times, you will want to create a WSS site that is not related to a project—for example, a department team site or a personal site for managing all your documents that allows access for others. In this situation, you can create a nonproject-related WSS site.

To create a nonproject-related WSS site, perform these steps:

1. In PWA, select the Admin tab.

2. Under the Actions menu select Manage Windows SharePoint Services.

3. Under Options, select Site provisioning settings.

4. In the main content window, under Windows SharePoint Services Central Administration Site, click the site URL link. This displays the Windows SharePoint Services Central Administration site, as shown in Figure 28.16.

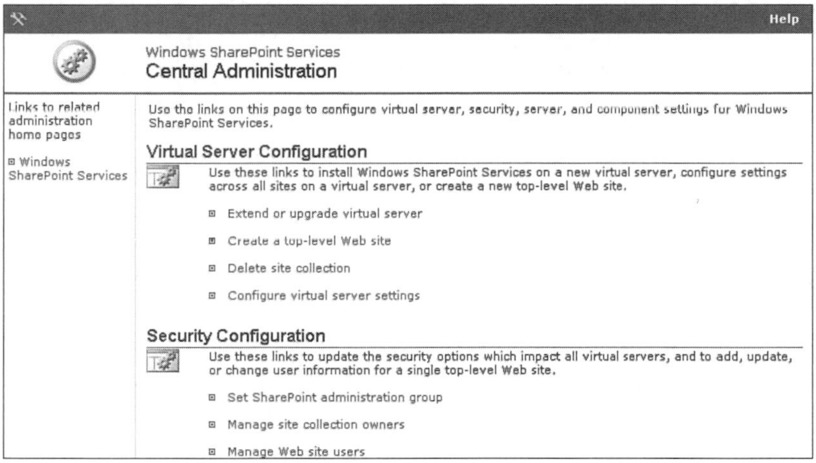

FIGURE 28.16   The WSS Central Administration site allows you to manage virtual server, security, server, and component configuration.

5. Under Virtual Server Configuration select Create a Top-Level WSS site. The Virtual Server List page displays.

6. On the Virtual Server List page, click the Default Web Site (or any other, if other templates have been created) link to use it as a template for your new site.

7. On the Create a Top-Level WSS Site page, fill out all the needed information such as the following:

- **Current Virtual Server**—Displays the current virtual server used for creating this site. You can click the Choose Virtual Server link to view all available virtual servers and a select a different one to use.

- **Web Site Address**—Allows you to create a name for the website or to create the URL at the root.

- **Site Collection Owner**—Enter the correct username in the format of *domain\username* and the user's email address. This user will be considered the site owner and administrator.

- **Secondary Owner**—Enter the correct username in the format of *domain\ username* and the user's email address. This user will be considered the secondary site owner and administrator.

- **Quota Template**—Allows you to select the quota template that indicates the maximum number of resources allowed for the site.

- **Site Language**—Select the language used for this site.

8. When you are finished entering all required information, click OK. If the site creation was successful, the Top-Level Site Successfully Created page displays, as shown in Figure 28.17.

FIGURE 28.17   Click the URL to create the site itself using one of the existing site templates.

9. Click the URL to select the template to apply to the new site.

   ▶ **SEE** "Web Pages," **PAGE 747**.

10. After you select the template to use as a base for your new site, click OK. The new top-level nonproject-related site is now created, as shown in Figure 28.18.

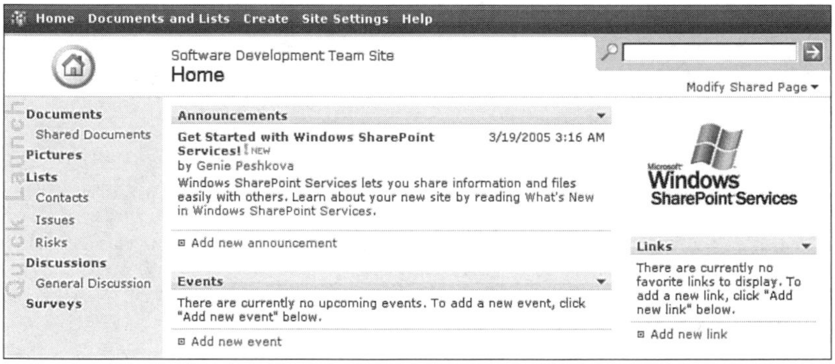

FIGURE 28.18   You can customize the new top-level site as you would a WSS project work-space site.

Server-Side WSS Customization Overview

In addition to WSS being highly customizable on the user end, you can customize WSS templates on the server. Customizing the server-side template allows you to globally change it in contrast with the user end, which is site specific. The WSS site template that resides on the server is referred to as the *site definition*. This section covers the general steps of how you can create, modify, and apply the site definition.

Server-side WSS customization is complex. This section is not meant to cover every detail of server-side customization, but rather introduce you to the concept and provide some guidance on where to begin.

In WSS, the site web pages can be generated using two methods. The first method consists of WSS retrieving the site data directly from the database and provides more of a static site. The second method is to dynamically generate the site pages based on the specified site definition. This method stores the changes made to the site from the definition in the database.

When you modify the site definition, the changes you make are global and are reflected on all WSS sites based on that definition.

You can find additional, detailed information on the site definition manipulation in the Windows SharePoint Services Software Development Kit (comes with WSS installation). You may also want to search for additional resources on MSDN.

Template Location and Structure

To perform any manipulation to the site definition, you need to locate the folder containing all the site definition files. Site definitions are located on WSS server: C:\Program Files\Common Files\Microsoft Shared\web server extensions\60\TEMPLATE\1033, as shown in Figure 28.19.

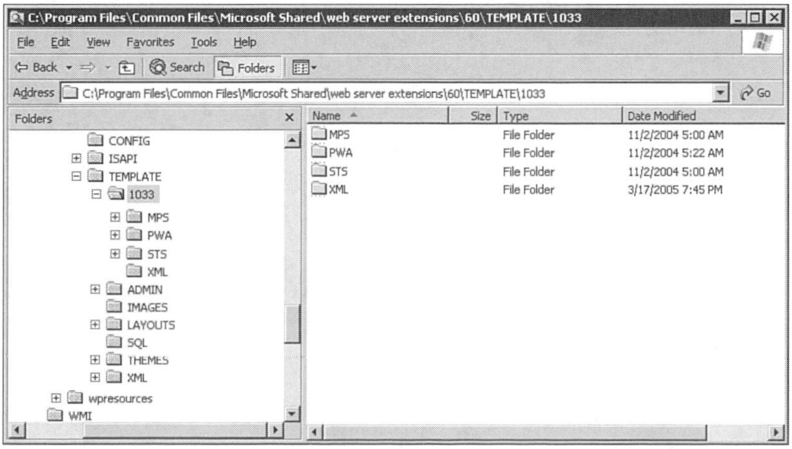

FIGURE 28.19 Physical structure of all WSS site definitions.

Each site definition is a folder stored under the 1033 folder. A site definition folder contains all files used for that site definition, including lists, document templates, libraries, and so on.

By default, the 1033 folder contains the following folders:

- **MPS (Meeting Workspace Project Site) folder**—Template folder that creates a team site used for planning, tracking, and organizing meetings. This template includes Objectives, Attendees, Agenda lists, and a Document Library.

- **PWA (Project Web Access) folder**—Template folder used for creation of project sites—WSS Project Workspace. This template includes Risks, Issues, Announcements, Contacts, Custom Lists, Discussions, Document Library, Events, Favorites, Image Library, and many others. The PWA template is used to create a new WSS site for each project published in Project Professional.

- **STS (SharePoint Team Services) folder**—Template folder used to create a team site used for team organization and collaboration. This template includes a Document Library, Announcements, Events, Contacts, and Quick Links.

- **XML folder**—Contains WSS definitions for sites—for example, a list of options for creating a new site.

By default, each PWA site definition folder contains the following folders:

- **DOCTEMP**—Contains the definitions of all document templates used on the WSS sites. For example, it includes the different file type formats accepted, such as Word, PowerPoint, Excel, XML, and so on.

- **DWS**—Used to initialize a new document workspace and includes the default.aspx file responsible for workspace creation.

- **LISTS**—Contains folders of all lists available for creation within the given site definition. These include Announcements, Contacts, Custom Lists, Discussions, Document Libraries, Risks, Issues, and so on. If you want to globally modify the items that appear in one of the lists of your WSS sites, you can modify that list template here.

- **XML**—Contains XML files that define the settings for the site definition, such as standard views, styles, and other preferences.

All list templates are stored in the LISTS folder under a particular site definition folder.

Each list template has a SCHEMA.XML file that defines all list fields, columns, views, and so on. You can modify the SCHEMA.XML file for the changes to the list to propagate to all WSS sites based on that site definition.

Creating a New WSS Site Definition

A WSS site definition is an XML-formatted schema file used to produce WSS sites' HTML and uses a method called *ghosting*.

> **TIP**
>
> *Ghosting* is a method of constructing WSS sites on-the-fly and is based off the template, including the changes that have been made to the site. Using ghosting reduces storage space by not storing redundant data for each site in the database and also may increase performance.

You can create a new site definition template to use in the creation of your WSS sites. This is a convenient method of standardizing lists, libraries, and other settings you frequently use for your WSS sites.

> **CAUTION**
>
> It is highly recommended to not modify the default WSS and PWA templates. If any problems occur during the template modification, you will no longer have the default one to refer to. This is also important if you ever install any service packs or upgrades that may overwrite the default WSS site definition template, and you could lose the changes you made. The best practice is to copy the default template and then make the desired modification to that copy.

To create a new WSS site definition, follow these steps:

1. Create a copy of the default WSS site definition folder under the 1033 folder by performing the following:

    - Locate the folder in the template directory named PWA that contains the default WSS project site definition. It is suggested to use a copy of this site definition for creating a new team/project site definition.

    - Make a copy of the PWA folder.

    - Use a meaningful name for your new site definition and always use capital letters for the template directory name, as shown in Figure 28.20.

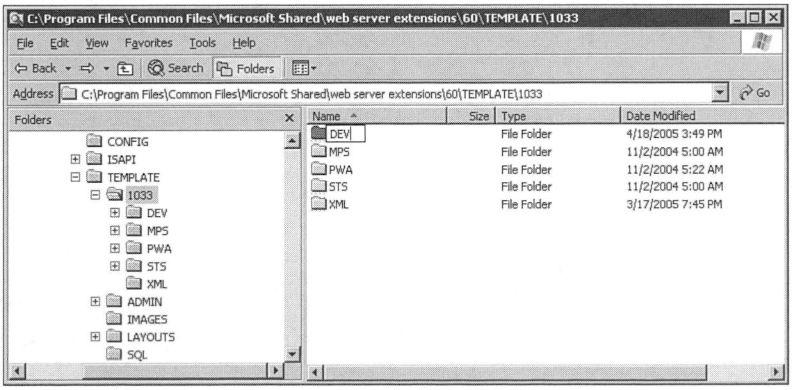

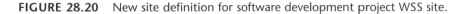

FIGURE 28.20   New site definition for software development project WSS site.

2. Modify the schema files, as follows:

- Modify XML site definition files. The most common modifications will be performed to lists. If you are creating a new list, copy the CUSTLIST folder located in the LISTS subfolder of the site definition.

- Modify the schema files.

NOTE

Schema files are written in XML and to modify their content you need to have sufficient knowledge of XML.

TIP

For detailed node definitions, parameters, and other details you need to modify the schema files. Refer to the MSDN documentation and the Windows SharePoint Services Software Development Kit (SDK), which can be downloaded from www.microsoft.com.

The schema file has one root XML node, named List. The MetaData child node contains a Fields node, where fields are defined, including names, types, choices, and so on. You can add a new field by adding new nodes. Figure 28.21 shows an example of a schema file.

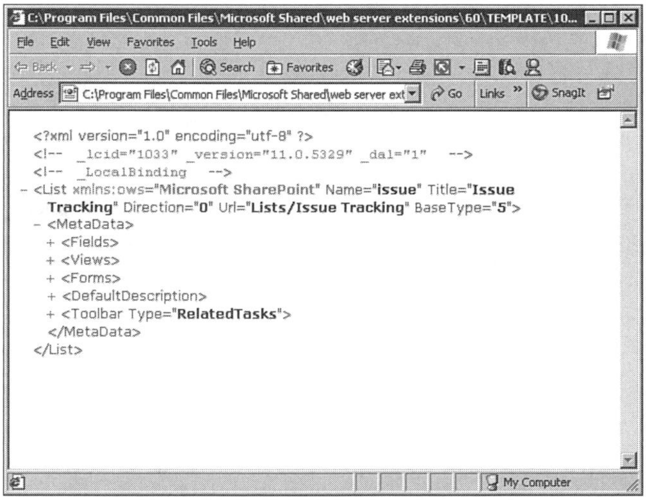

FIGURE 28.21   You can expand each node of the list—for example, Fields, Views, and so on—to view the details.

The simplest way to add a new node is by copying an existing node and modifying it. An example of modified field node is

```
<Field Type="Choice" Name="Status" DisplayName="Status" >
➥<CHOICES>
        <CHOICE>(1) Submitted</CHOICE>
<!-- For PWA Start -->
        <CHOICE>(2) Ready for Review</CHOICE>
<!-- For PWA End -->
        <CHOICE>(3) Final</CHOICE>
    </CHOICES>
<!-- For PWA Start -->
        <Default>(2) Medium</Default>
<!-- For PWA End -->
```

You can also add HTML for additional formatting, but for most purposes simply adding the field nodes should be sufficient.

The next node after Fields in the schema file is the Views node. The Views node contains definitions of all views available for the current list and fields they display. For the simplest operations, you can modify the ViewFields node to modify the fields displayed by the view. To add a new view, copy an existing view node and modify it to reflect the desired settings.

> **NOTE**
>
> When creating a new view node, make sure that the BaseViewID is unique. If the BaseViewID is not unique, the view may behave unexpectedly and not display properly.

When working with schema files, you also have to modify the ONET files. The ONET files are used for many different functions, but the most common one is adding links on the Actions pane of the page.

ONET.XML is located in the XML templates folder under 1033. If you have created a new list template and want it to appear as a template on a WSS site, modify the ONET.XML file by copying the existing ListTemplate node to a new node and modify the appropriate fields, such as name, display name, and so on. This operation displays the list template for users to choose from.

To create a link to the list in the quick launch bar, add the List node to the list of nodes under Configuration. An example of adding a new node is as follows:

```
<List Title="Shared Documents" Url="Shared Documents"
➥QuickLaunchUrl="Shared
Documents/Forms/AllItems.aspx" Type="101" />
```

Figure 28.22 shows an example of the Configuration node in the ONET.XML file.

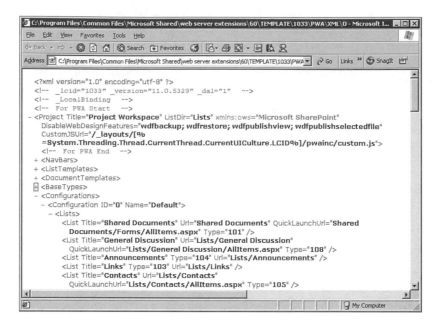

FIGURE 28.22   The Configuration node lists all links to lists and document libraries in the quick launch bar.

3. Reset Internet Information Services (IIS) for changes to appear on the user end.

You can also modify a site definition template using FrontPage.

> **CAUTION**
>
> Modifying a site using FrontPage removes its dependence on the site definition. Consequently, any changes made to the definition will not propagate to that site.

Setting Your New Definition to Be a Template Choice

After you have created a new site definition, you are now ready to make it appear as a selection when creating a new WSS site, such as a document or meeting workspace. You can also set the new site definition as the base template for all WSS sites created for new projects published using Project Professional.

To do so, follow these steps:

1. Access the XML folder under C:\Program Files\Common Files\Microsoft Shared\web server extensions\60\TEMPLATE\1033.

2. Locate the WEBTEMPP.XML file and make a copy.

3. Rename the copied file to WEBTEMPP<descriptive name>.XML—for example, WEBTEMPPDEV.XML.

> **NOTE**
>
> The filename must begin with WEBTEMPP for WSS to read the file.

4. Modify the file you just created to include appropriate settings, as shown in Figure 28.23. Some of the most common settings to modify are as follows:

   - **Template Name**—The exact name of the site definition folder you have created, for example, DEV.

   - **ID**—Represents the ID of the site definition and must be a unique integer. You can come up with the ID yourself; just make sure to check all other WEBTEMPP....XML files under the XML folder to ensure that your ID has not been used for another site definition.

   - **Title**—A descriptive title that will appear on the user end for your site definition.

   - **Description**—A detailed description of the purpose and contents of the site definitions. Description is a great place to specify the types of predefined lists and libraries the site definition includes.

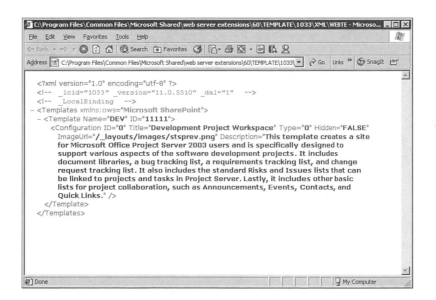

FIGURE 28.23   Modified DEV site definition WEBTEMPP file.

5. Reset Internet Information Services (IIS) to have the new site definition (template) appear in the PWA.

Changing the Template Used for Projects

Every time you create a new project in Project Professional and publish it, a WSS Project Workspace site is created. The WSS Project Workspace site is based on the specified site definition template. You can change the site definition used for all project sites by performing the following:

1. Access PWA, select Admin, and then select Manage Windows SharePoint Services.

2. In the quick launch bar under Options select Site Provisioning Settings.

3. Select the Site Template drop-down and then select the site definition you created, as shown in Figure 28.24.

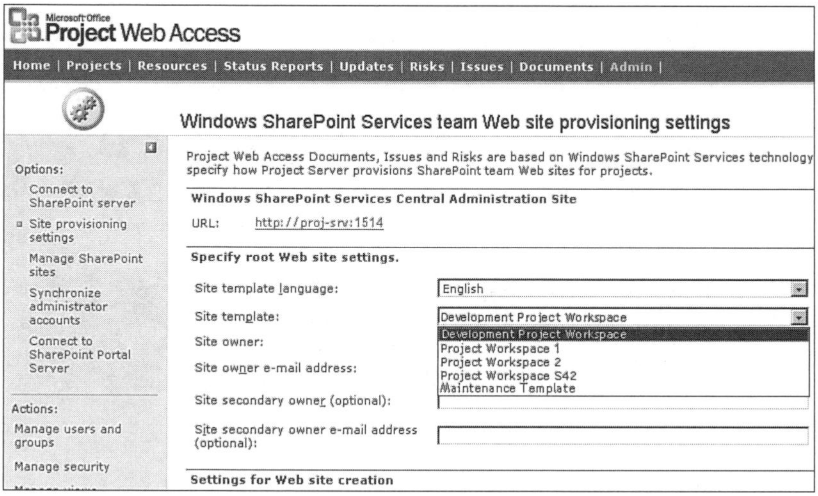

FIGURE 28.24   Development Project Workspace template name uses the DEV site definition that has been modified throughout this section.

4. Click the Save Changes button to apply your changes.

All new Project Workspace sites created from this point on will use the new template you have specified. However, this change will not affect any of the existing WSS sites.

Customizing PWA

You can customize PWA in many ways from simple modifications to changes that must be made by advanced programmers. This section progresses from simple customizations that can be made without coding to the structure of the ASP code the website is composed of and how to add new pages to it.

Unless otherwise noted, any files referenced will be referred to relative to the IIS Virtual Root for the PWA instance you are dealing with. The default Project Server installation places these files at C:\Program Files\Microsoft Office Project Server 2003\IIS Virtual Root.

URL Parameters

Three URL parameters can be used to modify the look and function of any page: SimpleUI, NoSaveLinkButton, NoMenu. These parameters can be added to the URL in the address bar of the user's browser by any user to affect the page temporarily. Or they can be added to the URL for the page in the menu structure in the database by a DBA to affect the page permanently for all users.

The SimpleUI parameter should be set to an integer value between 0 and 127 that represents bitmapped instructions about which parts of the user interface should be shown. The seven options that can be set are Indicator Click Disabled, No Grid Buttons, No Title Elements, No Tabs, No Action Pane, Collapsed Action Pane, and No Menu. A table of integer values showing all the combinations of these options and a thorough description of their function can be found on Microsoft's MSDN website.

The NoSaveLinkButton and NoMenu parameters are left over from Project Server 2002 and are now deprecated because their function is contained in the SimpleUI functionality. However, when only one of these options is needed, it can be more intuitive to use one of these parameters rather than look up their SimpleUI equivalents.

The Home page supports the NoBanter parameter. Setting this parameter to 1 hides the pane on the right side of the page, which by default contains a graphic and a Work with Outlook link.

Pages that support views, such as the Project Center, can be modified with a number of parameters that determine what data is displayed and how the grid is formatted. The simplest way to view and modify these parameters is to customize the view from the PWA interface and then click the Save Link button. When you click on the saved link in the Actions pane, the URL of that link is displayed in your browser's address bar. More information about the particular parameters available can be found on Microsoft's MSDN website.

Information on how to modify the menus in PWA to include any desired URL parameters will be given later in this chapter.

Modifying the Stylesheet

Modifying the colors and fonts of the website is an easy way to give PWA a custom feel, or make it match a corporate intranet site. Most of the styles you want to customize are defined in the file STYLES\1033\MSPROJECT.css. Styles that contain a gradient background color or other background colors based on browser settings make calls to functions in SHELL\SHELL.asp, and these functions may need to be modified to make some color changes.

Modifying Menus

The menus in PWA are created with a combination of database queries and JScript from ASP files. This section focuses on changing the menu structure stored in the database, which can affect the menu items across the top of all pages and in the Actions panes. Editing database tables and script is necessary for some modifications because the administrator's interface in PWA allows you to modify only the names of existing pages and not their URLs.

The two database tables that control the menu structure are MSP_WEB_SECURITY_MENUS and MSP_WEB_SECURITY_PAGES. These two tables link to MSP_WEB_CONVERSTIONS to provide localized text values and MSP_WEB_SECURITY_FEATURES_ACTIONS to provide security restrictions. The schema of these tables appears in Figure 28.25.

MSP_WEB_SECURITY_MENUS	
PK	**WSEC_MENU_ID**
	WSEC_MENU_NAME_ID
	WSEC_MENU_CUSTOM_NAME
	WSEC_MENU_PARENT_ID
	WSEC_MENU_SEQ
	WSEC_MENU_DESC_ID
	WSEC_MENU_CUSTOM_DESC
	WSEC_MENU_PAGE_ID
	WSEC_MENU_IS_CUSTOM
	WSEC_MENU_IS_TOP_LEVEL
	WSEC_MENU_LINKGROUP_NAME_ID

MSP_WEB_SECURITY_PAGES	
PK	**WSEC_PAGE_ID**
I2	WSEC_PAGE_MENU_ID
	WSEC_PAGE_URL
	WSEC_PAGE_CUSTOM_URL
	WSEC_PAGE_HELP_URL
I1	WSEC_PAGE_ACT_ID
	WSEC_PAGE_MASTER_PAGE_ID
	WSEC_PAGE_SESSION_SETTINGS
	WSEC_PAGE_DATABASE_SETTINGS
	WSEC_PAGE_CAN_OFFLINE

MSP_WEB_CONVERSIONS	
PK	**STRING_TYPE_ID**
PK	**CONV_VALUE**
PK	**LANG_ID**
	CONV_STRING

MSP_WEB_SECURITY_FEATURES_ACTIONS	
PK	**WSEC_FEA_ACT_ID**
	WSEC_FEA_ACT_NAME_ID
	WSEC_FEA_ACT_PARENT
	WSEC_IS_ACTION
	WSEC_ON_OBJECT
	WSEC_OBJ_TYPE_ID

FIGURE 28.25   Tables that need to be modified when customizing PWA menus.

An easy change to the menu structure is to add URL parameters to the existing pages to modify their look or function. For example, to remove the banter pane (right side of the page) from the Home page, find the entry for Home/homepage.asp in MSP_WEB_SECURITY_PAGES and change the WSEC_PAGE_URL field to Home/homepage.asp? NoBanter=1.

A more complicated change would be to add a new link to the Actions pane for an existing top-level menu item. As an introduction to the menu tables of the database, try adding a link to an existing PWA page. The same technique would be used to add a link to a new custom page.

For the sake of example, suppose that the administrators for your Project Server need to modify the settings for groups frequently and want to be able to access the group management page from the Home page. To enable this, add a link to the group management page to the top-level menu item for the Home section of PWA. This change requires adding an entry to MSP_WEB_CONVERSIONS for the link text, to MSP_WEB_SECURITY_MENUS so that the link appears under the Home top-level menu, and to MSP_WEB_SECURITY_PAGES. An entry for this page already exists in MSP_WEB_SECURITY_PAGES, but another entry is required to link it to the new entry in MSP_WEB_SECURITY_MENUS without removing the link from the Admin Actions menu.

`MSP_WEB_CONVERSIONS` contains string values related to both an ID and a language code to allow the user interface to be localized to different countries. The entries for menu items have a `STRING_TYPE_ID` of 5, and your new entry should follow this standard. `CONV_VALUE` is the ID used to refer to the new entry, so it must be unique among entries for the same language and string type. It should also be chosen to fit with the scheme used to identify other menu items. Make a new entry where `STRING_TYPE_ID` = 5, `CONV_VALUE` = 50107, `LANG_ID` = 1033, and `CONV_STRING` = "Manage Groups".

Add an entry to `MSP_WEB_SECURITY_MENUS` with the fields set as follows:

- `WSEC_MENU_ID` = an identity (this will be 10001 if this is the first new entry)
- `WSEC_MENU_NAME_ID` = the value used for `CONV_VALUE` for the link text entry in `MSP_WEB_CONVERSIONS` (50107 according to the previous instructions)
- `WSEC_MENU_CUSTOM_NAME` = NULL
- `WSEC_MENU_PARENT_ID` = the ID of the top-level menu item this item should fall under (100 because this link should appear on the Home menu)
- `WSEC_MENU_SEQ` = the order of this item in the menu (6 so that this item appears at the end of the menu)
- `WSEC_MENU_DESC_ID` = the value used for `CONV_VALUE` for the ToolTip entry in `MSP_WEB_CONVERSIONS` (leave this NULL because the link doesn't need a ToolTip)
- `WSEC_MENU_CUSTOM_DESC` = NULL
- `WSEC_MENU_PAGE_ID` = the value of `WSEC_PAGE_ID` for the page entry in `MSP_WEB_SECURITY_PAGES` (this entry links to a new entry that will get an identity value, so this should be set after the page entry is made)
- `WSEC_MENU_IS_CUSTOM` = 0
- `WSEC_MENU_IS_TOPLEVEL` = 0
- `WSEC_MENU_LINKGROUP_NAME_ID` = NULL

Add an entry to `MSP_WEB_SECURITY_PAGES` with all fields set to the same values as the existing entry for the group management page. The existing entry has a `WSEC_PAGE_ID` of 913. The new entry gets an identity value for the `WSEC_PAGE_ID`, which will be 10001 if this is the first new page entry. Change the field `WSEC_PAGE_MENU_ID` to be the `WSEC_MENU_ID` of the entry you just made in `MSP_WEB_SECURITY_MENUS` (the value will be 10001 if the item was the first new entry). After the entry is made, update the `WSEC_MENU_PAGE_ID` of the entry in `MSP_WEB_SECURITY_MENUS` that you made in the previous step to be the `WSEC_PAGE_ID` of the entry you made in this step.

At this point, you should be able to log in to PWA as an administrator and see a new link in the Actions pane from the Home page. If you were already logged in, you will need to log out and back in before the change will be visible. This is because the menu structure is loaded at login and cached for quick access on future page requests.

28

In the previous example, you used an existing feature action (the `WSEC_PAGE_ACT_ID` field in `MSP_WEB_SECURITY_PAGES`) to secure the page. In the following section, you learn how to add a new feature action to put custom security on a new custom page.

Adding New Pages Using ASP

The PWA website is a collection of ASP pages written in JScript, so the most intuitive way to add a new page is to use the same technology and take advantage of the architecture used for the existing pages. If you are not familiar with ASP and JScript, or if you want to use another technology to take advantage of other features, that is possible, and a method for implementing it is explained in the next section. This section focuses on using the existing PWA structure and provides a sample page to be used as a starting point for your own custom pages.

With the exception of a few special pages (the login pages, for example) all the pages in PWA include the file SHELL.asp, which renders the common content for all the pages and provides functions for customizing certain areas of the page, such as the menus and title area. To be consistent with the rest of the pages, any custom page should also include this file. The simplest of custom pages then only needs to set the ID and title of the page for the shell object, tell the shell to write itself, and then render the main content of the page. The following code does this and is a starting point for all other examples in this section.

```
<!-- #include virtual="/ProjectServerSAMS/Library/CommonIncTop.asp" -->
<!-- #include virtual="/ProjectServerSAMS/Shell/Shell.asp" -->

<%
oShell.SetCurrentPage(10002);
oShell.SetTitleText("Hello World Page");
oShell.Write();
%>

<!-- Put your content here and it will appear in
    the normal PWA shell inside a td -->
<h1>Hello World!</h1>

<!-- #include virtual="/ProjectServer/Shell/Bottom.asp" -->
```

To add this page to PWA, follow these steps:

1. Make a new folder in IIS Virtual Root called CustomPages.

2. Copy the preceding code into a text file, name it HelloWorld.asp, and place it in the new folder.

3. Add an entry to the menu for the Home page by following the instructions from the previous section and use CustomPages/HelloWorld.asp as the `WSEC_PAGE_URL` and 101 as the `WSEC_PAGE_ACT_ID`. (This is the feature action ID for the Home page.)

Now that it is working, examine the code. The first two lines include files needed to access all the code common to other PWA files.

Line 5 tells the shell object the ID of the page (WSEC_PAGE_ID) that it is rendering. The ID must be set so that the shell can load the correct menus and verify that the user has permission to view the page. If the ID is not set, the page will still be displayed but without the menu items in the Actions pane.

Line 6 sets the title to be displayed on the page. When the title of the page is not set, the title displayed is the same as the text for the link to the page.

Line 7 has the shell object write its content to the output stream. This is where most of the hard work for rendering the page takes place, and you don't have to do any of it.

Following the script block is the HTML that is the main content of the page. This content appears inside a td tag in the final page.

The last line includes a file that writes the remainder of the page to the output stream. This marks the end of just about the simplest custom page you could ever come up with.

The HelloWorld.asp page sets the title for the page, but some pages need to render more customized content in the title area. An example of this is the Project Center page, which places a drop-down list of views in the right side of the title area. This is accomplished by defining a function called Page_WriteHeader, which writes the HTML for that area. Adding the following code to the sample page (anywhere before the include of bottom.asp) renders a custom title area:

```
function Page_WriteHeader()
{
%>
  <!-- Put any content you want in the header here.
      The following is a piece of what other pages use to write
      the views drop down lists. -->
  <TABLE ID="idSectionButtonBarTable" CLASS="SectionButtonBarTable"
    CELLSPACING="0" CELLPADDING="2" STYLE="width: 100%; height: 100%;
    <%=(oPersist.bTitleElements ? '' : 'display: none;')%>">
    <TR><TD COLSPAN="2" STYLE="font-size: 60%;"> </TD></TR>
    <TR>
      <TD ID="idShellPageTitle" VALIGN=BOTTOM CLASS="page_title"
        STYLE="visibility: <%=(oPersist.bTitle) ? "visible" : "hidden"%>;">
          <%= "My Custom Page" %>
      </TD>
      <TD VALIGN="BOTTOM" ALIGN="RIGHT">
        This is where the view drop down usually goes.
      </TD>
    </TR>
  </TABLE>
<%
}
```

Notice that when providing this function, you are now responsible for rendering the title of the page in addition to any other custom content.

Now add a submenu to the page. An example of a submenu can be found on most Admin pages. For example, when you click on Manage Users and Groups, the items Users and Groups are in a submenu in the Actions pane. Submenus are rendered from the ASP code for the page, not from the menu structure stored in the database. Submenu items can either be links to other pages or links that call JavaScript functions from their `onclick` event. The following code adds a submenu that contains one of each type of menu item:

```
function FNThatWritesASubMenu(nPageID)
{
  //Special sub menu items are links that could be used
  //either with a valid url, or an onclick event
  oShell.AddNewSpecialSubMenu("idAdminManageScope", "Sub Menu For Something");
  oShell.AddNewSpecialSubMenuItem("idAdminUsers",➥
                          "Sub Menu1",➥
                          "The tooltip for Sub Menu1",➥
                          "Admin/sec_users.asp",➥
                          true, //true for selected, false for unselected➥
                          "SubmenuAction1_OnClick()",➥
                          "MenuStyle");
                          //The last parameter should be either
                          //"subTitle" or "subItem" for different affects
  oShell.AddNewSpecialSubMenuItem("idAdminGroups",➥
                          "Sub Menu2",➥
                          "The tooltip for Sub Menu2",➥
                          "Admin/sec_groups.asp",➥
                          false);
}
```

Now add a standalone menu. An example of a standalone menu is on the Project Center page, where the items Track Project Risks and Track Project Issues are in a standalone menu. Like submenus, standalone menus are rendered from the ASP code for the page, not from the menu structure in the database. Standalone menu items are links that call JavaScript functions from their `onclick` event. They cannot be links directly to other pages, but JavaScript could be used to redirect the browser. The code to add a standalone menu is as follows:

```
function FNThatWritesAStandaloneMenu() {
  //Standalone menu items are links with onclick events that call a function
  oShell.bWriteStandaloneDivider = true;

  oShell.sStandaloneSubhead = "Some actions related to My Page";
```

```
oShell.AddNewStandaloneMenu("idStandaloneAction1",➥
                            "Standalone Action",➥
                            "The tooltip for the standalone action.",➥
                            "StandAloneAction1_OnClick();");
}
```

To this point, the custom pages have contained only static content. Now you add code to render content gathered from a database query using helper functions provided by the PWA framework. The following code should replace the code that writes Hello World:

```
<%
oPJQuery.Connect();
var rsFields = oPJQuery.OpenRecordset(const_PjQuery_GetAllCategories);

for (i = 0; i < rsFields.RecordCount; i++)
{
  %>
  <tr>
    <td><%= rsFields.GetColumn(const_dbWSEC_CAT_NAME) %></td>
  </tr>
  <%
  rsFields.MoveNext();
}

rsFields.Close();
%>
```

Now that the page contains some sensitive information, you can change the permissions on it to use a user-defined feature action and make it so that only executives can see the link in the Actions pane for the home section. Feature actions are defined in MSP_WEB_SECURITY_FEATURES_ACTIONS, which links to MSP_WEB_CONVERSIONS entries with STRING_TYPE_ID of 9 for a localized name. Three feature actions are contained in the database out of the box that are intended to be used for defining custom permissions. Their names are User defined 1 through User defined 3, and they have IDs 150–152. For the purposes of this example, you can change the name of one of these feature actions and set the WSEC_PAGE_ACT_ID for your custom page to the ID of that feature action. After you've created a lot of custom pages and run out of predefined feature actions, you can follow the template of these user-defined feature actions to add your own new ones.

> **NOTE**
>
> When you create a new feature action, you must remember to add a reference to it to the MSP_WEB_SECURITY_ORG_PERMISSIONS table, or no users will ever really have access to that feature and your links will not appear.

Adding New Pages Using Another Language

If you want to add custom pages to PWA without using ASP, you will not be able to include SHELL.asp or any of the other files PWA provides you, so you will need another way to render the shell for the page. PWA lets you add links to external pages through the Admin interface, but out of the box this interface only supports absolute URLs, and it is often desirable to use a relative URL instead. This can be accomplished by making a small modification to SHELL/CUSTPAGE.asp as follows:

```
<!-- #include virtual="/ProjectServer/Library/CommonIncTop.asp" -->
<!-- #include virtual="/ProjectServer/Library/DataSpace.js" -->
<!-- #include virtual="/ProjectServer/Shell/Shell.asp" -->

<%
var sCustPageURL = "";
var nPageID = Number(Request.QueryString("PageID").Item);
if (!isNaN(nPageID)) {
  oShell.SetCurrentPage(nPageID);

  oPJQuery.Connect();
  var rsPage = oPJQuery.OpenRecordset(➥
    const_PjQuery_CustPageURLForPageID, nPageID);
  if(rsPage.RecordCount > 0)
  {
    sCustPageURL = rsPage.GetColumn(const_dbWSEC_PAGE_CUSTOM_URL);
    if (sCustPageURL == null) sCustPageURL = "";
  }
  rsPage.Close();
  oPJQuery.Disconnect();
}

if (sCustPageURL != "")
  sCustPageURL += (sCustPageURL.indexOf('?') == -1)➥
    ? "?InnerPage=1" : "&InnerPage=1";

//Added for customization
if (sCustPageURL != "")
{
  //If :// and :\\ are not present in the URL, prepend the application path
  if ( sCustPageURL.indexOf('://', 0) == -1 &&➥
    sCustPageURL.indexOf(':\\', 0) == -1)
    sCustPageURL = sAppPath + sCustPageURL;
}
//End of addition

oShell.Write();
%>
```

```
<A ID="idLinkHelper2" STYLE="display:none;"></A>

<DIV ID="idIframe">

  <IFRAME ID="idCustPageFrame" FRAMEBORDER="0" NAME="idCustPageFrame"
    SCROLLING="YES" STYLE="display: block; width: 100%; height: 100%;">
  </IFRAME>

</DIV>


<SPAN ID="D5D851A526ED41BFBB2D78C3625F3925" STYLE="display: none;"></SPAN>

<SCRIPT LANGUAGE="JScript">


function Ultimate_OnLoad()
{
  InitIFrameSrcAttributes();
}


function InitIFrameSrcAttributes()
{

  var e = new Error();
  var bParentWindowHasSentryGUID = false;

  try
  {
    bParentWindowHasSentryGUID =➡
      (typeof(window.parent.D5D851A526ED41BFBB2D78C3625F3925) != "undefined");
  }
  catch (e)
  {

  }


  if (window.self == window.top || !bParentWindowHasSentryGUID)
  {
    var link = unescape("<%=escape(sCustPageURL)%>");
    if (link == "")
    {
```

28

```
      return;
    }

    idLinkHelper2.href = link;
    var sProt = sProtocol + "://";
    if (idLinkHelper2.protocol != "")
    {
      sProt = "";
    }

    document.frames["idCustPageFrame"].window.location.href = sProt + link;
  }
}


</SCRIPT>


<!-- #include virtual="/ProjectServer/Shell/Bottom.asp" -->
```

With this page in place, PWA still supports adding external links, but it also allows you to specify root relative links to your custom pages so that the PWA cookies are available for your pages to use. Having the cookies available is important so that you can obtain a session and access any needed session variables, such as the ID of the current user.

When using a technology other than ASP, it probably is not possible to get direct access to ASP session state even after obtaining the session ID from the PWA cookie. One way to access session variables from another technology is to write a simple ASP page that receives the session ID as a query parameter and returns the desired variable as its output. The following is a page used to determine the current user's ID:

```
<%@ Language=JScript EnableSessionState=FALSE CODEPAGE=65001%>
<%
/*
This file takes PjSessionId in the query string and
writes the userID contained in the session it finds as a
response.  It is intended to be used by pages that are
added to PWA and need to know the logged in user's WRES_ID.
*/

var done = false;

function ReturnResult( result )
{
  Response.Write(result);
}

var session = null;
```

```
try
{
  session = GetObject( "pcs://SessionMgr?" +➡
    Request.QueryString("PjSessionID") );
}
catch(e)
{
  ReturnResult("No session found");
  done = true;
}

var userID;

if( !done )
{
  userID = session["userId"];
  if (typeof(userID) == "undefined" || userID.length == 0)
  {
    ReturnResult("No userID in session");
    done = true;
  }
}

if( !done )
{
  ReturnResult(userID);
}
%>
```

To use this page, browse to it from within your code. The following is some VB.NET code that does this:

```
Dim userIDUrl As String
userIDUrl = FullAppPath & "userID.asp"

Dim strUserID As String
Try
  If Request.Cookies("PjSessionId") Is Nothing Then
    Throw New Exception("No session cookie found." & _
      " You must be logged in to PWA to view this page.")
  Else
    Dim userIDRequest As HttpWebRequest = HttpWebRequest.Create( _
      userIDUrl & "?PjSessionId=" & Request.Cookies("PjSessionId").Value)
    Dim userIDResponse As HttpWebResponse = userIDRequest.GetResponse()
    Dim reader As New StreamReader(userIDResponse.GetResponseStream())
    strUserID = reader.ReadToEnd()
```

```
    Return Convert.ToInt32(strUserID)
  End If
Catch formatEx As FormatException
  ReportError("Response from " & userIDUrl & ":<BR>" & strUserID)
Catch webEx As WebException
  ReportError("Error while trying to acces " & userIDUrl, webEx)
Catch ex As Exception
  ReportError("Error while trying to determine userID.", ex)
End Try
```

When using the preceding code, you will receive a 401 unauthorized error unless userID.asp is allowed anonymous access from within IIS.

Although this method allows you to write custom pages for PWA in the language of your choice, it does have some significant drawbacks. It does not allow you to customize the title area for the page. It does not allow you to add submenus or standalone menus to the Actions pane. It does not allow you to set custom permissions for the page, so access to the page must be secured by your own custom code. Some of these drawbacks can be overcome by writing an ASP page that customizes the PWA shell and contains an IFRAME to hold the content of your custom page written in your language of choice.

How to Customize One Instance and Not Others

Multiple instances of Project Server can be hosted from a single server by creating new instances using the Edit Site utility. These multiple instances use different databases and have different Virtual Roots in IIS, but they all use the same set of web files. This can cause a problem when you want to customize the pages of one instance of PWA and leave the other unchanged.

To customize a single instance, you need to make a copy of the IIS Virtual Root folder (located at C:\Program Files\Microsoft Office Project Server 2003 by default) and point the Virtual Root in IIS to use this new root folder. In addition to this, you need to register the copied file PJDBCOMM.DLL with IIS as a Web Service Extension. Without registering this file, Project Professional will not recognize that instance as valid. To register the file, perform the following steps:

1. In IIS Manager, expand the Web Service Extensions node.

2. Double-click the Microsoft Office Project Server 2003 ISAPI entry in the right pane.

3. On the Required Files tab, click the Add button.

4. Browse to the file PJDBCOMM.DLL, located in the ISAPI folder of the new IIS Virtual Root folder and click OK.

It is important to note that included files in all the PWA pages are referred to with root relative URLs. This means that the pages in your custom virtual root will refer to files in the standard virtual root unless you change all the include lines in every file. In most cases it isn't necessary to change all those lines, but keep in mind that if you customize an included file, you need to change every file that refers to that file, or your changes will not be used.

Using VBA Macros

Microsoft Project 2003 gives you the ability to automate tedious, repetitive, or complex tasks through the use of macros. A *macro* is essentially a series of commands or instructions that you can save and run whenever you need to by pressing a key combination or by clicking an icon.

Each instruction or command within a macro is executed via a programming language called Visual Basic for Applications (VBA). Although this language is basically a watered-down version of Visual Basic, there is almost no limit to the types of tasks that can be performed within Microsoft Project and even beyond.

In fact, VBA is so powerful that it could almost be used to create standalone applications, aside from executing from within Project. You have the ability to reference binaries written in other languages, as long as it has objects exposed over the Component Object Model (COM).

All macros are stored as snippets of text called *modules*. These modules can reside in the Global template for use across all projects, or in individual project files. They can also be imported from and exported to Visual Basic style files.

Recording Macros

Of course you don't need to be a Visual Basic programmer to make simple macros. Project has the ability to translate all your keystrokes and mouse clicks into corresponding VBA code simply by using the macro recorder and performing the desired task manually.

Preparing to Record

Before recording your macro, it is best to have a plan of all the actions you need to perform. Because Project records all your keystrokes and clicks, any mistakes you make are recorded as well.

You also want to determine beforehand whether you want the macro available from a specific file and not globally. If this is the case, open the desired file before recording.

From the menu within Project, choose Tools, Macro, and then Record New Macro. The Record Macro dialog box appears, as shown in Figure 28.26.

> **TIP**
>
> The Visual Basic toolbar provides all the recording flow buttons (Record, Pause, and Stop). This is easier than going through the Options menu each time to control the recording process.

28

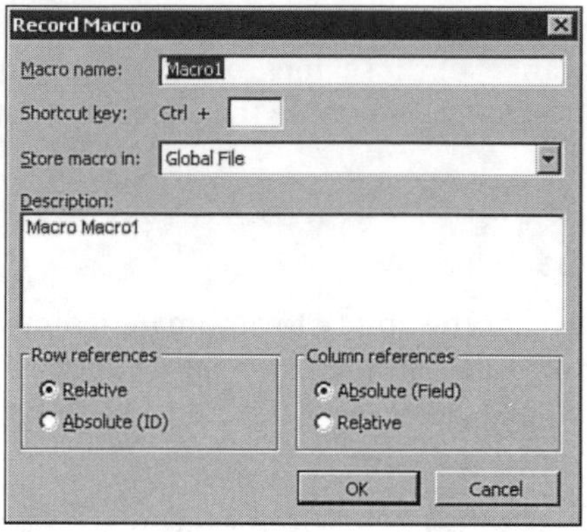

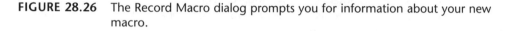

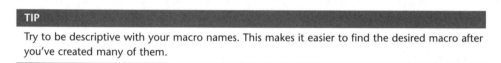

FIGURE 28.26   The Record Macro dialog prompts you for information about your new macro.

Give your new macro a name. Keep in mind that the name cannot contain any spaces or special characters. Also give your macro a brief description.

> **TIP**
>
> Try to be descriptive with your macro names. This makes it easier to find the desired macro after you've created many of them.

If you want, specify a shortcut key combination that can be used to quickly execute your macro (such as Ctrl+R).

Specify where you want the macro code to be stored, either in the global file or in the current project file. Keep in mind that if you specify the current project, the macro can be executed only when that project file is open.

The reference boxes specify how the macro recorder interprets selection changes on the view sheets. The Absolute options interpret any cell selection literally (such as A5), whereas the Relative options interpret selection changes in relation to the currently selected cell.

Record the Macro
After you click OK on the Record Macro dialog box, Project then translates any actions you perform into its VBA equivalent. If you need to pause the recording for any reason, you can do so either through the macro menu or on the Visual Basic toolbar if you added it. When you are finished, make sure that you stop the recording.

Testing the Macro
It's always good practice to test your macro immediately after recording to see whether any changes need to be made. Open the Macro dialog by clicking the Macro menu in Tools, Macro (or by clicking the Play button on the Visual Basic toolbar).

With your macro selected, click the Run button and watch as Project performs all tasks that you did in the recording process. Verify that the end result of running your macro is what you expect.

Assigning the Macro to a Toolbar Button

For macros that you execute frequently, specifying a shortcut key can sometimes be difficult to remember, especially when you frequently use many different macros. A good alternative is to assign your macro to a button on a toolbar.

To do so, open the Customize dialog box by selecting Tools, Customize, and select Toolbars (you can also right-click any toolbar and select Customize from there). Select the Commands tab, and find the All Macros option in the Categories list, as shown in Figure 28.27.

FIGURE 28.27   Macros can be dragged from the Customize dialog box to toolbars to create macro buttons.

Drag the desired macro to a convenient spot on the toolbar on which you want the button to reside. After the button is placed, you can click the Modify Selection button to bring up various options used to modify your new button. Some of the more useful options are

- **Name**—The text (if any) you want to display on the button.

- **Paste Button Image**—You can paste an image from the Clipboard onto the face of the button. The image must be properly presized.

- **Reset Button Image**—Select this if you've changed the button image and want to reset it to the default image.

- **Edit Button Image**—Brings up an image editing window on which you can draw a custom image for your button.

- **Change Button Image**—Select a button image from existing Office icons.

> **TIP**
>
> If you frequently use many macros, it may be convenient to create a whole new toolbar for your macro buttons. This can be done in the Customize dialog box on the Toolbars tab.

Using the same technique, you can also add your macros to the menu bar. Just drag the macro from the Customize window to the desired location on the menu bar. The menu automatically pops up as your mouse moves over it.

Any changes to toolbars, buttons, and menus are saved when that instance of Project is properly closed.

> **CAUTION**
>
> When creating a button or menu item from a macro, try to reference only those that reside in the Global template files. If a macro in a specific file is referenced, that file must be open for it to work.

Viewing and Editing VBA Code

When Project records a macro, it actually stores VBA code in a subroutine. You can view and edit this code. In fact, you are not limited to just creating macros; you can also create complex functions, classes, and even Windows forms.

The Office suite provides the convenient and powerful Visual Basic Editor, which can be opened from Project. This editor provides an easy way to write and debug code, transfer objects among open files, and even design Windows forms for your code to interact with the user. Open the editor through Project's menu Tools, Macro, Visual Basic Editor (or by pressing Alt+F11).

A specific macro can be opened by clicking the Edit button with the desired macro selected in the Macros dialog box. Open this dialog box by selecting Tools, Macros, and then Macros.

The Project Explorer and Basic Objects

By default, the Project Explorer is located on the upper-left quadrant of the editor and contains all open VBA files and objects. Each object usually resides in a Project file and is one of four types:

- **Module**—A text file containing global procedures and/or constants.
- **Class**—A class represents a programmable object with methods, properties, and variables.
- **Microsoft Project Object**—Special class representing the actual Project files themselves.
- **Form**—Special class representing a Windows form. You can use this to create a user interface that can be used for anything from prompting the user for information to simply displaying an image.

You can view any object in the Explorer simply by double-clicking it. Right-clicking an object brings up a menu with more options, as shown in Figure 28.28.

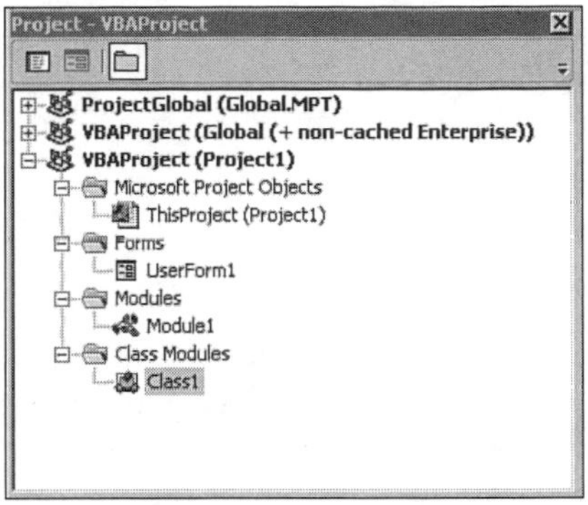

FIGURE 28.28   The Project Explorer behaves similarly to Windows Explorer.

The Explorer functions much like the left pane of the Windows Explorer. This makes dragging objects between different files easy and intuitive.

The Properties Window

Below the Project Explorer (by default) lives the Properties window. This window displays the properties of any selected object, whether it is an object in the Explorer window or a button on a user form.

Aside from clicking an object, its settings can also be displayed by selecting it in the top drop-down list of the Properties window, as shown in Figure 28.29.

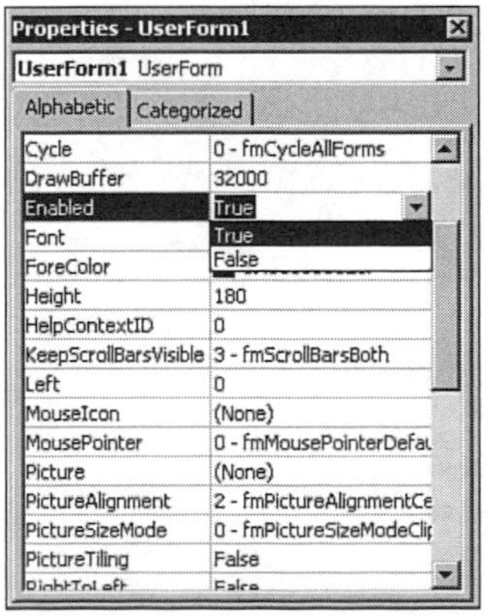

FIGURE 28.29   Some properties can be easily changed with a drop-down style list.

Each type of object has its own corresponding properties list, which can contain anything from the object's name to an image for it to display. Generally the property fields will be a text field or a drop-down list.

The actual list itself has two sorting modes, Alphabetical and Categorized. The Categorized mode groups similar properties together for convenience. Both modes display the same list, so it's a matter of preference which one you use.

TIP*

If ever in doubt of what a property is used for, simply select it and press F1 to bring up the Office help pane.

The Code Frame

The code frame contains all windows of code modules for any object that you have open, as well as the form designer for User Forms. This is where all your actual code and form editing takes place. Notice in Figure 28.30 the two drop-down boxes on the top of the Code windows. The drop-down on the left allows you to navigate through any objects located on the open module, like a form. The one on the right navigates through existing and potential subroutines and functions for the object selected on the right.

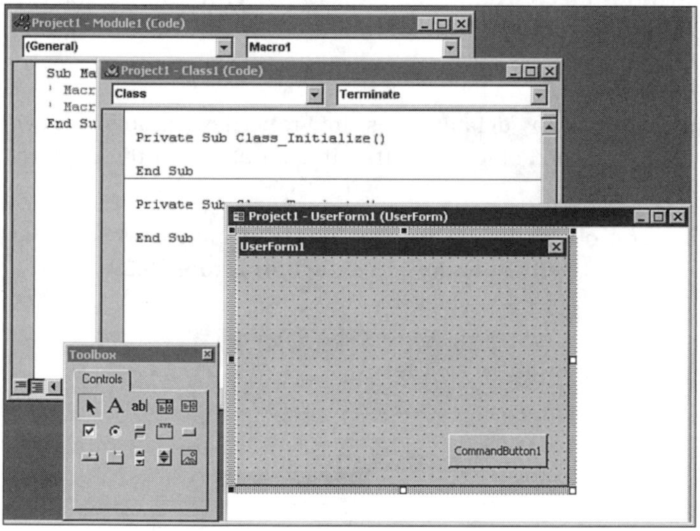

FIGURE 28.30   The Code window allows you to navigate through code, as well as drag controls to a user form.

Designing User Forms

Some VBA programs may require the user to input information, or may need to display pop-ups to the user. The Visual Basic Editor provides an intuitive Windows form editor to design Windows forms.

When you open a form by double-clicking it in the Project Explorer, it is displayed in the Form Designer. You can drag various controls from the controls toolbox (see Figure 28.30) onto your form to build a user interface. After a control is on the form, you can resize it and change its properties in the Properties window to get the desired look and feel.

You can change the properties of the child controls placed on a form by just selecting them and using the Object Properties window to change things such as caption and visibility.

After the control is placed on the form, you can set and view the code behind the control by double-clicking it. You'll notice when you do that the left drop-down box of the code window shows the name of the control, and the right one shows the subroutine you are in. This subroutine represents various events, such as when a button is clicked. The function is called by VB whenever the event is fired (if a subroutine is specified).

To display the user form from code, use the Show method as follows:

```
UserForm1.Show()
```

> **NOTE**
>
> When the Show method of a user form is called, program execution for that containing code segment is halted until the user form exits or is closed by the user.

Using this powerful editor, you can create what seems like an entire professional application within a Project file, or any Office document for that matter.

Debugging VBA Code

With any type of development, a great deal of time is spent debugging the code. The Visual Basic Editor provides a powerful and easy-to-use debugger.

Stepping Through Code

Stepping through the code line by line can strengthen your confidence that the code you've written functions as expected. While doing so, you are given a variety of tools to assess your code, and even the ability to change it without halting execution.

The following list provides the key combinations you can use to step through your code:

- **F9: Set Breakpoint**—This key can be pressed at design time or runtime. It tells the debugger to stop execution when the current line is encountered, as shown in Figure 28.31. Breakpoints can also be set by clicking on the bar to the left of the code.

- **Shift+F8: Step Into**—This command executes the current line and then stops at the next.

- **Ctrl+Shift+F8: Step Out**—This command executes the remaining code of the current procedure and halts at the line of code after the one in which the procedure was called.

28

- **Ctrl+F9: Set Next Statement**—This command tells the debugger to move to any line of code. This is useful if you need to rerun a previous line of code. You can also drag the yellow debug cursor to any line of code.

- **Shift+F9: Quick Watch**—This displays a convenient window showing the value of the currently selected variable.

FIGURE 28.31   Breakpoints halt execution at the specified line of code.

These keys give you the power to alter any code execution flow to help you assess your code's validity. These functions are also provided in the Debug menu, if you happen to forget which key combination you need.

The Immediate Window

The Immediate window is usually displayed as a long bar along the bottom of the Visual Basic Editor, which acts as a text entry box. If this is not displayed, you can enable it in the Views menu or by pressing Ctrl+G.

This window provides an easy way to find a value of a variable or the return value of a function. Just type a **?** followed by the variable or function you want to test.

TIP

Always test a function that simply returns a value in the Immediate window to verify that the function returns the expected result.

The Project Object Model

The core structure of Project is based on a hierarchy of objects, all representing different aspects of the Project application. The Project application itself is represented by an object, which contains things such as toolbars and projects. The Project object subsequently contains objects such as tasks and resources.

Each object contains various properties that can be altered, such as names of the object (like a task) or some type of state the object may be in. Objects also contain various methods or actions that can be invoked, such as Save() or Close().

The best way to browse an object's properties and methods is by typing the period character after an object's name. A list displays showing all properties and methods. This list is known as *intelli-sense* and is common in most programming environments. When more information about any object is desired, just search the online help by pressing the F1 key.

> **TIP**
>
> Pressing Ctrl+Space brings up the intelli-sense list, which can help you browse for an object you may not know the entire name of.

Auto-Methods

Included with the Project object model are various methods executed throughout various stages of normal editing of a document. These methods can be programmed by adding a subroutine labeled Auto*XXX*, where *XXX* is the name of the event to program (press Ctrl+Space to see a list of these). Add the code desired to accompany these events.

Security and Certificates

The closer you look at VBA's capabilities, the more it looks like a standalone development environment. However, the rich power and flexibility it provides is not offered free of risk. It also provides yet another avenue for malicious code to propagate itself and spread havoc across the Internet and intranet. The capability of Office applications to execute subroutines along with built-in events and triggers automatically makes matters worse.

Luckily this is easily preventable by properly setting macro security settings within Project and all Office applications. This can be done in the Macro menu under Security, as shown in Figure 28.32. Four different security levels are available:

- **Very High**—Only macros installed in trusted locations and digitally signed are allowed to run.

- **High**—Unsigned macros are disabled. The user is prompted if signed by a source not in the trusted list or with an invalid/corrupt certificate.

- **Medium**—All macros signed by a trusted source are allowed; the user is prompted to enable any others.

- **Low**—All macros are allowed.

The restrictive nature of these security settings can be a nuisance to VBA developers because their code may not be allowed to run on a client's computer. A common method to overcome this is to send out instructions on how to set macro security settings to low, with a recommendation to return them at the end.

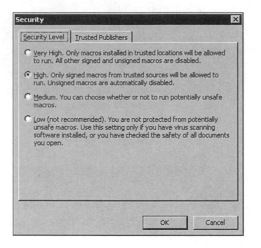

FIGURE 28.32   Restrict the code allowed to run by setting macro security.

This undermines the goal of macro security because it takes only one run of a virus to be detrimental. A safer way is to sign your code with a digital certificate.

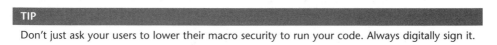

TIP

Don't just ask your users to lower their macro security to run your code. Always digitally sign it.

Digital Certificates

Think of a digital certificate as an electronic ID or passport carried along with a file or document. When opening or executing a file, this passport can be verified to ensure that the code's author is trusted, who signed the document when it was originally created.

The certificate's authenticity is ensured using a cryptographic method called *asymmetric encryption*. Asymmetric encryption uses two keys in the encryption and decryption process. A private key is used to encrypt data, and a public key is used to decrypt it.

If the information contained within a certificate is not decrypted properly (using the public key), the certificate is considered invalid. Due to the nature of the algorithm to generate the two keys, it is currently computationally impossible to generate a private key from a public key.

The certificate also contains hash codes created from the document it signs and the certificate itself. If these differ from on-the-fly generated hash codes, it suggests that the document or certificate was tampered with and is invalid.

Just about anyone can create a digital certificate. However, some digital certificates can be obtained from a certificate authority. An author must go through an application process that the certificate authorities use to verify an author's identity.

TIP

As a developer, getting a certificate issued by an established certificate authority is probably the most efficient method of signing your code. It gives your customers an easier way to verify the authenticity of your code in addition to boosting the professional feel of your company.

Creating a Certificate

You can create a new digital certificate yourself to sign code that you have created or for distribution throughout your organization. The Office suite contains a program to easily create a certificate named SelfCert.exe and located in the root office folder, as shown in Figure 28.33.

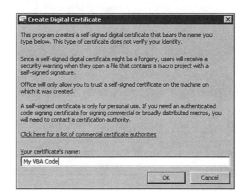

FIGURE 28.33   Certificates can be created using the SelfCert program.

This program is not installed on a typical installation, so you need to add it through Add/Remove programs. Look for the Office Tool named Digital Signature for VBA Projects to Run from My Computer.

After you click OK in the SelfCert window, a certificate is automatically created with that name and saved into the computer's certificate store.

NOTE

Notice in Figure 28.33 that a link is provided to a list of established certificate authorities. Follow this link if you are interested in applying for a certificate.

Exporting and Transferring Certificates

After a certificate is created (or installed from another location), it can be imported and exported through Internet Explorer. Simply go to IE's Properties page, click on the Content tab, and then click the Certificates button.

Clicking the Import and Export buttons brings up corresponding wizards that guide you through the process. Certificates are exported as a file that can subsequently be emailed or transferred like any other file.

Signing a VBA Macro

When certificates have been properly created or installed, it is easy to sign your VBA projects. From within the Visual Basic Editor, select the file that you want to digitally sign.

From the menu, select Tools, Digital Signature. A dialog box appears showing what certificate, if any, has signed the current document. Click the Choose button to display a list of certificates installed on the current computer, as shown in Figure 28.34.

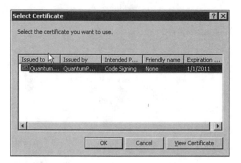

FIGURE 28.34   Select a certificate installed on your computer to digitally sign VBA code.

Click OK, and the current VBA project is signed. If the code is changed after it has been signed (on a computer other than the one used for the original development), the signature is automatically removed.

Adding a Trusted Certificate

An alternative to requiring users to lower their macro security settings is signing your VBA code and providing users instructions on trusting your certificate. With a security level set to high, they will still receive a security warning telling them the code and certificate are untrusted, as shown in Figure 28.35.

From this security warning, guide your users to click the Details button to view the signature. The Digital Signature Details screen contains a View Certificate button. Clicking this button brings up the Certificate dialog. From here, users can install the certificate as trusted by clicking the Install Certificate button.

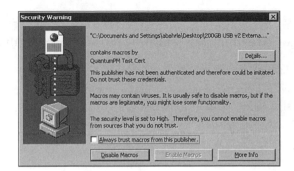

FIGURE 28.35   A security warning is displayed when a macro is signed with an untrusted certificate.

After the certificate is installed, the user must then reopen the file, and the user can check the Always Trust Macros from This Publisher box. Then when users click Enable Macros, the security warning does not display.

Even though it is possible to use SelfCert to sign VBA code, this is not entirely risk-free. If malicious developers get a copy of any document signed by this certificate, they will be able to sign their code, which will consequently be allowed to run automatically on your computer. It is strongly recommended to sign VBA code with a certificate issued from an established certificate authority.

The Tip of the Iceberg

This section has provided some of the basics when it comes to VBA macros but has just barely scratched the surface. If you are interested in pursuing further knowledge, you have the ability to record and view functions in Project (or other Office applications). Combine that with VBA help and the ultimate resource of the Internet, and you have all you need to become a verbose VBA developer.

Best Practices

- Take into consideration your current business processes when customizing WSS project sites.

- Use top-level sites for creating sites not related to a specific project. Use this site for team collaboration outside regular project work or for ongoing communication.

- Modify predefined WSS lists to provide meaningful fields for your project.

- Use WSS to improve project team collaboration, information management, and communication methods.

- Create a new IIS Virtual Root folder for your PWA instance and modify the copied pages in that folder, not the standard pages in the original folder.

- Remember to add entries for your custom feature actions to the `MSP_WEB_ SECURITY_ORG_PERMISSIONS` table so that users will have access.

28

- Avoid assigning macros not saved in the Global template to toolbar buttons.

- Take advantage of the Immediate window; test your functions there first if possible.

- Don't lower you macro security below high.

- Don't require your users to lower their macro security to run your code; always digitally sign it instead and require them to trust your certificate.

CHAPTER 29

Extending Enterprise Project Management Through Customization Overview

IN THIS CHAPTER

- Secure Access to Project Server Data Through the Project Data Service
- Extending the Cube
- SharePoint Portal Integration
- Best Practices

The Microsoft EPM solution is built as an extensible solution and, for the most part, the options are well documented. This chapter reviews a few of the different customization options, including the PDS API, SharePoint Portal integration, extending the cube, and a few third-party add-ons.

Secure Access to Project Server Data Through the Project Data Service

The Project Data Service (PDS) application programming interface (API) is another customization tool available to you. The PDS API is a component of a standard Project Server installation. You can create a client application that uses Simple Object Access Protocol (SOAP) to retrieve and set Project Server data without the need to directly access the Project Server database from your application.

> **TIP**
>
> SOAP is an XML-based protocol used to send messages between programs. This service is usually exposed over HTTP, but it generally can reside on top of any Internet protocol.

> **CAUTION**
>
> Updating the Project Server database directly could produce unwanted results. Various portfolio data is stored in different tables to allow efficient retrieval of the data for different clients such as Project Web Access (PWA) and Project Professional. Thorough testing should be conducted when updating the Project Server database directly in your customization application.

PDS methods allow you to programmatically log on to Project Server using the Project Server security model. You can then use PDS methods to access Project Server data using data access security consistent with Project Professional and PWA. Although the PDS API does not provide methods for all Project Server functionality, it does provide a way to perform many common tasks. In the compiled help module Project Data Service Reference for Microsoft Office Project Server 2003, available from the Project Server software development kit (SDK), the methods are broken down into the following categories:

- Project methods
- Enterprise project creation methods
- Resource methods
- Enterprise custom field methods
- Timesheet methods
- Version methods
- Administrative methods
- Project Server user maintenance methods
- Miscellaneous methods

Because not all methods are discussed in this book, consult the *Project Data Service Reference for Microsoft Office Project Server 2003* for details on all methods available in the PDS.

> **TIP**
>
> Accessing the Project Server database directly does not inherently provide you the same security model as Project Server. A combination of PDS and direct database access may be appropriate when data not accessible from the PDS is needed. In this case you could use the PDS to log on to Project Server, get necessary security access and details, and then directly make SQL requests from the database.

When to Use the PDS

The PDS can be useful in many situations. Although not a comprehensive list of uses for the PDS, the following is a starting point for customizations where the PDS would be practical:

- **Reporting**—You could use the PDS to extract the desired enterprise data and report the information in a custom reporting application. The `ProjectCodeValues` method of the PDS could be used multiple times to retrieve enterprise project fields and create a cross-project report on those fields.

  ▶ **SEE** Enterprise Global Codes," **PAGE 163**.

  ▶ **SEE** "Building Custom Enterprise Configuration," **PAGE 537**.

- **Enterprise resource management**—The PDS provides methods to add, delete, update, and attain details for enterprise resources. If you have a list of resources stored external to Project Server, the `ResourcesAdd` method could be used to add them to the Enterprise Resource pool. You would first programmatically extract the resource information from its current location, and then you would call `ResourcesAdd` to subsequently add the resource to Project Server.

- **Enterprise project fields management**—The PDS enables you to insert, update, and remove enterprise fields for a given project. The `ProjectCodeValuesUpdate` method is useful for updating enterprise field values. You could develop a custom application to allow the viewing and updating of enterprise fields for multiple projects by combining the functionality of the `ProjectCodeValues` and the `ProjectCodeValuesUpdate` methods.

> **NOTE**
>
> Not all enterprise fields are available with the `ProjectCodeValues` and `ProjectCodeValues Update` methods, as you might expect. Enterprise fields with graphical indicators are not updated, nor are the work, flag, and duration enterprise fields.

- **Enterprise global fields management**—The global template for the enterprise fields can be altered using the `EnterpriseCustomFieldsUpdate` method and the `OutlineCodeUpdateValues` method. The PDS would then allow you to build a custom application for managing the enterprise global template. This could be useful if one or more of your enterprise fields depends on an outside source for its available values.

- **Timesheet management**—The PDS allows you to get and save timesheet information for a given user, as well as send updates to the project manager. The `AssignmentsGet`, `AssignmentsSave`, and `AssignmentsProjectManagerUpdate` methods could be used to make a custom timesheet management application, when your current business practices require recording time against assignments in an application other than PWA.

How to Use the PDS

This section describes how to use the PDS, now that you know what the PDS is, and examples of when to use it. Because the PDS is a secure mechanism for retrieving data from Project Server, before you can use any of its methods you must programmatically log on to Project Server. After you are logged on to Project Server, the methods of the PDS API are available to you. To use the PDS follow these steps:

1. Log on to Project Server and collect the security cookie.

2. Form the PDS request with Extensible Markup Language (XML).

3. Send the request to the PDS and accept the XML-formatted response.

4. Check for errors in the response.

5. Use the data from the response.

6. Repeat Steps 3 to 5 as necessary.

The simplest PDS method is the PDSInfo method. This method allows you to make sure that you are using the PDS correctly and return information about the PDS. The following example shows you how to use the PDS to call the PDSInfo method, using the preceding six steps.

> **NOTE**
>
> The PDS example is written in C#. Any language that allows you to use SOAP can be used to interact with the PDS API. See the documentation for the language of your choice to use the PDS in that language.

Log On to Project Server and Collect the Security Cookie

The Project Server security model allows you to log on in two different ways: by Windows integrated authentication and Project Server authentication. When using Windows integrated authentication, the security credentials of the user are not required when logging on to Project Server. The following declaration and assignment are used for Windows authentication:

```
string sUrl;
sUrl = "http://yourserver/projectserver/LgnIntAu.asp";
```

With Project Server authentication, the preceding line of code would be replaced with the following:

```
sUrl = "http://yourserver/projectserver/LgnPSAu.asp";
sUrl += "?un=Administrator&pwd=";
```

> **TIP**
>
> Because the password when using Project Server authentication is sent as part of a URL string, you should check for reserved characters and replace them with their number representation. For example the # character would be replaced with %23 to allow the URL to properly send the string as a parameter.

After you form the proper URL, you then make the request:

```
HttpWebRequest myReq = (HttpWebRequest)WebRequest.Create(realURL);
CookieContainer conCookie = new CookieContainer();

myReq.CookieContainer = conCookie;
myReq.Credentials = CredentialCache.DefaultCredentials;

HttpWebResponse myRes = (HttpWebResponse)myReq.GetResponse();
XmlDocument XMLDoc = new XmlDocument();
XMLDoc.Load(myRes.GetResponseStream());

myRes.Close();

string sCookie;
```

The XMLDoc now holds the response from Project Server that looks similar to the following:

```
<?xml version="1.0"?>
   <Reply>
      <HRESULT>0</HRESULT>
      <Cookie>
      <![CDATA[svc={D8D06337-9C12-466D-84BF-57767FEDF8AD}
      &session={CCB39B94-A3D8-4C0B-AFA1-49604AF6C3D9}
      &prxy={EFBA0018-337F-4A35-9454-E7E1155F92A4}
      &org=projectserver]]>
   </Cookie>
</Reply>
```

Next, you parse the XMLDoc and put the cookie information into the sCookie string for use when making SOAP requests to the PDS.

Form the PDS Request
A PDS request is an XML string with the following form:

```
<Request>
   <MethodName>
       <Parameter1>value</Parameter1>
       <Parameter2>value</Parameter2>
       ...
       <ParameterN>value</ParameterN>
   </MethodName>
</Request>
```

29

In the example, the PDSInfo method does not have any parameters, so the request XML string is created like this:

```
String sRequest;
sRequest = "<Request>" +
               "<PDSInfo/>" +
           "</Request>";
```

With other methods of the PDS a more complex method of forming the request string may be required.

Send the Request to the PDS and Accept the Response

After the request string has been formed, you make the request to the PDS in the following manner:

```
localhost.PDS wsPDS = new localhost.PDS();

wsPDS.Url = "http://yourserver/projectserver/PDS.wsdl";

wsPDS.Credentials = CredentialCache.DefaultCredentials;
XmlDocument XmlDoc = new XmlDocument();
XmlDoc.LoadXml(sRequest);

string sResponse;
sResponse = wsPDS.SoapXMLRequest(sCookie, XmlDoc.InnerXml);
```

Notice the use of the security cookie in the SoapXMLRequest. Each time the SOAP request is made, the security cookie is used. If this security cookie is not present, the request fails.

Check for Errors in the Response

The response returned with a PDS method request is also formatted in XML. The template for the response takes this form:

```
<Reply>
    <HRESULT>0</HRESULT>
    <STATUS>0</STATUS>
    <UserName>Administrator</UserName>
    <MethodName>
        method-specific output
    </MethodName>
</Reply>
```

The HRESULT and STATUS values each have the value 0 when the method is called properly and no errors occur. The UserName value contains the name of the user who made the request.

At this point you would again parse the XML and check for the HRESULT and the STATUS values. The possible values and explanation of HRESULT and STATUS can be found in the "Error Codes" section of the *Project Data Service Reference for Microsoft Office Project Server 2003*.

The PDSInfo method returns an XML response similar to the following when successful:

```
<Reply>
    <HRESULT>0</HRESULT>
    <STATUS>0</STATUS>
    <UserName>Administrator</UserName>
    <PDSInfo>
        <ExeName>PDS</ExeName>
        <CompanyName>Microsoft Corporation</CompanyName>
        <FileDescription>Microsoft Project Data Service</FileDescription>
        <Comments/>
        <ProductName>Microsoft Project Server</ProductName>
        <Title>PDS</Title>
        <LegalCopyright>Copyright © 2000-2001 Microsoft
            Corporation.</LegalCopyright>
        <LegalTrademarks/>
        <Major>1</Major>
        <Minor>0</Minor>
        <Revision>728</Revision>
    </PDSInfo>
</Reply>
```

Use the Data from the Response

After you verify that the request is successful, you then parse the XML from the method-specific output to extract the necessary data. In the example the results from the request are not parsed but simply are written to the console:

```
Console.WriteLine("PDSInfo Results:");
Console.WriteLine(sResponse);
```

Repeat Steps 3 to 5 As Necessary

You can now repeat Steps 3 to 5 as many times as necessary for your customization application. You do not need to request a new security cookie each time a PDS method is called. You can simply use the same cookie, unless a different user is needed to make the request.

TIP

The Project 2003 SDK provides a sample application called the PDSTest. This application is useful for testing PDS methods without having to write any code. You simply input the XML request for a PDS method and the logon credentials. The PDSTest then makes the method call and returns the XML results. In this way, you can test the PDS methods and use the results for parsing algorithms and flow logic.

29

Limitations of the PDS

The PDS API is not a comprehensive interface to the Project Server data. Some of the functionality and usefulness of Project Server can be found only in the Project Professional and PWA interfaces. The PDS does, however, provide much of the essential functionality for a custom application. In the case that the PDS does not provide the necessary functionality for your application, PDS extensions can be created. A PDS extender allows you to use the same PDS interface but with customized methods for your particular situation. You can learn more about how to create a PDS extender in the "Writing a PDS Extender" section of the *Project Data Service Reference for Microsoft Office Project Server 2003*.

> **TIP**
>
> The Project 2003 SDK contains more examples of using the PDS. The SDK also includes an example of building a PDS extender. The *Project Data Service Reference for Microsoft Office Project Server 2003* comes with the SDK as well.

PWA Web Parts

Provided with Project Server 2003 are six custom web parts that can access Project Server data when added to a Project Workspace site, or with a few modifications to a SharePoint Portal Server (SPS) site. Additionally, using URL options to modify the appearance of PWA pages, you can quickly create customized web parts for your Project Workspace or SPS site for your own custom pages. The six Project Server web parts are Project Timesheet, Project Center, Project Report, Project Manager Updates, Project Resource Assignments, and Project Portfolio Analyzer.

Refer to the Microsoft download site for help on the custom web parts and the assemblies for them. The article's name is "Project Server 2003 Web Parts and URL Options."

In addition to the Project Server web parts, you can create your own custom web parts to integrate Project Server with SPS. The possibilities for useful web parts are limitless.

Extending the Cube

It is essential for any business to have some sort of insight into the health of its organization, including the health of its projects. Microsoft provides a tool capable of performing complex analysis of the data stored in a Project Server database. This analysis is supplied in a reporting service called the Portfolio Analyzer online analytical processing (OLAP) cube.

OLAP Cube Basics

The OLAP cube is a logical construct that brings together multiple dimensions of data and measures of that data that are organized to be displayed by the reporting service. This data is based on a fact table that resides in the project database itself.

Dimensions are used to summarize and display the data in the fact tables in a hierarchical manner, such as the work performed in given time periods. Each dimension can be visualized as one side of a three-dimensional cube (hence the name). However, a cube construct could contain just one dimension or many more than three.

The Data Warehouse

The *data warehouse* is a relational database that stores the underlying data used to build the cube. This is where all the facts, dimensions, and verified data values are stored for quick access.

The Purpose of Measures

Measures are numerical summarizations that use some given formula for the cube to display data within and across dimensions. Measures can be simple numerical values but also provide the capability to have calculated fields similar to formulated values in Excel. A simple example of a measure would be the count of all products sold in a given month or their equivalent dollar amount.

> **NOTE**
>
> Although most measures are simple summations, complex formulas can be used as calculated fields as well.

Overview of Fact Tables

The *fact table* is an independent table stored in the relational data warehouse that contains all the values used in the cube. The fact table contains at least one column as a key and one column as a value used for measures, or a fact.

A simple example would be a resource's name and a month as key columns and the amount of work that resource performed that month as a fact.

The fact table must contain rows that represent the lowest level of detail you would use for a measure. In other words, you would not use a fact table row to store aggregates of values.

Structure of Dimension Tables

The fact tables contain the data at the lowest level of detail, such as the amount of work performed by each resource. The *dimension tables* are used to store the hierarchical summaries of this data. This may be the work a particular resource performed in each month. One row in the dimension table corresponds to one leaf member for the dimension.

Dimension tables must contain at least one primary key column used to reference key columns in fact tables, such as resource unique identifiers. Although this primary key value must be unique in the dimension table, it may reference multiple rows in the corresponding fact table.

The dimension table also may have columns that represent parent members. In the resource table example given in the preceding section of this chapter, a parent member may be a department.

Multiple types of dimensions can be in a cube, such as key, time, and shared dimensions. References to the various types of dimensions can be found in the online documentation.

Description of the Analysis Server

At the core of Analysis Services is the analysis server. This server is the link between the reports you see in PWA and the data warehouse in the database. It is the entity responsible for extracting information from the data warehouse and constructing the cube itself.

The Portfolio Analyzer to Display Cube Data

The Portfolio Analyzer in PWA uses components in all three tiers of the Project Server application:

- **Database tier**—SQL Analysis Services uses data in a relational database to generate the cube.

- **Middle tier**—Fact and dimension tables are created based on data in other tables in the Project Server database (or beyond).

- **Client tier**—PivotTables and charts are used to display the cube data to the user in PWA.

The PivotTables and charts in PWA connect to the OLAP database through OLE, which then connects to Analysis Services on the server. The Analysis Services fetches the information from the database for the PivotTables and charts to display.

The Structure of the Default Portfolio Analyzer Cube

The out-of-the-box cube built with Project Server is labeled `MSP_PORTFOLIO_ANALYZER`. This cube is actually a virtual cube that contains two cubes: `MSP_ASSN_FACT` and `MSP_RES_AVAIL_FACT`. All the fact and dimension tables for these cubes reside in the same database read by Project Server.

TIP

The default cube fact and dimension tables in the Project Server database is a good, although complex reference for how information is stored in the data warehouse.

The two cubes are combined under one virtual cube so that the reports can more easily reference data from both cubes to display information side by side.

The `MSP_ASSN_FACT` cube contains assignment and timephased data for all enterprise projects. This cube contains data such as standard time, project versions, and resource status. It also contains dimensions for resources as well as enterprise project and resource outline codes.

The MSP_RES_AVAIL_FACT cube contains all resource availability and calendar information for all resources. This includes the standard time and resource dimensions, as well as dimensions for defined resource outline codes.

Cube Extension Build Process

The cube building process is generally kicked off in two ways—either on a scheduled basis or manually. Both are done in the Admin section of PWA under the Manage Enterprise Features tab.

When the cube build is kicked off, its first step is to create all staging tables (the data warehouse) referenced by the cube. Its second step is to build the actual cube structure, including all dimensions and measures. Project Server provides a method to insert functions to perform custom actions after each of these two steps, as shown in Figure 29.1. This is done by creating a custom library named MSPOLAPBREAKOUT.dll.

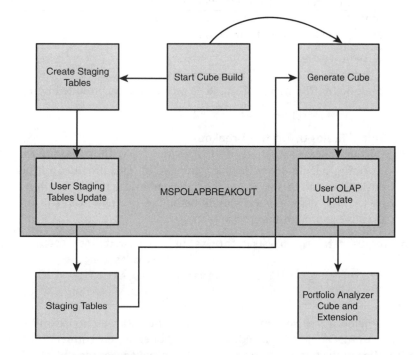

FIGURE 29.1   The MSPOLAPBREAKOUT object can be called to perform custom actions in the cube build process.

29

PWA then links the virtual cube to the staging tables, building all dimensions and measures referenced by the cube.

Overview of the Cube Build Breakout Object

When PWA builds a cube, it also checks for a registered dynamic link library (DLL) called MSPOLAPBREAKOUT. When this library is exposed over the component object model (COM), Project Server calls two methods involved in building the cube. One method sets up the staging tables used by the cube; the other sets up the cube itself. Refer to Figure 29.1 for an idea of where in the build process these methods are called.

Microsoft provides a Solution Starter that contains example cube extension code and the cube extension SDK. This Solution Starter is available from the Microsoft download center under the name "Microsoft Office Project Server 2003: Portfolio Analyzer OLAP Extensions."

NOTE

Although the Solution Starter that Microsoft provides is written in Visual Basic 6.0, the extension can be written in any language that can produce an ActiveX COM DLL, such as the .NET Framework. Make sure that the ActiveX class is labeled UserOptionalCode and that the proper methods are exposed.

To tell Project Server to break out to the MSPOLAPBREAKOUT code, you must register the DLL on the same computer. You can easily register a VB 6.0 created library by executing the following (specifying the full path of the DLL):

```
Regsvr32.exe .\MSPOLAPBREAKOUT.DLL
```

This can also be done in .NET by using the RegAsm.exe utility, provided by the framework.

Extending Staging Tables Using the Breakout

The UserStagingTablesUpdate method of the breakout COM allows you to execute custom code for filling staging tables during a cube build. This provides a foundation for your cube extension because this is where the data warehouse the cube will reference is populated. Note that the staging tables should be built separately from this process, such as through SQL calls or through Enterprise Manager.

```
Public Function UserStagingTablesUpdate(Byval o_dbConnection As ADODB.Connection,
➥                                        ByVal l_DBType As Long,
➥                                        ByRef l_errnum As long,
➥                                        ByRef s_errdesc As String) As Long
```

Two input parameters are passed: the connection to the data warehouse and the database type. Although an ADO object is passed, you should open a new connection to the database by using the connection string property of the m_dbConnection object. The database type can be ignored because it will always be a SQL server.

Two output parameters are given: an error number and error description. These provide essential bits of the information for debugging the cube extension build.

The functions should return a nonzero value on an error, which halts the rest of the cube build process.

Populate the staging tables using any SQL database connection library of your choice. The ADODB library is a logical choice because it is already used as one of the input parameters. See the cube extension Solution Starter for examples and the SDK for more information.

> **TIP**
>
> You are not limited to the Project Server tables for sources of information to be included in the cube. A common data source for cube information is WSS. Microsoft's Solution Starter kit provides an example of a risk cube and how to retrieve that information using WSS SOAP calls.

Building the Cube Structure with the Breakout Object

The UserOLAPUpdate method of the breakout object allows you to build your cube extension that relies on previously populated staging tables. This is where you can use Microsoft Decision Support Objects (DSO) to create objects such as measures, dimensions, and cubes themselves.

```
Public Function UserOLAPUpdate(ByVal sOLAPServerName As String,
➥                    ByVal sOLAPDatabaseName As String,
➥                    ByVal o_dbConnection As ADODB.Connection,
➥                    ByVal l_DBType As Long,
➥                    ByRef l_errnum As Long,
➥                    ByRef s_errdesc As String) As Long
```

The UserOLAPUpdate function has two additional input parameters than the staging tables update function, a server name and a database name. The server name is the name of the OLAP server machine, and the database name is the OLAP database name on that server (these values are both set in PWA's Admin page).

At the end of this function you kick off the actual cube build process for the custom cubes you've set up. The process is a command that is part of an MDStore object (the DSO object that represents a cube):

```
dsoCube.Process
```

> **CAUTION**
>
> In Microsoft's Solution Starter, the custom cube is always deleted before being built in the UserOLAPUpdate function. This should be avoided because doing so erases any custom security settings or any changes such as calculated fields.

MSDN provides a comprehensive reference for all the DSO objects. This reference combined with the Solution Starter should provide a good guide for building your custom cube. It may also help to first build the cube in SQL Analysis Manager to provide a plan before coding.

Debugging the Cube Extension

Debugging the cube extension build can be tedious. Elegant error handling within the breakout class itself is important to offer the debugger some sort of insight as to what is happening. Verbose event message reporting is recommended.

The Solution Starter kit provided by Microsoft includes a handy debugging application (along with the code) that you can use to test your custom MSPOLAPBREAKOUT library, as shown in Figure 29.2. You provide a connection string, the OLAP server name, and the OLAP cube name, and it runs the two exposed functions on the registered MSPOLAPBREAKOUT library.

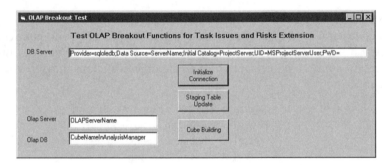

FIGURE 29.2   The Solution Starter kit provides a handy application to debug your custom cube extension.

The following list contains some common things to check while debugging a cube building problem:

- Make sure that the service packs for SQL Server and Analysis Server are the same versions. These must be applied separately from one another.

- Make sure that the OLAP repository was migrated to SQL Server (as opposed to an Access database) according to the *Microsoft Project Server Installation Guide*.

- Make sure that the account running in OLAP COM+ applications is an OLAP administrator.

- Make sure that your Project Server service account has access to the OLAP server and the particular cube, as well as the user viewing the data from PWA.

- Check that the cube name and OLAP server settings are correct in PWA's OLAP admin page, as well as the settings for a particular Portfolio Analyzer view.

- Use the cube extension test program to verify that your breakout functions are working properly.

SharePoint Portal Integration

SharePoint Portal Server (SPS) is Microsoft's enterprise-class portal solution. It facilitates collaboration, document management, enterprise consolidation, content targeting, and search across WSS sites, file shares, and intranet sites. SPS technology is built on WSS but gives you some important features not available in WSS, such as aggregated search, categorizing information into topics, personalization, and My Site. This section reviews some of the important integration points between SPS and the EPM solution.

> **NOTE**
>
> As a convention in this section, the term *project workspace* refers to a WSS site that has been automatically created for a project when the project is published to Project Server.

Connecting EPM to SharePoint Portal Server

Connecting EPM to SPS is a simple process that is easy and quick but gives you limited integration functionality. It creates a link to SPS search in your project workspace search result pages and a link to the portal prominently appearing on all your project workspace sites. Finally it gives you the ability to elevate content, such as annoucements, document libraries, risks, and issues from project workspaces to SPS areas. To set up the connection between SPS and Project Server, follow these steps:

1. In PWA, click the Admin tab.

2. From the Actions list on the side panel, click Manage Windows SharePoint Services.

3. When the browser refreshes, from the Actions list on the side panel, click Connect to SharePoint Portal Server.

4. On the Connect to SharePoint Portal Site screen, enter the URL and a name for the portal that is descriptive enough that users will know where this link will take them (see Figure 29.3).

When you complete the process to connect your project workspaces to SPS, one of the changes to your project workspace sites is a link that appears on the upper-right corner of all the pages in the project workspace sites, which gives an impression that SPS and the project workspace have tight integration. Additionally, when you execute a search on a project workspace, the search results screen has a convenient link to perform the search with your search terms on SPS. You can also create visibility in specified projects by elevating project workspace content to the portal by following these steps:

1. Open the project workspace content area (for example: Risks, Issues, Document Library, or Annoucements) that you want to see in the portal.

2. From the Actions list on the side panel, click Modify Settings and Columns.

3. When the browser refreshes, click the Select a Portal Area for this List link.

4. Change any of the settings on the Add Listing screen if you are not satisifed with the default values and click the Change Location link in the Location section to tell SPS where to put the new listing.

5. Click OK to accept your changes and have the new listing added to SPS.

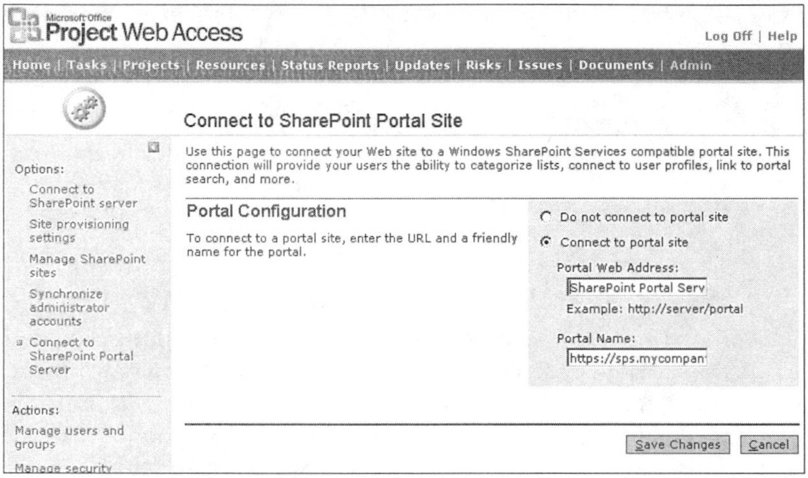

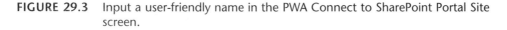

FIGURE 29.3   Input a user-friendly name in the PWA Connect to SharePoint Portal Site screen.

There are several things that you might expect to happen when you set up SPS in PWA. Unfortunately, the integration is not tight. Following is a short list of integration items that you might assume would happen but that do not happen:

- Automatic indexing of project workspaces is not set up.

- Project workspaces don't appear in the site catalog, which would give you a way to navigate to them directly—you could work around this limitation with a web part.

- Project workspaces don't automatically get added to Topics in SPS.

TIP

One way to set up search integration between SPS search and project workspaces is to create a stored procedure that returns a URL as a link to all your WSS sites to a hidden web page and then set up this hidden page as a content source for the SPS Indexer to index. Finally, you can set up a Project Workspaces scope that appears in the search sources drop-down list on the home page in SPS, giving users the option to narrow their SPS search to just project workspaces.

This approach to indexing/searching project workspaces might seem a little kludgy at first, but some conditions exist that make this the best approach. First, SPS, for performance reasons, should really reside on a separate computer from the EPM solution. Following are additional arguments for setting up SPS/WSS and Project Server/WSS separately:

- A separate server configuration allows clean division between project workspaces and WSS sites in the portal's site collection for archiving purposes.

- Cuts down on potential SPS clutter—old Project Workspaces don't have to be managed under the portal.

- When Project Server requests that WSS create a project workspace, it's going to get a number, not a name, which can't be changed. Thus, if you attempt to integrate WSS implementations, you'll end up with a bunch of ugly-named sites in your SPS catalog.

- SPS WSS sites are not static but can be easily reorganized on a corporate whim. This is not really the intention for project workspaces. If you separate the WSS implementations, there will be less breakage, and your user training will be easier and more consistent, with potential EPM users probably needing to be trained on only one application rather than two.

- If your organization is large, your system administrators will want to have the division of responsibility between the SPS team and the Project Server team. These teams can share knowledge but don't have to share the responsibility for both applications at once.

- Microsoft does not recommend installing SPS, WSS, and Project Server on the same computer for a production implementation, and doing so may have the following consequences: excessive memory usage, excessive paging to the hard disk drive, service performance degradation, and services delaying the start of other services.

Best Practices

- The PDS API should be used to access data when building a custom application.

- Classes with the base functionality of logging in programmatically, sending a SOAP request, and accepting the SOAP response should be implemented in the language the project will be written in.

- When the PDS API does not provide all data access needed for your application, a PDS extender should be written.

- Set up search integration between SPS search and Project Workspaces by creating a stored procedure that returns a URL as a link to all your WSS sites to a hidden web page; then set up this hidden page as a content source for the SPS Indexer to index.

29

- You can set up a Project Workspaces scope so that it appears in the search sources drop-down on the home page in SPS, giving users the option to narrow their SharePoint Portal search to just Project Workspaces.

- Use the Project web parts to display vital project information and create easy integration points between SPS and Project Server.

- Include detailed error handling and status updates as much as possible in all methods of your MSPOLAPBREAKOUT object. Report this to the event messages.

- Always utilize the test program included with the Solution Starter to test the cube build before testing from PWA.

- Designing your cube in Analysis Manager before developing the breakout code simplifies the development process.

Index

NUMBERS

6 Pillars of EPM (Enterprise Project Management), 19-20
  Artifact Management, plan development, 66-68
  Collaboration Management, plan development, 64-65
  Operational Principles, plan development, 69-70
  Organizational Readiness, plan development, 68
  Project Management, plan development, 58-61
  Resource Management, plan development, 61-63

A

About Microsoft Office Project Server 2003 page, 480, 534
Accept/Reject Task Column and Updates List option (Updates page), 339
accepting PDS requests, 798
Account Creation permissions (Server Configuration Features template), 146
Account Properties dialog (Enterprise Options feature), 539
accountability (Organizational Change tools), 17
Action bar
  PWA interface screen, 301
  Tasks page, 328
Actions menu (Documents and Lists page)
  Alert Me option, 739-740
  Export to Spreadsheet option, 739-740
  Modifying Settings and Columns option, 739-741

  Synchronize with Project Server option, 740-741
  View Reports option, 739-740
Active X components (Portfolio Analyzer), 397
ActiveX Controls (Internet Explorer), troubleshooting, 673
Actual work tracking method (Tasks page), 320, 326
actuals
  adjust actuals, troubleshooting, 288
  capturing, 254
AD (Active Directory)
  Enterprise Resource Pool management, 193
    synchronization, 199-201
  forest websites, 120
  synchronizing, 480
  Windows Server 2003, 652
Add button (Filter Enterprise Resources feature), 358
Add Category page (PWA), 489
Add Group page (PWA), 486
Add Version page (PWA), 521
Add Web Parts option (Modify Shared Page feature), 735
add-ins
  COM add-ins, 45-46
  portfolio management add-ins, 50
  process workflow management add-ins, 52
  project management add-ins, 51
  PWA add-ins, 47-50
  risk management add-ins, 51
adding
  columns in WSS, 451
  resources to Portfolio Analyzer views, 232

  Time dimension to Portfolio Analyzer views, 231
  versions (projects) to Manage Enterprise Features function (PWA Admin tab), 521
adjust actuals, troubleshooting, 288
Adjust Actuals feature (Resource Center), 391-392
Adjust Actuals in the Resource Center option (Updates page), 343
Admin tab (Project Server Health Monitor tool), 670
Admin tab (PWA), 35
  About Microsoft Office Project Server 2003 function, 480
  Clean Up Project Server Database function, 480
    deleting projects/to-do lists, 533
    deleting resource task changes, 532
    deleting resources, 533-534
    deleting status reports, 532
    deleting task assignment data, 531
  Customize Project Web Access function, 479
    Gantt Chart Formats function, 524-525
    Grouping Formats function, 525-527
    Home Page Format function, 528-529
    Notification and Reminders function, 529-530
    Tracking Settings function, 524
  functions, list of, 477

Manage Enterprise Features function, 479, 516
 Enterprise project check-ins, 520-521
 Enterprise resource check-ins, 521
 project versions, 521-523
 Update Resource Tables and OLAP Cube feature, 517-520
Manage Security function, 478
 category management, 488-490
 security template management, 491-494
Manage Users and Groups function, 478
 group management, 485-488
 user management, 480-485
Manage Views function, 479, 494
 adding Assignment views, 499-500
 adding Portfolio Analyzer views, 502-503
 adding Project Center views, 498-499
 adding Project views, 496-497
 adding Resource Center views, 501-502
 copying views, 505
 custom views, 506
 deleting views, 505
 managing Timesheet views, 503-505
 modifying views, 505
Manage Windows SharePoint Services function, 479, 512
 SharePoint site management, 514-516
 site provisioning, 513
 Windows SharePoint Server connections, 512-513
Server Configuration function, 479
 adding top-level menus, 510
 adding top-level sub-menus, 511-512

defining PWA menus, 509
 setting Enterprise features, 507-509
administration (EPK), 50
Administration area (Site Settings page), 749
 Configure Site and Workspace Creation option, 750
 Go to Site Administration option, 750-753
 Manage Sites and Workspaces option, 750
 Manage Users option, 750
administrative projects
 administrator selection, 242
 advantages of, 241
 company policies, 241
 creating, 241-245
 goal of, 240
 inactive resources, removing, 247
 maintenance, 247
 managing, 376-377
 overhead tasks, 245-246
 reporting cycle selection, 246
 special features of, 244
Alert Me function
 Documents and Lists page Action menu, 739-740
 Documents feature, 474-475
 Issues feature, 467
 PWA home page, 302, 305-308
 Risks feature, 460
 Tasks page, 328
 Updates page, 340
alerts
 document library notifications, 605
 email alerts in PWA, 302, 305-308
 message alerts, collaboration management, 64
 SharePoint project workspaces, 642
All Current and Future Projects option (Projects section), 155
All Current and Future Resources option (Resources section), 157

All Document Libraries feature (Documents feature), 472
all tasks, viewing in timesheets, 323
Allow Project Managers to Change the Default Method for Reporting Progress If a Different Method Is Appropriate for a Specific Project option (PWA customization), 702
Allow/Deny security feature, 145, 149, 153
analysis server (OLAP cube), 802
Analysis Server and Cube attribute (Portfolio Analyzer screen), 229
Analysis Services
 Project Server application layer, troubleshooting in, 671-672
 Project Server database tier (EPM solutions), 97-98
Analyze function (Portfolio Modeler), 435-436
Analyze Projects in Portfolio Analyzer feature
 Project Center, 371
 Resource Center, 390
Analyze Timescaled Data Wizard (Project Professional), 626
analyzing
 model data, 431-434
 resources, 390
And field (Filter Enterprise Resources feature), 357
Announcement lists, 744
Announcements feature (WSS project workspace home page), 734
annual cleanups (administrative projects), 247
application installation validation (Project Server)
 Project Server installation, 269-271
 SQL Server/analysis services installation, 264-265
 WSS installation, 266-268

application layer, troubleshooting, 668
- analysis services errors, 671-672
- EditSite.exe tool, 669
- Project Server Health Monitor tool, 669-671
- session manager errors, 672-673
- Views Processing errors, 673

application logs (Project Server), monitoring, 655

Application Server mode (Windows Server), terminal service installation, 677

Application tier (EPM solutions)
- data access, 91-92
- data retrieval, 93
- Office Project Server 2003, 88, 93-94
- PDS, 89-90, 93
- Project Server email layer, 95
- web-based front-end application layer, 87-88
- WSS, 89

Apply Filter button (Build Team for Project Name dialog), 568

Apply Theme to Site option (Customization area), 753

Approve Timesheet for Resources feature (Server Configuration Features template), 145

Approve Timesheets in the Resource Center option (Updates page), 344

Approve Timesheets option (Resource Center), 378

architectures
- EPM solutions, 99-100, 140
- Project Server, 33-34

archived status reports, 314-315

Artifact Management (Six Pillars of EPM), plan development, 20, 66-68

AS (Analysis Services)
- monitoring, 660-661
- Project Server, 653

As the Home Page to a New Outlook Folder option (Display Project Web Access Page in Outlook Web Page dialog), 621

As the Home Page to an Existing Outlook Folder option (Display Project Web Access Page in Outlook Web Page dialog), 620-621

ASP, PWA customization, 770-773

Assign Myself to an Existing Task page (PWA), 330

Assigned To field
- Issues feature, 464
- Risks feature, 457

assigning
- resources to project teams, 564
- yourself to tasks, 330

Assignment views, 202, 496
- adding, 499-500
- creating, 222
- modifying, 222-225

Assignment Work by Project view (View Availability function), 386

Assignment Work by Resource view (View Availability function), 386

assignment-centric views (Portfolio Analyzer view creation), 403-405

assignments (tasks), deleting, 531

AssignmentsGet method (PDS), 795

AssignmentsProjectManagerUp date method (PDS), 795

AssignmentsSave method (PDS), 795

Assume the Lead Role option (Delegate Tasks Wizard), 332

asymmetric encryption, 788

At or Below the Following Level in the Resource Breakdown Structure option (Choose Resources screen), 581

attachments
- issue file attachments, 465
- managing, 599
- shared attachments, creating document workspaces, 637

Attachments field (WSS), 449

augmentation areas (Project Server)
- budgeting/forecasting, 42
- governance, 44
- interdependency management, 43-44
- lightweight project management support, 44
- list of, 40
- methodology support, 43
- project initiation, 44
- project timesheets versus labor timesheets, 41-42
- resource commitment management versus usage management, 42
- standardization validation/support, 43
- strategic portfolio support, 42
- vendor management, 43-44

authentication
- EPM solutions, 103
- mixed, 493
- Project Server, 493
- Windows Server, 493

Auto Filter function (pivot table toolbars), 422

auto-methods (Project object model), 787

Autocalc function (pivot table toolbars), 422

Autofilter option (Filter/Group/Search tab), 350, 382

Automatically Detect Connection State option (Enterprise Options feature), 540

availability
- determining resource availability for project teams, 569-571
- EPM solutions, 101

filtering for resource availability, disabling, 576
resource availability, viewing, 360
work availability, selecting project team resources by, 569
Availability graph (View Availability function), 387
Availability page (Build Team feature), 360
Available Portfolio Analyzer Views, view restrictions, 159
Available Project Center Views, view restrictions, 158
Available to Work feature (Build Team for Project Name dialog), 569

B

Backup Enterprise Global Template function (Enterprise Options feature), 554
backups
    disaster recovery, 667
    Enterprise Global templates, 251-252, 554
    SQL Server database maintenance, 665-666
bandwidth, 114-116
Baseline Work field (Grid and Timesheet entry view), 321
baselines
    Project Professional scheduling, 30
    saved baselines, troubleshooting, 285
    SQL Server monitoring, 658
Basic Meeting Workspace option (Web Pages option), 748
basic Project Server configuration validation (Project Server), 260, 273
Basic Web Page option (Web Pages option), 747
Blank Meeting Workspace option (Web Pages option), 748

Blank Site option (Web Pages option), 748
booking condition (resources), changing, 354-355
booking proposed project team resources, 571
booking type (resources), changing, 359
breakout COM, 804-805
Budget Indicator Generic Enterprise custom field, customizing, 710
budgeting as Project Server augmentation area, 42
Build Team feature
    Build Team function, 355, 360
    PWA, 564-567
Build Team for Project Name dialog, 568-569
Build Team from Enterprise feature (Project Professional), 564
    adding generic resources to project teams, 571
    adding individual resources to project teams, 573
    determining resource availability, 569
    disabling filtering for resource availability, 576
    removing project team resources, 575
    replacing generic resources with individual resources, 573
    replacing individual resources, 575
    selecting project team resources, 566
    WAN, 576
Build Team function (Project Center), 353-355
    Build Team feature, 360
    Filter Enterprise Resources feature, 357-359
    Project Detail feature, 356, 360
build teams
    creating, 355
    resources
        adding, 358
        changing booking type, 359

matching, 359
removing, 358
replacing, 359
viewing availability, 360
business needs (capacity planning), 696
business process integration (EPM installation prerequisites), 141
business process validation (Project Server), 260, 274
business system integration (EPM installation prerequisites), 141

C

Calculated option (Optional Settings for Column section), 453
Calculated Totals and Fields function (pivot table toolbars), 422
Calculation tab (Enterprise Options feature), 546-547
Calendar (Outlook), viewing/reporting tasks, 332-333
Calendar tab (Enterprise Options feature), 544-545
Calendar views, creating in WSS, 454
calendars
    Company (Project Server), 248
    Enterprise (Project Server), 248-249
    EPM deployment, 138
    Resource (Project Server), managing, 249-250
    Standard (Project Server), 248
Calendars/Resource Pool settings, EPM deployment plans, 79
capacity planning
    application performance, 684-685
    approaches to, 683
    changing business needs, 696

data complexity, 684-686
defining, 683
federation, 696-698
goal of, 683
information life cycles, 696
PointCast Network, 684
software releases, 695
system customization, 696
system growth
  monitoring, 694-695
  planning, 693
system hardware/architec-
  ture instance design, 685,
  693
    client-side environments,
    691
    data complexity, 690-691
    data storage require-
    ments, 691-692
    network latency, 688-689
    peak/heavy usage scenar-
    ios, 687-688
    server environments, 689
    user location/connectiv-
    ity, 687
    user numbers/types, 686

**CART (Customer Architecture
Review Team), 115**

categories
  associating groups to, 160
  data permissions, setting,
  153-154
  managing via Manage
  Security function (PWA
  Admin tab), 488-490
  multiple category restrictions, 160
  My Direct Reports, 152
  My Organization, 152
  My Projects, 152
  My Resources, 152
  My Tasks, 152
  permissions
    building project teams,
    564
    skill-based scheduling,
    578
  project restrictions, 155-156
  Project Server 2003 security
  model, 106

resource restrictions,
156-158
resources, assigning to
groups, 161
as role-based names,
159-160
security, 151-153
view restrictions, 158-159

Categories attribute
  Modify View screen, 213,
  217, 221, 224
  Specify Views screen, 235

Categories page
  Project Center views,
  158-159
  Projects section, 155-156
  Resources section, 157-158

Category field
  Issues feature, 464
  Risks feature, 457

**Category is Models views, view
restrictions, 159**

**Central Administration site
(WSS), creating nonproject-
related WSS sites, 757-758**

**centralized binary logging log
file format, 656**

**Change Anonymous Access
option (Change Permissions
for This List field), 450**

**Change Booking Type button
(Filter Enterprise Resources
feature), 358-359**

**Change Column screen (WSS),
450-453**

**Change Field Order screen
(WSS), 453**

**Change Permissions for This
List field (WSS), 449-450**

**Change Site Title and
Description option
(Customization area), 753**

**"Chaos Report," The Standish
Group, 11**

**Chart (OWC), Project Analyzer
views, 228**

charts (Portfolio Analyzer)
  formatting, 409, 412-413
  views, changing, 233-234

**Check in My Projects feature
(Project Center), 375**

**Check Out field (Documents
feature), 473**

**Checked Out By column
(Resources Summary view),
380**

**checks (project schedule), QSA
add-in, 46**

**Choice option (Optional
Settings for Column section),
452**

**Choose Projects screen
(Resource Substitution
Wizard), 580**

**Choose Related Projects screen
(Resource Substitution
Wizard), 582**

**Choose Resources screen
(Resource Substitution
Wizard), 581-582**

**Choose Scheduling Options
screen (Resource Substitution
Wizard), 583**

**Choose Update Options screen
(Resource Substitution
Wizard), 585**

**Clean Up Project Server
Database page (PWA Admin
tab), 480**
  deleting projects/to-do lists,
  533
  deleting resource task
  changes, 532
  deleting resources, 533-534
  deleting status reports, 532
  deleting task assignment
  data, 531

client layer
  elements of, 668
  troubleshooting, 673-675

Client tier (EPM solutions)
  LOB applications, 87
  Office Outlook 2003, 85
  Office Project Professional
  2003, 85
  Office PWA, 86
  OWC, 86

**Close option (Modify Shared
Page feature), 737**

clustering projects within header groups, 362

clustering services (Windows Server 2003), 89

ClusteringOverview.doc website, 89

code masks (Enterprise Outline Codes), 163, 166

Code window (Microsoft Project 2003), viewing/editing VBA macros, 784

Collaborate tab (Enterprise Options feature), 548

Collaboration (Project Center)

documents management, 598-599

Go to Selected Project Workspace function, 367-370

issues management, 597

Manage Project Documents function, 367-369

overview of, 589-590

risk management, 597

Track Project Issues function, 367-368

Track Project Risks function, 367-368

Collaboration Management (Six Pillars of EPM), plan development

business processes, 65

technology items, 64-65

Collapse and Expand function (pivot table toolbars), 423

columns (WSS)

adding in, 451

changing order in, 453

customizing in, 451-452

deleting in, 453

COM (component object models)

breakout

UserOLAPUpdate method, 805

UserStagingTablesUpdate method, 804

third-party add-ins, 45-46

Commands and Options function

pivot table toolbars, 423

Portfolio Analyzer, formatting

charts, 409, 412-413

pivot tables, 406-408

views, 406-408

Comment field

Assign Myself to an Existing Task page, 330

Create a New Task page, 329

commenting on documents via web discussions, 642

communication

EPM organizational impact, 21-22

Organizational Change tools, 17

Communications plans (PWA), 32

Company calendar (Project Server), 248

Compare function (Portfolio Modeler), what-if analysis, 434

compelling threats, 16

compelling visions, 16

compiling status reports, 313

Complete Backup tab (Maintenance Plan Wizard), 665

complex data, defining, 691

Concept Phase (EPM deployment)

Concept Proposal Stage, 72-74

Planning Stage, 74-75

Concept Proposal Stage (EPM deployment), 72-74

configuration tools list, 668

Configure Site and Workspace Creation option (Site Settings page Administration area), 750

Connect to Project Server Using Microsoft Project 2002 feature (Server Configuration Features template), 145

Connect to SharePoint Server page (PWA), 513

Connection option (Modify Shared Page feature), 737

consolidated projects, 362

Contact lists, 744

Content area (PWA interface screen), 301

Contingency Plan field (Risks feature), 457

contract commitment, 42

cookies (security), collecting via PDS, 797

Copy function (pivot table toolbars), 422

Copy Picture to Office Wizard, 631

Copy View function, 505

copying

project objects, 552

views, 505

Cost field (Risks feature), 457

Create a New Personal or Shared To-Do List function (Project Center), 371-372

Create a New Task page (PWA), 329

Create page (WSS project workspace)

Custom Lists option, 742, 745

customizing, 742-749

Discussion Boards option, 742, 746

Document Libraries option, 742-743

Lists option, 742-745, 756

Picture Libraries option, 742-743

Surveys option, 742, 747

Web Pages option, 743

Basic Meeting Workspace option, 748

Basic Web Page option, 747

Blank Meeting Workspace option, 748

Blank Site option, 748

Decision Meeting Workspace option, 748

Document Workspace option, 748

Multiple Meeting Workspace option, 749

Project Workspace option, 749

Sites and Workspaces option, 748
Social Meeting Workspace option, 748
Team Site option, 748
Web Part Page option, 747

Create View screen (WSS), 454

cubes
MSP_ASSN_FACT cube, 802
MSP_PORTFOLIO_ANA-LYZER cube, 802-803
MSP_RES_AVAIL_FACT cube, 803
OLAP cubes, 800
analysis server, 802
creating, 518-520
data warehouse, 801
defining, 97
detail data, defining, 97
dimension tables, 801
dimensions, 400-401, 801-802
extension build process, 803-806
fact tables, 801
measures, 401, 801
Portfolio Analyzer, 225-228, 395-398, 802
staging table set (Project Server database tier), 96-98
summary data, 97
updating, 517-518
Windows Everyone security group, 398

Currency option (Optional Settings for Column section), 452

currency symbols, defining in Enterprise Global templates, 555

current tasks, viewing in timesheets, 323

Custom Filter option (Filter/Group/Search tab), 350, 381

custom filters
project resource selections, 568-569
resource matching, 574

Custom List in Datasheet View option (Custom Lists option), 745

custom lists (WSS), saving as templates, 754-755

Custom Lists option (Create page), 742, 745

custom Project Center views, 348

custom views
Manage Views page, adding to, 506
Resource Center views, creating, 385
Save Link button (Project Center), creating via, 352-354

Customization area (Site Settings page), 750, 753-754

Customization tabs (PWA), 339

Customize Enterprise Fields dialog (Project Professional), 556

Customize Filter button (Build Team for Project Name dialog), 568

Customize Home Page option (Customization area), 754

Customize Project Web Access function (PWA Admin tab), 479
Gantt Chart Formats function, 524-525
Grouping Formats function, customizing groupings, 525-527
Home Page Format function, 528-529
Notification and Reminders function, 529-530
Tracking Settings function, 524

Customize the PivotTable and Chart attribute (Portfolio Analyzer screen), 230

customizing
Budget Indicator generic enterprise custom field, 710
Create page (WSS project workspaces), 742-749

Documents and Lists page (WSS project workspaces), 738-741
enterprise custom fields, 709-710
enterprise generic outline codes, 705-707
enterprise global custom outline codes, 703-705
Enterprise Global templates, 555
adding custom objects, 560-561
enterprise custom fields, 558-560
Enterprise Outline Codes, 556-557
groupings, 525-527
home page (WSS project workspaces), 735-738
Portfolio Analyzer, 701-703
Project Area resource outline code714, 719
Project by Aircraft Type resource outline code, 716
Project Center views, 348-350
Project Funding resource outline code, 714
Project Life Cycle resource outline code, 727
Project Lifestyle resource outline code, 712
Project Location Enterprise Outline Code, 705
Project Location resource outline code, 711, 718, 726
Project Performing Division Enterprise Outline Code, 707
Project Phase resource outline code, 720-724
Project Portfolio by Area resource outline code, 727
Project Portfolio by Global Alliances resource outline code, 716
Project Portfolio Sector resource outline code, 715
Project Priority Enterprise Outline Code, 707

Project Scope resource outline code, 715

Project Sponsoring Division Enterprise Outline Code, 707

Project Status Enterprise Outline Code, 705-706

Project Status resource outline code, 711, 720-721, 726

Project Strategic Alignment resource outline code, 714

Project Type Enterprise Outline Code, 706

Project Type resource outline code, 713

Projects and Resources by Area of Capital Expenditures resource outline code, 719

Projects and Resources by Sector resource outline code, 718

Projects by Aircraft Type resource outline code, 716

Projects by Branch resource outline code, 717

Projects by Construction Component resource outline code, 722

Projects by Core Support Area resource outline code, 725

Projects by Core Technologies resource outline code, 724

Projects by Emerging Biopharmaceuticals resource outline code, 725

Projects by Healthcare Area resource outline code, 717

Projects by Type of Capital Expenditures resource outline code, 719

Projects by Types of Construction resource outline code, 722

PWA, 701, 766
  adding ASP pages, 770-773
  adding external pages, 774-778

Allow Project Managers to Change the Default Method for Reporting Progress If a Different Method Is Appropriate for a Specific Project option, 702

Force Project Managers to Use the Progress Reporting Method Specified Above for All Projects option, 702

locking down defaults, 702

Managed Time Periods option, 702

menu modifications, 767-769

NoBanter parameter, 767

NoMenu parameter, 767

NoSaveLinkButton parameter, 767

SimpleUI parameter, 767

single instances, 778

stylesheet modifications, 767

tracking settings, 702

views, 703

Resource by Skill Set resource outline code, 712-713, 716-717

Resource Center views, 380

Resource Distribution of Medical and Clinical Staff resource outline code, 725

Resource RBS resource outline code, 712

Resource Role resource outline code, 713

Resource Skill Set Classification resource outline code, 718

Resources by Certification outline code, 709

Resources by Construction Management Position resource outline code, 723

Resources by Core Construction Skills resource outline code, 723

Resources by Location outline code, 708

Resources by RBS outline code, 708

Resources by Skill Set outline code, 708, 720-727

Resources by Type outline code, 709

Schedule Indicator generic enterprise custom field, 709-710

Site Settings page (WSS project workspaces), 749-754

system customization (capacity planning), 696

timesheets, 324-325, 336

Updates page (PWA), 339

WSS project workspaces, 733

WSS site definitions
  changing project sites, 766
  creating, 761-764
  setting as base templates, 764-765
  template location/structure, 759-760

D

data
  access validation (Project Server), 273
  accuracy in Project Server, troubleshooting, 286-287
  analysis (OLAP), 800-806
  complex data
    capacity planning, 684-686
    defining, 691
    system hardware/architecture instance design, 690-691
  extraction, PDS requests, 799
  permissions, setting in categories, 153-154
  Portfolio Analyzer views, manipulating via Field List, 423
  restoration in Enterprise Global templates, 252
  storage requirements in system hardware/architecture instance design, 691-692

data warehouses, 801

database tier (EPM solutions)
  Analysis Services, 97-98
  database partitioning, 96
  OLAP cube staging table set, 96-98
  Project database table set, 95
  Project Server database table set, 96
  Views database table set, 96

databases
  maintenance (SQL Server), 663
    backups, 665-666
    Full Recovery model, 662
    integrity checks, 665
    optimization, 664
    report generation, 667
    Simple Recovery model, 662
  partitioning in Project Server database tier (EPM solutions), 96
  segmenting, EPM solution design, 113
  server performance (EPM solutions), 102

Datasheet views, creating in WSS, 454

datasheets
  documents, editing in, 472
  issues, editing in, 467
  risks, editing via Risks feature (PWA), 461

Date and Time option (Optional Settings for Column section), 452

Date Range option (View Options functions), 386

date ranges (timesheets), viewing, 324

Day-by-day tracking method (Tasks page), 320, 326

debugging
  OLAP cube extensions, 806
  VBA macro code, 785-786

Decision Meeting Workspace option (Web Pages option), 748

Default Group, Sort attribute (Modify View screen), 212, 216, 220, 224

Default View Settings attribute (Specify Views screen), 234

Delegate Task feature (Server Configuration Features template), 145

Delegate Tasks Wizard, 331-332

delegating tasks, 282, 331-332

Delegation tab (Tasks page), 331-332

Delete field (Documents feature), 473

Delete option (Modify Shared Page feature), 737

Delete Row button (Filter Enterprise Resources feature), 358

Delete View function, 505

deleting
  columns in WSS, 453
  document workspace documents, 639
  document workspace sites, 639
  project objects, 552
  projects, 533
  resource task changes, 532
  resources, 533-534
  status reports, 313-314, 532
  task assignments, 531
  to-do lists, 533
  versions (projects), 523
  views, 505
  WSS sites, 516

denies (soft), 145

Deny/Allow security feature, 145, 149, 153

deploying EPM
  calendars, 138
  capturing feature requirements, 78-80
  enterprise global codes, 138
  generic phases of deployment, 72-78
  implementation strategies, communicating, 80-81
  installation prerequisites
    business process integration, 141
    business system integration, 141
  communicating EPM benefits, 142
  establishing standards, 140
  incremental deployments, 140-141
  infrastructure design, 140
  pilot deployments, 141
  professional assistance, 138-139
  program management offices, 139
  training, 139
  rollout expectations, managing, 70-71
  security models, 137
  timesheets, 138
  views, 138

Description field (Risks feature), 457

Design and Development stage (EPM deployment), 75

Design phase (EPM implementation), 18

Design This Page option (Modify Shared Page feature), 736

desktop configuration controls (Operational Principles plans), 70

detail data (OLAP cubes), defining, 97

Diagnose phase (EPM implementation), 16-17

digital certificates
  SelfCert, 790
  VBA macros, 788-791

digital dashboards, displaying in Outlook (PWA/Outlook integration), 621

Digital Signature Details screen, View Certificates button, 790

dimension tables, 801

dimensions (OLAP cubes), 400-401, 801-802

disaster recovery, 667

disconnecting documents from document workspaces, 639

Discuss field (Documents feature), 474

Discussion Boards option (Create page), 742, 746

Discussion field (Issues feature), 465

Discussions feature (WSS project workspace home page), 734

Display Chart in Monochrome function (Portfolio Modeler), 432

Display Project Web Access Page in Outlook Web Page dialog, 620-621

DLL (dynamic link libraries), 804-806

document check-in/out (document libraries), 605

Document Information tab (Shared Workspace task pane), 640

document libraries
accessing, 469
documents management, 604
features of, 605
folder creation, 469
moving documents to, 642
My Projects group, 605
Other Projects group, 605
Public group, 605
subfolder creation, 471
viewing document lists, 471

Document Libraries option (Create page), 742-743

document lists, viewing, 471

Document Template field (Documents feature), 469

document versioning (document libraries), 605

Document Versions field (Documents feature), 469

Document Workspace feature (Office), 600-602

Document Workspace option
Documents and Lists page, 738
Web Pages option, 748

document workspaces, 636
creating, 637-638
making changes to, 638
managing, 638
saving changes to, 638

documenting Project Sever security settings, 146

documents
access, troubleshooting, 281
commenting on via web discussions, 642
creating, 470
datasheets, editing in, 472
document libraries, 469-471, 604-605, 642
editing without viewing, 473
moving to document libraries, 642
spreadsheets, exporting to, 475
uploading, 471
views, selecting, 474

Documents and Lists page (WSS project workspace)
Actions menu
Alert Me option, 739-740
Export to Spreadsheet option, 739-740
Modify Settings and Columns option, 739-741
Synchronize with Project Sever option, 740-741
View Reports option, 739-740
customizing, 738-741
Document Workspaces option, 738
managing
document libraries, 604
Document Workspace feature (Outlook), 600-602
email messages/file attachments, 599
Meeting Workspace feature (Outlook), 600
paper documents, 599
project team collaboration, 598-599
tips for, 601-603
Meeting Workspaces option, 739
Sites option, 738

Documents feature (PWA), 468
Alert Me option, 474-475
All Document Libraries feature, 472

Check Out field, 473
Delete field, 473
Discuss field, 474
document creation, 470
document folders, viewing contents of, 470
Document Template field, 469
Document Versions field, 469
documents
editing in datasheets, 472
exporting to spreadsheets, 475
uploading, 471
Edit in the Document Application field, 473
Explorer view, 474
Linking field, 471
Modify Settings and Columns feature, 475
Name and Description field, 469
Name field, 471
Navigation field, 469
Overwrite Existing File(s)? field, 471
Owner field, 471
Project Server synchronization, 475
Status field, 471
Upload Multiple Files field, 471
Version History field, 473
View Properties and Edit Properties field, 473

Documents feature (WSS project workspace home page), 734

Documents page (PWA), 32, 297

Documents tab
PWA, 66
Shared Workspace task pane, 640

dual NIC configurations (EPM solution design), 116

Due Date field
Issues feature, 465
Risks feature, 457

E

Edit button (Resource Center), 389

Edit in the Document Application field (Documents feature), 473

Edit Site utility, 131

Edit tab (Enterprise Options feature), 544

editing

Assignment views, 222-225

documents in datasheets, 472

documents window viewing, 473

event lists in Outlook, 645

issues in datasheets, 467

Portfolio Analyzer views, 228-235

Project Center views, 210-214

Project views, 215-218

projects in Project Center, 360

Resource Center views, 219-221

resources, 388-389

risks in datasheets via Risks feature (PWA), 461

status reports, 314

VBA macro code, 782-784

EditSite.exe, troubleshooting Project Sever application layer, 669

education and training (Organizational Change tools), 17

effort estimation (Project Professional scheduling), 30

email

alerts in PWA, 302, 305-308

attachments, creating document workspaces, 637

MAPI Email/Project Server integration, 622

messages, managing, 599

notifications

delegated tasks, 332

troubleshooting task assignment notifications, 281

reminders in PWA, 302, 305-308

email layer, Application tier (EPM solutions), 95

Email Notification field (WSS), 449

encryption (asymmetric), 788

enforced group policies, 677

Enterprise calendar (Project Server), 248-249

enterprise custom fields, 204

creating, 164-169, 205

customizing, 709-710

defining, 205-206

formula creation, 206

graphical indicators, 206

naming, 166

overview of, 205

Enterprise Custom Fields/Outline Codes, EPM deployment plans, 79

enterprise generic outline codes, customizing, 705-707

enterprise global codes, EPM deployment, 138

enterprise global custom outline codes, customizing, 703-705

Enterprise Global Resource Outline Codes

defining (resource management plans), 62

sing versus multivalue, 419, 422

Enterprise Global Resource Pool

defining (resource management plans), 62

Project Professional, accessing via, 35

resource management, 31

resource synchronization, 31

Enterprise Global standards, Operational Principles plans, 69

Enterprise Global templates, 542

backups, 251-252, 554

configuring, 37

customizing

adding custom objects, 560-561

currency symbols, 555

enterprise custom fields, 558-560

Enterprise Outline Codes, 556-557

data restoration, 252

EPM deployment plans, 79

modifying, 553

restoring, 554

transferring project file items to, 553

Enterprise Options feature (Project Professional)

accessing, 538

Account Properties dialog, 539

Automatically Detect Connection State option, 540

Backup Enterprise Global Template function, 554

Calculation tab, 546-547

Calendar tab, 544-545

Collaborate tab, 548

Edit tab, 544

General tab, 543

Import Project to Enterprise function, 554

Import Resources to Enterprise function, 554

Interface tab, 549

Manually Control Connection State option, 540

Microsoft Project Server Accounts function, 552

Open Enterprise Global Template function, 553

Open Enterprise Resource Pool function, 553-554

Project Server accounts, creating, 539

Project Server Accounts dialog, 540-541

How can we make this index more useful? Email us at indexes@samspublishing.com

Restore Enterprise Global Template function, 554
Save tab, 549
Schedule tab, 545-546
Security tab, 550
Spelling tab, 547
View tab, 542

Enterprise Outline Code option (Filter Enterprise Resources feature), 357

Enterprise Outline Codes
code mask definitions, 163, 166
creating, 164-169
defining/designing, 164
enterprise task outline codes, 202-204
lookup table hierarchies, 167
naming, 166
Project Analyzer views, defining, 226, 230
project outline codes, 169-173
resource outline codes
attribute assignments, 183-184
attribute edits, 184
attributes example, 178-179
creating, 177-179
defining, 176
multiple skills per resource, 181
multivalue skills, 181
planning, 174-176
RBS, 164, 185-190
resource matching, 177
skill definitions, 176
skill matching, 183
skill proficiency level definitions, 180
skill value assignments, 177
troubleshooting, 184
usage scenarios, 178

Enterprise projects
check-ins, 520-521
versions of, 521-523

Enterprise Resource Outline Codes, 564

Enterprise Resource Pool, 563
Active Directory management, 193
active project migration, 193
enterprise generic resources, 194-195
Enterprise Resource Outline Codes, 564
individual enterprise resources, 196
individual local resources, 196
local generic resources, 195-196
manual creation, 192
modifying, 553
opening, 389
Project Server upgrades, 193
PWA client creation, 194
resource additions, 192
Resource calendar, managing, 249-250

enterprise resources
Active Directory synchronization, 199-201
assignment views, 202
check-ins, 521
creating, 196-199
defining, 191
editing, 388-389
RBS code, 388
timesheet views, 203

enterprise task outline codes (Enterprise Outline Codes), 202-204

enterprise templates (Project Professional scheduling), 29

enterprise-level project management
enterprise custom fields, 204
creating, 164-169, 205
defining, 205-206
formula creation, 206
graphical indicators, 206
naming, 166
overview of, 205
Enterprise Outline Codes
code mask definitions, 163, 166
creating, 164-169
defining/designing, 164

enterprise task outline codes, 202-204
lookup table list hierarchies, 167
naming, 166
project outline codes, 169-173
RBS code, 164
resource outline codes, 174-190

EnterpriseCustomFieldsUpdate method (PDS), 795

EPK (Enterprise Project Knowledge) Suite, 41-50

EPK-Collaborate, 50

EPK-Portfolio, 45-48

EPK-Resources, 42, 47-49

EPK-Time, 44, 47-49

EPK-Timesheets, 41

EPM (Enterprise Project Management), 12
Application tier
Office Project Server 2003, 88
Office Project Server 2003, Session Manager service, 94
Office Project Server 2003, View Processing service, 93-94
PDS, 89-93
Project Server email layer, 95
web-based front-end application layer, 87-88
WSS, 89
architecture design factors
feature usage, 100
number of users, 98
project characteristics, 99
system users versus concurrent users, 99
usage patterns, 100
usage peaks, 99
availability, 101
Client tier, 85-87
configuring
Extranet, 124-125
Terminal Services, 126
for users in multiple geographic locations, 117-118

database server performance, 102
deploying
  capturing feature requirements, 78-80
  communicating implementation strategies, 80-81
  generic phases of deployment, 72-78
  managing rollout expectations, 70-71
  multiple domain deployment, 118
  nontrusted domains, 122-123
  single domain deployment, 118
  trusted domains, 119-121
designing
  database segmentation, 113
  developing user profiles, 110-111
  moving SQL 2000 Analysis Services, 113
  moving Views Publishing Services, 113
  network bandwidth, 114-115
  network latency, 115
  NIC cards, 115-116
  reviewing business requirements, 109
  server hardware infrastructures, 111-112
  system performance monitoring, 113
  WAN environments, 116-117
hyperthreading, 127
impact of, 13
implementing
  Artifact Management (Six Pillars of EPM), 20, 66-68
  benefits of, 22
  calendars, 138
  Collaboration Management (Six Pillars of EPM), 20, 64-65

enterprise global codes, 138
expectations of, 25-26
Microsoft workshops, 14
Operational Principles (Six Pillars of EPM), 20, 69-70
Organizational Change management, 15-18
Organizational Readiness (Six Pillars of EPM), 20, 68
organizational impact, 21-24
problem areas, 14
process versus technology, 18
Project Management (Six Pillars of EPM), 19, 58-61
Resource Management (Six Pillars of EPM), 19, 61-63
security models, 137
Six Pillars of EPM, 19-20, 58-70
timesheets, 138
views, 138
installation prerequisites
  business process integration, 141
  business system integration, 141
  communicating EPM benefits, 142
  establishing standards, 140
  incremental deployments, 140-141
  infrastructure design, 140
  pilot deployments, 141
  professional assistance, 138-139
  program management offices, 139
  training, 139
network performance, 102
process evaluation, 13
project manager's role in, 24
Project server database tier, 96-98

project servers, data usage/security, 102-103
scalability, 100-101
security
  Project Server 2003 security model, 105-106
  SSL implementation, 104-105
  user authentication, 103
SharePoint connections, 807
virtual infrastructures, 132
WSS
  Central Administration site, 757-758
  creating nonproject-related sites, 756-758
  custom lists, saving as templates, 754-755
WSS project workspaces
  accessing, 733
  Announcements feature (home page), 734
  Create page, customizing, 742-749
  Discussions feature (home page), 734
  Documents and Lists page, customizing, 738-741
  Documents feature (home page), 734
  Events feature (home page), 734
  home page, 733-738
  Links feature (home page), 735
  Lists feature (home page), 734
  manual, 733
  Modify Shared Page feature (home page), 735
  Pictures feature (home page), 734
  PWA Site Provisioning, 752
  quick launch bar, 733
  Site Settings page, customizing, 749-754
  Surveys feature (home page), 734

top navigation menu, 733

WSS site image feature (home page), 734

error checking PDS requests, 798-799

error events, components of, 655

Errors tab (Project Server Health Monitor tool), 671

establishing standards (EPM installation prerequisites), 140

estimates to complete, 317

event lists, 644-645, 744

Event Log Viewer, 654

Events feature (WSS project workspace home page), 734

EVM (Earned Value Management) solutions, 51

Excel

Export Grid option, 334

exporting Project Center data to, 365

exporting resource data to, 383-384

PivotTables, exporting Portfolio Analyzer tables to Excel, 625

Print Grid option, 334

project workspace integration, 645

importing spreadsheets, 646-647

publishing Excel lists, 646

synchronizing Excel lists, 647

PWA integration

displaying timescaled data in Excel, 626

exporting Portfolio Analyzer tables to Excel, 625

exporting PWA grids to Excel, 622-624

importing external data to Excel, 626

timesheets

arranging columns, 335

exporting to, 335

printing, 334-335

Excel lists, project workspaces

publishing to, 646

synchronizing with, 647

expectations of EPM implementation, 25-26

Explorer view (Documents feature), 474

Export Grid option (Excel), 334

Export Grid to Excel feature (PWA grids), 622-624

Export Project Data Wizard, exporting Gantt charts to project schedules, 633

Export to Excel function (pivot table toolbars), 423

Export to Excel link

Project Center, 365

Resource Center, 383-384

Export to Spreadsheet option (Documents and Lists page Action menu), 739-740

exporting

documents to spreadsheets, 475

Gantt charts to project schedules, 633

issues to spreadsheets, 467

Portfolio Analyzer tables to Excel, 625

Project Center data to Excel, 365

PWA grids to Excel, 622-624

resources to Excel, 383-384

risks to spreadsheets via Risks feature (PWA), 460-461

Visio timelines to project schedules, 629-630

extracting data from PDS requests, 799

Extranet, EPM solution configurations, 124-125

F

fact tables, 801

federation, 696-698

Field List function (pivot table toolbars), 423

Field Width attribute (Modify View screen), 211, 216, 220, 223

fields, removing from Grid and Timesheet entry view (Tasks page), 322

Fields attribute (Modify View screen), 211, 216, 220, 223

files

attachments, managing, 599

issues, attaching to, 465

Filter and Group Reports tab (PWA status reports), 315

Filter attribute (Modify View screen), 212, 217, 221

Filter Enterprise Resources feature (Build Team function), 355-359

Filter option (Filter/Group/Search tab), 349, 381

Filter/Group/Search tab

Project Center, 349-351

Resource Center, 381-383

Tasks page, 324

filtering

archived status reports, 315

custom filters, defining, 569

data in Portfolio Analyzer views, 233

issues, 466

Project Center views, 349

project team resource selections, 567-569

for resource availability, disabling, 576

Resource Center views, 381

risks via Risks feature (PWA), 460

Finish screen (Resource Substitution Wizard), 586

Force Project Managers to Use the Progress Reporting Method Specified Above for All Projects option (PWA customization), 702

forecasting as Project Server augmentation area, 42

Forester Research Report, 591-592

forest websites, 120

formatting
    Excel timesheet columns,
    335
    Portfolio Analyzer
        charts, 409, 412-413
        pivot tables, 406-408
        views, 406-409, 412-413
    timesheets, 320
forwarding archived status
    reports, 314
Framework of Organizational
    Change (EPM implementa-
    tion), 15
Full Recovery model (SQL
    Server database mainte-
    nance), 662
functional departments, 42

G

Gantt Chart Format attribute
    (Modify View screen), 212,
    216, 224
Gantt Chart Formats function
    (Customize Project Web
    Access function), 524-525
Gantt Chart Formats page
    (PWA), 524
Gantt Chart view, 363
Gantt charts
    bar styles, changing, 525
    blank task rows, adding, 632
    creating, 632
    Grid and Timesheet entry
        view (Tasks page), 322
    milestones, adding, 632
    model data, 430
    project schedules
        exporting from, 633
        importing to, 631
    renaming, 524-525
    task dependencies, creating,
        632-633
    zooming in/out of, 322
gap analysis documents, 73
Gartner Group, EPM imple-
    mentation expectations, 25

General tab (Enterprise
    Options feature), 543
generic resources
    enterprise generic, 194-199
    individual resources, replac-
        ing with, 573-574
    local generic, 195-196
    project teams, adding to,
        571
    resource matching, 574
geographical RBS (Resource
    Breakdown Structure),
    188-189
ghosting, 761
Giga, EPM implementation
    expectations, 25
global permissions
    assigning, 151
    building project teams, 564
    skill-based scheduling, 578
Global templates (Project
    Professional)
    Enterprise Global templates,
        542
        backups, 554
        customizing, 555-561
        modifying, 553
        restoring, 554
        transferring project file
            items to, 553
    locating, 538
global.mpt files, troubleshoot-
    ing duplications, 288-289
Go Offline function (PWA), 303
Go to Selected Project
    Workspace function (Project
    Center Collaboration),
    367-370
Go to Site Administration
    option (Site Settings page
    Administration area), 750-753
Go to Task icon (Gantt Chart
    view), 363
governance, 44
governance agreements, 70
GPMC (Group Policy
    Management Console), termi-
    nal services, 677-679
GPO (Group Policy Objects),
    677

graphical indicators (enterprise
    custom fields), 206
Graphical Indicators dialog
    (Project Professional), 560
Graphs dialog, determining
    resource availability, 570
Grid and Timesheet entry view
    (Tasks page), 321-322, 325
grids (PWA), exporting to
    Excel, 622-624
Group By function
    (Filter/Group/Search tab),
    350, 382
group policies, 677
grouping
    archived status reports, 315
    resources for project teams,
        skill-based selections, 566
Grouping Format attribute
    (Modify View screen), 212,
    216, 220, 224
Grouping Formats page (PWA),
    customizing/renaming group-
    ings, 525-527
Groupings in the Project
    Center in the Grouping for-
    mats page (PWA), 526
groups
    assigning
        to categories, 153
        resources to, 161
    associating to categories,
        160
    management via Manage
        Users and Group function
        (PWA Admin tab)
        deleting existing groups,
            488
        group creation, 485-487
        modifying existing
            groups, 487
    Project Center views, 350
    Project Server 2003 security
        model, 106
    Resource Center views, 382
    resources, 351
    security groups, 149-151
    setting category permis-
        sions, 153

Groups page (PWA), group management, 485

growth (capacity planning), 693-695

H

hard change, 15
Design phase (EPM implementation), 18
Diagnose phase (EPM implementation), 17
Implement phase (EPM implementation), 18
Sustain phase (EPM implementation), 18

help, PWA/Outlook integration, 617

Help function (pivot table toolbars), 423

Help option
Modify Shared Page feature, 737
Optional Settings for Column section, 453

Hide button (Tasks page action bar), 328

Hide Details and Show Details functions (pivot table toolbars), 423

histories (tasks), viewing, 342-343

home page (PWA), 302
Alert Me function, 302, 305-308
default functions table, 294-297
issues, displaying, 302
risks, displaying, 302
status reports, displaying, 302
tasks, displaying, 302
timesheets, displaying, 302
updates, displaying, 302
Work with Outlook link, 305

home page (WSS project workspaces), 733
Announcements feature, 734
customizing, 735-738

Discussions feature, 734
Documents feature, 734
Events feature, 734
Links feature, 735
Lists feature, 734
Modify Shared Page feature, 735-738
Pictures feature, 734
Surveys feature, 734
WSS site image feature, 734

Home Page Format page (PWA), 528-529

hotfixes, 70, 680-681

Hover Mouse over Bar Chart function (Portfolio Modeler), 432

Hyperlink or Picture option (Optional Settings for Column section), 453

hyperlinking to status reports, 313

hyperthreading, 127-128

I

IIS (Internet Information Services)
centralized binary logging log file format, 656
Microsoft IIS log file format, 656
NCSA log file format, 656
ODBC log file format, 656
Project Server
log file monitoring, 656-658
validation, 261
PWA, 652
W3C log file format, 656

Immediate window (Visual Basic Editor), debugging VBA macro code, 786

Impact field (Risks feature), 457

Implement phase (EPM implementation), 18

implementing EPM
Artifact Management (Six Pillars of EPM), 66-68
calendars, 138

capturing feature requirements, 78-80
Collaboration Management (Six Pillars of EPM), 64-65
communicating implementation strategies, 80-81
enterprise global codes, 138
generic phases of deployment, 72-78
installation prerequisites, 138-142
managing rollout expectations, 70-71
Operational Principles (Six Pillars of EPM), 69-70
Organizational Readiness (Six Pillars of EPM), 68
Project Management (Six Pillars of EPM), 58-61
Resource Management (Six Pillars of EPM), 61-63
security models, 137
Six Pillars of EPM, 58-70
timesheets, 138
views, 138

Import External Data feature, 626

Import New Assignments menu, 618

Import Project Data Wizard, 628-631

Import Project to Enterprise function (Enterprise Options feature), 554

Import Resources to Enterprise function (Enterprise Options feature), 554

Import Spreadsheet option (Custom Lists option), 745

Import Timeline Wizard, 629

importing
Excel spreadsheets to project workspaces, 646-647
external EPM data to Excel, 626
Gantt charts to project schedules, 631
project schedule data to Visio timelines, 628-629
project tasks to Outlook (PWA/Outlook integration), 618
task lists from Outlook (PWA/Outlook integration), 619-620

In the Selected Projects option (Choose Resources screen), 581

Include Proposed Bookings option (View Options functions), 386

incremental deployments (EPM installation prerequisites), 140-141

indicator field (Grid and Timesheet entry view), 322

Indicators column (Updates page), 340

individual resources, 194

adding to project teams, 572

individual enterprise, 196-199

individual local, 196

replacing, 575

replacing generic resources with, 573-574

resource matching, 574

information life cycles (capacity planning), 696

infrastructure design (EPM installation prerequisites), 140

Insert Notes button (Tasks page action bar), 328

Insert Row button (Filter Enterprise Resources feature), 358

Insight (Symphony Suite), 52

instance planning, system hardware/architecture instance design, 685, 693

client-side environments, 691

data complexity, 690-691

data storage requirements, 691-692

network latency, 688-689

peak/heavy usage scenarios, 687-688

server environments, 689

user location/connectivity, 687

user numbers/types, 686

Integrity checks (SQL Server database maintenance), 665

Integrity tab (Maintenance Plan Wizard), 665

intelli-sense list, 787

interdependency management (Project Server augmentation areas), 43-44

interface screen (PWA), 301

Interface tab (Enterprise Options feature), 549

Internet Explorer

ActiveX Controls, troubleshooting, 673

Project Server client layer, troubleshooting in, 673

PWA offline operation, setting options for, 303-304

Internet Security tab (Project Server), 673-674

involvement (Organizational Change tools), 17

Issue lists, 745

issue tracking (project team collaboration), 597

issues

access, troubleshooting, 281

creating, 463

datasheets, editing in, 467

displaying in PWA, 302

files, attaching, 465

filtering, 466

managing, 597

spreadsheets, exporting to, 467

summaries, 463

viewing reports, 466

Issues feature (PWA), 462

Alert Me option, 467

Assigned To field, 464

Category field, 464

Discussion field, 465

Due Date field, 465

issue summaries, 463

issues

attaching files to, 465

creating, 463

editing in datasheets, 467

exporting to spreadsheets, 467

filtering, 466

Project Server synchronization, 468

viewing reports, 466

Linking to Tasks, Risks, Other Issues, or Documents field, 465

Modify Settings and Columns feature, 468

Owner field, 464

Priority field, 465

Resolution field, 465

Status field, 464

Title field, 464

Issues module (Project Professional), 597-598

Issues page (PWA), 32, 296

Issues tab (PWA), 67

J - K - L

labor timesheets versus project timesheets, 41-42

LAP (Online Transaction Processing) Services

monitoring, 660-661

Project Server, 653

latency

EPM solution design, 115

system hardware/architecture instance design, 688-689

WAN environments, 116-117

Launch Phase (EPM deployment), Production Deployment Stage, 77

leadership teams, capabilities of (EPM organizational impact), 23-24

libraries (document)

accessing, 469

documents management, 604

features of, 605

folder creation, 469

moving documents to, 642

My Projects group, 605

Other Projects group, 605

Public group, 605

subfolder creation, 471

viewing document lists, 471

lightweight project management support (Project Server augmentation areas), 44

Link Documents button (Tasks page action bar), 328

Link Issues button (Tasks page action bar), 328

Link lists, 744

Link Project Risks button (View a Project page), 366

Link Risks button (Tasks page action bar), 328

linking

to PWA home page, 528-529

risks to project tasks, 366

risks to tasks via Risks feature (PWA), 458

to status reports, 313

Linking field (Documents feature), 471

Linking to Tasks, Risks, Other Issues, or Documents field (Issues feature), 465

Links feature (WSS project workspace home page), 735

Links tab (Shared Workspace task pane), 640

Lists feature (WSS project workspace home page), 734

Lists option (Create page), 742-745, 756

LOB (line of business) applications, Client tier (EPM solutions), 87

local resources, defining, 191

Lock Down Defaults, timesheets, 253

log files

formatting, 656

monitoring (Project Server)

IIS 6.0, 656-658

Windows Server 2003, 654

Logo function (pivot table toolbars), 422

Logon screen (PWA), 300

logons

Project Server via PDS, 796-797

PWA, 299-300

Lookup option (Optional Settings for Column section), 453

M

macros (VBA)

as modules, 779

Project object model, 787

recording, 779-780

security, digital certificates, 787-791

Toolbar button (Microsoft Project 2003), assigning, 781

VBA code

debugging, 785-786

viewing/editing, 782-784

maintenance

administrative projects, 247

EPM implementation requirements, 14

SQL Server database, 663

backups, 665-666

Full Recovery model, 662

integrity checks, 665

optimization, 664

report generation, 667

Simple Recovery model, 662

Maintenance Plan Wizard, 663-666

Manage Administrative Projects link (Project Center), 377

Manage Enterprise Features function (PWA Admin tab), 479, 516

Enterprise project check-ins, 520-521

Enterprise resource check-ins, 521

project versions

adding custom versions to, 521

deleting, 523

modifying, 523

Update Resource Tables and OLAP Cube feature, 517-520

Manage Enterprise Features permissions (Project Analyzer views), 227

Manage My Information area (Site Settings page), 750, 754

Manage My To-Do Lists function (Project Center), 371-373

Manage Project Documents function (Project Center Collaboration), 367-369

Manage Request option (Change Permissions for This List field), 450

Manage Security function (PWA Admin tab), 478

category management, 488-490

Project Server authentication mode, setting, 493-494

security template management, 491-493

Manage Sites and Workspaces option (Site Settings page Administration area), 750

Manage Users and Groups function (PWA Admin tab), 478-479

group management, 485-488

user management, 480-485

Manage Users option (Site Settings page Administration area), 750

Manage Views page (PWA Admin tab), 479, 494

Assignment views, adding, 499-500

Portfolio Analyzer views, adding, 502-503

Project Center views, adding, 498-499

Project views, adding, 496-497

Resource Center views, adding, 501-502

Timesheet views, managing, 503-505

views

copying, 505

customizing, 506

deleting, 505

modifying, 505

Manage Views permissions (Project Analyzer views), 227

Manage Windows SharePoint Services function (PWA Admin tab), 479, 512

SharePoint site management, 514-516

site provisioning, 513

Windows SharePoint Server connections, 512-513

Manage Windows SharePoint Services Sites page (PWA), 514

Managed Time Periods option

PWA customization, 702

Tasks page, 318

Managed Timesheets option (Resource Center), 378

Management and Statistics area (Go to Site Administration option), 751-752

managing

administrative projects, 376-377

categories via Manage Security function (PWA Admin tab), 488-490

delegated tasks, 332

document workspaces, 638

Enterprise calendar (Project Server), 248-249

EPM rollout expectations, 70-71

groups via Manage Users and Group function (PWA Admin tab), 485-488

portfolios via Project Center (PWA), 30-31

Project Professional views, 237

Resource calendar (Project Server), 249-250

resources via Enterprise Global Resource Pool (PWA), 31

security templates via Manage Security function (PWA Admin tab), 491-494

users via Manage Users and Group function (PWA Admin tab), 480-485

views via Manage Views function (PWA Admin tab), 494

adding Assignment views, 499-500

adding Portfolio Analyzer views, 502-503

adding Project Center views, 498-499

adding Project views, 496-497

adding Resource Center views, 501-502

copying views, 505

managing Timesheet views, 503-505

modifying views, 505

Window Server patches, 680

Manually Control Connection State option (Enterprise Options feature), 540

MAPI Email, Project Server integration, 622

master projects, 362

Match function (Filter Enterprise Resources feature), 359

matching resources, 574

MBSA (Microsoft Baseline Security Analyzer), 681

MDStore objects, 805

measurement (Organizational Change tools), 17

measures (OLAP cubes), 401, 801

Meeting Workspace feature (Outlook), document management, 600

meeting workspaces, 643-644

Meeting Workspaces option (Documents and Lists page), 739

Members tab (Shared Workspace task pane), 640

mentoring, 20

Menu tabs (PWA interface screen), 301

menus (PWA), customizing, 767-769

merging status reports, 283, 313

message alerts (collaboration management), 64

methodology support (Project Server augmentation areas), 43

Microsoft Configuration Planning Guide [ITAL] website, 99

Microsoft IIS (Internet Information Services) log file format, 656

milestones, adding to Gantt charts, 632

Minimize option (Modify Shared Page feature), 737

Miscellaneous Reports option (PWA status reports), 314

Mitigation Plan field (Risks feature), 457

mixed authentication, 493

mixed views (Portfolio Analyzer view creation), 403-405

Mobilize phase (EPM implementation), 16

Model Projects in Portfolio Modeler feature (Project Center), 371

models (Portfolio Modeler)

analyzing data in, 431-433

creating, 424-428

Gantt charts, 430

viewing data in, 429

what-if analysis, 433-434

modified organizational RBS (Resource Breakdown Structure), 188

Modify Settings and Columns feature

Documents feature, 475

Issues feature, 468

Risks feature, 462

Modify Settings and Columns option (Documents and Lists page Action menu), 739-741

Modify Shared Page feature (WSS project workspace home page), 735-738

Modify Shared Web Parts option (Modify Shared Page feature), 737

Modify Site Content option (Customization area), 754

Modify Template page (PWA), 492

Modify Timesheet View page, 504-505

Modify View function, 505

Modify View screen (PWA)

Categories attribute, 213, 217, 221, 224

Default Group, Sort attribute, 212, 216, 220, 224

Field Width attribute, 211, 216, 220, 223

Fields attribute, 211, 216, 220, 223

Filter attribute, 212, 217, 221

Gantt Chart Format attribute, 212, 216, 224

Grouping Format attribute, 212, 216, 220, 224

Outline Levels attribute, 212, 217, 220, 224

RBS Filter attribute, 221

Splitter Bar, 212, 216, 224

Table attribute, 216

View Name and Description attribute, 211, 216, 220, 223

View Type attribute, 211, 215, 220-222

modifying

Assignment views, 222-225

Portfolio Analyzer views, 228-235

Project Center views, 210-214

Project views, 215-218

Resource Center views, 219-221

versions (projects), 523

views, 505

WSS settings, 447

changing permissions, 449-450

general settings, 448

modules

Risk module (Project Professional)

accessing, 597

risk attributes, specifying, 596

risks, viewing, 597

VBA macros as, 779

monitoring

AS, 660-661

OLAP, 660-661

Project Server

application log monitoring, 655

log file monitoring, 654-658

real-time monitoring, 654-655

security log monitoring, 655

SQL Server 2000 monitoring, 658-660

system growth (capacity planning), 694-695

Monitors tab (Project Server Health Monitor tool), 670

moving documents to document libraries, 642

MPM (Micro-Frame Program Manager), 51

MSPOLARBREAKOUT.dll, OLAP cube build breakout objects, 804-806

MSP_ASSN_FACT cube, 802

MSP_PORTFOLIO_ANALYZER cube, 802-803

MSP_RES_AVAIL_FACT cube, 803

MSP_WEB_CONVERSIONS database tables, PWA menu customizations, 768, 773

MSP_WEB_SECURITY_FEATURES_ACTIONS database tables, PWA menu customizations, 768, 773

MSP_WEB_SECURITY_MENUS database tables, PWA menu customizations, 768-769

MSP_WEB_SECURITY_ORG_PERMISSIONS database tables, PWA menu customizations, 773

MSP_WEB_SECURITY_PAGES database tables, PWA menu customizations, 768-769

Multipage Meeting Workspace option (Web Pages option), 749

multiple configurations (virtual EPM solution infrastructures), 132

Multiple Lines of Text option (Optional Settings for Column section), 452

multiple projects, opening from Project Center, 362

multivalue Enterprise Global Resource Outline codes versus single codes, 419, 422

My Alerts on This Site option (Manage My Information area), 754

My Computer account (Project Professional), 538

My Direct Reports category, 152

My Network Places (Office), configuring project workspaces, 640-641

My Organization category, 152

My Projects category, 152

My Projects document library group, 605

My Resources category, 152

My Tasks category, 152

N

Name and Description field

Documents feature, 469

WSS, 449

Name field (Documents feature), 471

naming categories, 153

Navigation field

Documents feature, 469

WSS, 449

NCSA (National Center for Supercomputer Applications) log file format, 656

networks
>bandwidth, 114-116
>diagrams (Project Professional scheduling), 29
>latency, 115-117, 688-689
>management/security (Operation Principles plans), 70
>performance (EPM solutions), 102
>system validation (Project Server), 262-263
>WAN, 116-117

New and Changed Assignments option (Project Professional), 610

New Outlook Shortcut option (Display Project Web Access Page in Outlook Web Page dialog), 620

NIC (network interface cards) cards, 115-116

No further role option (Delegate Tasks Wizard), 332

NoBanter parameter, PWA customization, 767

nodes (Project Server), 89

NoMenu parameter, PWA customization, 767

Non-Managed Time Periods option (Tasks page), 318

nonproject time (manager notifications), 333-334

nonproject-related WSS sites, creating, 756-758

NoSaveLinkButton parameter, PWA customization, 767

Notification and Reminders page (PWA), 529-530

Notify tab (Project Server Health Monitor tool), 671

Notify Your Manager of Time You Will Not Be Available for Project Work page (Tasks page), 333

Number option (Optional Settings for Column section), 452

O

ODBC log file format, 656

Office (MS)
>add-ins website, 52
>Document Workspace feature, document management, 600-602
>My Network Places, configuring project workspaces, 640-641
>Shared Workspace task pane, 601, 638-640

Office Web Components. *See* OWC

OLAP (online analytical processing) cubes, 800
>analysis server, 802
>creating, 518-520
>data warehouse, 801
>defining, 97
>detail data, defining, 97
>dimension tables, 801
>dimensions, 400-401, 801-802
>extension build process, 803-806
>fact tables, 801
>measures, 401, 801
>Portfolio Analyzer, 225-228, 395-398, 802
>staging table set (Project Server database tier), 96-98
>summary data, defining, 97
>updating, 517-518
>Windows Everyone security group, 398

Only the Projects Indicated Below option (Projects section), 155

Only the Resources Specified Below option (Resources section), 157

Open Enterprise Global Template function (Enterprise Options feature), 553

Open Enterprise Resource Pool function (Enterprise Options feature), 553-554

Open model function (Portfolio Modeler), 429

opening
>consolidated projects, 362
>Enterprise Resource Pool (Resource Center), 389
>master projects, 362
>projects from Project Center, 361-362
>status reports, 313

Operational Principles (Six Pillars of EPM), 20, 69-70

OPM3 (Organizational Project Management Maturity Model), 12

opportunity (EPM organizational impact), 22

optimization, SQL Server database maintenance, 664

Optimization tab (Maintenance Plan Wizard), 664

Optional Settings for Column section (Change Column Screen), 451-453

Organizational Change Framework website, 15

Organizational Change management (EPM implementation), 15-18

organizational RBS (Resource Breakdown Structure), 187-188

Organizational Readiness (Six Pillars of EPM), plan development, 20, 68

Organizational structures (Organizational Change tools), 17

Organizer (Project Professional), 550-552

organizing saved links, 385

Other Projects document library group, 605

OU (Organizational Units), 677

Outline Code Definition dialog (Project Professional), 557

Outline Levels attribute (Modify View screen), 212, 217, 220, 224

OutlineCodeUpdatesValue method (PDS), 795

Outlook

Calendar, viewing/reporting tasks, 332-333

Client tier (EPM solutions), 85

integration

collaboration management, 65

project workspaces, 642-644

PWA integration, 305, 616-621

MAPI Email/Project Server integration, 622

Meeting Workspace feature, document management, 600

Overallocated Resources Only function (Portfolio Modeler), 431

overhead tasks, 245-246

Overwrite Existing File(s)? field (Documents feature), 471

OWC (Office Web Components)

Chart, Project Analyzer views, 228

Client tier (EPM solutions), 86

PivotTable, Project Analyzer views, 228

Portfolio Analyzer, 86, 397

Owner field

Documents feature, 471

Issues feature, 464

Risks feature, 457

P

partitioning databases, Project Server database tier (EPM solutions), **96**

passwords, changing in PWA, **302**

patches (Windows Server), managing, **680**

PDS (Project Data Services), 793

Application tier (EPM solutions), 89-90, 93

AssignmentsGet method, 795

AssignmentsProjectManager Update method, 795

AssignmentsSave method, 795

data access, 91-92

data retrieval, 93

EnterpriseCustomFieldsUpdate method, 795

limitations of, 800

methods of, 794

OutlineCodeUpdateValues method, 795

PDSInfo method, 796

Project Server logons, 796-797

ProjectCodeValues method, 795

ProjectCodeValuesUpdate method, 795

PWA web parts, 800

requests

data extraction, 799

error checking, 798-799

forming, 797

sending/accepting, 798

ResourcesAdd method, 795

security cookie collection, 797

usage guide, 796

uses of, 794-795

website, 93

PDS Info tab (Project Server Health Monitor tool), 670

PDSInfo method (PDS), 796

PDSTest, 799

Percent work complete tracking method (Tasks page), 320, 325

performance

applications, capacity planning, 684-685

EPM solutions, 102

systems, monitoring (EPM solution design), 113

permissions

category permissions, building project teams, 564

data permissions, setting categories, 153-154

global permissions

assigning, 151

building project teams, 564

group permissions, 153

Manage Enterprise Features, Project Analyzer views, 227

Manage Views, Project Analyzer views, 227

Project Server 2003 security model, 106

skill-based scheduling, 578

status reports, 308

View Portfolio Analyzer, Project Analyzer views, 227

View Project Center, Project Analyzer views, 227

WSS permissions

changing, 449-450

group permissions, 444

list permissions, 445

personal rights (WSS), 446

Personal View option (Modify Shared Page feature), 738

PI (portfolio items), 48

Picture Libraries option (Create page), 742-743

Pictures feature (WSS project workspace home page), 734

pilot deployments (EPM installation prerequisites), 141

Pilot Phase (EPM deployment), 76-77

Pilot Production Stage (EPM deployment), 76-77

pivot tables (Portfolio Analyzer)

custom formula creation, 414-415, 418

formatting, 406-408

toolbars, 422-423

PivotTable (OWC), 228

PivotTable and PivotChart Report feature, 626

PivotTables (Excel), 625

Planning Stage (EPM deployment), 74-75

Planning the Project Server 2003 Infrastructure website, 103

PMI (Project Management Institute), 12

PMO (portfolio management office)
enterprise custom fields, 204
  creating, 164-169, 205
  defining, 205-206
  formula creation, 206
  graphical indicators, 206
  naming, 166
  overview of, 205
Enterprise Outline Codes
  code mask definitions, 163, 166
  creating, 164-169
  defining/designing, 164
  enterprise task outline codes, 202-204
  lookup table list hierarchies, 167
  naming, 166
  project outline codes, 169-173
  RBS code, 164
  resource outline codes, 174-190
Enterprise Resource Pool
  Active Directory management, 193
  Active Directory synchronization, 199-201
  active project migration, 193
  enterprise generic resources, 194-195
  enterprise resource creation, 196-199
  individual enterprise resources, 196
  individual local resources, 196
  local generic resources, 195-196
  manual creation, 192
  Project Server upgrades, 193
  PWA client creation, 194
  resource additions, 192
PointCast Network, capacity planning, 684
Portfolio Analyzer, 86, 395
accessing, 371
Active X components, 397

Analysis server and Cube attribute, 229
charts, formatting, 409, 412-413
Commands and Options function, 406-409, 412-413
Customize the PivotTable and Chart attribute, 230
customizing, 701-703
Enterprise Global Resource Outline codes, single versus multivalue, 419, 422
Excel, exporting tables to, 625
OLAP cubes, 395-401, 802
OWC, 397
pivot tables, formatting, 406-408
Portfolio Analyzer Mode attribute, 230
project management, defining views, 60
Project Web Access Category permissions, 398
resource management, defining views, 62
resources, 390
SMS, 397
SQL Analysis OLAP cube permissions, 398
SQL Analysis Services, 395-397
troubleshooting, 287, 675
View Name and Description attribute, 229
View Type attribute, 229
views, 225-226, 496
  adding, 502-503
  adding resources, 232
  adding Time dimension, 231
  changing chart types, 233-234
  Chart, 228
  creating, 228-235, 402-405
  custom pivot table formula creation, 414-415, 418
  displaying data, 395

Enterprise Outline Codes, 226, 230
  filtering data, 233
  formatting, 406-409, 412-413
  manipulating, 422-424
  modifying, 228-235
  OLAP cubes, 227-228
  PivotTable, 228
  required user permissions, 227
  restrictions, 159
  typical views, 393
  user interaction with, 395
Portfolio Analyzer Mode attribute (Portfolio Analyzer screen), 230
Portfolio Modeler, 371
Analyze function, 435-436
Compare function, what-if analysis, 434
Display Chart in Monochrome function, 432
Hover Mouse over Bar function, 432
models
  analyzing data in, 431-433
  creating, 424-428
  viewing data in, 429
  what-if analysis, 433-434
Open model function, 429
Overallocated Resources Only function, 431
overloaded resources, 424
project management, 60
Project Professional Substitute Resources function, 437-438
Refresh function, 431
Select the Resources to Display function, 431
Timescale function, 431
Toolbox function, 436
troubleshooting, 287
typical views, 393
Portfolio view (Project Center), 348

portfolios

managing

Portfolios (ProSight), 50

Portfolios Bridge
(ProSight), 50

via Project Center, 30-31,
352

strategic support (Project
Server augmentation
areas), 42

Portfolios (ProSight), 50

Portfolios Bridge (ProSight), 50

**Post-Launch Evaluation Phase
(EPM deployment), 78**

Print Grid feature

Project Center, 364-365

PWA grids, 624

Resource Center, 383

Print Grid option (Excel), 334

printing

Project Center views,
364-365

Resource Center views, 383

timesheets via Excel,
334-335

**Priority field (Issues feature),
465**

**Probability field (Risks feature),
457**

**Process Manager (Symphony
Suite), 52**

**process workflow manage-
ment, third-party add-ins, 52**

**Production Deployment Stage
(EPM deployment), 77**

**professional assistance (EPM
installation prerequisites),
138-139**

**program management, third-
party add-ins, 51**

**program management offices
(EPM installation prerequisites), 139**

**progress reports, troubleshoot-
ing, 284**

Project

Project object model, VBA
macros, 787

Record Macro dialog,
779-780

software requirements, 128

system requirements,
129-130

troubleshooting

assigned tasks, 284

baseline saves, 285

document access, 281

group security permis-
sions, 280

issue access, 281

lost tasks, 284

progress reports, 284

Project Portfolio access,
279

Project Portfolio security,
280

resource additions, 284

risk access, 281

saving project schedules
as templates, 280

status report requests,
283

tasks, 281-283

timesheets, data entry
modes, 278

to-do list creation, 283

viewing resource infor-
mation, 279

web access, 277-279

**Project Area resource outline
code, customizing, 714, 719**

**Project by Aircraft Type
resource outline code, customizing, 716**

Project Center, 345

accessing, 346

Analyze Projects in Portfolio
Analyzer, 371

Build Team function,
353-360

Check in My Projects fea-
ture, 375

Collaboration, 367-370

Create a New Personal or
Shared To-Do List func-
tion, 371-372

default functions table, 295

Export to Excel link, 365

Filter/Group/Search tab,
349-351

functions of, 346-347

Gantt Chart view, 363

Manage Administrative
Projects link, 377

Manage My To-Do Lists
function, 371-373

Model Projects in Portfolio
Modeler, 371

portfolio management,
30-31

Portfolio view, 348

Print Grid feature, 364-365

project management, defining views, 60

Project view, 349

projects

editing, 360

opening, 361-362

resource management,
adding Enterprise Global
Resource pool resources to
build teams, 62

Revert function, 351

To-Do List Options func-
tion, 371, 374

View a Project page, Link
Project Risks button, 366

View Options tab, 348-349

views, 347

customizing, 348-354

filters, 349

groups, 350

portfolio management,
352

printing, 364-365

searches, 351

**Project Center views, 158-159,
495**

adding, 498-499

creating, 210

modifying, 210-214

**Project Codes (Project Server),
configuring, 37**

**Project database table set
(Project Server database tier),
95**

**Project Detail feature (Build
Team function), 356, 360**

**Project Explorer, viewing/edit-
ing VBA macros, 782-783**

**Project Funding resource out-
line code, customizing, 714**

**Project Guide (Project
Professional), 28, 53**

**project initiation (Project
Server augmentation areas),
44**

**Project Life Cycle outline code,
customizing, 727**

Project Lifestyle resource outline code, customizing, 712

Project Location outline code, customizing, 705, 726

Project Location resource outline code, customizing, 711, 718

project management

lightweight project management support (Project Server augmentation areas), 44

Six Pillars of EPM, 19-20, 58

Artifact Management, plan development, 66-68

Collaboration Management, plan development, 64-65

Operational Principles, plan development, 69-70

Organizational Readiness, plan development, 68

Project Management, plan development, 59-61

Resource Management, plan development, 61-63

project managers

new tasks, reviewing, 329-330

nonproject time notifications, 333-334

project team collaboration

Collaboration features, 589-590, 597-599

documents management, 598-604

issues management, 597

large organizations, 591-592

Project Professional, 593

PWA, 593

risk management, 594-597

small organizations, 590

solution websites, 593

updating project progress, 606-611

project teams, interaction with (EPM organizational impact), 24

role in EPM, 24

timesheets, update cycles, 319

Updates page (PWA), 336

Accept/Reject Task Column and Updates List option, 339

Adjust Actuals in the Resource Center option, 343

Alert Me option, 340

Approve Timesheets in the Resource Center option, 344

Baseline Work, 339

Customization tabs, 339

Indicators column, 340

rules for, 340-341

saving schedule changes, 338

Set Rules for Automatically Accepting Changes option, 341

time approvals, 337-338

time rejections, 338

Updates action bar option, 339

View History option, 342-343

View Timesheet Summary in the Resource Center option, 343

project outline codes (Enterprise Outline Codes)

attributes example, 172-173

creating, 173

defining, 170-171

planning, 169-170

troubleshooting, 173

Project Performing Division Enterprise Outline Code, customizing, 707

Project Phase outline code, customizing, 722-724

Project Phase resource outline code, customizing, 720

Project Portfolio, troubleshooting, 279-280

Project Portfolio by Area outline code, customizing, 727

Project Portfolio by Global Alliances resource outline code, customizing, 716

Project Portfolio Sector resource outline code, customizing, 715

Project Premier Partners, EPM installation, 139

Project Priority Enterprise Outline Code, customizing, 707

Project Professional, 33

Analyze Timescaled Data Wizard, 626

Build Team from Enterprise feature, 564

adding generic resources to project teams, 571

adding individual resources to project teams, 573

determining resource availability, 569

disabling filtering for resource availability, 576

removing project team resources, 575

replacing generic resources with individual resources, 573

replacing individual resources, 575

selecting project team features, 566

WAN, 576

Client tier (EPM solutions), 85

collaboration management, 65

compatibility of, 28

Customize Enterprise Fields dialog, 556

document libraries, features of, 605

enterprise custom fields, 204

creating, 164-169, 205

defining, 205-206

formula creation, 206
graphical indicators, 206
naming, 166
overview of, 205
Enterprise Global Resource
Pool access, 35
Enterprise Global templates
backups, 251-252
customizing, 555-561
data restoration, 252
locating, 538
Enterprise Options feature
accessing, 538
Account Properties dialog, 539
Automatically Detect
Connection State
option, 540
Backup Enterprise Global
Template function, 554
Calculation tab, 546-547
Calendar tab, 544-545
Collaborate tab, 548
Edit tab, 544
General tab, 543
Import Project to
Enterprise function,
554
Import Resources to
Enterprise function,
554
Interface tab, 549
Manually Control
Connection State
option, 540
Microsoft Project Server
Accounts function, 552
Open Enterprise Global
Template function, 553
Open Enterprise Resource
Pool function, 553-554
Project Server account
creation, 539
Project Server Accounts
dialog, 540-541
Restore Enterprise Global
Template function, 554
Save tab, 549
Schedule tab, 545-546
Security tab, 550
Spelling tab, 547
View tab, 542

Enterprise Outline Codes
code mask definitions,
163, 166
creating, 164-169
defining/designing, 164
enterprise task outline
codes, 202-204
lookup table list hierarchies, 167
naming, 166
project outline codes,
169-173
RBS code, 164
resource outline codes,
174-190
Enterprise Resource Pool
Active Directory management, 193
Active Directory synchronization, 199-201
active project migration,
193
enterprise generic
resources, 194-195
enterprise resource creation, 196-199
individual enterprise
resources, 196
individual local
resources, 196
local generic resources,
195-196
manual creation, 192
Project Server upgrades,
193
PWA client creation, 194
resource additions, 192
features of, 35
functions of, 28
Graphical Indicators dialog,
560
Issues module, 597-598
My Computer account, 538
New and Changed
Assignments option, 610
Organizer, project objects,
550-552
Outline Code Definition
dialog, 557
Project Guide, 28
project management,
Enterprise Global settings,
60

Project Server accounts
connecting to, 541
creating, 539
modifying properties,
540
selecting connection
type, 540
Project Server connections,
examples of, 541
project team collaboration,
593-597
Publish All Information
option, 610
Publish Project Plan option,
610
Republish Assignments to
Refresh Data on Members'
Tasks Page or Force and
Update Assignment
Information option, 610
Resources Substitution
Wizard, 438-439, 576-578
Choose Projects screen,
580
Choose Related Projects
screen, 582
Choose Resources screen,
581-582
Choose Scheduling
Options screen, 583
Choose Update Options
screen, 585
Finish screen, 586
functions of, 580
limitations of, 579
Review Results screen,
584
Substitute Resource
screen, 583
Welcome screen, 580
Risk module, 596-597
scheduling, 29-30, 279
software requirements, 128
Substitute Resources function, 437-438
system requirements,
129-130
Timesheet Update cycle, 319
troubleshooting, 674
Value List dialog, 559
views, creating/managing,
236-237

Visio integration
  exporting Gantt charts to project schedules, 633
  exporting Visio timelines to project schedules, 629-630
  importing Gantt charts to project schedules, 631
  importing project schedule data to Visio timelines, 628-629
  Visio WBS Chart Wizard, 627-628
project quality (EPM implementation), 14
project schedule checks (QSA add-in), 46
project schedule templates
  EPM deployment plans, 79
  saving, troubleshooting, 280
Project Scope resource outline code, customizing, 715
Project Server
  accounts
    connecting to, 540-541
    creating in Project Professional, 539
    modifying properties, 540
  Accounts dialog (Enterprise Options feature), 540-541
  AD, Windows Server 2003, 652
  adding node, 89
  administrative projects
    administrator selection, 242
    advantages of, 241
    company policies, 241
    creating, 241-245
    goal of, 240
    maintenance, 247
    overhead tasks, 245-246
    removing inactive resources, 247
    reporting cycle selection, 246
    special features of, 244

  application layer, troubleshooting, 668
    analysis services errors, 671-672
    EditSite.exe tool, 669
    Project Server Health Monitor tool, 669-671
    session manager errors, 672-673
    Views Processing errors, 673
  Application tier (EPM solutions), 88, 93-95
  architecture of, 33-34
  AS, 653, 660-661
  augmentation areas
    budgeting/forecasting, 42
    governance, 44
    interdependency management, 43-44
    lightweight project management support, 44
    list of, 40
    methodology support, 43
    project initiation, 44
    project timesheets versus labor timesheets, 41-42
    resource commitment management versus usage management, 42
    standardization validation/support, 43
    strategic portfolio support, 42
    vendor management, 43-44
  authentication mode, setting, 493-494
  client layer
    elements of, 668
    troubleshooting, 673-675
  Company calendar, 248
  Configuration Planning Guide website, 103-104, 115
  configuring
    administrative settings, 37
    Enterprise Global Resource Pool, 36
    Enterprise Global Templates/Project Codes, 37

  resource/project calendars, 36
  security model, 36
  time tracking methods, 36
  database tier (EPM solutions), 95-98
  databases, 662
  Deployment Resources website, 103
  disaster recovery, 667
  Documents feature synchronization, 475
  Enterprise calendar, 248-249
  EPM solutions
    data usage, 102-103
    server security, 102
  federations, 696-698
  Health Monitor tool, 669-671
  hotfixes, 680-681
  Installation Guide website, 118, 123-125
  Internet Security tab, 673-674
  issue synchronization, 468
  logons via PDS, 796-797
  MAPI Email integration, 622
  monitoring
    application log monitoring, 655
    log file monitoring, 654-658
    real-time monitoring, 654-655
    security log monitoring, 655
    SQL Server 2000 monitoring, 658-660
  multiple configurations, 131
  OLAP Services, 653, 660-661
  Outlook connections, 618
  Planning Configuration Guide website, 113
  Project Professional connections, examples of, 541
  published tasks, troubleshooting user assignment, 282-283
  Resource calendar, managing, 249-250

Risks feature (PWA) synchronization, 462

security
  adding categories, 153
  Allow/Deny feature, 145, 153
  assigning groups to categories, 153
  assigning resources to category groups, 161
  associating groups to categories, 160
  categories as role-based names, 159-160
  category restrictions, 154-160
  configuring via Server Configuration Features template, 145-146
  defining categories, 151-152
  design recommendations, 162
  identifying user groups, 147
  process flow diagram, 143
  RBS, 190
  naming categories, 153
  security groups, 149-151
  security model, 105-106
  security templates, 147-149
  setting category data permissions, 153-154
  setting category group permissions, 153

Security Group Guide website, 102, 552
service accounts, 262
service packs, 680-681
Session Manager, 653
SQL Server database maintenance, 662-667
Standard calendar, 248
terminal services, 675-679
third-party development information websites, 41
troubleshooting
  adjust actuals, 288
  application layer/client layer determination, 668
  data accuracy, 286-287

duplicate global.mpt files, 288-289
Portfolio Analyzer, 287
Portfolio Modeler, 287
published version deletion, 289
resource allocation process, 285-286
resource calendars, 289-290
Resource Substitution Wizard, 287
rule application, 288
task updates, 288
validation, 259-260
  basic configuration validation, 273
  business process validation, 274
  technology validation, 261-271
VP, 93-94, 653
workspaces, accessing, 442
WSS, 653, 809

Project Sponsoring Division Enterprise Outline Code, customizing, 707
Project Status Enterprise Outline Code, customizing, 705-706
Project Status outline code, customizing, 721, 726
Project Status resource outline code, customizing, 711, 720
Project Strategic Alignment resource outline code, customizing, 714
project teams
  collaboration
    Collaboration features, 589-590, 597-599
    documents management, 598-604
    issues management, 597
    large organizations, 591-592
    Project Professional, 593
    PWA, 593
    risk management, 594-597
  small organizations, 590
  solution websites, 593
  updating project progress, 605-611

project managers, interaction with (EPM organizational impact), 24
removing team members, 575
required global/category permissions, 564
resources
  adding generic resources, 571
  adding individual resources, 572
  assigning, 564
  determining availability, 569-571
  grouping resources, 566
  replacing generic resources with individual resources, 573-574
  replacing individual resources, 575
  selecting, 565-569
  skill-based scheduling, 577-578

project timesheets versus labor timesheets, 41-42
Project Type Enterprise Outline Code, customizing, 706
Project Type resource outline code, customizing, 713
Project views
  adding, 496-497
  creating, 215
  modifying, 215-218
  Show Outline Level option, 349
  Show Summary Tasks option, 349
  Show Time with Date option, 349
  Summary Rollup option, 349
Project Workspace option (Web Pages option), 749
Project Workspace templates, Team Member site group permissions, 445
project workspaces (PWA), 32
  configuring, 640-641
  documents, saving, 641
  Excel integration, 645-647
  Office integration, 640

Outlook integration,
642-644
templates, Team Member
site group permissions,
445
project workspaces (WSS)
accessing, 733
Create page, customizing,
742-749
Documents and Lists page,
customizing, 738-741
home page, 733
Announcements feature,
734
customizing, 735-738
Discussions feature, 734
Documents feature, 734
Events feature, 734
Links feature, 735
Lists feature, 734
Modify Shared Page fea-
ture, 735
Pictures feature, 734
Surveys feature, 734
WSS site image feature,
734
manual creation, 733
quick launch bar, 733
Site Settings page, customizing, 749-754
templates, PWA Site
Provisioning, 752
top navigation menu, 733
**project-centric views (Portfolio
Analyzer view creation), 403**
**ProjectCodeValues method
(PDS), 795**
**ProjectCodeValuesUpdate
method (PDS), 795**
projects
administrative projects
administrator selection,
242
advantages of, 241
company policies, 241
creating, 241-245
goal of, 240
maintenance, 247
managing, 376-377
overhead tasks, 245-246

removing inactive
resources, 247
reporting cycle selection,
246
special features of, 244
build teams
adding resources, 358
changing resource book-
ing type, 359
creating, 355
matching resources, 359
removing resources, 358
replacing resources, 359
viewing resource avail-
ability, 360
checking in, 375
clustering within header
groups, 362
consolidated projects, 362
deleting, 533
editing in Project Center,
360
linking risks to tasks, 366
management
lightweight project man-
agement support
(Project Server augmen-
tation areas), 44
Six Pillars of EPM, 19-20,
58-70
master projects, 362
objects
copying, 552
deleting, 552
list of, 550-551
renaming, 552
opening from Project
Center, 361-362
progress reports, trou-
bleshooting, 284
task insertion, troubleshooting, 282
versions
adding custom versions
to Manage Enterprise
Features function (PWA
Admin tab), 521
deleting, 523
modifying, 523
WBS, 555

**Projects and Resources by Area
of Capital Expenditures
resource outline code, customizing, 719**
**Projects and Resources by
Sector resource outline code,
customizing, 718**
**Projects by Aircraft Type
resource outline code, customizing, 716**
**Projects by Branch resource
outline code, customizing,
717**
**Projects by Construction
Component outline code, customizing, 722**
**Projects by Core Support Area
outline code, customizing,
725**
**Projects by Core Technologies
outline code, customizing,
724**
**Projects by Emerging
Biopharmaceuticals outline
code, customizing, 725**
**Projects by Healthcare Area
resource outline code, cus-
tomizing, 717**
**Projects by Type of Capital
Expenditures resource outline
code, customizing, 719**
**Projects by Types of
Construction outline code,
customizing, 722**
**Projects section (Categories
page), 155-156**
Projects tab (PWA), 59
**Properties window (Project),
viewing/editing VBA macros,
783-784**
ProSight, 42
ProSight Portfolios, 50
ProSight Portfolios Bridge, 50
**Prototype Phase (EPM deploy-
ment), 75**
Proxycfg.exe, 669
PSCOMPlus.exe, 669
psHealthMon.exe, 669
**public document libraries,
604-605**

Publish All Information option (Project Professional), 610

Publish Project Plan option (Project Professional), 610

published versions, deleting, 289

publishing

collaboration projects, 609-610

Excel lists to project workspaces, 646

PWA (Project Web Access), 33, 293

accessing, 299-300

Add Category page, 489

Add Group page, 486

Add Version page, 521

adding Office Project Server 2003 nodes, 89

Admin page, 35, 477

About Microsoft Office Project Server 2003 function, 480

Clean Up Project Server Database function, 480, 531-534

Customize Project Web Access function, 479, 524-530

functions list, 477

Manage Enterprise Features function, 479, 516-523

Manage Security function, 488-494

Manage Users and Groups function, 478-488

Manage Views function, 479, 494-506

Manage Windows SharePoint Services function, 479, 512-516

Server Configuration function, 479, 507-512

analysis server, 802

Appointment dialog, viewing assignment details, 619

Assign Myself to an Existing Task page, 330

Assignment views, creating/modifying, 222-225

Build Team feature, 564

resource type designations, 566

selecting project team resources via predefined filters, 567

selecting resources for project teams, 565

Category permissions, 398

Clean Up Project Server Database page, 532

client system requirements, 129-130

Client tier (EPM solutions), 86

client users, 192

collaboration management, status reports, 64

Communications plans, 32

Connect to SharePoint Server page, 513

Create a New Task page, 329

customizing, 701, 766

adding ASP pages, 770-773

adding external pages, 774-778

Allow Project Managers to Change the Default Method for Reporting Progress If a Different Method Is Appropriate for a Specific Project option, 702

Force Project Managers to Use the Progress Reporting Method Specified Above for All Projects option, 702

locking down defaults, 702

Managed Time Periods option, 702

menu modifications, 767-769

NoBanter parameter, 767

NoMenu parameter, 767

NoSaveLinkButton parameter, 767

SimpleUI parameter, 767

single instances, 778

stylesheet modifications, 767

tracking settings, 702

views, 703

Documents feature, 32, 66, 468

Alert Me option, 474-475

All Document Libraries feature, 472

Check Out field, 473

default functions table, 297

Delete field, 473

Discuss field, 474

document creation, 470

Document Template field, 469

Document Versions field, 469

Edit in the Document Application field, 473

editing documents in datasheets, 472

Explorer view, 474

exporting documents to spreadsheets, 475

Linking field, 471

Modify Settings and Columns feature, 475

Name and Description field, 469

Name field, 471

Navigation field, 469

Overwrite Existing File(s)? field, 471

Owner field, 471

Project Server synchronization, 475

Status field, 471

Upload Multiple Files field, 471

uploading documents, 471

Version History field, 473

View Properties and Edit Properties field, 473

viewing document folder contents, 470

Enterprise Global Resource Pool, 31

Excel integration

displaying timescaled data in Excel, 626

exporting Portfolio Analyzer tables to Excel, 625

exporting PWA grids to
Excel, 622-624
importing external data
to Excel, 626
features of, 34
functions, 294
Gantt Chart Formats page,
524
Go Offline function, 303
grids, 622-624
Grouping Formats page, 527
Groupings in the Project
Center in the Grouping
formats page, 526
Groups page, 485
home page, 302
Alert Me function,
305-308
default functions table,
294-297
linking to, 528-529
Work with Outlook link,
305
Home Page Format page,
adding PWA home page
links, 528-529
IIS 6.0, 652
interface screen, 301
Internet Explorer, setting
options for offline operation, 303-304
Issues feature, 462
Alert Me option, 467
Assigned To field, 464
attaching files to issues,
465
Category field, 464
creating issues, 463
Discussion field, 465
Due Date field, 465
editing issues in
datasheets, 467
exporting issues to
spreadsheets, 467
filtering issues, 466
issue summaries, 463
Linking to Tasks, Risks,
Other Issues, or
Documents field, 465
Modify Settings and
Columns feature, 468

Owner field, 464
Priority field, 465
Project Server synchro-
nization, 468
Resolution field, 465
Status field, 464
Title field, 464
viewing reports, 466
Issues page, 32, 67, 296
Logon screen, 300
Manage Windows
SharePoint Services Sites
page, 514
Modify Template page, 492
Modify Timesheet View
page, 504
Modify View screen
Categories attribute, 213,
217, 221, 224
Default Group, Sort
attribute, 212, 216,
220, 224
Field Width attribute,
211, 216, 220, 223
Fields attribute, 211, 216,
220, 223
Filter attribute, 212, 217,
221
Gantt Chart Format
attribute, 212, 216, 224
Grouping Format
attribute, 212, 216,
220, 224
Outline Levels attribute,
212, 217, 220, 224
RBS Filter attribute, 221
Splitter Bar, 212, 216,
224
Table attribute, 216
View Name and
Description attribute,
211, 216, 220, 223
View Type attribute, 211,
215, 220-222
navigating, 301
Notification and Reminders
page, 530
offline operation
resetting changes, 304
setting Internet Explorer
options, 303-304

online access, re-establish-
ing, 304
Operational Principles
plans, 69
Outlook integration, 305
displaying digital dash-
boards in Outlook, 621
displaying PWA in
Outlook, 620-621
help, 617
importing project tasks,
618
importing task lists from
Outlook, 619-620
installing PWA add-in,
616-617
Project Server/Outlook
connections, 618
Project Web Access Add-
in for Outlook
Integration Wizard, 616
reviewing project tasks,
618
updating/submitting
assignments, 619
passwords, changing, 302
Portfolio Analyzer, 395, 802
Active X components,
397
adding views, 502-503
charts, formatting, 409,
412-413
Commands and Options
function, 406-409,
412-413
creating views, 402-405
custom pivot table for-
mula creation in views,
414-415, 418
displaying view data, 395
Enterprise Global
Resource Outline codes,
single versus multi-
value, 419, 422
formatting views,
406-409, 412-413
manipulating views,
422-424
OLAP cubes, 395-401
OWC, 397
pivot tables, formatting,
406-408

project management,
defining views, 60
Project Web Access
Category permissions,
398
resource management,
defining views, 62
SMS, 397
SQL Analysis Services,
395-398
typical views, 393
user interaction with
views, 395
view creation, 402-405
Portfolio Analyzer screen,
229-230
Portfolio Analyzer views,
225-226
adding resources, 232
adding Time dimension,
231
changing chart types,
233-234
creating, 228-235
Enterprise Outline
Codes, 226, 230
filtering, 233
modifying, 228-235
OLAP cubes, 227-228
required user permis-
sions, 227
Portfolio Model
Analyze function,
435-436
Compare function, 434
Project Professional
Substitute Resources
function, 437-438
Toolbox function, 436
Portfolio Modeler
analyzing model data,
431-433
Display Chart in
Monochrome function,
432
Hover Mouse over Bar
function, 432
model creation, 424-428
Open model function,
429
Overallocated Resources
Only function, 431
overloaded resources,
424

Refresh function, 431
Select the Resources to
Display function, 431
Timescale function, 431
typical views, 393
viewing model data, 429
what-if analysis (models),
433-434
Project Center
creating views, 210
default functions table,
295
modifying views,
210-214
portfolio management,
30-31, 60-62
project management, user
security roles, 59
Project Professional, 33
collaboration manage-
ment, 65
compatibility of, 28
Enterprise Global
Resource Pool access,
35
features of, 35
functions of, 28
Project Guide, 28
project management,
Enterprise Global set-
tings, 60
scheduling, 29-30
project team collaboration,
593, 596-597
Project views, creating/mod-
ifying, 215-218
project workspaces, 32
Projects tab, 59
Request a Status Report
page, 308
Resource Center, 61
collaboration manage-
ment, timesheet sum-
maries, 65
creating/modifying
views, 219-221
default functions table,
295
resource management,
managing views, 62
risk management, 32
Risks page, 454
Alert Me option, 460
Assigned To field, 457

Category field, 457
Contingency Plan field,
457
Cost field, 457
default functions table,
296
Description field, 457
Due Date field, 457
editing risks in
datasheets, 461
exporting risks to spreadsheets, 460-461
filtering risks, 460
Impact field, 457
linking risks to tasks, 458
Mitigation Plan field, 457
Modify Settings and
Columns feature, 462
Owner field, 457
Probability field, 457
Project Server synchro-
nization, 462
risk creation, 455-457
risk summaries, 455
Status field, 457
Title field, 457
Trigger Description field,
457
Trigger field, 457
viewing reports, 460
viewing/reporting risks,
459
schedule data storage, 31
Site Provisioning, WSS project workspace templates,
752
Specify Views page, 495
adding Assignment views
to, 499
adding Portfolio Analyzer
views to, 502-503
adding Project Center
views to, 498-499
adding Project views to,
496
adding Resource Center
views to, 501-502
Categories attribute, 235
Copy View function, 505
Default View Settings
attribute, 234
Delete View function,
506

managing Timesheet views, 504

Modify View function, 505

SPS integration, 807-808

status reports, 307

  Alert Me function, 308

  archived reports, 314-315

  compiling, 313

  creating, 309-310

  deleting, 313-314

  editing, 314

  Filter and Group Reports tab, 315

  hyperlinking to, 313

  merging, 313

  Miscellaneous Reports option, 314

  opening, 313

  permissions, 308

  removing from PWA, 308

  requesting, 308-310

  Status Reports Archive option, 314

  submitting, 311-312

  viewing, 313

Status Reports Overview page, 308-309

Status Reports page, 32, 296

Tasks page, 317

  accessing, 318

  action bar, 328

  Actual work tracking method, 320, 326

  Alert Me function, 328

  current/all tasks, viewing, 323

  Day-by-day tracking method, 320, 326

  default functions table, 294-295

  Delegation tab, 331-332

  estimates to complete, 317

  Filter, Group, Search tab, 324

  Grid and Timesheet entry view, 321-322, 325

  Managed Time Periods option, 318

  Non-Managed Time Periods option, 318

Notify Your Manager of Time You Will Not Be Available for Project Work page, 333

Percent Work Complete tracking method, 320, 325

Remaining Work field, 325-327

Save Changes button, 327

Show Overtime Work option, 324

Show Scheduled Work option, 324

Show Summary Tasks option, 323

Timesheet Update cycle, 319

Update All button, 327

Update Selected Rows button, 327

View Options tab, 323

third-party add-ins, EPK Suite, 47-50

Timesheet view, 320

timesheets

  defining current tasks, 255

  Lock Down Defaults, 253

  specifying task progress report methods, 252

  time period settings, selecting, 253-254

updates, 297-298

Updates page, 336

  Accept/Reject Task Column and Updates List option, 339

  Adjust Actuals in the Resources Center option, 343

  Alert Me option, 340

  Approve Timesheets in the Resources Center option, 344

  Baseline Work, 339

  Customization tabs, 339

  default functions table, 296

  functions of, 606-607

  Indicators column, 340

rules for, 340-341

saving schedule changes, 338

Set Rules for Automatically Accepting Changes option, 341

time approvals, 337-338

time rejections, 338

Updates action bar option, 339

updating project team collaboration work-flows, 606

View History option, 342-343

View Timesheet Summary in the Resources Center option, 343

Versions page, 521

views

  EPM deployment, 138

  managing, 235

web parts, PDS, 800

Windows SharePoint Services Team Web Site Provisioning Settings page, 513

Workspace page, default functions table, 297

Q - R

QPA (Quantum Portfolio Auditor), 43

QSA (QuantumPM Schedule Auditor), 43-46

quick launch bar (WSS project workspaces), 733

RBS (Resource Breakdown Structure) enterprise resource outline code, 164, 388

  defining, 185-186

  geographical RBS code, 188-189

modified organizational RBS code, 188

modifying, 187

organizational RBS code, 187-188

organizational requirements, 186

Project Server security, 190

RBS Filter attribute (Modify View screen), 221

real-time monitoring (Project Server), 654-655

Record Macro dialog (Microsoft Project 2003), 779-780

recording VBA macros, 779-780

Refresh Data function (pivot table toolbars), 423

Refresh function (Portfolio Modeler), 431

RegAsm.exe utility, 804

Reject button (Tasks page action bar), 328

Remaining Availability view (View Availability function), 386

Remaining Work field (Tasks page), 325-327

Remove button (Filter Enterprise Resources feature), 358

removing

custom filters from project resource selections, 569

fields from Grid and Timesheet entry view (Tasks page), 322

resources from project teams, 575

team members from project teams, 575

renaming

Gantt charts, 524-525

groupings, 526-527

reordering columns (WSS), 453

Replace function (Filter Enterprise Resources feature), 359

report generation (Project Professional scheduling), 30

reporting

risks via Risks feature (PWA), 459

tasks in Outlook Calendar, 332-333

reporting structures (EPM deployment plans), 79

reports

issue reports, viewing, 466

viewing via Risks feature (PWA), 460

repositioning timesheet columns, 325

Republish Assignments to Refresh Data on Members' Tasks Page or Force and Update Assignment Information option (Project Professional), 610

Request a Status Report page (PWA), 308

Request Task Status button (Delegation tab), 332

requests

PDS requests, 797-799

status reports, 308-310

Resolution field (Issues feature), 465

resource assignment (Project Professional scheduling), 29

Resource by Skill Set resource outline code, customizing

air industry examples, 716-717

for research and development, 712-713

resource calendars

managing (Project Server), 249-250

troubleshooting, 289-290

Resource Center, 61

accessing, 379

Adjust Actuals feature, 391-392

Analyze Projects in Portfolio Analyzer feature, 390

Approve Timesheets option, 378

collaboration management, timesheet summaries, 65

default functions table, 295

Edit button, 389

Enterprise Resource Pool, 389

Export to Excel link, 383-384

Filter/Group/Search tab

Autofilter option, 382

Custom Filter option, 381

Filter option, 381

Group By function, 382

Search function, 383

Managed Timesheets option, 378

Print Grid, 383

resource management, managing views, 62

Save Link button, 385

uses of, 378

View Availability function, 385-387

View Options function, 381, 386

View Resource Assignments feature, 390-391

View Timesheet Summary option, 378

views, 158, 496

adding, 501-502

choosing, 386

creating, 219

custom view creation, 385

customizing, 380

filters, 381

groups, 382

modifying, 219-221

printing, 383

Resource Summary view, Checked Out By column, 380

searches, 383

resource commitment management versus usage management, 42

resource contention (EPM implementation), 14

Resource Details section (View Availability function), 387

Resource Distribution of Medical and Clinical Staff outline code, 725

Resource Freeze option (Choose Resources screen), 582

Resource Management (Six Pillars of EPM), 19
plan development, 61
plan development, business processes, 63
plan development, technology items, 62-63
resource matching, 177, 574
resource outline codes
attribute assignments, 183-184
attribute edits, 184
attributes example, 178-179
creating, 177-179
customizing
Project Area outline code, 714, 719
Project by Aircraft Type outline code, air industry examples, 716
Project Funding outline code, for government agencies, 714
Project Life Cycle outline code, information technology industry examples, 727
Project Lifestyle outline code, for research and development, 712
Project Location outline code, 711, 718, 726
Project Phase outline code, 720-724
Project Portfolio by Area outline code, information technology industry examples, 727
Project Portfolio by Global Alliances outline code, air industry examples, 716
Project Portfolio Sector outline code, air industry examples, 715
Project Scope outline code, for government agencies, 715
Project Status outline code, 711, 720-721, 726

Project Strategic Alignment outline code, for government agencies, 714
Project Type outline code, for government agencies, 713
Projects and Resources by Area of Capital Expenditures outline code, oil and gas industry examples, 719
Projects and Resources by Sector outline code, healthcare sector examples, 718
Projects by Aircraft Type outline code, air industry examples, 716
Projects by Branch outline code, healthcare sector examples, 717
Projects by Construction Component outline code, construction industry examples, 722
Projects by Core Support Area outline code, pharmaceuticals/biopharmaceuticals industry examples, 725
Projects by Core Technologies outline code, pharmaceuticals/biopharmaceuticals industry examples, 724
Projects by Emerging Biopharmaceuticals outline code, pharmaceuticals/biopharmaceuticals industry examples, 725
Projects by Healthcare Area outline code, healthcare sector examples, 717
Projects by Type of Capital Expenditures outline code, oil and gas industry examples, 719

Projects by Types of Construction outline code, construction industry examples, 722
Resource by Skill Set outline code, 712-713, 716-717
Resource Distribution of Medical and Clinical Staff outline code, pharmaceuticals/biopharmaceuticals industry examples, 725
Resource RBS outline code, for research and development, 712
Resource Role outline code, for research and development, 713
Resource Skill Set Classification outline code, healthcare sector examples, 718
Resources by Certification outline code, 709
Resources by Construction Management Position outline code, construction industry examples, 723
Resources by Core Construction Skills outline code, construction industry examples, 723
Resources by Location outline code, 708
Resources by RBS outline code, 708
Resources by Skill Set outline code, 708, 720-727
Resources by Type outline code, 709
defining, 176
multiple skills per resource, 181
multivalue skills, 181
planning, 174-176

RBS
    customizing, 712-713
    defining, 185-186
    geographical RBS code,
        188-189
    modified organizational
        RBS code, 188
    modifying, 187
    organizational RBS code,
        187-188
    organizational require-
        ments, 186
    Project Server security,
        190
    resource matching, 177
    skill definitions, 176
    skill matching, 183
    skill proficiency level defini-
        tions, 180
    skill value assignments, 177
    troubleshooting, 184
    usage scenarios, 178
**Resource Role resource outline
    code, customizing for
    research and development,
    713**
**Resource Skill Set Classification
    resource outline code, cus-
    tomizing, 718**
**resource substitution algo-
    rithms, 427**
**Resource Substitution Wizard,
    438-439, 576-578**
    Choose Projects screen, 580
    Choose Related Projects
        screen, 582
    Choose Resources screen,
        581-582
    Choose Scheduling Options
        screen, 583
    Choose Update Options
        screen, 585
    Finish screen, 586
    functions of, 580
    limitations of, 579
    Review Results screen, 584
    Substitute Resources screen,
        583
    troubleshooting, 287
    Welcome screen, 580
**resource tables, updating,
    517-520**

**resource tasks, deleting
    changes, 532**
**resource-centric views
    (Portfolio Analyzer view cre-
    ation), 403-404**
resources
    actual work, adjusting,
        391-392
    adding to projects, 358
    additions, troubleshooting,
        284
    allocation process, trou-
        bleshooting, 285-286
    analyzing, 390
    assigning
        to groups, 161
        to project teams, 564
    assignments, viewing,
        390-391
    availability
        determining for project
            teams, 569-571
        viewing, 360
    booking condition, chang-
        ing, 354-355
    booking type, changing, 359
    deleting, 533-534
    editing, 388-389
    Enterprise Resource Pool,
        modifying, 553
    exporting data to Excel,
        383-384
    generic resources, 571-574
    groups, 351
    individual resources,
        572-574
    information, viewing, 279
    managing via Enterprise
        Global Resource Pool
        (PWA), 31
    matching in projects, 359
    Portfolio Analyzer views,
        adding to, 232
    project teams, grouping for,
        566
    RBS code, 388
    removing from
        project teams, 575
        projects, 358
    replacing
        in projects, 359
        individual resources, 575

    selecting for project teams,
        565
        skill-based selections,
            566-567
        via custom filters,
            568-569
        via predefined filters, 567
        work availability, 569
    skill-based scheduling,
        577-578
    synchronizing via Enterprise
        Global Resource Pool
        (PWA), 31
**Resources by Certification out-
    line code, customizing, 709**
**Resources by Construction
    Management Position outline
    code, customizing, 723**
**Resources by Core Construction
    Skills outline code, customiz-
    ing, 723**
**Resources by Location outline
    code, customizing, 708**
**Resources by RBS outline code,
    customizing, 708**
**Resources by Skill Set outline
    code, customizing, 708**
    construction industry exam-
        ples, 722-723
    information technology
        examples, 727
    oil and gas industry exam-
        ples, 720-721
    pharmaceuticals/biopharma-
        ceuticals industry exam-
        ples, 725-726
**Resources by Type outline
    code, customizing, 709**
**Resources section (Categories
    page), 157-158**
**Resources Summary view
    (Resource Center), Checked
    Out By column, 380**
**ResourcesAdd method (PDS),
    795**
**resourcing (Organizational
    Change tools), 17**
**Restore Enterprise Global
    Template function (Enterprise
    Options feature), 554**
**restoring Enterprise Global
    templates, 252, 554**
**retitling document workspace
    sites, 639**

Revert function (Project Center), 351

Review Results screen (Resource Substitution Wizard), 584

reviewing tasks, 329-330, 618

rewards and recognition (Organizational Change tools), 17

risk management

project team collaboration, 594-597

PWA, 32

third-party add-ins, Risk+ (C/S Solutions, Inc.), 51

Risk module (Project Professional), 596-597

risk tracking (project team collaboration), 596-597

Risk+ (C/S Solutions, Inc.), 51

risks, 454

access, troubleshooting, 281

creating, 455-457

datasheets, editing in, 461

filtering via, 460

project tasks, linking to, 366

PWA, displaying in, 302

reporting, 459

spreadsheets, exporting to, 460-461

summaries, viewing, 455

viewing, 459

Risks page (PWA), 454

Alert Me option, 460

Assigned To field, 457

Category field, 457

Contingency Plan field, 457

Cost field, 457

default functions table, 296

Description field, 457

Due Date field, 457

Impact field, 457

Mitigation Plan field, 457

Modify Settings and Columns feature, 462

Owner field, 457

Probability field, 457

Project Server synchronization, 462

risks

creating, 455-457

editing in datasheets, 461

exporting to spreadsheets, 460-461

filtering, 460

viewing reports, 460

viewing summaries, 455

viewing/reporting, 459

Status field, 457

tasks, linking risks to, 458

Title field, 457

Trigger Description field, 457

Trigger field, 457

Risks lists, 745

role test cases, 273

rules, applying, 288

S

Save Changes button (Tasks page), 327

Save Link button

Project Center, custom view creation, 352-354

Resource Center, 385

Save tab (Enterprise Options feature), 549

saved links, organizing, 385

saving

baselines, troubleshooting, 285

document workspace changes, 638

documents to project workspaces, 641

Portfolio Analyzer view modifications, 424

schedule changes in Updates page (PWA), 338

WSS custom lists as templates, 754-755

scalability (EPM solutions), 100-101

schedule assessment (Project Professional scheduling), 30

Schedule Indicator generic enterprise custom field, customizing, 709-710

Schedule tab (Enterprise Options feature), 545-546

schedules (data storage), 31

scheduling

skill-based scheduling, 577-578

via Project Professional, 29-30

scope definition (Project Professional scheduling), 29

Search function (Filter/Group/Search tab), 351, 383

searches

Project Center views, 351

Resource Center views, 383

Sec_audit.asp, 669

security

Allow/Deny feature, 145

asymmetric encryption, 788

cookie collection via PDS, 797

EPM solutions

data usage, 102-103

deployment, 137

Project Server 2003 security model, 105-106

project servers, 102

SSL implementation, 104-105

user authentication, 103

passwords, changing in PWA, 302

PDS, 89-93

Project Server

administrative settings, 37

Allow/Deny feature, 153

categories, 151-161

configuring, 36, 145-146

design recommendations, 162

Enterprise Global Resource Pool, 36

groups, associating categories to, 160

identifying user groups, 147

logons, 796-797

monitoring security logs, 655

process flow diagram, 143

RBS, 190

resource/project calendars, 36

security groups, 149-151

security templates, 147-149

setup validation, 273

VBA macros, digital certificates, 787-791

security groups, creating, 149-151

security logs (Project Server), monitoring, 655

security models

EPM deployment, 137

Project Server, 36-37

Security tab (Enterprise Options feature), 550

security templates

creating, 147

denied features, 149

managing, 491-494

naming, 148

selecting permissions, 148-149

Select the Resources to Display function (Portfolio Modeler), 431

selecting

document views, 474

resources for project teams, 565

skill-based selections, 566-567

via custom filters, 568-569

via predefined filters, 567

work availability, 569

SelfCert digital certificates, 790

sending PDS requests, 798

Server Configuration Features template

Account Creation permissions, 146

Approve Timesheet for Resources feature, 145

Connect to Project Server Using Microsoft Project 2002 feature, 145

Delegate Task feature, 145

Project Sever security, configuring, 145-146

settings, documenting, 146

Timesheet Approval feature, 145

Server Configuration function (PWA Admin tab), 479

Enterprise features, setting, 507-509

PWA menus, defining, 509

top-level menus, adding, 510

top-level submenus, adding, 511-512

server maintenance (SQL Server database), 663

backups, 665-666

Full Recovery model, 662

integrity checks, 665

optimization, 664

report generation, 667

Simple Recovery model, 662

server operating system validation (Project Server), 261

server-side WSS customization, site definitions, 759

creating, 761-764

customizing, 764-766

template location/structure, 759-760

service accounts (Project Server), 262

service packs, 70, 680-681

session affinity, 95

Session Manager (Project Server 2003), 94, 653, 672-673

Set Rules for Automatically Accepting Changes option (Updates page), 341

SetTracing.exe, 669

shared attachments, creating document workspaces, 637

Shared View option (Modify Shared Page feature), 737

Shared Workspace task pane (Office)

Document Information tab, 640

document workspaces

creating, 601, 638-639

deleting workspace documents, 639

deleting workspace sites, 639

disconnecting documents from workspaces, 639

retitling workspace sites, 639

Documents tab, 640

Links tab, 640

Members tab, 640

project workspace integration, 640

Status tab, 640

Tasks tab, 640

SharePoint Alerts, project workspaces, 642

SharePoint folders, project workspace integration, 644

SharePoint Services, non-trusted domain environments, 123

Show As % function (pivot table toolbars), 423

Show Multi-Valued Fields option (View Options tab), 381

Show option (View Options tab), 381

Show Outline Level option

Portfolio view, 348

Project view, 349

Show Overtime Work option (Timesheet view), 324

Show Scheduled Work option (Timesheet view), 324

Show Summary Tasks option

Project view, 349

Timesheet view, 323

Show Time and Date option (View Options tab), 381

Show Time with Date option

Portfolio view, 348

Project view, 349

Show To-Do Lists option (Portfolio view), 348

Show Top/Bottom Items function (pivot table toolbars), 422

Side pane

project guide, 53

PWA interface screen, 301

signing VBA macro digital certificates, 790

Simple Recovery model (SQL Server database maintenance), 662

SimpleUI parameter, PWA customization, 767

Single Line of Text option (Optional Settings for Column section), 452

Site Collection Administration area (Go to Site Administration option), 753

Site Collection Galleries area (Go to Site Administration option), 752

site definitions, 758
  creating, 761-764
  customizing
    changing project sites, 766
    setting as base templates, 764-765
    template location/structure, 759-760

site group permissions (WSS), 444

site list permissions (WSS), 445

Site Provisioning (PWA), WSS project workspace templates, 752

site rights (WSS), 446

Site Settings page (WSS project workspace)
  Administration area, 749-753
  Customization area, 749-754
  Manage My Information area, 750, 754

Sites and Workspaces option (Web Pages option), 748

Sites option (Documents and Lists page), 738

Six Pillars of EPM (Enterprise Project Management), 19-20, 58
  Artifact Management, plan development, 66-68
  Collaboration Management, plan development, 64-65
  Operational Principles, plan development, 69-70

Organizational Readiness, plan development, 68

Project Management, plan development, 59-61

Resource Management, plan development, 61-63

skill-based scheduling, 577-578

SmokeTest.exe, 669

SMS (Systems Management Server), 397

SOAP (Simple Object Access Protocol), defining, 793

Social Meeting Workspace option (Web Pages option), 748

soft booking, 355

soft change (EPM implementation), 16-18

soft denies, 145

software
  new releases, capacity planning, 695
  Office Project 2003 requirements, 128

Solution Starter kit, debugging OLAP cube extensions, 806

Sort Ascending/Sort Descending functions (pivot table toolbars), 422

sort orders (timesheet columns), adjusting, 325

Specified Below option (Choose Resources screen), 581

Specify Views page (PWA), 495
  adding
    Assignment views to, 499-500
    Portfolio Analyzer views to, 502-503
    Project Center views to, 498-499
    Project views to, 496
    Resource Center views to, 501-502
  Categories attribute, 235
  Copy View function, 505
  Default View Settings attribute, 234

Delete View function, 506

managing Timesheet views, 504

Modify View function, 505

Spelling tab (Enterprise Options feature), 547

Splitter Bar (Modify View screen), 212, 216, 224

spreadsheets (Excel)
  exporting
    documents, to, 475
    risks to via Risks feature (PWA), 460-461
    issues to, 467
  importing from project workspaces, 646-647

SPS (SharePoint Portal Server)
  EPM connections, 807
  PWA integration, 807-808
  system hardware/architecture instance design, 692
  WSS integration, 809

SQL (Structured Query Language) Server, Project Server monitoring, 652

SQL Analysis Services
  moving (EPM solution design), 113
  nontrusted domain environments, 123
  OLAP cube permissions, 398
  Portfolio Analyzer, 395-397

SQL Profiler, 659-660

SQL Server, 33
  database maintenance, 663
    backups, 665-666
    Full Recovery model, 662
    integrity checks, 665
    optimization, 664
    report generation, 667
    Simple Recovery model, 662
  Operational Principles plans, backups/restores, 69
  Project Server
    database tier (EPM solutions), 97-98
    validation, 264-265

SQL Server Agent Service, 663

SSL (Secure Sockets Layer)
EPM solution security, 104-105
implementation website, 104

staging tables (OLAP builds), 804-805

Standard calendar (Project Server), 248

Standard views, creating in WSS, 453

standardization validation/support (Project Server augmentation areas), 43

Standish Group, The, 11

Status field
Documents feature, 471
Issues feature, 464
Risks feature, 457

status reports, 307
Alert Me function, 308
archived reports, 314-315
collaboration management, 64
compiling, 313
creating, 309-310
deleting, 313-314, 532
displaying in PWA, 302
editing, 314
Filter and Group Reports tab, 315
hyperlinking to, 313
merging, 283, 313
Miscellaneous Reports option, 314
opening, 313
permissions, 308
removing from PWA, 308
Request a Status Report page (PWA), 308
requesting, 308-310
requests, troubleshooting, 283
Status Reports Archive option, 314
Status Reports Overview page (PWA), 308-309
submitting, 311-312
viewing, 313

Status Reports Archive option (PWA status reports), 314

Status Reports Overview page (PWA), 308-309

Status Reports page (PWA), 32, 296

Status tab (Shared Workspace task pane), 640

sticky sessions, 95

storing schedule data, 31

strategic portfolio support (Project Server augmentation areas), 42

stsadmin command-line utility, document workspace management, 639

stylesheets (PWA), customizing, 767

subdating assignments in Outlook via PWA add-in, 619

subfolders (document libraries), creating, 471

Substitute Resources function (Project Professional), 437-438

Substitute Resources Options screen (Resource Substitution Wizard), 583

Subtotal function (pivot table toolbars), 422

summaries (issues), 463

summary data (OLAP cubes), defining, 97

Summary Rollup option (Project view), 349

Surveys feature (WSS project workspace home page), 734

Surveys option (Create page), 742, 747

Sustain phase (EPM implementation), 18

Symphony Server (Symphony Suite), 52

Symphony Suite (CMD Corporation), 43, 52

Synchronize with Project Server option (Documents and Lists page Action menu), 740-741

synchronizing
Active Directory, 480
Excel lists with project workspaces, 647
resources via Enterprise Global Resource Pool (PWA), 31

system customization (capacity planning), 696

system growth (capacity planning), 693-695

system hardware/architecture instance design (capacity planning), 685-686, 693
client-side environments, 691
data complexity, 690-691
data storage requirements, 691-692
network latency, 688-689
peaky/heavy usage scenarios, 687-688
server environments, 689
user location/connectivity, 687
user numbers/types, 686

system performance, monitoring (EPM solution design), 113

system requirements (Office Project 2003), 129-130

T

Table attribute (Modify View screen), 216

task lists, 619-620, 745

Task Name field (Create a New Task page), 329

task rows, adding to Gantt charts, 632

Task Start Date field (Create a New Task page), 329

task timesheets (collaboration management), 64

tasks
assigned tasks
deleting, 531
troubleshooting, 284
assigning
email notifications, 281
users to Project Server published tasks, 282-283
yourself to, 330
creating, 282, 329

current/all tasks, viewing in timesheets, 323

delegated tasks, 331

    email notifications, 332

    managing, 332

    troubleshooting, 282

displaying in PWA, 302

histories, viewing, 342-343

linking risks to via Risks feature (PWA), 458

lost tasks, troubleshooting, 284

overhead, 245-246

Project Server published tasks, 282-283

projects, inserting into, 282

reviewing, 329-330

timesheets, defining in, 255

updates

    displaying in PWA, 302

    rejected updates, 327

    troubleshooting, 288

viewing/reporting from Outlook Calendar, 332-333

Tasks page (PWA), 317

accessing, 318

action bar, 328

Actual work tracking method, 320, 326

Alert Me function, 328

current/all tasks, viewing, 323

Day-by-day tracking method, 320, 326

default functions table, 294-295

Delegation tab, 331-332

estimates to complete, 317

Filter, Group, Search tab, 324

Grid and Timesheet entry view

    Baseline Work field, 321

    Gantt charts, 322

    grid data, 321

    indicator field, 322

    moving separator bar, 325

    removing fields, 322

Hide button, 328

Insert Notes button, 328

Link Documents button, 328

Link Issues button, 328

Link Risks button, 328

Managed Time Periods option, 318

Non-Managed Time Periods option, 318

Notify Your Manager of Time You Will Not Be Available for Project Work page, 333

Percent work complete tracking method, 320, 325

Reject button, 328

Remaining Work field, 325-327

Save Changes button, 327

Show Overtime Work option, 324

Show Scheduled Work option, 324

Show Summary Tasks option, 323

Timesheet Update cycle, 319

Update All button, 327

Update Selected Rows button, 327

View Options tab, 323

Tasks tab (Shared Workspace task pane), 640

team collaboration

collaboration challenges, 592

Collaboration features

    documents management, 598-599

    issues management, 597

    overview of, 589-590

    risk management, 597

documents management

    document libraries, 604

    Document Workspace feature (Office), 600-602

    email messages/file attachments, 599

    Meeting Workspace feature (Outlook), 600

    paper documents, 599

    tips for, 601-603

issues management, 597

large organizations, 591

Project Professional, 593

PWA, 593

risk management, 594-597

small organizations, 590

solution websites, 593

updating project progress

    publishing projects, 609-610

    saving tasks, 607

    setting status dates, 609

    task changes, 607

    tracking changes, 605-606

    updating projects, 611

    workflow updates, 606-607

Team Site option (Web Pages option), 748

technology validation (Project Server), 260

application installation, 264

    Project Server installation, 269-271

    SQL Server/analysis services installation, 264-265

    WSS installation, 266-268

network systems, 262-263

server operating systems, 261

templates

Enterprise Global, 542, 553-554

    backups, 251-252

    customizing, 555-561

    data restoration, 252

    locating, 538

project schedules, saving as, 280

workspace templates, creating, 447

WSS custom lists, saving as, 754-755

terminal services

Application Server mode (Windows Server), 677

EPM solution configurations, 126

GPMC, 677-679

implementation considerations, 676

installation order, 677

Project Server benefits, 675-676

versus VPN, 675

websites, 126

Test field (Filter Enterprise Resources feature), 357

testing VBA macros, 780

Testing and Verification Stage (EPM deployment), 75

third-party add-ins, 45

COM add-ins, 45-46

portfolio management add-ins, 50

process workflow management add-ins, 52

project management add-ins, 51

PWA add-ins, 47-50

risk management add-ins, 51

third-party Project Server development information websites, 41

Time dimension, adding to Portfolio Analyzer views, 231

time reporting processes, EPM deployment plans, 79

time tracking

current/all tasks, viewing, 323

estimates to complete, 317

multiple tracking methods, 320-321

Project Server tracking methods, configuring, 36

Tasks page (PWA), 317

Actual work tracking method, 320, 326

Day-by-day tracking method, 320, 326

Filter, Group, Search tab, 324

Grid and Timesheet entry view, 321-322

Managed Time Periods option, 318

Non-Managed Time Periods option, 318

Percent work complete tracking method, 320, 325

Timesheet Update cycle, 319

View Options tab, 323

timesheets

formatting, 320

update cycles, 319

updating authority, determining, 319

timelines (Visio), project schedules

exporting data to, 629-630

importing data from, 628-629

Timescale function (Portfolio Modeler), 431

timescaled data, displaying in Excel, 626

Timesheet Approval feature (Server Configuration Features template), 145

Timesheet page, troubleshooting assigned tasks, 284

Timesheet Update cycle, 319

timesheet views

enterprise resources, 203

managing, 496, 503-505

PWA, 320

Show Overtime Work option, 324

Show Scheduled Work option, 324

Show Summary Tasks option, 323

timesheets

collaboration management, 64

columns

adjusting widths, 324

arranging in Excel, 335

formatting in Excel, 335

repositioning, 325

current tasks, defining, 255

current/all tasks viewing, 323

customizing, 336

data entry modes, troubleshooting, 278

date ranges, viewing, 324

displaying in PWA, 302

EPM deployment, 138

estimates to complete, 317

exporting to Excel, 335

formatting, 320

Grid and Timesheet entry view (Tasks page)

Gantt charts, 322

grid data, 321

labor timesheets versus project timesheets, 41-42

Lock Down Defaults, 253

nonproject time notifications, 333-334

printing via Excel, 334-335

project timesheets versus labor timesheets, 41-42

sort orders, adjusting, 325

summaries (collaboration management), 65

Task page (PWA)

Filter, Group, Search tab, 324

View Options tab, 323

task progress report methods, specifying, 252

time period settings, selecting, 253-254

tracking methods

Actual work tracking method, 320, 326

Day-by-day tracking method, 320, 326

multiple tracking methods, 320-321

Percent work complete tracking method, 320, 325

update cycles, 319

Title field

Issues feature, 464

Risks feature, 457

To-Do List Options function (Project Center), 371, 374

to-do lists

creating, 283, 372

deleting, 533

Project Center functions

Create a New Personal or Shared To-Do List function, 371-372

Manage My To-Do Lists function, 371-373

To-Do List Options function, 371, 374

visibility, selecting, 372

Toolbar button (Microsoft Project 2003), assigning VBA macros to, 781

Toolbox function (Portfolio Modeler), 436

top navigation menu (WSS project workspaces), 733

Track Project Issues function (Project Center Collaboration), 367-368

Track Project Risks function (Project Center Collaboration), 367-368

Track This Task option (Delegate Tasks Wizard), 332

tracking
   collaboration project changes, 605-606
   Project Professional scheduling, 30
   system growth (capacity planning), 694-695
   time
      current/all tasks, viewing, 323
      estimates to complete, 317
      multiple tracking methods, 320-321
      Tasks page (PWA), 317-326
      timesheets, 319-320
      updating authority, 319

Tracking Settings function (Customize Project Web Access function), 524

Transaction Log Backup tab (Maintenance Plan Wizard), 666

Trigger Description field (Risks feature), 457

Trigger field (Risks feature), 457

troubleshooting
   ActiveX Controls (Internet Explorer), 673
   enterprise project outline codes, 173
   enterprise resource outline codes, 184
   Portfolio Analyzer, 675

Project
   assigned tasks, 284
   baseline saves, 285
   document access, 281
   group security permissions, 280
   issue access, 281
   lost tasks, 284
   progress reports, 284
   Project Portfolio access, 279
   Project Portfolio security, 280
   resource additions, 284
   risk access, 281
   saving project schedules as templates, 280
   status report requests, 283
   tasks, 281-283
   timesheets, data entry modes, 278
   to-do list creation, 283
   viewing resource information, 279
   web access 277-279

Project Professional, 674

Project Server
   adjust actuals, 288
   application layer, 668-673
   client layer, 673-675
   data accuracy, 286-287
   duplicate global.mpt files, 288-289
   Portfolio Analyzer, 287
   Portfolio Modeler, 287
   published version deletion, 289
   resource allocation process, 285-286
   resource calendars, 289-290
   Resource Substitution Wizard, 287
   rule application, 288
   task updates, 288

tools list, 668

ViewDrop, 673

Views Notification service, 673

U

Update All button (Tasks page), 327

Update My Information option (Manage My Information area), 754

Update Project Web Access menu, 618

Update Resource Tables and OLAP Cube feature (Manage Enterprise Features function), 517-520

Update Selected Rows button (Tasks page), 327

Updates action bar option (Updates page), 339

Updates page (PWA), 336
   Accept/Reject Task Column and Updates List option, 339
   Adjust Actuals in the Resource Center option, 343
   Alert Me option, 340
   Approve Timesheets in the Resource Center option, 344
   Baseline Work, 339
   Customization tabs (PWA), 339
   default functions table, 296
   functions of, 606-607
   Indicators column, 340
   rules for, 340-341
   saving schedule changes, 338
   Set Rules for Automatically Accepting Changes option, 341
   time approvals, 337-338
   time rejections, 338
   Updates action bar option, 339
   updating project team collaboration workflows, 606
   View History option, 342-343
   View Timesheet Summary in the Resource Center option, 343

updating
　archived status reports, 314
　assignments in Outlook via
　　PWA add-in, 619
　OLAP cubes, 517-518
　patches (Window Server),
　　managing, 680
　project team collaboration
　　projects, 611
　　publishing projects,
　　　609-610
　　saving tasks, 607
　　setting status dates, 609
　　task changes, 607
　　workflow updates,
　　　606-607
　project team collaboration
　　projects, tracking changes,
　　605-606
　PWA, displaying in,
　　297-298, 302
　Resource tables, 517-520
　tasks
　　rejected updates, 327
　　viewing history of,
　　　342-343
　　timesheets, update cycles,
　　　319
**Upload Multiple Files field
　(Documents feature), 471**
uploading documents, 471
**usage management versus
　resource commitment man-
　agement, 42**
**user authentication, EPM solu-
　tions, 103**
**user groups, Project Server
　security, 147**
**user management via Manage
　Users and Group function
　(PWA Admin tab)**
　adding users, 480-481
　deactivating existing users,
　　484
　merging user accounts,
　　484-485
　modifying existing users,
　　482-483
**user role validation (Project
　Server), 273**
**UserOLAPUpdate method
　(breakout COM), 805**

**Users and Permissions area (Go
　to Site Administration
　option), 751**
**UserStagingTablesUpdate
　method (breakout COM), 804**

V

**validation (Project Server),
　259-260**
　basic configuration valida-
　　tion, 273
　business process validation,
　　274
　technology validation
　　application installation,
　　　264-271
　　network systems,
　　　262-263
　　server operating systems,
　　　261
**Value field (Filter Enterprise
　Resources feature), 357**
**Value List dialog (Project
　Professional), 559**
**VBA (Visual Basic for
　Applications) macros**
　debugging
　　Immediate window
　　　(Visual Basic Editor),
　　　786
　　stepping through code,
　　　785
　as modules, 779
　Project object model, 787
　recording, 779-780
　security, digital certificates,
　　787-788
　　adding trusted certifi-
　　　cates, 790-791
　　creating, 789
　　exporting/transferring,
　　　789
　　signing, 790
　Toolbar button (Microsoft
　　Project 2003), assigning,
　　781
　viewing/editing code
　　Code window (Microsoft
　　　Project 2003), 784
　　designing user forms,
　　　784

　Project Explorer, 782-783
　Properties window
　　(Microsoft Project
　　2003), 783-784
**vendor management (Project
　Server augmentation areas),
　43-44**
**Version History field
　(Documents feature), 473**
**versioning/baseline require-
　ments (EPM deployment
　plans), 79**
versions (projects)
　custom versions, adding to
　　Manage Enterprise
　　Features function (PWA
　　Admin tab), 521
　deleting, 523
　modifying, 523
　published versions, trou-
　　bleshooting, 289
Versions page (PWA), 521
**View a Project page (Project
　Center), Link Project Risks
　button, 366**
**View a Project view (Projects
　section), 156**
**View All option (Filter
　Enterprise Resources feature),
　357**
**View and Upload Documents
　page (Manage Project
　Documents function), 369**
view area (project guide), 53
**View Assignments view
　(Resources section), 158**
**View Availability function
　(Resource Center), 385**
　Assignment Work by Project
　　view, 386
　Assignment Work by
　　Resource view, 386
　Availability graph, 387
　Remaining Availability view,
　　386
　Resource Details section,
　　387
　Work view, 386
**View Certificate button (Digital
　Signature Details screen), 790**
**View History option (Updates
　page), 342-343**

View Information About Site Users option (Manage My Information area), 754

View Name and Description attribute
Modify View screen, 211, 216, 220, 223
Portfolio Analyzer screen, 229

View Options function (Resource Center), 386

View Options tab
Project Center
Show Outline Level option, 348-349
Show Summary Tasks option, 349
Show Time with Date option, 348-349
Show To-Do Lists option, 348
Summary Rollup option, 349
Resource Center, 381
Tasks page, 323

View Portfolio Analyzer permissions, Project Analyzer views, 227

View Processing service (Project Server 2003), 93-94

View Project Center permissions, Project Analyzer views, 227

View Properties and Edit Properties field (Documents feature), 473

View Reports option (Documents and Lists page Action menu), 739-740

View Resource Assignments feature (Resource Center), 390-391

View tab (Enterprise Options feature), 542

View Timesheet Summary in the Resource Center option (Updates page), 343

View Timesheet Summary option (Resource Center), 378

View Type attribute
Modify View screen, 211, 215, 220-222
Portfolio Analyzer screen, 229

ViewDrop tab (Project Server Health Monitor tool), 670, 673

viewing
assignment details, in Project Web Access Appointment dialog, 619
document lists, 471
event lists in Outlook, 644
issue reports, 466
model data, 429
reports via Risks feature (PWA), 460
resource assignments, 390-391
resource availability, 360
risk summaries, 455
risks via Risks feature (PWA), 459
status reports, 313
task histories, 342-343
tasks in Outlook Calendar, 332-333
timesheet date ranges, 324
VBA macro code
Code window (Microsoft Project 2003), 784
designing user forms, 784
Project Explorer, 782-783
Properties window (Microsoft Project 2003), 783-784

views
Assignment views, 496
adding, 499-500
creating, 222
modifying, 222-225
copying, 505
custom views, adding to Manage Views page, 506
deleting, 505
document views, selecting, 474
EPM deployment, 138
managing, 235, 494-505

modifying, 505
Portfolio Analyzer views, 225, 496
adding, 502-503
adding resources, 232
adding Time dimension, 231
changing chart types, 233-234
Chart, 228
creating, 228-235, 403-405
custom pivot table formula creation, 414-415, 418
displaying data, 395
Enterprise Outline Codes, 226, 230
filtering data, 233
formatting, 406-409, 412-413
manipulating, 422-424
modifying, 228-235
OLAP cubes, 227-228
PivotTable, 228
required user permissions, 227
restrictions, 159
typical views, 393
user interaction with, 395
processing, troubleshooting in Project Server application layer, 673
Project views, 495
adding, 496-497
creating, 215
modifying, 215-218
Project Center views, 347, 495
adding, 498-499
creating, 210
customizing, 348-354
filters, 349
groups, 350
modifying, 210-214
portfolio management, 352
printing, 364-365
searches, 351

Project Professional views, 236-237

Project Server security model, 106

PWA views, customizing, 703

Resource Center views, 496
    adding, 501-502
    choosing, 386
    creating, 219
    customizing, 380, 385
    filters, 381
    groups, 382
    modifying, 219-221
    printing, 383
    Resource Summary view, 380
    searches, 383

Timesheet views, 496, 503-505

in WSS, 453
    Calendar view creation, 454
    Datasheet view creation, 454
    Standard view creation, 453

Views database table set (Project Server database tier), 96

Views Notification service, troubleshooting, 673

Views Publishing Services, moving (EPM solution design), 113

virtual infrastructures (EPM solutions), 132-133

visibility (to-do lists), 372

Visio
    Gantt charts
        adding blank task rows, 632
        adding milestones, 632
        creating, 632
        creating task dependencies, 632-633
    Project Professional integration
        exporting Gantt charts to project schedules, 633
        exporting timelines to project schedules, 629-630
        importing Gantt charts to project schedules, 631
        importing project schedule data to timelines, 628-629
        Visio WBS Chart Wizard, 627-628
    WBS, 28

Visio WBS Chart Wizard, 627-628

Visual Basic Editor
    accessing, 782
    Immediate window, 786
    VBA macro code
        debugging, 786
        viewing/editing, 782

VP (Views Processor), 653, 673

VPN (virtual private network) versus terminal services, 675

W

W3C (World Wide Web Consortium) log file format, 656

WAN (wide area network)
    bandwidth, 116
    Build Team from Enterprise feature (Project Professional), 576
    EPM solution design, 116-117
    latency, 116-117

WBS (Work Breakdown Structure), 28, 555

WBS Chart Wizard (Visio), 627-628

Web access, troubleshooting
    administrator accounts, 277-278
    Project Professional schedule access, 279
    Windows-authenticated accounts, 278

Web Components (Office)
    Chart, Project Analyzer views, 228
    Client tier (EPM solutions), 86

    PivotTable, Project Analyzer views, 228
    Portfolio Analyzer, 86

web discussions, commenting on documents, 642

Web Pages option (Create page), 743
    Basic Meeting Workspace option, 748
    Basic Web Page option, 747
    Blank Meeting Workspace option, 748
    Blank Site option, 748
    Decision Meeting Workspace option, 748
    Document Workspace option, 748
    Multipage Meeting Workspace option, 749
    Project Workspace option, 749
    Sites and Workspaces option, 748
    Social Meeting Workspace option, 748
    Team Site option, 748
    Web Part Page option, 747

Web Part Page option (Web Pages option), 747

web parts (PWA), PDS, 800

Web-based front-end application layer, Application tier (EPM solutions), 87-88

Webb, Dan, project team collaboration, 592

Welcome screen (Resource Substitution Wizard), 580

what-if analysis, Portfolio Modeler models, 433-434

widths (timesheet columns), adjusting, 324

Windows 2000 Resource Kit website, 117

Windows Everyone security group, viewing OLAP cube data, 398

Windows Server
    Application Server mode, terminal service installation, 677
    authentication, 493
    clustering services website, 89

patch management, 680

Project Server

log file monitoring, 654

real-time monitoring, 654-655

Project Server AD, 652

SharePoint Services, 34

features of, 35

Operational Principles plans, site management, 70

Windows SharePoint Services Administrator Guide website, 441

Windows SharePoint Services Team Web Site Provisioning Settings page (PWA), 513

Windows, Operational Principles plans, 70

wizards

Analyze Timescaled Data (Project Professional), 626

Copy Picture to Office, 631

Delegate Tasks, 331-332

Export Project Data, exporting Gantt charts to project schedules, 633

Import Project Data

importing Gantt charts to project schedules, 631

importing project schedule data to Visio timelines, 628-629

Import Timeline, 629

Maintenance Plan Wizard

Complete Backup tab, 665

Integrity tab, 665

Optimization tab, 664

SQL Server Agent Service, 663

Transaction Log Backup tab, 666

Project Professional Resource Substitution Wizard, 438-439

Project Web Access Add-in for Outlook Integration, 616

Resource Substitution (Project Professional), 576-578

Choose Projects screen, 580

Choose Related Projects screen, 582

Choose Resources screen, 581-582

Choose Scheduling Options screen, 583

Choose Update Options screen, 585

Finish screen, 586

functions of, 580

limitations of, 579

Review Results screen, 584

Substitute Resources screen, 583

Welcome screen, 580

Visio WBS Chart, 627-628

work availability, selecting project team resources by, 569

Work Estimate field

Assign Myself to an Existing Task page, 330

Create a New Task page, 329

Work view (View Availability function), 386

Work with Outlook link (PWA home page), 305

workshops (EPM implementation), 14

Workspace page (PWA), default functions table, 297

workspaces (project), 32

accessing, 442

defining, 441

template creation, 447

WSS (Windows SharePoint Services), 635, 732

Administrator Guide website, 441

Application tier (EPM solutions), 89

Attachments field, 449

Central Administration site, creating nonproject-related WSS sites, 757-758

Change Column screen, 450

adding columns, 451

Help section, 453

Optional Settings for Column section, 451-453

Change Field Order screen, 453

Change Permissions for This List field, 449-450

columns

adding, 451

changing order of, 453

customizing, 451-452

deleting, 453

Create View screen, 454

custom lists, saving as templates, 754-755

document workspaces, 636

creating, 637-638

making changes to, 638

managing, 638

saving changes to, 638

Documents feature, 468

Alert Me option, 474-475

All Document Libraries feature, 472

Check Out field, 473

Delete field, 473

Discuss field, 474

document creation, 470

Document Template field, 469

Document Versions field, 469

Edit in the document application field, 473

editing documents in datasheets, 472

Explorer view, 474

exporting documents to spreadsheets, 475

Linking field, 471

Modify Settings and Columns feature, 475

Name and Description field, 469

Name field, 471

Navigation field, 469

Overwrite Existing File(s)? field, 471

Owner field, 471
Project Server synchro-
nization, 475
Status field, 471
Upload Multiple Files
field, 471
uploading documents,
471
Version History field, 473
View Properties and Edit
Properties field, 473
viewing document folder
contents, 470
downloading, 89, 441
Email Notification field, 449
Go to Selected Project
Workspace function
(Project Center), 369-370
installing, Project Server val-
idation, 266-268
Issues feature, 462
Alert Me option, 467
Assigned To field, 464
attaching files to issues,
465
Category field, 464
creating issues, 463
Discussion field, 465
Due Date field, 465
editing issues in
datasheets, 467
exporting issues to
spreadsheets, 467
filtering issues, 466
issue summaries, 463
Linking to Tasks, Risks,
Other Issues, or
Documents field, 465
Modify Settings and
Columns feature, 468
Owner field, 464
Priority field, 465
Project Server synchro-
nization, 468
Resolution field, 465
Status field, 464
Title field, 464
viewing reports, 466
modifying settings, 447
changing permissions,
449-450
general settings, 448
Name and Description field,
449

Navigation field, 449
nonproject-related sites, creating, 756-758
permissions, changing,
449-450
personal rights, 446
Project Server, 653
project workspace templates
PWA Site Provisioning,
752
Team Member site group
permissions, 445
project workspaces, 443
accessing, 733
Create page, customiz-
ing, 742-749
creating, 447
Documents and Lists
page, customizing,
738-741
home page, 733-738
manual creation, 733
quick launch bar, 733
Site Settings page, cus-
tomizing, 749-754
top navigation menu,
733
Risks feature, 454
Alert Me option, 460
Assigned To field, 457
Category field, 457
Contingency Plan field,
457
Cost field, 457
Description field, 457
Due Date field, 457
editing risks in
datasheets, 461
exporting risks to spreadsheets, 460-461
filtering risks, 460
Impact field, 457
linking risks to tasks, 458
Mitigation Plan field, 457
Modify Settings and
Columns feature, 462
Owner field, 457
Probability field, 457
Project Server synchro-
nization, 462
risk creation, 455-457
risk summaries, 455
Status field, 457

Title field, 457
Trigger Description field,
457
Trigger field, 457
viewing reports, 460
viewing/reporting risks,
459
sites
creating/customizing def-
initions, 759-766
deleting, 516
group permissions, 444
list permissions, 445
rights, 446
system hardware/architec-
ture instance design, 692
views, creating, 453-454
WSS Config DB (database), 662
WSS Content DB (database),
662
WSS Site image feature (WSS
project workspace home
page), 734

X - Y - Z

Yes/No option (Optional
Settings for Column section),
453

zooming in/out of Gantt
charts, 322, 363

www.quantumpm.com

QuantumPM is a project management consulting firm that provides solutions built for small, midsize and enterprise businesses. End-to-end project and portfolio management solutions include:

PROJECT KNOWLEDGE	• Project, Program and Portfolio Management • Enterprise Project Management (EPM) • PM Best Practice and Process Consulting • Training
TECHNOLOGY SOLUTIONS	• Integration and Development • Customized and Tailored Solutions • Hosting • Digital Dashboards • Project Management Tools and Technologies
BUSINESS & GUIDANCE	• Strategic Alignment • PMO Development • Project Audits • Corporate Health Measurement

Choose QuantumPM to help you guide your project-based business.
QuantumPM realizes that each business is unique. We take the time to listen to your specific needs and create solutions that enable your success. Our team is comprised of senior project management consultants who are experienced across a variety of industries. QuantumPM utilizes cutting edge technology and industry best practices to take you where you want to go.

Contact Us. To learn more QuantumPM solution offerings and how they can improve your business, visit **www.quantumpm.com**.

303.699.2334, 9085 E. Mineral Circle, Suite 235, Centennial, CO 80112

They say writing a book can either bring your team together or pull you apart. For *this* book, we brought our team together and pulled apart Microsoft Office Project 2003 to bring to your fingertips a comprehensive and relevant resource! We are all proud to be authors of this book and members of the QuantumPM team.

Signing off with approval for all your project management needs,
QuantumPM

Rose Blackburn

Kristen J. Catley

Steve

Greg

Jennifer Rollins

James V. Patterson

Russ

Karla L. Ferguson

Boris

Scott M. Footlik

Danny Dean Alt J.

Robert

Bruce Kohrn

Elham Young

Cristian

Herman N. Damon Jr.

Tony Black

Brian

Stewart

Esperanza Pashkova

Claudia

Adam Bohn

Laurie Dawkins

Crystal E. Zapata-Trevino

Our solutions are unique.
Our team is knowledgeable.
Our clients are satisfied.

303.699.2334, 9085 E. Mineral Circle, Suite 235, Centennial, CO 80112

License Agreement

By opening this package, you are also agreeing to be bound by the following agreement:

You may not copy or redistribute the entire CD-ROM as a whole. Copying and redistribution of individual software programs on the CD-ROM is governed by terms set by individual copyright holders.

The installer and code from the author(s) are copyrighted by the publisher and the author(s). Individual programs and other items on the CD-ROM are copyrighted or are under an Open Source license by their various authors or other copyright holders.

This software is sold as-is without warranty of any kind, either expressed or implied, including but not limited to the implied warranties of merchantability and fitness for a particular purpose. Neither the publisher nor its dealers or distributors assumes any liability for any alleged or actual damages arising from the use of this program. (Some states do not allow for the exclusion of implied warranties, so the exclusion may not apply to you.)

What's on the CD-ROM

The companion CD-ROM contains select source files to follow along in the book, trial software, webcast presentations on the EPM Workshop series, and this entire book in Adobe's Portable Document Format (.PDF) for fast and easy topic search.

Windows Installation Instructions

1. Insert the CD-ROM disc into your CD-ROM drive.

2. From the Windows desktop, double-click on the My Computer icon.

3. Double-click on the icon representing your CD-ROM drive.

4. Double-click start.exe and follow the on-screen instructions.

> **NOTE**
>
> If your version of Windows is set to hide known extensions, you may only see start instead of start.exe.
>
> If you have the AutoPlay feature enabled, start.exe will be launched automatically whenever you insert the disc into your CD-ROM drive.